USA West
a travel survival kit

Hawaii, the Pacific States & the Southwest

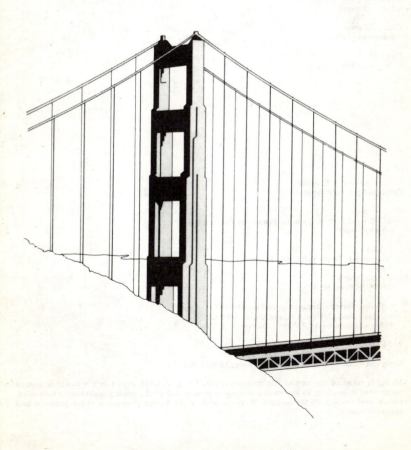

USA West – a travel guide to Hawaii, the Pacific states & the Southwest

Published by
Lonely Planet Publications
PO Box 88, South Yarra, Victoria 3141
Australia
Lonely Planet Publications
PO Box 2001A, Berkeley, CA 94702
USA

Printed in Singapore through
Hedges & Bell Printing (S.E. Asia)

Illustrations by
Judith Whipple

First published
November 1980

This edition
January 1985

National Library of Australia
Cataloguing-in-Publication data

Storey, Joan.
    U.S.A. west, a travel guide to Hawaii, the Pacific states &
    the southwest.

    2nd ed.
    Previous ed.: South Yarra, Vic.: Lonely
    Planet, 1980.
    Includes index.
    ISBN 0 908086 50 4.

    1. Pacific States – Description and travel – 1951-
    – Guide-books. 2. Hawaii – Description and travel –
    1981- – Guide-books. I. Reece, Daphne E. II. Title.

917.9'0433

Copyright © Joan Storey & Daphne E. Reece, 1980, 1985

Joan Storey was born and raised in Australia. A gypsy instinct made travel a must and the Katherine Dunham Company provided the opportunity when they visited Australia: she joined the company as stage manager in 1957 and traveled the world with them. She has since lived in New York and San Francisco, and now is a full-time travel writer. When not overseas she explores America in her '67 Chevy.

Daphne Reece is a cat-sitter and a freelance writer with a passion for travel and history. Born in Barbados, educated in England, she has long been a resident on the West Coast (she now lives in San Francisco) but wanders off whenever she can, usually to Europe, though she also lived in Hong Kong for a while.

ACKNOWLEDGMENTS

The compilation and writing of this guide reflects the generous aid and advice of many friends, associates and organizations. Our warm thanks are due to all of them for fielding our questions patiently and answering them fully. So many were kind that we regret we can express our gratitude individually to only a few of those who have helped.

First, we would like to thank Greyhound Bus Lines for assistance in travel in the Southwest. For assistance in Hawaii, our thanks to the Hawaii Visitors Bureau, particularly Lindy Boyes and Gene Wilhelm; World Airways; Tom McGarvey and Hawaiian Airlines; Betty Krauss and InterIsland Resorts; Sheila Donnelly and Amfac Hotels; Lori Sablas of Kaanapali Beach Resort; Vonnie Paine Lyons of Kailua-Kona Resort; Royal Rainbow and Tropical Rent-a-Cars.

To Peter and Jacqueline Samuels of Talisman Travel, San Francisco, for keeping us abreast of constantly changing travel facts.

To Timothy Mitchell for the use of his comprehensive Hawaiiana research library, and *Pacific Travel News* for invaluable research materials.

To Phyllis Elving, Diane Stevens, Beth Erickson, Edd Dundas, Chuck Maisel, San Francisco Convention & Visitors Bureau, San Luis Obispo Chamber of Commerce, Placerville County Chamber of Commerce, Arizona Office of Tourism and the Pacific Area Travel Association for use of their photographs.

To Judith Whipple for her illuminating sketches.

To Diane Stevens, Chuck Maisel and Steve Carroll for sharing their knowledge of Seattle and the Pacific Northwest.

To Edward and Ruth Gregg, who opened doors in New Mexico and helped in so many ways on the sidelines.

And to Helga Wall, not only for reading portions of the manuscript, but for her continuing encouragement and support.

Contents

Introduction

In writing *USA West* we have tried to present a broad picture of the western states, including Hawaii, as well as give you a really useful tool for planning and enjoying your trip. The great cities and attractions you've heard about are included; so are suggestions for skittering off the main tourist routes to out-of-the way places that give a real feeling for America. You will also find emphasis placed on the history, culture and legends of each area to enhance your understanding of the places you explore.

The introductory pages are intended to give you a general idea of the way things work in the US, providing a good deal of practical information about such down-to-earth matters as visa formalities, currency and where and how to shop, as well as your options in transportation, accommodation, the kinds of adventures you can plan for yourself (from backpacking into the crater of a Hawaiian volcano to running wild rivers), and where to go when you need very detailed information.

Each regional section begins with a write-up that will introduce you to its character, history, climate and major attractions. Then come our suggestions as to what to see, based upon the major cities. These are described sequentially, following specific itineraries. If many of the routes seem to demand the use of a car, remember that American life is based on a personal set of wheels, and rural areas are not well served by public transportation. Sections on Sightseeing Tours, Places to Stay, Places to Eat, Getting There, Getting Around, and Useful Addresses are included for each major city or region.

Facts and figures for costs and services are as up-to-date as inflation and entrepreneurial changes permit. But bear in mind, when you make any calculations, that no price included in this book can be regarded as firm; they are quoted purely for guidance.

We came to California from opposite directions – from Australia and from England. We were both bent on sampling life in the West as we imagined it to be after a youth spent assimilating Hollywood's export version in our local cinemas. Nearly 20 years and thousands of miles later, we find we have not yet moved on. The West is infinitely alluring. Welcome – and be warned!

Facts for the Visitor

PASSPORTS & VISAS

Before setting out for the United States you must have in your possession a valid passport with a visa, which you can obtain from any US embassy or consulate. Canadian citizens do not require a visa and, if entering from anywhere within the western hemisphere, do not require a passport, simply proof of Canadian citizenship.

CROSSING INTO MEXICO

Popping across the border for a quick trip to Mexico is easy to do, but there are a couple of things to remember. Although American citizens do not need a visa for entry to Mexico, some foreign nationals do. A re-entry permit for the US may also be required if you do not return within 30 days, so check with your consulate or US immigration authorities before you cross. See also the Driving in Mexico section in this chapter.

HEALTH

Presently there are no health requirements for entry to the US unless you are coming from an infected area. In that case, you should have proof of vaccination.

CUSTOMS

US Customs allow non-residents to bring in duty free their personal effects, 300 cigarettes (or 50 cigars or 3 pounds of smoking tobacco or proportionate amounts of each), $100 worth of gifts and one US quart (0.946 litre) of liquor. You may also bring in an additional US gallon (3.785 litres) of liquor as part of your $100 allowance if it is a gift. If you are under 21, you may not import that quart of liquor for your own use, but you are allowed to bring in a gallon as a gift. Note, though, that some states limit the amount of liquor that may be brought into the state. In those covered by this guide, the amount differs from that allowed by Customs only in Hawaii (one gallon) and Oregon (one quart).

Regulation Alert

As health and customs formalities are liable to change, we urge you to check with an American Embassy or consulate for the most recent information before you leave.

ACCOMMODATION

The West offers a wide range of accommodation at all price levels, from no-frills budget motels to deluxe resorts, by way of dude ranches, romantic country inns and renovated Victorian mansions. Their number, of course, is legion; we have therefore chosen to limit our suggestions to samplings from each category in major cities and prime tourist areas and to suggest authoritative accommodation directories. Rates quoted are for a double room occupied by two persons, breakfast not included. These are subject to change and are provided *only* as guidelines for planning.

Terms you may not have encountered before in connection with hotel charges are 'American Plan,' 'Modified American Plan,' 'European Plan' and 'Family Plan'. *American Plan* (AP) rates include breakfast, lunch and dinner. *Modified American Plan*

(MAP) includes breakfast and dinner. *European Plan* (EP) covers the cost of the room only. A *Family Plan* rate means that there is no charge for children when they occupy the same room as their parents (the hotels determine children's age limits). Most hotels will add an *extra person* charge if more than two persons occupy a double room (except for children). A local hotel tax is added to hotel bills throughout the West. Extra charges can amount to 21% for service charge and tax at some resorts.

Substantial savings on accommodation can often be achieved by purchasing a tour package with guaranteed transportation and accommodation included which may be worth the loss of flexibility. Those who prefer to rove at will can take advantage of off-season and extended stay tariffs to stretch the travel dollar. Hotels in areas which are primarily summer or winter resorts often lower their rates considerably out of season. Do ask about extended stay rates if you are planning to stay more than three days in one spot; many smaller hotels, particularly in the major cities, offer weekly and monthly rates. Another dollar-stretcher is the motel suite with well-equipped kitchen, including a refrigerator – for complete freedom in a home-away-from-home, simply add your provisions.

Hotels & Motels Expect a high standard of comfort and facilities in the famous-name chains such as Hilton, Hyatt Regency and Intercontinental. Rooms generally have a private bathroom, TV, radio and telephone and are air-conditioned. In major cities a double room in this category currently ranges from $60 to $105 on up to $250 per night for a luxury suite.

In the medium price range, look for such names as Sheraton, Ramada, Best Western, TraveLodge, Holiday Inn, Quality Inn, Red Lion, Thunderbird and Howard Johnson. A double room here runs around $55 to 75 a night in the city; on the road you may pay as little as $35 to 50 a night for a similar room. The difference between expensive and moderate accommodation is largely one of degree; you get similar facilities but in a simpler setting.

Conveniently located, inexpensive accommodation of good quality requires a little more research, but it does exist: enlist the aid of the local Visitors Bureau or Chamber of Commerce who issue accommodation lists. Invaluable guides are Mobil and the American Automobile Association regional handbooks which cover the entire range. (AAA handbooks are available to members only.) The most famous name in budget chains is Motel Six with more than 225 motels throughout the country. It's worth writing for a copy of the Motel 6 Directory from Motel 6 Inc, 51 Hitchcock Way, Santa Barbara, CA 93105. Other names to remember are Americana, Friendship, Ramada and Rodeway.

Many of the major hotel chains have nationwide, toll-free reservation service telephone numbers. These are listed in the phone book Yellow Pages, under 'Hotels & Motels – Out-of-Town Reservations'.

Bed & Breakfast – American Style Private homes offering rooms to let in the European style are not yet part of the mainstream American way of accommodation but the situation is changing. A pioneer in the field, Bed & Breakfast International, 151 Ardmore Rd, Kensington, CA 94707 maintains a roster of more than 200 private homes located in the San Francisco Bay Area, Monterey, Carmel, the Napa Valley Wine Country, Los Angeles, San Diego, Seattle and Hawaii which offer lodging. Prices currently range from $28 to 60 a night for a double room, including breakfast, with a 20% reduction for singles. Weekly and monthly rates can be arranged. If you write from outside the US for a brochure, include two international postal reply coupons.

The Bed & Breakfast League, 855 29th St, NW, Washington, DC 20008 is a membership organisation offering similar accomodation. On approval of membership and payment of an annual $25 fee, you will be issued a guest membership card and a directory of host homes in a number of metropolitan centres including Los Angeles, San Diego, San Francisco and Seattle. Charges for accomodation are currently from $25 to $35 per night single, $35 to $70 double.

Another source of information on accomodation in private homes is the local office of CONSERV (the National Council for Community Services to International Visitors). For a description of this organisation, see Meeting the Americans. Offices in the West are listed under Useful Adresses.

Two organisations whose members offer reciprocal hospitality are:

The Traveler's Directory, Tom Linn, Editor, 6224 Baynton St, Philadelphia PA 19144. Members of this international group offer free hospitality in their homes, information and a helping hand to fellow members. The annual $10 membership fee includes a copy of their directory describing the kind of hospitality offered by each member.

The Globetrotters Club, BCM/Roving, London WC1V 6XX, England, is a similar organization. Members receive not only a directory listing names and addresses of Globetrotters offering accommodation but a bi-monthly newsletter sharing travel information and updating membership data.

Rustic Charmers A widespread revival of interest in America's architectural heritage has generated a pleasing fallout for lovers of uncommon hotels. All over the West many old country inns and hotels have been restored to their former glory and the trend is spreading to the cities, especially San Francisco where several Victorian places have been converted to elegant bed and breakfast inns. These hostelries are usually small, with limited guest accommodation, and somewhat on the expensive side. Reservations should be made well in advance. Good supplements to our suggestions are *Country Inns of the West* (101 Productions) and Jim Crain's *Historic Country Inns of California* (Chronicle Books).

Youth Hostels Youth hosteling is an increasingly popular way of seeing the US, providing travelers of all ages with low cost, simple overnight accommodation in attractive locations that vary from big-city centers to mountain wildernesses and the ocean shore. American Youth Hostels, Inc operates some 52 hostels in the area covered by this guide, ranging in level of facilities provided from the very simple Shelter Hostel to the Superior Hostel which may offer bed linen rental, game rooms, common rooms, vending machines and laundry facilities. A spirit of camaraderie and mutual assistance pertains. Hostels operate on a self-help basis under the supervision of managers and you are required to share in such domestic chores as cooking and cleaning. Beds are equipped with a mattress, pillow and blanket so you must provide your own sleeping bag unless bed linen can be rented. Admission is, with very few exceptions, restricted to holders of AYH membership passes that cost $7 (junior and senior citizen), $14 (senior), $35 (three-year senior) and $140 (life membership). Passes are valid in any hostel in the world; members of foreign YHAs, of course, may use AYH hostels. For those who prefer to try the experience before committing themselves, the AYH offers a $2 Introductory Card valid for one night at a time.

Accommodation rates vary according to the grade of hostel, usually from $3 to $6 in summer and $4 to $8 in winter. A complete listing of hostels, their rates and facilities is published in the annually updated AYH Handbook issued free to members and available in book shops. For information, write to the American Youth Hostels Inc, National Administrative Office, 1321 I Street NW, Suite 800, Washington DC 20005.

Campus Lodging Contrary to popular belief, American universities are not a good source of inexpensive berths during vacation periods. Education is a year-round industry and the gaps between each semester are filled by short course sessions, seminars and conventions. As a consequence, campus lodging facilities are rarely unoccupied.

Budget Accommodation Directory *Where to Stay USA*, published by the Council on International Educational Exchange in cooperation with the American Revolution Bicentennial Administration, is *the* handbook for budget travelers. It lists accommodation throughout the US that costs from $1 to $15 per night.

OUTDOOR ADVENTURING

Organized Backpacking

Quite a number of outfitters are meeting the needs of those who would like to backpack but are diffident about their ability to go it alone or prefer the companionship of a group. Many organized backpacking expeditions include all food and equipment in the cost—an attractive feature for travelers who don't want to tote their own gear on a multi-faceted trip. Some outfitters provide packstock to carry your duffel, leaving you to hike free as a bird; others simply provide guide service – you carry everything you need. If you yearn for a hot meal and a shower at the end of the hiking day, check out camp-to-camp hiking in Yosemite National Park by contacting the Yosemite Park and Curry Company (see *Yosemite National Park*) and hiking from base camps with the Sierra Club; guest ranches often include guided day hikes in their programs. What all these possibilities have in common is the guidance of skilled professionals wise in the ways of the wilderness.

Expeditions vary in length from two to 10 days on average, and groups are usually limited to a maximum of 12 people. Costs depend on what the outfitter provides; if you are carrying all your own gear, the daily rate is between $25 and $35. Estimate an additional $20 if packstock are provided to carry duffel.

Two members-only organizations, the Sierra Club and the Wilderness Society, offer a wide range of wilderness trips that include backpacking and hiking from base camps. Their outings can cost as little as $20 a day. For membership information and outings catalogues write to:

Sierra Club Outing Department, 530 Bush St, San Francisco, CA 94108; tel (415) 981-8634.

The Wilderness Society, 1901 Pennsylvania Avenue, NW Washington, DC 20036; tel (202) 467-5810.

You might also look into the offerings of *Outward Bound*, the international self-discovery through-adventure organization at 165 W Putnam Avenue, Greenwich, CT 06830. Their toll-free number in the US is 800-243-8520.

John Hart's *Walking Softly in the Wilderness* (Sierra Club Books), the Sierra Club guide to backpacking, contains a wealth of indispensable information for both novices and seasoned backpackers. Everything you need to know, from gearing up to trail techniques.

Camping What better way to get away from it all for a while amid some of the grandest scenery on earth, economize on the budget and meet the Americans in an atmosphere particularly conducive to camaraderie than a camping trip through the West? Absolutely none. Thirty million Americans are doing it every year. But the very popularity of this kind of a vacation requires advance planning if you want to visit the most famous parks during the summer. Though most campsites in the National Park system are available on a first-come, first-served basis, reservations are required at certain campgrounds in the Grand Canyon, Yosemite and Sequoia-Kings Canyon between July and September. Reservations are often necessary for the lesser known state parks, particularly those along the California coast.

People pressure on the park system has also made it necessary to limit the number of persons permitted to enter ecologically fragile areas. A back country or wilderness permit must be obtained in advance. So, before you plan a primitive camping trip be sure to contact the appropriate park or forest authority for full, current information. Generally, permits are good for a single trip at a specified time (a separate permit is required for each trip you take) and are issued free. A reservation system has been set up enabling back-country hikers to pre-arrange a firm trail date. To obtain your, write to the Chief Ranger's office of the appropriate park. Provide alternative dates if you can.

National holiday weekends and the summer school vacation period from Memorial Day (May 31) to Labor Day (September 3) see the heaviest use of the parks. During March, April, September and October the crowds thin out, increasing again around Christmas and for the ski season in those parks which have winter sports facilities. In the desert regions of southern California and southern Arizona, the peak season is between December and February.

Campgrounds Campgrounds in the National Park Service, Forest Service and state park systems may be generally categorized as "developed" and "undeveloped". At developed sites expect to find flush toilets, showers, laundries, stores, parking, trailer hookups, fireplaces, table-and-bench combinations for outdoor meals – and your campsite. Some of the larger parks, like Grand Canyon and Mesa Verde, boast lodges, restaurants, coffee shops, stables, bicycle rentals and tour operations. In most, rangers conduct outdoor programs which include nature walks and campfire talks.

Facilities at undeveloped campgrounds are limited indeed. Water, chemical toilets, and a limited number of fireplaces and tables are the norm, though this does not always hold true in the remoter areas. Check the amenities against your requirements before heading for the distant hills: you may have to pack in everything you need.

Increasing demand for campsites has made it necessary to limit the number of days you may occupy a site in certain parks during peak seasons.

Costs Entrance fees are charged by the National Park Service and most state parks. If you plan to visit a number of national parks, it may be worth investing in a Golden Eagle Passport for $10, good for the calendar year in which it is issued and entitling the holder in a private vehicle to free entry to all areas of the NPS system where entry fees are charged. The pass *does not* apply to camping or other use fees, nor to the charges of the private concessionaires or other contractors operating within the parks.

Information Up-to-date information on the national parks in the West may be obtained by writing to the Regional Offices listed overleaf.

Rocky Mountain Regional Office, 655 Parfet, PO Box 25287, Denver, CO 80225 (tel (303) 234-3095).
Colorado, Utah, Montana, North and South Dakota, Wyoming.
Southwest Regional Office, PO Box 728, Santa Fe, NM 87501 (tel (505) 988-6340).
New Mexico, northeast corner of Arizona, Arkansas, Louisiana, Texas, Oklahoma.
Western Regional Office, Fort Mason, Building 201, San Francisco, CA 94123 (tel (415) 556-4122).
California, Nevada, most of Arizona, Hawaii.
Pacific Northwest Regional Office, Westin Building, Room 1920, Seattle, WA 98121 (tel (206) 442-4830).
Oregon, Washington, Idaho, Alaska.

Write to the field offices of the US Forest service about the National Forests and Wilderness Areas under their supervision. Maps of these areas are available at $1 each.
California Region, 630 Sansome St, San Francisco, CA 94111 (tel (415) 556-0122).
California.
Intermountain Region, 324 25th St, Ogden, UT 84401 (tel (801) 625-5182).
Idaho, Nevada, Utah, Wyoming.
Pacific Northwest Region, 319 SW Pine St, PO Box 3623, Portland, op 97208 (tel (503) 221-2877).
Oregon, Washington.
Rocky Mountain Region, 11177 W 8th Avenue, Box 25127, Lakewood, CA 80225 (tel (303) 234-4185).
Colorado, Nebraska, South Dakota, Wyoming.
Southwestern Region, 517 Gold Avenue SW, Albuquerque, NM 87102 (tel (505) 766-2444).
Arizona, New Mexico.

Reservations Presently advance reservations for certain campsites in Yosemite, Grand Canyon and Sequoia-Kings Canyon National Parks may be made in person at Ticketron sales terminals or by writing to Ticketron Reservation Office, PO Box 2715, San Francisco, CA 94126. Mail requests should be received by Ticketron at least two weeks in advance. They do not accept reservations by phone. You may also make reservations in person at the parks on the system and at National Park Service offices in San Francisco, Los Angeles, Phoenix, Denver, Atlanta and Philadelphia. As many campgrounds are filled long in advance, it's advisable to indicate alternate campgrounds and dates. Reservations may be made up to eight weeks ahead.

Ticketron also handles campsite reservations for certain US Forest Service campgrounds and for California state parks. These may be reserved up to eight weeks in advance. (Note that Ticketron's mailing address for Forest Service campground reservations is Ticketron Reservation Office, PO Box 26430, San Francisco, CA 94121). Certain Oregon and Washington State Parks accept reservations by mail only. Contact the appropriate agency at the address given above.

Private Campgrounds Several hundred privately-owned campgrounds add to your camping options throughout the West. Facilities range from simply a pleasant site on which to doss down for the night to comparatively luxurious complexes similar to the developed campgrounds of the publicly-owned systems. Fees are modest rarely exceeding $6 a night; you may be charged an additional fee for electricity, water, and sewer hookup. Most private campgrounds accept reservations.

Authoritative directories are Woodall's *Campground Directory* and AAA's *regional camping handbooks* (available to members only). Rand McNally covers the entire country with its *Campground & Trailer Park Guide*. All are updated annually. A name to remember as you are tooling along the freeways is KOA – Kampgrounds of America – a nationwide franchise that caters mainly to the needs of the RV (recreational vehicle) camper.

Caring for the Wild Places More than 350 million people are expected to visit the national parks alone during 1984. Though we all care about the impact of our visits, the sheer volume of our numbers threatens the wilderness with destruction. Park rules and regulations (which are suprisingly few) are therefore in our own best interests – please observe them. Stick to the trails. Pack out your trash. Think ecologically. The ideal wilderness traveler 'takes nothing but memories, leaves nothing but footprints.'

Bears, Bugs and other Beasts Observing wildlife in its natural habitat is one of the highlights of the wilderness experience; however, close encounters of any kind are not recommended. Please don't feed those cute bears hanging around for handouts; tragedy has resulted. Keep your food supplies outside your tent at night, preferably hanging 20 feet above ground from the limb of a tree. Lock them in the boot of your car if you don't mind risking scratches on the paint job.

Rattlesnakes are shy critters and the odds are against your encountering one. Nevertheless, it's wise to walk warily through long grass and be familiar with the latest first aid measures for snake bite. Bang your boots together before donning them in scorpion country; you may prevent an other-worldly experience. And don't forget that rabies is widespread in the West and Southwest, so even a nip from a chipmunk or a ground squirrel is potentially hazardous.

Insects are rarely a problem. The black widow is the one poisonous spider worth learning to identify. Ticks, however, are a pest in the California grasslands during spring and summer.

Horseback Trips
The romantic, traditional way to experience the West's great outdoors is to pack into the wilderness on horseback. There's no need to be an experienced rider for those sure-footed, wise and gentle creatures that will carry you over the trails are unflappable professionals, well-accustomed to the ways of novices. However, if you are really unsure of your seat, it is always possible to arrange a couple of day's riding lessons at the outfitter's lodge before setting out.

Most convenient of pack trip options is the *all inclusive* pack trip, usually two, six to eight, or 14 days long. You can, of course, arrange for longer periods. The outfitter provides camping equipment, food and pack and riding horses; wranglers take care of the cooking and packing, look after the stock and set up camp. All you do is bring a sleeping bag (and even that may be hired) and your personal gear in your own duffel bag, usually limited to 30 lbs. Rates are in the neighbourhood of $65 per person per day.

Another option is the *spot packing* trip. Here you furnish the camping equipment and food while the outfitter provides pack animals and a guide who will take you to your campsite and return to take you out again. For an additional fee, supplies and mail can be brought to you at intervals.

A *continuous hire* arrangement leaves all the organizing to you. The outfitter provides a guide and pack animals for the entire trip. You determine the length of stay in camps, supply food for your party and the guide – and provide the camping equipment. Rates are the same as spot packing.

To find an outfitter, contact:

High Sierra Packers Association, PO Box 123, Madera, CA 93637.

Professional Guides & Outfitters Association of New Mexico, Inc, Dode Hershey, President, PO Box 275, Pecos, NM 87552.

Wilderness Pack Trips, Box 71, Rogue River, OR 97537.

Float Trips

River running trips are a particularly satisfying way of coming to know the wilderness, combining the exhilaration of white water adventuring with onshore camping and time for independent exploration. More than 200 outfitters in the West offer package trips ranging from one-day runs to two week expeditions aboard craft as diverse as two-person doreys, rubber rafts, powered pontoon rigs, kayaks and canoes. Longer custom-designed trips may also be arranged.

The pace is unhurried, with stops for swimming, photography and hiking and camp is usually set up early – on average, you're on the water two to three hours at a stretch for six to eight hours per day. And there are no chores to worry about for boat crews take care of the cooking, camping and clean-up. Trips are limited in size, usually to 20 persons. As to safety, there is always an element of risk, of course, but on the whole river running with professional outfitters is not a dangerous sport. There is no upper age limit for participants; you should, however, be reasonably agile and healthy and, while the ability to swim is not required (everyone wears a Coast Guard approved life jacket on the water), it is recommended.

Outfitters generally provide all equipment and food; you bring only your personal duffel and camping gear. There is a weight limit, usually 35 lbs, on most trips. Camping gear may be rented for about $30 per person.

Costs currently run between $50 and $110 day per person, reflecting the degree of comfort built into the river experience. Some outfitters, as one wit observed, do everything but tuck you in at night, including such elegances as caviar, wine and cots. Do check whether or not transportation to and from the river is included: you could wind up with a ticklish transportation problem on your hands.

Inexpensive travel insurance covering baggage, accident and trip cancellation can usually be arranged through the outfitter.

Finding an Outfitter In addition to the guides and outfitters mentioned through the text, you may want to obtain the Western River Guides Association's free directory of member firms offering trips on more than 30 rivers in 10 Western States. Write to Western River Guides Association, Inc, 994 Denver, Salt Lake City, UT 84111; tel (801) 355-3388. Two non-profit organisations offering the river experience are the American River Touring Association, 1307 Harrison St, Oakland, CA 94612 and the Sierra Club Outing Department, 530 Bush St, San Francisco, CA 94108.

Houseboating

No matter what time of year you arrive, houseboating will be in season in California and the Southwest. Most popular areas are the mountain-ringed lakes of Whiskeytown-

Shasta-Trinity National Recreation Area (Lake Shasta and Trinity Lake) in northern California, the Delta Country between San Francisco and Sacramento, and stretches of the Colorado River, which has been dammed to form a series of lakes from Glen Canyon to the Gulf of California.

Lake Shasta and **Trinity Lake,** described in more detail elsewhere in this guide, are located about 235 miles north of San Francisco, near Redding. You can get to Redding by bus, air, or rail; some houseboat firms provide transportation to your boat.

The Cascade Range forms a distant backdrop for Lake Shasta, at 30,000 acres the largest impounded body of water in the state. Fishing is good year-round and so are water skiing conditions. In summer, temperatures hover in the 90°s during the day, dropping to the 70°s at night. Spring and autumn are cooler; in winter, daytime temperatures are in the 50°s and nights are chilly.

Trinity Lake, officially known as Clair Engle Lake, lies approximately 60 miles northwest of Redding, dominated by the dramatic Trinity Alps. About half the size of Lake Shasta, Trinity has a similar climate and also offers excellent fishing and water skiing.

For information on houseboat firms in this area, write to *Shasta-Cascade Wonderland Association*, PO Box 1988, Redding, CA 96001; tel (916) 243-2643.

The **Delta Country**, where the San Joaquin and the Sacramento Rivers converge in a labyrinthine series of waterways extending over 740,000 acres of low-lying land below Sacramento, gives those familiar with The Netherlands a curious sense of *deja vu*. Here the sky seems a vast bowl set over a limitless expanse of green, patterned with dykes – but with oaks and eucalyptus rather than willows, and weathered frame houses rather than squat brick farms. The Delta is rich in interesting old communities, including the only town in California built by the Chinese, Locke. Summer days are hot in this flat country, ranging between 60° and 90°. During the rest of the year it's cooler, between 45° and 75°, with some crisp days and morning and evening fog during the fall and winter months.

There are more than a hundred boating marinas scattered about the Delta. An excellent illustrated guide, providing a history and background of the region as well as charts, anchorage descriptions and a directory of rental agencies, is *Cruising the California Delta*, published by Aztez Corporation and distributed by Elsevier-Dutton. Other souces of information are:

Houseboat Owners Association, Route 1, Box 14, Antioch, CA 94509.

Greater Stockton Chamber of Commerce, 1105 N El Dorado, Stockton CA 95202; tel (209) 466-7066.

The stark beauty of the desert is the setting for houseboating on the **Colorado River** where dams have formed four great lakes that are popular watersports centers all year. Throughout the region summer daytime temperatures hover around the hundred mark and may reach 115 to 120° highs; evenings are mild to cool at the higher elevations. Winter ranges from the 40°s to the high 60°s, rarely freezing.

Northeast of the Grand Canyon is 186-mile-long **Lake Powell**, created by the damming of Glen Canyon. Here, some 3700 feet above sea level, you can explore hundreds of colourful and fjord-like side canyons, surrounded by mountain ranges. Fishing is good and boating can be varied by hiking the wilderness country surrounding the lake.

For information about the area and National Park Service facilities, write to the Superintendent, Glen Canyon National Recreation Area, Box 1507, Page, AZ 86040. Another source is the Page-Lake Powell Chamber of Commerce, PO Box 727, Page, AZ 86040; tel (602) 645-2741.

Lake Mead National Recreation Area, which extends about 177 miles along the Colorado from the Grand Canyon to a point 67 miles below Hoover Dam, includes two spectacular boating lakes, Lake Mead and Lake Mohave. **Lake Mead** is one of the largest man-made lakes in the world and, like Lake Powell, offers dramatic canyons to be explored. There's also the excitement of entering an unsurveyed portion of the Grand Canyon. **Lake Mohave** stretches for 65 miles from Davis Dam to Hoover Dam, confined by hills or sheer canyon walls for its entire length. Complete information on the area may be obtained from the Superintendant, Lake Mead National Recreational Area, 601 Nevada Highway, Boulder City, NV 98005.

Lake Havasu is the fourth major watersports area, located on the Arizona-California border south of I-40. Only three miles wide, this 46-mile-long lake leads to the bays and side canyons of Mohave Canyon, accessible only by water. Old London Bridge, transported block by block from the Thames in 1968, now stands on the lake at Lake Havasu City. For information on houseboat rentals and other attractions, contact Lake Havasu Area Chamber of Commerce, 2074 McCulloch Boulevard, Lake Havasu City, AZ 86403; tel (602) 855-4115. For a detailed description of the Colorado River recreation areas, see Colorado River Country under Arizona.

Houseboats These vary in size from about 25 to 50 feet long. Generally they are equipped with the essentials, including a full kitchen with cooking utensils. You provide bed linen, towels and food – though some agencies now include bedding and linen. All agencies will provide you with a check list of items to bring along.

The largest houseboats rent for around $1275 a week in peak season; however they sleep up to 10 persons, so the weekly per capita cost can be attractive indeed. Off-season discounts of up to 30% are customary. In the Southwest and the California Delta Country you can even hire a drive-on powered barge for your motor home. For budgeting purposes, estimate $120 for the first day and $50 each successive day, or $120 a week in peak season for these craft. Off season, rates can drop as much as $120 a week.

Expect to be asked for a deposit against breakages and cleaning. Insurance – property damage, special public liability and comprehensive – is sometimes required and may be included in the rental charge. Do check that out.

Ranch Vacations

Vacationing on a ranch offers the Old West experience minus the hardships and if you're really aching to participate in workaday chores a la 'Bonanza' there are farms and ranches where you may share in everything from milking to rounding up the dogies and baling hay. Most are located a considerable distance from public transportation facilities; arrangements can be made for pick-up at nearby bus, rail or air terminals.

Dude ranches provide a pretty plush environment for their guests. Candlelight dinners, luxurious accommodation, heated swimming pools, tennis courts and an extensive program of activities such as horseback trips, cookouts, steer roping and square dancing are the norm here.

Most operate on the American Plan which includes three full meals a day, participation in planned activities and the use of most facilities. In the medium price range, expect a comfortable room with private bath and maid service for between $200 to $275 per person per week. More luxurious establishments charge between $300 and $400 weekly.

Working ranches generally offer a simpler style of accommodation, but you can become part of the family and enjoy 'hands on' training in a host of new skills if you wish. Rates are less expensive, about $170 to $200 American Plan per person per week; horseback riding is not always included.

Off season and children's rates are available.

Peak Periods July and August are high season for northern and mountain ranches, January and February for those in desert areas. Reservations should be made several months in advance.

Finding Out About Ranch Vacations Best sources to supplement our suggestions are the tourism departments of the States of Arizona and New Mexico where dude ranching is a specialty. Their addresses:

State of Arizona Office of Tourism, 1700 West Washington, Room 501, Phoenix AZ 85007.

New Mexico Department of Development, Tourist Division, Bataan Memorial Building, Santa Fe, NM 87503.

Farm, Ranch & Country Vacations, 36 E 57th St, New York, NY 10022, publishes a comprehensive guidebook to guest ranches throughout the US.

THE AMERICAN WAY

FOOD

Although there are distinct regional styles, American cooking is basically 'no-nonsense' meat and potatoes, with salad on the side and coffee as lubricant. Throughout the country you'll find hamburgers and hot dogs, fried chicken, steak and baked potatoes, super-sized sandwiches, icecream and apple pie are the common denominators of restaurant menus. Where Mexican influence is strong, in Southern California and the Southwestern states, burritos, tacos and chilis are equally ubiquitous. Salads reach the highest levels of imaginative creativity in California.

Eating establishments vary widely in price and ambience and over-generous servings are the norm. Don't be embarrassed to ask for a 'doggy-bag' to take away your leftovers; America invented the concept and it's accepted practice in even the most elegant restaurants.

Breakfast is generally served from 7 to 10 am, lunch from 11 am to 2.30 pm and dinner from 5.30 to 10 pm; the 24-hour lifestyle, however, is reflected in the business hours of many restaurants. Most offer table d'hote and a la carte menus with daily specials. Particularly in San Francisco, you'll come upon small restaurants offering family-style dining; that means a pre-set menu, often with meals served at set hours only. And you share tables – one good way to meet the Americans. *Vin ordinaire* is normally included in the price of the meal.

A sales tax will always be added to the bill, but no service charge. You are expected to calculate the tip, normally 15% of the cost of the meal before tax is added.

For travelers in a hurry, a good rule of thumb is that fine fare will rarely be found near bus and rail terminals. Most large hotels have restaurants, and more often than not, a 24-hour coffee shop serving the basics. Fast food outlets providing on-the-premises or take-out light meals abound – 'Big Mac' is everywhere, but not unchallenged. Other good sources of take-out meals are delicatessens and small ethnic restaurants. Drugstores often contain a lunch counter or a snack-and-beverages self-serve center.

Having given the world the fast food franchises, Americans have rediscovered the delights of ethnic cuisines, gourmet cooking and dining as entertainment. Los Angeles, San Francisco and Seattle offer a veritable gazeteer of international cooking; you will also find the growing interest in healthful eating reflected in the number of natural food restaurants in the big cities where the emphasis is on the nutritive value of the ingredients.

The choice of restaurants is so wide that we can only list a few of the possibilities in this guide. We also recommend authoritative dining guides in the Places to Eat sections for Los Angeles, San Francisco, San Diego and Palm Springs; these books profile restaurants that offer good food at a reasonable price in attractive surroundings.

A word about the categories Expensive, Moderate and Budget used in describing the restaurants we have included. These are based on the cost of the main dinner, entree, with soup or salad included, but excluding dessert, wine, liquor and tips. Budget to $7; Moderate $7 to $14; Expensive over $14.

DRINK

California produces outstanding wines of every variety and good brandies. While grapes are grown throughout the state, the most famous wine districts lie just north of San Francisco, in Napa, Sonoma, and Mendocino counties. Try the red varietals produced from classic European grapes, such as Pinot Noir, or Cabernet Sauvignon. Fine whites and champagnes are also produced in the gravelly soils of the Livermore Valley east of San Francisco. Unique to California is Zinfandel, a red wine with a characteristic 'bramble' aroma. On average, prices for premium wines start around $6.95 a bottle. You can pick up very good jug wine for about $4 a half gallon.

Other western states are entering the wine picture. The Yakima Valley vineyards in Washington produce some notable cabernets, Oregon vintners have about 500 acres under cultivation, and New Mexico, historically the first western state to produce wine (early in the 17th century), has a few vineyards near Bernalillo and in the south. Good companions for oenophiles with some serious tasting on their minds are Leon D Adams' *The Wines of America* (Houghton Mifflin) and Sunset's *California Wine Country*.

Most American beers are light lagers, slightly on the sweet side and served icy cold. Draught beer – beer on tap – costs less than bottled beer. Leading brand names among beers brewed in the West are Coors, Olympia and Rainier, though of course, you'll find all the great Midwestern brews as well.

Drinking Throughout the country the way, means, hours and age when you may purchase and consume alcoholic beverages are regulated by state law and often by local ordinance as well. As a result you'll find places where you may only purchase your booze at the state liquor store, must sit down to drink or remain parched if you hit a 'dry' patch where Prohibition attitudes still obtain. Nevertheless, the average drinking day is a long one; bars usually stay open until at least midnight, sometimes for 23 hours. Keep an eye peeled for 'happy hour' signs – during those late afternoon periods prices are reduced to generate flow. And just one cautionary note; although Women's Lib has knocked down traditional barriers, in some settings discretion may still be the better part of valor as regards drinking unescorted.

In the states covered by this guide you must be 21 years of age to buy or imbibe alcohol, save in Arizona where the legal age is 19 years. If you look on the young side, you may be asked to offer proof of legal age and refused service if you cannot do so. Minors may not enter a bar but are allowed to enter licensed restaurants for meals.

The law is tough with those who drive under the influence of alcohol and casts a jaundiced eye on its presence in an automobile. In California, for example, an opened bottle may not be within reach of the driver. Keep the stuff safely locked away in the trunk.

GAMBLING

State laws regulate gambling as strictly as drinking. Nevada offers unlimited facilities for going broke, but even there you must be 21 years old to enter a casino or operate a one-armed bandit. Elsewhere no lawful opportunities exist save for Pari-mutuel betting at horse and dog racing tracks.

SHOPPING

The basic American shopping day runs from 9.30 am to 5.30 pm, though large downtown department stores often remain open until 9 pm several days a week and a few are open on Sundays from noon until 5 pm. Food supermarkets usually open their doors at 8.30 am and operate until 9 pm daily; some provide 24-hour service. Drug stores, which are in effect small department stores with a pharmacy thrown in for good measure have similar hours and in the larger centres there is always one with a pharmacist on duty until midnight. Additionally, you can count on small entrepreneurs, operators of 'ma & pa' corner grocery stores, to be open rather earlier and rather later than the norm. They usually stock a little of every essential, from toothpaste and bandaids to cold cuts, soft drinks, wine and spirits and fruit and vegetables.

Comparative shopping really pays dividends in the Land of Opportunity, especially if you are intent on purchasing records, photographic, recording or electronic equipment, clothing or a car. Discount and chain stores often offer substantial reductions. And look into secondhand stores associated with charitable associations – bargains in an astonishing variety of wares, from books to designer clothing.

Browse street fairs and flea markets as well as the galleries for works of American artists and craftspeople. You can pick up unusual handcrafted jewellery, leather and wooden goods at moderate prices. In the Southwest particularly you will be exposed to the artistry of the Indians. Especially prized are Pueblo pottery, Navajo weaving, Hopi basketry and Kachina dolls, and turquoise and silver jewellery created by Zuni, Hopi and Navajo silversmiths. Prices run high on the whole. And the buyer should always beware for the popularity of Indian crafts attracts imitation and fakery. Obtain advice: museums or the Chamber of Commerce in the community where you're shopping are excellent sources. New Mexico Magazine's modestly priced *The Indian Arts of New Mexico* Volumes I and II, are a mine of authoritative information.

MEETING THE AMERICANS

One of the most overworked phrases in the travel writer's armament is 'the natives are friendly'. In the United States none other will do. The Americans are surely the most hospitable and sociable of peoples and their generosity to strangers in need of guidance and assistance is proverbial. They even organise it. Across the country there are some 90 community member organisations of the *National Council for Community Services to International Visitors* (COSERV) whose main purpose is to help foreign visitors learn about America and the Americans. All COSERV affiliates extend a warm welcome and a helping hand, but the services provided by individual organisations aren't identical, ranging from introductions to members who share your interests or organising a visit to a factory to finding overnight accommodation for you in a member's home. Some even arrange sightseeing tours in cars driven by members. COSERV services for the most part are free; where charges must be made for accomodation and tours, the cost is usually quite low.

If you enjoy the great outdoors, you can meet your American counterpart by getting in touch with the local branches of two great national conservation associations, the *Sierra Club* and the *National Audubon Society*. Both welcome visitors on their scheduled outings.

USEFUL INFORMATION

COMMUNICATIONS

Postal Services Post Offices are open from 8.30 am until 5 pm, Monday through Friday and usually from 8.30 until noon on Saturday (the exceptions are sub-offices in metropolitan areas). Some main post offices and airport mail facilities remain open later – enquire locally. Additionally, most main post office lobbies contain scales, stamp vending machines and mail drops and rates are posted on the walls, enabling you to do it yourself after hours.

Express mail with guaranteed delivery within 24 hours (or your money back) to certain points in the US is available. The fee is fairly stiff.

Telephones The Bell Telephone System is very efficient, providing a level of service rarely encountered elsewhere in the world. The basic charge for a three-minute local call from a public telephone ranges from 10c in California to 25c in Oregon and Washington. Have a generous supply of dimes and quarters handy if you use a public call box for *toll* (within the area but outside the local zone) and *long distance* (outside the area) calls. Before calling distance to a hotel or business, determine whether it has an '800' (Wats, Zenith or Enterprise) number: these enable you to make your call free of charge. To find out, simply dial 800-555-1212.

Public telephone boxes all contain clear dialing instructions. Directories have usually been ripped off, so to obtain a phone number dial the appropriate information number listed below.

Local	411
Long Distance	Area Code + 555-1212
Overseas	O for Operator

If you have difficulty in locating a public telephone, try the lobbies of hotels, bars, or restaurants, restrooms in large department stores, or a drugstore. There is always a sign outside.

Calls placed from hotel rooms are usually subject to a surcharge imposed by the hotel. This can be substantial on a long distance call.

Telegrams-Telex Services Cables, internal telegram and telex services are provided by Western Union through their offices or by telephone. Should you phone from your hotel, the cost of the wire is charged to your account and subject to a surcharge. Telex service is also available in the major hotels.

MONEY

The US monetary unit is, of course, the dollar, divided into 100 cents. Coins are the cent (or penny); 5 cents (nickel); 10 cents (dime); 25 cents (quarter or 'two bits'); 50 cents; and the infrequently-encountered silver dollar. Notes are issued for $1, $2, $5,

$10, $20, $50 and $100. As all paper money is the same size and the same color (green, hence 'greenbacks'), it's worth acquiring the habit of calling the denominations of larger bills when making payment.

Credit Cards Carrying large sums in cash is neither recommended nor necessary in the land of the credit card. Most widely accepted cards are: American Express, VISA, Master Charge, Diners and Carte Blanche. Recognition of foreign cards is growing; you should have no difficulty with Baclaycard in the big cities, but you could run into wide-eyed disbelief elsewhere.

Checks Personal checks drawn on a foreign bank are almost impossible to negotiate, with or without identification. Travelers checks in dollar denominations, however, are every bit as good as cash, provided you have identification.

Identification A word about 'identification'. It is a tribute to the skill of America's bad-check artists that the number of proofs of identity required before a check is accepted has grown to ludicrous proportions. The standard unit of recognition is a valid driver's license. If you do not possess one, your passport should suffice; don't be surprised, though, if you encounter resistance and a request for an internationally known credit card as well. The reason simply is that merchants have found credit card organisations more helpful than governments in tracking down malefactors.

Banking Hours Banks are normally open Monday through Friday from 10 am to 3 pm and closed on Saturdays, Sundays, and state and national holidays. There is a growing trend toward a 9.30 to 4.30 banking day in the larger cities, with some staying open till 6 pm on Fridays.

Travelers checks can also be exchanged for US currency in foreign exchange offices and in the larger hotels as well as banks and savings and loan institutions.

ELECTRICITY
110 to 115 Volts, 60 cycles AC; plugs have two flat pins. If you plan to bring your electrical appliances and the voltage and prongs used in your country are differerent from those of the US. You should pack both a transformer and an adapter.

EMERGENCY MEDICAL SERVICES
The United States has no national medical program covering its citizens, let alone foreign nationals, and health care services are expensive. An example: recently an Australian citizen requiring two days in hospital for the removal of a cyst was asked to deposit $650 before being admitted. Adequate health insurance covering your time in the country is therefore recommended.

First aid and medical treatment can be obtained in hospital emergency rooms; a doctor is always on duty. Additionally the phone book Yellow Pages lists both medical and dental care referral services. Drugstores post a list of pharmacies open at night and on Sundays.

In any emergency you can obtain prompt assistance by dialing 'O' for operator. Ambulance, fire or police services may also be obtained by dialing direct: numbers are listed on the inside front cover of the telephone directory. All personnel are trained to administer first aid.

INFORMATION SERVICES

Convention and Visitors Bureaus and Chambers of Commerce throughout the country are the traveler's main source of information and assistance. Turn to them for the definitive word on accommodation, sightseeing attractions, restaurants, maps and touring within their areas. Their addresses and telephone numbers are listed in the white pages of the local telephone directory.

HATA Reservations HATA (Hotel, auto, tour, air) of Madison, Wisconsin, is a private company you should know about. It provides free information and reservations services for accommodation, car rentals, tours and airlines throughout the world at no cost to the consumer. Multi-lingual operators are on duty seven days a week from 7.30 am until 10.30 pm Central Time – all you do is dial toll-free 800-356-8392 for assistance, or write to them at PO Box 9428, Madison, Wisconsin 53715.

Highway & Weather Conditions Up-to-the-minute recorded information on highway conditions and weather reports may be obtained simply by dialing the local numbers listed in the directory.

Libraries In addition to the sources listed in this guide, you will find reference departments in American libraries gold mines of information and their librarians extraordinarily helpful in making the best use of them. All contain local directories, telephone books, area guide books, and local histories. Library notice boards will clue you in to a fascinating array of community happenings.

PUBLIC HOLIDAYS

Banks, government and business offices close on national and state holidays. Although the majority of shops close also, large department stores are usually open. Easter in the US is observed only on Easter Sunday – no bank holiday Monday here. National holidays are:

New Year's Day	January 1
Washington's Birthday	February 22*
Memorial Day	May 30*
Independence Day	July 4
Labor Day	September 3*
Veterans' Day	November 11
Thanksgiving Day	November 22
Christmas Day	December 25

*usually observed the preceding Monday

TIPPING

The practice of adding a comprehensive service charge to hotel, bar and restaurant bills is rarely encountered in the United States. As the art of tipping can be confusing, here are a few guidelines.

Airport bus baggage loader	None
Barber	$1 to $2
Bartender	10 to 15%
Beauty parlor staff	15 to 20%
Bell boy	50c per bag
Car park attendant	None

Valet car parking (hotels, restaurants)	$1
Cocktail waitress	10 to 15%
Doorman (hotels, restaurants)	$1
Hatcheck (wardrobe attendant)	50c for each garment
Maitre d'	Not required unless you wish to influence him
Restroom attendant	50c
Room service waiter	10 to 15% (never less than 25c)
Service station attendant	None
Sightseeing guide/driver	$1 minimum
Skycap (porter)	50c per bag
Taxi driver	15% of meter total (never less than 50c)
Theater usher	None
Waiter, waitress	15 to 20%

Getting There & Getting Around

Your way of getting to the the west and getting around there depends, of course, on where you're starting from, personal preferences, your travel budget and your travel plans. In this era of rapidly escalating transportation costs and world-wide inflation, your best course in our opinion is to enlist the aid of a top-notch travel agent to determine the way that's best for you. Travel agent's services cost nothing unless your plans necessitate expenses beyond those normally required to make the necessary reservations. Their hard-won expertise comes free. Your main options are outlined below.

AIR
Main gateway cities on the West Coast are Los Angeles, San Francisco and Seattle, served by direct flights from Australia, New Zealand, the Orient and Europe. Hawaii's gateway is Honolulu, on the routes of Air New Zealand, Qantas, Continental and Pan American between Australia and New Zealand and the West Coast. San Diego is linked to Honolulu by Continental, Western and United.

Domestic airlines connect you to most American cities from these points, including such major tourist destinations as the Grand Canyon (Flagstaff), Reno, Las Vegas, Lake Tahoe, Santa Fe (Albuquerque), Phoenix, Tucson and Santa Barbara.

Caught between the frying pan of deregulation and the fire of soaring fuel prices, few in the travel industry care to suggest what the cost of air travel to and within the United States will be tomorrow, let alone a few weeks hence. Fares change – usually upward – nearly every day. Regulations governing excursion fares seem to change almost as frequently. And increased competition between the airlines can mean very different fares over a given route. Comparative shopping is now the essence of the game and the following samples of options are given only as an indication of what's available as we go to publication.

Standby
The cheapest way to go if you don't mind hanging around airports. Vacant seats on flights are filled at boarding time by standby passengers on a first-come, first-served basis. Tickets are good for one year from the date of commencement of travel. Sorry, Down Under: standby fares are not available in your part of the world.

APEX (Advance Purchase Excursion Fare)
This discount fare is offered on a limited number of seats per flight. If you are flying from Britain, your ticket is valid for a minimum stay of seven days and a maximum stay of 180 days; additionally, you must make your reservation and pay for your ticket 21 days prior to departure.

There is no minimum-maximum requirement in Australia or New Zealand. Reservations and payment must be made 45 days in advance; 25% of the fare is non-refundable if you don't travel on the date and flight booked, *but* you have the option of changing your return date 30 days beforehand without penalty.

Economy Class
Good for one year from date of purchase, the standard (interline) economy fare permits

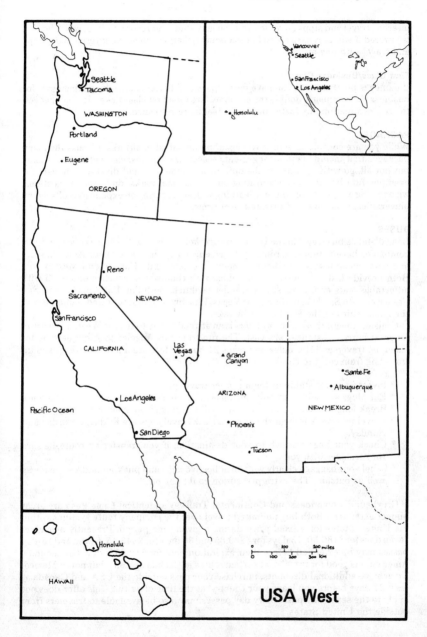

USA West

interline travel and stops en route. And you may alter your reservations at will. The cost is lowered if you purchase an on line economy ticket: you make no intermediate stops and travel with one airline only.

First Class/Business Class

If money is no object you can have more space and better service by paying more for business class or nearly double the economy fare for a first class ticket. It won't get you to your destination any faster but you'll feel more refreshed.

PACKAGES

While you are consulting your travel agent on the latest in airfares, discuss the many packages that include land arrangements – accommodations, car rentals, etc. Some, but not all, go with the airfare: the options are numerous and diverse. You can, for example, find bus tours concentrating on the national parks, dude ranch vacations, wine tasting weekends, or combine learning with adventuring on expeditions offered by universities, museums and private travel firms.

BUSES

Long distance bus travel in the US means *Greyhound* and *Continental Trailways*. Both companies have nationwide route systems, encompassing every major American city and many small towns. Greyhound's network extends into Canada and Mexico, too. Both provide fast scheduled service aboard air-conditioned coaches equipped with adjustable seats and, in most cases, toilet facilities. Both link Los Angeles and San Francisco with San Diego, Reno, Las Vegas, Phoenix, Albuquerque and Santa Fe, and the major cities of the Pacific Northwest.

Cruising aboard these freeway liners is an attractive way to see the West, if you are in no great hurry – distances are vast. The run from Los Angeles to Albuquerque, for example, traverses 1150 miles and takes 21 hours. Here are a few tips we picked up travelling from coast to coast.

* Invest in an inflatable or foam rubber travel pillow.
* Ear plugs are helpful in reducing noise; a sleep mask obliterates headlight glare.
* Break long distance journeys with a solid night's sleep every other day.
* Travel mid-week to beat the crowds. Peak travel days are Friday, Saturday and Sunday.
* Check your bags through to your destination; if you transfer en route, be sure they transfer with you.
* Label your baggage clearly with an adhestive tag – and put your address inside as well as outside. The extra precaution could pay off.

Greyhound's **Ameripass** and Continental Trailway's identical **Eagle Pass** are great budget extenders. Both buy unlimited travel over the company route systems within the United States for a fixed price during a given time period. Presently available: seven days for $186.50, 15 days for $239.85 and 30 days for $346.45. Seven and 15-day passes may be extended before their expiration date for $10.65 a day. Greyhound's Ameripass is good for travel over certain routes in Canada as well – but not in Mexico. To achieve additional discounts, purchase your pass outside the USA and Canada at least 21 days before you leave your country; at the time of writing, this offer does not apply to the seven day pass. Sixty day passes may also be available to travelers from outside the United States.

CAR RENTAL

Renting a car is simplicity itself if you are over 21 and hold a valid driver's license from your country (or an International Driver's Licence) and an internationally recognized credit card such as VISA, American Express or Master Charge.

As the car rental situation is getting more and more competitive every day, you can save money by looking beyond the world-wide 'Big Two', Avis and Hertz. National, Budget Rent-A-Car, Econo-Car and Thrifty Car are national operations offering good service and attractive promotions such as weekend rates, one-way vacation rates and special monthly rates. Rent-A-Wreck specialises in born again used cars. You will find local firms by thumbing through the Yellow Pages of the telephone directory.

Though all kinds of rental contracts are available, the *unlimited mileage* arrangement is probably the most economical for even a liberal free mileage allowance is rapidly consumed by the distances you inevitably cover in the US. And then those cents per mile start adding up. Specify a sub-compact if you require a small, gas-economical car.

Insurance is included in the rental cost. You will, however, have to pay a substantial portion of the repair costs of any damage to the car unless you take out a full collision waiver. Personal accident insurance is also available.

Drop-off charges are levied by some agencies when you turn in your car at a different point from where you hired it. Avis quotes $265 for cars picked up in San Francisco and relinquished in Santa Fe, New Mexico.

DISTANCES BY ROAD (Miles)

Los Angeles to		San Francisco to	
Grand Canyon	513	Big Sur	156
Las Vegas	287	Los Angeles	460
Palm Springs	119	Mendocino	125
Phoenix	390	Monterey	130
San Diego	137	Portland	672
San Francisco	460	Reno	233
Santa Barbara	95	Sacramento	97
Santa Fe	867	San Simeon	224
Sequoia Kings Canyon		Seattle	852
National Park	235	South Lake Tahoe	209
Tucson	506	Wine Country (Napa)	46
		Yosemite National Park	193

Freeways permit rapid travel and distances 'shrink' as a consequence. Driving time between Los Angeles and San Francisco averages 7¾ hours without stops.

If you are unfamiliar with the abbreviations SR and I used in conjunction with highway numbers throughout this guide, know that SR stands for State Route and I for Interstate Highway.

AUTOMOBILE ASSOCIATIONS

American Automobile Association With over 20 million members, 'Triple A' is the largest automobile association in the country. Membership benefits include: insurance (US and Mexican automobile, accident and homeowners); dividend benefits; 24 hour emergency road service nationwide/towing by AAA contract stations; garages for services and repairs at competitive prices; check cashing privileges; and comprehensive touring services. Their touring services are a powerful incentive for joining and include maps, tour and accommodation handbooks, camp and trailer directories, auto-license, registation and transfer, and traffic and citation aid services. AAA also has full-service travel agencies, arranges car rental and all reservations.

Membership dues are $26 a year, with a first enrollment fee of $12. Annual associate memberships are $9 for the member's spouse, $12 for dependent children between 16 and 20 years. A temporary membership card entitling you to all benefits is issued immediately. For further information write to American Automobile Association, 8111 Gate House Rd, Falls Church, VA 22047 or to the California State Automobile Association, 150 Van Ness Avenue, San Francisco, CA 94101.

National Automobile Club Although considerably smaller, the National Automobile Club provides similar benefits and services, with two notable exceptions: automobile and home-owner insurance. Mexican automobile insurance is available through NAC, however. Annual membership costs $40 for principals, $52 for principal spouse, and $12 for each dependent. Write to the home office at One Market Plaza, San Francisco, CA 94105 for particulars.

Reciprocal Services Membership in a national automobile association in your own country may entitle you to AAA or NAC services if there is a reciprocal agreement between the clubs. Reciprocity does not necessarily entitle you to all services provided by the American association, however – only to those specified in the agreement.

DRIVING TIPS

Though traffic regulations do vary from state to state, two basic points to remember are that you drive on the right hand side of the road and the maximum speed limit is 55 mph. The majority of Interstate highways have a minimum speed limit, too, which you should observe as carefully as the maximum. AAA's *Digest of Motor Laws* is a useful, authoritative source of more detailed information for the whole country; they can also supply you with copies of driving regulations in each state.

Motoring in the West can pose some challenges if you are unaccustomed to mountain and desert driving or negotiating ice and snow-bound roads. A few tips to bear in mind:

Desert Driving During the hottest period of the day, between 11 am and 4 pm, temperatures of 123°F in summer and over 100°F in spring and fall are common. Plan to avoid travelling at that time if you can. Experienced desert drivers recommend carrying a three-gallon container of water against emergencies, especially if you drive back roads. Tire pressure should be checked at intervals: if it increases abnormally, stop for a while to let the tires cool. Never release air as this will result in under-inflation when they are cool. Keep an eye on the temperature gauge, especially on long uphill grades, and take care not to overwork your engine.

Torrential rains and sandstorms occur frequently, often without warning. If you get caught, pull off the highway as far as you can and wait until the storm stops. Don't pick a dry wash, one of those broad depressions in the desert floor that looks as though it is an old river bed. It is, and you could find yourself engulfed by a flash flood after a rainstorm.

Mountain Driving It is important to remember that car engines lose power at high altitudes; keep your radiator full. If a vapor lock develops in the fuel system, place a damp cloth over the fuel pump for a few minutes. This will cool the fuel in the pump.

On long downgrades, don't ride the brakes. Use the engine by shifting down to second or low gear. And *always* keep as far to the right as possible. The most common cause of accidents on mountain roads is straying onto the wrong side of the dividing line. Should you encounter another vehicle on a steep road where neither can pass, the rule is that the vehicle facing downhill must back up until the vehicle going uphill can pass.

Winter Driving Safety in winter requires special precautions and techniques. Skidding is the chief hazard and the California State Automobile Association (AAA) has kindly permitted us to pass on these tips from their pamphlet *How to Negotiate Safely Through Ice & Snow:*

1 Keep speed well below dry road speed.
2 Keep car moving steadily.
3 Take curves cautiously.
4 Avoid turning or swerving suddenly.
5 Avoid applying brakes too suddenly or too hard.
6 Avoid accelerating or decelerating suddenly.

If you do get into a skid, *avoid braking.* Steer in the direction in which the rear end is skidding. As the car begins to straighten, straighten the front wheels also. When you are again moving in the desired direction, then either lightly pump your brakes to slow down slightly or gently accelerate to continue moving.

CSAA also recommends that you get the feel of the road. Find out just how slippery or slick the road is and adjust your speed accordingly. Follow at a safe distance for it takes from three to 12 times as far to stop on snow and ice as it does on a dry pavement. Fast up-and-down pumping is the best technique for stopping on snow or ice. Check periodically for an accumulation of slush under the fenders; if it freezes solid, you may not be able to steer. And be sure to have good tread and tire chains.

Emergencies If you have a breakdown, pull over off the highway and raise the hood of your car – it's the recognised distress signal. Although new cars are fitted with flashing emergency lights, keep a few flares handy too.

DRIVING IN MEXICO
Motorists visiting Mexico need a car permit which must be obtained at the border from the Mexican customs officials, and Mexican automobile insurance. Under Mexican laws persons involved in a traffic accident who are unable to produce an acceptable insurance policy may be held by authorities pending an investigation, determination of liability and payment of fines and damages. A number of agencies offer this insurance; our recommendation is that you obtain it from either the AAA or NAC.

If you are driving a rental car or a car registered in another person's name be sure you have proper documentation authorizing you to take the car into Mexico (in the case of someone else's car, a notarized letter will do). Should you be driving your own car, proof of car ownership – car registration or an authorised bill of sale – must be presented. Current plates and a valid driver's licence are also required.

RAIL
Passenger rail service connecting over 500 cities in the US is operated by Amtrak, a 23,000 mile network operated by the National Railroad Passenger Corporation. Trains are spacious and very comfortable; all are air-conditioned and seats are individually adjustable, most with leg-rests that ensure a very relaxed ride. As most trains are long distance, you can expect to find a bar, dining and lounge cars; special glass-domed 'sightseer' cars are in service on scenic routes.

Travelling coach is the basic way to go. At additional cost you can obtain private rooms, ranging from a single with private toilet and washing facilities to a family bedroom which can accommodate two adults and three children. Amtrak has even introduced a specially designed bedroom for the handicapped on its Superliner from Seattle to Chicago.

Scenic Routes Amtrak routes in the West are particularly scenic. The *Coast Starlight* from Seattle to Los Angeles traverses much of the loveliest scenery in southern Washington, Oregon and California. Between San Luis Obispo and Santa Barbara the train runs close to the Pacific most of the way. The *San Francisco Zephyr* follows the tracks of the pioneers between San Francisco and Chicago, crossing the Sierra Nevada via the 7018-foot Donner Pass; it stops at Truckee for Lake Tahoe, and at Reno and Sparks. You can get to Las Vegas from Los Angeles aboard the new *Desert Wind* which crosses the Mojave Desert. Seven trains a day presently link Los Angeles to San Diego along the coastal route. And then there's the *Southwest Limited* from Los Angeles to Chicago via Flagstaff and Albuquerque, which cuts across the Mojave to ascend the plateau south of the Grand Canyon. From Flagstaff to Lamy, New Mexico (where we got off) you enjoy magnificent vistas across the high desert, given scale by the abrupt upthrust of brilliantly tinted mesas. The run from Los Angeles to Lamy takes about 20 hours.

Costs Over competitive routes, rail fares are considerably lower than those charged by bus and airline companies. The one-way coach fare between Seattle and Los Angeles on the *Coast Starlight* (1400 miles) is $123; the additional cost for a private room starts at $47. Round trip excursion fares offer considerable savings; that same run costs $173 round trip coach, starting at $247 round trip with a private room. Family fares and Senior Citizen discounts are also available. To obtain a Senior Citizen discount, simply offer documentary proof of being 65 or older (a driver's licence, passport, birth certificate or similar official document is acceptable).

Amtrak's **USA Rail Pass**, available outside North America only, is similar to the widely-known Eurail pass in offering unlimited travel for specified periods of time. Current costs (for adults): seven days, $220; 14 days, $330; 21 days, $440; 30 days, $550.

Amtrak vacation packages are worth investigating. One, combining accommodation and car rental at 61 different locations across the country, may be particularly appealing to USA Rail Pass users.

Meals and snacks are reasonably priced, but do not expect *haute cuisine*. A substantial breakfast of eggs, coffee and rolls runs around $3; a dinner consisting of entree, salad, coffee, costs around $5.50. Drinks cost about the same as in the local bar – $1.50 for bottled beer, $2.00 on up for cocktails.

Reservations & Information Don't count on hopping aboard trains European-style. For one thing, service is nothing like as frequent. More importantly, after decades in the doldrums, rail travel in the US is once again regarded as a viable alternative to the automobile. Trains are often booked several weeks in advance. And, as routes, schedules and fare changes are anticipated in 1984, it may be well to be primed with the latest information. Your travel agent should know, or write to the National Railroad Passenger Corporation, 400 North Capitol St, NW, Washington, DC 20001. In the US, call the local toll-free 800 number. In Arizona, Oregon, Nevada, New Mexico, and Washington, it's 800-421-8320; in California call 800-648-3850 from all points save Los Angeles, which is not toll-free. There you dial (213) 624-0171.

California

California is the American Dream realised, a vast and lovely land of alluring climate, varied topography and distinctive lifestyle, looking back on a past full of adventure and color and toward a future that may set the pattern for the rest of the country. With more than 20 million inhabitants, it is the most populous state in the nation and the most cosmopolitan. Here, side by side with descendants of Indians who entered the country across the Bering Straits at least 25,000 years ago, you'll find people of every race and nationality on the globe living in remarkable harmony. Together they have built the state into the world's sixth most powerful economic unit and enjoy a higher per capita income than any other people.

To savor the interest of California to the full, look beyond the immediate 'American-ness' of what you see. Take note of the diversity of cultural heritages reflected in architectural styles – the onion dome of a church that would be at home in Russia; the characteristic Spanish grouping of buildings about a plaza in towns like Sonoma and San Juan Bautista; the New England flavor of homes at Sutter Creek and Nevada City in the Gold Country. The pattern of immigration may be traced through place names and local customs, too: north of Sonoma, town names are Anglo-Saxon; centuries-old Oriental festivals mark the passage of the year in San Francisco and Los Angeles. Simply looking around you on a big-city bus gives a sense of how much California is a part of every race and nationality.

History

The idea of California seized the imagination of Spanish explorers long before its discovery. In the 16th century, Garcia Ordonez de Montalvo wrote of a land 'close to the Terrestrial Paradise' inhabited by a race of lovely Amazons whose queen was named Califia; for lack of any other metal, these warrior maidens fashioned their armour from pure gold. Although Montalvo's island, Queen Califia and her maidens were wholly imaginary, California acquired sufficient substance to inspire voyages of exploration, and half a century after Columbus had landed in the West Indies, Juan Rodriguez Cabrillo sailed into San Diego Bay on September 28, 1542.

Cabrillo's voyage opened up the Pacific coast to a point 50 miles north of present-day Santa Barbara and established Spanish sovereignty which was challenged only by Sir Francis Drake during his circumnavigation of the globe. Halting at Point Reyes to repair the *Golden Hind* in 1579, Drake found the land attractive and took possession of it in the name of the Queen Elizabeth I. Nothing came of the gesture. And California received little attention from Spain for more than 150 years in spite of the urgings of Sebastian Vizcaino who sailed as far north as Cape Mendocino in 1602. Not until 1768, when Russian settlements in Alaska and on the northern California coast posed a serious threat to their claim, did the Spanish colonize the golden land.

The Franciscans were the first settlers. Under the vigorous leadership of Father Junipero Serra a chain of 21 missions was begun that in time extended from San Diego to Sonoma some 600 miles north. The primary duty of the missionaries was to convert the Indians to Christianity and bring them the benefits of civilisation; while so doing, the Franciscans laid down the bases of California's first industries. And they brought with them the grape vines now so important to the state's economy. The Spanish plan also called for the establishment of *presidios,* military garrisons to protect the missions against foreign invasion, at San Diego, Santa Barbara, Monterey and San Francisco. Small settlements grew up around the *presidios* and in time they acquired a civic character, but California's first true towns were the *pueblos* of San Jose (1777), Los Angeles (1781) and Santa Cruz (1797) which were organised under a civilian government from their foundation.

In 1822 the Mexican Revolution ended Spanish rule. Of the colonizing nations who eyed California's wealth, the United States was best placed to catch the rich prize should it slip from Mexico's uncertain grasp. From the 1820s onward a steady stream of American immigrants had flowed across the Sierra Nevada from the frontier settlements of the Mississippi valley and the greater part of California's foreign trade was in Yankee hands. In June 1846, unaware that the United States was at war with Mexico, a group of American settlers staged the Bear Flag Revolt in Sonoma and for 23 days California became an independent republic. Less than a month later two American sloops of war entered Monterey Bay and by August, California was in American hands.

Booms – and busts – marked California's rise to prominence. Discovery of gold at Coloma in the Sierra Nevada foothills in 1848 set off the greatest migration in history: more than half a million frenzied adventurers poured into the state in search of easy wealth. As the main port of entry, the little town of Yerba Buena became San Francisco almost overnight, transformed into the cultural and financial center of the state. When the main gold veins were exhausted, many of the miners remained to try again in San Francisco as farmers. Statehood was achieved in 1850 and Sacramento became the state capital in 1854.

With the completion of the transcontinental railroads in 1869, more immigrants headed west, lured by the promise of cheap land and the certainty of a beneficent climate. Southern California's era of growth, centered on Los Angeles, began in the 1880s, stimulated in part by agricultural and oil booms and by the advent of movie industry pioneers in 1910. In WW II wartime production dominated the economy; defense-related industries, shipbuilding and the aircraft-aerospace industry still play a leading role. Today the balance of political and economic power lies in the south, where 60% of the state's population resides.

California remains 'near the Terrestrial Paradise' in spite of the problems that have accompanied a phenomenal growth. Their high standard of living has given Californians time to look around them and the habit of optimism and innovation that came with the gold seekers has given rise to a philosophical pioneerism. Californians were in the vanguard of the environmental movement with legislation to preserve the natural beauty of their state. They are tolerant of ideas, however 'far out', and do not hesitate to experiment. It is no accident that New Age philosophies are born on the West Coast and move eastward, nor that political power is shifting to the West.

Geography

Bold contrasts and a remarkable variety of land forms are a stimulating aspect of travel in California. Much of the state's 158,693 square miles are mountainous: south of the Cascades the 450-mile-long Central Valley merges with a succession of transverse ranges north of Los Angeles. Beyond the deserts come into their own. And elevations range from 282 feet below sea level to 14,495 feet on Mt Whitney, the highest point in the US outside Alaska. Californians recognize the diversity of their land with an informal geography that ignores boundary lines and defines the distinctive character of the region.

Up north is the mountainous **Redwood Empire** extending from the Oregon border to Leggett. This is big timber country, domain of the coastal redwoods, the world's oldest living things. Large stands are preserved in Redwood National Park and several state parks lining the Redwood Highway US 101. Old lumbering communities and ports hereabouts retain the flavor of early California. East of the principal ranges, the Klamaths, Siskiyous and the Cascades, the landscape alters radically, dropping away to open range land and extensive lava fields in the northeastern corner of the state.

Although the grape is cultivated throughout California today, the historic **Wine Country** lies immediately north of San Francisco, centered on the Napa and Sonoma Valleys. As far as the eye can travel, vineyards clothe the hillsides and valley floors; tended with minute care, they produce the country's finest table wines. Small towns with a strong Victorian ambience cluster along the main north-south highways, catering to the wine industry and vacationers who would combine their winetasting and outdoor sports. There are plenty of opportunities for fishing, boating and backpacking in the mountains that bound the eastern Wine Country. The **Russian River Region,** a popular recreation area, forms a scenic buffer zone between the redwoods and the wine regions.

Centered on San Francisco, the **Bay Area** encloses a lovely stretch of the Coastal Range between Point Reyes and San Jose. Although densely populated around San Francisco and San Pablo bays, the wilderness experience is only minutes away for much of the coastlands lie within the Golden Gate National Recreation Area.

The **Gold Country,** also known as the Mother Lode Country for the vein of gold-bearing quartz that lured the Argonauts, takes in a 259-mile stretch of the western Sierra Nevada foothills from

Sierraville to Mariposa. Varying in altitude from a few hundred feet above sea level to the 6500-foot elevation, this is superb outdoor vacationing country. Its swift rivers are particular favorites with 'white water' boaters. For the visitor with a taste for historic structures, antiquing and legends, almost any community will do: evocative reminders of the gold seekers and their turbulent era are everywhere to hand.

The **High Country** encompasses the rugged beauty of the Sierra Nevada peaks, young mountains by geological standards, and marvellously sculpted by glaciers during the Ice Age. Large areas are set aside as national parks and wilderness areas, including the incomparable Yosemite and Sequoia-Kings Canyon National Parks. Lake Tahoe straddles the California-Nevada state line, offering and resort vacationing and immediate access to the wilderness.

The **Desert Country** lies in Southern California, reaching east of the Sierra Nevada beyond the Nevada border and south into Mexico. Los Angeles and San Diego are the main gateways to this vast land of widely spaced mountain ranges and broad basins containing the lowest and hottest place in the US, Death Valley. Winter sun seekers will find the Desert Country most attractive between November and May, particularly after the winter rains when the land springs to life with a profusion of wildflowers.

California's 1264-mile coast is incredibly varied. There are interminable stretches of fine sand beaches in the south; there are impressive promontories like Point Reyes; there are long reaches near the Oregon border where the forest spills down the mountains to the Pacific's edge. But only one section has come to be called a country and that is **Big Sur,** running roughly from just below Carmel to Lucia. 'This is the face of the earth as the Creator intended it to look' – the phrase is novelist Henry Miller's – with magnificent seascapes that alter dramatically with the shifting humors of the sun and coastal fogs.

There are other countries, as you will discover – the Delta Country, formed by the confluence of the Sacramento and San Joaquin Rivers, the Feather River Country, the new wine countries growing up south of Monterey, the Channel Islands off the southern coast. Each is an excellent reason for lingering in the Golden State.

Climate

California's generally pleasent climate, varying with the elevation, is a strong factor in the state's popularity with vacationers. Somewhere the sun will be shining, somewhere you can swim, somewhere you can retreat to a refreshing coolness, at any time of year. The following regional generalities may be useful in planning your visit.

Southern California (from San Diego to San Luis Obispo) is characteristically sunny year-round, at its warmest between June and September when temperatures range between the high 60s and mid-70s along the coast. In the desert areas, expect highs in excess of 100°. Between January and May, rain does fall and at all times nights are cool enough to warrant packing a light jacket.

Northern California's coastal regions from Monterey to the Oregon border are far cooler in summer than you might expect: morning and evening fogs keep the averages around 50° in January and low 60s in September. During the winter months (November-January) in the San Francisco Bay Area count on some brisk days in the high 40s and periodic rains. But on the whole, days are sunny.

Away from the coast, temperatures are more extreme: the Central Valley, between the Coast Range and the Sierra Nevada, is markedly cooler in winter above about 4000 feet, contrasting with comfortably warm summers. Up among the High Country peaks the range is from below zero in January to summer highs in the mid-70s.

FESTIVALS & EVENTS

January	*Pasadena* – New Year's Day Tournament of Roses Parade in conjunction with the Rosebowl Football Game.
	Pebble Beach – Bing Crosby Golf Tournament classic.
February	*San Francisco* – Chinese New Year (first full moon after January 21). Week-long festivities culminate in the Golden Dragon Parade through Chinatown.
March	*San Diego* celebrates St Patrick's Day with its Darts Tournament. In *San Francisco,* the annual Snake Race precedes the big parade on Market St.
Easter Day	*San Diego* – Easter Promenade, with prizes awarded to best-dressed men and women.
	Los Angeles – Disneyland Parade.
April	*Borrego Springs* – Pegleg Liars Contest, rewarding tellers of the tallest tales.
	San Francisco – Cherry Blossom Festival, Japantown. Folk and classical dancing, martial arts, concerts, exhibits and traditional costumes.
	Los Angeles – University of California students celebrate Mardi Gras.
May	*Angels Camp* – Jumping Frog Jubilee, celebrating Mark Twain's *Jumping Frog of Calaveras County.*
	San Diego – Fiesta de La Primavera. Strolling mariachis, troubadours, Spanish dancers, exhibits recall the days of the Dons in the Old Town.
	San Francisco – Latin America Fiesta Parade through the heart of old Mission District.
June	*San Diego* – Kool Jazz Festival.
	San Francisco – Gay Freedom Day Parade on Market St, the only Gay community parade in the country.
	Mission Santa Ysabel – Fiesta commemorating the foundation of the mission, with procession of Caballeros del Camino Real.
July	*Salinas* – The California Rodeo, largest in the state.
	Placerville – Week-long Wagon Train Days Festival commemorates original Sierra Nevada crossing with a 60-mile covered wagon trek from Round Hill, Nevada to Placerville on the old Emigrant Trail.
	Pollock Pines – Pony Express Re-Run over a portion of the Pony Express Riders' route.
	San Diego – Blessing of the Animals and Blessing of the Bells at Mission San Diego de Alcala.
	Mission San Luis Rey Fiesta, re-creating the journey of Father Junipero Serra by the Caballeros del Camino Real.
	Fourth of July celebrations.
August	*Santa Barbara* – Old Spanish Days Festival.
	Los Angeles – Nisei Week, Little Tokyo.
	Redondo Beach – International Surf Festival.
September	*Solvang* – Danish Days, two day fiesta affirming Solvang's Danish heritage.

Sonoma – Valley of the Moon Vintage Festival, with pageant at Mission San Francisco de Solano.

San Diego – Cabrillo Festival, re-enacting Cabrillo's landing in 1542

Santa Rosa – Scottish Gathering and Highland Games, one of the oldest events of this kind in the West.

San Francisco – Aki Matsuri, Japantown. Japanese Fall Festival celebrated with dances, martial arts and the tea ceremony among the events.

San Francisco – Mexican Independence Day (September 15) festivities. Traditional Grito Ceremony on the steps of City Hall.

September/
October

San Francisco – Columbus Day Celebration and Parade, North Beach. Italian community commemorates the discovery of the American continent by Columbus with week-long festivities.

October

San Francisco – Madonna del Lamme Celebration (Blessing of the Fleet), October 1, Church of St Peter and St Paul, Washington Square and at Fisherman's Wharf.

November

El Cajon – Mother Goose Parade anticipates the holiday season with floats, clowns, bands, all geared to entertain children.

December

San Diego – Christmas Light Boat Parade, San Diego Harbor. Fleet of gaily decorated boats parades along the Embarcadero and past Harbor and Shelter Islands.

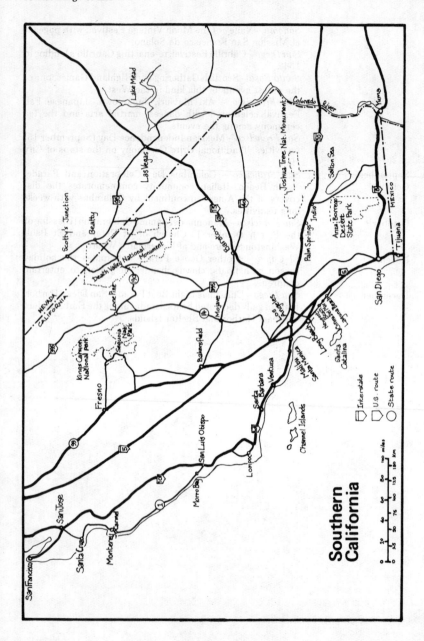

Southern
California

San Diego to LA

SAN DIEGO

San Diego, southernmost gateway to California, sits in the southwest corner of the state, just 15 miles north of the Mexican border. San Diego County spreads eastward 80 miles from the Pacific Ocean and northward from the Mexican border 100 miles. The city and its environs are bounded to the west by the Pacific shoreline, the natural San Diego harbor and man-made Mission Bay and to the east by rolling foothills of the Coast Range.

San Diego fulfills the dream of California. Red-roofed homes cover the undulating hills and valleys in seemingly ever spreading waves as more and more people discover and settle in its salubrious climate (which evoked a salute in *Holiday Magazine* from a group of meteorologists as the 'only area in the US with perfect weather'). Its residents enjoy life at a pleasurable pace, taking full advantage of their outdoor opportunities.

For visitors, however, its appeal lies not only in alfresco activities, but equally in the fascination of its historic locales, for San Diego is the birthplace of California.

History

The discovery of San Diego harbor and eventual settlement of Alta California by the Spanish was triggered by their search for the elusive Straits of Anian – the legendary Northwest Passage that was believed would provide a link to the Indies. Hernando Cortes, conqueror of Mexico, believed the passage would be found near the 'California Islands' and, starting in 1532, he dispatched expeditions to search for it. In 1533, an expedition discovered the Baja California and their reports of the wealth in pearl-beds led to the founding of a settlement there in 1535 which was abandoned two years later.

On September 28, 1542, Juan Rodrigues Cabrillo, a Portuguese in the service of Spain, sailed into San Diego harbor, then continued up the Californian coast, laying claim to the whole area for Spain. But still he found no sign of the Northwest Passage.

By the turn of the century, the search for the straits was no longer the only objective of exploration. The Philippine trade, which had begun in 1565, was exacting a heavy toll. By the time Mexico-bound galleons heavily laden from Manila reached the Californian coast provisions had run short and crews were decimated by scurvy; a supply base was needed.

On his exploration voyage north in 1602, Sebastian Vizcaino renamed the Bay of San Diego in honor of his patron saint, and continued up the coast to discover Monterey Bay, which he selected as the perfect site for settlement. 167 years passed before the next development in 1769. In 1769, charged with the combined missions of resupplying the Manila galleons, Christianizing the Indians and forestalling southern expansion by foreigners, four units of military and clergy were dispatched to colonize Alta California. The group led by Gaspar de Portola, governor of Baja California and the Franciscan friar, Father Junipero Serra, reached San Diego on July 1. On July 16 they established the Mission San Diego de Alcala and the Presidio– the former for the spiritual conversion of the Indians and the latter to guarantee protection of the colony.

Life in the fledgling colony centred around the Mission, which was moved in 1774 to its present location six miles east up Mission Valley from the Presidio out of a need for fresh water and to be nearer Indian grounds. The Christianizing of the Indians was relatively successful with the exception of a brief and isolated setback; in 1775 a mob of disgruntled Indians swept down on the San Diego mission, killing two colonists and martyring a missionary, Father Jaime. But as with other missions in the chain, San Diego de Alcala flourished with the help of Indian labor, producing crops and livestock which became the envy of the secular segment of the colony centred around the Presidio.

The declaration of Mexican independence from Spain in 1821 had little effect on the Californians who, though they swore formal allegiance to the new government, evinced some contempt for the ineptness of Mexican administration.

Meanwhile pressure was growing to secularize the missions and in 1834 Governor Jose Figueroa ordered implementation of secularization. Although mission property was intended to be divided between the Indians and the religious establishment, much of it fell into the hands of administrators and rancheros and by the 1830s the ranchos replaced the mission as the leading institution and social life revolved around the adobe homes proliferating in what is now Old Town. In August of 1834, Governor Figueroa decreed the Pueblo of San Diego, making it the oldest municipality in the state of California.

The beginning of the 19th century saw the first Americans sailing into San Diego Bay intent on trading fur pelts and, by the 1820s, hide and tallow for which San Diego was becoming a center.

When the United States declared war on Mexico in 1846, the San Diegans sent word to Commodore Stockton, who had five US ships in Monterey Bay under his command, to send a force to occupy the San Diego Presidio. The *Cyane* duly arrived in San Diego harbor on July 29, 1846 and a small force marched to the Presidio which offered no resistance. The Mexican flag was lowered and the Stars and Stripes raised above the Plaza in Old Town while all of Southern California was proclaimed for the President of the United States.

Following the cession of California to the US in the treaty ending the Mexican War in 1848, the County of San Diego was organised February 18, 1850 (the first county in California), San Diego was chartered March 27, 1850 and on September 9 of that year, California was admitted as the 31st state in the Union.

Still life progressed with little change in San Diego until the arrival in 1867 of Alonzo E Horton who founded New San Diego, now the heart of downtown. The coming of the Santa Fe railroad in 1885 quickened the pace of growth. But San Diego remained a quiet backwater into the 20th century, protected by its location from the chaotic urban sprawl experienced by many other American cities.

WW II naturally brought many changes and an enlivened pace to this headquarters of the 11th Naval District, but through the postwar years, even up to today, San Diegans seem to march to a measure markedly less frenetic than their fellow Americans.

Orientation

Several ways suggest themselves to get your bearings. You might drive the 52-mile Scenic Drive, marked by a white seagull sign – join it anywhere along the course. You can rent a Tote-a-Tape at either Mission Bay or Seaport Village Information Centres for a 2½ hour self-guided scenic tour for $10, plus a returnable $20 deposit. Or you can view the city from the bay on one of the harbor cruises or by chartered boat.

The San Diego Culture Loop narrated bus tour provides an interesting orientation to the city's areas and attractions. The complete loop covers Sea World, Old Town, Hotel Circle, Balboa Park, the Embarcadero, Harbor and Shelter Islands and Ocean Beach. It takes 2½

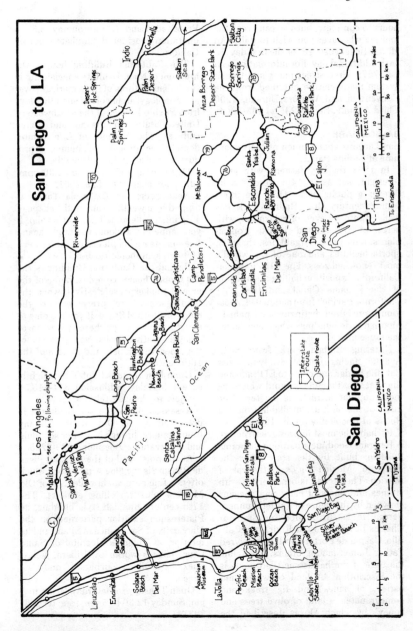

hours to complete, but you can break the journey whenever you wish to dally. An all-day ticket costs $8 for the first day, $3 each additional day. For information, call 232-7579. Free street maps and transit system maps can be obtained from the Convention and Visitors Bureau, 1200 Third Avenue, Suite 824; tel 233-3004.

BALBOA PARK

San Diegans spend much of their spare time at Balboa Park.

In 1868 the city fathers, with great foresight, set aside 1400 acres 'to be forever a public park'. Over the intervening century-plus, Balboa Park has evolved into a haven of relaxation, with acres of tree-shaded lawns, tropical plants, museums, art galleries, theaters, sports facilities and one of the world's most renowned zoos. The 1915 Panama-California Exposition hailing the opening of the Panama Canal and the 1935 California-Pacific International Exposition contributed distinguished Spanish-Moorish style buildings which now house the museums.

Entering Balboa Park from Sixth Avenue (facing Laurel St), you cross Cabrillo bridge and come to El Prado and the Plaza de Panama, around which the most popular attractions cluster. Free maps of the park are available from the **House of Hospitality** on the Plaza.

Perhaps the most impressive structure is Bertram Goodhue's baroque **California Building**, built by the state after the design of Mexico City's Cathedral of Mexico. The facade is ornamented with statues and busts of early San Diegans crowned by the figure of Father Junipero Serra. He is surrounded by Emperor Charles of Spain, Juan Rodriguez Cabrillo, Gaspar de Portola, and the martyred Father Jaime, among others. Encircling the base of the handsome tiled dome is the inscription: 'A land of wheat and barley, of vines and fig trees and pomegranates, a land of olive trees and honey', by which Moses described the Promised Land (Deuteronomy 8:8), a quotation considered exquisitely apt by Californians!

The California Building houses the **Museum of Man**. Exhibits specialising in the Indian cultures of the Americas cover anthropology, archaeology and ethnology from Pueblo Indians of the southwestern United States to Mayan and Aztec cultures. The 'Wonder of Life' exhibit depicts the process of human reproduction and birth in multimedia.

Open daily 10 am to 4.30 pm; admission charge; tel 239-2001.

Next door, the **California Tower** is topped by a weather vane in the shape of a Spanish galleon, tribute to Cabrillo. If you happen by at noon, you might hear a five-minute recital played on the Tower's 100-bell symphonic carillon.

Behind the California Building is the **Old Globe Theater** complex, home of the annual Shakespeare Festival, when the bard's works are presented on the outdoor Festival Stage. If you're going to a performance, do get there by 7.45 pm to enjoy the festival revels – young artists set the mood with music and dances of the 16th century.

Open June through September, nightly except Monday; admission $14-$15.50 (subject to change); tel 239-2255.

A season of contemporary drama is presented by the Old Globe company from January through May. For schedule and reservations, telephone 239-2255.

At the north end of the arcaded Plaza de Panama is the **Fine Arts Gallery**, which offers a fine permanent collection of Old Masters plus travelling exhibits. The 17th century Spanish-style building, its Plateresque exterior patterned on the University of Salamanca in Spain, and its interior on Toledo's Hospital of Santa Cruz, houses works by Ribera, Velasquez, Murillo, Zurbaran and El Greco.

Open Tuesday to Saturday 10 am to 5 pm; Sunday 12.30 to 5 pm; free; tel 232-7931.

Across the Plaza is the **House of Charm**, featuring a model railroad (Sunday 1 to 4.30 pm; Friday 7 to 11.30 pm; free) the **San Diego Art Institute** (Tuesday to Saturday 10 am to 5 pm; free) and a sports museum. **The Hall of Champions** honors athletes of San Diego who have achieved national and world recognition (open Monday to Saturday 10 am to 5 pm; Sunday noon to 5 pm; free; tel 234-2544).

One of the park's – and San Diego's – most popular attractions is the **Reuben H Fleet Space Theater and Science Center**. The theater shows an audio-visual, electronically projected by 80 projectors on a tilted hemispheric screen, which gives the sense of image and sound surrounding you while you hurtle through space. The adjacent science center offers do-it-yourself exhibits demonstrating your sensory perceptions.

Open daily 9.45 am to 5 pm, 7 to 9.30 pm winter; 9.45 am to 10 pm summer; admission charge; tel 238-1168.

Other museums in that area include the Natural History and the Aero-Space museums. The **Natural History Museum** has extensive exhibits and a research library detailing Southern Californian animal, reptile, plant and marine life from prehistory until today. Bi-monthly nature walks are conducted and a self-guided nature walk around the Prado is available.

Open daily 10 am to 5 pm; admission charge; tel 232-3821.

The **Aero-Space Museum and International Aerospace Hall of Fame** was destroyed by arson in early 1978, but the exhibits honoring accomplishments of aviation and space heroes have been reconstructed in a new building. Displays record the history of flight from the Wright Brothers to space missions. Included is a replica of Lindbergh's *The Spirit of St Louis*, dear to the hearts of San Diegans because the plane was designed and built by a local firm and Lindbergh departed on the first leg of his historic flight to Paris from North Island Naval Air Station, Coronado, in 1927.

Open daily 10 am to 4.30 pm; free; tel 234-8291.

A lily pond fronts the **Botanical Building**, housing over 500 species of tropical and subtropical plants and seasonal floral displays.

Open daily except Friday 10 am to 4.30 pm; free.

San Diego is one of the few cities in the world which has such an even climate it allows for an outdoor organ and the **Spreckels Organ Pavilion**, to the west of the Plaza, houses a beauty. With approximately 3500 pipes, ranging from an inch and a half to 32 feet long, it is the world's largest organ. A Corinthian peristyle frames the theater, where a free organ recital is played many Sundays at 2.30 pm.

The **San Diego Zoo** has been acclaimed as one of the world's finest. An extraordinary collection of animals lives in surroundings approximating as closely as possible their natural habitat. Exotic birds fly through a tropical rain forest; koalas nap in eucalyptus trees, rousing themselves occasionally to munch leaves and somnambulantly consider their excited audience; jungle cats pace freely behind wide moats. Try riding a Skyfari gondola high above the denizens roaming sections with fanciful names such as Monkey Mesa, Stock and Crane Canyon and the Horn and Hoof Mesa. From the tramway's highest point, you also enjoy superb views of Balboa Park, the city and the sparkling blue Pacific.

Youngsters love the **Children's Zoo**, where they can pet and feed baby animals, watch newly-born being cared for by surrogate human mothers, perhaps even hitch a ride on the back of a forbearing Galapagos turtle.

Open daily 9 am to dusk, admission charge; tel 231-1515.

Not-so-young children indulge in nostalgia by riding the hand-carved animals on a turn-of-the-century merry-go-round beside the zoo's parking lot; it operates weekdays through the summer and on weekends year-round.

What does Balboa Park offer sports enthusiasts? Archery, both field and target, baseball, bicycling, golf, tennis – San Diego has been tennis-crazy since a 16-year-old local girl named 'Little Mo' made good in 1951, winning both the world title and national title three years in a row. The Parks & Recreation Department maintains 96 public courts, 70 of them night-lighted, plus jogging, lawn bowling, shuffle-board, horseshoes and badminton. If all this sounds too active, you might settle for people-watching at an alfresco cafe or picnicking on the lawns. For information on any of these, telephone 239-0512.

Places to Eat

Cafe Del Rey Moro Dine alfresco in gardens of replicated Moorish palace, the park's House of Hospitality. Known, too, for Sunday champagne brunch and box lunches. (B) Lunch daily, dinner Tuesday to Sunday. 1549 El Prado; tel 234-8511.

Hob Nob Hill Hospitable family restaurant renowned for home cooking for almost four decades. Day-long breakfast a specialty with home-made rolls, breads. (B/M) Breakfast, lunch, dinner daily. 2271 First Avenue; tel 239-8176.

OLD TOWN

Following San Diego history is enlightening and pleasant in Old Town, a six-and-a-half block State Historic Park which recreates early Mexican and American days in restored adobes. Not only does history come alive, but you rub shoulders with locals browsing and buying from remodeled shops, sipping margaritas and lunching on Mexican burritos and chile rellenos in a courtyard setting under spreading pepper trees.

Life in Old Town centered around the **Plaza Vieja** on San Diego Avenue, where

the Stars and Stripes was first raised. The inner streets of the area are closed to traffic now, so the options are to stroll through, following the green line on the road, or to take an inexpensive horse-and-buggy tour. **Park headquarters** on Wallace St features exhibits describing the early history of the area and a free folder including a map and descriptions of the casas and museums. The Park Service also conducts a free walking tour every afternoon at 2 pm.

Headquarters open daily 10 am to 6 pm summer; 10 am to 5 pm winter; free; tel 237-6770.

In addition, the San Diego Historical Society operates a free tour, departing the Whaley House on San Diego Avenue each Saturday at 1.30 pm – Saturday is a good day, as the old arts of bread baking in an outdoor oven, brick making, candle dipping and wool spinning are demonstrated in the gardens of **La Casa de Machada**. The restored adobes hint at the affluent lifestyle of the rancheros who benefited from secularization of the missions.

Casa de Estudillo, on Mason east of San Diego Avenue, has been extensively restored – note the curved roof tiles, formed in pre-mould days by the workman shaping soft clay over his thigh.

Open daily 10 am to 6 pm summer, 10 am to 5 pm winter; admission charge (includes Seeley Stable on Calhoun St, restoration of stables built in 1869 to serve US Mail Stage Line); tel 294-5182.

Casa de Bandini was variously the home of wealthy Don Juan Bandini, a stage-coach station, and Commodore Stockton's headquarters. It now is home to a good alfresco restaurant.

Within the Old Town State Historical Park there are several museums in restored buildings: **The Historical Museum of Old California** features a scale model of Old Town in the 1870s (open daily except Monday 10 am to 5 pm). The San Diego Union **newspaper museum** in Casa de

Altamirano is restored as an early printing office, displaying the paraphernalia for printing a newspaper in 1868 (open daily except Monday 10 am to 5 pm). The **Old San Diego Drug Store Museum** brings a 19th century pharmacy back to life (open Wednesday-Sunday 10 am to 4 pm). The **American Presidents Museum** has presidential campaign memorabilia, including commemorative buttons for the George Washington inaugural (open daily 10 am to 4 pm, admission charge). The **Antique Appliance Museum** displays an 1864 clothes washer, as well as other old-time implements (open daily 9 am to 6 pm except between noon to 1 pm on weekends). The **Roscoe Hazard Museum** in the Seeley Stables offers a collection of horse-drawn vehicles and other artifacts from the old West (open daily 10 am to 5 pm).

Besides adobes, the **Whaley House** on San Diego and Harney, just outside the park, shows early American-style architecture. It was the first brick structure in Southern California and has served many diverse functions including a funeral parlor, a saloon and a Sunday School! Little wonder that it is reputed to be haunted. Next door the **Derby-Pendleton House** is an example of the prefabricated New England houses that were shipped around Cape Horn and sold off sailing ships to be fitted together with wooden pegs on site in the mid-19th century.

Both houses open for viewing Wednesday-Sunday 10 am to 4.30 pm except holidays; admission charge; tel 298-2482.

Places to Eat
Hamburguesa Hamburger Heaven, popular with families. Hamburgers in a score-plus of imaginative variations, served in a garden setting. Steaks and Mexican dishes too, and omlets at weekends. (B)

Lunch, dinner daily. Bazaar del Mundo, Old Town; tel 295-0584.

Casa de Bandini Early California and Mexican cuisine enhanced by splendid surroundings of Don Juan Bandini's 1829 home. (M) Lunch, dinner daily. Mason and Calhoun Sts; tel 297-8211.

Presidio Hill Rising above the Old Town, Presidio Hill bears only grassy mounds to mark the original presidio and old American garrison known as Fort Stockton. The ruins are now being excavated by students. A green line on the road marks a scenic drive to the summit, crowned by the **Serra Cross** and the handsome **Serra Museum**. Home of the San Diego Historical Society, the museum's exhibits and artifacts housed in a mission-style white adobe delineate San Diego's heritage through early days from missionaries to first Americans. Best time to climb Presidio Hill is when the setting sun tinges the museum's Moorish arches – and the panorama of Old Town, Mission Valley and the Pacific – with a rubric glow.

Open daily 9 am to 5 pm Monday to Saturday, noon to 5 pm Sunday; free; tel 297-3258.

MISSION SAN DIEGO DE ALCALA
Drive a few miles up Mission Valley on I-8 to visit the Mission San Diego de Alcala on the site where it was relocated in 1774. Stop at the **visitor centre**, where a mural depicts San Diego's history, for a tote-a-tape which guides you at your own pace through the mission's reconstructed Indian village and olive grove. On Sundays, you can attend services in the original chapel.

Open daily 9 am to 5 pm; admission charge; tel 281-8449.

Within the mission grounds is the **Father Luis Jaime Museum,** Southern California's only permanent collection of ecclesiastical art, plus mission relics and records, including some in the hand of Father Junipero Serra himself.

Open daily 10 am to 5.30 pm; admission charge.

DOWNTOWN

In 1867 Alonzo Erastus Horton, an enterprising entrepreneur from San Francisco, bought 960 acres of barren land edging San Diego Bay – for the grand sum of $265, or 27½ cents an acre, considered at that time a generous price – and proceeded to build his New Town, today's downtown.

Start your exploration at **Horton Plaza Park**, focal point for the city's transportation system – and for the current restoration project which is turning the center of town from a somewhat seedy 'navy town' look into an attractive area befitting San Diego's status as a major tourist destination.

Notice Mr Horton's careful planning: the rather short blocks provided him more top-dollar corner lots to sell, and the stretch of Broadway running to the Embarcadero allowed water views for guests in his hotel, which stood where the US Grant Hotel is now!

The **US Grant Hotel** was built in 1905 by the Civil War general and president's son, Ulysses S Grant Jr, a San Diego resident. The US Grant Hotel is, at writing, closed and undergoing restoration. It will reopen as a first-class hotel.

Across from the US Grant is the luxurious **Little America Westgate Hotel**, definitely a must to walk through to admire the lobby, recreation of a Versailles anteroom, and such rare decorations as Aubusson tapestries and Baccarat crystal chandeliers, which adorn the interior. You can't help but feel Mr Horton most definitely would have approved.

A block north is the attractive **Charles C Dail Concourse**, a four-block mall embracing the City Administration Building, a Convention Hall and the **Civic Theatre**, home of the San Diego Symphony, San Diego Opera Company and the San Diego and California ballet companies.

Walk west on C: at 5th, you'll see the famous **Jessop's Calendar Clock**. You are now in the main shopping section of downtown. The area south of Broadway on 5th is part of the **Gaslamp Quarter**, where property owners are restoring their turn-of-the-century and 1920s buildings in line with the Horton Plaza restoration project, a plan which is doing much to revitalize the downtown area. Gaslamp Quarter tours are offered Fridays at noon and Saturdays at 10 am and 1 pm; tel 233-5227 for information. On 7th look for the **Farmers Bazaar**, selling farm-fresh produce and distinctive local arts and crafts. It's located in the historical Western Metal Warehouse.

If you are still on an historical bent, the **San Diego Public Library** on 8th and E will take you back four thousand years with its Sumerian cuneiform tablets! It is one of the best stocked libraries in the country.

Open Monday to Thursday 10 am to 9 pm; Friday to Saturday 9.30 am to 5.30 pm; tel 236-5800.

At the foot of Broadway, on Kettner, the restored Santa Fe Depot is the starting point for Amtrak, the San Diego Trolley and Mexicoach. There's an Information Booth inside.

Places to Eat

Marios Strolling singers perform showtunes and light opera to accompany good Italian food. (M) Dinner closed Sunday. 2604 5th Avenue; tel 234-1822.

Frenchy Marseilles' Popular sidewalk cafe, serving traditional bistro fare. (M) Lunch Monday to Friday, dinner Tuesday to Saturday. Corner 8th and C Sts; tel 233-3413.

Fat City Fanciful decor highlights dining in this historical Art Deco landmark. Menu offers wide choice. Plush turn-of-the-century bar links it to *China Camp* adjoining: Dine here in the style of an 1880s gold mining camp on California Chinese cuisine. Both restaurants (M). Lunch Monday to Friday, dinner nightly. 2137 Pacific Highway; Fat City tel 232-

0686; China Camp tel 232-1367.

WATER-ORIENTED SAN DIEGO

Much of San Diego life is attuned naturally to the waters of the Pacific, San Diego Bay and man-made Mission Bay. Walk down to the **Embarcadero** and you see San Diego Bay bustling with craft: naval ships, tuna fishing boats, pleasure boats, harbor cruisers. There are even antique sailing ships moored along Harbor Drive.

The **Maritime Museum** on the Embarcadero vividly represents nautical history with three floating exhibits: *The Star of India,* an iron-hulled merchantman launched at England's Isle of Man in 1863, sister ship of San Francisco's *Balclutha;* the 1898 San Francisco Bay ferryboat *Berkeley;* and a vintage luxury steam-yacht *Medea.*

Open daily 9 am to 8 pm, admission charge; tel 234-9153.

At the historic Coronado ferry landing, **Seaport Village** is a 22-acre shopping and restaurant complex with a turn-of-the-century look. Its architecture reflects Old Monterey and early California styles, and a highlight is an authentic 1880s carousel, with hand-carved wooden animals.

Harbor Cruises Several narrated harbor cruises offer opportunity for close-ups of the busy bay, including perhaps aircraft carriers, nuclear submarines and other naval vessels in port. One-hour and two-hour cruises sail from Broadway Pier. The shorter cruise leaves at 45-minute intervals and shows you the bay from Shelter Island to near the San Diego-Coronado Bridge. The two-hour cruise sails twice a day and covers a 25-mile loop past Harbor Island and Shelter Island, and along Point Loma past the naval submarine base. Circling the naval air station at North Island on Coronado's tip, you catch a glimpse of the venerable Hotel Del Coronado. Along the Spit, you pass the mothball fleet. Telephone 234-4111 for information and seasonal timetable changes.

To go aboard a naval vessel, call 235-3534 to enquire when the navy is holding a weekend 'open house'. Both the navy and marine corps welcome guests at colorful Friday afternoon military reviews. They are scheduled at 2.30 pm at the Naval Training Center, Point Loma and at 3.30 pm at the Marine Corps Recruiting Depot, off Pacific Highway.

The 365-ton classic schooner yacht *The Invader* offers two-hour cruises daily at 10 am and 1 pm for $6.50 per person; twilight dinner sails for $29.50 per person; half-day city tours for $24.50 per person and whale watching tours in season for $10 per person; tel 298-8066 for information.

Newest addition to the San Diego waterways is *Duck Tours,* which has hourly guided tours of Mission Bay aboard WW II amphibious landing craft. Rate of $7 per adult includes pick up at major hotels; tel 273-DUCK, 273-3828 for information about combined Mission Bay and Sea World tours.

Places to Eat

Lubach's Renowned seafood restaurant on the Embarcadero overlooking harbor. Established over a quarter century. Jacket required. (E)

Lunch Monday to Friday, dinner Monday to Saturday. 2101 North Harbor Drive; tel 232-5129.

Anthony's Fish Grotto Less posh of two sister restaurants on waterfront, serving same fresh seafood. (B/M) Lunch, dinner. Closed Monday. 1360 North Harbor Drive; tel 232-5103.

Coat and tie required at the more elegant *Star of the Sea Room* (M/E).

Shelter & Harbor Islands

San Diego Bay contains two 'islands' – both of which are actually attached to the mainland. **Shelter Island,** connected to Point Loma by a causeway, has a South Seas flavor imparted by the Polynesian-style architecture. Explore its winding paths for great views and a nautical atmosphere.

Harbor Island, opposite San Diego International Airport has numerous hotels and restaurants, many of which have stunning views of the city skyline by night.

Places to Eat

Bombay Bicycle Club Fine Indian cuisine served in Victorian Raj atmosphere. (M) Lunch Monday to Saturday, dinner nightly. 2806 Shelter Island Dr; tel 224-2483.

Tom Ham's Lighthouse Early California decor and spectacular view add to enjoyment of excellent food, unusual menu in this genuine lighthouse. (M) Lunch Monday to Friday, dinner nightly, Sunday brunch. 2150 Harbor Island Dr; tel 291-9110.

The Reuben E Lee An authentic riverboat with two restaurants – the Seafood Room and Sternwheeler – plus several bars and dancing. (M) Lunch, dinner daily. 880 E Harbor Island Dr; tel 291-1870.

MISSION BAY

Prime lure for San Diegans at leisure is Mission Bay, an aquatic sportsperson's Eden. The 4600-acre playground boasts 27 miles of beach and designated areas for sailing, waterskiing, swimming, power boating, paddle boating and fishing. All manner of boats are available for rent. If you're a landlubber, you might play a round of golf instead, or rent a bicycle and pedal the marked trails. And if all this sounds too energetic, you can dine and dance aboard an old-fashioned stern-wheeler or take a sunset or moonlight cruise on the paddlewheeler *Bahia Belle* from the Bahia Hotel or the *Lady Hilton,* a 47-foot pleasure yacht, from the Hilton Hotel.

Mission Bay also boasts five resort hotels and a 42-acre campground. An **Information Center** right off I-5 (freeway signs point the way) will fill you in on all the details (tel 276-8200).

Sea World Undoubtedly the main attraction on Mission Bay is Sea World, acclaimed as one of the country's finest marine parks, which features shows and exhibits on marine life from around the world. Star performer is Shamu, a three-ton killer whale who flings his weight around with remarkable agility and the panache of a veteran entertainer. Other performers include a trained elephant seal, a skating penguin, a waterskiing chimpanzee and dolphins displaying their intellect in an amazing quiz show. The shows, included in the park admission fee, average 20 minutes each and start on the half-hour, so you can catch them all. The latest offering is Penguin Encounter, featuring Antarctic emperor and Adelie penguins.

Sea World's aim is to involve you; it educates with feel-touch-learn experiences, as well as entertaining. You can feed and pet lumbering, friendly walruses, docile dolphins and playful seals, and explore tidepools, studying their denizens. There's so much to see and do you should schedule a full day here. Apart from applauding marine performers, you can ride up to the Sky Tower for 360° views, go behind the scenes to see the feeding and care of animals, wander through an exotic Japanese village where diving women will retrieve your very own pearl. Sea World is designed to be exceptionally accessible for wheelchair travelers.

Sea World is located at Perez Cove on the Sea World Drive. Open daily 9 am to dusk, admission adults, 90-minute tour, $2.50; tel 225-1221.

Point Loma

The high promontory separating Mission Bay is Point Loma, where San Diego's history began with Cabrillo's landing in 1542. At the point's tip, the **Cabrillo National Monument** draws more visitors than even the Statue of Liberty. Cabrillo's statue, a gift from his homeland, Portugal, faces Ballast Point where he actually set foot. An 1854 lighthouse, replete with period furniture, appears untouched since the keeper left years ago.

Open daily 9 am to 5.15 pm; (summer 8.30 am to 7.45 pm); admission free; tel 293-5450.

Cabrillo's landing is re-enacted anually – on Shelter Island – as a climax to the week-long **Cabrillo Festival,** held in the early fall. Telephone 293-5450 for dates and information.

Whale Watching The Cabrillo Monument is a great vantage point for whale watching from Christmas through mid-February, when the behemoths head south for the warm Baja waters to procreate, then in March to mid-April when they make the return journey. The Monument Visitor Center has a glassed-in observatory and volunteers are there to answer questions.

Other ways to view the giants are on excursions on sportfishing boats and cruise boats (out of Mission Bay call 224-3383, and out of San Diego Bay call 222-1144 or 232-3101). Trips are also offered by the San Diego Natural History Museum (tel 232-3821, ext 22). Adult prices range from $6 up for whale-watching cruises.

Sports Fishing boats are docked along Scott St, off Harbor Drive, at Point Loma.

Places to Eat

Halcyon Basque family style. Soup, salad, fresh vegetables and garlic bread accompany entree of the night. Dancing nightly. Dinner only. 4258 W Point Loma Boulevard; tel 225-9559.

LA JOLLA

For the uninitiated, that's pronounced La Hoy-a! The name is said to be derived from the Spanish word for 'jewel', an apt description for this delightful residential community much favored by artists, just a 15-minute drive by freeway from downtown San Diego.

La Jolla sits on a promontory, with seven miles of sea-swept rocky shore and cliffs, broken by stretches of sandy beach. The main shopping area on **Girard Avenue** is testament to the affluence of this community, with elegant boutiques and branches of exclusive stores such as Saks Fifth Avenue lining its tree-shaded sidewalks.

La Jolla is something of a gourmet's paradise, too, with numerous fine restaurants, including the popular Mexican *Su Casa* on La Jolla Boulevard (be warned, though, its margaritas which come by the pitcher are so good, their temptation can prove devastating!). Restaurants on **Prospect St,** where it curves inland, range from family-style eateries to smart dining rooms. A long-time village landmark is the charming 1920s vintage **La Valencia Hotel** on the corner of Prospect and Coast Boulevard – drop by to admire the art deco lounges and the view from the outdoor dining patio.

On Prospect is the **La Jolla Museum of Contemporary Arts,** which shows the work of today's top artists and indicates directions currently being taken in the visual arts.

Open Tuesday to Friday 10 am to 5 pm, Wednesday 7 to 10 pm, Saturday to Sunday 12.30 to 5 pm; admission free; tel 454-0183.

La Jolla Cove Coast Boulevard loops down around La Jolla Cove, one of the most attractive areas along the whole Southern California coast. The **Ellen Browning Scripps Memorial Park,** an expanse of well-manicured lawns and palm-lined paths, fronts the ocean and is a rendezvous for strollers, frisbee fans and sunbathers. At the north end of the park, a sea wall hides from view popular **La Jolla Cove Beach,** nestled under sandstone bluffs. Its gentle surf and underwater gardens lure swimmers and divers. The protected cove is also great for sunbathing – except when the tide comes in and the beach all but disappears!

Places to Eat
Top O' the Cove A celebrity favorite with outlook over La Jolla Cove. Unusual menu of fine continental dishes. Reservations a must. (E) Lunch, dinner daily. 1216 Prospect; tel 454-7779.

Clay's Texas Pit Barbecue There's a genuine Texas taste to spareribs and other choices barbecued over oakwood firepit. Try the sweet potatoe pie to follow. Take-out, too. (M)

Lunch Tuesday to Saturday, dinner nightly. 623 Pearl St; tel 454-2388.

La Jolla Shores Drive La Jolla is famed worldwide for oceanographic studies, conducted at the **Scripps Institution,** along La Jolla Shores Drive, since 1912. A visit to the Institution's **Thomas Wayland Vaughan Aquarium-Museum** fascinates with marine specimens from all around the globe.

Open daily 9 am to 5 pm; admission free; tel 452-4087.

Continuing on La Jolla Shores Drive, you come to the **University of California at San Diego** campus (of which Scripps is now a part), set amid eucalyptus groves atop the Torrey Pines mesa.

TORREY PINES
The **Salk Institute for Biological Studies** is at 10010 N Torrey Pines Rd. The Institute, named for the discoverer of the polio vaccine, was founded in the belief that scholars from differing disciplines, including the arts, should explore together a deeper understanding of life. The building's architectural design provokes controversy and lively discussion amongst all who visit it.

Tours Monday to Friday 10 am to 2 pm; admission free; tel 453-4100.

The cliffs in this area are a favorite location for sail planing. You'll also see hang-gliders intrepidly swooping low over the waves and up the cliff faces.

Golfers will want to stop at the par-72 municipal golf courses, home of the Andy Williams Open. These courses stretching along the cliff tops are just two of 70 which have earned San Diego the sobriquet 'Golfland USA'. The complex's Torrey Pines Inn has a motel and the only restaurant atop the mesa which has splendid ocean views (more enjoyable than the cuisine).

Adjoining is the 887-acre **Torrey Pines Reserve,** habitat of the rare torrey pine. The gnarled trees, descendants of pre-Ice Age forests, grow naturally only here and on Santa Rosa Island, off the coast of Santa Barbara. The park numbers hiking trails and tidepools (check the tide charts so you don't get caught!) among its lures for nature lovers. And all this is but a 30-minute freeway drive from downtown San Diego.

Open daily, 8 am to 10 pm April to October; 8 am to 5 pm in winter; free.

CORONADO
The tiny town of Coronado, at the end of the soaring blue bridge which links it to San Diego, is a seaside resort, much of it redolent of a more gracious era.

A popular misconception is that Coronado is an island. It is actually a peninsula connected to the mainland by a long narrow man-made stretch known as the Strand, which includes the **Silver Strand State Beach.** This five-mile-long ocean beach draws locals for clam digging and surfcasting, as well as swimming and picnicking at units which include fire rings for barbecues. Swimming and waterskiing are also popular across the road on the quieter bay side, reached by subway paths. At the south end of the bay is a marine biology area for study of the leas and tern, among other inhabitants.

The Queen Anne architectural confection, the **Hòtel Del Coronado,** opened its doors in 1888. In the decade following, sugar magnate John D Spreckels promoted it into a mecca for royalty, entertainers and politicians. The grand hotel has hosted 10 US presidents, including all but one since President Kennedy. It was the setting for that fateful meeting when the Duke of Windsor (then Prince of Wales) was introduced to Wallis Simpson. Many films have been made here, including Marilyn Monroe's *Some Like it Hot.* Now designated an Official Landmark, the Del Coronado conducts a tour of the premises every Saturday at 2 pm, as well as Tote-Tours.

Glorietta Bay Spreckels' 1908 mansion is heart of the **Glorietta Bay Inn** across from the Del Coronado on Glorietta Bay, and favorite with sailors for its sheltered waters. If you would like to take a turn around the bay yourself, the dock next to the Victorian-style boathouse is the place to rent sailboats, outboards and paddleboats or a Hobie Cat, at rates varying from $2.50 a half-hour (paddleboat) to $12 an hour, two-hour minimum for a 22-foot Catalina. Sailing lessons are available for an additional $10 an hour, on weekends only. Fishing and sightseeing charters are also possible for up to six people at rates ranging from $350 for a half-day to $700 for a full day.

For land-oriented sportspeople, Coronado has golf, tennis, volleyball and bicycling. The latter can either be rented in Coronado or in San Diego; the public bus from the city has racks on the back for free carriage of bikes.

Many of the Eastern tycoons who came to Coronado to enjoy the Del liked the town so well they built their own mansions, some designed by famed turn-of-the-century architect, Irving Gill. A pamphlet and map for a self-guided tour of the notable homes is available at a nominal fee from Victorian Corner in the shopping arcade of the Del Coronado, or at Central Federal Saving and Loan in Coronado, Plaza.

Places to Eat
Chuey's Cafe Longtime local hangout.

Authentic Mexican food served in setting of old Quonset hut. (B)

Lunch, dinner daily. 1910 Main St; tel 234-6937.

Bula's Pub & Eatery 'Bula' is Fijian for hello, welcome – which you'll feel here where friendliness and good Continental food provide a happy experience. (M)

Lunch, dinner daily. 170 Orange Avenue; tel 435-4466.

Places to Stay
A surge of new hotel buildings and extensions to existing hotels has greatly increased the choice for the traveler throughout the San Diego area, and more projects – both renovations and new properties – are under way.

Hotels tend to be clustered in different areas. Rates are lower away from tourist areas; for instance, suburban East San Diego motels run around $20 to $30 double and some have family units with kitchens. Access to downtown is fast by freeway. The Bed & Breakfast phenomenon is just starting in San Diego, and there are five youth hostels – see accommodation in the Facts for the Visitor section for information on these. (There are also two youth hostels in Julian in the Back Country.)

The San Diego Convention and Visitors Bureau issues a booklet listing hotels and motels in San Diego County and Baja Mexico; write 1200 Third Ave, Suite 824, San Diego CA 92101.

A handy service is offered to San Diego visitors by a group called **A-A Referral Service,** who will make accommodation and rental car reservations on a daily, weekly or monthly basis, all without charge. Write to them at 6235 El Cajon Boulevard, San Diego CA 92115; tel (619) 583-1811.

Listed below is a selection of places to stay in the main tourist areas. Prices quoted are for comparison purposes only, since they change rather frequently without notice. A 6% room tax must be added.

Downtown San Diego – Top End

Westgate Hotel (1055 2nd Ave, San Diego CA 92101; tel (619) 238-1818, toll free 800-522-1564). Luxurious downtown hostelry renowned for plush antique-furnished public rooms, individual period decor in guest rooms. Free transportation to major attractions, airport pickup. Rates from $89 double.

Holiday Inn at the Embarcadero (1355 N Harbor Drive at Ash St, San Diego CA 92101; tel (619) 232-3861). On Embarcadero with sweeping views of the city and harbor from many rooms. Pool, parking, entertainment, airport pickup. Rates from $75 double.

Downtown San Diego – Mid-Range

Friendship Inn Town House Lodge (810 Ash St, San Diego 92101; tel (619) 233-8826, toll free 800-453-4511). Near Balboa Park. Air conditioned rooms and suites with fully equipped kitchens. Heated pool. Complimentary morning coffee. Parking. Rates from $41 double.

Pickwick Hotel (132 W Broadway, San Diego CA 92101; tel (619) 234-0141). 150 units in heart of downtown. Restaurants, shops, tour desk, 24-hour room service, parking. Greyhound depot in building. Rates from $32 double, weekly rates available.

Downtown San Diego – Bottom End

Golden West Hotel (720 4th Avenue, San Diego CA 92101; tel (619) 233-7596). A few blocks north of downtown, 325 units popular with senior citizens. Rates from $16.50 double. Weekly and monthly rates available.

Hotel Churchhill (9th & C St, San Diego CA 92101; tel (619) 234-5186). 100 units, no restaurant. Top floor lounge with bay view. Rates from $26 double.

Places to Stay – Hotel Circle

In Mission Valley, close to Old Town, this is an area of new hotels and motels as well as the Fashion Valley Center shopping mall, one of the country's largest. Hotels located here tend to be resort style with all facilities. Golf courses are nearby.

Top End

Quality Royale (1433 Camino Del Rio South, San Diego CA 92108; tel (619) 260-0111; toll free 800-228-5152 (national, 800-268-8990 (California only). Newly opened, 265-room luxury hotel with valley views, color TV, swim-up bar. Rates from $75 double.

Mid-Range

Interstate 8 Motel 444 Hotel Circle No, San Diego CA 92108; tel (619) 291-1883). 110-room motel with waterbeds. Rates from $34 double.

Circle 7/11 Motel 2201 Hotel Circle So, San Diego CA 92108; tel (619) 291-2711). 178 units with color TV, courtesy coffee, pool. Some kitchens; coffee shop. Rates from $39 double.

Places to Stay – Mission Bay

The area surrounding the bay itself is the setting for a number of resort hotels, while the beach areas – including Mission Beach, Ocean Beach and Pacific Beach – offer many family-style motels and cottage units which tend to be rented in summer on a weekly basis to families.

Top End

Hyatt Islandia (1441 Quivira Rd, San Diego CA 92109; tel (619) 224-2541; toll free 800-228-9000; telex 697-844). High rise resort hotel with views of bay or ocean. Some kitchens. Boat rentals, sportfishing, marina, jacuzzi. Rates from $90 double.

Vacation Village (1404 W Vacation Rd, San Diego CA 92109; tel (619) 274-4630; toll free 800-542-6275 (California only); 800-854-2179 nationwide). Across from Sea World. Tennis, marina, bicycle and boat rentals. Kitchen units available. Rates from $72 double.

Mid-Range

Cresta Arms Apartment Motel (3314

Mission Boulevard, San Diego CA 92109; tel (619) 488-6097). One and two-bedroom apartments, kitchens. Weekly and monthly rates available. Rates from $35 double.

Santa Clara Motel (839 Santa Clara Place, San Diego CA 92109; tel (619) 488-1193, 583-1811). 17-unit motel within block of bay and ocean. Some kitchens. Rates from $35 double.

Mission Bay Motel (4221 Mission Boulevard, San Diego CA 92109; tel (619) 488-2895). 50-unit motel, with color TV, courtesy coffee, some kitchen units. Rates from $45 double.

Bottom End

Western Shores Motel (4345 Mission Bay Drive, San Diego CA 92109; tel (619) 273-1121. 40-unit motel, color TV. Night-lighted golf opposite. No restaurant. Rates from $27 double.

Point Loma/Shelter Island/Harbor Island

Harbor Island, almost directly opposite the airport, is particularly convenient for arriving air passengers, though most hotels arrange free pickup from the airport. Shelter Island is patronised mostly by sailing aficionados and vacationers, while Point Loma accommodation tends to be moderately priced and popular with sport fishing buffs.

Top End

Ebb Tide Hitching Post (5082 W Point Loma Boulevard, San Diego CA 92107; tel (619) 224-9339, 583-1811). 22 units with color TV, courtesy coffee, free TV movies, kitchen units. Within block of bay and ocean. Rates from $50 double.

Half Moon Inn (2303 Shelter Island Drive, San Diego CA 92106; tel (619) 223-3411, toll free 800-854-2900; California only 800-532-3727). It's a 136-room hotel with Polynesian-style decor set in tropical garden. Some kitchens. Marina, putting green. Rates from $85 double.

Kona Kai Club (1551 Shelter Island Drive, San Diego CA 92106; tel (619) 222-1191). Luxurious rooms with water views. Beach, tennis, racquetball, health spas. Kitchen units. Rates from $87 double.

Mid-Range

Vagabond Motor Hotel-Point Loma (1325 Scott St, San Diego CA 92106; tel (619) 224-3371, toll-free (800) 854-2700; (800) 522-1555), California only. On Fisherman's Wharf, Point Loma, with harbor view. Sport fishing, no restaurant. Kitchen units. Rates from $45 double.

Ocean Manor Apartment Hotel (1370 Sunset Cliffs Boulevard, San Diego CA 92107; tel (619) 222-7901, 224-1379). Rooms, studios and apartments on cliffs overlooking ocean with steps down to the sea. It's near beaches and fishing pier and there's no restaurant. Rates from $40 double.

Bottom End

Loma Lodge Motel (3202 Rosecrans St, San Diego CA 92110; tel (619) 222-0511). 43-unit motel with courtesy coffee and donuts, color TV, pool. Rates from $23 double.

Point Loma Youth Hostel (3790 Udall St, San Diego CA 92107; tel (619) 223-4778). Family accommodation available with advance reservations. Rental linen $1. Rate $4.

Places to Stay – Coronado

Coronado's accommodation offerings range from the prestigious Hotel del Coronado through condominiums to motels.

Top End

Hotel del Coronado (1500 Orange Avenue, Coronado CA 92118; tel (619) 435-6611. Grand 19th century seaside resort. Tennis, pool, health spas. Rates from $68 double.

Glorietta Bay Inn (1630 Glorietta Boulevard, Coronado CA 92118; tel (619) 435-3101). Modern hotel built around the turn-of-century Spreckels mansion.

Bay views, some kitchens, no restaurant. Rates from $70 double.

Mid-Range

Crown City Motel (520 Orange Avenue, Coronado CA 92118; tel (619) 435-3116). 32-unit motel. Some queen-size beds. Rates from $42 double.

Places to Stay – La Jolla

Several properties in La Jolla have ocean views although only one is right on the beach.

Top End

La Valencia Hotel (1132 Prospect St (PO Box 269), La Jolla CA 92037; tel (619) 454-0771). Gracious old hotel with ocean-view rooms set in pleasant gardens. Some oversize beds, kitchens, private balconies. Rates from $90 double.

Mid-Range

La Jolla Cove Apartment-Motel (1155 Coast Boulevard, La Jolla CA 92038; tel (619) 459-2621, toll free 800-647-4783). Studio, one-bedroom and two-bedroom apartments with kitchens and oceanfront balcony overlooking La Jolla Cove and park. Rates from $45 double, mid-June to early September, lower balance of year. Recommended – worth the commute to San Diego.

Bed & Breakfast

If you'd care to select bed & breakfast lodgings, you can obtain a directory by sending $6 to: *Carolyn's Bed-and Breakfast,* PO Box 84776, San Diego CA 92138; tel (619) 435-5009, or (619) 481-7662. The directory includes some 30 homes, ranging from $20 double up.

Other possibilities are:
Britt House, 406 Maple St, San Diego CA 92103 (vicinity of Balboa Park); tel (619) 234-2926; rates from $65 to 95 double. *Bed & Breakfast of Del Cerro* (referral service), 5649 Linfield Avenue, San Diego CA 92120; tel (619) 466-2794;

rates from $30 double-weekly rates available.

Places to Eat

The San Diego Convention & Visitors' Bureau's free booklet *Dining & Entertainment* lists restaurants offering 15 different types of cuisines, as well as nightclubs, lounges and fast food outlets, so there is sufficient variety to please any taste. Another publication provides detailed information on the dining scene: *San Diego Guide,* which includes 120 restaurant reviews plus discount coupons for major attractions – its on sale at newsstands, supermarkets and book stores.

Entertainment

The entertainment scene in San Diego emanates largely from the big hotels around Mission Bay, Shelter and Harbor Islands and the Hotel Circle area. These offer live entertainment, piano bars and often dancing until 2 am.

The *Old Globe* theater company, which mounts a Shakespearean Festival in the summer and offers contemporary dramas and comedies from October to April is well-patronised (tel 239-2255). The *Civic Theater* downtown hosts the *San Diego Symphony* (season November-April plus weekend performances at various alfresco venues July and August; tel 239-9721); and the *San Diego Opera* (spring season May-June, fall season October-November; tel 237-7636).

The *Civic Light Opera* performs June-September in Balboa Park's Starlight Bowl where unfortunately the lyrics are sometimes drowned by the roar of planes coming in to land at Lindbergh Field! For further information call 280-9111.

Getting There

Air San Diego's Lindbergh International Airport is presently served by 20 airlines, with direct air service from Hawaii and other US cities by major airlines, and by several commuter airlines.

Lindbergh Field, as it is still known to San Diegans, sits on the edge of San Diego Bay across from Harbor Island, a five minute drive from downtown San Diego. The new West Terminal building is used by American, Delta and Western while the other airlines use the East Terminal.

Arriving at West Terminal you take the pedestrian bridge in the front of the building to the baggage claim area; Travelers Aid, hotel reservation facilities and the car rental desks are also located there. In the East Terminal, these facilities are located in the central area between the two piers.

Restaurants and cocktail bars are on the first floor of the West Terminal and central section of the East Terminal; gift shops, the Harbor Police and Lost and Found are in the same area. Taxis and airport limousines are located at the central divider in the street fronting both terminal buildings.

Rail Amtrak run seven trains daily north to Los Angeles, 128 miles up the coast, all called the *San Diegan.* The trains depart from Santa Fe Station downtown at 1050 Kettner Boulevard. No seat reservations are taken and with the fuel shortage increasing the number of riders, it is best to reach the station early. For schedules and fares (at writing, fare is $17 one-way to Los Angeles), telephone toll free (800) 648-3850.

Bus Continental Trailways bus depot at 201 West Broadway (tel 232-2001) and Greyhound Bus depot at 120 West Broadway (tel 239-9171) have services connected to their nationwide networks.

Getting Around
Public Transportation The *San Diego Transit* system covers San Diego from San Ysidro on the Mexican border north to Oceanside and Rancho Bernardo, and from the Pacific east to El Cajon. Within that system, frequent bus sevice costs

only 80c local and $1 express with free transfers system-wide. Transfers intercity, connecting with north county bus systems are also available. Monthly passes and a Senior Citizen pass allowing half-fare are offered at the Transit office, 235 Broadway (tel 239-8161). Route maps are obtainable at the Transit Office, the Convention and Visitors' Bureau, or telephone 233-3004.

The *San Diego Trolley* runs from city center to the Mexican border, within walking distance of Tijuana (it's known as the 'Tijuana Trolley'). It departs from Santa Fe Depot, the Amtrak station, and makes seven city and 11 suburban stops in the 40 minute journey. One-way fare is a maximum of $1.50 (50c senior citizens and handicapped).

Car Rental Rental cars are available at the airport; the San Diego Convention & Visitors' Bureau also issues a list of some 30 car rental agencies serving the San Diego area.

The highway system is excellent and clearly marked. I-5 and I-15 running north-south and I-8 running east provide speedy cross-city access. A toll bridge (60c) connects San Diego and Coronado.

Taxis Taxis are plentiful and their fares, set by city council, are moderate (at writing, $2 for the first mile and $1.20 for each additional mile).

Tours A great many sightseeing tours are available not only throughout San Diego city and county, but also into neighbouring Baja California. The Gray Line, 1670 Kettner Boulevard, San Diego (tel (619) 231-9922) offers a variety of tours to the major tourist attractions with pickup and drop-off services to most hotels included. A Convention and Visitors' Bureau folder lists sightseeing tour operators.

A tour of the Grand Canyon is possible by small plane. Contact National Air

College, 3760 Glen Curtiss Rd; tel (619) 279-4908 or 279-4595 for information.

ACROSS THE MEXICAN BORDER TO TIJUANA

Tijuana, across the Mexican border in Baja California, is only 17 miles from San Diego and is a popular day trip. It provides a brief look at Mexican living; bear in mind though, that being a border town, it is not typical of the rest of the country. Remember to check visa requirements and car insurance. For information, telephone toll free 800-522-1516 or 684-2126.

Tijuana offers shopping, of course, plus jai alai, horse and greyhound racing and *coridas* at the two bullrings from late spring to early fall. English is widely spoken and US dollars are accepted – most willingly.

First stop in Tijuana should be the **Tijuana Cultural Center**, a massive new complex just across the International Bridge. Its Omnitheater film presentation (shown in English at 2 pm daily) thrills as the images of Mexico, shown on a 180° screen, seem to wrap around you. An adjoining museum introduces the regions of Mexico.

Avenida de la Revolucion between 2nd and 9th Sts is the center of Tijuana. As gaudy, crassly commercial and dilapidated as it may be, still the aura of gaiety and color endemic to Mexico comes through. **Avenida Constitucion**, parallel to Avenida de la Revolucion, where the Mexicans shop, is slightly less frenetic.

Visit the **Fronton Palacio** for dazzling displays of skill and strength in jai alai, fastest of all ball games (tel 903-385-1612). Thoroughbred horse racing is featured at **Agua Caliente** Saturday and Sunday year-round and greyhounds race there Wednesday through Sunday nights.

The bullfight season runs from May through mid-September; fights are scheduled the first Sunday in May and each Sunday from July through the first Sunday in September. Venue for the first half of the season is **El Toreo de Tijuana** on Boulevard Agua Caliente and for the balance of the season **Plaza Monumental** at Playas de Tijuana, the fast-develoing beach resort six miles west of town via Mexico 1-D. Bullfighting tickets, ranging in price from $10 to $20 can be obtained from Espectaculos Taurinos de Mexico, 1494 5th avenue, San Diego CA 92101; tel (619) 232-4588, 239-4112.

Tijuana's restaurants, nightclubs and discotheques all vie for tourist dollars, as do curio and handicraft shops. For good regional Mexican cooking, try the *Guadalajara Grill* across from the Abraham Lincoln statue on Diego Rivera Boulevard. Don't forget you will have to declare purchases returning to the US so check your customs allowance before you go.

Be careful of drinks with water or ice, and eating from sidewalk vendors' stalls.

ESENADA

A scenic four-lane toll road runs 65 miles south from Tijuana to the holiday town of Ensenada on the bay of Todos Santos, popular with fishermen. Parallel to the toll road is the old Ensenada Libre (free) road, which is slower but allows a closer look at life along the way.

En route, the Rosarito Beach Hotel in **Rosarito**, favorite hideaway of an earlier generation of Hollywood moguls, may have fallen on less affluent times, but its slightly shabby splendor recalls when secret assignations and high-powered deals were the order of the day.

Oenophiles can tour one of Mexico's most famous wineries in Ensenada; the **Mision de Santo Tomas** conducts free tours twice a day.

For information contact Bodegas de Santos Tomas, Avenida Miramar no 666, Ensenada, Baja California; tel 903-398-2509.

Getting There

Bus service from San Diego to Tijuana

includes *Mexicoach,* which leaves San Diego seven times a day from Santa Fe station at the foot of Broadway; tel (619) 232-5049 for schedule and fare information. Mexicoach serves downtown Tijuana, plus the Tijuana airport, Agua Caliente racetrack, the jai alai fronton and the bullfights, in season. *Greyhound Bus* also serves Tijuana; or you can take the *San Diego Transit* bus or the popular *San Diego Trolley* to the border, walk across, then hail a taxi (settle the fare ahead with the driver though, so you won't be overcharged).

If you decide to drive, you can take 1-5 close to the Mexican border. Remember that you will need Mexican insurance. Car traffic on the 25-lane gateway arch separating California and the Baja can be agonizingly slow, whereas special lanes speed the border crossing for bus traffic.

THE BACK COUNTRY ROUTE

Beyond San Diego, lower California is divided into three regions: the South Coast, a strip of coastal ledge backed by mountains running from San Diego to Laguna Beach; the mountainous Back Country, covering most of San Diego County; and the Colorado Desert, which stretches to the mighty Colorado River in the east, and northward to Palm Springs.

The Back Country offers a cornucopia of tourist pleasures too often bypassed by travelers intent on heading north to Los Angeles. If time allows, a day or two browsing back roads rewards with Indian lore, trails of the early emigrants, a sleepy town which basks in the remembered glory of a brief gold rush, and several missions, including the only one which still ministers to Indians. A network of reservoirs provides recreationland where you can fish, sail, swim and camp. Rugged mountains forested with pine and oak promise occasional stunning vistas across sun-burnished desert, the chance to visit

a world-famed observatory, and moments of rare quiet in silence broken only by birdsong.

EL CAJON
Heading east on 1-8 into Mission Valley you come to El Cajon. This area has three country clubs and six 18-hole golf-courses, along with a new 80-acre shopping mall, **Parkway Plaza**. For a look backward at the Old West, **Big Oak Ranch-Frontier Town** recreates a Wild West Town, complete with mock gun-fights and the 'Red Garter Saloon'. Open daily, admission charge; 1723 Harbison Canyon Rd; tel (619) 445-3047.

Places to Eat
Pinnacle Peak Old West atmosphere; kerosene lanterns. Steaks charbroiled over mesquite firepit. Very informal (they've been known to cut off the ties of men wearing them and pin them to the wall!!). Highly recommended. Get there early or you're in for a long wait. (M) Dinner, opens 5 pm nightly. Bradley and Magnolia Avenues; tel 448-8882.

SUNRISE HIGHWAY
San Diegans seeking peace and quiet often head for Cuyamaca Rancho State Park on SR 79 north of I-8. For an interesting scenic loop, continue on I-8 to Pine Valley, then head north on country Route S 1 to Mt Laguna. Rocky lowlands yield to mountain slopes forested in oak and sycamore which mantle the slopes in fall with brilliant golds and reds. Higher up, you're in pine country. This is the **Sunrise Highway**, one of the most scenic drives in southern California. From the shade of cool pines on Mt Laguna, you look out over the sunbaked wilderness of the Anza-Borrego Desert. Complete the loop by joining SR 79 and heading south to I-8.

Laguna Mountain Recreation Area, part of the Cleveland National Forest, and **Cuyamaca State Park** both offer camping, hiking trails, nature walks, picnicking, fishing, horse riding and winter sports. From atop Mt Cuyamaca on a clear day, the vista spans from the Pacific Ocean all the way to the Salton Sea and from the Mexican border north to San Bernardino.

Cuyamaca's park headquarters on SR 79 shares an old stone ranch house with an interesting museum of Indian artefacts, detailing the life of the Indians who lived in the surrounding canyons until they were driven from the area during a short-lived gold rush in the 1870s.

JULIAN

Center of the gold rush was Julian, now a sleepy village nestled in the foothills some eight miles north of Cuyamaca. Hard to believe that this quiet farming and orchard center once rivaled San Diego for county seat, losing by only one vote in 1873. That was before the gold gave out! Today Julian is a charming town of false-front stores, white frame cottages and orchards famed for semi-sweet apples which ripen in the fall, drawing thousands of visitors to buy them fresh from the trees. Popular with the visitors are Julian's homemade fruit pies, fresh apple cider from the roadside stands, real sarsaparilla served at the Drug Store's old-fashioned soda fountain.

Another event which attracts crowds to Julian is the unique **Weed Show & Art Mart**, a two-week festival held each August in the town hall. Locals compete with imaginative arrangements of weeds, rocks, desert wood and pods, and works of local artists are on display. Julian also hosts a **Fall Harvest Festival** in October.

The story of Julian's golden days is told in exhibits at the **Memorial Museum** (open weekends and holidays 10 am to 4 pm). The **Eagle Mine** features a guided tour, including an explanation of how gold was mined – just follow the signs from C St (open daily from 8 am to 4 pm). At the **George Washington Mine**, reached by a footpath at the end of Washington

St, an assay office and blacksmith shop have been reconstructed.

The **Julian Gold Rush Hotel** was established in 1887 by freed slaves from Georgia and claims to be the oldest continuously operating hotel in Southern California. A rocker on the front porch accentuates the sense of nostalgia and it seems entirely appropriate to retire to a four-poster bed in a room lacking such 20th century amenities as radio and television, with facilities down the hall labelled 'Ladies' and Gentlemen's Necessary Rooms'.

Julian also has two youth hostels, if you are looking for budget accommodation.

If you happen to be in this area on Memorial Day (the final Monday in May), take a detour to Banner to join in the **Malki Springs Fiesta** on the Morongo Indian Reservation – it's one of the few regularly sceduled Indian events held in California. Banner is located on SR 78, the road east to Anza-Borrego.

SANTA YSABEL

At the junction of SR 78 and SR 79 is Santa Ysabel: its claim to fame resting mainly in the ovens of **Dudley's Bakery**, which turns out 20 varieties of freshly baked bread and mouth-watering pastries made with pure well water and natural ingredients. Pick up the rest of your supplies for a picnic and head for the Mission Santa Ysabel's tree-shaded picnic tables. The mission was built as an *assistencia* (branch) of Mission San Luis Rey in 1818. Its whitewashed stucco chapel was rebuilt in 1920. It's a pleasant place to dally a while, maybe to toss a coin in the wishing well.

San Diego Wild Animal Park

SR 78 west leads to San Pasqual, location of the renowned **San Diego Wild Animal Park**.

The 1800-acre wildlife sanctuary's chaparrel terrain provides a habitat where almost 3000 animals roam freely. Many of them are numbered amongst rare and endangered species and some have given birth, unusual in captivity. Ride the Wgasa Bushline Monorail – best time to view the animals is early morning and late afternoon, and binoculars are an advantage. For close-ups, Nairobi village presents free animal shows, ideal for photography. You can pet the less exotic animals in a kraal and an animal nursery, and wander through a free-flight aviary.

The 1½-mile Kilimanjaro Hiking Trail offers spectacular views and photographic subjects as well as picnic sites. The Wild Animal Park is a must and you should allow plenty of time to enjoy it all. This park is particularly thoughtful of the needs of handicapped visitors. You can reach the park from San Diego in a 40-minute drive up I-15, or from Oceanside on the coast, even if time does not permit back country exploring. The park's open daily from 9 am to 5 pm (summer 9 am to 9 pm, November to February 9 am to 4 pm), admission $9.35 includes monorail; tel (619) 231-1515.

The San Pasqual Valley is wine country, too, with several vineyards offering tasting.

Eight miles southeast of Escondido a marker commemorates the **San Pasqual battlefield**, where the bloodiest battle of the Mexican War took place in 1846, ending in the defeat of General Kearny's Army by General Pico and his native Californian troops.

ESCONDIDO

Continuing west on SR 78, you come to Escondido, touted as the 'avocado capital of the world'. You might stop for a meal at *Lawrence Welk's Country Club Village* – it's on Champagne Boulevard, naturally!

MT PALOMAR

From Escondido Highway S6, the Highway to the Stars, leads to the famous observatory atop 5500-foot Mt Palomar. The Observatory can be reached also from Santa Ysabel by taking SR 79, then SR 76 past Lake Henshaw to its junction with S 6. (SR 79 continues to **Warner Springs**, site of a popular dude ranch and hot springs resort).

Palomar Observatory houses America's largest telescope; its 200-inch-diameter captures on film stars billions of light years from earth. During the conducted tour, you view the 500-ton telescope from a gallery while guides describe how it is penetrating ever deeper into the secrets of the universe. Open daily 9 am to 4 pm; admission charge; tel 757-3651.

MISSION SAN LUIS REY

From its junction with S6, SR 76 loops northwest to Pala, then follows San Luis Rey River down to its mouth at Oceanside. The Mission San Luis Rey, four miles from the coast, was founded in 1789 on a hill overlooking a lovely valley and became the Americas' largest Indian mission. Now a seminary, it is one of the most attractive in the chain of missions, with a beautifully proportioned facade, lofty ceilings and interesting paintings executed by local Indians. California's first pepper tree, imported from Peru in 1830 still stands in the grounds and you can explore an early cemetery and a small museum to get the feeling of the 18th century mission life.

Museum open Monday to Saturday, 9 am to 4 pm, Sunday 1.30 to 4 pm; admission charge.

San Antonio de Pala was built inland in 1815 as an assistencia of Mission San Luis Rey. Situated on the Pala Indian Reservation, the restored chapel is the only one still used by a predominantly Indian congregation. It features Indian frescoes on the walls and an attractive campanile stands near it. Highlight of the year on the reservation is the festive **Corpus Christi Fiesta**, held in late May or early June. A 9.30 am mass outside the mission campanile celebrating the primarily religious festival is followed by a colorful procession and carnival in the afternoon. For information, telephone (619) 742-3317.

From Pala, you can return to San Diego quickly on I-15 or take SR 76 out to I-5 on the coast to head south to San Diego or north to Los Angeles. (See description of the coastal route from San Diego to Los Angeles.)

RANCHO BERNARDO
Off I-15 south of Escondido is Rancho Bernardo, worth the detour a mile or so east on S 5 to visit the **Mercado**. Artists and craftspeople create and sell their wares in studios and shops grouped around a central courtyard while musicians enliven the atmosphere with a Spanish beat.

FRONTIER MUSEUM
The Frontier Museum Historical Center recreates the history of the Old West from the post Civil War era to the turn of the century. You'll see the gunfight at the OK Corral in diorama, stagecoaches, weapons and you can stroll through a frontier town, peopled by effigies of Buffalo Bill, Wyatt Earp and the like.

At 27999 Front St, Temecula; tel (714) 676-2260. It is open daily 9.30 am to 5 pm; admission charge.

Places to Stay
Back country accommodation ranges from budget motels to posh resorts, country clubs and even dude ranches. Tariffs, of course, vary as widely. Summer rates – printed below – are usually slightly higher than winter.

Places to Stay – Escondido
Pine Tree Lodge (425 W Mission at Centro City Parkway, Escondido CA 92025; tel (619) 745-7613). 38 units, some with kitchens at an extra $4 to $6 charge, some with oversized beds, adjacent coffee shop. Rates from $40 double.
Lawrence Welk's Village Inn (8868 Champagne Boulevard, Escondido CA 92026; tel (619) 749-3000). 90 units, oversized beds, private patios, jacuzzi,

restaurant. Some efficiencies. Rates from $53 double.

Places to Stay – Julian
Julian Hotel (Box 856, Julian CA 92036; tel (619) 765-0201). Restored 1887 gold rush hotel. Victorian decor, wood-burning stove in lobby. Some private bathrooms. Bed & breakfast. Rates from $38 double.
Pine Hills Lodge (PO box 71, Julian CA 92036; tel (619) 765-1100). Rustic lodge rooms and cabins; restaurant and bar; Friday & Saturday dinner theater; brunch Sunday 10 am to 2 pm. Rates from $85 double.

Places to Stay – Mt Palomar
Lazy H Steak Ranch & Motel (PO Box 155, Pauma Valley CA 92061; tel (619) 742-3369). On SR 76 near Mt Palomar. Golf, fishing, hiking and horse riding.

THE COLORADO DESERT
The 4000-square-mile Colorado Desert is shaped like a hand coming from the Colorado River at the southeast corner of California, with an outstretched finger pointing up the center of the state. At its base is the Imperial Valley, the knuckles are covered by the Salton Sea, the pointed index finger is the Coachella Valley with Palm Springs at the fingertip, while the Anza-Borrego Desert State Park reaches out to the west like loosely clenched fingers.

In summer, the Colorado Desert is one of the hottest places on earth, reaching temperatures between 105 to 110°F. But the six-month winter brings mild, sunny days and crisp, clear nights, which have made Palm Springs and its environs in the Coachella Valley one of the country's most popular resort areas. Rapidly increasing in popularity is the Anza-Borrego Desert region.

THE IMPERIAL VALLEY
There is not much to see or do here, except perhaps for those interested in the

reclamation of a desolate desert into a prime agricultural area, producing vast crops of sugar beets, melons and lettuce.

The major urban center, **El Centro,** billed as the 'largest city below sea level in the Western Hemisphere', functions primarily as an administrative and shopping center for valley residents.

Brawley is a farmworkers' town and **Calexico** is a gateway to Mexicali, Mexico.

THE ANZA-BORREGO DESERT

In the Anza-Borrego Desert you can experience one of California's most primitive, undeveloped areas. The history of settlement in this region probably began with the San Dieguito Indians, who lived here over 9000 years ago when grasslands and streams supported hunting and fishing. The opening of the Anza Trail signalled permanent change with the coming of Europeans. But even today you will see almost exactly the same landscape that those first visitors from Mexico saw; changed only by nature through the intervening 200 years.

You encounter reminders that this was traditionally a transportation corridor, first between Mexico and Alta California and later for pioneers from the east. Discovery of gold in California in 1849 triggered the gold rush and easterners streamed across what had become the Southern Emigrant Trail to seek their fortune. From 1858 to 1861, the route was used by the famous Butterfield Overland Mail Stage, connecting St Louis with Los Angeles and San Francisco.

Anza-Borrego State Park

The nearly half million acres embraced by the Anza-Borrego State Park offer below sea level stretches to the 6000-foot San Ysidro Mountain, scenic canyons, oases and the spectacularly incised Borrego Badlands.

Although the sabertooth cats, camels, giant turtles and other animal life that roamed the region in the Pleistocene Epoch are long gone, the park still harbors more than 250 types of animal, as well as 600 species of plants and over 150 varieties of birds – including the singular roadrunner which can achieve a speed of 30 miles per hour when it elects to run rather than fly!

Best place to start your exploration is park headquarters at **Borrego Palm Canyon.** Rangers will give you maps showing which park roads are negotiable by ordinary car and which require jeep or four-wheel drive. They also have brochures describing self-guided automobile tours and self-guided walks on nature trails, including information on geology, history and plant life. The rangers conduct nature walks and auto tours, too, as well as campfire programs on weekends and holidays from October to May. For information, park headquarters telephone is (619) 767-5311.

Borrego Palm Canyon is the site of the largest campground, situated at the mouth of the canyon. On a 1½-mile self-guided nature walk up the trail into the canyon, you may be lucky enough to see bighorn sheep (*borrego* is Spanish for bighorn) drinking at the fan palm-shaded spring.

The **Borrego Badlands,** etched through eons by water and wind into twisted, undulating mountains of rock through which rushing flash floods have incised deep canyons, present one of the park's most breathtaking sights.

A good vantage point from which to view the Badlands is **Font's Point,** off S 22. En route you pass **Peg Leg Smith Monument,** commemorating Thomas Long Smith, whose claims to have found and lost again a fabulous gold mine were buttressed when a few black pebbles he carried to Los Angeles in 1828 turned out to be almost pure gold. Since his death in 1866, Peg Leg's lost gold mine has evolved into one of the Southwest's best-known legends, fortified by occasional claims (one as recently as 1965) to have re-discovered the black gold source. Perpetuating the legend is the annual campfire celebration of the **Peg Leg Liar's Contest**, held at the Monument the first Saturday in April and open to all who have a tale to tell about Peg Leg's lost mine.

Borrego Springs

Borrego Springs, a quiet resort community, sprawls across the Borrego Valley in the shelter of San Ysidro Mountain, just outside the park. Its year-round population of around 1100 expands to 3000 in the winter season – October through May – when it becomes hub for park activity. Being mostly a community of retired people, nightlife is limited but there are a few restaurants and cocktail lounges in the valley to relax in after a day of golf or tennis, perhaps.

THE SALTON SEA

If you tire of desert scenes and feel like indulging in some water sports, head east from Borrego Springs on S 22 to the Salton Sea.

A thousand years ago, freshwater Lake Cahuilla filled the below-sea-level basin left by the receding waters of the Gulf of California. Then 500 years ago it disappeared, leaving only high-water marks on the surrounding land to show its existence.

In 1905, the flooding Colorado River burst through poorly constructed irrigation headgates and for two years poured into the Salton basin, inundating farms, communities and the Southern Pacific railroad track until 1907, when the breach was sealed. In the ensuing years, leaching has turned the freshwater lake into an inland sea, which is becoming more salty each year. The Salton Sea is presently 40 miles long, 16 miles wide and 40 feet deep at its deepest spot, with an average depth of only 10 feet.

Salton City, on its northwest shore, was developed as a seashore resort and has

lodging and restaurants. But most of the water sports are centered on the 16,000-acre **Salton Sea State Recreation Area** off SR 111 on the northeast shore. Popular are swimming, motor boating and water skiing, although strong winds can whip up 10-foot-high waves at times.

Places to Stay

Anza-Borrego State Park and the Salton Sea State Recreation Area both offer a range of camping areas, plus a selection of resorts and motels for the non-camper.

A complete list of the campgrounds can be obtained by writing to Anza-Borrego Desert State Park, Borrego Springs CA 92004, tel (619) 767-5311; reservations can be made with them or through any Ticketron outlet in California.

Non-camper visitors to Anza-Borrego have a choice of resort-style apartment hotels and motels in Borrego Springs. A complete list of accommodation can be obtained from Borrego Springs Chamber of Commerce, Borrego Springs CA 92004, telephone (619) 767-5555. Reservations should be made directly with the hotel, particularly in season (October-May). Some samples of what's there:

Borrego Springs - Top End

La Casa Del Zorro (Yaqui Pass Rd at Borrego Springs Rd (PO Box 127), Borrego Springs CA 92004; tel (619) 767-5323). Resort rooms and deluxe cottages, some with kitchens. Golf and tennis available. Rates from $40 double.

Borrego Springs - Mid-Range

Stanlund's Resort Motel (2771 Borrego Springs Rd, Box 278, Borrego Springs CA 92004; tel (619) 767-5501). 21 units, some kitchens, air-conditioned, color cable TV. Pool. Rates from $26; reservation deposit required.

Getting There

Borrego Springs is served by commuter airlines, with scheduled flights linking it to San Diego, Palm Springs and Los Angeles. Rental cars are available at the airport (there is no bus or taxi service in town).

THE COACHELLA VALLEY
The Coachella Valley has become one of the world's richest fruit and vegetable growing regions, famous for its acres of date palms and succulent grapefruit.

At the valley's northern tip, a string of recreational communities has grown up along SR 111, where it loops from SR 86 at Indio to join the main east-west freeway I-10 further west. The towns from Indio to Palm Springs are gradually overlapping, now being separated only by golf courses for the most part. Though Palm Springs is the most populous and fashionable, frequent visitors often prefer the quieter, less glamorous ambience of Palm Desert or Indio.

PALM SPRINGS
The glamorous aura attached to Palm Springs and the prospect of rubbing shoulders with celebrities lure visitors to the city – and more often than not they are disappointed.

True, celebrities abound. But they tend to remain out of public sight behind the walls of exclusive hostelries and private country clubs. Stargazers must pay the price of expensive dining at one of the more elegant restaurants if they hope to catch sight of a former president, Old Blue Eyes, or the honorary mayor of Palm Springs, Bob Hope.

But visitors do find a resort town soaking in sun (350 days of sunshine a year), smart shops, fine hotels and restaurants, and an abundance of opportunities for golf, tennis and swimming – there is one pool for every five residents!

The town centers on Palm Canyon Drive, actually SR 111S, which is lined with fashionable department stores – branches of those in Beverley Hills – boutiques and restaurants. The more affluent homes are set away from downtown, in the foothills, while the huge estates are secluded behind high walls a distance from downtown.

Palm Springs Aerial Tramway
The most popular way to gain an overview of Palm Springs and its environs is from the Aerial Tramway which, in a 15-minute ride, transports you from the heat of the desert floor to alpine coolness 8516 feet above on Mt San Jacinto. (Temperatures can be 40° lower up there so carry a sweater.) At the top are the Alpine Restaurant and cocktail lounge, a coffee shop, picnic area, gift shop and a 54-mile network of hiking trails, sprinkled with campgrounds. Snow conditions permitting, a Nordic ski center is open from mid-November to the end of April. Mule rides are available from noon to dark daily when there's no snow.

The cable tramway departs from Tramway Drive-Chino Canyon, off SR 111N, every half-hour from 10 am to 7.30 pm daily; round trip fares are $8.95 adults, $4.95 age three to 11. A special Ride 'n' Dine rate applies from 4 pm which includes dinner in the Alpine Restaurant: $12.95 adult, $8.50 children; tel (619) 325-1391. (The Tramway closes in September for maintenance.)

Agua Caliente Indian Reservation
The Agua Caliente Mission Indians' reservation covers Palm Canyon and several smaller canyons. The tribe, descendants of the Cahuilla Indians who inhabited the area a thousand or so years ago, periodically allows visitors to explore their sanctuary after payment of an entrance fee at a toll gate. The reservation is closed to the public in summer, so check dates ahead - the **Palm Springs Convention and Visitors Bureau** located in the lobby of the Municipal Airport Terminal will advise you. They are located in Suite 315, Airport Park Plaza, 255 North El Cielo Rd, Palm Springs CA 92262; tel (619) 327-8411.

The Desert Museum

The Desert Museum documents how the Cahuilla Indians survived the inhospitable land that was their home. From October to June, nature walks, bird watching walks and hiking trips are conducted.

At 101 Museum Drive, Palm Springs, it is open daily (except Mondays) 10 am to 4 pm Tuesday to Friday, 10 am to 5 pm weekends; closed June 6-September 20; admission charge. Tel (619) 325-7186.

LIVING DESERT RESERVE

The Living Desert Reserve in Palm Desert provides self-guided and escorted walks through the park, which encompasses six different desert habitats.

It is at 47-900 Portola Avenue, Palm Desert, south of SR 111S; open daily 9 am to 5 pm closed June 1 to September 1; admission charge; tel (619) 346-5694.

MOORTEN'S DESERT BOTANICAL GARDENS

A botanist's delight, Moorten's Desert Botanical Gardens offers over 2000 species of cacti, including indigenous desert varieties in their natural habitat, Indian relics and a wide variety of wildlife.

At 1701 S Palm canyon Drive, Palm Springs, it is open daily 9 am to 5 pm all year; admission fee; tel (619) 327-6555.

CABOT'S OLD INDIAN PUEBLO MUSEUM

This is a fascinating testament to one man's dream. Cabot Yerxa, adventurer and traveler *extraordinaire*, built his Hopi Indian style home alone over a 20 year period, using pueblo cliff dwellings as his inspiration. It has 35 rooms, 150 windows and 65 doors – and he left behind the plans for 200 more rooms when he died in 1965! The museum contains Yerxa's considerable memorabilia and relics of his far-flung travels.

The address is 67-616 Desert View Avenue, Desert Hot Springs; open daily 9.30 am to 5.30 pm; admission charge; tel (619) 329-7610.

Things to See & Do

Hot air ballooning affords an exciting way to view the valley, clear down to the Salton Sea. Several companies operate; we found *Sunrise Balloons* dependable, and they have a helicopter to fill in when conditions preclude ballooning. They take off from the Indio side of the valley; tel (619) 346-7591 for directions. Season is from October to May; a 40-minute flight is currently $60 per person.

Apart from desert viewing, golf, tennis, riding – bicycle and horse – usually occupy the time of Palm Spring's citizens.

Bicycles are available for rental by the hour or day. Popular sources are Mac's Bike Rentals, 700 E Palm Canyon Drive and Tramview Bike Shop, 67-911 SR 111. Many of the hotels also have a supply for guests. A network of bike trails, marked by blue and white signs, is laid out around Palm Springs and bicycle trail maps, detailing a number of pedal tours taking in points of interest, can be obtained from the Leisure Services Department at City Hall.

Golfers will find a number of public golf courses; in addition, some private clubs offer reciprocal playing privileges to members of other clubs and to some local hotel guests.

Over 100 golf tournaments are held annually in and around Palm Springs, including the Bob Hope Desert Golf Classic in early February. This one draws not only the cream of the players but also lures the celebrated to the gallery, where they in turn become an attraction. The women's equivalent is the Nabisco Dinah Shore Invitational, played in early April at Mission Hills County in Rancho Mirage. If you're tempted to join the gallery for either of these, make your hotel reservations well in advance or you might find yourself commuting from Imperial Valley!

There are **tennis courts** at nine hotels and several dozen public courts, some lit for night playing. **The Palm Springs Tennis Center** has nine lighted courts with automated machines which allow practice without a partner. At 1300 East Baristo Rd, it is open daily 7 am to 11 pm.

Tennis highlight is the **Congoleum Tennis Games**, which draws 64 of the world's top players every March.

Horse riding is popular from September to May. Smoke Tree Stables 2500 Toledo, has horses for hire, lessons, trail rides and special events such as hayrides, breakfast rides and moonlight cookout rides from time to time; tel (619) 327-1372.

Polo fans have the opportunity to watch games played at the Eldorado Polo Club, on Cook St in Indian Wells. You might even be lucky enough to catch sight of stars from the sports and entertainment worlds, who occasionally participate or watch. The polo season is from December to April and games are held on Wednesday, Friday, Saturday at 1 pm; Sunday 11 am and 1 pm.

If **baseball** interests you, drop by the Angels Stadium while the California Angels are in spring training here in March. It is at Sunrise Way near Ramon Rd; games 1 pm; admission charge.

Perhaps the most unusual classic is the annual **Sled Dog Races**, held in the San Jacinto Wilderness at the top of the Aerial Tramway in January.

Festivals: A Look at Local Life

Coachella Valley derives its living from dates, mineral spring spas and citrus fruits for the most part. So it's not surprising that the annual **National Date Festival**, held in Indio for 10 days in February to celebrate the multi-million dollar industry, is the highlight of the local folks' year. If you are planning to be in that part of the world at the time, be sure you've reserved your accommodation well in advance, then join in the fun. Apart from displays of dates and citrus, the festival offers many shows and exhibits, including a Gem and Mineral Show rated as one of the five best in the world, and hilarious camel and ostrich races. Entertainment

includes the extravagant Arabian Nights Pageant, presented nightly in an outdoor theater.

If you happen to be in Palm Springs in January, you'll catch the popular **Palm Springs Police Rodeo**, sponsored by the illustrious Palm Springs Mounted Police, whose main mission is search-and-rescue. A colorful parade through the business district is followed by a two-day rodeo featuring professional rodeo riders.

Places to Stay

Accommodation in the Palm Springs area ranges from exclusive, and expensive, resorts for the jetset to comfortable motels.

The high season tariffs are almost double low season (high season runs from around December 15 to the end of April). Rates decrease in the fall and are even lower again in the summer, though some hotels close down altogether in the summer months.

Secondly, rates are inclined to be lower the further away you get from Palm Springs, except for the exclusive country club properties; i.e. Indio rates are generally less than, say, Palm Desert.

The prestigious and expensive hotels generally offer a choice of rooms, suites or even villas. They also have facilities like pools, jacuzzis, spas and usually tennis and golf, which cost extra. Rate reductions and special packages are often available.

Palm Springs – Top End

Americana Canyon Hotel & Golf Resort (2850 S Palm Canyon Drive, Palm Springs CA 92262; tel (619) 323-5656). Rates from $95 double in season; closed mid June to mid September.

Ingleside Inn (200 W Ramon Rd, Palm Springs CA 92262; tel (619) 325-0046). Rates from $95 double in season; $60 double summer.

La Mancha Villas & Court Club (444 N Avenida Caballeros, Palm Springs CA 92262; tel (619) 323-1773). Elegant one, two and three-bedroom villas with private terrace, whirlpool spas, many private swimming pools. Tennis, restaurant. Convertible cars for use by guests with three-night stay. Rates from $235 double in high season.

Palm Springs Hilton Rivera Hotel (1600 N Indian Avenue, Palm Springs CA 92262; tel (619) 327-8311, toll-free (800) 472-4395). Rates from $85 double, $40 off-season.

Palm Springs Spa Hotel (100 N Indian & Tahquitz Drive, Palm Springs CA 92262; tel (619) 325-1461). Rates from $110 double, $45 off-season.

Sheraton Plaza (400 E Tahquitz-McCallum Way, Palm Springs CA 92262; tel (619) 320-6868). Rates from $95 double, $60 off-season.

Palm Springs – Mid-Range

Golden Palm Villa (601 Grenfall Rd, Palm Springs CA 92262; tel (619) 327-1408). Small motel set in landscaped grounds in quiet area. Color TV, pool, whirlpool, BBQ, some oversize beds. Under 18s not accepted. Rates from $38 double in season; closed July 1 through early September.

Mira Loma Hotel (1420 N Indian Avenue, Palm Springs CA 92262; tel (619) 320-1178). Charming 12 room hotel decorated with antiques. Personalized service. Six rooms with kitchen, one with fireplace. Pool, complimentary bicycles. Rates from $40 double October-April, $30 June to September.

Ramada Inn North (1177 North Palm Canyon Drive, Palm Springs CA 92262; tel (619) 325-5591). Centrally located 78 room hotel with pool, jacuzzi, restaurant and cocktail lounge. Rates from $68 double, $32 off-season.

Palm Springs/Indio – Bottom End

Palm Shadow Motel (80-761 Highway 111, Indio CA 92201; tel (619) 347-3476). 18-unit motel set in citrus and date palm grove. Pool, some kitchenettes. Rates from $24 double.

Versailles (288 Camino Monte Vista, Palm Springs CA 92262; tel (619) 325-6248). 16 air-con units, some kitchens (two-day minimum). Two oversize beds, color TV, pool, therapy pool. No restaurant. Rates from $28 double, kitchens extra.

Motel 6 (95 E Palm Canyon Drive, Palm Springs CA 92262; tel (619) 327-2044). 126 air-con rooms, pool, adjacent cafe. Rates from $19.95 double.

Places to Eat

Palm Springs and its environs are noted for fine restaurants offering every type of cuisine – there are nearly 200 in the immediate area.

Restaurants, both expensive and inexpensive, line the city's main street, Palm Canyon Drive. Nearby, a restaurant row has grown up on SR 111 between Frank Sinatra Drive and Bob Hope Drive in Rancho Mirage. You'll find Japanese, Continental, Mexican, Italian and Yugoslav cuisines, as well as America's favored steak-and-seafood.

A handy guide to dining and entertainment is *Palm Springs Life's Guide,* a free monthly publication distributed in select hotels and popular visitor attractions. A second complimentary publication, *Key Magazine,* also gives dining information.

Many hotel restaurants feature entertainment, ranging from dazzling Las Vegas-style revues to low-key supper club acts. Favorite entertainment is often discreet star-gazing, particularly in chic hotel dining rooms, where celebrities may be seated at the next table. Among them:

Melvyn's Restaurant, in the Ingleside Inn, is all elegant indoor and patio dining and champagne brunch weekends, popular with the in-crowd. (E) lunch, dinner daily. 200 W Ramon Rd; 325-0046.

Perry's in the Americana Canyon Hotel. Very fashionable. Serves haute cuisine, frequently to the stars. (E)

Lunch, dinner; closed June to September. 2850 S Palm Canyon Drive; tel 323-5656.

Less expensive restaurants abound, too. Some samples:

Hank's Cafe Americain in the Sheraton Oasis Hotel. Continental-style menu; entertainment nightly. (M) Breakfast, lunch, dinner daily. 155 S Belardo; tel 325-1301.

Tony Roma's Features barbecues, including ribs; entertainment evenings. (B)

Lunch, dinner daily. 450 S Palm Canyon Drive; tel 320-4297.

Elmer's Pancake & Steak House serves typical American menu, from pancakes to steaks. (B/M)

Breakfast, lunch, dinner daily. 1030 E Palm Canyon Drive; tel 327-8419.

Getting to Palm Springs & Getting Around

Air Palm Springs Municipal Airport, 15 minutes from downtown, is served by scheduled and commuter airlines. Ground transportation service is available, tel (619) 320-0044.

Car Car rental firms with desks at the airport are Avis (619) 325-1331, Budget (619) 327-1404, Hertz (619) 327-1523, National (619) 327-4100 and Dollar (619) 325-7334. Among those with off-airport premises are Thrifty (619) 325-2261, Ajax (619) 320-7441 and Aztec (619) 325-2294.

Bus *Greyhound Bus* serves Palm Springs.

Public minibuses called Sun-Liners – carpeted, air-conditioned and equipped with stereophonic music, as you would expect in such a posh community – provide transportation throughout Palm Springs for only 50c. They are a good way to explore the town.

Tours The two major tour operators offering guided sightseeing tours of the area are Gray Line (tel (619) 325-0974) and Tramway Transportation & Tours (tel (619) 325-2682, 325-2472).

THE COAST ROAD TO LOS ANGELES

Heading north from San Diego I-5, the Santa Ana Freeway runs up the coast to Orange County and from there inland, through Los Angeles, and through the central valleys all the way to the Pacific Northwest.

In fact, I-5 does not actually edge the ocean but runs slightly inland, bypassing the beach communities. The Pacific Coast Highway S 21 connects the beach towns; if you have the time, take this road to see the towns, beaches and the better ocean views.

DEL MAR

Fifteen miles up the coast from San Diego is the charming village of **Del Mar**, famed for its racetrack, where top thoroughbred horses compete from late July to mid-September, often for high stakes. Del Mar's groves of eucalyptus shelter the houses of San Diego executives who commute.

Places to Eat

Dini's Unpretentious spot featuring fresh seafood, steaks, Saturday and Sunday brunches. (B)

Breakfast, lunch, dinner daily. 526 Camino del Mar; tel 481-9111.

Bully's North Locally popular hideaway serving generous portions prime rib, cracked crab. Lively atmosphere. (B)

Lunch, dinner daily. 1404 Camino del Mar; tel 755-1660.

Jake's Del Mar Beachfront dining, alfresco if you wish. Extensive menu for snack or full dinner. (M) Lunch Tuesday to Friday, Sunday brunch, dinner nightly, closed Monday. 1660 Coast Boulevard; tel 755-2002.

Rudi's Hidden Acres Family-style German cooking, with home-made soup and salad included. (B/M)

Lunch, Sunday brunch, dinner nightly, closed Monday. 3700 Carmel Valley Rd; tel 481-9656.

ENCENITAS

Continuing up the coast from Del Mar, through Solana Beach and Cardiff-by-the-Sea, bursts of brilliant color (at least in springtime) mark the way to Encenitas, self-claimed 'flower capital of the world', which daily sends truckloads of cut flowers out across the country. December displays of poinsettia herald the Christmas season here with dazzling crimson.

Places to Eat

La Costa Cantina Fine Mexican specialties, served in charming atmosphere, to mariachi music. (B) Lunch, dinner daily. Village Square I, 1476 Encinitas Boulevard; tel 753-1488.

LEUCADIA

Leucadia's hills, rising steeply from the beach are treasure troves for lovers of succulent avocados. If you're passing through on the weekend, stop at the Flea Market, set up under the ubiquitous eucalypts on a lot off old Highway 101 near Leucadia Boulevard, for bargains and works of local artists.

CARLSBAD

Next is Carlsbad, named after Karlsbad in Germany for the simarity of their mineral waters; the **Alt Karlsbad Hanse House** was built over the spring. Now a gift shop, the old European-style building has paintings and a replica of Bohemian King Karl IV's crown. (It's at 2802 Carlsbad tel 729-6912).

Places to Eat

Pisces Restaurant Extraordinary seafood, served in glittering art deco decor. Jackets required (tie optional). (E) Dinner nightly, closed Wednesday. La Costa Plaza, 7640 El Camino Real; tel 4369362.

Java Murni Indonesian specialties served buffet style or a la carte in converted lagoonside house. Wine, beer only. (M) Dinner nightly, closed Monday. 4509 Adams; tel 434-4131.

Twin Inns Family-style meals featuring country fried chicken dispensed on blue-willow plates in a tradition since 1919. (M) lunch Tuesday to Saturday, Sunday brunch, dinner nightly, closed Monday. 2978 Carlsbad Boulevard; tel 729-4131.

OCEANSIDE

Crossing the mouth of the San Luis Rey River, you reach Oceanside, longtime beach resort and gateway to Camp Pendleton, a major US Marine Corps base. You can explore the replica Cape Cod village on the beach or take a dip in the bracing surf.

Places to Eat

Cafe Europa Owner-chef prepared Continental specialties are memorable. (M) Lunch Tuesday to Friday, dinner nightly; closed Monday. 1733 S Hill; tel 433-5811.

SAN CLEMENTE

You have a choice now of driving through Camp Pendleton on Vandergrift Boulevard, which heads inland to the historic ranch house of Pio Pico, last Mexican governor of California. Or you can take I-5 which follows the coastline through the military reserve to emerge at **San Clemente,** the quiet seaside community which was catapulted into fame as the home of Richard Nixon.

Swimming is good at the **San Clemente State Beach** and camping is allowed on the edge of the bluff, but campsite reservations must be made well in advance through Ticketron or by writing to Orange Coast State Parks, 3030 Avenida del Presidente, San Clemente CA 92672 (Orange County starts at the northern fence of Camp Pendleton).

San Onofre State Beach, off I-5 inside Camp Pendleton, is also good for swimming. You can't see it from the highway, but take the Basilone Rd exit and you'll see the signs by the nuclear generating plant. There is a visitor centre at the power plant.

SAN JUAN CAPISTRANO

A few miles north of San Clemente, after I-5 turns inland, take the turnoff for the lovely village of San Juan Capistrano, setting of the seventh mission in Father Junipero Serra's chain, which he founded in the year of America's independence, 1776. Completed in 1806, the **Mission San Juan Capistrano** suffered terrible damage in an 1812 earthquake. The adobe chapel where Father Serra said mass still stands and four bells retrieved from the fallen bell tower now ring out from a bougainvillea-draped campanile. Almost tame pigeons and swallows – they have brought lasting fame to the mission with their faithful return each year around St Joseph's Day (March 19) – splash in the fountains, strut possessively through the lush gardens and nest in the ruined walls. If you're there on October 23, the day of the mission's patron St John, you'll see the swallows depart for their flight south. It is open daily, 7 am to 5 pm, admission charge.

The village itself is worth exploring, too. On Main St, a row of original adobe houses has been converted into restaurants and shops, and the late 19th century railroad museum and restaurant, using the structure and fittings in a novel way (waiting for your table you sit oh the old shoeshine stand!). The 19th century **Richard Egan mansion** on Camino Capistrano is open weekends for a small fee, which contributes to the restoration and upkeep of the place. You can pick up a map for a walking tour of historical sights at the Chamber of Commerce, El Paseo Real Plaza, 31882 Camino Capistrano.

DANA POINT

Back on the coast, Dana Point until recently was known primarily as the Point San Juan of Richard Henry Dana's *Two Years Before the Mast*. In this book he describes the practice of hurling hides over the cliffs to traders waiting below, who took them to San Diego for pro-

cessing in the surf. Today Dana Point has a 2000-berth marina, restaurants and shops in the attractive **Mariner's Village**, a motel and fine sport fishing. You can indulge in boat-watching to your heart's content here, or rent one for the day, if you'd rather.

LAGUNA BEACH

Laguna Beach is one of California's most renowned art communities. Its lovely setting along cliff-tops poised between sea and mountains first attracted artists around the turn of the century. Best way to explore is to park and stroll, browsing shop windows and inside artists' galleries, jewellery stores featuring original designs, ceramics and leather-goods studios.

Festivals are a year-round thing in Laguna Beach. The famed **Festival of Arts and Pageant of the Masters** draws some 300,000 spectators each summer, from mid-July to late August. Multiple art shows are highlighted by the nightly performance at 8.30 pm at Irvine Bowl of the Pageant of the Masters which recreates art masterpieces with living models in a two-hour tableau. Tickets for these performances sell out months in advance. To apply for tickets, write Festival of Art, 650 Laguna Canyon Rd, Laguna Beach CA 92651.

If you're not there in the summer, you might be lucky enough to catch the **Winter Festival** held in February and March, or the **May Fair**.

NEWPORT BEACH

Newport Beach and its twin community of Balboa are prosperous waterfront resort towns offering a number of diversions. Dubbed the Gold Coast for the high-priced real estate, both communities' waterfronts are lined by large houses with private marinas containing some of the world's great yachts. You can take a look at the posh residential area of **Lido Isle** by crossing the humpbacked bridge on the Via Lido to Balboa Peninsula, then wandering through Lido Village, where shops and patios huddled behind the seawall to form one of the more unusual cityscapes in California.

Newport Beach's **dory fleet** ranks as one of the most unusual historic landmarks in the country. If you rise at dawn, you can watch this picturesque fleet of small wooden craft setting out to sea to work the fishing grounds for mackerel, flounder, sea trout, sand dabs and halibut. By noon, the fishermen head for shore and the beach becomes a large open-air fishmarket.

If you want to go fishing yourself Davey's Locker in Newport at Balboa Pavilion will take you out for $30 on a day-trip, share boat. This company operates sightseeing and Whale Watching cruises, too. The address is 400 Main St, Balboa; tel (714) 673-1434.

Inland from Newport Beach, you can inspect a totally planned community. Developed in the 1960s by the Irvine Company, owners of an 83,000-acre mountains-to-ocean ranch, **Irvine** was designed to integrate housing, business sites, shopping centres and wildlife preserves into a planned environment. The University of California at Irvine campus is part of the master plan.

From Irvine, you can take either I-405, the San Diego Freeway, or I-5 into Los Angeles. Or, if you wish, you can continue up the coast to Santa Monica, then take I-10, the Santa Monica Freeway, to downtown Los Angeles.

Places to Stay
Each coastal community offers a fairly wide range of motels, from budget to expensive. Except for the peak summer school holidays (July-August), it's usually fairly easy to get what you want without prior reservations. There are three noted resorts, however, for which reservations are recommended.

La Costa Motel & Spa (Costa del Mar Rd, Carlsbad, CA 92008; tel (619) 438-9111,

toll-free 800-421-0652, California only 800-252-0063). Luxurious resort including golf, tennis, horseback riding. Health spa: Roman salon, diet supervision, herbal wraps and whirlpool. Rates from $125 double.

The Newporter (1107 Jamboree Rd, Newport Beach, CA 92660; tel (619) 644-1700). Spacious resort in landscaped grounds. Sauna, massage, whirlpool; golf and tennis extra. Rates from $100 double.

The Inn at Rancho Santa Fe (Linea del Cielo at Paseo Delicias (PO Box 869), Rancho Santa Fe, CA 92067; tel (619) 756-1131). Lodge and cottages in lush garden setting. Putting green, tennis, beach cottage at Del Mar for guests. Gracious service. Rates from $40 double.

Useful Addresses
San Diego Convention & Visitors Bureau (1200 Third Avenue, San Diego, CA 92101); tel (619) 232-3101).

Automobile Club of Southern California (AAA) 16558 Bernardo Circle Drive, San Diego, CA 28598; tel (619) 487-6350.)

Mission Bay Information Center (2688 E Mission Bay Drive, San Diego, CA 92109; tel (619) 276-8200.)

Tijuana Convention & Visitors Bureau (PO Box 1831, Tijuana, Baja California, Mexico; tel (903) 385-8692.)

Palm Springs Convention & Visitors Bureau (Airport Park Plaza No 315, 255 N El Cielo Rd, Palm Springs, CA 92262; tel (619) 327-8411.)

Indio Chamber of Commerce (82503 Highway 111, Indio, CA 92201; tel (619) 347-0676.)

Automobile Club of Southern California (AAA) (300 S Farrell Drive, Palm Springs, CA 92262; tel (619) 327-8511.)

Laguna Beach Chamber of Commerce, (205 N Coast Highway, Laguna Beach CA 92651; tel (714) 494-1018.)

Meeting The Americans
Sierra Club (1549 El Prado, House of Hospitality, San Diego, CA 92010; tel (619) 233-7144.)

HUNTINGTON BEACH TO MALIBU

Follow the Pacific Coast Highway from Newport Beach to Malibu and you discover part of the appeal of living in the Greater Los Angeles Area – mile after mile of beaches and a stretch of the Pacific warm enough to swim in most of the year (wet suits required in winter). Freeways debouching in the beach cities will get you to downtown Los Angeles with surprising speed; driving time from Long Beach, for example, is approximately 40 minutes.

LONG BEACH

Past the oil-and-surf riding city of Huntington Beach you reach **Long Beach,** one of California's five largest cities, with a 5½mile beach, gaily-painted off-shore oil derricks and the **Queen Mary.** The venerable monarch of the seas rests alongside Pier J, at the southern end of the Long Beach Freeway.

You can explore much of the great Cunarder on a self-guided tour which includes the bridge, officers' quarters, engine rooms, the aft steering station and the upper decks. There's also the Queen Mary museum, Jacques Cousteau's Living Sea and a tank with five sharks. Highlight of the Queen's daily entertainment program is a re-enactment of the Changing of the Guard ceremony (given on the hour). In addition to these attractions, there are some 40 specialty shops and three restaurants on board, plus the new Marysgate Shopping Village ashore. This is a West Coast version of an Elizabethan English village. And if you would like to spend the night in one of the original first class cabins, contact the **Queen Mary Hotel** people (tel (213) 435-3511 or toll-free 800-421-3732). Rates are from $76 to $86 double. It is open daily, 10 am to 5 pm. Admission $6.75 includes tour; $3 boarding only. Tel (213) 435-4747.

Joining the world's largest passenger liner on Pier J in 1983 is the largest wooden aircraft ever built. Howard Hughes' *Spruce Goose,* designed in the 1940s to transport cargo, has a 320-foot wingspan and is 219 feet long. The great plane flew only once (with Hughes at the controls) in 1947.

Long Beach has two old buildings worth seeing. **Rancho Los Cerritos** (1844), 4600 Virginia Rd, is one of the most attractive old adobes in the Los Angeles area, with a garden that has changed little in nearly a century. It was built by one of those early Yankee immigrants to Alta California, Don Juan Temple, who opened the first general store in the Pueblo de Los Angeles. Open Wednesday to Sunday, 1 to 5 pm; closed major holildays, admission free; tel (213) 424-9423.

The other, **Rancho Los Alamitos,** 6400 Bixby Hill Rds, belonged to Don Abel Stearns, who married the daughter of one of Alta California's Spanish aristocrats. The house has undergone alterations over the years, but the oldest portions are believed to date from around 1806. There is a complete blacksmith shop in the grounds. Open from Wednesday to Friday, 1 to 5 pm; closed major holidays, admission free; tel (213) 431-2511).

SAN PEDRO

San Pedro, the Port of Los Angeles stands on a portion of one of the earliest land grants in California. Richard Henry Dana knew it as the foremost hide shipping port on the Pacific Coast, but found it 'designed in every way for wear and tear on sailors'. Today, with the adjacent port of Long Beach, it comprises the world's largest man-made harbor, handling an estimated two million tons of cargo each month.

The chief attractions for the visitor here are two shopping and restaurant complexes on the main channel of the harbor. **Ports O'Call** takes as its theme an early California seaport; **Whaler's Wharf** is patterned on the 19th century whaling town of New Bedford, Connecticut, complete with elm shade trees, gaslit streets and New England Colonial architecture. It is open daily from 11 am to 9 pm; closed Christmas Day, admission free.

A harbor cruise is particularly fascinating here and you can take one with **Los Angeles Harbor Cruises** for $3. (Call (213) 831-0996 for schedules and reservations.)

Another popular maritime attraction is the *SS Princess Louise*, at Berth 94, San Pedro. This luxury liner of the 1920s, which formerly plied between Vancouver, Canada and Skagway, Alaska, is now an entertainment-shopping complex with a restaurant that serves both lunch and dinner daily. (Phone (213) 831-2351 for reservations.) There's disco dancing daily on the forward deck, and you'll also find renovated rooms maintained as they were in the vessel's heyday, boutiques and replicas of the British Crown Jewels.

You might like to round off your visit to this huge port area by touring the house of the man who began its development in the middle of the 19th century. The **General Phineas Banning Residence Museum** stands at 401 E M St, Wilmington, surrounded by a large park. Banning built this romantic Greek Revival mansion in 1864 with the help of ship's carpenters whose captains traded their services for tar from the La Brea tar pits. The rich interior is furnished with period antiques, some of them contributed by the Banning family. Admission is by guided tour only.

Open Wednesday, Saturday and Sunday, 1 to 4 pm. Admission free. Tel (213) 548-7777.

SANTA CATALINA ISLAND

Discovered by Juan Rodriquez Cabrillo in 1542 and for long a hideout for buccaneers and smugglers who found its calm coves and mountainous hinterland ideal for their trade, Santa Catalina Island lies 22 miles off the California coast. Its great natural beauty, sunny climate and clear waters abounding in game fish have been attracting visitors since the 1880s when enterprising businessmen developed the resort town of Avalon and opened a ferry service from the mainland. A one-day excursion is both feasible and worthwhile.

Avalon, the island's one sizeable town and port, is the center for touring. Your first stop should be the **Chamber of Commerce** on Green Pleasure Pier (213) 510-1520) where you can pick up everything you need to know about the island's attractions. The Chamber can also help you make airline, boat and hotel reservations. Since visitors may not bring cars onto the island, and even cars and bicycles rented in Avalon are not permitted much beyond the town limits, sightseeing tours are the best way to explore.

Among the offerings are the *Inland Motor Tour* (3¾ hours $11) along the coast, with a stop at El Rancho Escondido to watch a performance by pure-bred Arabian horses – and you may see goats, deer, boar and buffalo which roam the backcountry unhindered. *Skyline Drive* (1¾ hours, $6) goes into the interior of the island, offering grand views and a chance to see something of the island's unusual vegetation. *Scenic Terrace Drive* (50 minutes, $4) is a jaunt into the hills around Avalon, including a visit to the home of chewing-gum millionaire William Wrigley who did so much to develop the island as a resort.

There are some cruises too. Most popular are the *Two Harbours Tour* (5¼ hours, $9), a 14-mile run along the coast with a four-hour stop in Two Harbors, location for many movies, and the *Glass Bottom Boat Tour* (40 minutes, $3.75), of the Underwater Gardens. Enquire about the special combination ticket enabling you to purchase three tours at a reduced rate.

Getting There
Boat *Catalina Cruises,* 330 Golden Shore Boulevard, Long Beach provides year-round service from its Long Beach and San Pedro terminals. Five departures daily in summer and two in winter. Current fares are $9.25 one way; $18.50 round trip. Call (213) 775-6111 from Los Angeles; 832-4521 from the harbor area; (714) 527-7111 from Orange County.

Air You can also get to Santa Catalina by air with *Helitrans.* The one way fare is currently $44, $80 round trip. For information call (213) 548-1314.

Palos Verdes Peninsula
Palos Verdes Drive follows the coast much of the way from San Pedro across the Palos Verdes Peninsula, offering splendid vistas of rugged cliffs and coves and of some palatial homes. At Portuguese Bend overlooking the Pacific, is the **Wayfarer's Chapel.** Designed by Frank Lloyd Wright's son, Lloyd Wright, this handsome glass and redwood chapel is a memorial to the Swedish philosopher-mystic Emmanual Swedenbord. Open daily 1 to 4 pm; admission free; tel (213) 377-1650.

A mile or so further is **Marineland** the famous showcase for dolphins, whales and sealions with show-biz leanings (see Theme Parks).

MARINA DEL REY
Journey on through the beach cities, past Los Angeles International Airport, to Marina Del Rey, home port for more than 10,000 pleasure craft and setting of the very popular **Fisherman's Village** complex of speciality stores and restaurants. The style here is Old New England whaling village. Among the attractions is the *Perseus,* fitted out as a nautical museum. For information on daily harbor cruises – Fun Fleet Cruises, tel (213) 882-1151.

VENICE
Venice-by-the-Sea, bordering Marina Del Rey, is the sad remnant of an ambitious development launched in the last decade of the 19th century. Abbot Kinney, a wealthy mid-Western manufacturer, sought to build a replica of the City of the Doges that would also become a great cultural center. Canals, bridges, gondolas with singing gondoliers, Italian Renaissance homes – the elements were all there, but Kinney's buyers preferred the bathing beaches to watching Bernhardt in *Camille.* Today, Venice has become a last bastion of the counter-culture.

SANTA MONICA
Eight public beaches, a fine climate and all the fun of an old-fashioned pier are the main lures of this attractive residential-resort city. Santa Monica has been a mecca for sun worshippers since the 1870s and for a while in the 1930s it was a popular playground for Hollywood's stars. For people-watching, fishing, boating and swimming, head for **Santa Monica Pier.**

Will R Rogers State Historical Park
The former home of that humorous philosopher Will R Rogers lies in the hills a few miles east of Pacific Palisades, at 14235 Sunset Boulevard. You'll find mementos of a career that included periods as cowboy, trick rider and artist before he became famous around the world as a 'cracker barrel' philosopher. A guide is on hand to answer questions.

Near the house is the stable area with corrals, a riding ring and roping arena, just as Rogers left it. Riding and hiking trails which he laid out in the surrounding hills offer pleasant walking.

Grounds open daily 8 am to 5 pm; admission free. House open daily 10 am to 5 pm; small charge. Tel (213) 706-1310.

MALIBU
Malibu lies at the northern end of Santa

Monica Bay, dreaming of days when it was *the* retreat of Hollywood's stars. Posh homes, restaurants and motels front the ocean, nevertheless you can enjoy good swimming at the very popular public beaches stretching some 27 miles along the coast. **Paradise Cove** and **Malibu Pier** are the place to go for sport fishing from party boats, bait and tackle shops and water skiing; **Surfrider Beach** has a reserved area for the big-board set; and hang-gliders hover above the sunbathers at **Torrance** and **Dockweiler** beaches.

J Paul Getty Museum

Looking down on it all is oil tycoon John Paul Getty's spectacular re-creation of the *Villa Dei Papyri* in Pompeii which houses his magnificent collection of Greek and Roman antiquities, Western European paintings and French decorative arts of the 18th century. The Mazarin *Venus* and Lansdowne *Herakles* are displayed here.

The Getty Museum is located at 17985 Pacific Coast Highway, just north of Sunset Boulevard. If you're going to the museum by car, be sure to obtain a parking reservation beforehand (at least a week).

Open Monday to Friday from June to September, 10 am to 5 pm; Tuesday to Saturday from 10 am to 5 pm; orientation lectures; admission free. Tel (213) 459-8402.

Los Angeles

Laid-back LA, city of turquoise swimming pools, smog, 3.2 million cars, bronzed nymphets, inflated egos, far-out religions and philosophies, where individualism has gone wild and excess passes for appropriate behaviour – that image, while containing more than a pinch of truth, obscures the fact that Los Angeles is a vital, exciting metropolis, splendidly situated between the Pacific and a semicircular wall of mountains. It is California's largest city, sprawling over 464 square miles. It contains some of the country's leading cultural and educational institutions. It is the center of the entertainment industry. And it has a climate just this side of perfection which has given rise to the California stereotype: orange blossoms and eternal sunshine.

History

There was a time when Los Angeles was an Indian village where the Spanish expedition searching for Monterey Bay camped overnight on August 1, 1769. Father Crespi who accompanied the explorers, named the river near the village the Porciuncula and noted in his diary that the region had 'all the requisites for a large settlement'. That settlement began very humbly 12 years later in response to the threat of Russian incursions; it was given the resounding name of 'El Pueblo de Nuestra Senora de La Reina de Los Angeles de Porciuncula'.

Despite a brief period as capital of the province of Alta California, Los Angeles remained for decades the traditional sleepy little pueblo where, grumbled mission friars, more attention was paid to gambling and playing the guitar than to tilling the land and educating children. The plain supported thriving cattle ranches and enterprising Yankees established a brisk seaborne trade, but even annexation by the Americans and the explosive gold rush period that followed barely altered the Angelenos' lifestyle.

LA's transformation from cattle town to metropolis began with the completion of the transcontinental railroads in 1869; $1 tickets from Kansas City to Los Angeles brought thousands of land-hungry settlers to the south-land and communities mushroomed across the plain. Discovery of oil in the 1890s and the arrival of two New York motion picture producers seeking a surer source of sunshine than Brooklyn increased prosperity – and the population. By the beginning of WW I many industries were making the city their western headquarters and WW II brought even greater prosperity and growth as LA's airplane factories boomed, laying the foundation of its important role in the aerospace industry. Tourism, entertainment, petroleum and space-age industries, and world trade are the bases of LA's thriving economy today.

Much of the interest in visiting here lies in observing Angelenos invent their future. No longer 'suburbs in search of a city', LA's 78 component communities surround a gleaming new center confidently rising 38 stories in earthquake country. Past visions are an eternal source of delight to connoisseurs of fantastic architecture. And where else can you eat in a drive-in hamburger? Or a bowler hat?

Climate

That near-perfect weather, give or take a little smog, means mild winters with average daytime temperatures of 60° to 75° and cool nights. LA's 14 inches of rain annually falls mainly between November and March, sometimes until May. The hottest months are from August through November. Lightweight clothing is suitable most of the year, but in winter sweaters or light coats may be needed. Remember too, night-time temperatures can plummet 20°.

CIVIC CENTER

One good place to begin a tour of Los Angeles is 27 stories above the city on the observation deck of **City Hall tower**, 200 Spring St, open 10 am to 4 pm weekdays. Smog permitting, there is a magnificent panorama of the city from the encircling mountains, dominated by Mt Wilson, to the Pacific, Los Angeles harbor and the Palos Verdes Peninsula. Below you is the **Civic Center** complex, the largest concentration of government buildings in the West, surrounded by pleasant gardens. Free City Hall tours are given Monday to Friday (by reservation only); call 485-4423 at least two days in advance. After your orienteering course, stroll across to the 60-foot tall **Triforium** at Temple and Main Sts – there's a taped music show here at 11.30 am and 1.30 pm weekdays (2.30 weekends) and again at 5.30 pm, enhanced by lights.

LITTLE TOKYO

Nearby, at First St, is Little Tokyo, focus of the Japanese-American community. This area is chock full of teahouses, restaurants, sushi bars and shops displaying everything from kimonos to woks. August is high holiday season, when Nisei Week celebrations include bonsai exhibits, sports and dollmaking displays and the age-old Ondo parade features brilliantly costumed performers who snake dance through the streets. Little Tokyo is also the setting of traditional spring and fall festivals.

EL PUEBLO DE NUESTRA SENORA DE LOS ANGELES

Just north of Hollywood Freeway is the birthplace of Los Angeles. El Pueblo De Nuestra Senora de Los Angeles is now a 42-acre State Historic Park undergoing restoration that is bringing new life to the cluster of early 19th century buildings surrounding the plaza laid out by Governor Felipe de Neve in 1781. The pueblo can only be explored by foot, and Tuesday through Saturday you can join a free tour (conducted hourly from 10 am to 1 pm) by signing up at the visitor information center, 130 Paseo del Plaza. (Call 628-1274 for reservations and information.)

Day and night, the pueblo is full of life and color. In the summer there are open-air concerts in the iron-lace bandstand at the center of the **plaza**, setting of fiestas throughout the year. Lining the plaza, between Main and Los Angeles Sts, are the **Masonic Hall** (1858); the **Pico House** (1869), built by the last Mexican governor of California which, with its bathtubs and gaslighting, was considered the grandest hotel in the southwest in its day; and the **Merced Theatre** (1870), Los Angeles' first theatre. Both the Pico House and the Merced Theatre will in future function in their original roles. At Los Angeles St is **Firehouse No 1** (1884), housing one of the first fire engines used in the city.

West of the plaza, the Church stands on the site of a tiny chapel put up in 1784. The present rather plain building was begun about 1818 with funds raised by the sale of brandy donated by the padres of Mission San Gabriel. Its bronze bells still ring out the Angelus, as they did more than 150 years ago.

Olvera St's old buildings look down on the booths of as colorful a market as you will find in Mexico. Browse here for vanilla and pecan fudge, silver jewellery, sandals and serapes. You'll probably find craftspeople at work, fashioning wrought iron and clay ollas, even blowing glass, and you can take your ease in attractive small restaurants with outdoor dining areas. The cuisine is authentically Mexican. Summer evenings are most attractive, when colored lanterns light the shops and music spills into the streets from the bodegas – **Casa La Golondrina**, in the historic Pelanconi house, offers an all-Mexican cabaret.

The long, low **Avila Adobe** (1818), 14

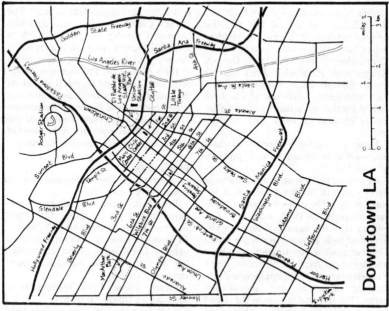

Downtown LA

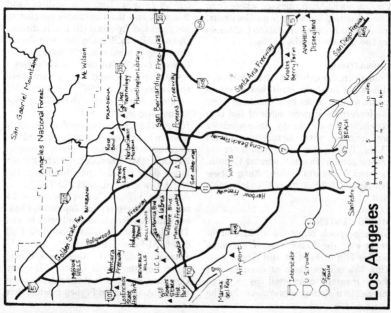

Los Angeles

Olvera St, was the home of Don Francisco de Avila, son of one of Los Angeles' original settlers. It is the city's oldest house, at various times occupied by Commodore Robert Stockton, General Kearny and 'Pathfinder' John Charles Fremont. Meticulous restoration and period furnishings, some of which were owned by the Avila family, offer an intimate glimpse of early 19th century life.

Open Tuesday to Friday, 10 am to 3 pm; weekends 10 am to 4.30 pm; admission free.

Cross over to the south side of Alameda St to view the last great symbol of the Railway Age. The **Union Passenger Terminal**, completed in 1939 at a cost of $11 million, is in the Spanish Colonial style, with vast halls finished in marble and a 135-foot clock tower. Readers who have weathered the comforts of British Rail's Victorian terminals will appreciate its individual armchairs and tree-shaded patios. The terminal stands on the site of the famous El Aliso vineyard where Jean Louis Vignes, a cooper from Bordeaux, introduced French varietals to California for the first time in the 1830s.

CHINATOWN

Chinatown, bounded by Broadway and Hill Sts, is not large but it has a certain exotic appeal, at its most fetching when the lanterns and neon signs of **Gin Ling Way** light up the night sky. Shop windows are jammed with merchandise from China, Taiwan and Japan, and there are several good restaurants serving Cantonese and Mandarin dishes. **Kong Chew Temple** at 215½ Ferguson Alley is worth a visit.

MUSIC CENTER

Glittering pools offset the striking architecture of the Music Center crowning Bunker Hill at First St and Grand Ave. This $35 million complex composed of three theaters connected by a large piazza, is a fitting centerpiece for the entertainment capital of the country. The **Dorothy Chandler Pavilion**, named for Mrs Norman Chandler who did so much to foster the Music Center's development, is the largest of the three theatres and home of the Los Angeles Philharmonic Orchestra and Civic Light Opera. It also hosts the Academy Awards presentations, opera, recitals and dance performances. The circular **Mark Taper Forum** and the **Ahmanson Theater** put on a broad range of plays, including experimental drama.

Places to Eat

Backstage Cafe Sandwiches and salads in this deli-style cafe. (B)

Breakfast, lunch and dinner. Open daily (from 4 pm Sundays). 135 Grand Avenue (Music Center); tel 972-7525.

El Paseo Restaurant Informal, popular place on Los Angeles' oldest street offering Mexican dishes. Flamenco dance shows nightly. (B)

Lunch, dinner. Open Wednesday to Monday. 11 Olvera St; tel 626-1361.

Golden Dragon Dim sum addicts head this way, and the Cantonese specialties are good too. Informal (B) lunch, dinner. Open daily until midnight. 960 North Broadway, Chinatown; 626-2039.

General Lee's What can you say about a restaurant that's been serving Cantonese specialties since 1880? Enjoy it! (M)

Lunch, dinner, daily. 475 Gin Ling Way, Chinatown; tel 624-1825.

Hungry Tiger Seafood Oyster Bar Attractive modern setting seafood specialties. Located in the Music Center's Chandler Pavilion. (M) Breakfast, lunch, dinner. Open daily (from 4 pm Sundays). 135 North Grand Avenue; tel 272-7322.

Japanese Village Plaza There are 14 restaurants here serving Japanese, Chinese and American food at all price levels. The plaza is at 327 East Second St. Call 620-8861 for information.

Pavilion Restaurant Luxurious dining room atop the Music Center's Dorothy Chandler Pavilion featuring truly regal buffets. Accent is on French cuisine. Prix fixe menu. (E) lunch, dinner. Open daily. 165 North Grand Ave; 972-7333.

San Antonio Winery LA's only producing winery has an attractive dining room and garden area. Sandwiches as well as Italian dishes. (B) lunch, dinner, open daily. 737 Lamar St; 223-1401.

Thousand Cranes Traditional Japanese cuisine in a charming room overlooking the garden-in the-sky. (E)

Breakfast, lunch, dinner. Open daily. New Otani Hotel, 120 South Los Angeles St; tel 629-1200.

DOWNTOWN LOS ANGELES

Downtown Los Angeles is on the way up in more ways than one. New skyscrapers crowd the skyline and a much-needed facelifting is transforming a rather seedy Victorian area which centered on Pershing Square.

Arco Plaza and the **Bonaventure Hotel**, facing each other across Fifth St between Figueroa and Flower Sts, ride the wave of futuristic architecture. Arco Plaza's twin towers soar above a monumental sculpture by Herbert Bayer set in a reflective pool; underground are three floors of restaurants, shops and galleries where art exhibits, fashion shows and concerts are regularly held. The Los Angeles Convention & Visitors Bureau and RTD Information Center are on the C level.

The five gleaming cylinders of the new Bonaventure Hotel enclose a vast atrium lobby characteristic of John Portman's architectural style. Cocktails in the comfortably upholstered pods overhanging its one-acre lake several stories below are a heady experience. Six balconies of shops line the atrium and a pedestrian skywalk links the hotel to the 38-acre **World Trade Center** where you'll find more restaurants, shops and two handy banks for exchanging currency.

The **Biltmore Hotel**, fronting Pershing Square, harks back to the ebullient 1920s. Its public rooms are on a magnificent scale, decorated by the Italian artist Giovanni Smeraldi in the Renaissance style of European palaces. To get the full impact of their splendor, enter the hotel through the lobby lounge on Olive St and ascend the twin staircase into the Galeria Real, Smeraldi's *tour de force*. Meeting rooms lining the gallery are equally impressive – you may have seen the Crystal Ballroom before; it has been used as a set in many films, including *The Last Tycoon*. And it was here that the Oscar awards were born in 1927 when the biggest names in Hollywood gathered to celebrate the formation of the Academy of Motion Picture Arts and Sciences.

Bradbury Building

Another architecturally impressive structure which has featured in many movies and TV is the historic **Bradbury Building** at 304 S Broadway, in the heart of the Mexican quarter north and east of Pershing Square. Built in 1893, it is renowned for its center court, flooded with light falling from the glass roof five stories above. Amber-toned brick walls, Mexican tile floors and rich wood paneling counterpart a wealth of ornamental cast iron. The ornate workmanship of the open-cage elevators and stair railings is particularly impressive.

The Bradbury is open to public viewing Monday to Saturday during normal office hours. A small admission fee is charged.

Grand Central Market

Across the street is the Grand Central Market which you should not miss. Stalls are heaped with unusual produce from across the border – hunks of panocha, tamarinds, scarlet and green peppers, fragrant spices, sweet stubby bananas, and an astonishing variety of beans. Cheese lovers will find cheeses from as far away as Greece and South America. The market is a mecca for LA's Mexican housewives who debate quality in liquid syllables, but you won't have to speak Spanish; the signs are all bilingual.

Places to Eat

Arco Plaza contains several restaurants in its seven underground acres – from fast food to elegant. Worth checking out. 505 South Flower St.

Bernard's Simply elegant, and considered one of the finest French restaurants in the country. Wine list features rare California wines. Reservations recommended. (E)

Lunch, Monday to Friday; dinner, daily. In the Biltmore Hotel, 515 South Olive St, downtown LA; tel 624-0183.

Italian Kitchen Restaurant Informal place with a cozy atmosphere serving pizzas, Italian and American dishes. (B)

Breakfast, lunch, dinner. 420 West 8th St; tel 622-9277.

Pacific Dining Car Famous for its steaks and seafood, this pleasant, informal restaurant has been serving Los Angelenos since 1921. (M/E)

Breakfast, lunch, dinner. Open 24 hours. 1310 West 6th St; tel 483-6000

EXPOSITION PARK

South and slightly to the west of downtown Los Angeles (and rather beyond comfortable walking distance) is Exposition Park, a green oasis bounded by Exposition Boulevard, Figueroa St and Menlo and Santa Barbara Ave. At its center is the **Sunken Garden** where, from late spring through the fall, more than 16,000 rose bushes bloom. The massive **Memorial Gateway** on Exposition Boulevard commemorates the 10th Olympic Games held in the Memorial Coliseum in 1932. Today the coliseum, with a seating capacity of nearly 95,000 is used for home football games by the University of Southern California. It's also the setting for rodeos, pageants and track meets and will host Olympian events and pageantry during the 1984 Olympic Games.

Also within the park are two interesting science museums. The **California Museum of Science and Industry**, 700 State Drive, contains do-it-yourself exhibits which could keep you pressing buttons for hours. The idea here is to celebrate the accomplishments of American technology and demonstrate how it impinges on our daily lives. Displays focus on energy, electricity, communications, automotive technology, finance, and even animal husbandry.

It's open daily, 10 am to 5 pm; closed Thanksgiving and Christmas Days; admission free; tel 794-0101.

The collections of the **Natural History Museum**, west of the Sunken Garden, trace the history of mankind and the earth. The Pre-Columbian and the American History halls give a comprehensive picture of cultural evolution on the American continent. First-rate arts and crafts from around the world are for sale in the museum's Ethnic Arts shop, which also hosts the annual American Indian Artistry Exhibit and Sale in December. Craft demonstrations, traditional dance performances, films and lectures supplement. Open Tuesday to Sunday, from 10 am to 5 pm; closed Thanksgiving and Christmas Days; admission charge; tel 746-3775.

Adjacent to Exposition Park is the **University of Southern California**, founded in 1880 under the sponsorship of the Methodist Conference of Southern California. It is California's largest private university, with an enrolled student body of some 27,000. The buildings are a pleasant blend of early Italian Renaissance and modern architectural styles and near the entrance to the administration building you'll find an eight-foot statue of a Trojan Warrior, the university's symbol.

WATTS TOWERS

Watts Towers soar above the community where black frustrations exploded in violence in August, 1965. This trio of intricate structures, reminiscent of the work of Antonio Gaudi, was fashioned of scavenged junk metal, glass bottles, stone, tile and seashells by an Italian tilesetter who came to Watts from Rome. It took Simon Rodia 33 years to create his masterpieces – and when they were completed in 1954, he abandoned them. After two decades of neglect and vandalism, the towers are now maintained by the City of Los Angeles as a cultural landmark.

Watts Towers are located at 1765 E 107th St and Wilmington Ave. Open daily from 9 am to 5 pm; admission charge; tel 569-8181.

WILSHIRE BOULEVARD

Lined by some of the costliest real estate in the city, Wilshire Boulevard runs 16 miles from downtown Los Angeles near Grand St to the Pacific at Santa Monica. In part it follows a stretch of the old Spanish road to the La Brea Tar Pits and the Camino Real, but its history begins in the real estate boom of the 1920s when forward-looking developers conceived of a 'Miracle Mile' between La Brea and La Cienaga Ave. Today Wilshire Boulevard has something of New York's Fifth Avenue, combining elegant boutiques, department stores, restaurants and grand hotels with plush apartment buildings and parks.

First of the famous-name hotels are the Los Angeles Hilton and the Ambassador, separated by **MacArthur Park,** a pleasant oasis with a small lake and an open-air theater for Shakespearean performances and musicals. Charlie Chaplin made his earliest movies here when the park was known as Westlake Park.

RANCHO LA BREA TAR PITS

Hancock Park, west of La Brea Avenue, encloses the Rancho La Brea Tar Pits, where brea, crude oil, still oozes out of the ground. The Spanish used the tar to waterproof their adobe houses and it was not until 1906 that scientists appreciated that the pits were also an extraordinarily rich source of prehistoric fossils. All manner of prehistoric mammals, birds and amphibians were entrapped over the millennia, including the saber-toothed tiger, mastodon, giant ground sloth, giant

vulture, imperial elephant and prehistoric camel. Life-sized replicas of some of the more dramatic-looking animals and birds stand in the pits, which still disgorge Ice Age fossils.

The **George C Page Museum** at the east end of the park, near Fairfax Ave, houses the La Brea collections, numbering over 1,500,000 specimens. Among the exhibits are reconstructed skeletons and films and slideshows on the tar pits. Watching the paleontologists at work in the glass enclosed laboratory is one of the museum's most popular features; you can also observe excavation in progress at the nearby Rancho La Brea Project viewing station. The museum is open Tuesday to Sunday, 10 am to 5 pm; viewing station 10 am to 4 pm; guided tours; admission charge; tel 936-2230.

LOS ANGELES COUNTY MUSEUM OF ART

The three buildings and sculpture garden of the Los Angeles County Museum of Art, actually float on a three-foot-thick concrete slab atop the tar pits a little farther west. The **Ahmanson Gallery** houses the permanent collections which are particularly rich in impressionistic paintings; you'll also find a notable assemblage of prehistoric objects from the Near East and Central Asia as well as 19th and 20th century sculpture. Contemporary art and temporary exhibitions are featured in the **Frances and Armand Hammer Wing** and the **Leo S Bing Center** contains a theatre, cafe and art rental gallery.

It is open Tuesday to Friday, 10 am to 5 pm; weekends 10 am to 6 pm. Closed Thanksgiving and Christmas days. Guided tours; admission charge; tel 937-4250.

FARMERS MARKET

Fairfax Avenue leads north from Wilshire Boulevard to the Farmers Market at 6333 West Third St, and it's well worth turning aside here for an hour or so to stroll its aisles. The market began in 1934, during the depression, when farmers set up stalls in a vacant field on what was then the edge of town in an effort to sell their produce. From such simple beginnings has grown a vast market place for the world's wares and gastronomic items, interspersed with open-air cafes and restaurants. It is open Monday to Saturday, 9 am to 6.30 pm (October to May), 9 am to 8 pm (June to September), 933-9211.

Places to Eat
The Cape Cod Seafood is the specialty of this informal restaurant in the Sheraton Townhouse. (B/M)Breakfast, lunch, dinner; open daily except Monday. 5814 Wilshire Boulevard; tel 933-5596.
The Egg and the Eye Very popular restaurant-cum-art gallery with more than 50 different omelets to choose from, plus Continental dishes. (M)

Lunch, dinner; daily except Monday. 5814 Wilshire Boulevard; tel 933-5596.
Farmers Market There are 26 restaurants in this great market at the corner of Fairfax and Third Sts. It is open daily except Sunday, 9 am to 8 pm in summer; 9 am to 6.30 pm October to May.
Robaire's Fine French fare in an attractive bistro setting. (E) dinner only. Closed Monday. 348 South La Brea; 931-1246.

BEVERLY HILLS
Beverly Hills, as everyone knows, is the epitome of the Hollywood dream. Luxurious homes and a handful of the West's finest hotels and boutiques line its handsome streets. A stroll along **Rodeo Drive** and adjacent side streets running between Wilshire and Santa Monica Boulevards will give a fair sampling of local affluence.

Beverly Hills' most celebrated mansion is **Pickfair** at 1143 Summit Drive which was the home of Mary Pickford from 1919 until her death in 1979. It is not open to public viewing. Another impressive residence is **Greystone Mansion**, Loma Vista and Doheny Rd, built by Edward Doheny, a key figure in the Teapot Dome scandal, at a cost of $4 million. You can enjoy the beautiful grounds any day between 10 am and 6 pm; the house is no longer open to view.

If you are interested in modern architecture, a detour from Wilshire Boulevard via the Santa Monica Freeway and the Avenue of the Stars to **Century City** is worthwhile. This strikingly futuristic development of skyscrapers interconnected by parks and plazas is built on the old 20th Century Fox lot (before that it was cowboy star Tom Mix's ranch). Although Welton Becket & Associates were the project architects, Minoru Yamasaki designed the dramatic **Century Plaza Hotel**. It was here that the Presidential State dinner honouring the first men to walk on the moon was held. Across the street is the **ABC Entertainment Center**, where you'll find the Shubert Theater and two movie houses in a complex of offices, shops, restaurants and clubs.

Places to Eat
Cafe Rodeo Sidewalk cafe on Beverly Hills' famous shopping street. Salads are a specialy of the house.(M) Lunch, dinner daily (no dinner Sundays). 360 North Rodeo Drive, Beverly Hills; 273-0300.
Chasen's Award-garnering restaurant popular with show-biz celebrities.(E) Reservations recommended. No credit cards. 9039 Beverly Boulevard, Beverly Hills; 271-2168.
Garden Restaurant Renowned for its cuisine and lovely garden setting.(M/E) Breakfast, lunch, dinner, open daily. In the Century Plaza Hotel, 2025 Avenue of the Stars, Century City; 277-2000.
Magic Pan Branch of the well-known chain producing superlative crepes, omelets and blintzes.(M) Lunch, dinner, daily. 9601 Brighton Way, Beverly Hills; 274-5222.
Old World Restaurant In the Heart of the shopping area. Fresh home-made food is

made food is featured. Beer and wine only. (BM) Breakfast, lunch, dinner; open daily. 216 Beverly Hills Drive, Beverly Hills; tel 274-7694

WESTWOOD/UNIVERSITY OF CALIFORNIA, LOS ANGELES

The University of California's largest campus covers 411 acres of terraced hillside overlooking the community of Westwood (between Beverly Hills and Santa Monica). The university began as the Los Angeles State Normal School, founded in 1881, and in 1919 was incorporated into the statewide University of California system. Today, UCLA is a leader in the fields of chemistry, medicine, drama, music and environmental design – and has so much to offer in the way of sightseeing that we recommend your first campus stop be the **Visitors Center**, 1215 Murphy Hall, at the south end of Dickson Plaza. Here you can pick up a free brochure and map describing two self-guiding campus tours and obtain information on the several free guided tours. These range from a general walking tour of the central and northern section of the campus, including the famous Sculpture Garden and fine Arts area, to those with a special-interest theme, such as a tour of the Molecular Biology Institute, Botanical Gardens or the Dance Department. Open Monday to Friday, 8 am to noon and 1 to 5 pm. Call 825-4321 for schedule information. Reservations required for some tours.

Information is also available at the James E West Alumni Center, facing Westwood Plaza, and the Office of Public Information, 1104 Murphy Hall.

UCLA's best-known sights lie a few minutes' walk north of Murphy Hall. The **Franklin D Murphy Sculpture Garden** is a lovely tree-shaded area displaying major works by Jean Arp, Alexander Calder, Barbara Hepworth, Jacques Lipchitz, Matisse and Rodin, to name just a few of the masters represented. Immediately to the northwest is the **Dickson Art Center**

which contains the Frederick S Wight Art Gallery displaying collections of the Grunwald Center for the Graphic Arts and the Museum of Cultural History in rotating exhibitions. The Center is an important research institute, numbering among its resources the Princeton Index of Christian Art and the Elmer Belt library on Leonardo Da Vinci.

The gallery is open during exhibitions, Tuesday to Friday, 11 am to 4.30 pm; weekends 1 to 5 pm; tel 925-1461.

For a good view of the campus and metropolitan Los Angeles, take the elevator to the observation deck of **Ralph J Bunche Hall**. Ackerman Union's Kerckhoff Coffee House is the place for quick, moderately-priced meals. And in the **Botanical Gardens** at Hilgard and LeConte Ave in the southern part of the campus, you can enjoy a stroll through eight acres of exotic and native plants. Open Monday to Saturday, 8 am to 5 pm; Sunday, 10 am to 4 pm. Closed University holidays.

HOLLYWOOD

The legend is potent still. Although many of the studios have moved to the San Fernando Valley and there hasn't been a full-blown premier at Grauman's Chinese Theater in years, Hollywood is still the mecca of the filmgoer's universe. Confronted by the sheer ordinariness of Hollywood Boulevard today – the porno shops, the massage parlors and the pimps and prostitutes who patrol the sidewalks – you may have to draw heavily on your imagination as you tour the artefacts of the most magnificent, stupendous, colossal, super-special dream factory in the world.

It all began in 1911 when two New York movie-makers seeking a better source of sunlight than Brooklyn rented an old barn in the sheep ranching village of Hollywood, a community with so strong a bias toward right living that when the local hotel applied for a liquor licence, the city fathers refused in horror. The movies changed all that, and for an eloquent portrait of Hollywood's scandal-ridden heyday, we commend you to Kenneth Anger's *Hollywood Babylon*.

The famed intersection of **Hollywood and Vine** (Hollywood Boulevard and Vine St) is the traditional center of the film community. Nothing much to catch the eye here – it was *who* crossed the intersection that counted. One block north is the **Capitol Records Building**, the first circular office building in the world.

But look down as you stroll Hollywood Boulevard: the sidewalk from Sycamore to Gower is studded with bronze medallions engraved with the names of the stars and leading character actors. This is the **Walk of Fame**, commemorating those who made Hollywood an international word.

Grauman's Egyptian & Chinese Theaters

Two fantastic landmarks of the golden years are the **Egyptian Theater**, 6712 Hollywood Boulevard, and **Mann's Chinese Theater**, 6925 Hollywood Boulevard, both built by master showman Sid Grauman. The Egyptian Theater, dedicated to Thespis, is a replica of a Theban palace, its long forecourt dominated by an effigy of Osiris. Grauman staged Hollywood's first movie premier here in 1922, a silent version of *Robin Hood*, and by all accounts it was a marvellous show. In its heyday a 'Libyan sheik dressed in desert garb' patrolled the walls of the Egyptian all day, and beautiful usherettes dressed like Cleopatra's handmaidens, received the public.

So successful was the Egyptian that Grauman built his masterpiece, the lavish Chinese Theater, 10 years later. Here he combined Chinese architecture with such unrelated attractions as a Polynesian village in the forecourt and Napoleon's carriage. The carriage and the Polynesian village are gone, but you can still enjoy his stroke of genius, the foot and handprints of the stars preserved for posterity in concrete.

Hollywood Wax Museum

One block east of the Chinese Theater, at 6767 Hollywood Boulevard, is the **Hollywood Wax Museum** containing more than 200 figures and tableaux, a Chamber of Horrors, and the Oscar Movie Theater with a filmed history of Academy Award presentations. There's a clip of just about everyone who was anyone, from Mary Pickford to John Wayne. It is open daily, 10 am to midnight (Friday until 2 am); admission $4, tel 462-8860.

Sunset Strip

Sunset Boulevard, immortalized by Gloria Swanson in the movie of that name, runs from the plaza in downtown LA to the Pacific. Its most famous section is the **Sunset Strip**, a 20-block section between Fairfax and Coldwater Canyon, which once drew the fans to the doors of Ciro's, the Trocadero and the Mocambo in the hope of spotting the famous. But the Strip, too, has lost its glamour – celebrity-spotting is better done in Beverly Hills these days. One landmark remains at the intersection of Laurel Canyon and Sunset Boulevard. **Schwab's Drugstore** is hallowed as the place where Lana Turner was discovered sipping a soda; it's still the rendezvous for show-biz folk.

Where the Stars Live

There are maps, there are tours, there is even a brochure put out by the Los Angeles Visitors and Convention Bureau, but the fact is, you will probably see very little of these palatial domains screened from view by high walls, hedges and thickets of stately trees. Nevertheless, a pleasant hour or so can be spent tooling around Beverley Hills, Bel Air and Topanga Canyon – the houses you see may not belong to the stars but they are impressive. *Gray Line* and *Starline Sightseeing* have tours focusing on the theme; see Tours for more information.

Will Roger's house in Pacific Palisades is open to the public, however. See the Pacific Palisades section for details.

Hollywood Cemetery

You might round off your tour of moviedom's most famous sights with a visit to the **Hollywood Cemetery** at 6076 Santa Monica Boulevard, where the unidentified 'Lady in Black' still lays a wreath at the crypt of Rudolph Valentino on the anniversary of his death. Among the famous buried here are John Gilbert, Peter Lorre, Douglas Fairbanks Sr, Tyrone Power and Marion Davies. It is open every day between 8 am and 4.30 pm.

Barnsdall Park

Hollywood does have places of interest which have nothing to do with the film colony. In Barnsdall Park, crowning Olive Hill, you may visit Frank Lloyd Wright's Mayan-style **Hollyhock House**, built for the heiress Aline Barnsdall between 1916 and 1920. This was Wright's first work in the Los Angeles area. It is open Tuesday and Thursday; guided tours between 10 am and 2 pm (last tour at 1 pm) also open the first Saturday of every month, admission charge, tel 662-7272.

The **Los Angeles Municipal Art Gallery** nearby, offers changing exhibits of works by contemporary artists; in summer the All City Outdoor Art Festival is held here. You can visit here between Tuesday to Sunday, 12.30 to 5 pm (until 8 pm on Wednesdays); admission free; tel 662-8139.

Hollywood Bowl

Chaparral-covered hills frame the Hollywood Bowl at the end of Bolton Rd, a block south of the Cahuenga Boulevard-Highland Ave intersection. This 60-acre natural amphitheater, with a sound shell designed by Frank Lloyd Wright, has been the summer home of the Los Angeles Philharmonic since 1922. The orchestra's summer 'Symphonies under the Stars' opera and the famous Easter Sunrise Service are held here. To find out what's on, where to park and how to get to the Bowl by RTD, just dial 87-MUSIC.

Studio Tours

Three movie and TV studios have opened their doors to the public and you can get a very good impression of what goes on in front of the camera and behind scenes by visiting one of them. Private tour com-

panies also include studio tours as part of their package.

Burbank Studios VIP Tour, 4000 Warner Boulevard, Burbank; tel (213) 954-6000, extension 1744.

A two-hour visit to Columbia Pictures and Warner Brothers' combined studios includes the special effects department, sound complex, the historic back lot, and actual film production. By reservation only. Tours Monday to Friday, 10 am and 2 pm; admission $16; free parking.

NBC Television Studio Tour, 3000 W Alameda Boulevard, Burbank; tel (213) 840-3572, extension 2468.

Backstage at this major TV studio, home of Johnny Carson's *Tonight* show, you'll see sets under construction, learn how costumes are designed and visit color stages. The tour lasts about an hour. Open daily, with continuous tours from 10 am to 5 pm; admission fee for tour; free standby tickets for shows, free parking.

Universal Studios Tour, 100 Universal City Plaza, Universal City; tel (213) 877-1311.

Some 2½ million visitors enjoy this tour annually, so make your reservations early. The two-hour-plus guided tour by Glamor Tram explores 420 acres of movie making magic, taking you to the stars' dressing rooms, Sound Stage 32 and several sets. You'll take on armed cyclons in the Battle of Galactica and suffer an attack by the shark from *Jaws.* At the new **Visitors' Entertainment Center,** where the Glamor Tram ends the tour, you can browse the movie museum in the Cinema Pavilion, watch makeup artists and stunt men demonstrate their skills, or watch members of the audience participate in a show at the Screen Test Theater. There are several outdoor dining areas offering food and drink.

Open daily with continuous tours from 8 am to 6 pm in summer; 10 am to 3.30 pm weekdays, 9.30 am to 4 pm weekends the rest of the year. Closed Thanksgiving and Christmas Days. Admission $9.75.

Television Show Tickets

Free tickets are available for a number of TV shows but you'll have to write several months in advance, enclosing a self-addressed envelope with the appropriate US postage affixed or with international postal coupons. You will receive coupons redeemable for tickets – depending on availability – at the time of your arrival. The following studios invite the public to their productions: *CBS-TV* 7800 Beverly Boulevard, Hollywood 90036 (852-1222); *NBC-TV,* 3000 W Alameda Boulevard, Burbank 91505 (845-7000); and *ABC-TV,* 4151 Prospect Avenue, Los Angeles 90027 (213) 663-3311).

Tickets are sometimes available at the Los Angeles Visitors & Convention Bureau.

Places to Eat

Antonio's Restaurant Mexican cuisine in attractive rooms. Roving mariachis add a romantic touch. (M/E) Lunch, Dinner; closed Monday, no lunch Saturday. 7472 Melrose Avenue, Hollywood; 655-0480.

Aware Inn Garbo was among the first patrons. Extensive menu includes vegetarian dishes. Reservations recommended. (M) Dinner only, closed Monday. 8828 Sunset Boulevard; West Hollywood; tel 652-2555.

Don the Beachcomber Exotic decor, hula music, a relaxed atmosphere and delicious seafood South Seas style. Reservations recommended. (M/E) Lunch, dinner, open daily. 1727 N McCadden Place , Hollywood; tel 469-3968.

Yamashiro! Superlative view of LA from this mountaintop restaurant in a replica of a Japanese palace. Continental cuisine and Japanese specialties. (M/E)

Lunch and dinner, open daily; no lunch Saturday and Sunday. 1999 N Sycamore, Hollywood; tel 466-5125.

HOLLYWOOD HILLS
Forest Lawn Memorial Park

It is written that on New Year's Day, 1917 the banker Hubert C Eaton stood on a hill overlooking an old Glendale cemetery he had acquired by foreclosure and was inspired by a vision 'of what this tiny God's Acre might become'. And lo, there was **Forest Lawn Memorial park**, so deftly satirized by Evelyn Waugh in *The Loved Ones*. The park is a maddening blend of good and execrable taste, with sylvan glades and emerald lawns, piped music wafting through the trees beside an ornamental lake, and expensive reproductions of famous European sculptures at every turn. The **Little Church of the Flowers** is a copy of Stoke Poges church in England where Grey conceived his *Elegy in a Country Churchyard;* the **Wee Kirk O' the Heather** replicates Annie Laurie's place of worship in Glencairn, Scotland; and Leonardo da Vinci has been upstaged in the **Memorial Court of Honor** with a larger-than-life stained glass reproduction of *The Last Supper*. A celestial baritone relates the history of this masterpiece at regular intervals daily. Don't miss it.

Other Forest Lawn attractions include a huge painting of the *Crucifixion,* dreamed by Paderewski and painted by Jan Styka, and the museum housing an eclectic collection of gems, bronze sculptures, copies of Michelangelo sketches and originals of every coin mentioned in the Bible.

Forest Lawn is included in a number of sightseeing tours; if you're getting there on your own, the address is 1712 South Glendale Ave, north of the Glendale Freeway-San Fernando Rd intersection.

Open daily, 10 am to 5 pm; admission to grounds and churches is free; small entry fee to the Memorial Court of Honor; tel 241-4151, 254-3131.

GRIFFITH PARK

Los Angeles has more than a hundred parks within its boundaries and, at 4063 acres of the eastern Santa Monica Mountains, **Griffith Park** is the largest – indeed, the largest park within a city in the country. Here you'll find more than a hundred miles of hiking and bridle trails, tennis courts, a swimming pool, picnic areas, a bird sanctuary, a wilderness and half a dozen golf courses within a 20-minute drive of the downtown area. The park is named for its donor, Colonel Griffith J Griffith, who also gave the City a trust fund to build two of the park's popular attractions, the **Greek Theatre**, an open air stage set in a canyon, where music dance and drama are performed, and the **Griffith Observatory and Planetarium** crowning Mt Hollywood. You may use the observatory's twin refracting telescope on clear evenings (between 7 and 10 pm, Tuesday to Sunday) or catch a show that takes you hurtling through the cosmos – there are five different extra-terrestrial events annually. Showings are given daily in summer, Tuesday through Sunday the rest of the year. For information, dial 664-1191. The **Laserium** features a cosmic light show-cum-concert in the evenings Tuesday through Saturday (Monday to Saturday in summer); for information on its program, call 997-3624. Tickets cost $3.50. There are also permanent displays on astronomy and the physical sciences in the **Hall of Sciences**.

Open daily, 1 to 10 pm summer, 2 to 10 pm rest of year, free admission; tel 664-1191.

Other attractions within Griffith Park: the **Los Angeles Zoo**, with more than 2000 mammals, birds and reptiles, and a petting zoo for children. Open 10 am to 5 pm daily, save Christmas Day; entry fee.

Travel Town, a museum of antique planes and locomotives (open daily 9 am to 5 pm, admission free); and **The Ferndell,** a lush and lovely setting for 20 different species of fern from around the world.

Main entrances to Griffith Park are at Ferndell, Vermont Canyon and Riverside Drive, all intersecting with Los Feliz Boulevard. You can also enter from the Golden State Freeway. Open daily, 5 am to 10.30 pm (mountain roads close at dusk). Visitors Center 4730 Crystal Springs Rd; tel (213) 665-5188.

SOUTHWEST MUSEUM

For an excellent introduction to the arts and artifacts of the West's Indian peoples spend a couple of hours browsing the Southwest Museum at 234 Museum Drive and Marmion Way. Of particular importance are the basketry exhibits and Indian paintings – there is a work by Sitting Bull himself executed shortly before his assassination. The Northwestern Indians Room displays some impressive totem poles. Open daily (except Mondays) 1 to 4.45 pm; closed August 16 to September 16 and major holidays; tel 221-2163.

Close by, at the Avenue 43 exit of the Pasadena Freeway, is **El Alisal**, home of the museum's founder, Charles Fletcher Lummis. Lummis, who arrived on the Los Angeles scene in the 1880s after a 3500-mile cross-country trek, was a prominent writer, archaeologist, editor and, for a time, the city librarian. He built El Alisal with his own hands, helped only by an Indian boy. Open Sunday to Friday, 1 to 4 pm; admission free; tel 222-0546.

HERITAGE SQUARE

The Cultural Heritage Board of Los Angeles has rescued several Victorian homes from destruction and relocated them attractively at 3800 Homer St, not far from El Alisal. Here you can explore the way Los Angelenos lived between 1865 and 1914 in a variety of environments, among them the French Second Empire-style Valley Knudsen Garden Residence and Hale House, a Queen Anne-Eastlake home furnished with period antiques. Guided tours are offered.

Open first and second Sunday and third Wednesday of each month, 11 am to 3 pm. Nominal admission charge. Tel (213) 222-3150.

Places to Eat

Lawry's California Center, 586 San Fernando Rd, is an ideal spot to restore the flesh and the spirit. The famous packaged food firm offers an enchanting dining experience in its 12-acre garden center daily between May and November, featuring mariachi music, Mexican cuisine and a steak fiesta. Call (213) 225-2491.

GREATER LOS ANGELES

Los Encinos State Historic Park

Located in the outskirts of Encino between Moorpark and La Maida Sts north of Ventura Boulevard, Los Encinos State Historic Park is where Gaspar de Portola's pathfinding expedition camped at a large Indian settlement in 1769. The grounds are part of the 4460-acre Rancho El Encino granted to three Indians in 1845 who sold it to Don Vincente de la Osa, four years later. The Osa adobe (1849) and the Garnier sheep-ranch buildings (1872) are of considerable interest, with many rooms furnished with period antiques.

Grounds open Wednesday to Sunday, 8 am to 5 pm; admission charge; tel 784-4849 for current home tour hours.

Calabasas

Some nine miles west of Encino is the historic community of Calabasas, worth seeking out for its old buildings. The town's origins go back to the late 18th century; both the Gaspar de Portola and de Anza expeditions halted here, and after the establishment of Mission San Fernando in 1897, the padres found it a convenient way station on their journeys along El Camino Real. The site of the Hangman's Tree near the corner of Ventura Boulevard and El Cajon Drive recalls Calabasas' heyday as the toughest frontier town in Southern California, a haven for the notorious Tiburcio Vazquez gang and cattle rustlers.

The **Miguel Leonis Adobe**, 23537 Calabasas Rd, was built in 1869 by a Basque sheep rancher whose giant stature, strength and contentious disposition secured him a place in local mythology. It's a fine example of an old California ranch house, furnished to period and set in a semi-tropical garden with a grape arbor. Open Wednesdays and weekends, 1 to 4 pm; free admission; tel 346-3683.

Mission San Fernando

Southwest of San Fernando, at 1515 San Fernando Mission Rd between the San Diego and Golden State freeways, is the valley's oldest settlement; **Mission San Fernando Rey De Espana** was founded by Father Lasuen in 1797. The present church, built in 1818, is decorated with paintings by the mission Indians. The long, low convento or 'House of the Fathers' with its massive square pillars supporting the arches of the loggia along the facade is more interesting. The handiwork of Indian blacksmiths can still be seen in the wrought iron mouldings of the doors and windows, and in the cellars you'll find old vats used for making wine. The grounds enclose the ruins of the first church, the cemetery and the walls of the Indian quarters.

Across the street is the **Memory Garden** dominated by a statue of Father Junipero Serra.

Open daily, 9 am to 5 pm; admission charge; (213) 361-0186.

Two blocks south of the mission, at 10900 Brand Boulevard is the **Andres Pico Adobe**, a faithful restoration of the building put up in 1834 for relatives of California's last Mexican governor. It is the second oldest home in Los Angeles. Open Saturday to Sunday, 1 to 4 pm; tel 365-7810.

PASADENA

Affluent and dignified, Pasadena lies at the base of the San Gabriel Mountains 11 miles northwest of downtown Los Angeles. It's known around the world, of course, for the **Rose Bowl** football game, where the champions of the East and West leagues fight it out, and for the spectacular **Tournament of Roses** parade held every New Year's Day. The parade, inspired by the Carnival of Flowers in Nice, France, was first held in 1890 as a simple celebration of the mid-winter flowering season. Today, both the parade and the game attract a nationwide audience, courtesy of the TV networks.

Pasadena is also the home of the **California Institute of Technology**, one of the country's leading scientific research centers, and its Jet Propulsion Laboratory – the faculty once included Albert Einstein. The laboratory is control center for missions to the planets. Space science buffs should make reservations for one of the free guided tours; call (213) 354-2337. On the last Sunday of each month, it's open house from 1 to 5 pm.

Norton Simon Museum of Art

At the intersection of Orange Grove and Colorado Ave is the Norton Simon Museum. It houses one of the West's most important art collections, encompassing six centuries of European painting from the early Italians to the present, sculpture from India and Southeast Asia and from European and American schools of the 19th and 20th centuries. On display are notable works by Filippino Lippi, Raphael, Tiepolo, Rembrandt, Hals, Reubens and Goya. The museum is particularly rich in works by the French Impressionists and moderns – the Degas gallery contains 88 examples of his work, including the famous *modele* set of bronzes. Important paintings by Picasso, Juan Gris and Georges Bracques highlight the collection of modern works. In the sculpture collection you will find works by Rodin, Henry Moore, Matisse, Brancusi, Picasso and Giacometti. Open Tuesday to Sunday, noon to 6 pm; admission charge; tel (213) 449-6840.

Three Stately Homes

On either side of the Norton Simon Museum is Orange Grove Boulevard with its impressive array of stately homes. Three of these may be visited.

The Gamble House, 4 Westmoreland Place (off N Orange Grove Boulevard) is perhaps the best known Craftsman style bungalow in the country. Built in 1908 for the Gambles of Procter & Gamble by Charles and Henry Greene, it is an extraordinarily harmonious structure with obvious Japanese influences. The Greene brothers also designed the furnishings and Tiffany glass work. Admission is by guided tour only. Open Tuesday and Thursday, 10 am to 3 pm and first Sunday of the month noon to 3 pm. Closed holidays. Admission charge. Tel 793-3334.

Located at 470 W Walnut Boulevard (Orange Grove intersection), the **Pasadena Historical Museum (Fenyes Mansion)** was built in 1905 for the Fenyes family and for many years it served as the Finnish Consulate. There's an interesting collection of Pasadena history in the basement; the main floor retains its original furnishings and memorabilia of the Fenyes family; and in the grounds you will find a replica of a 16th century Finnish farmhouse containing Finnish folk art. Open Tuesday, Thursday and last Sunday of every month from 1 to 4 pm. Admission free. Tel 577-1660.

Tournament House, 391 S Orange Grove Boulevard, is an impressive mansion from the early years of this century, surrounded by broad lawns and landscaped gardens. Formerly the home of William Wrighley, Jr, it is now the headquarters of the Tournament of Roses Association. Memorabilia of Rose Bowl games is a feature of the house tours. Gardens open daily. House tours February 1 to September 30, Wednesdays from 2 to 4 pm. Admission free. Tel 449-4100.

A good place to recover from museum prowling is the grand old **Huntington Hotel** at the intersection of Oak Knoll and Wentworth Aves. This rambling Spanish Mission style resort was put up in 1906 by the magnate Henry E Huntington and its spacious gardens with their lily ponds are pleasant for alfresco drinking.

SAN MARINO
Huntington Library, Art Gallery & Botanical Gardens

On Oxford Rd in San Marino, another affluent residential community just south of Pasadena, is the former home and 200-acre estate of Henry E Huntington which has become one of the country's leading cultural institutions. Huntington's palatial home is now an art gallery, devoted mainly to British art of the 18th and 19th centuries. Best known of the paintings is Gainsborough's *Blue Boy;* others of note are Constable's *View of the Stour* and Lawrence's *Pinkie.* The gallery also contains a wealth of French 18th century decorative art – sculpture, tapestries, porcelain and furniture.

A selection of the library's remarkable collection of rare books and manuscripts spanning a period from the 11th century to the present is always on view. You can see the Gutenberg Bible, the first book printed in Europe with movable type, a 'First Folio' of Shakespeare's plays and the Ellesmere manuscript of Chaucer's *Canterbury Tales.*

The Huntington's grounds are of unusual beauty, with grand views of Los Angeles framed by California live oaks. There are 12 specialised gardens. If your time is short, do not miss the Japanese Garden beyond the Rose Garden and the 12-acre Desert Garden (in the south-east corner of the grounds) which contains the world's largest outdoor collection of desert plants. The Shakespeare Garden displays the flowers and shrubs mentioned by the Bard in his works.

Open Tuesday to Sunday, 1 to 4.30 pm; closed Mondays, major holidays and October 1-31. Sunday visitors must have advance reservations. For information, call 681-6601 (from Los Angeles) or 792-6141 (from San Marino-Pasadena); admission and parking free.

Mission San Gabriel Arcangel

South of San Marino at 530 W Mission Drive, San Gabriel (some nine miles east of downtown Los Angeles) is the fourth of the missions established by Father Junipero Serra. Mission San Gabriel Arcangel was founded in 1771 on a site overlooking the Rio Hondo five miles south and moved to its present location in 1776. Under a succession of talented leaders, the mission became one of the wealthiest in the chain, with extensive lands running from the mountains to the ocean and a famous distillery of fine wines and brandy. The church, begun in 1791 and completed in 1803, is massively constructed, with flying buttresses to support the walls and the unusual feature of an outdoor staircase leading to the choir loft. To the rear is the bell tower pierced with arches corresponding to the different sizes of the bells.

There is one particularly interesting treasure within the church, a 17th century oil painting of *Our Lady of the Sorrows* which, according to Father Palou, quieted a band of hostile Indians who sought to interfere with the founding of the mission. In the museum you will find an early series of the Stations of the Cross executed on sailcloth by the mission Indians. Open daily, 9.30 am to 4 pm; admission charge; tel (213) 282-5191.

AROUND LOS ANGELES

After a few days in the city, you may be needing a change of scene and you can do no better than follow the old injunction, 'head for the hills'. That ring of mountains separating Los Angeles from the deserts of the north and east is a summer and winter playground of grand design, much of it untouched wilderness only to be explored on foot. Here chaparral, oaks, willow, pepper trees and eucalyptus clothe the lower slopes, leaving the high country to pines and incense cedar. Wildflowers add rich color in spring and summer. And here, too, you may be fortunate enough to sight California cougar, bobcat, coyote, even the rare bald eagle.

Resorts and campgrounds are plentiful but in summer you would be wise to make reservations in advance. For information on the San Gabriel Mountains which fall within the boundaries of Angeles National Forest, write to the Supervisor. Angeles National Forest, 150 Los Robles Ave, Pasadena, CA 91101; tel (213) 577-0050. The San Bernardino Mountains are the province of the Supervisor, Bernardino National Forest, 144 N Mountain View Ave, San Bernardino, 92408; tel (714) 383-5588.

San Gabriel Mountains

A one-day excursion by car will give you an impression of the San Gabriels' rugged beauty. Follow the **Angels Crest Highway** (SR 2) from La Canada up through the peaks to **Mount Wilson Observatory**. This famous observatory welcomes visitors to the 100 inch Hooker telescope and two other telescopes as well as to the museum. Open daily, 10 am to 4 pm, admission free; tel (213) 577-1122.

SR 2 twists across the spine of the San Gabriels in a northeasterly direction to descend into the Mojave desert at Big Pines. You can return to Los Angeles, however, via SR 39 which intersects SR 2 roughly five miles beyond Buckhorn Forest Ranger Station. The distance between La Canada and Azusa at the mouth of the San Gabriel Canyon is only 70 miles but it's mountain driving at its most demanding – and scenically rewarding.

San Bernadino Mountains

Equally popular with wilderness vacationers are the **San Bernadino Mountains** which are accessible via SR 18 and SR 330 running north from the San Bernardino Freeway. Here the peaks are higher than those of the San Gabriels, many reaching over 10,000 feet. They enfold three great lakes – Silverwood, Arrowhead, and Big Bear.

For spectacular views and a reasonably easy drive, follow SR 18, the famous Rim of the World Drive, leading to the most popular mountain resort areas. **Lake Arrowhead** offers theaters, restaurants, motels, stores, private cabins, a marina with water skiing instruction, and excellent swimming in the man-made lake. It's open in winter too, for skiing.

Big Bear Lake, 22 miles east, offers similar facilities. Snow Summit ski resort operates its lifts in summer, affording views of the lake and mountains from an 8300 foot elevation. **Silverwood Lake,** northwest of Lake Arrowhead, is not so well developed.

THEME PARKS

Alligator Farm, 7671 E La Palma Avenue, Buena Park 90620; (714) 522-2615.

More big, sharp teeth than in your wildest nightmares are displayed in this jungle-like park across the street from Knott's Berry Farm. Over a thousand saurians and reptiles show off their attractions year-round, including the largest crocodile in captivity in the world. Open daily 10.30 am to 5 pm (September to June); 10.30 am to 8 pm (July to August). Free parking. Admission $4.50.

Disneyland 1313 Harbor Boulevard, Anaheim 92803; (714) 999-4565.

To put it simply, the greatest. Uncle Walt's world of fantasy is divided into seven theme areas – Main St, Adventureland, Frontierland, New Orleans Square, Bear Country, Fantasyland and Tomorrowland. You get around by monorail and a number of different craft including the stern-wheeler *Mark Twain,* log rafts and submarines. Space doesn't permit description of all the attractions – they range from a marvellously Haunted Mansion at the edge of New Orleans Square to evocations of Walt Disney's best films and exploration of the cosmos on the new Space Mountain. The Horseshoe Revue takes you back to the 19th century with a lively old-time music hall show, complete with can-can girls, and there's more entertainment in the Fantasyland and Carousel theatres. You really shouldn't miss it! Open daily 9 am to midnight mid-June-Labor Day. Rest of year hours vary. Usually 10 am to 6 pm weekdays, 9 am to 7

pm weekends. Check the hours before you go.

General admission $8. Best buy is a ticket book covering general admission and attractions of your choice. The Big 11 book gives you 11 choices and admission for $9.25, the Passport unlimited use of the attractions and admission for $10.25. Disneyland is also included on many sightseeing tours – check the Los Angeles sightseeing section.

A monorail or tram ride away is the *Disneyland Hotel,* a fantasyland in its own right with a myriad attractions set in 60 acres of lush, tropical gardens. On the lagoon is one of the most popular seaports of the Pacific, evoking romantic ports-of-call like Bali, Hong Kong and Bangkok. Laze on a white sand beach, swim in one of the pools, stroll the aqua gardens, feast at one of the restaurants, but try not to miss the magical Dancing Waters show held twice each evening. To find out show times, call (714) 778-6600. To find out about staying there, turn to the Hotels section.

Knott's Berry Farm, 8039 Beach Boulevard, Buena Park (south of the Santa Ana Freeway); (714) 827-1776.

The Old West lives on in this famous park which began as a berry farm in 1920. You can ride a Butterfield stage coach, walk through a ghost town, pan for gold and indulge in a number of hair-raising thrill rides that include the Sky Tower, a parachute dropping you 20 stories at what seems to be the speed of light. Free daily entertainment featuring big names in the Good Time Theater and dancing in the Cloud Nine ballroom. And that's not all by any means. Open 9 am to midnight daily in summer; Friday to Tuesday 10 am to midnight (9 pm Sundays) rest of year. Closed Christmas Day. Unlimited use ticket book $9.50; 11-ride ticket book $8. Free parking.

Lion Country Safari, 8800 Irvine Center Drive (off San Diego Freeway), Irvine; (714) 837-1200 or (213) 485-8951. You're just a windshield away from the world's largest collection of lions, rhinos, giraffes, elephants, zebras and other denizens of the African veldt in this fascinating 485-acre wildlife reserve. A free taped narration is available to illuminate your drive. Windows must be closed and convertibles are forbidden (but rental cars are available). The adjacent **Safari Camp** features Zambezi River Cruise, an auto trek and a bazaar selling authentic African handicrafts. Open daily, April 1 to October 31; 9.45 am to 5 pm in winter. Admission $6.50.

Magic Mountain, Magic Mountain Parkway, Valencia; (213) 367-2271.

200 acres of thrill rides and attractions, plus the Showcase Theater where you can catch top-name performers. There's a Wizard's Village and a petting zoo for children. Magic Mountain's newest attraction is the Colossus, advertised as the fastest wooden roller coaster in the world – it hits 60 mph and there are blenching 100-foot drops . . . Magnificent views from the 384-foot Sky Tower observation decks. Open daily in summer 10 am to midnight; variable rest of year. Admission $10.95.

Marineland, 6600 Palos Verdes Drive S, Rancho Palos Verdes; (213) 541-5663. Whale shows, dolphin games, sea lions and a 540,000-gallon tank which houses more than 3000 fish, head the bill of attractions at this famous oceanographic park. A new feature is **Baja Reef**, the country's first swim-through aquarium, for which there's an extra charge. Open daily 10 am to 7 pm in summer; Wednesday to Sunday 10 am to 5 pm rest of year. Admission $8.50. Parking fee.

Movieland of the Air Museum, Orange Co Airport, Santa Ana (714) 545-1193. Follow the history of aviation from the days when pilots flew by the seat of their pants to the space age in one of the best antique aircraft collections in the country. More than 50 planes, many originals, some reproductions. Open daily 10 am to 5 pm (closed Mondays in winter). Admission $2.25.

Movieland Wax Museum and Palace of Living Art, 7711 Beach Boulevard, Buena Park (714) 522-1154.

Scenes from movies and TV featuring over 200 stars, among them the upside-down scene from the *Poseidon Adventure*, the future world of *Star Trek* and *Hello Dolly*.

The adjoining **Palace of Living Art** contains reproductions of famous works of art, such as Michelangelo's *David* and the *Pieta*. Open daily in summer from 9 am to 9 pm (until 10 pm Friday to Saturday); 10 am to 8 pm rest of year (until 10 pm Friday to Saturday). Admission $6.95.

Places to Stay

You have an unusual variety of environments to choose from in a city that extends over mountains and broad valleys and includes a long stretch of the Pacific coast. And because you can get about LA so rapidly by car on the freeways, it's perfectly feasible to select a hotel in, say, Pasadena or San Marino in the foothills of the San Gabriel Mountains, or a beach city like Santa Monica, or a waterfront marina like Marina del Rey – and still be within a half hour's drive of the downtown area. We've confined our suggestions to the downtown, Wilshire-Beverly Hills and Hollywood districts and to Anaheim, Disneyland City.

Some of the West's most famous (and expensive) hostelries are to be found in the Wilshire-Beverly Hills area but you'll find equally elegant addresses downtown and in Hollywood. Budget hotels handy to the attractions are a little harder to come by in this affluent city so if these are your preference, you would do well to make a reservation in advance. In between, you've a wide choice of moderately-priced motels and hotels, most of them with swimming pools. The *Accommodations Guide* of the Greater Los Angeles Visitors and Convention Bureau is an invaluable extension to our suggestions. To obtain a copy, write to the

Bureau at ARCO Plaza, Level B, 505 South Flower St, Los Angeles 90071.

Central Los Angeles-Wilshire District – Top End

Ambassador Hotel, 340 Wilshire Boulevard, Los Angeles 90010; (213) 387-7011; 800-252-8385.

This famous resort hotel has entertained everyone, from Charlie Chaplin to Madam Chiang Kai-Shek and six American presidents. Among the amenities: Olympic-sized swimming pool, putting green, health club, tennis courts and a running track for joggers. Air-conditioning, color TV, two dining rooms, coffee shop, entertainment. Rates from $90 double.

Biltmore Hotel, 515 S Olive St, Los Angeles 90013; (213) 624-1011; 800-421-0156 (outside California), 800-252-0175 (inside California).

Historic grand hotel at the heart of the downtown area. Air-conditioning, color TV, coffeeshop, entertainment. Restaurants include Bernardo's. Airport bus at door. Rates from $105 double.

Wilshire Hyatt House, 3515 Wilshire Boulevard, Los Angeles 90010; (213) 381-7411; 800-228-9000.

On 'Miracle Mile' at Normandie Avenue not far from the Los Angeles County Art Museum. Heated pool, air-conditioning, color TV plus dining rooms. Entertainment in the Carnival nightclub. RTD airport bus at door. Rates from $94 double.

Mid-Range

Best Western Kent Inn, 920 S Figueroa St, Los Angeles 90015; (213) 626-8701; 800-528-1234.

Olympic Boulevard with courtesy limousine service. Heated pool, sauna, restaurant, cocktail lounge. Air-conditioning, color TV and complimentary coffee. Rates from $54 double.

Figueroa Hotel, 939 S Figueroa St, Los Angeles 90015; (213) 627-8971; 800-331-5151).

Next to Convention Center and within walking distance of ARCO Plaza, major department stores and restaurants. Air-conditioning, color TV, swimming pool, and gardens. Cafe and cocktail lounge. Airport bus at door. Rates from $48 double.

Mayflower Hotel, 535 S Grand Avenue, Los Angeles 90071; (213) 624-1331; 800-532-8800.

Built in the 1920s, it retains its period decor and 'other era' feeling. Excellent location, just across street from the Biltmore. Air-conditioning, color TV, dining room and cocktail lounge, of course. Airport bus stops at door. Rates from $80 double.

InnTowne Motor Hotel, 925 S Figueroa St, Los Angeles 90015; call collect (213) 628-2222 for reservations. Heated pool, dining room and coffee shop in this superior motel. Air-conditioning, color TV. Rates from $50 double.

Bottom End

Rainbow Hotel, 536 South Hope St, Los Angeles 90071; (213) 627-9941. Totally renovated, this former budget special is still very moderately priced for its convenient location in the heart of the downtown area. The airport bus stops at the Mayflower Hotel behind the Rainbow. Rates from $42 double.

YMCA, 1006 East 28th St, Los Angeles 90011; (213) 232-7193. Men only. Swimming pool and cafe on premises. Rates: $15.75 per person, single or double.

YWCA, Clark Residence, 306 Loma Drive (corner of Third St), Los Angeles 90017; (213) 483-5780. Not far from the Music Center with TV room, library and rec room. Rates from $23 per person, including breakfast and dinner.

Beverly Hills, West Wilshire, Westwood – Top End

Beverly Hills Hotel, 9641 Sunset Boulevard, Los Angeles 90210; (213) 276-2251.

Celebrities have been flocking to this

pink-and-green palace for nearly 40 years. The famous Polo Lounge is here and a staff of 400 takes care of 275 guests. Every amenity imaginable including an olympic-sized pool in 12 acres of landscaped gardens, two dining rooms and a coffeeshop. Rates from $120 double.

Beverly Wilshire, 9500 Wilshire Boulevard, Los Angeles 90212; (213) 275-4282; 800-282-4804.

Another of LA's gran'luxe hotels. Gas lights from Edinburgh castle line the cobblestone entrance, leading to an interior gleaming with carrara marble, mosaics, Louis XVI chandeliers and immense mirrors. A favourite with monarchy. Heated swimming pool, and oh yes, air-conditioning and color TV. Restaurants include La Bella Fontana. RTD airport bus at door. Rates from $168 double, the Christian Dior-designed suite, $1000 a night.

Mid-Range

Beverly Crest Hotel, 1255 S Spalding Drive, Los Angeles 90212; (213) 274-6801.

In Beverly Hills, a block south of Wilshire Boulevard, this small comfortable hotel has a swimming pool. Rates from $55 double.

Century Wilshire, 10776 Wilshire Boulevard, Los Angeles 90024; (213) 474-4506.

One and two-bedroom housekeeping apartments and some motel units. Air-conditioning and color TV, plus a heated swimming pool. Rates from $55 double.

Royal Palace Hotel, 2528 S Brand Boulevard, Los Angeles 90064; (213) 477-9066; 800-528-1234.

Award-winning member of Best Western chain, near intersection of San Diego and Santa Monica freeways. Charming garden heated swimming pool, health spa and Finnish sauna. Soundproof rooms, some housekeeping apartments. Weekly and monthly rates available. Rates from $55 double; suites from $75.

Bottom End

Beverley Vista, 120 S Reeves, Los Angeles 90212; (213) 276-1031.

Located a block from Wilshire Boulevard and Beverly Drive, this small hotel is in European *gasthaus* tradition. Daily maid service, phones in the rooms and color TV in the lobby. Rates from $35 double with bath or shower. Weekly rates available.

Hollywood – Top End

Hyatt on Sunset, 8401 Sunset Boulevard, Los Angeles 90069; (213) 656-4101; 800-228-9000.

Close to Sunset Strip and Restaurant Row with views over the city and toward the mountains. Heated rooftop swimming pool and sundeck plus all the mod cons of a conventional top-line hotel – air-conditioning, color TV, restaurants, coffeeshop and the Red Roulette Room, a favorite with Hollywood entertainers. Rates from $90.

Mid-Range

Best Western Holywood, 6141 Franklin Ave, Los Angeles 90028; (213) 464-5181; 800-528-1234.

Located two blocks east of Vine St and just minutes to downtown Los Angeles and Universal Studios, this comfortable motel has a number of kitchen units, coffeeshop, heated swimming pool, air-conditioning and some color TV. Rates from $49 double.

Farmer's Daughter Motel, 115 S Fairfax Ave, Los Angeles 90036; (213) 937-3930.

Opposite the Farmers Market. Small swimming pool, air-conditioning, color TV. Reservation deposit required. Rates from $45 double.

Wilshire Dunes Motor Hotel, 4300 Wilshire Boulevard, Los Angeles 90010; (213) 938-3616.

Convenient location for Beverly Hills, Hollywood and downtown Los Angeles, with a heated pool, air-conditioning and color TV. Rates from $38 double.

Bottom End

Howard's Weekly Apartments, 1738 N Whitley St, Hollywood, 90028; call collect (213) 466-6943.

Comfortable air-conditioned apartments, half a block from Hollywood Boulevard in the heart of Hollywood. Weekly maid service, private baths and light food preparation facilities. Weekly rates $84.95 for one person, $99.95 for two, plus $12.50 a week for roll-aways (three persons per appartment maximum). There are a limited number of kitchenette apartments at $119.95 per week for two persons.

There are Howard's Weekly Apartments at two other locations. One is at 1225 N El Centro, Hollywood 90038; (213) 464-0948 or call collect 92130 845-1863.

Rates differ slightly from those quoted for the N Whitley St location. Ask about the three day/three night mini-week rate, subject to room availability. Reservation and security deposits are required in advance. The latter are refundable under specified circumstances.

YMCA, 153 Hudson Avenue, Los Angeles 90028; (213) 467-4161.

Hotel for men and women, with swimming pool, sauna, sports facilities and cafe. There is a 30 day limit on stay. Key deposit $2. Rates: $24.50 double, $16 single.

Anaheim (Disneyland-Knott's Berry Farm) – Top End

Anaheim Hyatt, 1700 S Harbor Boulevard, Anaheim 92802; (714) 772-5900.

Close to Disneyland main entrance, with heated swimming pool, air-conditioning, color TV, suites. Dining room and entertainment. Rates from $75 double.

Disneyland Hotel, 1150 W Cerritos Avenue, Anaheim 92803; (714) 635-8600.

Resort hotel in beautifully landscaped gardens. Features include two heated pools, putting green, health spa, paddleboats, mini-golf, tennis and Dancing Waters show, six restaurants, shopping mall. On Disneyland monorail. Reserve deposit required. Rates: from $84 double.

Grand Hotel, No 1 Hotel Way, Anaheim 92802; (714) 772-7777.

Just across from Disneyland, within minutes of main entrance. Heated pool, dinner theaters, air-conditioning, color TV, two restaurants. Some suites. Reserve deposit required. Rates from $60 double.

Mid-Range

Anaheim Friendship Inn, 426 W Ball Rd, Anaheim 92805; (714) 774-3882. Comfortable motel within short distance of Disneyland and Knott's Berry Farm. Small heated pool, air-conditioning, color TV. Substantial discounts between mid-September and mid-May. Rates from $45 double.

Alpine Motel, 715 W Katella Ave, Anaheim 92802; (714) 535-2186.

Not far from Disneyland south entrance, opposite Convention Center. Some rooms feature steam baths. Heated pool, air-conditioning, color TV. Reserve deposit required. Lower rates between mid-September and mid-May. Rates from $38 double (high season).

Candy Cane Motel, 1747 S Harbor Boulevard, Anaheim 92802; (714) 774-5284.

Surrounded by attractive grounds, near main and southern Disneyland entrances. Some family units. Lower rates between mid-September and mid-May. Air-conditioning and color TV. Reserve deposit required. Rates from $38 double (high season).

Park Vue Motel, 1570 S Harbor Boulevard, Anaheim 92802; (714) 772-5721. Free shuttle bus tickets to and from Disneyland, free transportation to and from Anaheim airport coach terminal, Greyhound and Continental bus depots. Family units, kitchenettes, heated pool, air-conditioning, color TV and restaurant among the conveniences offered. Substantial discounts from early September to the end of May. Rates from $41 double (high season).

Bottom End

Motel 6, 921 Beach Boulevard Anaheim 92804; (714) 827-9450
Member of the famous budget chain. Rates from $19.95 double.

Sixpence Inn, 2020 Via Burton, Anaheim 92806; tel (714) 956-9690.
No frills accommodation, like the Motel 6s, but with everything you really need. Rates from $16.95 double.

Places to Eat

Your options in Los Angeles are almost overwhelming in their diversity; like San Francisco, the city's restaurants reflect a history of immigration from every quarter of the globe. Proximity to the Mexican border and the largest Chicano population of any Californian city account for the very large number of Mexican style restaurants.

Atmosphere, always an important element of a good dinner, has received particularly imaginative attention in the City of the Angels. You may take your choice of such settings as a Pacific Railroad car, bicycles, King Arthur's Camelot (with furnishings from the movie set), a flaming fire where waitresses bustle around in asbestos aprons and the organist plays *A Hot Time in the Old Town Tonight,* and more conventional decors. Perhaps the Brown Derby started it all.

Los Angeles also scores heavily with good moderately-priced chain eateries. Names to watch for: *Carl's Jr's* (there's one in the Bonaventure) *Hamburger Hamlet, Soup 'n' Such, Numero Uno* and *Magic Pan.* The *Thinnery* and *Gazebo* restaurants are for those who take their calories seriously. Not chain outlets but very famous locally for their specialties are *Pink's Hot Dogs* in Hollywood and *Patio Burgers* in the Wilshire District.

Inexpensive ethnic cuisine is to be had in Chinatown, Little Tokyo and Olvera St.

Eat your way around the world at the Farmers Market different restaurants. Handy for downtown shoppers are the cafes and restaurants of ARCO Plaza, Broadway Plaza and the World Trade Center. And if you'd like to enjoy a fudge sundae in the ice-cream parlor where Judy Garland once waited table, hie yourself over to *C C Brown* at 7007 Hollywood Boulevard. Celebrity spotters agree that *Ma Maison, Chasen's La Scala, Michaelangelo's* and the *Polo Lounge* of the Beverly Hills Hotel are excellent bets.

Informality is a characteristic of the Los Angeles lifestyle; nevertheless, a good rule of thumb is, the more glamorous and expensive the restaurant, the more formal is the dress code. We would not recommend dropping by *Beaudry's, L'Escoffier* or the *Scandia* without a jacket and tie.

The 'Happy Hour' is in force at a dizzying array of cocktail lounges. If you enjoy a view with your drink consider the *Top of Five* cocktail lounge on the 34th floor of the Bonaventure Hotel, *Angel's Flight* atop the Hyatt Regency or the pubs in Marina Del Rey's Fisherman's Village overlooking the harbor. *The Celebrity* in the Ambassador Hotel, *Zindebad Bar* in the Beverly Wilshire, the *Portuguese Bar* of the Sheraton Universal, and the *Polo Bar* in the Beverly Hills Hotel offer glamorous settings.

Most portable of the wining-dining guides to the Greater Los Angeles area are Camarro Press' *Hidden Restaurants of Southern California* and *Little Restaurants of Los Angeles.*

Shopping

In a metropolitan area extending over 464 square miles you can find *everything* from haute couture boutiques and top-line department stores to discount marts and import bazaars where you can pick up some astonishing bargains. Our suggestions are confined to the downtown Los Angeles area and Beverley Hills merely for the sake of convenience.

Downtown Los Angeles Two shopping complexes, pleasantly spiced with cafes and restaurants, head our recommendations here. Arco Plaza, 505 S Flower St, is subterranean, air-conditioned and pleasingly decorated with plants and flowers. Boutiques offer good browsing in books, art, fashion, jewellery, and you may even find a fashion show or concert in progress as you step off the escalator. Well placed maps help you keep your sense of direction in this charming labyrinth.

Broadway Plaza, sandwiched between the Hyatt Regency and a high-rise at Seventh and Hope Sts, is a two-level shopping mall offering a similar range of wares. Always something going on in the way of entertainment at noon, and you have easy access to the Hyatt's patio cafe. One of the city's largest department stores, the Broadway is part of the complex.

From Flower St to Grand Avenue, Seventh St is lined with well-known stores – Bullock's, Robinson's and the May Company have branches here.

Six tiers of speciality shops surround the atrium of the *Bonaventure Hotel,* selling everything from books to gift items. A pedestrian skyway leads from the hotel to the World Trade Center where you'll find more of the same.

On the northern fringe of the downtown area you can blend sightseeing and shopping in LA's foreign quarters. Grand Ave, lined with Latin music stores, is a colourful way to reach Grand Central Market's display of fruits, vegetables and exotic foods. Olvera St, at the center of the pueblo, is a Mexican market where you can pick up huaraches, pottery, decorative tinware, all manner of baskets, and jewellery from south of the border. *Little Tokyo* and *Chinatown* (new and old), display wares from the Orient – bronzes, chinaware, silk kimonos, jade, and figurines in ivory are just some of the temptations.

Wilshire Boulevard's Miracle Mile Between La Brea and Fairfax Ave, branches of big-name department stores line Wilshire Boulevard. *Ohrbach's* is the one where you will find copies of French high-fashion clothing. Try the 'Egg and the Eye' for unusual gifts.

Beverley Hills of course is *the* place for luxury shopping. In the area bounded by Wilshire and Santa Monica Boulevards and Doheny Drive, you'll find an array of prestigious stores which enjoy the patronage of international celebrities. Rodeo Drive has become the center of high fashion – Hermes, Gucci, Courreges, Ted Lapidus are here. So is Giorgio (couturier clothing), Jax (elegant casual wear) and Bijan (high fashion for men). Other famous names you'll spot include Victor Sassoon, Elizabeth Arden and Van Cleef & Arpels. Chances of spotting a celebrity are high, too.

Along Wilshire Boulevard, Bonwit Teller, Saks Fifth Ave, Nieman Marcus, Tiffany and I Magnin enhance the glamor. A useful aid in shopping in Beverly Hills is *Beverly Hills: The Where-It's-At and How-To-Get-There Guide* offered at no charge by the Chamber of Commerce, 239 South Beverly Drive.

Art lovers would do well to pick up a copy of the Camarro *California Gallery Guide,* a wonderful navigational aid to an ocean of well-known names. For antiques hie yourself to Melrose Avenue, between La Cienega and Robertson Boulevards in West Hollywood – more than a hundred antique shops. If Culver City is not too far a diversion from your path, the Antique Guild in the Old Helms Bakery Building, Venice Boulevard at Helms Avenue, has three acres of antiques under one roof. Internationally famous fine art auctioneers Sotheby Parke Bernet have a branch in that area too.

Other names to know about: for *records,* the Wherehouse and Tower Records, with branches all over Los Angeles; for *stereo components,* Pacific Stereo and the Radio Shack, for *photographic equipment,* Henry's.

Nightlife & Entertainment

Los Angeles is second only to New York in the variety of its entertainments. There's a wide range of night spots from discos and clubs where you can catch the top names in pop, rock and country/western to posh supper clubs in the big hotels that offer dancing and entertainment. Theatrical presentations cover the spectrum – classical drama, experimental, even turn-of-the-century vaudeville can be found somewhere in the LA area at any time – 'little theater' is often a chance to see film stars honing their skills on the stage. Music lovers can take their pick from a broad range of recitals, concerts, celebrity series, musicals and opera.

Because it's one of the centers of the record and music industries, you will find excellent live music and cabaret. **Jazz** buffs should head for Donte's in Hollywood, the Hong Kong Bar of the Century Plaza Hotel, and Concerts by The Sea in Redondo Beach. For **pop**, try Doug Weston's Troubador and The Roxy; punk and power rock flourish at The Whiskey and Starwood; and for country/western, it's the Palomino. All these are in Hollywood.

The **Music Center** theaters head the list of Los Angeles showcases with a diverse bill of concerts, opera, musicals, dance and drama. The Dorothy Chandler Pavilion presents concerts, dance and opera as well as being the home of the Los Angeles Philharmonic Orchestra. This is where you may pick up the New York City Opera or Isaac Stern on tour, or find the Los Angeles Civic Light Opera season in progress.

The Mark Taper Forum tends toward contemporary drama, while the Ahmanson Theater is home for the experimental Center Theatre Group. **Other important forums** include the Greek Theatre in Griffith Park which offers a summer season of concerts, opera, dance and plays; the Universal Amphitheatre, an outdoor theatre in Universal City presenting leading artists of the pop musical world; the Hollywood Palladium – everything from big-name bands to boxing; the Shubert, Century City, for musicals; and the Hollywood Bowl, where the Los Angeles Philharmonic presents its summer concert season 'Under the Stars'. For something rather different, try the Mayfair Music Hall in Santa Monica, an elegantly refurbished turn-of-the-century opera house now offering old time vaudeville and musicals.

Disco spots with great music and transcendental lighting are Dillon's Downtown, Crazy Horse West, Gazzarii's, and you can do it in the Genji Bar of the New Otani. Live orchestras for dinner dancing at L'Escoffier in the Beverly Hilton, the Joint Venture Room of the Hyatt Regency, the Cabaret in the Bonaventure and the Cafe Carnival of the Wilshire Hyatt House.

Baedeker of Baedekers for what's on in town is the Sunday *Los Angeles Times* 'Calendar' section (there's a section for Singles activities too.) Also useful are *Los Angeles Magazine, Where* and *Key*. Major ticket agencies are Al Brooks Theatre Ticket Agency, with branches at 900 Wilshire Boulevard (213) (626-5863) and the Century Plaza Hotel (213) 556-3556), and Ticketron. You'll find Ticketron outlets in all Sears, Montgomery Ward and Broadway department stores.

Getting There
Los Angeles International Airport

Located on the coast 15 miles due west of the city center, Los Angeles International Airport is the West Coast's major gateway, with an annual passenger flow of more than 35 million. There are nine terminal buildings used by scheduled and commuter airlines ranged around a central parking area, plus the Western Imperial Terminal. WIT is roughly 10 minutes by car from the airport proper.

Expect to walk a fair way between the plane and US Customs and Immigration at LAX; distances between terminal buildings are such that you will probably want to use the airport shuttle. Keep hand baggage as light as possible – pre-arranged wheelchair service (through your carrier) is of real value to the handicapped here. Baggage carts are available in each terminal.

Airport Shuttle buses (trams in LAX terminology), operating at 10-minute intervals except WIT. Labeled 'Airline Connections', they're colored green, white and blue. A shuttle bus runs between the main terminal and WIT every 30 minutes. Stops are located on islands outside baggage claim areas.

These islands are also pick-up points for buses into Los Angeles, airport trams to the parking lots, and courtesy shuttles. from hotels and car agencies.

Yellow and brown **information kiosks** on the sidewalk outside baggage claim areas provide tickets and schedule in-information on airport bus service into Los Angeles and can assist you con-cerning public transportation to towns in the greater Los Angeles area. If the kiosks are not manned, call the information numbers listed under Transportation.

Services
The Los Angeles Department of Airports puts out a meticulously detailed guide to Los Angeles International's services and facilities which you can pick up on arrival. Here are the basics:

Baggage Carts In each ticketing and satellite complex area.

Baggage Lockers Each satellite complex and ticketing areas 4, 5, 6 and 7.

Car Rental Counters Ticketing areas 2 through 7. If the counters are not staffed a 24-hour telephone service is provided.

Off-airport car rental firms are listed in the phone book Yellow Pages. Consult your aircraft cabin steward about inflight car rental service.

Emergencies and Information Use the White Courtesy phone system. Tele-phone numbers are posted by each phone, but just in case:

Police   646-2256
Medical/First Aid   646-6254
Greater LA Convention and Visitors' Bureau, 201 World Way (in the Theme Building). Tel 215-0605 or 215-0606.

Foreign Currency Exchange Six bureaus, located adjacent to the International Terminal and in satellite complexes 2 and 3, ticketing areas 5 and 6, and West Imperial Terminal.

Hours:

International 2	9 am to 9 pm daily
Satellite 2	7 am to 11 pm daily
Satellite 3	7.30 am to 12.30 and 4 to 5.30 pm daily
Ticketing Area 5	7.30 am to 6 pm daily
WIT	Two hours before flights

Hotel-Motel Information Baggage claim areas in ticketing areas 2 through 7 and West Imperial Terminal. Pick-up/direct dial phone service.

Insurance Counters Ticketing areas 2 and 3; satellite complexes 4, 5, 6 and 7, and West Imperial Terminal. Self-service vending machines on the lower level of each satellite complex.

Lost and Found Baggage lost in flight and in the airport should be reported to your airline.

Shopping Gift shops located in each satellite complex and West Imperial Terminal. Tax free shops are located in satellites 2, 3, 4 and 5, ticketing area 2 and West Imperial Terminal; all pur-chases must be made 45 minutes before flight departure.

Postal Services Stamps and mail drop facilities in each building.

Wheelchairs/Aid to the Handicapped Check with your airline for wheelchairs and special services for the handicapped. Airport restrooms and telephones have been designed with the handicapped in mind.

Parking
Central Terminals Seven parking lots in the area surrounded by World Way.

Lots C and VSP Off-airport locations, linked to terminals by trams marked 'Parking Lot C' and 'Parking Lot VSP'. You can save 80 to 85% on long-term parking by using these lots which allow three hours free parking. Lot C is located at the intersection of Sepulveda Blvd and 96th St, Lot VSP at 111th St and La Cienega Blvd.

West Imperial Terminal Adjoins the WIT Terminal. Take the tram marked 'Western Imperial Terminal' which runs each half hour, 7.30 am to 11.30 pm.

For information on parking at these lots, call A-I-R-P-O-R-T.

Transportation (On-Airport)

Terminal Trams provide free transportation between airline terminals, at frequent intervals. They're marked 'Airline Connections' and you board at signs marked 'Airport Tram Stop'. Take the tram marked 'Western Imperial Terminal' for WIT; it operates every half hour. Trams to the parking lots also stop at airport tram stops and are marked for Lots C and VSP.

Transportation (Off-Airport)

Airport Service Fast, frequent and direct service to downtown LA and the Wilshire District (stopping at the major hotels); Hollywood and Universal City; Beverly Hills, Westwood and Century City; and West LA/San Fernando Valley. Buses stop at the shelters in front of Terminals 2, 3, 4, 5, 6, and 7. Tickets and information from the booths in front of the baggage claim area. If these are not manned, give the bus driver the exact fare. Current fare to downtown LA is $4. 24 hour information (213) 646-4716 (LAX); 723-4636 (LA); 855-1727 (Beverley Hills).

Airport Service also provides express service to Disneyland; Orange County Airport, Orange County inland and coastal cities, Long Beach, Pasadena and other cities nearby.

Antelope Valley Bus serves Newhall, Palmdale and Lancaster (morning arrival, evening departure, weekdays only). Information and tickets at the booths in front of baggage claim areas. Information (213) 365-8555; (805) 948-8421.

Crown Airport Commuter Van service to Glendale and Burbank Airport. Information (213) 245-0937.

Culver City buses provide frequent service to Westchester, Culver City, Santa Monica and West Los Angeles between 6 am and 9.40 pm. Pick them up at RTD bus stops. Information (213) 559-8310.

FlyAway Bus Service has non-stop service to the Van Nuys Bus Terminal, connecting point of San Fernando Valley services. Buses stop at the shelters. Information (805) 499-1995.

Norwalk Transit runs six trips daily to Norwalk from Parking Lot C – catch the Parking Lot C tram at any airport tram stop. Information (213) 393-9231.

RDT (City Bus) operates seven direct lines, connecting service to all Greater LA areas, from the transfer depot at 98th and Vicksburg. Pick up the connecting Airport Shuttle (No 608) outside the airport terminals. Shuttle service operates from 5 am to 1 am daily. Tel (213) 626-4455. **Santa Monica Flight Line** provides van service between LAX and Santa Monica hotels. Information (213) 393-9231.

Taxis Board cabs bearing the Los Angeles City franchise seal – they're the only ones authorised to solicit fares. On long hauls, do ascertain the fare in advance. Typically it's $19 to downtown LA, $17 to $19 to Hollywood and Beverley Hills. Should you need to call one, try:

Checker Cab – 258-3127

City Cab – 769-3333

Independent Cab – 385-8294

United Independent Cab – 653-5050

Yellow Cab – 481-2910

Getting Around

Los Angeles is best toured by car. You

can visit the major attractions by sightseeing coach or Southern California Rapid Transit District buses, but distances are great and the freeways were designed to get Angelenos where they want to go in the shortest possible time – so a rented car is a good investment. We've listed the leading car rental agencies under the Los Angeles International Airport section.

A word or two about driving in LA. Don't be intimidated by the heavy traffic. Whatever you may have heard, Angelenos are courteous, skilful Jehus and the freeways were not designed by engineers on an acid trip. Drive positively and keep up with the traffic flow; the LA style does not allow for hesitancy. 'When in doubt, accelerate.' And before you leave the rental parking lot, take a few minutes to study your route carefully – overshooting the turnoff can mean driving many unnecessary miles.

Airport Bus Service See Los Angeles International Airport section.

Bus *Southern California Rapid Transit District* buses cover Los Angeles, Orange, Riverside and San Bernardino counties. The basic fare is 65c a ride (85c if you transfer), so their 'Dollar a Day' tourist pass entitling you to unlimited travel over the network is a genuine travel bargain. Passes are issued for a minimum of three days to a maximum of 15 days and proof of residence outside the area is required. They're available at the airport ticket and information booths and RTD ticket agencies.

RTD's *Minibus Shuttle* is a particularly convenient way of touring the downtown area. Buses follow a circle route through the main shopping district and pass the major attractions – the Music Center, Civic Center, El Pueblo de Los Angeles State Historic Park, Olvera St, Chinatown and Little Tokyo.

For information, route maps and passes visit the *RTD Information Center* in the subterranean shopping complex at ARCO Plaza, Level B, 505 South Flower St (between 5th and 6th Sts). Hours are from 7.30 am to 4.30 pm. For 24-hour information, call (213) 626-4455 or 973-1222.

Limousine Service Always the plush way to go, some LA firms have added little touches to help while away the duller stretches of the freeways – color TV, built-in bars and tape decks. Firms advertise in the phone book Yellow Pages and rates begin around $30 an hour.

Taxis Rates are presently $1.90 at flag drop and $1.40 a mile thereafter. The fare from downtown Los Angeles to LA International won't cost less than $19.

Tours

The ubiquitous Gray Line Company heads a long list of companies offering sightseeing tours to LA's attractions and American Express offices and the Greater Los Angeles Visitors and Convention Bureau are excellent sources of information on the full range.

Bus *Gray Line,* 1207 W 3rd St, Los Angeles; (213) 481-8400, 800-4218921. City sightseeing tours cost $2.25 (half day). Hollywood, movie stars' homes and Beverley Hills half day tours run $13.50 all day in Disneyland is $27; and an all day tour of Marineland and the *Queen Mary.* An all day tour to $30 and an all day shopping spree in Tijuana, Mexico for $36 are among others.

Reservations (required for all tours) may be made at your hotel or motel and prices include free pickup and return from your hotel.

Starline Sightseeing Tours, Inc, 6845 Hollywood Boulevard, Hollywood, 90028; (213) 463-3131.

These include a Stars Homes tour (two hours), $8.50, Universal Studios (five hours), $21.75; and a nightclub tour, $40.

You should also know about *California Parlor Car Tours* which operate two to six-day package tours. Several run one-way in either direction between Los Angeles and San Francisco. The three-day San Diego-Palm Springs-Las Vegas tour, taking you to Mission San Juan Capistrano, La Jolla, Indio and the Great Mojave desert on the way, costs $258. (Prices quoted are based on double occupancy, American Plan.) For information in Los Angeles, write: California Parlor Car Tours, 3400 Wilshire, Los Angeles 90010; (213) 381-3925, (800) 622-0895. Its main office in San Francisco is in the Cathedral Hill Hotel, Van Ness at Geary, San Francisco 94101; (415) 495-1444.

Useful Addresses

Greater Los Angeles Visitors and Convention Bureau, 505 South Flower St, (subterranean ARCO Towers Complex), Level B, Los Angeles 90071; (213) 628-3101 (see also Los Angeles International Airport).

Free brochures on sightseeing attractions, maps, tour services, accommodation, entertainment, restaurants and tickets to some television shows. Open Monday to Friday, 9 to 5; Saturday 10 am

to 6 pm. 'Welcome Line' (taped information on events), tel (213) 628-5857. Additional information available from:

Beverly Hills Chamber of Commerce, 239 S Beverly Drive, Beverly Hills 90212; (213) 271-8126.

AAA/Automobile Club of Southern California, 2601 S Figueroa St; (213) 741-3111.

Services to members only, Monday to Friday 8.45 am to 5 pm (Saturday until 1 pm).

Miscellaneous

Foreign Currency Exchange (downtown Los Angeles).

American Foreign Exchange, 350 S Figueroa St; (213) 626-0255. Open Monday to Friday, 9 am to 5 pm.

Deak Perera of California Inc, 677 S Figueroa St; (213) 624-4221. Open Monday to Friday, 9 am to 5 pm.

Meeting the Americans

Sierra Club, Angeles Chapter, 2410 W Beverly Blvd, Los Angeles, 90057; (213) 387-4287.

Las Vegas & Death Valley

LAS VEGAS

The city of Las Vegas rises out of the mountain-ringed desert like a fantastic illusion. Situated in the southwestern corner of Nevada, it is 330 miles from Los Angeles and 595 miles from San Francisco.

Briefly a Mormon settlement from 1855 to 1857, then devoted to ranching and sporadic mining, Las Vegas' catalyst for growth to its present stature came in 1931, when the Nevada State Legislature legalized gambling – or 'gaming' as Nevadans prefer to call it. Gaming taxes now provide 40% of the state's revenue, and Las Vegas attracts over 12 million visitors annually.

Vegas is a 24-hour town where circadian rhythms cease to function. Night rivals day, with the blaze of neon and fluorescent lights replacing the sun. Breakfast, lunch and dinner are all served 24 hours a day. The cacophony of slot machines, jackpot bells, croupier calls, clattering dice and incessant music contrast with the silence of the desert.

Gambling is the *raison d'etre* for everything. Hotel and restaurant prices are less than you might expect; you can see spectacular shows and the top stars of show business performing less expensively than almost anywhere else – everything is designed to draw you to the tables, day and night. Slot machines greet you in laundromats, in supermarkets – even at times in the bathroom!

Climate

From May to September, Las Vegas is hot, but dry. Temperatures soar over the century mark through June, July and August but humidity stays relatively low. However, universal air-conditioning often reduces building interiors to near-Arctic temperatures, so you should carry a sweater. Winter temperatures are usually mild by day with cold nights.

The Casinos

The casinos and resort hotels center on two areas: Casino Center downtown and the famed Strip.

Downtown Casinos and hotels crowd the blocks around the intersection of downtown's Fremont St and Casino Center (also the name of a street). This area is, if anything, gaudier than the Strip; it is certainly more informal.

The **Mint Hotel** at 100 E Fremont is a good place for novice gamblers to start. Its casino conducts free tours every half hour; you see the money-counting room, the inside workings of a slot machine and you look down from a gallery onto the casino floor through a one-way security mirror. Tours Monday to Friday 10 am to 5 pm, free. Reservations (702) 385-7440, required for the tour; persons under 21 not admitted.

Binion's Horseshoe Casino at 128 Fremont St inspires gamblers by offering a look at $1 million in cash! In a bullet-proof showcase sit 100 US banknotes, each worth $10,000. Open daily, 24 hours.

The Strip The Strip is 3½ miles of Las Vegas Boulevard South, a six-lane highway lined with hotels, motels and casinos, some opulent, some modest, all wooing customers with huge neon signs. Among them:

Caesars Palace at 3570 Las Vegas Boulevard South. An incredibly ornate, kitsch tribute to ancient Rome. Acres of plush; Roman tiled casino and showrooms; mini-toga clad cocktail waitresses and keno runners scurrying hither and yon.

MGM Grand, 3645 Las Vegas Boulevard South. The studio's original venture into hotel building, executed with the

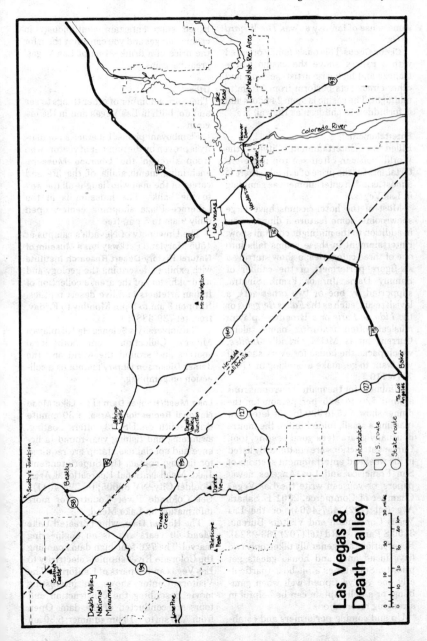

Las Vegas &
Death Valley

Interstate
U.S. route
State route

same sense of fantasy as was *The Wizard of Oz*.

Circus Circus This one's family oriented with a gallery above the casino where trapeze and high wire artists, clowns and other circus acts perform from 11 am to midnight. The casino is open 24 hours and is forbidden to children as they all are.

Entertainment
Billed as 'Entertainment City of the World' you can often see top-name entertainers for the price of a drink – there is almost as much entertainment as gambling in Las Vegas.

Most of the hotel-casinos have large showrooms; some feature a dinner show in addition to the midnight cocktail show. Entertainment in these rooms falls into one of three categories: a show starring a six-figure performer, of the caliber of Sammy Davis Jnr or Frank Sinatra, supported by one or two other acts; a lavish revue, such as the *Folies Bergeres* or the *Lido de Paris* or a Broadway play or musical, often featuring name talent. Current hit is MGM Grand's *Jubilee*, which packs the house for every show. If you want to go, make a booking on (702) 731-4110.

Minimum for the main showrooms runs around $20 to $25 per person for the dinner show, $15 to $20 for the late show (passing a small, folded bill to the maitre d' usually guarantees good seating, too). Current attractions are customarily listed in the weekend entertainment sections of San Francisco and Los Angeles newspapers, or you can write the Las Vegas Chamber of Commerce, 2301 E Sahara Ave (tel (702) 457-4664), or the Las Vegas Convention and Visitors Bureau, 3150 S Paradise Rd (tel (702) 733-2323). Reservations are generally taken only two days in advance and house guests get priority. Sometimes a pit boss (particularly one you've tipped well when gambling) or a bell captain can be helpful in arranging reservations.

Up and coming performers and estab-lished stars entertain continuously in casino lounges and you can enjoy them for the price of a drink – one of Las Vegas' great bargains.

Other
There are a number of other things to see and do, both in Las Vegas and in the environs.

Flamboyant pianist Liberace's popularity is proven by the number of visitors who troop through the **Liberace Museum**, enshrining memorabilia of the life and career of the man who 'laughs all the way to the bank'. The museum is in the Liberace Plaza shopping center, open daily 9 am to 5 pm, free.

The University of Nevada's campus at 4505 Maryland Parkway has a **Museum of Natural History-Desert Research Institute** with exhibits describing the geology and natural history of the area, a collection of Indian artefacts and live desert reptiles. Its open 8 am to 5 pm Monday to Friday, free; tel 739-3381.

The university's **Science Hall** displays a Mineral Collection from both local sources and around the world and the **James Dickinson Library** maintains a collection on gambling.

Lake Mead/Hoover Dam The **Lake Mead National Recreational Area**, a 30-minute drive south on US 93, offers boating, swimming and fishing year-round (a licence and special use stamp are required for fishing; contact the Superintendent, Lake Mead National Recreational Area, Boulder City, NV 89005; tel 293-4041). See Colorado River Country for more information on Lake Mead.

The **Hoover Dam**, which created Lake Mead 40 years ago, is an engineering marvel. The 726-foot-high dam spanning the Colorado River supplies electricity to Las Vegas and to parts of California. The Visitors Center shows an interesting movie describing the construction and tours are conducted of the dam. Open from 7.30 am to 7.15 pm summer; 8.30 am to 4.15 pm after Labor Day; movie every half hour; admission charge; tel 293-8367.

En route, in Henderson, is **Old Vegas**, a re-created Old West town featuring mock gunfights and hangings and the honky-tonk of a ragtime piano. It's free and open daily from 10 am to 5 pm, tel 564-1311.

The Spring Mountains Within an hour's drive west from the Strip, the forested slopes of the Spring Mountains provide a refreshing change of pace, with shaded picnic spots and hiking trails allowing enjoyment of crisp mountain air and spectacular scenery. **Mt Charleston**, highest peak at 11,918 feet, is particularly attractive in fall, when groves of aspen flash brilliant gold amongst the pines.

All shades of red, from salmon pink to deep ochre, color **Red Rock Canyon** at the southernmost extension of the mountain range. A 28-mile paved road, off Charleston Boulevard west of Las Vegas, loops the canyon, giving fine views of the vivid multicolored sandstone rock formations.

Southern Nevada's only ski area, **Lee Canyon**, is in the northern Spring Mountains. Ski season usually runs from early December to March or April. In summer, the chair lift operates for scenic rides. Take I-95 north for 28 miles, then SR 52 west.

Sports Las Vegas is a favourite with **golfers** because of the sunny weather and excellent courses. There are public and semi-private courses and several Strip hotels with championship courses. Best public course is probably Municipal Golf Course at Washington Ave, and Decatur Boulevard (tel 878-4665).

Tennis courts abound in Strip hotel grounds, mostly open to the public.

Major **boxing** bouts can often be seen at Caesar's Palace and the Aladdin Hotel. Unknowns fight bouts every Wednesday at the Showboat downtown (tel 385-9123).

Jai alai play continues all year at the MGM Grand fronton (tel 739-4682).

The annual **Helldorado**, a nine-day celebration held late May to early June, features a rip-roaring rodeo.

Weddings Las Vegas' other claim to fame is that couples over 18 (or 16 with parental consent) can get married on the spot, without any blood test or waiting period. The Las Vegas Marriage Licence Bureau is open round the clock, with the brief exception of the hour from 2 to 3 am! If you're interested: Clark County Courthouse, 3rd & Carson Sts (tel 385-3156).

Tours Tours to Lake Mead, Hoover Dam, Mount Charleston – even to Death Valley and the Grand Canyon – are run from Las Vegas, as well as evening tours taking in several casinos and shows. Major operators are *Gray Line Sight-Seeing Tours* (384-1234), American Sightseeing (873-6000), Greyhound (382-2640), and Las-Vegas-Tonopah-Reno Stage Lines (384-1230).

Lake Mead Ferry Service (736-6180) operates combination bus-yacht tours, including a lake cruise.

At publication time, five airlines are offering flight tours to the Grand Canyon, including *Scenic Airlines* (739-1900), *Air Nevada* (736-8900) and *Air Cortez* (739-6657). Cost runs from $155 round trip, including lunch. One-day flights are also offered to Disneyland and motorcoach tours to London Bridge in Arizona and Zion-Bryce parks in Utah.

Places to Stay

The major hotels along the Strip are all resort hotels; they offer landscaped grounds, sports facilities, restaurants and coffee shops, in addition to the casinos and showrooms. Biggest and most plush are the *MGM Grand, Las Vegas Hilton* (actually not on the Strip, but adjacent to the Convention Center a block away), *Caesars Palace* and the *Desert Inn Hotel.* The *Riviera* and the *Sands* are more elegant and less frenetic than most. Reservations are easier to obtain for mid-week and almost impossible for a Saturday night-only booking.

Since they all offer basically the same resort facilities (only the *Desert Inn,*

Dunes, Sahara and *Tropicana* have golf, all for an extra fee), they are listed below without description. Rates are added for comparative purposes only, as these are ever changeable, with special packages on offer. In Las Vegas, rates are generally the same for single and double occupancy.

Top End

Caesars Palace 3570 Las Vegas Boulevard South, Las Vegas NV 89109; tel (702) 731-7110. Rates from $95 double.

Sahara 2535 Las Vegas Boulevard S, Las Vegas NV 89109; tel (702) 737-2111. Rates from $45 double.

Desert Inn 3145 Las Vegas Boulevard South, Las Vegas NV 89109; tel (702) 733-4444. Rates from $55 double.

Dunes 3650 Las Vegas Boulevard South, Las Vegas NV 89109; tel (702) 737-4110. Rates from $48 double.

Frontier 3120 Las Vegas Boulevard S, Las Vegas NV 89109; tel (702) 734-0110. Rates from $42 double.

Las Vegas Hilton 3000 Paradise Rd, Las Vegas NV 89109; tel (702) 732-5111. Rates from $49 double.

MGM Grand 3645 Las Vegas Boulevard S, Las Vegas NV 89109; tel (702) 739-4111. Rates from $59 double.

Riviera 2901 Las Vegas Boulevard S, Las Vegas NV 89109; tel (702) 734-5110. Rates from $49 double.

Sands 3355 Las Vegas Boulevard S, Las Vegas NV 89109; tel (702) 733-5000. Rates from $60 double.

Flamingo Hilton 3555 Las Vegas Boulevard S, Las Vegas NV 89109; tel (702) 733-3111. Rates from $45 double.

Tropicana 3801 Las Vegas Boulevard S, Las Vegas NV 89109; tel (702) 739-2222. Rates from $60 double.

Mid-Range

Hacienda 3950 Las Vegas Boulevard S, Las Vegas NV 89109; tel (702) 739-8911. Rates from $34 double.

Bottom End

Circus Circus 2880 Las Vegas Boulevard

S, Las Vegas NV 89109; tel (702) 734-0410. Rates from $18 double.

Mini-Price Motor Inn 4155 Koval Lane, Las Vegas NV 89109; tel (702) 731-2111. Rates from $25 double.

Downtown

Hotels and motels in the Casino Center area generally are in the moderate class, though you can find low rates:

Safari Motel 2001 E Fremont St, Las Vegas NV 89109; tel (702) 384-4021. Rates from $19 double.

Places to Eat & Drink

One of the best tips in Las Vegas is to try the buffet lunches and dinners served by virtually all the Strip hotels and most of the downtown hotels – they're 'all-you-can-eat' at budget prices! Locals recommend the downtown hotels for gourmet dining.

The second tip is that if you like your drinks to be not too weak, order them straight in the showrooms!

As you might expect there is a plethora of restaurants from fast-food to gourmet from which you can choose. Some of the more notable:

Bacchanal Room In Caesars Palace. Elegant seven-course feast including three wines. Fine service. (E)

Dinner nightly. Reservations required; tel 731-7110.

Don the Beachcomber In the Sahara Hotel. Polynesian surroundings and cuisine in one of noted chain. (M)

Dinner nightly. Reservations required; tel 737-2111.

Alpine Village Inn German Rathskeller with European atmosphere, German and Swiss cuisine. (M) Dinner nightly; closed November 22 to December 25. Opposite Las Vegas Hilton, tel 734-6888.

Facciami's Library Library-cum-English pub in setting of old mansion. (M)

Breakfast, lunch, dinner daily. 200 W Sahara Avenue. Reservations recommended; tel 384-5200.

El Burrito Cafe Tiny restaurant serving authentic Mexican dinners. (B) 1919 E Fremont St. Reservations required, tel 385-9461.

For hearty, inexpensive breakfasts, try the *Stardust Hotel* or *Food Fantasy* in the Flamingo Hilton.

Getting There

Air McCarran International Airport, three miles south of downtown Las Vegas, is served by major trunk and commuter airlines. Limousine and bus service is available to the Strip and downtown.

Bus Both Greyhound Lines, 200 S Main St and Continental Trailways, 217 N 4th St, serve Las Vegas, as well as Las Vegas-Tonopah-Reno Stage Lines, 922 E Stewart Ave.

Car Major access route by car is I-15 from San Diego and Los Angeles, which runs parallel to the Strip, with exit ramps leading to the Strip and downtown.

Getting Around

Bus The *Las Vegas Transit System* covers most of the city by bus. Fare is 80c with one free transfer. A 10-ride discount ticket costs $5.25 (Schedule information: 1550 Industrial Rd, tel 384-3540).

Car Rental The major rental agencies are all represented at McCarran Airport and on the Strip. Numerous other agencies are listed in the Yellow Pages of the phone book.

Being basically built on a grid pattern Las Vegas is easy to get around and parking is seldom a problem.

Taxis Cabs are easily obtained at the airport, hotels and taxi stands. Fare depends on mileage and number of passengers, but basic rate is $1.40 first sixth of a mile, 20c each additional sixth of a mile. Standard tip is 15-20%.

DEATH VALLEY

California's Death Valley, 160 miles northwest of Las Vegas, is actually a fault basin lying between the Sierra Nevada mountains to the west and Nevada's Amargosa Desert to the east. More than 550 of the nearly 3000 square miles in the **Death Valley National Monument** lie below sea level. Two points west of Badwater are 282 feet below sea level, making them the lowest points in the western hemisphere. The Monument also encompasses four mountain ranges – the Cottonwood, Panamint, Black and Funeral Mountains. Highest peak is 11,049-foot Telescope Peak in the Panamints.

Evidence of each of the four major eras of geologic history of the earth is visible within Death Valley. Interesting features are the remarkable striation of canyon outcroppings and weird, swirling patterns on the valley floor, as though a giant primordial wave of minerals is frozen in space. Wind-rippled sand dunes and striped buttes, colorful water-polished rock betraying the former presence of a sea, salt creeks and mineral springs as well as mine ruins, ghost towns, and century-old charcoal kilns – all lie within easy access of Furnace Creek and Stove Pipe Wells, the two main stopping places in the Monument.

Death Valley belies its name by the life it supports. Within the Monument are some 600 plant species, 50 types of mammal and nearly 400 species of resident and migrant birds. Best bird-watching is around Furnace Creek Ranch from September to May. Wildflowers carpet many areas in the early spring; particularly attractive are Daylight and Jubilee Passes.

History
Death Valley was discovered by whites in 1849, when a group of miners en route to the Californian gold rush took what they expected to be a short cut through it. Several died in the attempt and it was not until precious ores were found in the 1870s that fortune seekers again ventured into the barren wasteland. The discovery of borax in 1873 brought the major activity to the valley and led to its development as a tourist attraction. Borax

mines flourished and towns boomed, only to go bust five to six years later, leaving ghost towns which now invite exploration. During the heyday of the borax mining the famous 20-mule team was born. It was used to haul special 36½-ton wagons over the 165-mile route to the Mojave railhead. The original wagons can be seen today at the Furnace Creek Ranch.

Climate
Death Valley is a winter resort. From November to March, temperatures are typically around the 60°s and 70°s F at midday, in the 40°s at night. Humidity is usually low; Furnace Creek boasts the nation's lowest average rainfall, 1½ inches annually. Summer temperatures, on the other hand, top the 90° mark and often hit the 110 to 120° range. If you cross the valley in summer, you should carry extra water and preferably travel by night.

FURNACE CREEK
Furnace Creek is the focal point for most visitors. The **National Park Service Visitor Center,** located here, maintains a museum and offers hourly slide presentations detailing the history and natural history of the Monument. Maps and guided walks, self-guided auto tours, horseback tours and trail leaflets are available. In winter, naturalist programs are presented each evening. It's open daily November to mid-April 8 am to 9 pm, balance of year 8 am to 5 pm, free; tel (619) 786-2331.

Ranger stations are also maintained at Wildrose, Emigrant, Grapevine and Rhodes Well (winter only).

The borax story is told at the **Borax Museum,** an outdoor exhibition of implements and transportation used in the mining. Smaller displays are in the 1883 mining office-bunkhouse nearby. The original 20-mule-team wagons are two miles north at the site of the Harmony Borax Works.

Things to See
Sightseeing highlights within easy reach

of paved roads are: **Artist's Drive**, a narrow, winding paved one-way road (entered from the south 7½ miles north of Badwater). The drive gives exciting vistas over salt flats and multi-colored clay hills. **Artist's Palette** at midway point is the best vantage point and late afternoon light most enhancing.

Sunrise and sunset are spectacular at **Dante's View**, a mile-high lookout above Badwater, the salt flats and the valley's lowest points. The panorama includes the Panamint peaks and, in the distance, the Sierra Nevada with Mt Whitney, highest point on the continent.

Zabriskie Point in the rugged Black Mountains overlooks sharply incised yellow mudhills rising out of ancient lakebeds.

An improved dirt spur road leads to the **Devil's Golf Course**, a jumble of sharp spires and ridges of crystallized salt, some two feet high, which covers 200 square miles of valley floor.

Scotty's Castle

One of the best-known landmarks in Death Valley, this Moorish mansion in Grapevine Canyon near the Monument's northern boundary is named for Walter Scott, 'Death Valley Scotty'. A prospector and one-time rough rider with Buffalo Bill's Wild West Show, he charmed a Chicago millionaire into building this home for him. The lavishly furnished castle is now operated by the National Park Service, who conduct tours through it. Open daily from 9 am to 5 pm; with tours every hour on the hour, admission charge.

A visit to Scotty's Castle can be combined with a look at **Ubehebe Crater** five miles beyond the castle turnoff. Ubehebe, which the Indians called 'Duhveetah's Carrying Basket', is one of several craters, from one of which rises an almost perfect volcanic cone.

Around Death Valley

One of the most interesting ghost towns, Rhyolite, is actually in Nevada off SR 58, just outside the Monument's boundary. Rhyolite boomed from 1905 into one of Nevada's finest towns, with 12,000 people. Three years later, the mine closed. Ruins along Golden St, the old jailhouse and Boothill cemetery are testament to Rhyolite's past but the main attraction today is the **Bottle House**, constructed from 51,000 beer bottles, which dispenses food and souvenirs.

Also outside the Monument's border is **Marta Becket's Amargosa Opera House** in Death Valley Junction at the junction of SR 190 and SR 127, 29 miles southeast of Furnace Creek. Marta Becket presents a one-woman mime-ballet weekends mid-October to April 30, Saturdays only in May and early October. You are joined in the 'audience' by 260 Spanish courtiers and commoners – a full-sized mural, also the product of Becket's talents. The 20-room *Amargosa Hotel* next door serves pre-show dinner and dessert afterwards.

For reservations, necessary for both hotel and theater, write Amargosa Opera House, Death Valley Junction CA 92328; to telephone, ask operator for Death Valley Junction toll station no 1 for hotel, no 8 for theater.

Places to Stay

The main accommodation is at Furnace Creek, with one hotel at Stove Pipe Wells. Easter, Thanksgiving, and the weekend of the Death Valley '49ers Annual Encampment in early November are booked out a year ahead; otherwise reservations are easy to obtain.

Furnace Creek Inn (Death Valley, CA 92328; tel (619) 786-2361). Luxurious winter resort set amid palms. Air-conditioned, pool, tennis, golf and riding extra. Dining room (reservations necessary for non-guests); cocktail lounge, entertainment. Open October to April only. Rates from $130 double. Reservations and deposit required.

Furnace Creek Ranch (Death Valley, CA 92328; tel (619) 786-2345).

Modest resort, air-conditioned cottages and motel units. Pool, tennis, store, gas station, trailer park, and light aircraft landing strip. Golf and riding extra. Coffee shop, cafeteria and steak house (closed in summer). Ranch open year-round. Rates from $41 double.

Stove Pipe Wells Village (Death Valley, CA 92328; to telephone dial (619) and ask operator for 181, Stove Pipe Wells). 79-unit motel, air-conditioned, heated mineral pool, service station, grocery store. Restaurant, cocktails. Conducted tours; evening talks in season. Open year-round. Rates from $33 double.

There are *campgrounds* at Furnace Creek, Stove Pipe Wells and seven other sites throughout the Monument. Reservations should be made through Ticketron or Death Valley Monument Supervisor, Death Valley, CA 92328; tel (619) 786-2331.

Getting There

Nearest commercial airport is Las Vegas. Driving from there, you can take US 95 N to Lathrop Wells, cut over to Death Valley Junction on SR 127 and take SR 190 N to Furnace Creek. Or you can continue on US 95 to Beatty and take SR 58 through Daylight Pass to join SR 190 near the Stove Pipe Wells Hotel. From San Francisco or Los Angeles, you take I-5 to US 395 (see below), then cross the Panamints

on SR 190. Greyhound links Las Vegas with Death Valley Junction, Furnace Creek and Scotty's Castle with daily service November through April.

The Sierra's Back Door

Heading west out of Death Valley, over the Panamint Range, SR 190 runs around Owens Lake to connect with US 395 in the vicinity of Mt Whitney, which at 14,495 feet is the continental US's highest peak. US 395 runs up the eastern side of the Sierra Nevada, from San Bernardino in southern California all the way north to the Canadian border.

This route provides access through the spectacularly scenic Tioga Pass (closed through the winter) to Yosemite; on SR 08 to Sonora, gateway to the Gold Country and to the San Francisco Bay Area (this particularly attractive drive is possible only in summer, too); and to Mammoth Lakes, Lake Tahoe, Carson City and Reno. It passes through numerous small towns, giving a look at country life, and lush ranchlands en route to Lake Tahoe. There are motels and restaurants in towns like Bishop, Independence and Lone Pine. From Independence, the turn-off for the Kearsage Pass leads to the Sierra high country and from Lone Pine, you come to the hiking trails which lead you to the wonders of Sequoia and Kings Canyon National Parks.

Los Angeles to San Francisco

Beyond Santa Monica SR 1 traces the old route of the Spanish conquerors and missionaries to Santa Barbara through Malibu, Oxnard and Ventura. Out to sea loom the Channel Islands, a chain of eight small islands which are the eroded peaks of ancient mountain ranges. These islands were among the first parts of California to be explored by the Spanish: Cabrillo anchored off Anacapa in 1542 and 60 years later the Vizcaino expedition used them as a source of wood and water. Their sporadic inhabitation by the Chumash Indians continued until the mid-1800s. Today, Santa Cruz and Santa Rosa are in private hands, used for ranching. Three were set aside in 1938 as the Channel Islands National Monument to preserve their rare plant and animal life.

CHANNEL ISLANDS NATIONAL MONUMENT

Anacapa, Santa Barbara and San Miguel islands constitute Channel Islands National Monument, offering an opportunity to escape to the desert island lifestyle for a while. Here you can see California sea lion, harbor seal, sea elephant and a large number of different sea and land birds, including the brown pelican so close to extinction a few years ago. Plant life is dominated by the giant coreopsis or tree sunflower which can grow up to 10 feet in height (they bloom in early spring), and the clear island waters contain a wondrous range of marine life, from microscopic plankton to sharks and killer whales – sport fishing, scuba diving and underwater photography are popular activities in the monument.

Closest to the mainland is **Anacapa**, actually a chain of three separate islets, each about 700 acres in area, lying roughly 11 miles south of Oxnard. Camping is confined to East Island; as there is a limit to the number of persons who may use it,

advance registration with Monument Headquarters in Ventura is required. Advice and trail booklets are available at the ranger station on East Anacapa.

Santa Barbara Island, 38 miles west of Los Angeles' San Pedro Harbor, is particularly interesting to observers of wildlife. Sea mammals and birds abound, and during late summer or early fall you may even come upon sea elephants. Primitive camping, limited to 14 days, is permitted near the ranger quarters only, and, as on Anacapa, advance registration with Monument Headquarters is required.

Farthest west and smallest of the islands is **San Miguel,** owned by the US Navy but managed by the National Park Service. Somewhere on its windswept reaches is the grave of the navigator Juan Rodriguez Cabrillo who died here in 1543. Access to San Miguel is by permit only – the navy still uses the island for target practice.

When to Visit

Summer is the most popular season, of course. Days are usually sunny and the ocean temperature is an acceptable 68°F (20°C). Winter brings high winds and rains which turn the islands a brilliant green and cleanse the air, allowing spectacular views. Temperatures seldom fall below 40°F (4°C) and you can expect quite a few sunny days too. Spring is the best time to see wildflowers and the giant coreopsis in bloom.

Because the ecology of the islands is extremely fragile, there are quite a few restrictions on what you can do there. For example, hiking is limited to established trails and access to the water is permitted only in the landing coves. Visitors who plan to fish or dive for abalone, lobster and scallops must observe the California fish and game laws and obtain a valid fishing licence. Information on current conditions and regulations is available from Monument Headquarters, 1699 Anchors Way Drive, Ventura, CA 93003; tel (805) 644-8157.

Getting There

The uncomplicated way is chartering your own boat – and there are many charter boat outfits in southern California ports who will be delighted to help you.

Public transportation to the islands is trickier. Presently there is only one regularly scheduled operation running between Ventura and Anacapa Island. The *Island Packers Co* operates trips daily in summer, normally leaving Ventura at 9 am and returning at 5 pm. Weather and water conditions permitting, that leaves you some three hours to enjoy the nature trail. On the way back you cruise past points of interest. Reservations may be made not less than three days and not more than 30 days in advance. Current fare is $22 and you must bring your own lunch. If you plan to camp on Anacapa, note that two reservations must be made – one day to go out and one day to come back. For this reason, the fare is doubled.

Island Packers also operates a Saturday service to Santa Barbara Island (again, summer only), leaving Ventura harbor at 7 am and returning about 8 pm. The round trip fare is $37. You may be able to tag along with a group charter if Saturdays are not feasible. Island Packers will put you in touch with a group if you write giving the month you would like to go – then it's up to you to make the arrangements with the group. For information, write Island Packers Co, PO Box 993, Ventura, CA 93001; tel (805) 642-1393 or 6452-3370.

SANTA BARBARA

Prosperous, lovely with a warm, sunny climate, Santa Barbara looks southward over the Pacific from a plain at the foot of the Santa Ynez Mountains. Your first impression may be that you have been transported to a Mediterranean coastal city as the glistening white buildings with red tile roofs take form and you approach the center of town along streets lined with palms. And this is not inappropriate for Santa Barbara was founded by the Spanish and carefully nourishes its Hispanic traditions. It was the earthquake of 1925, however, that paved the way for the Spanish look. Down went a number of architecturally undistinguished buildings, and the Architectural Review Board responsible for rebuilding the city decided that all new construction would conform to a Mediterranean style. The result is a singularly harmonious community of great beauty.

Though Cabrillo and Vizcaino anchored in the channel on their voyages up the coast and Gaspar de Portola's expedition camped in the area in 1769, Santa Barbara's history begins with the decision of the indefatigable Father Junipero Serra to establish three intermediate missions between San Luis Obispo and San Gabriel. In 1782 Governor Felipe Neve at last granted permission and Serra hastened southward to the Santa Barbara Channel. After founding Mission San Buenaventura (modern Ventura), he continued to the large Indian village near a wide crescent bay remarked by the earlier explorers, and a very favorable site for the presidio was found within view of the beach. The building of the mission, however, was postponed until the end of 1786.

In the opinion of one early traveler, a philosophy of 'dolce far niente' governed Santa Barbara's growth. The Barbareno cattle barons led a gracious and urbane existence based on a profitable trade in hides and tallow which even the arrival of the Americans changed little. During the gold rush years they waxed even richer as great herds of cattle were driven north to feed the Argonauts.

This halcyon era ended with the drought that began in 1864; most of the herds died of thirst and the vast rancheros were divided into small farms. With the advent of the Southern Pacific railroad Santa Barbara began its transformation into a wealthy resort and residential community – those brightly painted oil rigs floating offshore help support the economy but otherwise impinge little on a way of life that draws greatly on old-world traditions. There's no better expression of those traditions than the 'Old Spanish Days' fiesta held during the August full moon period when modern Barbarenos don costume and the streets are filled with music, dancing and pageantry.

Pueblo Viejo

A good place to begin a tour of Santa Barbara is Pueblo Viejo (Old Town), the core of the city which grew up around the Presidio. Bounded by Victoria, Chapala, Ortega and Santa Barbara streets, the area is a historic preserve – no buildings may be altered, torn down or built here without city approval. Bronze markers in the sidewalks indicate the Presidio limits and plaques identify the structures. It's worth while picking up a copy of the *Red Tile Tour* from the Santa Barbara Chamber of Commerce at 1301 Santa Barbara St (tel (805) 965-3201) as a supplementary guide.

A stroll along **El Paseo**, between State and Anacapa St, immediately takes you back to Santa Barbara's early days. This attractive pedestrian arcade, lined with art galleries, boutiques and outdoor cafes, is built around the adobe home of the de la Guerra family. The **Casa de la Guerra** (1827) built by Jose Antonio Julian de la Guerra y Noriega, Commandante of the Presidio, with the aid of Indians, was the center of social life and many distinguished visitors enjoyed the hospitality of the congenial Don in its rambling rooms. Richard Henry Dana was here in 1834 and again in 1859; he painted a vivid portrait of de la Guerra in *Two Years Before The Mast*. It's fitting that one of Santa Barbara's most popular restaurants now occupies part of the house.

Nearby, on east Canon Perdido St, you'll find the two oldest buildings in town. **El Cuartel**, No 122, was built in 1782 as housing for the Spanish garrison and is part of the Presidio's original quadrangle. Open Monday to Friday, 9 am to noon, 1 to 4 pm; admission free; tel (805) 966-9719.

Just across the street is **La Caneda Adobe**, dating from the same period. The **Hill-Carrillo Adobe**, 11 E Carrillo St, is another old home accessible to the public. Daniel Hill of Massachusetts built it for his Spanish bride in 1826 and it boasted Santa Barbara's first wooden floor. Fully restored, the adobe now houses the Santa Barbara Foundation.

Santa Barbara Historical Society Museum

The Santa Barbara Historical Society houses many treasures in its adobe building at the corner of de la Guerra and Santa Barbara Sts. In the wing devoted to the Mexican and Spanish periods of local history, you'll find paintings of California missions executed between 1875 and 1890 by Edwin Deakin and relics of Richard Henry Dana's visits to the city. The museum is open Tuesday to Friday; noon to 5 pm; weekends 1 to 5 pm. Closed holidays. Guided tours Wednesday and Sunday 1.30; admission free; tel (805) 966-1601;

Around the corner at 715 Santa Barbara St is the former home of Mexican artist and illustrator Miguel Covarrubias. **Casa de Covarrubias** (1817) was the scene of the last meeting of congress under the Mexican flag in 1846. The **Historic (Fremont) Adobe** (1836) shares the museum grounds. Farther down Santa Barbara St is the **Rochin Adobe**, built of bricks from the original Presidio chapel.

Santa Barbara County Courthouse

Set in lush gardens and occupying a whole city block between Anapuma and Figueroa Sts is the Santa Barbara County Courthouse, a remarkable essay in the Spanish-Moorish style. The courthouse was built in 1929 on the site of the first encampment in the area by the Gaspar de Portola expedition (1769); two-story-high murals by Dan Dayre Groesbeck in the **Assembly Room** depict Santa Barbara's history. For an excellent view across the city, take the elevator to the observation deck of **El Mirador**, the courthouse's 70-foot tower. It's open 8 am to 5 pm weekdays; 9 am to 5 pm weekends, holidays, admission free. Free guided tour Fridays at 10.30 am.

Santa Barbara Museum of Art

At the corner of State and Anapuma Sts, the Santa Barbara Museum of Art is a showcase for Greco-Roman, Egyptian and oriental antiquities and western art. European and American painting is well represented with works by Eakins, John Singer Sargent, Edward Hopper and Georgia O'Keefe among the collections. Also of interest is the display of American glass. The Santa Barbara Museum of Art is open Tuesday to Saturday, 11 am to 5 pm; Sunday, noon to 5 pm. Guided tours 1.30 weekdays, 2 pm weekends, admission free; tel (805) 963-4364.

Santa Barbara Mission

Overlooking the city from a hilltop site chosen by Father Junipero Serra in 1784, Santa Barbara Mission is the 10th in the chain of Franciscan foundations. Serra did not live to see the construction of 'The Queen of Missions'; the work was carried out under the direction of Father Fermin Lasuen who consecrated the building in 1786. Within five years this church was replaced by a larger structure which was so badly damaged by the 1812 earthquake that it was decided to build again. The present church, completed in 1820, is massively constructed of sandstone, with six feet thick walls supported by buttresses eight feet square. Even so, it suffered considerable damage in the 1925 'quake, necessitating a complete restoration.

Plates illustrating a Spanish translation of Vitruvius' work on architecture inspired the classical facade set between Colonial towers and the decoration of the church's ceiling. (The work is still in the mission archives.) Many of the interior furnishings date from the Colonial period, including oil paintings brought from Spain in the last years of the 18th century.

Follow the arcaded corridor to view three of the original mission rooms which display furnishings, paintings and statues of the 18th and 19th centuries as well as artefacts of the Chumash Indians. A Roman archway decorated with two authentic skulls and crossbones to the right of the church leads to the mission cemetery, planted with roses and rare plants.

Part of the irrigation system built in 1806 is still in use: the ornate Moorish fountain in front of the mission is fed by water from Pedregosa Creek two miles away, brought down via a stone aquaduct to a reservoir in what is now Mission Historical Park on the hillside behind. This reservoir remains part of the city water system. The large octagonal basin by the fountain was used by Indian women to do the family wash.

The view of the mission from the reservoir area is worth the walk; in addition, you can see ruins of the old grist mill and kiln where utensils, bricks and tiles were made. Open Monday to Saturday, 9 am to 5 pm; Sunday 1 to 5 pm; admission free; tel (805) 682-4713.

Santa Barbara Museum of Natural History

On Puesta del Sol, just north of the mission, is the Santa Barbara Museum of Natural History, with collections focusing on western phenomena. On the grounds is the **Gladwin Planetarium**. Here a closed circuit television system permits a view of the heavens through the planetarium telescope after the 8 pm show on the second and fourth Thursday of each month. It's open Monday to Saturday, 9 am to 5 pm; Sunday 10 to 5 pm (10 am to 5 pm in summer); closed major holidays.

Santa Barbara Botanic Garden

There are more than five miles of trails in the Botanic Garden's 65 acres, leading you through sections devoted to California's native trees, shrubs and wildflowers. Every different kind of environment in the state is represented, from cool redwood groves to the desert. The **Historic Trail** illustrates how Indians lived off the land, using plants to make medicines, food, drink and even soap. Within the grounds is the old mission reservoir (see above). Open daily from 8 am to sunset; guide tour Thursday, 10.30 am; admission free.

Things to Do

Santa Barbara's superb climate and environment are a continuing invitation to play outdoors. Golf enthusiasts have half a dozen public courses to choose between – try the Santa Barbara Community Course (18 holes) at Las Positas Rd and McCaw Avenue (tel 687-7087) and Sandpiper Golf Course (18 holes) at 7925 Hollister Avenue, Goleta (tel 968-1541). Rates are $6.25 and $8 for 18 holes respectively (slightly higher at weekends).

Plenty of tennis courts, too. You'll find municipal courts at Salinas St and US 101; Oak Park; Las Positas, 1002 Las Positas Rd; Pershing Park, Castillo St and West Cabrillo Boulevard. Pick up a permit at the Chamber of Commerce. In addition there are several private tennis clubs and courts at each country club.

Horseback riding is a popular local activity. Two stables offering escorted trail and beach rides are San Ysidro Stables, 900 San Ysidro Lane (tel 969-2157) and Gene O'Hagen Stables, Circle-Bar-B Ranch, Refugio Canyon. Reservations required.

You can zip around the area on a set of self-powered wheels rented from Open Air-Bicycles, 8 W Cabrillo Boulevard (tel 963-25240. They've got three and 10-speed bikes, mopeds and roller skates. A deposit is required and don't forget your ID card.

For boating and fishing, head for the Breakwater. *Shoreline Cruises, West Beach Marine*, offer one-hour Santa Barbara Bay trips daily. Phone 963-5600 for their schedule. *Sea Landing, Bath* and *Cabrillo* (tel 963-3564) can help you enjoy the excellent local fishing. Food and drink are sold on board and rental equipment is available. You should obtain a fishing licence at the Breakwater – ask about the special three-day non-resident license. You'll also find inboards, outboards and sailboats for rent at the Breakwater. Phone *Santa Barbara Boat Rentals* (962-2826) and West Beach Marine Co (963-5600) for their current hourly rates and deposit requirements.

Literally miles of free public beaches in the Santa Barbara area; Leadbetter Beach Park and Arroyo Beach Park are both accessible by MTD buses. Carpinteria State Beach lies 12 miles south of Santa Barbara; El Capitan and Refugio beaches are 17 and 23 miles north of the city respectively. Good surfing, campgrounds, and a lifeguard on duty in summer at the state beaches.

Places to Stay

Santa Barbara has no lack of good hotels, including three of California's most prestigious resorts. Book well in advance for a summer stay as the city is very popular.

Top End

Mariott's Santa Barbara *Biltmore* 1260 Channel Drive, Santa Barbara 93108; tel (805) 969-2261, 800-228-9290.

One of the West's most famous resort hotels, amid 21 acres of palm-studded gardens in the posh Montecito area. Private beach, two heated swimming pools, putting green. Rooms and cottages with color TV, and the kind of service that goes with the coveted five star rating. Rates from $115 double.

San Ysidro Ranch 900 San Ysidro Lane, Santa Barbara 93108; tel (805) 969-5046.

A 500-acre retreat high in the Santa Ynez Mountains, this legendary guest ranch opened its doors in 1893. Over the years, Winston Churchill, President Kennedy and Rex Harrison have signed the guest register. One, two and three-room cottages, furnished with antiques. No TV. Amenities include heated pool, tennis, riding stables and restaurant. Rates from $84 double.

Mid-Range

Miramar Motor Hotel Resort 1555 S Jameson Lane (PO Box M), Santa Barbara 93102; tel (805) 969-2203, 800-4474470. Overlooking the Pacific, with 14 acres of gardens, two swimming pools, tennis courts and a private beach. Most accommodation is in cottages with kitchens. Air-conditioning, color TV and entertainment. Reserve deposit required. Rates from $42 double.

El Prado Motor Inn 1601 State St, Santa Barbara 93101; tel (805) 965-4586.

Central location, near Plaza and Performing Arts Center. Heated pool. Air-conditioning, color TV, complimentary morning coffee. Rates from $36 double.

Polynesian Motel 433 W Montecito St, Santa Barbara 93101; tel (805) 963-7851. Three blocks from the beach, with heated swimming pool. Some kitchen units (four-day minimum stay required). Color TV. Rates from $34 double.

Tropicana Motel 223 Castillo St, Santa Barbara 93101; tel (805) 966-2219. Two blocks from the beach. Heated pool. Color TV. Some kitchen units (three-day minimum stay required). Rates from $36.

The Upham 1404 De La Vina, Santa Barbara 93101; tel (805) 962-0058.

Established in 1871, this is Santa Barbara's oldest hotel. Not large, but of great charm, with an attractive garden. Most rooms with bath or shower. B&W TV and a color TV room. Rates from $28 double.

Bottom End

Motel 6 3505 State Street, Santa Barbara 93105; tel (805) 687-5400.

This one also has a swimming pool. Again, reservations recommended. Rates from $19.95 double.

Hotel de Riviera 125 W Carrillo St, Santa Barbara 93101; tel (805) 965-9141.

Attractive little inn in European tradition, surrounded by garden and only a block from bus station. No meals, but close to city center's restaurants and coffee shops. Rates from $28 double (without bath).

Places to Eat

Chanticleer Restaurant Dine indoors or in the courtyard on fine French cuisine. Live entertainment nightly. Strict about jackets for dinner. (E)

Lunch, dinner. Open daily. 1279 Coast Village Rd, Montecito; tel 969-5959.

El Encanto In the El Encanto Hotel, overlooking the city and the coast. Renowned for 'nouvelle cuisine' and gracious service. (M/E)

Breakfast, lunch, dinner, open daily. 1900 Lasuen Rd; tel 965-5231.

Good Earth Restaurant The accent is on natural foods in this cozy restaurant with a bakery on the premises. (B/M)

Breakfast, lunch, dinner. Open daily. 21 West Canon Perdido; tel 962-4463.

The Feed Store, Steaks, seafood and Italian amidst a decor redolent of the past. Live entertainment nightly. (M/E)

Lunch, Monday to Friday; dinner daily. 110 Santa Barbara St; tel 966-2435.

The Mandalay Restaurant & Coffeehouse Step back into the atmosphere of the British Raj and enjoy scones, high tea and authentic curries. Pop and Jazz from the 1930s and '40s nightly after nine. (B/M)

Breakfast, lunch, dinner. Open daily. 21 W Victoria St; tel 965-5497.

Suishin Sukiyaki Excellent Japanese fare, enhanced by Japanese music and shoji screens. Booths for those who prefer not to scrumple up on the tatami matting. (M)

Lunch, dinner. Open daily. 511 State St; tel 962-1495.

Nightlife & Entertainment

Santa Barbara's events calendar covers the whole spectrum of entertainment from piano bars to symphony concert seasons. *This Week In Santa Barbara,* which you can pick up at the Chamber of Commerce along with their events schedule, profiles the nightspots, and you can also check out the Santa Barbara News Press entertainment section.

The *Lobrero Theatre,* 33 E Canon Rerdido St (tel 963-0761) and the *Arlington Center for the Performing Arts,* 1317 State St (tel 963-3686) feature leading performers in dance, drama and music. The Center offers annual concert seasons by the Los Angeles and Santa Barbara Symphony Orchestras and there's a Summer Festival Series at the *Music Academy of the West* in Montecito. Local college campuses are also a good source of outstanding cultural events.

Getting There

Air Santa Barbara Airport, located six miles from the city near Goleta, is presently served by Airport limousine service to the downtown area.

Bus *Greyhound's* terminal is at Carrillo and Chapala Sts. For information, call (805) 963-1351.

Rail Amtrak service. The train depot is at 209 State St. Call toll free 1-800-252-0001 for information and reservations.

Getting Around

Public Transportation *MTD* buses serve the South Coast area from Isla Vista to Summerland. Information and schedules from the Transit Center, 1020 Chapala St (adjacent to the Greyhound terminal) or by phoning 965-5184.

Taxi Yellow Cab, tel (805) 965-5111.

Useful Addresses

Santa Barbara Conference & Visitors Bureau 1301 Santa Barbara St/PO Box 299, Santa Barbara 93102; tel (805) 965-3021, open Monday to Friday, 8 am to 5 pm; Saturday and Sunday 9 am to 4 pm.

Meeting the Americans

Sierra Club Los Padres Chapter, PO Box 30222, Santa Barbara 93105.

SANTA YNEZ VALLEY

Some six miles north of Santa Barbara, SR 154 turns away from US 101 to follow the old stage coach route through the Santa Ynez Mountains. It is an attractive detour, taking you past massive peaks, through the San Marcos Pass, into the verdant Santa Ynez Valley which has been cattle country since the Portola expedition passed that way in 1769.

Lake Cachuma

Lake Cachuma is the center of a 9000-acre county park giving fine views of the surrounding peaks. Stocked with rainbow and Kamloops trout, it's a popular spot with anglers and picnickers drawn to the shade of the great oaks lining the grassy banks. No swimming permitted for the lake is principally a reservoir, but there's a pool at the Recreation Center. The Marina rents boats and has a bait and tackle and snack shop, and just beyond Vista Point you can hire horses at the Riding Stable. Developed campsites are available on a first-come, first-served basis – camping permits per night, per vehicle cost $5.

SOLVANG

Solvang is more Danish than Denmark itself. Pretty windmills, simulated thatched roofs, simulated storks and cobblestone walks attest the authentic Scandinavian mementos, gourmet and delicatessen foods and gifts, plus unvang in 1911 as a place to educate immigrants from Denmark. Tourism is the economic staple today. Plenty of Scandinavian mementoes, gourmet and delicatessen foods and gifts, plus unarguably excellent Danish pastries and fudge and good, but usually crowded restaurants. In mid-September each year the town reaffirms its ties to the Old Country with the two-day **Danish Days** festival, a lively affair of folk dancing, parades, and unforgettable aebleskiver and medisterpolse breakfasts. The open-air **Solvang Festival Theatre** puts on a season of plays and musicals from July to early September.

Of interest is **Bethania Church** on Atterdag Rd: it is patterned on a typical rural Danish church, right down to a scale model of a fully-rigged ship hanging from the ceiling. The **Lutheran Home** farther along Atterdag Rd has a famous wind chiming harp.

MISSION SANTA INES

In a beautiful setting north of the Santa Ynez River is Mission Santa Ines, founded in 1804 as a center of instruction for Chumash Indians whose descendants still live on the Santa Ynez Indian Reservation four miles east of the town. Most of the original structures were destroyed in the 1812 earthquake, rebelling Indians fired others in 1824, and an unusually wet winter in 1884 badly damaged the old adobe walls. What you see today is largely a skilful reconstruction. The **chapel**, paved with brick, still has the original sanctuary and some notable paintings, including the 'Ecce Homo' painted by Miquel de Santiago in 1623. In the **museum** is a rich array of early vestments, brass and silver vessels, and massive old tomes bound in rawhide. Not the least of the mission's attractions is the lovely flower-filled garden. The mission is open daily from 9.30 am to 4.30 pm weekdays; noon to 5 pm Sundays. Admission charge; tel (805) 688-4815.

Places to Stay
Solvang is well endowed with good hostelries and the Visitors Bureau at 1623 Mission Drive (tel (805) 688-3317) supplies a list for the entire Santa Ynez Valley. Among them are:

Hamlet Motel (1532 Mission Drive, Solvang CA 93463; tel (805) 688-4413). Central location, color TV, quiet rooms. *Meadowlark Motel* (2644 Mission Drive, Solvang, CA 93463; tel (805) 688-4361). Air-conditioning; color TV and a swimming pool. Some units with kitchens. Rates from $18 double.*Three Crowns Inn* (1518 Mission Drive, Solvang CA 93463; tel (805) 688-4702). A friendly place, right in the center of everything. Air-conditioning, color TV. Complimentary continental breakfast at the Danish Village Bakery opposite. Rates from $31 double.

Places to Eat
The Danish Inn Bountiful smorgasbord served daily in this pleasant restaurant. (E)
Dinner. Open daily. 1547 Mission Drive; tel 688-4813.
The Belgian Cafe Sidewalk cafe specialising in Belgian waffles, plus a wide array of crepes, home-made soups, salads and sandwiches. Open-air patio. (M)
Open daily, 8 am to 4 pm. 475 First St, Solvang Mall; tel 688-6316.
The Elegant Egg 35 varieties of omelette – soups and salads, too. (B)
Open daily, 8 am to 8 pm. Mission Drive; tel 688-6830.

BUELLTON

SR 154 rejoins US 101 at Buellton, place of pilgrimage for lovers of Andersen's split pea soup. The shrine stands near the highway, identified as Pea Soup Andersen's Restaurant; it's open until 2 am daily.

MISSION LA PURISIMA CONCEPCION

Fifteen miles west of Buellton via SR 246, is one of the most interesting experiments in historical reconstruction in California. Mission La Purisima is the only one of the Franciscan mission chain to be restored as a complete mission establishment – under the direction of the State Parks System, it re-creates the life style of the padres and the Indian neophytes with fascinating authority. A self-guiding trail leads you through the gardens and outbuildings to the mission's soap factory, tannery, padres' residence and the handsome mission church with its stately colonnade.

Though one of the most prosperous of the missions, La Purisima did not have a tranquil history. In 1787 Father Lasuen established it at a site half a mile south of what is now central Lompoc, but in 1812 the buildings were totally destroyed by an earthquake. (A few fragments of the walls remain at the south end of F St.) A new church was promptly erected on the present site. Twelve years later, the mission was seized in a revolt by the Indians who held it for several weeks before soldiers from Monterey were able to disperse them. After Secularization, neglect, vandalism and the elements took a heavy toll until the Civilian Conservation Corps and the National Park Service undertook its restoration in the mid-1930s. Open daily, 9 am to 5 pm. Closed Christmas, New Years' and Thanksgiving days. admission charge; tel (805) 733-3713.

LOMPOC VALLEY & SAN LUIS OBISPO BAY

Aside from its fragments of the first Mission La Purisima, Lompoc has little to detain the visitor. But beyond is the Lompoc Valley, which raises 75% of the flower seeds grown in the country. The fields are a riot of color between May and September. No tiptoeing through the blossoms, though, except in June, when the annual Flower Festival includes a guided tour of the fields.

Beyond the flower fields, SR 1 treks independently northward through the Santa Maria Valley and its oil fields to rejoin US 101 at Pismo Beach on San Luis Obispo Bay. Clean white sand beaches, a warm ocean and excellent sport fishing make this stretch of the coast a popular vacation area. **Pismo Beach**, renowned for its clams and vast expanse of dunes, is one place to overnight within sound of the waves – and it's one of the few spots in California where you can still enjoy the old-fashioned thrill of driving along the beach. Watch out for the sand yachts.

Some 10 miles further, within the northern arc of the bay is **Avila Beach**, a charming old seaside resort where the water rarely drops below 60°F and even rises into the low 70s. About half a mile east of the town is **Cave Landing**, a natural pier used by the padres of Mission San Luis Obispo for shipping tallow and grain. From the beach you can see Robbers' Cave, believed to be the hiding place of pirate treasure, but it's probably more profitable to hunt for tiny moonstones washed up along the shore of Moonstone Bay.

SAN LUIS OBISPO

Historic San Luis Obispo, situated at the base of the Santa Lucia mountains, is seven miles from the sea. As the story goes, when Father Junipero Serra established the fifth of the Franciscan missions here in 1772, he named it after St Louis, Bishop of Toulouse, because two of the volcanic peaks which surround the valley suggest a bishop's mitre. The Mexican pueblo that grew up around the mission is now a prosperous business and educational centre for the agricultural Central Valley, with an important Mozart Festival of music held annually in August, but you'll find much evidence of a rich past scattered throughout the town. A green line marks the route of a self-guided tour of the old central district – for a free copy of a descriptive brochure on 19 of the most interesting sights, stop by the San Luis Chamber of Commerce at 1039 Chorro St.

Mission San Luis Obispo de Tolosa overlooks an attractive modern plaza in the center of the city. Its adobe church, used today as a parish church, was built between 1792-94 to replace Father

Serra's wooden structure. The first roof tiles manufactured in California were made here for the original tule-thatched roofs were too easily set alight by the incendiary arrows of hostile Indians; after 1784 all the missions adopted this technique of roofing. Within the church are some notable paintings and statues dating from the early 1800s, including a statue of the patron, St Louis, above the altar. Two of the mission bells were cast in Peru in 1818, during the Mexican war of independence from Spain. The mission is open daily, 9 am to 5 pm in summer; 9 am to 4 pm rest of year; closed Thanksgiving, Christmas and New Year's days; tel (805) 543-6850.

Recreated in 1971, **Mission Plaza** is a pleasant tree-shaded center for the city's many fiestas and cultural events. Grouped round the perimeter are the **Murray Adobe,** a privately-owned residence open for viewing between noon and 4 pm on Monday, Wednesday and Friday; the **San Luis Obispo County Historical Museum** (open Wednesday to Sunday, 10 am to noon, 1 pm to 4 pm), and the **Art Center.**

San Luis Obispo has a number of old adobe homes worth tracking down. Of particular interest is the **Dallidet Adobe** on San Luis Creek at 1185 Pacific St, built by the French vineyardist Pierre Hyppolite Dallidet in 1853. (Open Sunday, 1 pm to 4 pm, summer only). The iron-shuttered **Ah-Lee Store,** 800 Palm St, served as bank, post office and general store for Chinese laborers who built Southern Pacific's railroad tunnels through Cuesta Pass a century ago.

A modern architectural landmark which should not be overlooked is the **Madonna Inn** at the intersection of Madonna Rd and US 101. This extravagant building in conflicting styles, materials and colors is the creation of millionaire Alex Madonna who opened the motel in 1958 and has continued to add unconventional architectural statements ever since. The *piece de resistance*

is the main men's room: a bell sounds at intervals to permit the 'second' sex a view of its unusual furnishings.

Places to Stay
The term 'motel' was coined in San Luis Obispo back in the 1920s by the architect Alfred Heineman for the 'Milestone Mo-Tel' (still operating today as the *Motel Inn*), and there is a good choice of hostelries. Prices for a double room currently begin around $20 in the simpler establishments, and $30 for a berth at a motel with color TV and a swimming pool.

Campus Motel (404 Santa Rosa St, San Luis Obispo 93401; tel (805) 544-0881). Near California Polytechnic State University. Heated pool, color TV, and in-room coffee. Rates from $34 double.

Lamplighter Motel, 1604 Monterey St, San Luis Obispo 93401; tel (805) 543-3709. Small with color TV and air-conditioning. Rates from $26 double.

Madonna Inn (100 Madonna Rd, San Luis Obispo 93401; tel (805) 543-3000). Highly individual decor, with no two rooms alike, plus dining room, cocktail lounges, coffee shop and boutiques. Located just outside the city. Rates from $50.

Motel Six, 1443 Calle Joaquin, San Luis Obispo 93401; (805) 544-8400. Outside the downtown area, off Freeway 101 (Los Osos Rd turnoff). TV, pool, air-conditioning. Rates from $19.95 double.

Places to Eat
Apple Farm Old California country charm and home-style cooking. (B/M)
Breakfast, lunch, dinner. Open daily. 2015 Monterey St; 544-6100.

Cigar Factory Not far from the mission, in a former Victorian cigar factory. International cuisine. Early bird specials 5.30 to 7.30 pm and nightly entertainment (M).
Dinner, open daily. 726 Higuera St; tel 543-6900.

1865 Prime rib is the specialty of this

pleasant loft restaurant with hanging gardens and folk rock music. (M)

Lunch, Monday to Friday; dinner, daily. 1865 Monterey St; tel 544-1865.

MORRO BAY

An attractive way station on the coastal route, the fishing port of Morro Bay lies within the curve of Estero Bay some 13 miles northwest of San Luis Obispo. At the harbor entrance is **Morro Rock**, towering 576 feet above the Pacific. It is the haunt of sea birds, sometimes of sea lions, and you can walk out to it across the causeway at the north end of town.

Morro Bay's charm lies not only in its seascapes and beaches, but in the excellent seafood restaurants along the waterfront. Have a meal at sundown and you'll catch one of the West Coast spectaculars as the sun's last rays throw Morro Rock into dramatic relief against the darkening sky.

North of Morro Bay

The coast waters as far as Monterey Bay are the domain of the enchanting sea otter and you stand an excellent chance of sighting them as the road runs very close to the water much of the way. These puckish little creatures were hunted almost to extinction during the 19th century for one pelt fetched up to a hundred dollars in the China Trade. But one small herd survived along the Monterey coast and today their numbers are estimated at around a thousand. They are protected by law and the penalty for harming one in any way is stiff.

HEARST-SAN SIMEON STATE HISTORICAL MONUMENT

The world largely ignored the tiny whaling village of San Simeon until 1919 when William Randolph Hearst chose to erect a home on a coastal knoll that was part of his father's vast ranch holdings. Here, until 1947, the newspaper magnate – Orson Welles' *Citizen Kane* – and his architect Julia Morgan created La Cuesta Encantada (The Enchanted Hill), a group of buildings in the Spanish Renaissance style where he entertained the famous of the world and governed his vast empire. La Casa Grande, with its cathedral-like facade and twin towers housing carillon bells, dominates the hill; there are, too, three guest 'cottages' of 10 to 18 rooms and two Olympic swimming pools. All the buildings are furnished with priceless art objects from around the world – even Cardinal Richelieu's bed is there.

Hearst Castle is so large that there are three different guided tours, each lasting two hours. They are so popular that reservations are necessary. If time is short, take Tour 1 which includes the famous public rooms. Contact any Ticketron agency, or write to Ticketron, PO Box 26430, San Francisco, CA 94126 at least 30 days in advance. Parking is provided off SR 1 and a shuttle bus runs visitors up to the Castle. If you want to have a good look it's open daily, 8 am to 4 pm, June 1 to August 31; 8.30 am to 3.30 pm rest of year. Closed Thanksgiving, Christmas and New Year's Days. Admission $7 each tour.

MISSION SAN ANTONIO DE PADUA

Shortly beyond Gordo, a dirt road runs eastward over the peaks into Hunter Liggett Military Reservation, offering a worthwhile detour into the past. In many ways Mission San Antonio de Padua is one of the most evocative of the Franciscan foundations. It stands remote from anything hinting of our time, in an oak-studded valley backed by the Ventana range; no effort is required to shed the centuries separating you from that day in 1771 when Padre Junipero Serra rang the bells and loudly called upon the Indians to receive the faith of Christ.

The buildings you now explore date from a later period. The first church stood 1½ miles away and the present structure was begun in 1810; it is one of the largest and also loveliest the Franciscans ever built, constructed of burnt brick, with three arched doorways giving entry to the handsomely proportioned interior. To the left are the cloisters, enclosing a patio where the padres once had their garden.

The mission suffered greatly from neglect after Secularization, and the 1906 earthquake undid much of the restoration work begun in 1903. Aided by the Hearst Foundation, the Franciscan Order began a complete restoration in 1948, which has only recently been completed. San Antonio is one of only four missions still in the hands of the founding order.

It is possible to drive on through the Ventanas to Carmel Valley along a dirt road, but for all its beauty, it's a slow, demanding route, without gas stations or much hope of aid if you break down. The round trip to the Mission from the SR 1 turnoff is approximately 40 miles.

LUCIA

Lucia perches on the cliff edge some six miles beyond the turnoff. There are some old-fashioned motel cabins and a little restaurant overlooking the Pacific which sells possibly the best homemade apple crumble in the West.

At Sunset, the place to be is *Nepenthe's Patio*, several hunred feet above the ocean. The food here is good, the helpings generous, and if the weather's good, the views down the coast are stupendous. The Nepenthe turn-off is less than half a mile north of the Big Sur Inn.

PFEIFFER-BIG SUR STATE PARK

Pfeiffer-Big Sur is the most popular of the area's state parks, so if you would like to stop over amid its majestic Coastal Redwoods, make arrangements in advance. There are three developed campgrounds, a restaurant and coffee shop, and the Big Sur Lodge (tel (408) 667-2171).

The park is not large, but its trails lead up through the redwoods into the magnificent peaks of Los Padres National Forest and the Ventana Wilderness. Here are cougars, racoons, deer and wild boar – the last have no understanding of brotherly love and are best avoided.

POINT LOBOS STATE RESERVE

The superb natural beauty of Point Lobos is the climax of a run along the Pacific Coast. Here, on the southern cusp of Carmel Bay, granite cliffs rise sheer above the surf. A web of reefs and kelp forests slow the headlong rush of the sea, mantling crags and offshore islands with pale foam; and up on the headland, stands of Monterey cypress seem, as Robert Louis Stevenson observed, to flee before the wind.

The reserve protects a wealth of rare plants, trees, animals and birds. Amid the turgid kelp forests you are likely to sight sea otters – the best time is early morning or late afternoon; both Steller's and California sea lions live on the offshore crags; and brown pelicans, gulls and cormorants are everywhere, particularly Pelican Point. Deer come down from the Santa Lucias on occasion, and your picnicking will probably be shared by an importunate colony of squirrels who hang around the parking lots.

With a permit from the park headquarters, you may dive the waters but as all animal and plant life is protected, nothing may be removed or injured. A network of walking trails covers the park – please stick to them to protect the fragile ecology. Open daily, 9 am to sunset; admission charge; no camping.

CARMEL-BY-THE-SEA

Sheltered by the Monterey Peninsula to the north, Carmel is a pleasant, rather self-conscious seaside resort enjoying a broad beach of clean white sand and a reputation as a center of the arts. At the turn of the century several prominent writers and artists, drawn by the grandeur of the scenery and the mild climate, built homes among the pines: the poet George Sterling was the first, and he was soon joined by Mary Austin, Jack London, Chris Jorgensen, the pioneer painter of Yosemite, Arnold Genthe, renowned for his photographs of San Francisco's Chinatown before the 'quake, and Upton Sinclair. Later, Robinson Jeffers was to live here for many years. Tor House, his home on Carmel Point, may be toured on Fridays and Saturdays (by reservation only). Write to Tor House Foundation, PO Box 1887, Carmel CA 93921; tel (408) 624-1813.

Today Carmel's art galleries, boutiques and good restaurants make it a popular vacation spot. The annual July **Bach Festival** is one of California's most important musical events.

Mission San Carlos Borromeo

Two centuries before Carmel was established, Father Junipero Serra selected a site overlooking the mouth of the Carmel River for 'A stone church, large and beautiful'. Mission San Carlos Borromeo retains barely a wall of the buildings Serra erected in 1770, but it has been meticulously restored, and the present church (completed in 1796) contains his remains, marked by a handsome sarcophagus with a bronze effigy of Serra and three mourning padres. Two other eminent missionaries, Fathers Crespi and Lasuen, are also buried here.

The mission was in the care of Father Serra himself, and you can see the cell believed to be one in which he lived and died – it contains a crude raw-hide bed; his scourge and the small bible he used lie upon the table. The mission museum has a notable collection of relics. It's open daily, 9.30 am to 4.30 pm; Sundays 10.30 am to 4.30 pm; tel (408) 624-3600.

Places to Stay

Carmel and Carmel Valley boast many excellent hostelries ranging from inexpensive guest houses to luxurious resorts. *The Carmel Business Association*, on San Carlos between Ocean and 7th, (tel (408) 624-2522), puts out a free guide which includes a full listing of member inns for the area. Among those which have given us pleasure over the years are: *Carmel River Inn* (26600 Oliver Rd, Carmel 93921; tel (408) 624-1575). Motel and cottages in attractive grounds near the river. Swimming pool, complimentary coffee, TV. Rates from $30 double.

Green Lantern (Casanove & 7th, Carmel 93921; tel (408) 624-4392). Quiet, comfortable, close to shops and beach. Family cottages. Some housekeeping units. TV. Rates from $35 double.

Highlands Inn (Highway 1 (Box 1700), Carmel Highlands 93021; tel 408 624-3801). Renowned luxury resort overlooking the dramatic coast between Point Lobos and Yankee Point. Garden cottages and Lanai rooms. Reservations recommended. Rates from $140 double, including any two of the three meals they serve.

Pine Inn (Ocean Ave (Box 250), Carmel 93921; tel (408) 624-3851). Carmel's oldest. Pleasing Victorian decor and centrally located. Popular dining room, TV. Rates from $45.

Places to Eat

Carmel Butcher Shop Cosy, popular restaurant specialising in prime beef, steaks and seafood. Early bird menu from 4.30 to 6 pm. Reservations recommended. (M/E)

Dinner, open daily. Ocean Avenue between Lincoln and Dolores; tel 624-2569.

Hog's Breath Inn Clint Eastwood's restaurant is in a courtyard and offers family style American cooking. (M/E)

Lunch, dinner. Open daily. San Carlos, between 5th and 6th; tel 625-1044.

Scandia Scandinavian specialties, plus fish and steaks in a quiet, attractive dining room. Wine and beer only. (M) Lunch, dinner. Open daily. Ocean Avenue between Lincoln and Monte Verde; tel 624-5959.

Spinning Wheel Informal, welcoming family restaurant that's especially good at breakfasts. (B)

Breakfast, lunch, dinner. Open daily. Monte Verde, near Ocean Avenue; tel 624-7548.

SEVENTEEN MILE DRIVE

Although SR 1 will take you to Monterey in a matter of minutes meandering along the scenic Seventeen Mile Drive's is a far better way to go. This famous toll road traverses a particularly lovely private community, Del Monte Forest, where groves of Monterey cypress and pine look down on a shoreline of unsullied natural beauty. From Carmel, enter via the Carmel Gate, bear left, and follow the 17-Mile Drive signs to Pebble Beach. A little beyond the famous golf links, home course of the Crosby National Pro-Am Tournament, is The Lodge at Pebble Beach, one of California's major resorts. There are several restaurants here as well as specialty shops. Pescadero Point, the Lone Cypress and Cypress Point are famous vista spots. At Seal and Bird Rocks picnic area and Point Joe the chances of seeing seals, sea lions and sea otters in the water and on the offshore rocks are good; the golf course south of Point Joe is popular with the forest deer; and you can count on gulls, cormorants, and ground squirrels to put on a good show along the length of the shoreline route.

Seventeen Mile Drive ends in **Pacific Grove**, a pleasant little town three miles short of Monterey. Founded in the 1870s as a summer camp by the Methodist Church, it has become famous as the breeding grounds of Monarch butterflies which mass on the pine trees of Lighthouse Ave from late October to March.

MONTEREY

Monterey's superb setting mitigates but cannot erase the effects of urban sprawl on the former Spanish and Mexican capital of Alta California. When Robert Louis Stevenson stayed here in 1879, he found the Peninsula 'the greatest meeting place of land and water in the world', but today it is too often the rendezvous of automobiles circling in search of parking spaces. Because the town is a popular vacation and convention destination, it's advisable to stop first at the Visitors Bureau, 380 Alvarado St, to enlist their aid in finding accommodation. Then set out on foot with the Bureau's map of walking tours through the historic district.

The bay was first sighted by Sebastian Rodriguez Cermeno in 1595; seven years later Sebastian Vizcaino landed and took possession of the country for the Spanish crown. No interest was displayed in the new province until 1769, when Gaspar de Portola's expedition, charged with rediscovering and peopling the bays of San Diego and Monterey, opened up the land as far as San Francisco Bay. On the outward journey Portola failed to recognize Vizcaino's harbor, but the following year he established a presidio here, and Father Junipero Serra dedicated the second mission in Alta California on the site where San Carlos Church is today. Mission San Carlos Borromeo was soon relocated to a hill overlooking the mouth of the Carmel River. Monterey remained the capital until the Americans annexed California in 1846.

Things to See

The **Old Custom House,** one of a cluster of carefully restored adobes near Fisherman's Wharf, is the oldest government building in California. The central portion dates from 1814. The collection of import duties was its prime purpose, but the old building often doubled as the setting of Monterey's grandest balls and fiestas. It's open daily, 9 am to 5 pm; admission fee good for all Monterey State Historic Park units.

Of Monterey's many fine old buildings, five should not be missed. California's first theater stands at the corner of Pacific and Scott Sts. Built in 1846 as a lodging house and saloon, its British owner Jack Swan loaned it to some soldiers from Colonel Stevenson's New York Volunteers for dramatic presentations. Swan's ghost reputedly still haunts the building. Open daily except Mondays, 9 am to 5 pm; admission fee good for all Monterey State Historic Park units.

Follow Pacific St to Jefferson St and you will find two houses which figured prominently in California history. **Colton Hall**, the scene of the Constitutional Convention in 1849, is now the city museum. Directly behind is **Casa Vasquez**, a picturesque adobe which was once the home of Dolores Vasquez, sister of California's most ruthless bandit. Tiburcio Vasquez himself once lodged for a while in the one-story jail in the Colton Hall grounds. The hours are from 10 am to noon, 1 pm to 5 pm Tuesday to Sunday; tel (408) 646-3851 or 375-9944.

The **Larkin House**, on the corner of Calle Principal and Jefferson St, was the home of Thomas Oliver Larkin who came to Monterey in 1832 and was appointed American consul in 1843. Larkin's house set an architectural fashion widely copied throughout California; its priceless antiques and furnishings can only be viewed on tours. Open daily except Tuesdays' tours hourly, 9 am to 4 pm, except at noon. Garden open 9 am to 5 pm; admission fee good for all Monterey State Historic Park units.

Robert Louis Stevenson boarded at the French Hotel on Houston St in 1879 while pursuing his American love Fanny Van der Grift Osbourne. Now known as the **Stevenson House**, the gracious old adobe displays many of his possessions, including his sea chest marked for Suva. During his stay in Monterey, Stevenson wrote *The Pavilion on the Links*, gathered material for *The Old Pacific Capital* and began *The Amateur Emigrant*. Stevenson House is open daily, 9 am to 5 pm; tours on the hour, except at noon; admission

fee good for all Monterey State Historic Park units.

Fisherman's Wharf & Cannery Row

Fisherman's Wharf and John Steinbeck's Cannery Row are both metamorphosized into congeries of shops and restaurants where abalone is a powerful draw. Cannery Row lies about ¾ mile beyond Fisherman's Wharf – the way is clearly posted.

Steinbeck enthusiasts should know that his childhood home in Salinas may be visited. This Queen Anne Victorian house at 132 Central Avenue, where he wrote *The Red Pony*, is run as a luncheon restaurant by the Valley Guild (open Monday to Friday; reservations required). Tours of the Steinbeck Home are only available to restaurant patrons. Call (408) 424-2735. The *John Steinbeck Library* at 110 West San Luis St, Salinas, houses memorabilia, first editions and letters as well as taped interviews with people who knew Steinbeck when he lived in the area.

Open Monday to Thursday, 10 am to 9 pm; Friday to Saturday, 10 am to 6 pm; tel (408) 1-758-7311.

Royal Presidio Chapel

The Royal Presidio Chapel of San Carlos de Borromeo stands on Church St, occupying the site chosen by Father Junipero Serra for the first Mission San Carlos Borromeo. It's the only one of California's four presidio churches still standing, a little gem of Spanish-Mexican baroque, built in 1794. The dead trunk of the massive oak tree under which Vizcaino claimed Alta California for Spain in 1602 and Serra established the mission in 1770 is preserved in the garden behind the church.

For all its historic treasures, Monterey does not dwell exclusively on the past. Each September it's the setting of the celebrated *Jazz Festival*, highlight of a year-long calendar of festivities that includes the *Salinas Rodeo*, California's biggest, in July and Laguna Seca's *Grand Prix* in October. These events are held only a short drive from Monterey.

Places to Stay

The Monterey Visitors Bureau provides a comprehensive pamphlet listing the Peninsula's motels and hotels – on the whole, rates are lower in **Pacific Grove**. Many Monterey hostelries are right on the water and the local motel row is Munras Avenue. Some suggestions:

Casa Munras Garden Inn (700 Munras Ave, Monterey; tel (408) 375-2411). Centrally located, with swimming pool, color TV, entertainment. Rates from $64 double.

Cypress Gardens Motel (1150 Munras Ave, Monterey 93940; tel (408) 373-2761). On Carmel Hill, in attractive grounds. Color TV, pool, free continental breakfast. Rates from $32 double.

Doubletree Inn of Monterey (2 Portola Plaza, Monterey 93940; tel 800-528-0444 or (408) 649-4511). Handsomely appointed resort hotel right at Fisherman's Wharf. Ocean views, pool, tennis courts, two restaurants among the amenities. Rates from $68 double.

El Padre Motor Hotel (1288 Munras Avenue, Monterey 93940; tel (408) 375-2168). Swimming pool, color TV, waterbeds, complimentary coffee. Substantially reduced winter rate. Rates from $30 double (peak season).

Monterey Peninsula Youth Hostel (404 El Estero, Monterey 93940). For information call YMCA Office at (408) 373-4166 as this hostel will be relocated in 1983.

Motel 6, 2124 Fremont St (old Highway 1), Monterey 93940; (408) 373-3500. Outside the downtown area, inland. TV and pool. Rates from $19.95 double.

Places to Eat

Bruised Reed Gallery & Vegetarian Restaurant Carefully prepared vegetarian dishes amid elegant surroundings. (B/M)

Lunch and dinner, Thursday; Sunday to only Friday. Closed Saturdays. 375 Alvarado; tel (408) 649-3462.

Clock Garden Restaurant Informal dining in a flower-filled garden enhanced by fountains. Early bird specials 5.30 to 7 pm. Reservations recommended. (M/E)

Lunch and dinner, open daily. 565 Abrego St; (408) 375-6100.

Neil de Vaughn's Well known dinner house overlooking the water, specializing in steaks, lobster and fish. Informal. Reservations recommended. (E)

Dinner, open daily. 654 Cannery Row; tel (408) 372-2141.

Plazatree Restaurant Attractive cafe-restaurant in the Doubletree Inn serving American cuisine. Large servings. (B/M)

Breakfast, lunch, dinner. Open daily. Doubletree Inn, 2 Portola Plaza; tel (408) 649-4511.

Sancho Panza Mexican Restaurant Opportunity to dine in one of Monterey's oldest homes, the historic Gutierrez Adobe. Beer and wine only. (B)

Lunch, dinner. Open daily. 590 Calle Principal; tel (408) 375 0095.

Triples Continental fare in a charmingly restored Victorian house near the historic Custom House. Wine, beer and aperitifs only. (M/E)

Lunch and dinner, Monday to Saturday. 220 Olivier St; (408) 372-4744.

Getting There

Air Monterey Peninsula Airport, located approximately six miles east of downtown Monterey, is served by Monterey Peninsula transit buses (see below) and Airport Limousine (tel (408) 372-5555).

Bus *Greyhound's* depot is at 351 Del Monte Avenue. Tel (408) 373-4735 or 424-1626.

Coastlines run a daily, all-year service between Monterey and San Luis Obispo along SR 1, leaving you free to enjoy 153 miles of spectacular coastal scenery. Stops include Carmel, Big Sur and Hearst Castle. For information, call (408) 649-4700.

Rail Amtrak's nearest station is in Salinas. Monterey Peninsula Transit buses meet the trains. Call 800-648-3850 for Amtrak information.

Getting Around
Public Transportation Monterey Peninsula Transit provides bus services to the six Peninsula cities, including Monterey, Pacific Grove and Carmel, and as far south as Big Sur (Nepenthe). Call (408) 899-2555 or 424-7695.

Tours *Grayline Tours* (tel (408) 373-4989 or 625-5233) and *Monterey Peninsula Tours* (tel (408) 375-1550) offer a variety of tours covering Peninsula attractions and Hearst Castle. *Surtreks* (tel (408) 649-1131), a division of Coastlines, has daily tours of Big Sur ($25) and Hearst Castle ($40); both these tours include lunch at Nepenthe.

Taxis *Black & White Cab Co*, tel (408) 646-1234.

Useful Addresses
Monterey Peninsula Chamber of Commerce and Visitor and Convention Bureau, 380 Alvarado St, Monterey, CA 93940; tel (408) 649-3200. Open daily.
AAA, 53 Soledad Drive, Monterey, CA 93940; tel (408) 373-3021. Open Monday to Friday, 8.30 am to 5 pm.

Meeting the Americans
Sierra Club (Ventana Chapter), PO Box 5667, Carmel, CA 93921; tel (408) 624-8032.

MONTEREY TO SAN FRANCISCO
North of Monterey, SR 1 skirts Fort Ord infantry training center to traverse broad acres of artichoke fields surrounding Castroville, self-styled artichoke capital of the world. After crossing the Salinas River, a decision must be made; you may either continue up the coast on SR 1 to Santa Cruz and San Francisco, or veer inland to SR 156 which joins US 101 at Prunedale. This takes you to San Francisco via Gilroy and San Jose.

If you choose the latter route, SR 156 offers an attractive short detour when it leaves US 101 and turns south for San Juan Bautista.

SAN JUAN BAUTISTA
Lying in a valley between golden hills, the quiet old town of San Juan Bautista grew up around the mission founded by Father Lasuen in 1797. Its buildings stand on the west side of the plaza, handsomely restored after a long period of neglect following secularization in 1834. The mission church, its thick adobe walls supported by massive buttresses, dates from 1803 and is the only one in Alta California to be built with three aisles. The plain interior perfectly complements a handsome reredos and altar – this altar is also unique in that it is the only one ever decorated by an American, Tom Doak, who was Alta California's first American settler.

The church and mission museum contain some rare treasures including old illuminated musical scores and registers signed by Father Lasuen.

Grouped around the plaza are several notable early buildings, now given the status of a state historic park. On the south side is the **Plaza Hotel**; the lower story was built in 1813 for the use of the mission guard and in 1858 Angelo Zanetta added the second story. The hotel was an important stop on the stage coach route from the Gold Country to Monterey.

Next door is one of the finest examples of early California adobe buildings. The **Castro House** (1825) was the home of a family prominent in early California history and for a period in the 1840s it served as headquarters for General Jose Castro, commander of the California forces. In 1848 the house was purchased by the Patrick Breen family, survivors of the Donner Pass tragedy, whose descendants held it until 1933. At the back is an exquisite, common garden, shaded by a 150-year-old pepper tree.

The **Plaza Stable** has been restored to its 1870s glory when the Coast Line Stage Company kept its horses there. On display are carriages and wagons, tack, and the paraphernalia of the blacksmith's shop.

Beside the stable, the **Zanetta House** occupies the site of the old mission nunnery, built in 1815. Angelo Zanetta used bricks from the nunnery to construct a two-story building in 1868; he reserved the ground floor as his residence and rented the upper storey as a public hall.

THE COAST HIGHWAY

After Castroville, SR 1 strikes across the fertile Pajaro Valley to Watsonville, center of a prosperous fruit and vegetable growing region, and then turns northwest past the seaside resorts of Aptos, Soquel and Capitola before fetching up in Santa Cruz, a distance of some 30 miles. From the highway you can see remnants of the first redwood forests seen by Europeans, discovered by Portola on his march north in 1769.

SANTA CRUZ

Santa Cruz is a popular seaside city of broad, safe beaches lying at the foot of the Santa Cruz Mountains. The **Boardwalk** has been the center of amusement for a century, offering the simple pleasures of sticky comestibles, slot machines, souvenirs and a famous roller coaster offering breath-taking views of the bay.

Up on Mission Hill is a small scale replica of the original **Mission Santa Cruz** consecrated by Father Lasuen in 1791. The mission prospered for more than 20 years; then came a long era of misfortune culminating in its destruction by the 1857 earthquake. Within the present structure are many of the original altar furnishings, sacred statues and richly ornamented vestments.

Nearby, on School St, is the **Neary-Hopcroft House** which was formerly

headquarters of the mission guard. It may date from the 1790s, and has a charming old garden to the rear. On the whole, 'progress' has not dealt kindly with Santa Cruz' early buildings, but you will notice a large number of Victorian Gothic homes still stand.

ANO NUEVO STATE RESERVE

Ano Nuevo's windswept dunes have a spare beauty enhanced in summer by the flowering of iceplants, however the headlands are most interesting between December and March when large numbers of elephant seals come to the area to breed, birth and nurse their pups. Most remain on Ano Nuevo Island, but since 1975 more pups have been born on land. For this reason you may visit the reserve only on guided tours during this period – and do observe the law requiring you to remain at least 20 feet from the animals. Elephant seal bulls weigh in around three tons, are notoriously irritable, and for all their bulk, they can move rapidly on dry land. Tele-lenses and binoculars are useful adjuncts here.

You must make a reservation for a guided tour. To do so, apply in person at Ticketron outlets or write to Ticketron at PO Box 2715, San Francisco, CA 94126. For recorded information about the reserve, call (415) 879-0227. To get to the reserve, turn off SR 1 at New Year's Creek Rd and drive till you come to a parking lot where park rangers are on duty.

PIGEON POINT

Six miles north the slim, white tower of Pigeon Point Light rises above the rocks which claimed the clipper *Carrier Pigeon* in 1853. The light station is open to visitors on summer weekends from 1 to 4 pm, and tidepool buffs will find much of interest along the shore. Some of the lighthouse station buildings have been converted to a *Youth Hostel* with several family rooms. Two weeks advance reservation is recommended if you plan a weekend there. The rates are $4.50 members, $6.50 non-members, per night. Write to Pigeon Point Lighthouse, Pescadero, CA 94060; tel (415) 879-633.

Between Moss Beach and Montara on SR 1, some 25 miles south of San Francisco, there is another oceanside hotel. *Montara Lighthouse Hostel,* housed in a Victorian structure built in 1883, has one family room; nightly rates are the same as those at Pigeon Point and advance reservations are recommended in summer. The address is PO Box 737, 16th St at Cabrillo Highway, Montara, CA 94037; tel (415) 728-7177.

San Francisco

Situated on steep hills at the northern tip of a peninsula, between the Pacific Ocean and the broad expanse of San Francisco Bay, San Francisco has an irresistible appeal to everyone who goes there. It is a city of magnificent views and brilliant light, of cool wreaths of fog that steal in from the ocean, and tall skyscrapers overshadowing a wealth of old buildings that line streets laid out in the horse and buggy age. To the north lie Marin County's green and golden hills, rising abruptly from the waters of the narrow Golden Gate, and to the east, Contra Costa's cities rim the horizon, linked to the city by the Golden Gate and Bay bridges.

But San Francisco's fascination lies as much in a cosmopolitan society where ethnic differences are encouraged as in the remarkable beauty of its setting. Here for two centuries peoples from around the world have settled, maintaining their languages and customs: as a result you'll hear a medley of tongues as you stroll the streets and foreign quarters of distinctive character – North Beach's 'Little Italy', Chinatown, the Spanish Mission District, Japantown – and find a diversity of restaurants that makes dining in the city an international trip.

History

The navigators of the Great Age of Discovery missed the landlocked harbor, so often wreathed in layers of tule fog, and the story of San Francisco does not begin until 1769 when Jose de Ortega discovered San Francisco Bay. Seven years later, the Anza expedition arrived from Monterey to found the Mission San Francisco de Assis and Presidio.

Spanish colonial policy encouraged neither foreign trade nor foreign settlement and it was not until the first decades of the 19th century, when Alta California was ruled by Mexico, that foreign nationals were permitted to settle in the village which had grown up on the shores of Yerba Buena Cove. By 1846 the presence of Americans was well established, and in that year Captain John B Montgomery took possession of Yerba Buena and the northern frontier in the name of the United States government.

The boom years which followed the discovery of gold in the Sierra Nevada foothills in 1848 changed Yerba Buena's fortunes and gave birth to San Francisco. The Bay became a forest of masts as adventurers poured through the Golden Gate, bound for the gold fields – by the end of 1849 the population had swelled to 50,000. Gold and silver millionaires raised their palaces on the slopes of Nob Hill and introduced a way of life that still excites the imagination. By the end of the 19th century San Francisco was well established as the gateway to the Orient and a cultural and economic metropolis.

Then, at 5.12 am on April 18, 1906, the city was shaken by an earthquake that measured 8.4 on the Richter scale. For 74 hours after the shocks, fire raged through the streets, destroying about one-third of the buildings. From the 'damnedest finest ruins' a new city quickly arose; in spite of the setback, San Francisco has progressed steadily.

Today, San Francisco pleasingly combines the old and new. Downtown, the Financial District and Embarcadero are showcases for stylish modern architecture. Old San Francisco survives on the hilltops the fire never reached and the residential neighbourhoods west of Van Ness Avenue are particularly rich with Victorian homes. There is a certain joie de vivre in the air that few other American cities match – the city is for strolling, for listening to street musicians, for taking your coffee in open-air cafes.

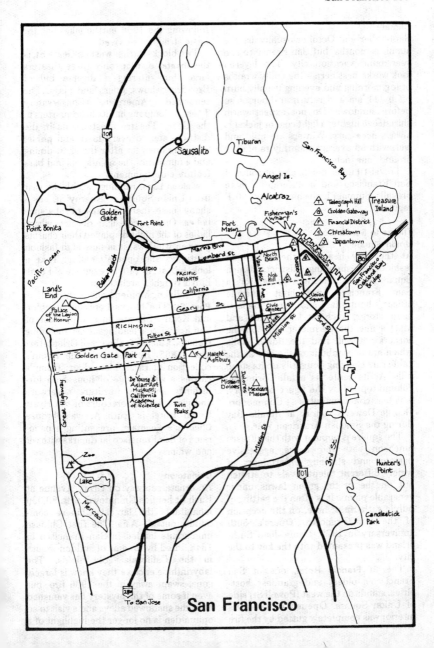

San Francisco

Climate

September and October usually are the sunniest months, but San Francisco is a year-round vacation city. The layered look works best here – the chilly wraiths of fog morning and evening usually burn off by 11 am and return an hour or so before sundown. Do not expect warm shirtsleeve nights; a light coat or jacket is always necessary. Winters are mild and wet, with an average monthly rainfall of around four inches.

Travel 10 miles north, east or south of San Francisco and a different climate prevails. Summer highs hit the low 100°F regularly.

Things to See & Do
Union Square

At the very heart of the hotel and fashionable shopping district, Union Square is an excellent base for a San Francisco walkabout. Airline offices, boutiques and large department stores, such as I Magnin's and Macy's line the perimeter, and on the corners you will find the flower stalls which are as symbolic of the city as the cable cars clanging doughtily up its steep hills. At its center is a tall Corinthian column topped by the figure of Victory, which commemorates Commodore George Dewey's victory at Manila Bay during the Spanish American War.

The square is popular with the alfresco luncheon set who brave aggressive pigeons and strolling entertainers of widely different talent levels to stretch out on the bright green lawns under venerable palms. It is often the setting of public gatherings; here, on the occasion of the San Francisco Opera's 50th anniversary in 1972, Dame Joan Sutherland was presented with the key to the city.

The **St Francis Hotel**, one of San Francisco's oldest and grandest hostelries, stands on the west (Powell St) side of Union Square. Opened in 1904, its interior was completely gutted by the fire following the 1906 earthquake, but the basic structure survived.

Two blocks farther west on Geary St, is the **theater district**, only three theaters large, but offering a diverse bill of Broadway shows, opera and plays. The renowned American Conservatory Theater Company has its headquarters in the Geary Theatre. Restaurants in the district cater to every taste and purse; many are open for after-the-show dining and a number of the nightspots and bars feature entertainment.

Maiden Lane, running two blocks east from Union Square to Kearny St, has a shady past that its present elegance belies. Once a red-light district, where ladies of the night displayed their charms at open windows, it is now high-fashion boutiques and open-air eating. Take a look, too, at No 140, an example of Frank Lloyd Wright's architecture.

Paralleling Maiden Lane to the north is **Post St**. The blocks between Stockton and Kearny Sts are lined with some of San Francisco's leading stores, including Gump's, a mecca for lovers of Oriental art since 1865. Besides the Jade Room's collection of rare objets d'art, Gump's carries a wide range of household furnishings, antiques, furniture, silverware and glass. In the forecourt of the Hyatt Union Hotel is Ruth Asawa's bronze **Children's Fountain**, presenting a panorama of San Francisco landmarks with wit and whimsy.

Chinatown

An ornate gateway on Grant Avenue at Bush St heralds Chinatown, with 80,000 inhabitants the largest Chinese community outside Asia. The first Chinese immigrants landed in San Francisco in 1848, lured by dreams of sudden wealth in the California gold fields. The labyrinthine enclave they knew is largely gone, swept away in the 1906 fire, but even if some of the mystery has vanished from the shadowed alleys and a visit to an opium den is no longer the highlight of a

Chinatown tour, colorful is still the appropriate adjective here.

Dragon-entwined street lamps mark the eight blocks of exotic stores, restaurants and gabled buildings which predate the 'quake. At Chinese New Year (the first full moon after January 21) Lion Dancers prance from door to door amid pungent smoke and the thunder of exploding firecrackers, beginning a round of celebrations that culminates in the great Dragon Procession.

Arrive here early, if you can, as the sun pokes long shadow fingers down the side streets, to catch the Tai Chi practitioners at exercise in St Mary's Square. Then, simply meander, for the sidewalks are a browser's heaven. Notice the variety of unusual fruits and vegetables, the live carp lazily circling the fish tanks as they await their fate, the apothecary shops stuffed with dried sea-horses and herbs, the flattened silhouettes of ducks strung up like washing on the line. Tantalizing aromas steal from an abundance of restaurants offering every kind of Chinese cuisine, though the Cantonese style predominates. (For a little bit of everything, try a dim sum lunch house where you make your selection from a myriad of pastry-encrusted delicacies brought around on trays.) You'll find a number of stores displaying antiques, furniture and silk brocades interspersed among the souvenir shops.

Worth visiting are **Old St Mary's Church** (on California St at Grant), San Francisco's first cathedral, twice gutted by fire but faithfully rebuilt to the original 1853 plan; **Tien Hou Temple** (4th floor, 125 Waverly Place), dedicated to the Queen of Heaven; and the **Kong Chow Temple** at Clay and Stockton Sts, housed in the headquarters of the oldest Chinese family association in the country. The story of the Chinese in the West is portrayed in artefacts, documents and photographs at the **Chinese Historical Society of America**, 17 Adler Place (between Grant and Columbus Avenues).

Open Tuesday to Saturday, 1 to 5 pm; closed Christmas and New Year's Days; admission free; tel 391-1188.

Portsmouth Square

East of Grant Avenue, bounded by Clay, Washington and Kearny Sts, is Portsmouth Square, center of the city when Spain and Mexico ruled California. Here, to the tune of 'Yankee Doodle' played by the ship's band of one drum and a fife, Captain John B Montgomery of the USS Portsmouth raised the American flag on July 9, 1846.

The adobe Custom House put up on the northwest corner by the Mexican government in 1844, the city's first public school house, the noisy saloons, gambling houses and theaters – all are long gone. But a few gold rush-style buildings still stand to remind you of the boisterous days when the square was the setting of fetes and fiestas and summary justice meted out by the Vigilance Committee. During his stay in San Francisco in 1879, Robert Louis Stevenson could often be found wandering among the crowds which provided him with rich material for The Wreckers.

Today the cradle of San Francisco is a pleasant park, a tree-shaded oasis for Chinatown residents who come to relax and enjoy mahjong and checkers at the open-air tables.

A plaque on the building at the corner of Clay and Kearny Sts commemorates the opening of the world's first cable car railway in 1873. The Clay St Hill Railroad, progenitor of the city-wide system still in use today, was the invention of a local wire manufacturer, Andrew S Hallidie. Revolted by the suffering of horses flogged up San Francisco's steep hills, Hallidie applied the principles of overhead cable conveyors used in mining to design a street car with a grip capable of grasping and releasing the activating cable running in a slot beneath the street. The inventor himself operated the grip on that first, hazardous run down Clay St hill; but the true test came in the public trial that afternoon when, carrying far more than its capacity of 14 passengers, the little car struggled pluckily up the steep grade. The cable cars have been in continuous operation ever since – more than a century – and were declared a National Landmark in 1964. (For the whole story, visit the **Cable Car Barn and Museum** on Nob Hill).

The **Chinese Cultural Center** in the Holiday Inn (3rd floor) on the east side of Portsmouth Square was founded to promote better understanding and appreciation of Chinese arts and culture. The Center's program includes not only rotating exhibitions and a performing arts program, but a Chinese Heritage Walk for which advance arrangements must be made. The charge for the walk is $6; admission to the center is free. It's open Tuesday to Saturday, 11 am to 4 pm; closed major holidays; tel 986-1822.

Round off your walk through Chinatown with a visit to **Buddha's Universal Church** at Washington and Kearny Sts. The church, the largest Buddhist place of worship in the country, is open to the public on the second and fourth Sundays of the month; you'll se a Bodhi tree grown from a slip taken from the tree under which Buddha found enlightenment.

Places to Eat

Globos West Japanese home cooking in simple surroundings. Lunch and dinner. Open daily except Sunday lunch. (B)

419 Grant Avenue; 982-3656.

Hang Ah Tea Room Popular, noisy center for lovers of dim sum. Also serves traditional Cantonese dishes. Lunch and dinner. Closed Mondays. (B)

1 Pagoda Place (off Sacramento St, near Stockton); tel 982-5686.

Kan's Classical Chinese cuisine is the forte of this restaurant which has consistently garnered awards over the years. Lunch weekdays, dinner nightly (E).

708 Grant Avenue; 982-2388.

Obrero Hotel & Basque Restaurant Hearty Basque fare served family-style at long tables where world travelers and locals mingle congenially. Dinner only, served at 6.30 pm. Open daily. Reservations required – please call by noon; 5 pm latest (M).

1208 Stockton St; 986-9850.

Yah Su Yuan Outstanding Northern Chinese cooking and budget-priced lunchtime specials make this a popular restaurant indeed. Reservations recommended. Lunch and dinner. Closed Tuesdays (M/E).

683 Pacific Avenue; 986-7386.

NORTH BEACH

Garish Broadway divides Chinatown from Italian North Beach (so named for the bathing beach long swallowed up by wharves) with a strip of nightspots both tawdry and respectable. During the city's first years, the district was home to Irish, French, Germans, Italians and Latin Americans, but during the last decades of the 19th century waves of Italian immigrants began to overwhelm the other nationalities. North Beach retains its predominantly Italian character although Chinatown is encroaching on its southern flank.

Like Chinatown, North Beach rewards the stroller. The side streets between Telegraph and Russian Hills are lined with bay-windowed Victorian homes, espresso cafes, small shops, family restaurants and delicatessans perfumed with the aroma of freshly roasted coffee and salami. Always the haunt of San Francisco's Bohemians, North Beach watched the rise and fall of the Beatnik movement in the 1950s. You'll find poet Lawrence Ferlinghetti's **City Lights Bookstore** at 261 Columbus Avenue, just east of the Broadway intersection. Cafes where Ginsberg and Kerouac read their works still provide havens for the *cognoscenti* on Grant Avenue's upper reaches.

At the intersection of Columbus and

Vallejo Sts, is San Francisco's first parish church, the **Church of St Francis of Assisi**, tracing its origins to a little chapel put up by the city's French residents in 1849. The present Victorian Gothic building, dedicated in 1859, suffered considerable damage in the 1906 fire; its restored interior contains a series of frescoes portraying the life of St Francis and an ornate reredos.

Two blocks farther is Washington Square, a pleasant old fashioned park overshadowed by the slender spires of **St Peter and Paul Church**. Crowds foregather here on Columbus Day (October 12) for a special mass honoring Christopher Columbus, followed by a pageant at Fisherman's Wharf where local citizens in 15th century costume re-enact that momentous landing on the shores of Santo Domingo.

Places to Eat
Cafe Puccini Ambrosian coffee, home-made pastries and gargantuan sandwiches make this a popular pit stop. Open daily.
411 Columbus Avenue; 989-7034.
Caffe Sport Enjoy Italian home cooking and seafood specialties in a fantasy of Sicilian folk art. Lunch, dinner. Closed Sundays and Mondays. (M)
574 Green St, 981-1251.
Cafferata Ravioli Factory Twenty-seven different kinds of pasta are just part of the menu in this 1886 ravioli factory overlooking Washington Square. Informal and very North Beach. Lunch, Monday to Saturday, dinner Wednesday to Sunday. (M)
700 Columbus Avenue (at Filbert); 392-7544.
Cherry Flower Vietnamese Restaurant Unassuming small restaurant offering very good Vietnamese food and friendly service. Lunch weekdays; dinner daily (B/M)
124 Columbus Avenue; 398-9101.
Enrico's San Francisco's oldest, most famous sidewalk cafe. Great for people

watching the nightclub belt. Deli meals, too. Open daily. (M)
504 Broadway; (415) 392-6220.
Greek Taverna Strong men lift tables with their teeth and belly dancers perform in this famous old gathering place for San Francisco's Greek community. Tasty Mediterranean cuisine – dinner daily except Sundays. (M)
256 Columbus Avenue; 362-7260.
Vesuvio's Cafe Funky murals draw the eye to this famous haunt of Beat writers that's still a favourite with the city's Bohemians. Open for morning coffee as well as drinks until the wee hours. Open daily.
255 Columbus Avenue (near Grant); tel 362-3370.

TELEGRAPH HILL
You may either catch the No 39 Coit bus on the Union St side of Washington Square or climb the steep grade up Filbert St to the crest of Telegraph Hill for a panorama of the city and the Bay. You'll gain another 200 feet or so in height by paying the 50c admission fee to **Coit Tower's** observation deck (open daily 10 am to 4.30 pm). This San Francisco landmark was built in 1933 with a bequest from Lily Hitchcock Coit, firebuff extraordinary, who, as a child in the 1890s, was the mascot of Knickerbocker Engine Company No 5. The tower's murals portraying the California Scene of the 1930s were executed by San Francisco painters as the first project of the Public Works of Art Project during the Depression.

For an intimate glimpse of some of San Francisco's most attractive homes and gardens, follow Filbert St steps down the hill's eastern flank to Sansome St. Julius' Castle, anchored to a notch in the cliff where Montgomery St plunges into space, is a landmark restaurant offering superb views. At the bottom of the hill, turn left for Fisherman's Wharf or follow Battery St back to Jackson Square and the Financial District. Opposite is *Levi's*

Plaza, a handsome group of red brick buildings surrounding a plaza, which was built by Levi Strauss & Company (the blue jeans people) as its headquarters. You can walk through the plaza fountain, refresh yourself at one of the cafes, or take a stroll alongside the little stream in the park bordering the Embarcadero.

FISHERMAN'S WHARF

The authentic smack of the sea has long faded from Fisherman's Wharf, sprawling three blocks deep along the waterfront from Hyde to Powell St. Shortly after sun-up it is still possible to recapture the feeling of the days when San Francisco housewives drove down in buggies to purchase Bay shrimp and crab from the brightly painted vessels moored alongside the piers. But as the crab cauldrons begin to steam and the walk-away shrimp cocktail signs are set out on the sidewalks, 20th century commercialism governs.

Oases of good taste among the souvenir stands, commercial museums and fish restaurants are **The Cannery** and **Ghirardelli Square** on Beach St near the cable car terminal. These 19th century buildings, respectively a former fruit cannery and a chocolate factory, have been converted into stylish groups of art galleries, restaurants, shops and little theaters – even the street musicians must audition before performing in the courtyards.

For those who love the lore of wine, as well as for those who simply like beautiful things, the **Wine Museum of San Francisco** opposite The Cannery is very rewarding. The only museum of its kind in the country, it sets out the history of wine with a fine display of old photos, prints and artefacts. The exquisite glassware of the Sichel Collection alone is worth the visit. It's open Tuesday to Saturday, 11 am to 5 pm; Sunday, noon to 5 pm; closed major holidays; admission free; tel 673-6990.

Of particular interest are the **National Maritime Museum's** collections housed in the Art Deco building on Beach St, opposite Ghirardelli Square. Here you'll find ship models, painted figureheads and an outstanding assemblage of scrimshaw and photographs. Open daily, 10 am to 5 pm; tel 556-8177.

At Hyde St Pier (Hyde and Jefferson Sts) you can embark on a voyage through Pacific Coast maritime history aboard the five vessels of the **Historic Ships Museum.** The lumber schooner *C A Thayer* (1895), the coaster *Wapama* (1915), the *Eureka,* a San Francisco side wheel ferry boat, the *Eppleton Hall,* and the little scow *Alma,* have all been restored to near-mint condition. Open daily, 10 am to 6 pm; closed major holidays; admission charge; tel 556-6435.

As you follow Jefferson St east from Hyde St Pier toward the Embarcadero, you come to a small harbor where the last of San Francisco's fishing fleet rides at anchor. Walkways lead out to the piers affording romantic views of the Bay, and here, on the first Sunday in October, you can observe the colorful Blessing of the Fleet. A little farther, the prow of the *Balclutha* soars proudly above Pier 43. This steel square-rigger, relic of the Cape Horn fleet, was built in Scotland in 1886. Below decks, she has been furnished to recreate life aboard in the late 19th century. The *Balclutha* is open daily, 9 am to 11 pm; admission charge; tel 982-1886. Latest comer to San Francisco's array of historic vessels is the *Pompanito,* moored alongside Pier 45. This WW II submarine of the Balao class contains most of her original equipment. Open daily, 10 am to 10 pm; admission $3; tel 673-0300.

The Embarcadero is headquarters for sightseeing jaunts on and above the Bay; it is also the site of a new pleasure development, Pier 39.

Places to Eat

Buena Vista Cafe In a Victorian house

overlooking the bay, the 'BV' is one of San Francisco's oldest bars, crushingly popular with visitors and locals alike. Light meals. Breakfast, lunch, dinner. Open daily.

2765 Hyde St (at Beach St); 474-5044.

Castagnola's Popular seafood restaurant with attractive view over Fisherman's Wharf's innermost harbor. Reservations recommended. Breakfast, lunch, dinner. Open daily. (M/E)

286 Jefferson St; 776-5015.

The Mandarin Exquisite Northern Chinese cuisine prepared by award-winning chefs. Epicures flock to this informally elegant restaurant. Reservations advised. Lunch, dinner. Open daily. (E)

Ghirardelli Square; 673-8812.

Mildred Pierce's Step back into the 1940s in this pleasant cafe at the foot of the Telegraph Hill. Breakfasts are outstanding. Breakfast Monday to Friday until 2.30; dinner Tuesday to Saturday (B).

1300 Battery; 392-4850.

Pier 23 Cafe Waterfront view and Dixieland jazz to go with your drinks Wednesday to Sunday. Pleasant place to watch the sun go down and wait for it to rise again. Open daily.

Pier 23, The Embarcadero; 362-5125.

RUSSIAN HILL & PACIFIC HEIGHTS

The hills rising behind Fisherman's Wharf offer pleasant, if demanding, walks through San Francisco's older and elegant residential neighbourhoods. No sightseeing musts here, unless you really want to descend the 'Crookedest St in the World'. It's the 1000 block of Lombard St, between Hyde and Leavenworth. The Hyde St cable car stops at the corner.

More rewarding are vistas of the Bay and city framed by the angular protuberances of ornate Victorians, and serendipitous moments earned along alleys threading the slopes of Russian Hill. Artists and writers gathered here

before the turn of the century, among them the acerbic Ambrose Bierce, poet George Sterling and the painter Maynard Dixon. The Bohemian tradition is kept alive in the **San Francisco Art Institute** at 800 Chestnut St, near Jones. You can view the Diego Rivera mural in the art gallery any day between 10 am and 4 pm. The Institute has two other galleries open to the public which display changing shows of contemporary art. There's no admission fee.

Private palaces crown the bluffs of Pacific Heights west of Van Ness Avenue, locally the most prestigious of addresses. Widely differing architectural styles mingle comfortably along Broadway, Jackson and Pacific Sts, reflecting the highly individual tastes of San Francisco's nabobs who moved here during the first decades of this century. At 2080 Washington St is the **Spreckels Mansion**, commanding a magnificent view of the Bay and the Marin Hills. This handsome French-style mansion was built about 1912 for a son of the sugar magnate, Claus Spreckels, by George Applegarth who later designed the California Palace of the Legion of Honor in Lincoln Park. There's an exact copy of Marie Antoinette's Petit Trianon in Versailles on the corner of Washington and Maple Sts.

Open to public viewing is the **Haas-Lilienthal House** at 2007 Franklin St. This is one of San Francisco's stateliest homes, a showplace of the 19th century Queen Anne style. It still has most of the furnishings collected by the Haas and Lilienthal families between 1886 and 1972. Open Wednesdays midday to 4 pm; Sundays 11 am to 6 pm (4.30, October to April); admission charge; tel 441-3004.

A few blocks west, at 2090 Jackson St is the **California Historical Society**, housed in a fine example of 19th century brownstone opulence. The Society's collection of early Californiana is of great interest. Open Wednesday, Saturday and Sunday, 1 to 5 pm entry fee includes a tour at 1.30 pm; tel 567-1848.

A useful companion on a drive or walkabout through Pacific Heights is the Peregrine Smith *Guide to Architecture in San Francisco and Northern California*.

NOB HILL

The splendor of Nob Hill's Mansions excited the admiration of the world in the days of the Bonanza Kings. Here San Francisco's 'Big Four' – Mark Hopkins, James C Flood, James G Fair and Leland Stanford – vied with each other in extravagant display, far above the counting houses of Montgomery St. The only survivor of the 1906 fire which destroyed their lavish houses is the brownstone Flood Mansion (1886), now the Pacific Union Club. In their place are luxury apartment houses, four of the city's most famous hotels (the Mark Hopkins, Stanford Court, the Fairmont and the Huntington) and a handful of expensive restaurants.

Grace Cathedral, seat of the Episcopal Bishop of California, stands on the site of the Crocker mansion at California and Taylor Sts. Rising 265 feet from the foundations to the gold-leafed cross surmounting the spire, the cathedral is one of the largest church buildings in the West. Though the foundation stone was laid in 1910, changes in plans delayed construction until 1928 and it was not until 1964 that the building was considered ready for consecration. Contrary to tradition the cathedral is oriented west – a consequence of San Francisco's prevailing westerly winds.

The cathedral was built of reinforced concrete. Its Gothic architecture is modeled on French patterns – you will notice something of Notre Dame in Paris and elements of the cathedrals of Amiens and Chartres. The overall length of the building is 320 feet and the transeptal width is 165 feet.

Among Grace Cathedral's many treasures is a 15th century Flemish reredos from the Abbey of Hambye in France, a bas-relief by Mino di Giovanni Fiesole (1431-1484) and 16th century Flemish tapestry. The magnificence of the stained glass windows of American and French manufacture cannot be overstated. The 44-bell carillon is from England, and the Ghiberti doors of the east portal were cast directly from molds taken from the 'Doors of Paradise' at the Baptistry in Florence.

Across California St is the **Masonic Auditorium** containing some notable murals. Not far away, down the slope of Mason St at Washington, is the **Cable Car Barn** and control center for the cable car system. On display are scale models of every type of cable car used over the past century, photographs and cable car relics. You can watch the operation of the system from the spectator's gallery – special lighting has been installed for photographers. Open daily 10 am to 6 pm, except major holidays; admission free; tel 474-1887.

JACKSON SQUARE

Leafy alleys and weathered brick buildings harking back to the mid-19th century characterize elegant Jackson Square, showplace for the wares of art and antique dealers and the interior decorating trade. It's all very decorous today, but a century ago the blocks bounded by Pacific, Montgomery, Washington and Battery Sts earned an internationally infamous reputation, first as Sydney Town, haunt of Australian outlaws, then as the Barbary Coast.

At that time the waterfront ran along Montgomery St to the foot of Telegraph Hill. Sailors swarmed ashore looking for action in the Coast's saloons, brothels and dance halls, and often found more than they had bargained for at the hands of the hoodlums and rowdies who roamed the gas-lit streets. Lord of an unsavory fief was 'Spider' Kelly whose saloon stood at 574 Pacific Avenue. No one knows how many men he murdered, nor how many blackjacked sailors dropped through his trapdoors to wake up in the holds of vessels far out to sea. Even his appearance inspired fear – San Francisco mothers of the time had only to invoke his name to bring their errant offspring into line.

Kelly and his kind gave the words *hoodlum* and *shanghai* to the English language, but as you stroll Pacific Avenue, you may encounter a gentler shade, Joshua A Norton, self-styled Emperor of the United States, Protector of Mexico, and prospective consort of the British Queen. Norton strode around the city in cape and plumed hat, issuing imperial decrees and scrip which were honoured by San Francisco merchants, tolerant of an old man who had lost his mind on suffering financial disaster. When Norton died in 1868, his bereaved subjects subscribed to a funeral royalty might have envied.

Jackson Square was proclaimed a Historic District in 1972. Its 17 designated landmarks include the **Lucas, Turner & Co Bank Building** on the corner of Montgomery and Jackson Sts where William Tecumseh Sherman of *Marching Through Georgia* fame once presided as manager, and Domingo Ghirardelli's first chocolate factory.

The **A P Hotaling Distillery** at 451 Jackson survived the 1906 fire almost intact, giving rise to the irreverent ditty:

If, as they say, God spanked the town
For being over-frisky,
Why did He burn His churches down
And spare Hotaling's whiskey.

Hitching posts and ivied walls enhance the charm of **Hotaling Place**, running between Jackson and Washington Sts. In its days as Jones' Alley between 1847 and 1910, it echoed to the clatter of drays and Wells Fargo coaches hauling their cargoes down to vessels moored along the Broadway Wharf. Later it was the setting of the city's first open-air art show in 1941. Around the corner on Montgomery St is the **Belli Building** which housed California's first Masonic Lodge in 1849. It now contains the offices of the 'King of Torts', attorney Melvin Belli.

Embarcadero Center
In complete contrast are the nearby highrises and townhouses of the Golden Gateway and Embarcadero Center, a stunning new $300 million complex of offices, shops and restaurants dominated by four skyscrapers. Never any need to come down to earth here – you can cross from plaza to plaza by pedestrian bridges high above the city traffic, shop at three levels, and take your ease on lawns, lulled by the splash of fountains. A particularly attractive feature is the important sculpture dominating the courtyards; you'll find Louise Nevelson's 200-foot 'Sky Tree' towering above the open-air restaurants at the east end of Embarcadero Three.

Just across Drumm St is the **Hyatt Regency Hotel**. John Portman's eye-catching architecture is most dramatic in the enormous lobby – here amid trees and ivy trailing from the balconies, you can sit beside an ornamental pool, dabble your fingers in a sculpted stream. The effect is sheer Hanging Gardens of Babylon.

The exit at the east end of the lobby leads to **Justin Herman Plaza**, a popular venue for vendors of leather belts, buckles, and hand-crafted jewellery, dominated by Jacques Vaillancourt's controversial walk-through fountain.

At the foot of Market St, half hidden by the overhead Embarcadero Freeway, is the **Ferry Building**, its clock tower modeled on the Giralda Tower in Seville. It's the terminal for ferries to Sausalito and Larkspur, and also contains the World Trade Center and the State Division of Mines' mineral exhibits.

MONTGOMERY ST
Montgomery St, a canyon of corporate skyscrapers and brokerage houses cutting across the Financial District from Market St to the Bay, has little in the way of early buildings to detain the sightseer

although it is the historic center of the west's financial wheelings and dealings. From that day in 1849 when Sam Brannan ran its length to Portsmouth Square shouting the news that set off the greatest gold rush in history, Montgomery has seen the rise and fall of generations of millionaires. The wealth of the Mother Lode and Comstock mines flowed through its counting houses and in an atmosphere that bordered on clinical dementia, fortunes were made and lost in the San Francisco stock market. They still are, but in the Computer Age, manners, alas, have changed for the less colorful.

As you walk north from Market St, the first of the Montgomery skyscrapers is the **Crocker Building**, set back from the street behind a tree-shaded plaza. This is very popular on sunny noon-hours with Financial District brownbaggers and street entertainers. The lower level, screened by wrought iron and dubbed the 'Bear Pit', contains shops and restaurants; stairs lead down to the BART subway station. Weekdays, a belt-buckle-and-jewellery street market flourishes at the foot of the Wells Fargo Building opposite.

Around the corner at 130 Sutter St, is one of the earliest glass and steel structures in the country. The **Hallidie Building**, named for the inventor of the cable car, was designed in 1918.

Head and shoulders above the skyline is the new **Bank of America World Headquarters** at California St. Designed by Pietro Belluschi, who found his inspiration in basalt columns of the Devil's Postpile in the Sierra Nevada, this 52-story building of polished carnelian and bronze-tinted glass soars 700 feet above street level. Construction began in 1967 and the building was completed in 1969. Ground floor galleries display rotating art exhibits, and the city's finest view is part of the menu in the top-floor Carnelian Room, open to the public for cocktails and dinner. In the plaza is Masayuke

Nagare's abstract granite sculpture, known around town as 'the banker's heart'.

Few business enterprises have ever caught the public imagination as did Wells Fargo & Co, bankers and express shippers to gold rush California. Organised in New York in March, 1852 by Henry Wells and Willim H Fargo, the company rapidly dominated western commerce and handled countless millions in gold and silver through its agencies in the mining towns of California and Nevada. Its lively, romantic history has been portrayed in story and film, but perhaps never so evocatively as in the exhibits and memorabilia of the **Wells Fargo Bank History Room** at 420 Montgomery St. Among the exhibits is a scarlet and buff Concord coach, the gold spike which Leland Stanford drove to join the two sections of the first transcontinental railway at Promontary, Utah, in 1869, paintings, prints and contemporary photographs. A poster recalls the period between 1877 and 1883 when the fortunes of Wells Fargo and that most gentlemanly bandit, Black Bart, were inextricably entwined.

Disappointed in his quest for wealth in the California gold fields, the mild little man opted for a more certain method. For a time Charles E Boles worked as a clerk in staging offices. Then, in August, 1877, 'Black Bart' put his knowledge of routes and schedules to good use in at least 28 robberies. Between holdups, he lived in San Francisco as Charles Bolton, something of a socialite, a pleasant fellow with business interests in the mines. His double life ended when he accidentally dropped a handkerchief while escaping from a holdup near Copperopolis – the laundrymark was traced to a customer of a San Francisco laundry.

Bart never harmed any of his victims – indeed, he possessed no ammunition for his shotgun. After serving a six year sentence, with time off for good behavior, he was released from San Quentin and slipped silently into the realm of legend, whereabouts unknown.

The pyramid-shaped skyscraper rising 48 stories above street level on the corner of Washington St arrived on the San Francisco scene in 1972. Designed by William L Pereira & Associates, the **Transamerica Building** occupies the site of the Montgomery Block, in 1853 the largest building on the Pacific Coast. The 'Monkey Block' was first the venue of the legal profession, and then of artists and writers. In the 1860s, Mark Twain was often to be found hunched in an alcove of the main stairway, scribbling notes on the personalities who passed him by; later, Kathleen and Frank Norris, George Sterling and Charles Dobie had their studios here. A link to that period is the Bank Exchange Saloon on the ground floor, lineal descendant of the celebrated saloon where Frank Nichol invented Pisco punch. Nichol took his secret to the grave, but a potent brew employing his basic ingredient, Peruvian brandy, continues the tradition.

Places to Eat

Clown Alley Hunger-stopping hamburgers charcoal grilled exactly the way you want them from breakfast time till 3 am. Open daily (B).

42 Columbus Avenue at Jackson; 421-2540.

Cornucopia A cheerful spot, specializing in health foods. Especially good on sandwiches and salads which you can eat there or take out. Breakfast, lunch. Closed weekends. (B).

408 Pacific Avenue; 398-1511.

London Wine Bar Popular Financial District rendezvous where you can sample California's finest vintages along with the best in French cheeses. Light deli-style meals. Lunch and cocktails. Closed weekends. (M).

415 Sansome St; 788-4811.

Schroeder's Cafe They've been serving German home-cooking in a vast, noisy hall reminiscent of Munich's **Hofbrauhaus** since 1893. Friendly waiters dispense good advice to the unitiated. (B/M) Lunch, dinner. Closed weekends.

240 Front St; 421-4778.

MARKET ST

All downtown streets converge on Market St, the city's broad boulevard running diagonally from the Bay to Twin Peaks some five miles distant. Long before Jasper O'Farrell plotted the new city of San Francisco in the 1840s, Mexican carts laden with cargoes for the sailing vessels in Yerba Buena Cove had worn a rough trail from the southern ranchos. This was paved with planks by the Forty Niners, and by the end of the century, San Franciscans could with some justification rank Market St among the great boulevards of the world. The 1906 fire destroyed most of the ornate earlier buildings and Market St lost something of its glamor. But as the current renewal program, begun in the 1960s, proceeds, and more glittering highrises go up above the newly-planted trees lining the wide sidewalks, Market St is coming into its own again.

A striking series of new skyscrapers, set back in plazas and garden courts, share the blocks from the Hyatt Regency Hotel to First St with a few neo-Classical survivors of the post-quake period.

At the headquarters of the Pacific Gas & Electric Company, the West's largest utility company tells the story of energy with multi-media presentations and do-it-yourself exhibits. The entrance to **Energy Expo** is just off Market St at 77 Beale St. It's open Monday to Friday, 9 am to 4.30 pm; closed holidays; admission free; tel (415) 481-4211, ext 4248.

In the lobby of its 555 Market St building, the Standard Oil Company of California similarly presents the drama of oil production, from exploration to finished product. Open Monday to Friday, 9 am to 4 pm; closed holidays; admission free. tel (415) 894-4940.

The **Sheraton Palace Hotel** on new Montgomery St at Market retains something of the 19th century's elegant style. Its Garden Court Restaurant is the reconstructed garden entrance of the legendary Palace Hotel built by William C Ralston in 1875. Ralston, founder of the Bank of California and a Comstock Lode millionaire, intended the Palace to be the most splendid hotel the world had ever seen, and he succeeded magnificently. The Palace covered 2½ acres, boasted the first elevators in the West, and contained 800 rooms. Artesian wells drilled on the spot supplied 760,000 gallons of water for the storage reservoirs and celebrated 'noiseless' water closets. Ralston even financed factories to supply the hotel's needs. For 30 years its luxuries, conveniences and opulent cuisine drew the famous of the world to its doors, until the 1906 fire destroyed all but its shell.

As you walk west toward Civic Center, don't forget to take a look at the cast-iron shaft on the island formed by the intersection of Market, Third and Geary Sts. **Lotta's Fountain** has little aesthetic appeal, but it recalls one of the most successful entertainers of the last century. Lotta Crabtree, the little girl befriended by Lola Montez in Grass Valley in 1853, had a long and immensely successful theatrical career; the fountain was her gift to the city that adored her. The bas-relief portrait of Louisa Tetrazzini was added later to commemorate that Christmas Eve in 1910 when thousands massed around the fountain at midnight to hear the great soprano sing 'The Last Rose of Summer'.

Between Third and Seventh Sts, department stores, discount shops and boutiques attract large crowds of shoppers. **Hallidie Plaza**, adjoining the Powell St cable car terminal, is a signal instance of the city's efforts to refurbish an area which had in truth fallen far from its former grandeur. During the day, the plaza is a lively place, attracting street musicians, gospel singers and preachers who exploit a captive audience waiting to ride the cable cars. On the lower level is the **Visitors and Convention Bureau** information center and the BART station entrance.

Turn aside at Fifth St for the **Old Mint**, an impressive example of 'federal classical' architecture near Mission St. Constructed in 1870-73 to replace the first branch mint established in 1854, it's now a museum with a particular appeal for numismatists. Among the treasures is a pyramid of gold bars currently valued at more than $9½ million and the 201-troy ounce Fricot nugget. The government's Special Coins and Metals Division caters to every need of the serious coin collector, a movie relates the Old Mint's history, and there's an 1869 press where you can strike a souvenir medal of your visit. Open Tuesday to Saturday 10 am to 4 pm; closed major holidays; admission free; tel 974-0788.

South of Market, Moscone Convention Center (bounded by Third and Fourth Sts) is beginning to change the character of the district. Older buildings are sprucing up, and new restaurants, shops and hotels rise on the perimeter. The Convention Center is named for Mayor John Moscone, shot to death in City Hall in 1978.

Places to Eat

Brasserie Chambord/Crepe Escape An *Ile de France* on the corner of Kearny and Sutter Sts offering outstanding French cuisine. Attractive atmosphere and attentive waiters. Reservations recommended. Breakfast daily; lunch, dinner weekdays only. (M/E)
150 Kearny St; 434-4449.
Delices de France Dazzling display at the food counter, exquisite fare at the tables. French country cooking. Hard to leave without purchasing a little souvenir to munch on later. Lunch, dinner. Closed Sundays. (M/E)
320 Mason St; 433-7560.

Cha-Ya Popular little Japanese restaurant serving outstanding sushi. Takeaway meals, too. Lunch Monday to Friday; dinner Monday to Friday and Sunday. Closed Saturdays (B/M)

323 Grant Avenue; tel 781-6730.

John's Grill Old San Francisco chophouse frequented by Dashiell Hammett and his detective, Sam Spade. One place in town where you can sample a gold rush era Hangtown Fry. Lunchtime reservations advised. Lunch, dinner. (M/E)

63 Ellis St; 986-0069.

La Bourgogne Classic French cuisine meticulously presented has earned this elegant restaurant a reputation as one of the city's finest. Reservations recommended. Dinner. Closed Sundays. (E)

330 Mason St; 362-7352.

Lefty O'Doul's Informal, popular restaurant. Gallery features hundreds of photos of sportsworld greats. Lunch, dinner. Open daily. (B)

333 Geary St (at Union Square); 982-8900.

Marco Polo Gourmet Chinese specialties, exotic international dishes and great steaks, all served in very generous portions. Hurry! Lunch, dinner. Open daily. (B/M)

619 Taylor St (near Post); tel 775-1028.

CIVIC CENTER

Approaching Civic Center from Market St along the promenade that begins at the United Nations Fountain, you get a fine view of the dome of City Hall silhouetted against the sky. As you draw closer, the grand scale of the French Renaissance buildings surrounding spacious piazzas is seen to best advantage. The principal buildings (in clockwise order) are the **Civic Auditorium**, linked to subterranean **Brooks Hall** beneath your feet, which provide the city with convention and exhibition facilities; **City Hall**; the **State Building**, housing California state government offices, and the **Main Public Library**.

City Hall, begun in 1913, is the centerpiece of the complex, replacing an earlier structure destroyed in the 1906 earthquake. Built of gray California granite, with blue and gold burnished ironwork, the building covers two city blocks and rises four stories high. The dome – as Mayor James Rolph was quick to boast – is 13 feet 7¾ inches higher than the National Capitol in Washington, DC. The interior, with its magnificent staircase and three acres of marble tile flooring, is richly finished in California marble, Indiana sandstone and oak.

Across Van Ness Avenue are Louise M Davies Symphony Hall, the Opera House and the Veterans Building, forming the San Francisco War Memorial and Performing Arts Center.

The **Opera House** opened on October 15, 1932, with the great Claudia Muzio singing 'Tosca', and in 1945 it housed the conference that gave birth to the United Nations; the charter was signed in the adjacent Veterans Building. As the home of the San Francisco Opera Company and the San Francisco Ballet Company, the building plays host to the world's greatest singers and dancers.

Louise M Davies Symphony Hall, home of the San Francisco Symphony Orchestra, was completed in 1980 and opened its doors to the public on September 13 that year. The Henry Moore sculpture near the Van Ness entrance anticipates the handsome design of the hall.

The four-story **Veterans' Building** houses the San Francisco Museum of Modern Art and a small auditorium for concerts. On the ground floor is a memorial hall with mementos of the two world wars.

The San Francisco Museum of Modern Art has a notable collection of modern painting and sculpture, including works by Matisse, Klee, Calder and Jackson Pollock. It is also devoted to promoting the works of local artists and photographers through changing exhibitions.

There are guided tours daily at 1.15 pm and at 7.15 pm on Thursdays. Open 10 am to 6 pm, Tuesday, Wednesday, Friday; 10 am to 10 pm Thursday; 10 am to 5 pm Saturday and Sunday; closed major holidays; admission charge to special exhibition galleries; tel 863-8800.

Returning to Civic Center along McAllister St, you'll pass the **Society of California Pioneers** building, No 456. The small, but interesting collection of early Californiana prior to 1869 includes a Concord stage coach and the original Vigilance Committee bell. Open Monday to Friday 10 am to 4 pm; closed holidays and all July; admission free; tel (415) 861-5278.

A visit to the **Main Public Library**, facing Civic Center Plaza on Larkin St, is not a sightseeing must, but the California History Room on the top floor contains unusually interesting local history exhibits. Check opening hours by calling 558-3191.

ALONG THE SHORE

Wide open spaces and that wilderness feeling are within a 30 minute bus ride of Union Square. From Fort Funston, at San Francisco's southernmost limit, to Olema 60 miles north in Marin County, the Golden Gate National Recreation Area encloses 35,000 acres of supremely beautiful terrain, including some of San Francisco's most popular attractions – Alcatraz, Angel Island, Fort Point and the cliffs at Land's End.

To enjoy some of the city's finest marine views, we suggest you follow GGNRA's three-mile **Golden Gate Promenade** along the shore from Fort Mason at the foot of Van Ness Avenue, past the Marina Yacht Basin and Chrissy Field, to Fort Point below the Golden Gate. Beyond the bridge, the trail continues another six miles or so along Baker Beach, the Land's End cliffs and Ocean Beach to Fort Funston. You can reach all the attractions on the route by car,

following the blue and white seagull signs that mark 49 Mile Drive.

Fort Mason

Fort Mason, occupying the site of an old Spanish battery at the foot of Van Ness Avenue, formed part of the Presidio of San Francisco until 1972 when it was turned over to the National Park Service as headquarters of the Golden Gate National Recreation Area. Parking, guidance and an excellent free map are available at the headquarters building facing the fort's Bay St entrance. Open 8 am to 4.30 pm weekdays; tel (415) 556-0560.

Several attractive homes from the 1860s cluster along Franklin St leading to Black Point and romantic views of the Bay. Here, shaded by eucalyptus trees, is the site of **Bateria San Jose**, built by the Spanish in 1795. Below, to the east, is a club-shaped pier formerly used to embark prisoners to Alcatraz. The old army piers and warehouse buildings are the setting for Fort Mason's renaissance as a cultural, recreational and educational center for San Francisco – drop by the Center offices in Building A for a copy of the monthly events calendar. You may catch a jazz concert, a play or an Indian arts festival complete with traditional foods and dancing.

Good for browsing are the **San Francisco Museum of Modern Art's** Rental Gallery and the **Mexican Museum** in building 'D' which displays Hispanic and Mexican art from pre-Columbian times to the present day. The second Saturday of the month, the museum's guided walk features Mission District's famous murals; executed by local artists, they are brilliant examples of contemporary folk art. Open Wednesday to Sunday, noon to 5 (non to 8 Thursdays); closed major holidays; tel 441-0404.

The Marina

West of the fort, Marina Green and its yacht basin, home to a proud gathering of sleek yachts, is a pleasant stretch of green sward popular with joggers and sunbathers alike. In 1915 the area was the site of the Panama-Pacific International Exposition, a $50 million celebration of the opening of the Panama Canal. Above the rooftops looms the terracotta dome of the **Palace of Fine Arts** at 3601 Lyon St, all that remains of the array of splendid pavilions that reached from Fort Mason to the Presidio. This impressive structure, with curving colonnade and rotunda in the Roman Classical style, is the work of Bernard Maybeck. The buildings behind the rotunda house **The Exploratorium**, an unusual science museum where you may tinker with the exhibits to your heart's content. 'Explainers' are on hand to help you understand and use them.

Open Wednesday to Sunday, 11 am to 5 pm, 7 to 9.30 pm. Wednesday evenings. Tel 563-3200 (recorded information).

The Presidio

The main entrance to the Presidio of San Francisco, headquarters of the US 6th Army, is on Lyon St at Lombard, but you can also enter via SR 1 at the south end of the Golden Gate Bridge. This is one of the oldest military stations in the country, for Juan Bautista de Anza chose the site in March, 1776, and by July, Spanish troops under the command of Lieutenant Jose Joaquin Moraga were constructing the first buildings. Nothing remains of them; their sites have been marked, and the Officers Club incorporates the walls of the adobe *commandante* headquarters built in the 1820s. Bronze cannons cast in Madrid in the 17th century flank its entrance.

This old building is associated with one of San Francisco's most romantic episodes. In 1806, Count Nikolai Rezanov sailed through the Golden Gate to negotiate with the Spanish authorities for Russian settlements to the north. Rezanov was a frequent guest in the home of the Presidio *commandante,* Don Jose

Dario Arguello, where he met and fell passionately in love with Arguello's daughter, Concepcion, by all accounts the most beautiful woman in California. He won her heart, but the Czar's permission for the marriage was necessary, and Rezanov set out on the arduous journey back to Moscow. Concepcion waited long, refusing all suitors, before she took the veil; it was 36 years before she learned that her lover had died when thrown from his horse in the Siberian steppes. She lies buried in St Dominic's Cemetery in Benicia on the shores of Suisun Bay.

The Presidio's wooded hills are pleasant to stroll through, and scattered around the grounds are some good examples of Victorian military architecture. The **Presidio Army Museum** (on Lincoln Boulevard at Funston Avenue) is housed in the Old Station Hospital, dating from 1857. Here the military presence in San Francisco from 1776 to the present day is interestingly displayed. Open 10 am to 4 pm Tuesday to Sunday; closed major holidays; admission free; tel 561-4115.

Fort Point

Beyond the Marina, the trail along the waterfront leads across Chrissy Field, the West's first airstrip, to Fort Point National Historic Site, clinging to the rocky promontory under the south tower of the Golden Gate Bridge. Never a shot was fired in battle from this redbrick Civil War fort occupying the site of the Spanish Castillo de San Joaquin. As a consequence, you can explore a remarkably well preserved and unaltered example of 19th century military architecture, complete with cannon. There are dramatic views of the Golden Gate from the top floor barbette gun emplacements, and the little museum contains Civil War memorabilia and armaments. Fort Point is open daily, 10 am to 5 pm except Christmas Day; free admission and tours; tel 556-1693.

GOLDEN GATE BRIDGE

The statistics of San Francisco's most famous landmark are staggering. The Golden Gate Bridge spans the 3½ mile narrows with enough steel wire to girdle the globe three times. Its twin towers rise 746 feet. The largest ships afloat can pass beneath the deck which soars 16 stories above the water at mid-span. More than 95,000 vehicles cross it each day. And it was built in only four and a half years, between 1933 and 1937. It may now be only the second largest single-span suspension bridge in the world, but for sheer grace and beauty of line, the Golden Gate Bridge remains unsurpassed.

There's no best time for viewing. The bridge is lovely in all its moods, at every hour of the day. Dress warmly if you decide to walk the 1½ miles from abutment to abutment (permitted from dawn to sunset only). There are vista points and car parks on both sides. Muni and GGT buses stop at the southern toll gate; GGT's Sausalito-bound buses will take you across, too, but they do not stop at the bridge's northern vista point. Fort Baker's entrance, about a mile further on, is the first chance to get off.

BAKER & PHELAN BEACHES

West of the bridge are Baker and Phelan Beaches, offering a mile or so of shoreline and exhilarating views. Baker Beach is not recommended for swimming, and it's advisable to keep an eye open for sudden huge waves if you're strolling close to the surf. Phelan Beach (still known locally by its old name, China Cove) has changing facilities and sun decks, and a lifeguard is on duty there from April to October.

LINCOLN PARK

El Camino del Mar leads from Phelan Beach through Sea Cliff's elegant residences to the broad meadows of Lincoln Park. There's a municipal golf course here, and the trail to the right of the Sea Cliff entrance to the park follows the rim of 500-foot cliffs to Land's End. The area

has been allowed to remain a wilderness of cypress, pine and wildflowers. Its small coves are the haunt of sea lions, and the views up the coast toward the Point Reyes Peninsula are superb.

The **California Palace of The Legion of Honor** crowns the summit of the slopes rising behind the cliffs at the west end of Lincoln Park. This replica of the Palace of the Legion of Honor in Paris houses an all-French collection spanning the 16th to the 20th centuries, with works of Corot, Degas, Manet, Monet, Pissarro and Renoir permanently on view. Sculptures by Rodin stand in the forecourt. Open Wednesday to Sunday, 10 am to 5 pm; tours; admission charge; tel 558-2881.

Refreshments and a close view of Seal Rocks' colony of California sea lions and harbor seals are available at the **Cliff House**, one of San Francisco's oldest attractions, about a mile west of the museum. Ocean Beach, magnificent at sunset, runs due south to Fort Funston, an old Civil War fort, where hang gliders now strive to emulate Icarus. Ocean Beach Boulevard provides access to Golden Gate Park and the San Francisco Zoo.

GOLDEN GATE PARK

Extending from Ocean Beach to Stanyan St, Golden Gate Park is a sylvan retreat of some 1017 acres where San Franciscans can get away from it all right in the heart of the city. Lakes, rhododendron groves, broad meadows, wooded hills and formal gardens produce a landscape of great beauty and pastoral charm that even a network of asphalt roads cannot impair. The wonder of it all is that every inch of the park is man-made, patiently reclaimed from 'a dreary waste of shifting sandhills where a blade of grass cannot be raised without four posts to support it and keep it from blowing away'.

Laid out in 1870 according to the principles of Frederick Law Olmstead, designer of New York's Central Park, Golden Gate Park today is largely the product of one man's devotion. John McLaren, appointed superintendent in 1887, spent 55 years in its service. He dealt with encroaching sand by planting a North European sand grass, Australian ti-trees and Australian acacia, and by pressing San Francisco's horses to his task – needing fertilizer, he obtained the rights to all sweepings from the city streets. When forced to accept the gift of cast-iron statues he considered worthless, he banished them behind screens of shrubbery. This stubborn, doughty Scot was still superintendent when he died in 1943 at the age of 96, leaving a legacy of more than a million trees that includes a redwood forest he started from seed.

There's a great deal to see and do in 'Uncle John's' domain. At the center of the park is the **Music Concourse**, an outdoor auditorium with a bandshell where concerts and opera are performed during the summer season. On the northwest side is the **M H De Young Memorial Museum**. Here European and American art and the traditional arts of Africa, Oceania and the Americas are displayed with classical objects from Egypt, Greece and Rome. Superb furniture and tapestries from mediaeval Europe add to the rich feast for the eyes. The De Young is also the setting for most of the major travelling exhibitions that include San Francisco on their itineraries. Open Wednesday to Sunday, 10 am to 5 pm; tours; admission charge; tel 558-2887.

The **Asian Art Museum**, housing Avery Brundage's renowned collections of Oriental jades, porcelains and art, is a recent addition to the De Young. In addition to the Brundage bequests, you'll find a notable collection of the arts of the Middle East, India, Nepal, Afghanistan and Southeast Asia. It's open daily, 10 am to 5 pm; tours; admission charge; tel 558-2993.

Across the concourse are the buildings of the **California Academy of Sciences**, the West's oldest scientific institution. Pre-historic fossils, minerals, ecological anthropology displays, the Laserium, Steinhart Aquarium and Morrison Planetarium are gathered under one roof here, relating the story of the earth and man from the dawn of time to the present. Open daily, 10 am to 5 pm (later in summer); admission charge; tel 221-4241.

Those who like horticulture and architecture should not miss the ornate **Conservatory**, brought around The Horn from London in 1879, or **Strybing Arboretum's** 6000-strong collection of species. And in spring and summer, there's no lovelier place to refresh yourself than the **Japanese Tea Garden**, a relic of the Midwinter Exhibition in 1894. The park's best seasonal bets are cherry blossom, rhododendrons and azaleas in March and April; roses and the Shakespeare Garden in June and July.

Recreational facilities include riding and boating on Stow Lake. Bike and roller skate rental agencies are to be found on Stanyan and Fulton Sts near the gates. To reserve your horse, call the Golden Gate Equestrian Center at 664-9877.

ISLANDS IN THE BAY

Out in the Bay, two islands offer completely different experiences. **Alcatraz**, the grim federal prison, closed its doors to convicts in 1963, but you can view some of the facilities that housed America's criminal elite on guided tours led by National Park Service rangers. Among the former residents were Al Capone, 'Machine Gun' Kelly and Robert Stroud, the 'Birdman of Alcatraz'. In November, 1969, about a hundred Indians occupied Alcatraz to establish a cultural center for their people; they defied all attempts to remove them until March 1971. You may still see fading Red Power symbols on the walls near the landing dock.

Ferries to Alcatraz leave daily at 45-minute intervals between 9 am and 3 pm from Fisherman's Wharf, Pier 41. Tickets cost $3.75, and both reservations and warm clothing are recommended. Call 546-2805 for recorded information.

Even on a sunny weekend when all San Francisco seems to be streaming aboard the ferry, **Angel Island State Park** is an ideal spot to play Robinson Crusoe for a day. Ayala Cove (the ferry terminal) has a number of shady picnic sites. If you lack the gregarious spirit, just follow the circle road in either direction, for paths lead to secluded coves and grassy slopes carpeted in summer with a profusion of wildflowers. The central peak gives magnificent views around the Bay. There's plenty of wildlife – all harmless – including black-tailed deer and the rare brown pelican – but do beware of poison oak along the trails.

About halfway around the island road, the abandoned mid-Victorian buildings of **Fort McDowell** and **Camp Reynolds** look out across the Bay. At the turn of the century, Fort McDowell was a detention and quarantine camp for soldiers returning from the Philippines; now under restoration, the buildings are open to public viewing. A little farther on, **Hospital Cove** was the site of the immigration center known until 1943 as the 'Ellis Island' of the West. The fishing is good from its old piers.

Refreshments and island tours by elephant train are available in summer only. Ferry service is provided from San Francisco by the Red and White Fleet, Pier 43½, Fisherman's Wharf (546-2815) and from Tiburon (daily from mid-June to Labor Day; weekends only the rest of the year).

Union St

Slightly off the beaten tourist path and very popular with the locals, is Union St, between Van Ness Avenue and the Presidio, a mellow aggregation of cafes, restaurants, pubs and boutiques housed in refurbished Victorian buildings. A century or so ago only dairy farm buildings stood here, earning the street its nickname 'Cow Hollow'. Today, antique shops, art galleries and decorator showrooms put Union St high on a browser's list, and after dark music adds to the attractiveness of the bistros.

As you stroll west from Van Ness Avenue, you'll come upon an unusual small house set back from the street behind a white picket fence. The **Octagon House**, (1861), its entrance on Gough St, is one of two remaining examples of San Francisco homes designed on the premise that an eight-sided structure is lucky. Now the property of the National Society of Colonial Dames of America, it's open to the public on the first Sunday and second and fourth Thursday of each month, from 1 to 4 pm. Call 885-9796 for information.

Two other Cow Hollow buildings are of unusual architectural interest. **The Vedanta Society's Old Temple** at 2963 Webster St (down a block from Union St, at the corner of Filbert) was built in 1905. The various elements of its design – Oriental, Queen Anne, Colonial and Mediaeval – express the Vedanta belief that all religions are but pathways to the same goal. At 2727 Pierce St (a block south of Union St) is the opulent **Casebolt House**, an Italianate mansion built in 1865 for Henry Casebolt, a Virginia blacksmith who settled in San Francisco in 1851. In the days when Pierce St was just a country road, the house stood in an impressive setting of broad acres, overlooking an ornamental lake.

Two blocks away, at 2301 Union, there's a charming example of Victorian ecclesiastical architecture, **St Mary the Virgin**, built in 1891 for Pacific Heights' Episcopalians. The courtyard has some handsome murals, and the fountain rises from an artesian spring held sacred by the Indians for its curative powers long before the Spanish set foot in California.

Places to Eat

Balboa Cafe Restaurant Off Union, at the corner of Fillmore and Greenwich, this is a cheerful, popular place serving tasty Continental dishes until 10 pm. Reservations recommended. Lunch, dinner. Open daily. (M)

3199 Fillmore; tel 922-4595.

Coffee Cantata One of 'Cow Hollow's' more attractive cafes. Gets crowded, so go on off-hours or be prepared to stand in line. Open daily, 11.30 to 2 am. (B/M)

2030 Union St; tel 931-0770.

Perry's Popular pub'n'grill with a reputation for good food and a friendly ambience. Breakfast, lunch, dinner. (M)

1944 Union St; tel 922-9022.

Doidge's Renowned for their brunches and very busy at weekends. Reservations recommended. Breakfast, lunch. Open daily. (B/M)

2217 Union St; tel 921-2149.

JAPANTOWN (Nihonmachi)

Local wits will tell you the quickest way to Japan is to hop the outbound No 38 Geary bus, and get off in Japantown a few blocks west of Van Ness Avenue. On the way, at the crest of Cathedral Hill, at Gough St, you'll pass the glistening white marble bulk of **St Mary's Cathedral,** mother church of the Roman Catholic Archdiocese of San Francisco, which replaces the 72-year-old cathedral destroyed by fire in 1962. Its spectacular design is the work of Pier Luigi Nervi, Belluschi and local architects Angus McSweeney, Paul A Ryan and John Michael Lee. The interior is restrained but impressive: the vast, column-free nave can seat 2400 worshippers. Above the sanctuary is a free-hanging cascade of 7000 anodized aluminium rods, symbolizing the infinite flow of divine grace and the ascent of prayer. Four stained glass windows dividing the ceiling represent the four elements – earth, fire, air and water. To the right of the sanctuary is a Ruffati organ considered one of the finest in the world.

Japantown, San Francisco's own 'Nihonmachi', lies on the lower slopes of the hill, bounded by Fillmore, Post and Laguna Sts. Japanese immigrants settled the area during the early 1900s, creating a miniature Ginza that was eventually dismembered in WW II by the evacuation of Japanese-Americans to barbed wire 'relocation centers' in the West's badlands. Modern Japantown arose from the bulldozed splinters of the depressed neighbourhood just over a decade ago.

It's a handsome showcase for the city's 13,000-strong Japanese community. A torii gate on Post St opens the way to the **Japanese Center** where you can shop for just about everything from bonsai trees to samurai swords in a $16 million complex of shops, restaurants and tempura bars dominated by Yoshiro Taniguchi's serenely beautiful **Peace Pagoda.** The courtyard is the setting of brilliant pageantry during the spring Cherry Blossom festival and Aki Matsuri in autumn. Try the small family restaurants lining the side streets for some of the best and least expensive Japanese meals in town.

About a mile west of Japantown, on Presidio Avenue at Bush St, is the **San Francisco Fire Department Pioneer Memorial Museum.** Equipment, photographs and memorabilia of San Francisco's 'smokies' from 1849 to the present day are on show here, and a large exhibit honors Lillie Hitchcock Coit, the city's most famous fire buff. Open daily, 1 to 5 pm; admission free; tel 861-8000, ext 210.

HAIGHT-ASHBURY

If you are wondering what happened to the 'Hashbury', take heart. It's still there, sans the Flower Children, in its pre-60s role of residential neighbourhood. Haight St, while good for inexpensive counterculture clothing, headshops and underground movies, is on its way to being another Union St, with antique shops, cafes and fashion boutiques. Sidestreet after sidestreet are the delight of photographers with a fancy for exuberant Victorian architecture.

MISSION DISTRICT

The patois and traditions are Spanish in the venerable Mission District, radiating east and west of San Francisco's oldest thoroughfare. **Mission St** once linked the Presidio to Mission San Francisco de Asis; now it's the heart of a busy residential and business community, a great place for aficionados of Mexican cooking.

Local artists have enhanced many buildings with brilliant murals. Some of the best of these are to be found within a few minutes' walk of BART's 24th St station, between Mission and York St, especially in Balmy Alley and Garfield Square just off 24th St. The Mexican Museum features a guided mural walk on the second Saturday of the month – call 441-0404 for information. A self-guiding tour map is available from the museum.

Mission Dolores

Overshadowed by a modern basilica, the small church with thick adobe walls standing at Dolores and 16th Sts is probably the city's oldest structure. Mission Dolores (Mission San Francisco de Asis) was founded by Father Junipero Serra in 1776, but the present church dates from 1782, replacing a much simpler structure. Architecturally, the Mission combines Corinthian, Moorish and Mission styles, and both Spanish and Mexican influences can be observed in the interior decorations executed by Indian craftspeople. Notice the ceiling, strikingly painted with triangular designs between the heavy beams. The churrigueresque reredos behind the main altar was handcarved in Mexico before 1800, and the three bells above the portico, also of Mexican manufacture, date from 1780.

Near the north side altar is the tomb of Don Jose Joaquin Moraga, first commandant of the Presidio and leader of the Spanish settlers who crossed the continent from Arizona to settle Yerba Buena in 1776. A walkway leads to a small museum of Mission treasures and a cemetery where several of San Francisco's early notables are buried, including Don Luis Antonio Arguello, governor of Alta California from 1822 to 1825.

Open daily 9 am to 4.30 in summer; 10 am to 4 pm November through April; voluntary donations are appreciated.

Places to Stay

San Francisco's compactness means that no matter where you select a hotel within the city limits, you are rarely more than a 30 minute ride by public transportation from the major attractions. BART, AC Transit and Golden Gate Transit extend your options to Oakland and Berkeley in the East Bay and Sausalito on the Marin County shore just across the Golden Gate Bridge.

Most convenient for sightseeing, shopping, entertainment and transportation are the hotels clustered around **Union Square**, heart of the downtown area bounded by Mission, Leavenworth, Bush and Montgomery Sts. Tucked between the luxurious giants, especially along O'Farrell, Sutter, Pine and Bush Sts within a five minute walk of the square, are many good, moderately-priced and budget hotels. **Nob Hill**, four blocks north, is the setting of several of the city's most exclusive hostelries. Among the famous names are the Mark Hopkins and the Fairmont. Further removed from the downtown area but still within a very short bus ride is **Civic Center**; the blocks between 7th and 9th Sts south of Market St are a good source of budget hotels and motels. **Fisherman's Wharf** is a popular, rather pricey area on the waterfront. A conveniently located alternative to the Wharf is the **Lombard St-Van Ness Avenue** area, an L-shaped district running from Civic Center to Fort Mason and west to the Presidio. Moderately-priced motels set the accommodation-style here.

Different and very attractive are San Francisco's bed-and-breakfast hotels, where you can put up in style in a converted Victorian or turn-of-the-century home. Most are located in the city's prime residential areas – Pacific Heights, Jackson Heights and Union St – about 10 minutes' drive from the downtown area. Rates for these little gems are comparatively expensive. Advance reservations are definitely recommended.

For a complete list of member hotels, write to the San Francisco Convention and Visitors Bureau, PO Box 6977, San Francisco, CA 94101. Ask for the current *San Francisco Lodging Guide*.

Rooms in Private Houses If you would like to stay with a family in the Bay Area, check out what *Bed & Breakfast International* has to offer, 151 Ardmore Rd, Kensington CA 94707; tel (415) 525-4569. They'll try to fix you up with people who share your interests if you tell them something about yourself and the purpose of your visit when you ask for a reservation. Lodgings range from Victorian flats in San Francisco to places in the Berkeley Hills overlooking the Bay, and all are close to public transportation. (See *Guest Houses* in the Facts for the Visitor section for this organisation's listings throughout the West.) Rates include breakfast and currently are $28 to $60 for a double room with a 20% reduction for singles; most are between $34 to $44. A minimum stay of two nights is required. When writing for reservations, please include two international reply coupons, your expected arrival time and place of arrival.

American Family Inn/Bed & Breakfast San Francisco provides a similar service with listings in the San Francisco Bay Area, Carmel, Monterey, the Wine Country and the Gold Country. And they also have yachts. There's no minimum stay requirement and rates for a double room are currently between $45 and $55. Give as much advance notice as you can, of course, but they'll do their best to help even if you call the morning you arrive.

Address inquiries to 2185-A Union St, San Francisco, CA 94123; or call (415) 931-3083 (8 am to 10 pm).

San Francisco – Top End

The Bed & Breakfast Inn (4 Charlton Court; tel (415) 921-9784). On a cul-de-sac off Union St in two ivy-covered Victorian buildings. Good public transportation. Fresh flowers and fruit in all rooms, each of which is decorated differently. Rates from $53 with shared bath; $85 with private bath.

Fairmont Hotel & Tower (California and Mason; tel (415) 772-5000; 800-527-4727). One of the great ones, located atop Nob Hill, with a breathtaking view of the Bay. Opulent decor, six restaurants, six cocktail lounges, two orchestras for dancing, and international supperclub talent in the Venetian Room. Rates from $110 double.

Westin St Francis (Union Square; tel (415) 397-3000; within California 800-228-3000). Grand old hostelry, serving the city since 1904. Opulent decor, central location. Family plan; pets (on approval). Rates from $105 double.

Travelodge at the Wharf (250 Beach St; tel (415) 392-6700, 800-255-3050). On Fisherman's Wharf. Many rooms with private balconies and Bay views. Swimming pool. Family plan. Rates from $96 double.

San Francisco – Mid Range

Air Terminal Hotel (415 O'Farrell; tel (415) 928-6000, 800-854-3380). Convenient location near the downtown airline bus terminal and four blocks from Union Square; Family plan. Rates from $39 double.

Americania Motor Lodge (121 7th St, near Market St; tel (415) 626-0200; 800-227-4368; within California, 800-622-0797). Close to Greyhound, Civic Center, with courtesy shuttle to and from airlines terminal. Kitchenettes, swimming pool, family plan. A Best-Western motel. Rates from $59 double.

Bedford Hotel (761 Post St; tel (415) 673-6040, 800-227-5642; within California, 800-652-1889.
Quiet, comfortable. Two block walk to Union Square. Rates from $55 double.
Beresford (635 Sutter St; tel (415) 673-9900); within California, 800-227-4048).
Handy for Union Square, art galleries and a clutch of good restaurants. Rates from $46.
Manx Hotel (225 Powell St; tel (415) 421-7070; within California, 800-652-1535).
The big stores and the theater district are just around the corner. Family plan. Rates from $55 double.
King George Hotel (334 Mason; tel (415) 781-5050; 800-227-4240). Recently renovated, attractive hotel in the theater district. Offers English high teas with live piano music in the Bread and Honey Tea Room. Rates from $48 double.
Laurel Motor Inn (444 Presidio Avenue at California St; (415) 567-8467). Half an hour by bus from Union Square, in quiet Pacific Heights residential neighbourhood. Good public transportation nearby. Kitchenettes. Rates from $52 double.
Seal Rock Inn (545 Point Lobos Avenue (end of Geary Boulevard); tel (415) 752-8000). Overlooks the Pacific, close to the Cliff House and Sutro Heights Park. Requires two-day minimum stay. Coffee shop. Deposit required. Rates from $41 double.
Hotel York (940 Sutter St; tel (415) 885-6800; within California, 800-227-3608). Good hotel about six blocks from Union Square. Many rooms with wet bars and refrigerators. The elegant Plush Room is on the premises. Rates from $50.

San Francisco – Bottom End

Brazil Hotel, (875 Post St at Hyde; tel (415) 775-1864). Small family-operated hotel, five minutes by bus from Union Square. No elevator or restaurant, but quiet and recently renovated. Some rooms with private bath, all with phones. Weekly rates. Deposit (one night) required. Rates from $25 double without

bath; $30 with bath.
Carroll Plaza (245 Powell St; tel (415) 421-4525). On cable car lines in heart of downtown shopping area. Hostel type accommodation. Family plan, student rates. $5 a night for Youth Hostel members.
Embarcadero YMCA Center (166 The Embarcadero; tel (415) 392-2191). The waterfront Y boasts a swimming pool. All rooms without private bath. From $28 double.
Red Victorian Bed & Breakfast Inn (1655 Haight St; tel (415) 864-1978). Near Golden Gate Park, this 1904 family resort hotel now offers a meditation room and funky atmosphere – plus a continental breakfast with home-made rolls served in bed, bath or the Pink Parlor. Most rooms share bath; family plan. Rates from $34 double.
Obrero Hotel & Basque Restaurant (1208 Stockton St; tel (415) 989 3960). Located on the edge of Chinatown. Immaculate rooms. Traditional Basque family-style dinners nightly for $9.50 plus tax, including wine. Rates from $32 double includes such a hearty breakfast that the table groans.
San Francisco International Hostel (Building 240, Fort Mason; tel (415) 771-7277). An AYH Superior hostel located in a parklike setting, close to the Bay and Fisherman's Wharf attractions. Dormitory style except for a few family rooms. Maximum stay allowed is three nights. Ask them about additional hostels in the Bay Area. Rates are $7 a night with Hostel pass; $9 without.
YMCA Hotel (351 Turk St; tel (415) 673-2312). The men's Y takes women too. On the edge of a tough neighbourhood, close to Civic Center. Swimming pool. Rates from $28 double. Rooms without private bath $3 to $4 less.
Youth Hostel Central (116 Turk St; tel (415) 346-7835). In the heart of the Tenderloin. Offers dormitory style accommodation for $6 a night; some private rooms at $15 for two persons. Weekly and

monthly rates. Kitchen facilities.

Be warned: these two hostels are in one of San Francisco's toughest areas.

Places to Eat

It is a local article of faith that few cities in the world can rival the quality and variety of San Francisco's eating establishments, great and small. City chefs, drawing on a tradition of old as the gold rush when immigrants from every quarter of the globe streamed through the Golden Gate, offer a dizzying array of international cuisines that omits none of the major ones and only a few of the more rarified. Yes, it is possible to dine poorly in San Francisco, but you will have to work harder to do so than anywhere else in the country. On your way to a steady date with Weightwatchers International, we suggest you sample at least these local specialties: crusty sourdough French bread (the starter may have come north with the Mexican miners in 1849); cioppino, the local Italian retort to bouillabaisse; sand dabs; Rex sole; wines from Napa, Sonoma and Mendocino counties and the Livermore Valley; and Pisco punch, a 19th century invention born of Peruvian brandy in the old Bank Exchange Saloon on Montgomery St.

Very San Francisco are lingering brunches with champagne cocktails or Ramos fizzes, dim sum lunches in Chinatown and family-style dining at North Beach's small Basque and Italian restaurants. Although the city's generally informal, quite a few restaurants require jackets, ties and reservations. Several feature live entertainment and the Hyatt Regency has brought back the thé dansant to its famous lobby.

Good, inexpensive little restaurants and coffeehouses abound. Particularly rewarding areas to browse for these are **Clement St.** between 19th and 26th Avenues, the 1800-2000 blocks of **Union St** and its sidestreets, **Polk St** between Geary and Union, **North Beach** (particularly the side streets off Columbus Avenue and between Broadway and Washington Square), and, of course, **Chinatown and Japantown.** Increasingly, local pubs are offering light meals or hearty sandwiches along with the libations. In the 'fast food' category, names to remember are *Salmagundi,* and *Zims,* with locations scattered around the city.

Enjoying a superlative view with your meal or drink is another San Francisco tradition. *Ghirardelli Square, Fisherman's Wharf* and the *Embarcadero* restaurants offer many different aspects of the Bay. If you prefer a room at the top, there are several sky rooms: try the *Carnelian Room* on the Bank of America Building's 52nd floor, the *Top of the Mark* in the Mark Hopkins Hotel, the Fairmont's *Fairmont Crown* or the Hyatt Regency's *Equinox,* the city's only restaurant that revolves. Cross the Bay to Sausalito, Tiburon, Berkeley or Oakland for spectacular views of San Francisco. The prices match the exalted elevation.

With more than 2600 restaurants and 3000 watering holes to choose from, investment in a guide is recommended.

Shopping

San Francisco rivals New York, Paris and London in the quality and variety of its shops, and has a distinct advantage by virtue of its compact size. Large department stores, high fashion boutiques and specialty shops center conveniently on **Union Square** and its environs. Macy's I Magnin, Nieman-Marcus, J Magnin and Saks Fifth Avenue are just a few suggestions. Look for those internationally famous names in household furnishings, china, glass and silverware in the 100 and 200 blocks of **Post St,** where you'll find a number of luxury stores such as Gump's, Dunhill's, Shreve, Crump & Low, Christian of Copenhagen and Gucci. Eddie Bauer's is headquarters for high quality outdoor gear. Photographic equipment suppliers cluster on the first two blocks of **Kearny St.**

Chinatown is showcase for a bewildering array of wares imported from the Orient. Japan's arts and crafts may be comfortably browsed in **Nihonmachi,** surrounding the Japan Center on Geary St.

For antiques, browse **Jackson Square, Union St, Haight St,** and **Sacramento St** between Lyon and Spruce. The show rooms of fine art auctioneers Butterfield & Butterfield and Sotheby Parke Bernet are worth a visit. And if it's rare books you're after, seek out John Howell Books and the Albatross Bookstore downtown. A leader in the discount record field is Tower Records.

Art galleries abound. Among the leading names are Paule Anglim, John Berggruen, Braunstein, Fuller Goldeen, William Sawyer and Van Doren. The San Francisco Art Dealers Association publishes a helpful directory, available from any member gallery.

The Fisherman's Wharf area is crammed with boutiques and specialty shops. Some of the best are to be found in the Cannery and Ghirardelli Square. Nearby Cost Plus, a rambling emporium of the world's goods is just the place to look for unusual and inexpensive trophies.

Tax-free stores are to be found on O'Farrell St, near Powell, and on Geary St, near Union Square.

Nightlife & Entertainment

The City can offer you a little bit of everything in the way of nightlife and entertainment – internationally renowned concert artists, opera-singers, dancers, cabaret stars. The Opera House is home of three famous institutions, the San Francisco Opera Company, the San Francisco Ballet and the San Francisco Symphony Orchestra; major Broadway shows on tour pause at the Curran and Orpheum; at the Geary the American Conservatory Theater offers broadbased repertory and a host of little theaters run the gamut from musical revues to serious drama. Celluloid buffs will find the

world's classics at the Pacific Film Archive and the Film Festival is firmly established on the international scene.

Jazz is alive and well (Earthquake McGoon's is a civic institution) and the biggest names in showbiz play the Fairmont's Venetian Room and the Hotel York's Plush Room. There are dozens of cafes where you can drop by for live music – Union St bistros are particularly rewarding.

The Singles Scene flourishes behind the plate glass and dangling ferns of a number of attractive watering holes citywide: presently, it's *Victoria Station, Perry's, Cafe Balboa* and *Henry Africa's.* The Gay World hangs it all out along Polk and Castro Sts – pick up a copy of the *Advocate* for the inside view.

North Beach's rather raunchy establishments faintly echo the entertainments of the Barbary Coast, but the Live Male and Female Acts should not deter you from discovering the charm of Tosca's, Vesuvio's and Banducci's for after-the-show nightcaps in colorful surroundings.

Best sources of up-to-the-minute information are the Sunday Chronicle-Examiner's *Datebook* – the 'Pink' section – and the weekly *Bay Guardian.* Reservations for shows can be made through ticket agencies listed in the phone book's Yellow Pages. For Opera House attractions, it's the Opera House Box Office at Civic Center.

Entertainment Calender

San Francisco Opera Fall season, from mid-September through November, is an international event with heavy advance sales – book well in advance. The new annual Summer Festival, from the end of May through early July, is also very popular. Promising young artists perform in the San Francisco Opera Center's Showcase (March) and in Western Opera Theater performances between September and December in the Bay Area; they also perform at Stern Grove in July and in Saratoga in August.

San Francisco Symphony, regular season December through May. Again book well ahead – Thursday and Saturday night are best bets. In summer, the Symphony plays for the *Municipal Pops Concerts* (July) and the free, open-air *Midsummer Music Festival* (mid-June-August, Sunday afternoons, Sigmund Stern Grove).

American Conservatory Theater, October-May. The City's resident repertory company plays the Geary and Marines Memorial Theatres.

San Francisco Ballet, January through May. One of the country's leading dance companies.

Civic Light Opera, beginning in May, offers four productions, each with six-week runs, at the Orpheum Theater.

San Francisco International Film Festival, October, presents afternoon and evening showings daily for a two-week feast of US and foreign films.

Getting There
San Francisco International Airport

Located 15 miles south of San Francisco on the shores of the Bay, San Francisco is one of the most convenient, compact and up-to-date airports in the country. All **Arrival** facilities are located on the lower (ground floor) level; **Departures** use the upper deck. Terminals are about 200 yards apart, linked by walkways and brown airport shuttle buses which operate at three-to-five minute intervals. The walk from the plane to the US Customs & Immigration area is quite a hike and includes a flight of stairs; for the elderly or handicapped, reserving a wheel chair through your airline is definitely worthwhile.

Services

Most passenger services are maintained around the clock. In addition to the usual cocktail lounges, coffee shops and snack bars in each terminal, and the Central Terminal restaurant, you will find:

Baggage Lockers Both levels in each terminal building.

Car Rental Counters Arrivals level, all terminals; 24-hour service. If the counters are not staffed, telephone service is provided.

Avis	(415) 877-6780
Budget	(415) 877-4477
Dollar	(415) 952-6200
Hertz	(415) 877-1600
National	(415) 877-4745

Off-airport car rental firms advertise in the phone book Yellow Pages. You may also be able to arrange for car hire on the plane – consult the aircraft cabin steward.

Emergencies & Information White Courtesy Phones system throughout the airport provides immediate assistance and information. Telephone numbers are posted beside each phone.

Foreign Currency Exchange South Terminal, Departures level. Bank of America – open daily, 7 am to 10 pm. Deak-Perera of California Inc – open daily, 7 am to 11 pm.

Hotel-Motel Information Arrivals level, all terminals. Pick-up/direct dial service to a number of airport and downtown hostelries. Insurance desks in the South Terminal building also provide reservation service.

Insurance Counters Departures level, all terminals.

Lost and Found Baggage lost in flight should be reported to your airline. For items lost in the terminal public areas, use the White Courtesy Phone, 6-2161.

Medical Service Available at any time – ask a policeman or call 7-0444 on the White Courtesy Phone. New electric mini-ambulances are stationed within two minutes of any spot in each terminal.

Shopping Gift shops are located on the Departure level, all terminals. Tax-free shopping in the International Departures area, South Terminal.

Post Office Arrivals level, Central Terminal.

Wheelchairs/Aid to the Handicapped
Wheelchairs are provided by the airlines – ask the customer representatives on the plane. Throughout the airport, restrooms and telephones have been designed to aid the handicapped. Curbs are ramped and elevator service is available in all terminals.

Parking
Airport Garage 24-hour service and patrolled by security officers. Valet service (for an additional $8) on the Departures level.
Economy Parking Lot Lowest rates and free-24-hour shuttle service between the lot and airline terminals. Located near San Bruno Avenue East exit from US 101 and the North Terminal, it too is patrolled by security officers.
Off-Airport Lots Anza (415) 348-8800) on Airport Boulevard, Burlingame, and Park 'N Fly (415) (877-0304) in South San Francisco both provide low-cost airport parking and 24-hour shuttle bus service between the lots and airport terminals.

Transportation (On-Airport)
Airport Shuttle Brown buses operate continuously on Arrivals and Departures levels. Pick them up at the central traffic islands.
Parking Lot Shuttles Identified by company symbols, also operate continuously. They stop on demand at the central traffic islands, Arrivals and Departure levels.
Transportation (Off-Airport)
SFO Airporter (Airport Bus Service) Daily 24-hour non-stop service between the airport and San Francisco downtown terminal at Ellis and Taylor Sts. Buses

operate approximately every 10 to 15 minutes between 5.15 am and 9 pm; every 30 to 40 minutes thereafter. Current fare is $4. Additional direct service to Fisherman's Wharf and other areas. Limited service is also provided to Oakland International Airport (fare $5). For information on fares and schedules call (415) 673 2432. Bus stops are in front of the Arrivals area at each terminal.
Greyhound Limited service between airport and Bay Area cities. Tel (415) 433-1500.
Sam Trans Frequent service from the airport to Peninsula cities and San Francisco. Buses to San Francisco depart from Arrivals level stop between Central and South terminals. Exact fare required.

On weekdays only they also offer a connecting service between the airport and the Daly City BART station. At airport, call (415) 726-5541; in San Francisco (415) 761-6000.
Mini-bus Lorrie's Travel & Tours provides mini-bus transportation between SFO and downtown San Francisco points for $6.50 one way. Advance reservation required to airport; inbound, telephone for pick-up on arrival. Tel (415) 885-6600.
Additional Services In addition to the transportation services listed above, a number of bus and limousine companies link SFO with Napa, Sonoma, Marin, Contra Costa and Alameda countries, and Sacramento.
Limousine Service Fare to San Francisco averages $40, to Oakland $90. Drop-off service to all major downtown hotels. Prior reservation may be necessary through your carrier or travel agent.

SFO Helicopter Airlines operates flights connecting SFO with Oakland International. Fare is currently $39. Passengers connecting with other airline flights may be able to obtain a special joint fare. On-airport, use white courtesy phones for information; off-airport, call (415) 877-0165.

Taxis Be sure to negotiate the fare to your destination *in advance.* Fare to downtown San Francisco is approximately $20. Pick up near baggage claim areas, Arrivals level. For information, call (415) 876-2209.

Getting Around

Public transportation in the San Francisco Bay Area is good: equipped with the Metropolitan Transportation Commission's *Regional Transit Guide* and MUNI's street and route map (both available in bookstores), you can navigate within a block or two of most sights aboard the systems described below.

San Francisco Municipal Railway The MUNI's network of bus, street car and trolley lines provides 24-hour service over many routes; the popular cable cars are out of service for system repairs, possibly until 1985. Basic fare is 60c at press time; no change is given by bus drivers so have the exact amount ready as you board. Check the destination sign on the front of the bus before you get on. If it's marked 'L' (Limited) or 'X' (Express), ask whether it stops at your destination, for buses so marked halt at specific points only. Ask for a **Transfer** if you need to change buses en route. Transfers are free and currently afford unlimited travel in either direction for a limited period of time (usually 90

minutes). The tear line indicates the expiration time.

The MUNI Metro (street car lines J, K, L, M and N) functions as a subway in the downtown area, sharing station locations with BART from Civic Center to the Embarcadero.

Information (415) 673-MUNI (24-hour service).

AC Transit provides rapid, convenient bus service from San Francisco to East Bay cities via the Bay Bridge from the Transbay Terminal at First and Mission Sts. Call (415) 653-3535 for information.

BART's ultra modern subway system links San Francisco to the East Bay via a tunnel under the waters of the bay. BART operates from 6 am (9 am on Sundays) to midnight.

Minimum fare 60c; free one-way transfers are available from East Bay stations to AC Transit buses. BART riders transferring to the San Francisco MUNI can purchase a two-ride pass for 60c. In San Francisco, call (415) 788-BART for information.

Golden Gate Transit operates the bus service between San Francisco and Marin and Sonoma counties via the Golden Gate Bridge. No central San Francisco terminal, but you can catch the buses at convenient points around the city (see the system maps in the Yellow Pages of the San Francisco phone book, or pick up a free Transit Guide from one of the ticket agencies listed therein). Exact fare required.

Ferry Service GGT also operates daily ferry service aboard high-speed vessels equipped with bars and refreshment counters between San Francisco and Sausalito (30 minutes, $2.50 one way, weekdays; $3 weekends) and San Francisco and Larkspur (45 minutes, $2 one way, weekdays. No weekend service). In San Francisco board ship at the Ferry Building terminal, foot of Market St. Information (415) 332-6600.

Sam Trans buses serve all communities in San Mateo County between San Francisco and Palo Alto, and also San Francisco International Airport. Buses leave from First and Mission Sts, in front of the Transbay Terminal. Exact fare required. Information 761-7000 (in San Francisco).

Southern Pacific Commuter-oriented train service between San Francisco and Peninsula cities as far as San Jose from the depot on 4th and Townsend Sts. Information (415) 495-4546 (6.30 am to 7 pm).

Limousine Service Chauffeur-driven limousines are available for hire by the hour, day, week or month. Firms advertise in the phone book Yellow Pages. Sample tariffs: between San Francisco and San Francisco International, $40; tours, $30 per hour with a three-hour minimum basic charge.

Taxis At press time, San Francisco taxis charge $1.30 at flag drop and $1.30 per mile. Fare from downtown San Francisco to San Francisco International (15 miles) is around $20; to Oakland Airport (14 miles), around $28.

Self-Drive Car Hire Most of the major international automobile rental agencies such as Hertz and Avis maintain desks at San Francisco International and Oakland airports. For off-airport and downtown locations, consult the Yellow Pages of the local telephone directory.

Tours

Bus *Gray Line of San Francisco* 1st and Mission Sts; tel (415) 771-4000, has tours of San Francisco and Chinatown ($12.75), the Napa Valley Wine Country ($29.75), Monterey-Carmel ($38.75), and Muir Woods-Sausalito ($12.75). You'll find a representative and shuttle bus parked opposite the St Francis Hotel on Union Square from 8 am to 8 pm daily; pick up service from the San Francisco Hilton.

Great Pacific Tour Co 2276 Bush St; tel 929-1700. You can scoot around the city in minibuses for ($12.75). Also offered: Muir Woods-Sausalito $15; Wine Country $42; Monterey-Carmel $45.

Maxi Tours 1961 Chestnut St; tel 563-2151, has a program which includes City Tour $13; Muir Woods-Sausalito $13; Wine Country $29.50; and Monterey-Carmel $32.50. Transportation in 14-seat minibuses. Reservations required.

Bay Cruises Cruises around San Francisco Bay operate every day of the year (weather permitting) from piers at Fisherman's Wharf. Reservations are recommended during summer.

Alcatraz Tour (2½ hours) – Pier 41, Fisherman's Wharf; tel (415) 546-2805. $3.75.

Blue & Gold Fleet (1½ hours) – Pier 39, Fisherman's Wharf; tel (415) 781-7877. $8. *The Red & White Fleet* (1½ hours) – Pier 43½, Fisherman's Wharf; tel (415) 546-2810. $8.

Sacramento River Cruises *Delta Travel Agency,* 1240 Merkley Ave (PO Box 813) West Sacramento, CA 95691; tel (916) 372-3690.

Between April and October, 500-passenger riverboats ply the old Forty Niner river route between San Francisco and Sacramento, traversing the waterways of the Delta and the Sacramento River. The Delta is one of California's wonders – 886 islands ranging from five feet above sea level to 21 feet below, reclaimed by

Chinese laborers a century ago. It's now some of the richest farmland in the world – the province, too, of egrets, waterfowl and small game. As only 12 miles of the 91-mile route are paralleled by roads, the sights – old river ports, the US Navy's 'Mothball Fleet', and isolated farms – are rarely seen.

One and two-day cruises are offered from both San Francisco and Sacramento. One-day cruise fare of $33 includes return trip by bus to point of origin; two-day cruise fare of $81 includes hotel room (based on double occupancy), boat cruises and bus transfers. Reservations should be made as far in advance as possible.

Flights *Helicoptours* (five to 30-minute tours), Pier 46, Fisherman's Wharf; tel (415) 495-3333. $15 for a five-minute flight. Tickets also available at all major ticket outlets and Ghirardelli Square booth (Woollen Mill). Courtesy shuttle service to heliport from Ghirardelli Square, Hyatt Regency Hotel and Ferry Building with parties of 8 or more.

Commodore Helicopter Tours Four-minute tours; longer by arrangement), Pier 43, Fisherman's Wharf; tel (415) 981-4832; $12.

Napa Valley Balloons PO Box 2860, Yountville, CA 94599; tel (707) 253-2224. Drift above the Wine Country for approximately an hour for $110 per person, including a champagne reception, instant photos and a balloon pin. These trips are very popular, so make your reservations as soon as you can.

Walking Tours *City Guides* San Francisco History Room, San Francisco Public Library, Civic Center; tel (415) 558-3770. Volunteers lead free tours of North Beach and Pacific Heights on Saturday and Sunday mornings.

Foundation for San Francisco's Architectural Heritage 2007 Franklin St; tel (415) 441-3046.

Two architectural walking tours tell the story of San Francisco's development from frontier town to sophisticated metropolis. Telephone for recorded information on times, cost, meeting places.

Street Walkers of San Francisco 66 Geary St, 15th floor; tel (415) 457-9218. Five-hour tours offer the comprehensive San Francisco experience. Chinese lunch included. Groups limited to 10 persons, so reservations are required. Walks begin in Union Square, end in Ghirardelli Square.

Chinese Culture Center Holiday Inn (3rd floor), 750 Kearny St; tel (415) 986-1822. 2½ hour walk through Chinatown focuses on the Chinese community's cultural heritage and achievements. Advance arrangements necessary. $6 per person.

Mexican Mural Walk Mexican Museum, Bldg D, Fort Mason; tel (415) 441-0404. Guided tours of the Mission District murals on the second Saturday of each month. $2.50 per person.

Guided Plant Walks Strybing Arboretum, 9th Avenue & Lincoln Way, Golden Gate Park; tel (415) 661-1316.

One-hour guided walks daily, 1.30 pm. Also at 10.30 am Thursday through Sunday. No charge. Meet at the information kiosk.

AROUND THE BAY AREA
SAUSALITO

Sailing across the bay to Sausalito is one of the nicest things you can do while visiting San Francisco. Ferries leave from the Ferry Building at the foot of Market St, hug the Alcatraz shoreline, then spurt across open water, to dock within a short walk of everything Sausalito has to offer.

In the main, Sausalito has a sunny, Mediterranean-type climate and atmosphere. Though the town can trace its origins to 1838 when Captain William Richardson, mate of the whaler *Orion*, was awarded Rancho Saucelito by the Mexican authorities, few early buildings remain to recall the days when Sausalito was known as Monte Carlo of the West. Today, the houses of most local residents cling to the steep hills overlooking the bay; fine old palms shade a small park where the local young hang out around the fountain with pizza, pop and pot; and houseboats cluster at the far end of Bridgeway, upstaging the yachts in the harbor.

Sausalito, simply, is a place to take your ease and potter. You can shop for the usual assortment of tourist mementos and antiques in converted Victorian buildings along the waterfront and in the Village Fair, an attractive beehive of boutiques tucked into the cliffside behind the **Marina**. If you're there on the seventh Sunday after Easter, you can join the crowds celebrating **La Chamarita**, when descendants of Portuguese fishermen who settled here foregather for the Feast of the Holy Ghost. There is a small museum of local history in City Hall on Litho St, but the pleasant aroma of espresso coffee and good food emanating from the parade of waterfront bistros are most powerful lures.

Places to Stay
Sausalito and East Bay Hotels

Alta Mira Hotel (125 Bulkley Avenue, Sausalito; tel (415) 332-1350). Cliffside hotel with sweeping views of the Bay and renowned restaurant. Easy walk to the San Francisco ferry. Rates from $45 double.

Casa Madrona (801 Bridgeway, Sausalito; tel (415) 332-0502). Former lumber baron's mansion (1885) amid hillside gardens overlooking the water. Rates from $60 double without bath; $70 with bath. Three cottages on the grounds, $140-160 double occupancy; additional persons $10 each.

Sausalito Hotel (16 El Portal, Sausalito; tel (415) 332-4155). Romantic waterfront retreat, near the ferry. One room boasts the bedroom furniture of General Ulysses S Grant. Rates from $40 without bath; $60 with bath.

Claremont Resort Hotel & Tennis Club (Ashby at Domingo Avenue, Oakland; tel (415) 843-3000). Grand old resort in the Berkely Hills with swimming pool and tennis courts. Family plan. Rates from $90 double.

Places to Eat

Alta Mira Hotel Continental cuisine and a truly spectacular view from this Sausalito landmark set on the cliff's edge. (M)

Breakfast, lunch, dinner. Open daily. 125 Bulkley Avenue; tel (415) 332-1350.

Moti Mahal Flute and sitar players add their cachet at dinners here from Thursday to Sunday. The cuisine is authentically Indian. (M)

Dinner. Open daily except Monday. 2650 Bridgeway; tel (415) 332-6444.

Ondine This elegant waterfront restaurant with a San Francisco view gathers awards for its cuisine. (E)

Dinner. Open daily. 558 Bridgeway; tel (415) 332-0791.

The Sweetshop Informal, friendly cafe with its back to the water so you can concentrate on the good fare. (B)

Breakfast, lunch, dinner. Open daily. 680 Bridgeway; tel (415) 332-1454.

TIBURON

Not so long ago Tiburon was a roistering railroad town; its present decorously prosperous air is fitting in a community that owns some of the costliest homes in the bay area. There's good shopping in the architectural award-winning **Boardwalk Center** and outstanding views of Angel Island and San Francisco from cafes clustered around the yacht harbor. *Sam's Anchor Cafe* is a local yachting tradition.

Daily in summer (weekends only the rest of the year), the Angel Island Ferry at the end of Main St will run you across Raccoon Strait to Angel Island's Ayala Cove. Call (415) 435-2131 for information. At Ayala Cove, you could then pick up the ferry to San Francisco. GGT buses serve Sausalito and Tiburon at frequent intervals.

Places to Eat

Sam's Anchor Cafe This classic waterfront restaurant and bar has been a Berca for the yachting crowd since the 1920s. Outdoor dining on the deck. (M)

Lunch, dinner. Open daily. 27 Main St; tel (415) 435-4527.

Sabella's A huge menu, generous portions and a marvellous view. Reservations recommended at weekends (B/M).

Lunch Saturday and Sunday; dinner daily. 9 Main St; tel (415) 435-2636.

BERKELEY

Twelve miles across the bay (eight of them via the Oakland-Bay bridge) lies Berkeley, home of the University of California and radical philosophy. Standing on hills overlooking the Bay and San Francisco, the campus is a pleasant place of smooth green lawns, eucalyptus groves and old oaks that frame an imposing array of buildings reflecting Berkeley's growth from a small college in 1860 to UC's largest. The southern entrance, **Sather Gate**, is the hub of the student universe – at noon you'll still find debates in full swing around the fountain. The **Student Union Building** nearby is the starting point of a free 1½ hour walking tour held Monday through Friday (except University holidays) at 1 pm – for information, call 642-5215. On your own, you could hop on the campus bus, Humphrey Go-Bart, at the Bank of America building opposite BART on Shattuck Avenue. It runs weekdays only, between 7 am and 7 pm; most buses terminate at Mining Circle but every half hour there's an express bus right up to the Lawrence Hall of Science which stops at the Botanical Gardens.

Get off at Moffit Avenue for the **Bancroft Library**, adjacent to the Main Library building, which contains the largest and most important collection of books, manuscripts and pamphlets on the history of California. The galleries of both libraries always have interesting displays.

Opposite is the **Campanile** (Sather Tower) where you can ride up to the observation deck for a superb view. Its 36-bell carillon plays a concert of light music daily at noon. Farther on up the slopes in Strawberry Canyon is the 25-acre **Botanical Garden** which specialises in orchids, cacti, succulents and tropical exotica. Opening hours are 9 am to 5 pm daily. Free tours on Saturdays and Sundays at 1.30 pm. The **Lawrence Hall of Science** on Centennial Drive offers scientific diversions and displays – here you can play computer games, watch movies or take in a planetarium show. The hall is open daily 10 am to 4.30 pm (9 pm Thursdays); admission $1 weekdays; $2.50 weekends; tel 642-5132.

If you want to take a look at the rarified world of atomic physics, the **Lawrence Berkeley Laboratory** is open to view on Tuesdays (on other days by prior arrangement). Guided tours include the Bevatron, a cloud chamber and other subatomic research tools. Call 486-4017 for necessary reservations.

Off the main campus at 2626 Bancroft Way, is the striking new **University Art Museum** which concentrates on contemporary works of art. Exhibits change frequently. Open 11 am to 5 pm; Wednesday to Sunday; free admission; tel 642-0848.

Places to Eat

Chez Panisse Gourmets flock to this charming restaurant in a converted Victorian home near the campus. Prix fixe menu offers a different entree nightly from a vast repertoire of French and continental dishes. Reservations advised. (E).

Lunch, dinner. Open Tuesday to Saturday. 1577 Shattuck Avenue; tel 548-5525.

Dock of the Bay Creole specialties highlight a wide choice of dinner entrees at this elegant restaurant on the water. (M/E)

Lunch, dinner. Open daily. Berkeley Marina (route posted); tel 845-7656.

Larry Blake's Comfortable 'ratskeller' atmosphere and a wide range of American and continental dishes. (B)

Lunch, dinner. Open daily. 2367 Telegraph Avenue, near Sather Gate; tel 848-0886.

OAKLAND

'There is no there, there', quipped Gertrude Stein of her native city. A nice aphorism, and perhaps an appropriate one at the time Ms Stein set off for Paris. Today there is a lot of 'there' in and about the thriving East Bay city. Oakland has taken over San Francisco's role as Northern California's major port and entrepot for Pacific commerce, and the new airport attracts an ever-increasing share of international and internal traffic. And corporate highrises attest its status as California's third city.

For visitors, though, **Jack London Square** is Oakland's main attraction. This waterfront complex of small shops, restaurants and congenial pubs with romantic views of San Francisco and the Bay Bridge is a pleasant place to spend a few hours. At the foot of Broadway you'll find the log cabin which was Jack London's home during the Alaska gold rush. In the 'First and Last Chance Saloon' nearby there are many souvenirs of Oakland's most famous son who frequented the bar in his days as an 'oyster pirate' on the bay. Also worth a visit for their attractive Victorian style buildings and boutiques are **Bret Harte Boardwalk** on Fifth St and **Embarcadero Cove Marina**, on the waterfront about a mile south of the square.

Oakland Museum, located at 10th and Oak Sts, is an important center for the study of California history and regional art. It also contains displays illustrating the state's natural history and ecology, and is open Tuesday to Saturday, 10 am to 5 pm; Sunday, 10 am to 7 pm; tel 834-2431; admission free.

Two fine examples of Victorian mansions worth a visit are **Camron-Stanford House** and **Dunsmuir House**. Not far from Oakland Museum on the banks of Lake Merritt at 1418 Lakeside Drive, the Camron-Stanford House (1876) is the last of the great homes that used to line the lake shore. It has been restored to illustrate life in an upper middle class household at the end of the 19th century, and is open 11 am to 4 pm Wednesdays; 1 to 5 pm Sundays; tel 836-1976.

Dunsmuir House (1899) was built by Alexander Dunsmuir as a wedding gift to his wife. Considered one of the finest examples of Greek Revival architecture in the West, it is splendidly situated in extensive gardens at the foot of the Oakland hills. Access to the house is by tour only, between Easter and Labor Day. Open noon to 4 pm Sundays, Easter to September 30. 2960 Peralta Oaks Court; tel 562-7588.

Getting There
Oakland International Airport

The Bay Area's second airport is situated on San Francisco Bay 20 miles east of San Francisco via the Oakland-Bay Bridge and seven miles from downtown Oakland. Though considerably smaller than San Francisco International, it carries a full complement of services. These include a gift shop and duty-free shop, flight insurance, foreign exchange, food and beverage services, a dining room and five car rental counters, all concentrated in one terminal building. There is also an 8th floor cocktail lounge in the Tower, giving fine views around the bay.

Emergencies and Information Use the White Courtesy Phone System. Additionally, there is an Information Booth near the Baggage Claim area.

Parking Conveniently located near the

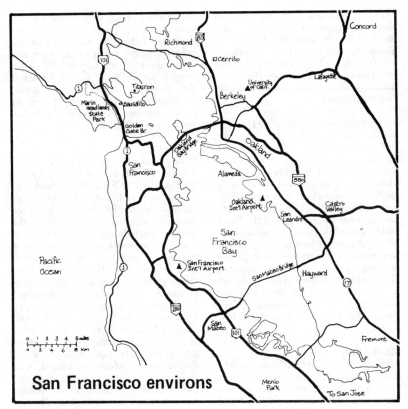

San Francisco environs

Terminal Building.

Transportation

Excellent public transportation links Oakland International to San Francisco and East Bay cities.

Oakland Air-BART operates from 6 am to midnight, Monday to Saturday, and 9 am to midnight on Sunday, connecting the airport with BART trains at the Coliseum/Oakland Airport station – service on demand or every seven to 10 minutes. For information call 788-2278 (in San Francisco), 465-2278 (in Oakland/East Bay area).

SFO Airporter provides service between the airport and downtown Oakland (Jack London Square), downtown San Francisco and San Francisco International Airport. Call 673-2434 for the schedule. The fare to downtown San Francisco is presently $5.

AC Transit's Line 57 provides local bus service crosstown Oakland, connecting at major intersections with intercity express buses. Basic fare 60c, with additional zone charges for longer trips to East Bay cities. Tel (415) 653-3535.

SFO Helicopter Airlines operates flights between Oakland and San Francisco International Airports. Fare is currently $39, time 6½ minutes. Passengers using them to connect with flights may be able to obtain a special joint airfare. Call 430-8815.

Taxis If you are traveling any considerable distance by cab, do negotiate the fare before boarding. The fare to downtown San Francisco is currently around $28. Call Associated Cabs (893-4991) or Yellow Cab (839-5110).

THE PENINSULA

The peninsula cities lining the old Spanish Camino Real from San Francisco to San Jose are not merely dormitory communities for their large neighbor to the north. Many began as agricultural communities in the fertile Santa Clara Valley; others served as centers for the lumber industry which drew on the dense redwood forests that formerly clothed the hills between the Pacific and the Bay to build – and rebuild – San Francisco in the 1850s. Attracted by the sunny climate and scenic countryside, many pioneer millionaires established vast estates near Hillsborough and Menlo Park. Today, the area is dominated by space-age electronic industries which earned the area south of San Carlos the nickname 'Silicon Valley'.

MENLO PARK

Menlo Park, south of San Francisco on US 101, is an attractive, affluent small town, home of the publishers of *Sunset Magazine,* arbiter of the West's lifestyle for more than 75 years. The **Lane Magazine and Book Company** at Willow and Middlefield Rds, welcomes visitors to their test kitchens, editorial offices and experimental gardens each weekday. Free tours begin at 10.30 am – phone 321-3600 for information.

WOODSIDE

Woodside provides an opportunity to view the opulence of Bay Area grandees at the turn of the century. **Filoli,** a magnificent early 20th century mansion set in 17 acres of gardens laid out in the Italian Renaissance style, was designed by Willis Polk for the millionaire William Bourn II. Tours include the Carriage House which preserves seven carriages in mint condition. To get there from San Francisco, follow US 280 south about 30 miles to Edgewood Rd. Exit right and then turn right on Canada Rd. After roughly a mile, there is a well-marked gate. Tours are conducted from Tuesday to Saturday at 10 am and 1 pm, by reservation only. Admission $3 to house recorded information.

PALO ALTO

Photographic history was made in Palo Alto back in 1872 when Senator Leland Stanford invited Edward Muybridge to take a series of instantaneous photographs of trotting racehorses at his seven thousand acre stock farm. In 1887, the railroad magnate and his wife founded **Stanford University** on the farm as a memorial to their only child who died of typhoid fever in his 16th year. The main driveway of the spacious campus, University Avenue, leads to the principal buildings ranged around vast quadrangles. Colonnades, arches, fountains, and patios add grace to the rather massive mission style structures. On the southern side of the inner quadrangle you'll find the imposing **Memorial Chapel** with elaborate mosaics of Venetian origin and some notable stained glass. **Hoover Tower,** named for President Herbert Hoover who graduated with Stanford's first class in 1895, provides a good view over the campus.

Important works by Rodin highlight the **University Museum of Art's** collections. It also contains an important assemblage of Oriental art as well as American Indian antiquities. Open 10 am to 5 pm Tuesday to Friday; 1 to 5 pm Saturday and Sunday; admission free. Tel 497-4177 for information on guided tours.

The **Library** contains the Hoover War Library, the gift of Herbert Hoover, the most important and valuable collection of WW I documents and publications outside France.

Mountain View

A further five miles south is Mountain View, home of one of NASA's leading research centres. **Ames Research Center** at Moffett Field is open to the public, but advance reservations are necessary as tours are primarily for groups – they try to accommodate individuals, however, so call the Tour Office at 965-6497. Open Monday to Friday 8 am to 4.30 pm; closed Federal holidays; admission free.

San Jose

Rivalling Los Angeles in speed of urban sprawl, San Jose is an historic place. It was the first pueblo to be established in Alta California, founded in 1777 three miles south of the Mission of Santa Clara. For a brief period in 1849 San Jose was the capital of California – on the east side of City Hall Square there's a tablet marking the site of the state capitol which first did duty as an hotel. Modern San Jose, however, barely has time to look back as it hurtles into the future as a center for space age industries. But for people who like the esoteric, two attractions are worth a diversion from the freeway.

The **Rosicrucian Park** and headquarters of the Ancient and Mystical Order of the Rosy Cross for the Western Hemisphere stand at 1342 Naglee Avenue, catching the attention immediately with the Egyptian manner of its architecture. Within the grounds are the Oriental Museum, displaying a good collection of Middle Eastern antiquities, and a replica of an Egyptian temple hung with tapestries said to be from temples in Cairo and Luxor. Artificial moonlight enhances the mystique. It's open daily but hours vary. Call (408) 287-9171 for times.

On the western edge of the city, on Highway 280 at Winchester Boulevard, is the 160-room **Winchester House**, which has been described as 'the externalization of a psycopathic mind'. It is the creation of Sarah Winchester, heiress to the rifle millions, who built as though her life depended on it. In fact, she believed it did, for a seer had convinced the unhappy woman that she would live as long as the house was under construction. So room after room and stair after stair were added throughout her long life, using costly materials and employing occult principles. Gutted of furniture and allowed to fall into partial ruin on her death in 1922, the huge Victorian Gothic mansion is now being carefully restored and refurnished. A museum of 19th century antiquities and Winchester firearms and a gift shop-restaurant complex add to the diversions. Open daily from 10 am to 4 pm; admission $6.50; tel (408) 247-200.

Theme Parks

There are two well-known amusement parks in the Peninsula area. Closest to San Francisco is **Marine World/Africa USA**, off US 101 on Marine World Parkway, Redwood City. Allow six hours to tour the lavish 65-acre complex featuring exotic wildlife, killer whales and dolphins. Open 9.30 am to 6.30 pm daily, Memorial Day-Labor Day; check hours during remainder of the year; admission $9.95; tel (415) 365-7446 for taped information.

Off US 101 on Great America Parkway near Santa Clara is **Marriott's Great America**, a family entertainment center with five theaters, thrill rides and recreations of historic American areas. Also featured: a new Skytower and the giant-screen movie, *To Fly*. It's open daily, 10 am to 10 pm, Memorial Day to Labor Day; check admission hours during fall and spring seasons. Closed late November through March; admission $13.95; tel (408) 988-1800 for taped information.

Useful Addresses

San Francisco Convention and Visitors Bureau (Hallidie Plaza, Powell and Market Sts (BART station level); tel (415) 626-5500); 24-hour recorded events 391-2000.

Free maps, brochures and descriptive pamphlets. Open Monday to Friday, 9 am to 5 pm; Saturday 9 am to 3 pm; closed Sunday.

Redwood Empire Association (360 Post St, Suite 201 (Qantas Building); tel (415) 421-6554). Covers Northern California coastal counties from San Francisco to the Oregon border. Free maps and brochures. Open Monday to Friday, 9 am to 5 pm.

California State Automobile Association (150 Van Ness Avenue; tel (415) 565-2012). Services to members only; Monday to Friday, 8.30 am to 5 pm.

Miscellaneous

Foreign Currency Exchange (see also San Francisco International Airport).

AFEX (Associated Foreign Exchange), 251 Montgomery St; tel (415) 781-7683. Open weekdays, 8.30 am to 6 pm.

Deak Perera of California Inc 100 Grant Avenue; tel (415) 362-3452. Open Monday to Friday, 9 am to 5 pm. Saturday 10 am to 2 pm.

Meeting the Americans

International Visitor Center (312 Sutter St, 4th floor, tel (415) 986-1388). Member of COSERV. They will arrange coffee-and-conversation visits in members' homes, and also provide Bay Area maps and descriptive brochures. A week's advance notice for home visits is appreciated.

Sierra Club (530 Bush St; tel (415) 981-8634). Headquarters of the nationwide conservation association. Bookstore and Information Center dispenses authoritative know-how on backpacking and other outdoor adventure activities in the West. Visitors welcomed on local outings – ask for the Bay Area Chapter activities schedule ($1.25). They're open Monday to Friday, 10 am to 5.30 pm.

Wine Country

California's classic wine regions lie about an hour's drive north of San Francisco, enfolded by steep ridges of the Coast Range. Sonoma and Napa Counties produce their aristocratic vintages in broad valleys that enjoy a dry, sunny climate tempered by moist breezes from the Pacific. Frosts and summer rains, bane of the vintner, are rare. The rich soil, well watered by a number of small rivers, is perfectly suited to the cultivation of *Vitis vinifera* grapes from Europe's celebrated wine districts: today more than 125 varieties thrive in the valleys, with new varieties constantly being developed.

History

The first grapes to be planted were the 'Mission' grapes introduced by Franciscan missionaries at Mission San Diego in 1768 to provide sacramental wines. After secularization of the missions in 1834, General Mariano Guadaloupe Vallejo, Commandante General of the Mexican forces, obtained the vineyards of Sonoma's Mission San Francisco Solano and successfully produced wine on a commercial scale. It was not until 1856, when Vallejo invited Count Agoston Haraszthy to taste a wine of which he was rather proud, that European stocks were first introduced to the area.

Haraszthy is an extraordinary figure in the history of California winemaking. Born of a Hungarian aristocratic family which had, for generations, engaged in the production of Tokay wine, he fled to America in 1840 under sentence of death for rebelling against the Hapsburgs. According to legend, he brought the beginnings of the California wine industry with him in a black satchel – cuttings from the family vineyards. Haraszthy tried unsuccessfully in Wisconsin, San Diego and Crystal Springs, near San Francisco, to cultivate his stocks; in Sonoma he found the proper soil and climate. He purchased several hundred acres from Vallejo and named his new vineyard Buena Vista as a gesture to his friend. The first wines, bottled in 1857, changed the history of California winemaking.

Haraszthy's successes, industry and talent for promotion attracted French, German and Italian winemakers to the area. His winery became the center of distribution of viticultural knowledge and a nursery of foreign vines for the whole state. At his own expense he journeyed through Europe in 1861, bringing home cuttings of every attainable variety, including the unique zinfandel, a variety whose origin remains uncertain to this day. Haraszthy died mysteriously in Central America in 1869, his reputation secure as the father of the California wine industry.

The worldwide blight of phylloxera in the 1880s and the Prohibition years both hampered the growth of California wines, but since the 1940s a renaissance in techniques and interest has placed California wines on tables all around the world.

Getting Around

There are many escorted tours of the Wine Country from San Francisco, but exploring by car is probably best as it reveals the full charm of the countryside. A network of backroads patterns both the Sonoma and Napa valleys, threading between the vineyards and crossing the mountains in several loop trips, any of which may be easily accomplished in an afternoon.

The most attractive route from San Francisco is via US 101 over the Golden Gate Bridge to SR 37, near Ignacio. That road takes you east across the water-meadows of the Petaluma River to Sears Point and the junction with SR 121 which runs north toward Sonoma. Seven miles along SR 121, turn left on SR 12 that leads directly into Sonoma's plaza, and joins US 101 at the northern limits of the Valley of the Moon.

SR 121 continues to Napa to join SR 29, the classic winetaster's route traversing the length of the Napa Valley. Some 60 wineries line the route, several of which open their tasting rooms daily. The Silverado Trail, paralleling SR 29 east of Napa, is the old stagecoach highway made famous by Robert Louis Stevenson in The Silverado Squatters. It is lightly traveled, with fine views across the Mayacamas between Oakville and Glen Ellen. You can also cross the ranges at St Helena and Calistoga at the northernmost end of the Napa Valley. These are 'slow' roads but the reward is superb views across the vineyards.

Wine Country tasting rooms and aging cellars welcome visitors year-round, but the harvest does not usually begin until late August. To be sure of seeing the production of wine from the gathering of grapes to the first crush, plan your visit for September or October. Harvesting may continue until early November when the highest vineyards yield their grapes. Avoid the tasting rooms on summer weekends when facilities are taxed to their limits by the press of visitors. And before setting out, scan the entertainment section of the paper: many wineries present open-air concerts of jazz, opera and chamber music throughout the summer.

SONOMA

Sonoma developed as a garrison town on Mexico's northernmost frontier. Father Jose Altimira had established the last of the Franciscan missions in the fertile valley on July 4, 1823; 10 years later, the threat of Russian cannon at Fort Ross 45 miles to the northwest seemed sound

reason to the Mexican authorities to establish a pueblo there and troops were sent up from the Presidio of San Francisco under the command of General Mariano Guadaloupe Vallejo, who was to play a leading role in the transition of California from Mexican to American rule.

Vallejo laid out much of the heart of the town and presided over its most exciting era. In 1841 the Russians withdrew from Fort Ross, but within a few years Vallejo found himself faced with a more formidable threat from Americans who had settled in the Napa and Sacramento valleys. Inspired by the example of the Texans, they decided to throw off Mexican rule and on the morning of June 14, 1846, a small army of 33 American settlers rode into Sonoma, captured Vallejo and declared the independent Republic of California. Above the plaza they raised the famous Bear Flag that flutters from the mastheads as the state symbol today. Outbreak of hostilities between Mexico and the United States terminated their independence movement – within a month Commodore John D Sloat of the USS Portsmouth had taken Monterey and San Francisco for the American government. A monument in the corner of the plaza near the mission marks the spot where the Bear Flag was first hoisted.

Many of the buildings surrounding the Plaza constitute a state historic park. At the north-east corner of the square, on Spain St are the **Sonoma Barracks,** put up in 1837 to house the Mexican garrison and later occupied by American forces until 1852. Recently gutted by fire, they are presently being restored.

First St separates the barracks from **Mission San Francisco Solano,** founded without benefit of proper church authority by Father Jose Altimira in 1823. The mission suffered greatly from neglect and decay after Secularization, but the church and padres' quarters have been restored. The adobe church has some

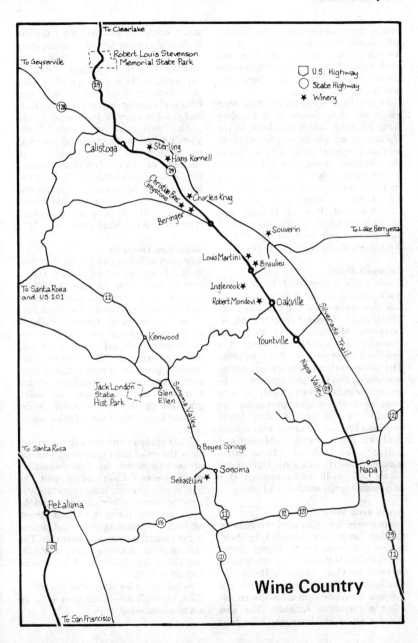

To Clearlake

Robert Louis Stevenson
Memorial State Park

To Geyserville

29

128

Calistoga

★ Sterling
★ Hans Kornell

29

Christian Bros.
Greystone

★ Charles Krug

Beringer

★ Souverin

To Lake Berryessa

Louis Martini ★

★ Beaulieu

To Santa Rosa
and US 101

12

Inglenook ★

Robert Mondavi ★

Oakville

Silverado Trail

Kenwood

Yountville

Napa Valley

29

Jack London
State
Hist Park

Glen
Ellen

Sonoma Valley

121

To Santa Rosa

Boyes Springs

Sonoma

Napa

Sebastiani ★

12

121

Petaluma

116

12

121

101

121

12

29

12

To San Francisco

☐ U.S. Highway

◯ State Highway

★ Winery

Wine Country

notable frescoes painted by the Mission Indians and the little museum recreates the life of the inmates authoritatively. Each September the old buildings are the setting of a brilliant pageant during the two-day **Vintage Festival**.

Across the street is the old **Blue Wing Inn**, a two-storey adobe with a gallery along its front, which was built in the 1840s. Among the famous who stayed here were General Grant, Kit Carson and the notorious bandit, Joaquin Murieta. Several other early adobe buildings front the plaza, some of them encased in wood but retaining the characteristic Spanish-style balconies. Particularly handsome are the **Swiss Inn** at 18 West Spain St and **Salvador Vallejo's home** at 415-417 St West, both dating from the 1840s.

Lachryma Montis

About a mile northwest of the plaza (the route is plainly signed) at the end of a long lane running toward the foothills from Third St, is General Vallejo's house, **Lachryma Montis**. Vallejo built this charming Carpenter Gothic place in 1851 and lived there until his death in 1890. The museum contains many interesting memorabilia and old photographs. In the grounds stands a Swiss chalet, formerly used as a stable and storehouse, an example of the prefabricated frame buildings brought by sailing ship around the Horn. Together with the Mission and Barracks, the Lachryma Montis forms Sonoma State Historic Park. Open daily, 10 am to 5 pm (6 pm in summer). One admission charge admits to all units.

Buena Vista Winery

Grapes were first planted in Sonoma on mission lands now occupied by Sebastiani Vineyards, but the oldest winery in the Valley is **Buena Vista**, established in 1857 by Count Agoston Haraszthy, who found the foothills a mile or so east of Sonoma perfectly suited for the cultivation of premium varietals. The two massive stone buildings which he con-structed still stand on the flank of the hill; their cool storage tunnels running deep into the limestone clearly display the pickaxe strokes of Chinese laborers. Arrows point the way along a self-guided tour between huge aging casks and displays relating winemaking methods and the life story of the Count. In the tasting room you can sample Buena Vista's range: an unusual (and pleasing) red is *Lachryma Montis*, blended from zinfandel every five or six years. Shaded public picnic tables stand in the lee of the ivy-shrouded buildings, overlooking the fountain courtyard. At 18000 Old Winery Rd; tel (707) 938-8504 it's open daily, 9.30 am to 5 pm retail sales.

Sebastiani Vineyards

The story of Sebastiani Vineyards begins in the Piedmont region of Italy over a century ago when Samuele Sebastiani learned the art of winemaking from his father. After some years in San Francisco, Samuele purchased General Vallejo's former vineyard on the northeastern edge of Sonoma and set about producing zinfandel wine in 1904. Today, Sebastiani's produces a wide range of reds, whites and roses as well as sherry, vermouth and champagne. Samuele's grandson was the first California vintner to make Beaujolais in the French *nouveau* style.

Daily guided tours through the winery show the small hand crusher and basket press with which the first Sebastiani made wine, as well as a modern plant. The high point of the tour is the opportunity to view the largest collection of carved casks in the country, the work of Earle Brown who came to Sonoma to retire and instead found himself reviving an ancient art. The tasting room displays family portraits and the winery deed signed by General Vallejo in 1865.

Sebastiani Vineyards, 398 Fourth St East; tel (707) 938-5532; open daily, 10 am to 5 pm; retail sales.

Places to Stay

Sonoma Hotel (110 W Spain St, Sonoma 95476; tel (707) 996-2996). For connoisseurs of the singular inn, a century-old hostelry furnished with European and California antiques. Only 17 rooms here – reservations recommended. Rates from $35 double.

Places to Eat

Au Relais Outdoor dining on the brick patio, Art Nouveau decor throughout the interior in this outstanding French restaurant. Extensive wine list features European and local vintages. (M/E)

Lunch, dinner. Wednesday to Monday. Closed Tuesdays. 691 Broadway; tel (707) 996-1031.

Capri Excellent fare in this small, tastefully furnished restaurant overlooking the Plaza. Lavish Sunday brunches. (M)

Lunch, dinner. Open daily. 101 East Napa St (corner of Plaza); tel (707) 996-3866.

Depot 1870 Hotel This former home of General Vallejo is an important stop for Bay Area gastronomes – reservations recommended. (M/E)

Lunch, dinner. Open daily. 241 First St West; tel (707) 938-2980.

Gino's of Sonoma Relaxed, friendly place on the Plaza offering a wide selection of sandwiches, salads and steaks. (B)

Open daily, 11 am to 1 am. 420 First St East; tel (707) 996-0319.

Sonoma Cheese Factory Deli, wine store and sandwich spot on the north side of the Plaza where you can watch cheese being hand made by traditional methods. (B)

Open daily 2 Spain St; tel (707) 938-5225.

VALLEY OF THE MOON

The road to Glen Ellen, site of Jack London's Beauty Ranch, runs north of Sonoma through Boyes Hot Springs, Fetters Hot Springs and Agua Caliente, resorts which in their 19th century heyday attracted the San Francisco fancy to sip the bitter mineral waters and restore their equanimity gazing out on the splendid line of the Sonoma Mountains to the west. The towns are still popular recreation centers in summer and winter alike. One of the oldest resort hotels in the area is the **Sonoma Mission Inn** in Boyes Hot Springs, surrounded by tree-shaded lawns. It has a world class spa and three restaurants among its amenities.

Glen Ellen stands on the banks of Sonoma Creek, below Sonoma Mountain. There's a shopping-gallery-restaurant complex, housed in General Vallejo's old grist mill, a couple of good restaurants, and some pleasant Victorians on the edge of town. Local dogs flout tradition with cheerful bandanas in lieu of collars and happily lead the way to antique stores filled with promising bric-a-brac. A pleasant place to while away some time before visiting nearby **Jack London State Historic Park.**

The park is a fraction of London's 1500-acre Beauty Ranch which he acquired not simply as an idyllic retreat but as a proving ground for his agricultural theories. 'Everything I buy is for the years to come', he wrote, and **Wolf House,** overlooking the Valley of the Moon, was to be the climax of his dreams. The magnificent structure was almost completed on August 8, 1913, when the Londons were aroused at 2 am with the news that the house was ablaze; in a few hours it was gutted. London died three years later. His ashes lie on the hillside near the ruins of Wolf House, under a boulder of red lava.

The **House of Happy Walls** was Charmian London's home thereafter, until her death in 1955. Under the terms of her will, it is used as a museum housing many of her famous husband's personal effects. It's open daily from 10 am to 5 pm (6 pm daylight time at weekends); closed Thanksgiving, Christmas and New Year's Day. Admission charge. Tel (707) 938-5216.

A Place to Stay
London Lodge (13740 Arnold Drive, Glen Ellen 95442; tel (707) 996-6306). Overlooking Sonoma Creek at the foothill entrance to Jack London State Park, this comfortable hostelry boasts a popular restaurant offering American and Continental dishes. They have a swimming pool, too. Rates from $37.

Places to Eat
Glen Ellen Inn Omlets are the house specialty of this attractive little place where the dinner menu varies daily. (B/M)

Lunch, Wednesday to Sunday. Dinner, Thursday to Saturday. 13670 Arnold Drive; tel (707) 938-3478.

NAPA
Napa stands at the southern entrance to the most famous wine district in the United States. This thriving business center can trace its history back to the 1840s when Harrison Pierce, a member of the Bear Flag Party, surveyed the original town site and the burgeoning community soon carried on a considerable water-borne trade with San Francisco. Some handsome Victorian buildings have survived Napa's explosive growth over the past decade, and Tulocay Cemetery on the east side of the Napa River contains the tomb of San Francisco's notorious voodoo queen, Mammy Pleasant. Well endowed with restaurants and motels, the town is a pleasant center for exploring the 60 wineries that lie ahead.

The Christian Brothers Winery
The Christian Brothers, a lay brotherhood of the Roman Catholic Church dedicated to the education of the young, began making wine in California toward the end of the last century as a means of supporting their schools. In 1930 they moved their operations from Martinez to Mont La Salle near Napa and 20 years later purchased the Greystone Cellars just north of St Helena as additional aging cellars. Today their operations are the largest in the Napa Valley. All the crushing, fermenting and bottling are carried out at a new plant south of St Helena, which is not open to visitors, but you can tour and taste at both the Mont La Salle and Greystone wineries.

Mont La Salle, some eight miles northwest of Napa, is headquarters of their genial empire. The Mission-style novitiate and old stone winery built by a German wine-maker in 1903 stands on the slopes of the Mayacamas Hills overlooking 200 acres of vines. Spacious gardens enhance the charm of the setting. On Redwood Rd (off Highway 29); tel (707) 226-5566, it's open daily, 10.30 am to 4 pm; retail sales.

Places to Stay
Downtown Motel (2nd and Coombs Sts, Napa 94558; tel (707) 226-1871). Located mid-way between the Valley's two main highways, in the heart of the business district. Swimming pool. Reservations recommended. Rates from $32 double.

Motel Six (3380 Solano Avenue, Napa 94558; tel (707) 226-1811). Member of the famous budget chain. Air-conditioning and swimming pool privileges. No credit cards. Rates are $19.95 double.

Silverado Country Club (1600 Atlas Peak, Napa 94558; tel (707) 255-2970). Luxurious 1200-acre resort in the eastern foothills. Nucleus is an 1870 mansion built by General John Miller. Apartments here are privately owned but rented out by management for their owners. Air-conditioning, color TV, bar, fireplace and kitchen in each unit. Five swimming pools, two Robert Trent Jones golf course, eight tennis courts. Grill room. Reservations recommended. Rates from $127 to $154 (one bedroom unit) to $270 (two bedroom unit).

YOUNTVILLE
Yountville is named after the first

American settler in the Napa Valley. George Yount had roved the continent as a trapper, soldier and frontiersman before arriving in Sonoma in 1833. There he struck up a lifelong friendship with General Vallejo who granted Yount 11,814 acres of land in the upper Napa Valley. American settlers of the 1840s found the master of Rancho Caymus a generous source of help and by 1855 a small village had grown up on the southern tip of his lands. When Yount died in 1879, the settlers changed its name from Sebastopol to Yountville in his honour.

The massive red brick walls of Yountville's **Vintage 1870** rise east of the highway just beyond the Yountville exit. Gottlieb Groezinger's former winery has been transformed into an attractive complex of restaurants, delicatessens and specialty shops. Throughout the summer a local repertory company plays the small theater and nearby you'll find a hot air balloon launching pad – champagne aloft adds to the exhilaration of the views. (See also San Francisco tours section.)

Places to Stay
Burgundy House (6711 Washington St, Yountville 94599; tel (707) 944-2855). Century-old inn with friendly staff, antique furnishings and views of the hills and vineyards. Limited number of rooms, so make reservations well ahead. Rates from $78 double.
Magnolia Hotel (6529 Yount St, Yountville 94599; tel (707) 944-2056). Only seven bedrooms in this 1873 gem which once did service as a bordello. All have antique furnishings, air-conditioning and private bathrooms. Swimming pool. The hotel restaurant is an award winner. Prixfixe menu with a single entree, changed nightly. Ask the patron about his unusually comprehensive selection of wines, which includes local rarities. Reservations necessary for this small dining room. Rates from $75-145 double.
Napa Valley Lodge (Highway 29, Yountville 94599; tel (707) 944-2468). Mission-style motel, all rooms with a view. Soundproofed, color TV, air-conditioning. Reservations recommended. Rates from $74 double.

Places to Eat
The Diner Traditional counter-style cuisine featuring the noble hamburger, french fries and milkshakes. For the takeaway trade there's a delicatessen counter. (B)
Open daily except Mondays from 7 am. 6476 Washington St; tel (707) 944-2626.
Domaine Chandon The French champagne people, seeking a showcase for their California wines, opened this beautiful restaurant with an outdoor terrace. The cuisine of Champagne is presented by a disciple of Paul Bocuse. Reservations necessary. (E)
Lunch, dinner, Wednesday to Sunday. California Drive; tel (707) 944-2467.
The French Laundry Friendly, elegant, family-owned and operated restaurant in a turn-of-the-century laundry. French country cooking with but a single entree nightly, so phone ahead. (E)
Dinner, Wednesday to Saturday. 6640 Washington St; tel (707) 944-2380.
Magnolia Hotel Restaurant – see Magnolia Hotel.
Mama Nina's Cocktails on the terrace in summer, hearty Italian cooking in the restaurant. They make their own pasta. Casual, very popular. Reservations recommended. (M/E)
Dinner, Thursday to Tuesday. 6772 Washington St; tel (707) 944-2112.

OAKVILLE
Oakville is the home of the **Robert Mondavi Winery**, founded in 1966 by Robert Mondavi, scion of a celebrated family of wine makers. The Mission-style buildings, set back from SR 29 among the vineyards, were designed by Cliff May and house an ultra-modern plant that produces more than a million gallons of

wine annually. Small groups and a friendly informality characterize the tours here, and each Sunday in summer the winery plays host to the greatest names in jazz in a concert series of the lawns. In winter, a classic film festival (with wine tasting at intermission time) is held in the Vineyard Room. Located at 7801 St Helena Highway, Oakville; tel (707) 963-9611; it's open daily, 10 am to 5 pm. Retail sales.

RUTHERFORD

Just before you reach the small town of Rutherford, a sign points out **Inglenook Vineyards** at the end of a private road to the left of the highway. Here in 1879 Gustave Niebaum of Helsinki, retired sea captain and fur trader, turned his large fortune and enterprising talents to creating the finest winery in California. Within 10 years his wines had won awards for overall excellence at the Paris Exposition, and they continued to do so until his death in 1908. Highlight of the winery tour is the Captain Neibaum tasting room, oak panelled and richly furnished in the baronial manner, where crystal stemware shimmers in the light let in by stained glass windows. These vineyards on Highway 29, Rutherford; tel (707) 963-7184 are open from 10 am to 4 pm daily. Gift shop and retail sales.

Beaulieu Vineyards date from 1900 when a young Frenchman, Georges de Latour, purchased a wheat farm at Rutherford and set about realizing his ambition of producing great wines. None but the finest varietals were planted and Latour journeyed regularly to France to obtain his cuttings. Beaulieu's French connection continued until 1969 when Georges' granddaughter, the Marquise de Pins, sold the historic winery.

The handsome new Visitors' Center at Rutherford Square is the starting point of a tour through BV's ivy-covered buildings, the oldest of which dates from 1885. In addition to the tasting room where you can sample the celebrated cabernets,

there's a theater where films on wine making are shown. Beaulieu Vineyard at 1960 Highway 29, Rutherford; tel (707) 963-2411 is open from 10 am to 3.15 pm daily; retail sales.

ST HELENA

St Helena manages to convey a Victorian village air that almost conceals its role as business center for a concentration of famous wineries in the upper valley. The first you'll come to is the **Louis Martini Winery** on the southern edge of the town, built by a former fisherman who got his start in the business selling his father's backyard vintages door-to-door in San Francisco's Italian quarter before the 1906 'quake. Martini survived Prohibition by manufacturing a grape concentrate; in the 1940s his fine table wines created something of a sensation throughout the industry. The full line is available for tasting. At 254 St Helena Highway, St Helena; tel (707) 963-2736 it's open daily from 10 am to 3.30 pm; retail sales.

The tasting room of **Beringer Winery** is in the ornate Rhine House, a replica of the Rhineland home in which Frederick and Joseph Beringer lived before emigrating to California in the middle of the 19th century. The brothers founded their enterprise in 1876, engaging Chinese laborers to dig the famous tunnels in the hillside where the wines are aged. Among the redwood tanks are many fine old casks decorated by German master carvers. At 2000 Main St, St Helena; tel (707) 963-7115. It's open daily, 9.30 am to 4.30 pm; gift shop, retail sales.

An avenue of elms leads to the Christian Brothers' **Greystone Cellars,** largest in the world when William Howard Bourn built them at a cost of $2 million in 1888. The massive stone walls are handcut sandstone, and you'll find huge white oak tanks in the aging cellars dating from that time. Among the early winemaking equipment on display is a selection of Cellarmaster Brother Timothy's renowned collection of corkscrews.

On the third floor, champagne is produced by the Charmat method. At 2555 Main St, St Helena; tel (707) 963-2719. These cellars are open daily, 10 am to 4 pm; gift shop and retail sales.

Perhaps the oldest winery in the Napa Valley is **Charles Krug**, set back from the highway amid a grove of oaks about a mile or so north of St Helena. The founder, Charles Krug, came to San Francisco from Prussia in 1852. There he met Count Agoston Haraszthy, and later General Vallejo, who influenced him to plant vines in Sonoma. In 1860 Krug moved to St Helena and opened the present winery, which is at 2800 Main St, St Helena; tel (707) 963-2761; retail sales.

St Helena is a most attractive spot to weekend in the wine country, with a number of good boutiques, restaurants and inns. Of interest to lovers of Robert Louis Stevenson's works is the **Silverado Museum** at 1490 Library Lane, housing several original manuscripts, autographed letters and family photos. It's open Tuesday to Sunday, noon to 4 pm; closed holidays; tel (707) 963-3757.

On Lodi Lane, you can drop into **The Barrel Builders** workshop where coopers assemble casks for California vintners and hedonistic 'hot-tubbers'.

Bale Grist Mill State Historic Park

About three miles beyond St Helena is a romantic old wooden structure with a 40-foot waterwheel. The **Bale Grist Mill** was built in 1846 by Edward Bale, an English physician who had jumped ship in Monterey in 1837 and found employment as surgeon-in-chief to the Mexican forces. Bale married a niece of Captain Salvatore Vallejo in 1839 and was granted nearly 9000 acres of land in the northern Napa Valley. Because of the increased amounts of grain produced by settlers in the valley, Bale replaced the small mill he had built in 1842 with the present structure, which was restored in 1967. There are picnic tables under trees and it is open daily.

Places to Stay

El Bonita Motel (195 Main St, St Helena 94574; tel (707) 963-5216). Located on SR 29, just south of town. Comfortable, with air-conditioning, TV and swimming pool. Six luxury garden rooms with optional kitchenette facilities. Reservations recommended. Rates from $28 double.

Places to Eat

Abbey Restaurant Situated in the Freemark Abbey Winery and very busy at lunchtime. Continental cuisine and a good wine list featuring Freemark wines. (M)

Lunch, dinner Wednesday to Sunday. 3020 St Helena Highway; tel (707) 963-2706.

La Belle Helene Informal elegance and French provincial cuisine in a handsome 19th century stone building. Superlative cooking. (E).

Lunch, dinner Wednesday to Saturday; 1345 Railroad Avenue; tel (707) 963-1234.

Miramonte Hotel Restaurant Renovated old hotel offers pleasing ambience; entertainment at weekends. (M)

Dinner Thursday to Monday. 1327 Railroad Avenue; tel (707) 963-3970.

CALISTOGA

Calistoga marks the end of the wine-taster's trail, its half dozen spas offering mud baths and hot springs to undo whatever damage pleasuring hath wrought. Sam Brannan, the flamboyant San Francisco millionaire, founded the town in 1860 with the intention of developing the West's most fashionable resort. He lost his fortune in the process. His home on Washington St still stands, refurnished as a cultural center for the town.

Lincoln Avenue Airpark is a magnet for gliding and skydiving enthusiasts; you can arrange a soaring trip above the Napa Valley by telephoning *Calistoga Soaring Center*, (707) 942-5592. Railroad buffs won't want to miss the **Calistoga Steam Railroad** on the Silvarado Trail. There's an authentic 19th century depot and locomotives built for the 1915 Panama-Pacific Exposition in San Francisco.

Just north of town are two natural phenomena which have been attracting visitors since the 1860s. The **Old Faithful Geyser** on Tubbs Lane erupts approximately every 40 minutes, thereby earning its name. Five miles or so to the west, on Petrified Forest Rd, are the fallen trees of **Petrified Forest**, opalized and silicified by the volcanic flow from Mt St Helena millions of years ago. Excavation has revealed a transmutation so perfect that the texture and fiber are completely preserved. Admission fees are charged for both attractions.

'Bubbly' is the specialty of **Hanns Kornell Champagne Cellars** three miles north of Calistoga. Kornell, who fled from his native Germany in 1939, has built a solid reputation among wine lovers, using the traditional *methode Champagnoise*. The light, dry Sehr Trocken should not be missed if it's offered in the tasting room. At 1090 Larkmead Lane, Calistoga; tel (707) 963-2334, the cellars are open daily, 10 am to 4 pm; gift shop, retail sales.

The brilliant white structure crowning a steep hill east of SR 29 owes its inspiration to chapels built in the Greek islands by mediaeval crusaders. **Sterling Vineyards** was founded in 1964 by the principals of a San Francisco paper company. You can park your car at the foot of the hill and take the aerial tram to the winery for a fee or walk up. Both routes have great views down the valley.

A self-guided tour through the buildings show not only the operations of this impressively modern winery, but the bells of St Dunstan's-in-the-East, London, which hang now in the bell towers. The winery is at 111 Dunaweal Lane, Calistoga; tel (707) 942-5151; open daily, 10.30 am to 4.30 pm; gift shop, retail sales.

Places to Stay

Calistoga Spa (1006 Washington St), Calistoga 94515; tel (707) 942-6269). Kitchenette facilities and free use of the outdoor mineral pools are included in the rates of this spa-cum-motel. Treatments available. Reservations recommended. Rates from $37 double.

Dr Wilkinson's Hot Springs (1507 Lincoln Avenue, Calistoga 94515; tel (707) 942-4102). Well equipped spa with rooms and kitchenette facilities available for daily and weekly stays. Air-conditioning, color TV. Swimming pool. Reservations recommended. Rates from $33 double.

Pachetau's Hot Springs (1712 Lincoln Avenue, Calistoga 94515; tel (707) 942-5589). Century-old palms line the approach to this venerable spa located on the site of Sam Brannan's original bathhouse. House-keeping cottages, Olympic-sized pool. Reservations recommended. Rates from $33 double.

Triple S Ranch (4600 Mountain Home Rd, Calistoga 94515; tel (707) 942-6730). Tree-shaded cabins available by day or week in the grounds of a stately ranch high in the mountains. Spotless interiors. Swimming pool. Country cooking in the converted barn restaurant (dinners only); full bar. Rates from $25 double.

Places to Eat

Cinnabar Restaurant This cosy little place specializes in omlets – create your own from the ingredients list. (B)

Open daily, 8 am to 10 pm, 1440 Lincoln Avenue; tel (707) 942-6989.

Palacio The Mexican vittles are worth waiting for - don't dilute your appetite for their generous servings. Informal atmosphere. (B)

Open daily, 11 am to 11 pm. 1400 Lincoln Avenue; tel (707) 942-5139.

Silverado Restaurant & Tavern Popular for its hearty fare and impressive wine list. On Wednesdays, the big draw is the inexpensive buffet. Reservations recommended. (M)

Open daily, 7 am to midnight, 1374 Lincoln Avenue; tel (707) 942-6725.

MOUNT ST HELENA

Beyond Calistoga, SR 29 twists northeastward through steep foothills to Mt St Helena, soaring above the Mayacamas range. Many romantic tales are told of this volcano which was thrice named Helena by explorers of three nations, none aware that others had found and christened the peak before them. It was here in 1880 that Robert Louis Stevenson and his bride Fannie Van der Grift Osbourne lived for two months in a deserted miner's cabin near the old Silverado Mine. Stevenson loved the great mountain, which he called the Mont Blanc of the Coast Range, and celebrated it in his delightful *The Silverado Squatters*. Vestiges of the mine remain but the cabin is long gone, its site marked by a granite monument near the entrance to the state park which bears his name.

LAKE COUNTY

North of Calistoga are the lakes and forested mountains of Lake County, a popular vacation area for Californians as far back as the time of the Pomo Indians who came to bathe in the hot springs in the shadow of their holy mountain, Konocti. Wild flowering trees color the back roads to historic little townships, farms and cattle ranches tucked within the ranges, but for modern vacationers, it's the lakes that really count.

Clear Lake This lake is used by powerboat enthusiasts, yachtsmen and waterskiers because of its expanses of open water, and it is the second home of Australia's traveling waterskiing team on their annual tour of the United States. The lake's 100-mile shoreline is studded with resorts, backed up by a plethora of motels and recreation facilities that include five golf courses, championship tennis courts, boat and canoe rentals, and tackle shops where you can get the latest word on local trout and bass fishing. There's hunting in the surrounding national forests, and rock hounds flock to the area in search of Lake County 'diamonds', semi-precious gems of volcanic origin, onyx, jasper and obsidian.

Dominating the western shore is **Mt Konocti**, the home of the Great Spirit. By Indian tradition, the mountain is the fallen body of water god Konocti who would not allow Kah-Bel, the forest god, to marry his daughter. The angry Konocti hurled a huge rock which shattered Kah-Bel's skull, the blood dyeing the slopes of Red Mountain. But as he died, Kah-Bel loosed an arrow into the heart of Konocti. The bereaved girl wept tears that formed Little Borax Lake, then threw herself into Soda Bay and drowned – rising bubbles still show where her body sank. Thereafter Kioto, the Great Spirit, chose Konocti for his home.

SR 29 skirts the base of the mountain, but at Kelseyville you can pick up a road leading to the summit. It's a short walk from the parking lot to a sublime view over the lake and mountains.

Lakeport is the chief town hereabouts, a busy nerve center for a region that bases its economy as much on fruit farming and grapes as on countless resorts and vacation spots. The Lake County Museum adjacent to the Courthouse is quite interesting with its displays on local history. The Chamber of Commerce and Visitors' Bureau at 875 Lakeport Boulevard and SR 29 will provide you with brochures on accommodation and an excellent map. Their phone number is (707) 263-5092.

Blue Lakes Some six miles west of Upper Lake on SR 20, Blue Lakes appeals to those who enjoy leisurely vacationing. Mountains rise abruptly from the water's edge, and the area is shaded by great stands of oak, bay and pepperwood trees. There are numerous resorts, the swimming is sublime, and trout fishing in the tributary streams is the major sport.

Lake Pillsbury The most rugged and remote countryside in Lake County surrounds Lake Pillsbury, constructed to supply electricity for the city of Ukiah in Northern California. It's 'big sky' country where you can swim, fish, hunt, and hike the trails of Mendocino National Forest, or ramble along the banks of the Eel River.

Pillsbury is popular and there are only three resorts, so be sure to check the accommodation situation in advance.

There are plenty of first-come first-served camp sites available in the National forest, however. The Upper Lake Ranger Station on Middle Creek Rd can advise you. Call (707) 275-2361 or write PO Box 96, Upper Lake 95485.

To get there, follow Middle Creek Rd north for 30 miles from Upper Lake. You must return the same way to Upper Lake and SR 20 unless you'd like to adventure over Forest Service roads to the village of Elk Creek and pick up SR 162, which joins I-5 at Willows.

Gold Country

I-80 is the fast road from San Francisco to the Gold Country, the Sierra Nevada and Lake Tahoe, cutting across the northern portion of the vast Central Valley that extends from the Cascades to the Tehachapis to follow the old immigrant trail over the Donner Pass into Nevada. The land is lowlying, fertile and watered by the great Sacramento and San Joaquin Rivers whose tributaries rise high in the peaks of the Sierra Nevada. A veritable cornucopia of agricultural crops is raised in the valley – rice, figs, walnuts, peaches, apricots, grapes, tomatoes, to name but a few – a cattle ranching plays an important role.

Summer temperatures often rise over 100°F at noon. Schedule your passage for early morning or late afternoon if you can. Breaking the journey at the highly popular Nut Tree; a complex with restaurants, cocktail bars and a gift shop, is an established bay area tradition. You can also refresh yourself at the Coffee Tree opposite, or the Black Oak a little farther on.

SACRAMENTO

Sacramento, the state capital, lies 85 miles east of San Francisco at the confluence of the American and Sacramento Rivers. It's an interesting place to pause or stop over for a night or two before heading for the hills, rich in history and old buildings dating from pioneer days. A building renaissance is changing the face of the downtown area and you'll find some attractive modern architecture along the K St Mall.

Sutter's Fort

Sutter's Fort, 1701 L St, is where the story of Sacramento began. Here, in 1839, the Swiss adventurer John August Sutter set about realizing his ambitious dream of a New Helvetia on 48,000 acres of land granted him by the Mexican government. Sutter's interests in the fur trade, agriculture, fisheries and the brandy distillery he established brought him considerable wealth. But the dream was never realised; paradoxically, the discovery of gold at his Coloma lumber mill in 1848 ruined him. He failed to acquire the mineral rights and unscrupulous land developers following the frenzied tide of gold seekers swindled him out of many of his holdings. Debts piled up and when Sutter died in Pennsylvania in 1880, he was penniless.

The fort has been restored to illustrate the self-sufficient lifestyle of Sutter's day. In the grounds is the **State Indian Museum** interpreting the culture of California's Indians. Their skill as artisans and artists is well displayed in exhibits covering every aspect of their lives. The museum is open daily from 10 am to 5 pm, except Thanksgiving, Christmas and New Year's days; admission charge also admits to Governor's Mansion the same day; tel (916) 445-4209.

Old Sacramento

The tent city that sprang up near Sutter's Fort was soon replaced by brick and masonry structures. **Old Sacramento's** congeries of restored buildings near the river vividly recreate the atmosphere of the days when as many as 428 sailing vessels a year docked at the Embarcadero, and Sacramento grew rich supplying the Argonauts with provisions. Strolling its gas-lit boardwalks you'll find a plethora of boutiques, restaurants and drinking establishments housed in the 19th century buildings. Particularly interesting are the **B J Hastings Building**, terminus of the Pony Express; the **Old Eagle Theater** (melodrama at weekends);

and the burgeoning **Railroad Museum**, sited on the first terminus of the Central Pacific Railroad.

The **State Capitol** stands at the center of a 40-acre park at 10th St and Capitol Mall. After six years of careful restoration, the grandeur of this ornate 1860s structure can be fully appreciated once again. You may walk through the building on your own (be sure to include the Senate Chamber, which may be viewed from the 3rd floor gallery) or take one of the free tours offered on the hour from 9 am to 4 pm daily. When the Legislature is in session you may watch the action from the public galleries.

Open daily, 9 am to 5 pm; closed major holidays; tel (916) 324-0333.

In the southwest corner of Capitol Park, the **Crocker Art Museum** displays European paintings and drawings acquired by Judge E B Crocker and his family in the middle of the last century and a good though small collection of works by prominent contemporary California artists. Built in the Italianate style between 1869 and 1873, the Crocker is the West's oldest public museum and considered a particularly good example of early American museum architecture. The former ballroom with its fluted columns, elaborate plasterwork and brilliant hues, alone is worth the nominal admission fee.

California's **Old Governor's Mansion** at 16th and H St is no longer occupied by the chief executive of the state – Governor Ronald Reagan and his family were the last to reside there. Built in 1877 for a prosperous Sacramento merchant, Albert Gallatin, in Victorian Gothic style it is both architecturally and historically interesting. It's open 10 am to 5 pm daily, by tour only; last tour 4.30 pm; admission fee also admits to Sutter's Fort on the same day; tel (916) 445-4209.

Tours
Delta Travel, 1540 West Capitol Avenue, operates riverboat cruises between Sacremento and San Francisco. For details, see San Francisco Tours; for information call (916) 327-3690.

Places to Stay
Sacramento's 8000-plus hotel and motel rooms range from the economical to the presidential suites with separate living rooms, wet bars, color TV and sunken whirlpool baths. Room rates are up to 50% lower than you'd expect to pay for similar accommodation in other cities.

Many big-name chains are represented. You'll find Americana, Best Western, Holiday Inn, Host International, Rodeway and Travelodge hostelries in convenient locations for touring state capital sights. Among them:

Mid-Range
Mansion Inn (700 16th St, Sacramento 95814; tel (916) 444-8000). Beautiful landscaped gardens, swimming pool and color TV in every room – plus an ideal location directly opposite the Old Governor's Mansion. Air-conditioned. Rates from $45 double.
Mansion View Lodge (711-16th St, Sacramento 95814; tel (916) 443-6631). Across from Governor's Mansion. Air-conditioning, color TV. Rates from $26 double.
Marina Inn River Hotel (West Capitol Avenue and 2nd St, Broderick 95605; tel (916) 371-7700.) Convenient location on banks of Sacramento River, opposite Old Sacramento. Air-conditioned, airport limousine service, restaurant, pool and TV. Rates from $39 double.
Downtown Travelodge (1111 H St, Sacramento 95814; tel (916) 444-8880). Three blocks from State Capitol, air-conditioned, color TV, airport limousine service. Rates from $33 double.

Places to Eat
Sacramento's dining possibilities don't match those of larger cities in ethnic variety but you can eat very well here these days. Plenty of choice in the

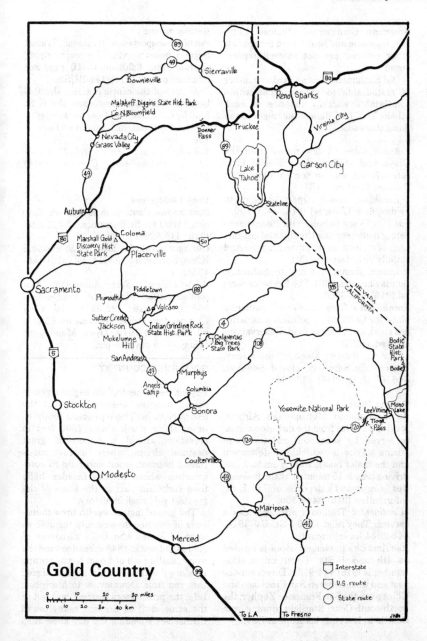

Gold Country

Scale: 0 10 20 30 miles / 0 10 20 30 40 km

Interstate

U.S. route

State route

American, Continental, Mexican, Chinese, Japanese and health food categories; other cuisines are not so well represented.

Old Sacramento has a sizeable number of restaurants to choose from within comfortable walking distance of each other. You can dance the night away down there too.

Cossack Cafe A few paces from the Greyhound station, this cheerful little cafe offers American home cooking with Russian overtones. (B)

Breakfast, lunch. Open Monday to Friday, 629 'L' St; tel (916) 442-7159.

Fat City Very popular Old Sacramento eating house serving Continental cuisine. Lots of stained glass, Tiffany lamps. And sinfully rich desserts. (M)

Lunch, dinner Monday to Saturday; Sunday brunch. 1001 The Embarcadero; tel (916) 466-6768.

Frank Fat's This renowned gathering place for California's political luminaries has steak and Chinese food. Reservations advised. (M/E).

Lunch, dinner Monday to Friday; dinner only Saturday; closed Sundays. 806 'L' St; tel (916) 442-7092.

Getting There

Air Sacramento Metropolitan Airport, located 12 miles from the downtown area, is served by scheduled airlines. Limousine service is available to downtown and the major hotels from 5 am to 1 am; driving time is 15 minutes to the freeway.
Bus *Greyhound's* depot is at 715 L St. Information (916) 444-6800.

Continental Trailways also provides a service. They're at 1129 I St. Call (916) 443-2044 for information.

Rail *Amtrak's* passenger depot is located at 4th and I Sts. Local information number is (916) 444-9131. Direct service east and west between San Francisco and Chicago on the San Francisco Zephyr; the north-south Coast Starlight running from Seattle to Los Angeles stops at Davis.

Getting Around

Public Transportation Regional Transit System buses serving the major sights operate from 6.30 am to 10 pm. For information call (916) 444-BUSS.

A turn-of-the-century tram shuttles between Old Sacramento and the K St Mall from 10.30 am to 4 pm weekdays; 10 am to 6.30 pm on Sundays. Fare is 15c.

Taxis *Greyhound Taxi Co* (tel (916) 443-3961); *Yellow Cab Co* (tel (916) 444-2222).

Useful Addresses

Sacramento Convention & Visitors Bureau, 1100 14th St, Sacramento 95814; tel (916) 449-5291.

Old Sacramento Visitors Center, 2nd and K Sts, Sacramento 95814; tel (916) 446-4314.

AAA-California State Automobile Association, 4333 Florin Rd, Sacramento 95823; tel (916) 422-6511, and 4745 Chippendale Drive, Sacramento 95841; rel (916) 331-7610. Open Monday to Friday, 8.30 am to 5 pm.

GOLD RUSH COUNTRY

Beyond Sacramento, I-80 begins a gentle ascent into the western slopes of the Sierra Nevada. These peaceful foothills, never rising much above 2500 feet in elevation, enfold a region of great pastoral charm, where narrow roads thread between wood and field to communities whose drowsy facades belie their turbulent past as the focus of the greatest gold rush in history.

The lure of instant wealth drew thousands of frenzied dreamers to the area as word of James Marshall's discovery of gold at Coloma in 1848 spread around the world, and a rash of boom towns sprang up along the Mother Lode, the belt of gold that ran from Downieville to Mariposa. Life, the prospectors learned, was not of the same stuff as dreams: many found themselves spending the day knee-deep in icy streams panning for elusive particles, or shovelling the dirt into cradles, or laying into the earth with picks. The labor was always backbreaking. At the end of the day, they could look forward to a narrow, flea-ridden straw mattress in a boarding house, if among the lucky ones. Prices were unbelievable: breakfast eggs cost not a penny less than $3 each.

Isolation, frustration and loneliness were constant companions. When they could, miners compensated extravagantly in the gaudy brothels, fandango halls and saloons that brightened the main streets of the richer camps: for $16 they could dance with a 'hurdy-gurdy' girl; $600 bought female companionship for a whole night. If there was anything left in their pockets after the bartenders had taken their 'pinch', gaming tables, bear baiting, horse racing and traveling variety shows offered infinite diversion.

But, with luck, they could make a fortune, and many did. The Argonauts kept coming for more than a decade. When the placer and surface gold were used up, they turned to hydraulicking and deep quartz mining, and thrived for another 30 years. Toward the end of the century the Gold Country began its evolution to an economy based on agriculture, ranching and lumbering. There's still gold in the hills and streams, but for the most part modern mining is for weekend adventuring.

Today, though less than half those mining camps remains, the Gold Country is rich in reminders of its youth. Many gold rush era buildings still stand and deserted mines are scattered throughout the foothills. Authentic ghost towns are rare, however, victims in their own time of the miners' need for lumber or of latter-day vandalism. the best of them is **Bodie**, now a state historic park in the desert, east of Yosemite.

The Golden Chain Highway, SR 49, follows the line of the Mother Lode, a distance of some 232 miles. You can obtain a sense of this historic region on a three-day side trip from San Francisco to some of the communities described below; to explore in any depth requires at least a week, and preferably two. We follow the traditional division of the Gold Country into the Northern and Southern Mines with I-180 as the boundary line.

AUBURN
Auburn, located at the intersection of I-80 and SR 49, marks the dividing point between the Northern and Southern mines. The dome of its handsome **County Court House** thrusts above a huddle of older buildings, promising rather more than can in fact be offered for Auburn has suffered many conflagrations. The Chamber of Commerce at 1101 High St offers its *Map & Guide to Historic Old Auburn* free of charge, leading you through the old center to some interesting survivors which include **Lawyers Row** on Commercial St and the **Joss House**, amid a group of old Chinese houses on Sacramento St. The **Placer County Historical Museum** in the Agricultural Fairgrounds is a good introduction to the history of the area; among its collections are gold mining tools, antique photographs and artefacts from early Chinese settlers. Open Monday to Friday 10 am to 4 pm; Saturday to Sunday 10 am to 5 pm; closed major holidays; admission free.

Nearby, off Pacific Avenue, is the **Auburn Dam Construction Overlook,** where you can watch the construction on the American River of the world's longest double-curvature, thin arch concrete dam.

COLOMA
SR 49 winds southward through grassy foothills patterned with stands of oak and pine to Coloma, on the South Fork of the American River. It all began here on the morning of January 24, 1848 when a young carpenter from Missouri looked up from the tailrace of John Sutter's sawmill and shouted, 'Boys, by God, I believe I

have found a gold mine!'

James Marshall hurried to Sutter with samples of the gold which, after careful testing, proved to be pure. Although the men agreed to keep the news secret, word soon leaked out and the rush to the Sierra foothills began. Coloma celebrates the anniversary every January with parades, mock shootouts and old-time melodrama.

The discovery site is part of the 220-acre **Marshall Gold Discovery State Historic Park**, which includes an excellent museum portraying the lives and times of Marshall and Sutter (movies on gold mining and the gold discovery are shown at weekends), Marshall's cabin and gravesite, a Chinese store, old mining machinery and a number of early buildings restored to their original appearance. The original sawmill was dismantled by miners needing lumber for their operations, but an exact replica stands near the river. Open daily, 10 am to 5 pm; closed major holidays; admission charge to museum; tel (916) 622-3470.

Opposite the old pioneer cemetery on the southern edge of town is **Vineyard House**, a handsome home of the 1880s which has been converted into an hotel-restaurant. Its romantic air is enhanced by tales of a haunted bedroom and the winery ruins in the gardens.

PLACERVILLE

Journey on to Hangtown, modern Placerville, which began as the tent city of Old Dry Diggin's in 1848 and became 'Hangtown' after a number of necktie parties at the huge white oak that stood on Main St until 1857. During the gold rush era this busy city prospered both as a placer mining camp and as a transportation center on the routes between the northern and southern mines and Sacramento and Carson City. It's still an important stop for travelers bound for South Lake Tahoe's resorts via US 50.

A number of pioneer buildings predating the disastrous 1856 fire remain in downtown Placerville, among them the **Placerville Hardware Store** on Main St which has been continuously in business since 1856. Farther along is the **Ness Building** at 524 Main, dating from 1852. A plaque at 549 Main marks the site of the store where 'Wheelbarrow' John Studebaker made miner's barrows in the 1850s. He returned to South Bend, Indiana with his savings to found the largest wagon factory in the country; in time it became the now defunct automobile manufacturer, the Studebaker Corporation. Wheelbarrow races are held at the annual El Dorado County Fair to commemorate him. Other Placerville purveyors who moved on to greater things were meat-packing king Phillip Armour and the railroad magnates, Collis P Huntington and Mark Hopkins, who both operated stores here during the gold rush. **Cedar Ravine** contains some notable Victorian Gothic houses.

Placerville's numerous antique stores offer pleasurable browsing. Popular refreshment stops are the old-fashioned soda fountain in the **John Pearson Soda Works** and the venerable **Raffles Hotel** on Main St.

You can walk down two shafts of the famous **Gold Bug Mine** in Beford Park, 1½ miles north of town. It's a little damp and cool – but authentic. Near the mine is a giant stamp mill which was used to crush the gold ore. Open daily 8.30 am to 4.30 pm; free.

Also of interest to the gold rush buffs are the displays in the **El Dorado County Historical Museum**, located in the fairgrounds west of the city center. You can see them from 10 am to 4 pm Wednesday to Saturday; 12.30 to 3.30 pm Sunday; donation.

The Hangtown Chamber of Commerce, 542 Main St, offers a free historical and recreational map describing walking and driving tours of the city. Annual events of interest are the **Golden Vineyard Spring Festival** held in May and the July **Wagon Train Days** celebration when horsedrawn wagons rumble into

town from Lake Tahoe, commemorating the pioneer trains which followed the Overland Trail across the Sierra Nevada.

To see Placerville and its environs from a differant point of view, ask *Sierra Western River Guides* about their one and two-day trips on the American River. Write to PO Box 7129, University Station, Provo, UT 84602 or call toll-free (800) 453-1482. *Chili Bar Whitewater Tours* have two to three-hour runs daily from Chili Bar, Placerville to Coloma between April 1 and October 1. Call (916) 622-6104, or write to them at 1669 Chili Bar Court, Placerville, CA 95667.

FIDDLETOWN

At Plymouth, 20 miles south of Placerville, you can turn east to Fiddletown, a small village tucked in a fold of the hills beside a rivulet. Nothing much goes on in Fiddletown; let's hope it never will. Sleepiness is the essence of its charm. At the western end of the tree-shaded main street is a rammed earth adobe constructed in the early 1850s that was once a Chinese herbalist's home and store. The **Chinese Museum** is only open on Sundays or by appointment (tel (209) 245-6225), but by pressing against the panes you can see the personal memorabilia of the last member of the largest

Chinese settlement outside San Francisco. Opposite is the Chinese gambling house dating from the same period. Farther down is the former blacksmith's forge, now an antique shop, and the **Schallhorne Blacksmith and Wagon Shop**, built around 1870.

Fiddletown's stock in trade appears to be the breeding of amiable kittens and puppies to grace front porches. In fact, it is the center of a prosperous dry farming area producing grapes, walnuts and pears, still farmed by the descendants of Missouri pioneers who came here in 1849.

The adventurous way back to SR 49 is over an isolated dirt road through ranch country of uncompromised loveliness; check the route locally and be prepared to ford a stream – don't try it in wet weather. The metalled road east from Fiddletown climbs over steep grades to **Daffodil Hill**, a prime tourist attraction from the end of March until the last week of April when the slopes are carpeted with golden blooms.

VOLCANO

A steep three-mile descent is the prelude to Volcano, nestling in a bowl of hills which was mistaken by settlers for a volcanic crater. But they had caught the spirit of the place, which enjoyed as lively a history as any of the roaring camps up and down the Mother Lode. Two theaters, three dozen saloons, 17 hotels, 20 restaurants, three breweries and fandango halls catered to a population of 8000 miners. For those with cultural aspirations, there was a literary and debating society, a public library and an astronomical observatory – all of them the first to appear on California's cultural scene.

Volcano was the center of a very rich placer and hydraulic mining area that produced some $90 million in gold between 1849 and 1865. There's still gold mining in the hills, but for the most part Volcano is rapt in the past – do not be surprised if you run into buckskinned Mountain Men or Civil War soldiers in full uniform performing the maneuvers of their forebears.

The vine-covered **St George Hotel**, a notable example of the gold rush architectural style, should not be missed. It was built in 1862. Other historic buildings are the **Masonic Hall** (1854), the **Old Jail House** (1872), the **Assay Office** (1871), and the **Union Hotel**, now a private residence, on Consolation Rd. Two old cemeteries laid out in the 1850s yield some fine epitaphs.

Places to Stay
St George Hotel (Box 275, Volcano 95689; tel (209) 296-4458). One of the most appealing of the Gold Country inns. Shared bathroom on each floor – modern annex has rooms with private baths. Dining room serves breakfast and dinners only. Every Monday/Tuesday rest of the year. Rates from $27 to $40 double.

Getting Away
Three scenic routes lead back to SR 49. We suggest taking either the road that follows the river between steep wooded hills to Sutter Creek, or the Volcano-Pine Grove Rd which passes Chaw-Se Indian Grinding Rocks State Historic Park to join SR 88 to Jackson at Pine Grove.

Chaw-Se Indian Grinding Rocks State Park preserves an unusual monument to prehistoric Indian life. Centuries before the gold rush, Miwoks of the western Sierra foregathered here each autumn to use the vast limestone outcropping as a communal grist mill. Its surface is pitted with 1158 holes which served as mortars for pulverizing acorns into meal. You'll also find more than 300 petroglyph designs. Modern Miwoks continue the tradition with dancing and games at a ceremonial 'Big Time' held annually on the fourth weekend in September.

Near the grinding rocks are replicas of bark teepees, an Indian football field and a round house used for meetings and religious rites. The new Indian Cultural Center within the park preserves the Miwok heritage. Open daily, year-round; facilities include campsites and a picnic area.

AMADOR CITY
A few miles south of Plymouth on SR 49 is Amador City, dominated by the rusty headframe of the Keystone Mine. A stroll along the wooden sidewalks leads past a wealth of antique stores housed in historic structures to the **Amador Hotel** (1856), a survivor of the 1878 fire which consumed much of the town. Two doors away is the **Fleehart Building,** dating from 1851. Formerly the Wells Fargo Agency, it now displays the collections of the Indian and Gold Rush Era Museum.

Just beyond the town, the **Mine House Inn** overlooks the highway from the hill to your right. The buildings formerly served as business offices for the Keystone Mine which operated for more than a century. The inn's attractive accommodation ranges in price from $40 to $50 double occupancy, and there's a swimming pool in the gardens.

SUTTER CREEK
Sutter Creek takes its name from the Swiss adventurer John Sutter who es-

tablished a lumber camp here in 1846. It got its start, the story goes, when early miners pitched a community tent for use on rainy days when they could not reach Drytown or Jackson. Today, it's a very solid little town, with a number of charming homes, antique stores and old buildings. Notable on Main St are the **Brinn Malatesta Store** (1860), the **Brignole Building** (1859), complete with iron doors and shutters, the **Masonic and I O O F Hall** (1865), and the **Methodist Church** (1862), an elegant example of the Greek Revival style. **Knight's Foundry** at 13 Eureka St welcomes visitors around noon each Friday to watch molten metal poured into casts much as it was done a century ago. It's the only water-powered foundry in the country, in continuous operation since 1873.

Downs Mansion on Spanish St was once owned by Leland Stanford who struck it Bonanza-rich at the Union Lincoln Mine just outside Sutter Creek. Stanford went on to become a railroad king, U S Senator, Governor of California, and founder of Stanford University. The mine also counted among its owners Hetty Green, 'Witch of Wall Street', the richest woman in the world.

Places to Stay

Sutter Creek has several hospitable inns in mellow settings. Among them:

Bellotti Inn (53 Main St, Sutter Creek 95695; tel (209) 267-5211). Original furnishings circa 1900 are part of the charm of this old hotel which opened its doors in 1858. Some rooms with private baths. Lunch and dinner served daily in the restaurant. Rates from $25 double.

Sutter Creek Inn (75 Main St, Sutter Creek 95695; tel (209) 267-5606). The former home of California Senator E C Voorhies has a New England air, a gentle ghost, and rooms furnished with antiques. All have private baths. No children. Serves breakfast only. Rates from $72 (weekends); $52 (weekdays) double.

JACKSON

Jackson is a bustling place with a number of important relics of gold rush days. Its prosperity depended in large measure on the **Argonaut** and **Kennedy** mines which worked the rich quartz deposits on the northern outskirts of the town from the early 1850s until 1942. Their shafts were among the deepest in the world, the Argonaut's reaching 6300 feet into the earth. Two of the giant wooden tailing wheels, built to lift waste from the Kennedy Mine, are still standing in the park on Jackson Gate Rd.

Nearby is **St Sava's Church,** a small gem of late Victorian architecture built in 1894. It is the mother church of Serbian Orthodox Christians in North America.

Jackson Gate Rd leads to the center of town, but turn left onto Oneida St leading into Church St for one of the most evocative museums in the Gold Country. The **Amador County Museum** is housed in the historic George Brown House built in 1859. Open from 11.30 am to 4 pm daily save Tuesday and Wednesday; donation; tel (916) 223-2884.

Among the more interesting buildings that line the busy streets of Old Town, Jackson's Center, is the **Independent Order of Oddfellows Hall** which was, in its day, the tallest three-story building in the country. A sidewalk plaque a few steps farther marks the site of the old **Hanging Tree**. The **National Hotel** is a Gold Country landmark, rivaling its Nevada City namesake as the oldest continuously operating hostelry in California. The National opened for business in 1863 on the site of the Louisiana Hotel; it has a century-old bar, and has been frequented by such diverse personalities as Presidents Hoover and Garfield and Black Bart. You'll find an antique store and a dining room in the cellar. They'll put you up for $22 a night, double, with a private bathroom, 2 Water St, Jackson 95642; tel (209) 223-0500.

Jackson offers a wide choice in both restaurants and places to stay. The

Amador County Chamber of Commerce is located at 80 S Highway 49 and 88, Jackson. Open from 9 am to 5 pm, or call (209) 223-0350.

MOKELUMNE HILL

Roughly eight miles south of Jackson is Mokelumne Hill, a popular weekend spot for San Franciscans who head for the tastefully renovated splendors of the old Hotel Leger, which was built in 1852. 'Mok Hill' has a great deal of charm, some good architecture, art galleries and a nice selection of romantic ruins that photograph well at sunset.

The town was not always a placid retreat. Mokelumne Hill got off to a violent start in 1848 with at least one murder a week for a 17-week stretch, and racial disputes – common enough in the Gold Country – provoked two 'foreign wars' within three years. In 1849 armed conflict broke out between the Americans and Chileans who, it was claimed, used illegal peon labor to work their claims. A full-blown war between Chile and the United States was narrowly averted. Two years later, the 'French War' broke out when French miners celebrating a rich strike raised the tricolor above their diggings. Excusing themselves on the grounds that 'the Frogs' were defying the US government, the Americans drove the French from the hill and seized their claims.

Places to Stay

Hotel Leger (Mokelumne Hill 95245; tel (209) 286-1401). Elegantly restored in the 1960s, this fine old hotel maintains a century-old tradition of luxurious comfort. The dining room offers continental cuisine. Rates from $26 with shared bath to $44 for parlor room with private bath (double occupancy).

ANGELS CAMP

Mark Twain assured Angels Camp of a place in American literary history with a hilarious yarn called *The Celebrated Jumping Frog of Calaveras County*, and every May contestants pour into this quiet little town to compete in the commemorative jumping frog jubilee. For $2 anyone can enter a frog (the required minimum length is four inches from nose tip to tail base). If your frog has aspirations, the prize money for breaking the world record jump of 20 feet 3 inches presently stands at $1200. There are imposing monuments to both Twain and the frog in the park. The historic **Angels Hotel**, where Twain is supposed to have been told the tale by a bartender, still stands.

Also of interest: **Angels Camp Museum** containing early artefacts and a mineral collection; the iron-shuttered **Peirano Building**; and **Utica Park**, site of the famous Utica mine.

At Altaville you can turn aside to visit the nearest grove of giant sequoias to San Francisco in Calaveras Big Trees State Park (there are three other stands of these huge trees in Yosemite National Park). The round trip along Murphys Grade Rd is approximately 40 miles.

Places to Stay

Gold Country Inn (Box 188, Angels Camp 95222; tel (209) 736-4611). Open all year. Air-conditioning, color TV. Rates from $30 double.

MURPHYS

Murphys is a picturesque little village some seven miles east of Altaville, with several stone gold rush era buildings worth browsing. The **Old Timers Museum** in the Traver Building is rich in memorabilia, but the main attraction is the **Murphys Hotel**, the hostelry Bret Harte wrote about in *A Night in Wingdem*, his novel of life in the mining camps in the 1850s. Real bullet holes in the doorway, and don't forget to take a look at the old guest register to see the signatures of General Ulysses S Grant, Horatio Alger and Mark Twain. Black Bart checked in as 'Charles Bolton, Silver Mountain'. Opposite is Murphys' one room jail.

Legend of Joaquin Murieta

Up and down the Gold Country you'll probably hear many references to Joaquin Murieta, the handsome young Mexican bandit of the 1850s who emerges from a tangle of myth and fact as a western Robin Hood. Historians debate the truth of his reality, but for old-timers, Murphys was the place where Yankees tied Joaquin to a tree, ravished his wife and murdered his brother. His oath of vengeance extended to all who mistreated his people as he roamed the state from Sonoma to Los Angeles tracking down his persecutors, and, like Robin, he robbed the rich to aid the poor. In 1853, according to the legend, Joaquin was shot to death in southern Mariposa County by a law agent named Harry Love who pickled the bandit's head in a bottle of alcohol as proof to claim the $5000 reward. On dark nights along the back roads you may hear the thunder of hooves and the moaning cry 'Where is my head? Where is my head?' as the decapitated shadow of Joaquin gallops by.

Places to Stay

Murphys Hotel (457 Main St, PO Box 329, Murphys 95247; tel (209) 728-3444). Modern and historic rooms; open year-round. Restaurant on premises. Rates from $35 double (weekdays), $40 weekends.

CALVERAS BIG TREES STATE PARK

The first giant sequois to be discovered by white Americans stand in two groves surrounded by pine forests 15 miles east of Murphys. The state park preserves about 100 of these awesome relics of the age of dinosaurs, some of which show traces of a fire that raced through the groves more than a thousand years ago. An easy one-mile trail meanders through the North Grove near the park entrance. If you have the time walk the extra miles to the larger South Grove which is more remote and primitive in feeling.

Open year round, the park offers two developed campgrounds and several picnic spots, and swimming and fishing in the North Fork of the Stanislaus River. Park rangers lead guided walks through the big trees in summer.

COLUMBIA

Now a State Historic Park, Columbia is steeped in carefully nurtured charm and contains a wealth of historic buildings beautifully refurbished with gold rush artefacts and furnishings. The town began as Hildreth's Diggings in 1850 when Dr Thaddeus Hildreth and a party of prospectors discovered rich placer deposits of gold near Kennebec Hill. Within a decade Columbia was the largest town in the Southern Mines, with a population of 10,000. As early as 1860, when the placer gold ran out, the town began to decline, but it was never completely deserted and retains much the same appearance as it had in its heyday.

Strolling tree-lined Main St, you can easily slip back into the mid-19th century, for park concessionaires preserve the flavor of the period with stage coach rides, a working blacksmith's shop, and emporiums where you can purchase such gold rush era delicacies as homemade sarsaparilla, elderberry vinegar, horehound drops and candy concocted from old family recipes.

For a glimpse of Victorian elegance, pop into the **City Hotel**, one of Columbia's largest buildings back in 1857. The hotel is operated now as a training center for students of the Columbia Junior College Hotel Management Course whose culinary prowess has earned it a coveted five-star rating – reservations for lunch and dinner are a must. The interior decor and furnishings reflect the opulent taste of the 1870s.

The **William Cavalier Museum's** collection of gold rush artefacts is housed in the building across the street which once served as Sewell Knapp's Miners Supply Store. Two doors up is the **Chinese Herb Store**, complete with a temple.

'Bellying up to the bar' is a fine old Gold Country tradition. You'll find the **St Charles Saloon** an inviting place to whet your whistle and reflect on the turbulence of gold rush life – the bar was the scene of a notorious murder in the 1860s.

A turn along Washington St brings you to one of Columbia's most impressive buildings. **Fallon House**, built after the 1857 fire, drew such famous entertainers as Edwin Booth, Lotta Crabtree and Lola Montez. Today the University of the Pacific brings the old theater back to life with a season of plays during June and July.

Other notable buildings around the town are **St Anne's Church** on Kennebec

Hill, probably the first brick church in California; the **Magendie Building's** Fandango Hall (melodramas staged every afternoon in summer); the **Wells Fargo Building**, boarding point for stage coach rides; and the old **Schoolhouse** at the northern end of town which was restored with funds raised by schoolchildren all over the state. In summer, the **Quartz Mine** on Italian Bar Rd is open to visitors.

Places to Stay
City Hotel (PO Box 1870, Columbia 95310; tel (209) 532-1479). Beautifully appointed small luxury hotel dating from 1857. Award-winning restaurant. Rates from $33 to $45 double double with continental breakfast.

SONORA
Turn down any of the narrow lanes hemmed in by steep-walled ravines and you'll find a number of old buildings belonging to Sonora's rowdy youth, when liquor ran freely in the saloons and bull-and-bear fights were popular entertainments. The town was originally settled by Mexican miners in 1848; the advent of race-conscious Americans made fights commonplace, but it was not until the introduction of the iniquitous $20-a-month tax on foreigners in 1850 that Sonora lost its Latin flavor. Today Sonora is an attractive, bustling little city that makes its living as an agricultural and lumbering center, recapturing its flamboyant past with the colorful Mother Lode Round Up every Mother's Day weekend and the Mother Lode Fair in July.

Gunn House, built in 1850, is the oldest structure still standing in the town. It has since been remodelled as a motor hotel. Other notable buildings include the **Higgins Home** on Washington St, which was constructed of lumber brought around the Horn in the 1850s, the **Oldfellows Hall**, and **St James Episcopal Church** (1860), possibly California's oldest Episcopal church, located at the northern end of Washington St.

Tuolumne County Museum once served as the town jail. Today – among others – it has a good collection of antique firearms – the Chamber of Commerce is also in the building – and it's open daily 9 am to 5 pm in summer; weekdays only rest of the year.

Nearby, on Piety Hill, is the site of the **Big Bonanza Mine**, reputedly the richest pocket mine ever discovered in Mother Lode; in one day $160,000 in gold was taken from the ground.

Places to Stay

The Gunn House Motor Hotel (286 So Washington, Sonora 95370; tel (209) 532-3421). Historic inn with antique furnishings. Pool and restaurant. Rates from $30 double.

Sonora Gold Lodge (480 W Stockton, Sonora 95370; tel (209) 532-3952). Tree-shaded motel with air-conditioning, color TV. Rates from $34 double.

MARIPOSA

Don't rush through Mariposa to Yosemite. This attractive small town has California's oldest courthouse, a fine church and a notable museum along with several other early Victorian buildings worth seeing. **Mariposa County Courthouse**, a two-story frame building put up in 1854, retains its original wooden pegs, square nails and old clock brought around Cape Horn; the second floor courtroom still has its original furnishings. It's open daily, Easter-Labor Day, 9 am to 5 pm weekdays; 9.30 am to 4.30 pm weekends, holidays. Open Monday to Friday rest of year. Tel (209) 966-2005. Beyond Sonora, SR 49 curves gently through the remaining Southern Mines past Jamestown, Chinese Camp and Coulterville to Mariposa which effectively marks the southern limits of the Gold Country.

If you are bound for Yosemite National Park, turn east at Mariposa onto SR 140;

the park entrance is at El Portal.

A pleasant loop trip back to San Francisco can be made by following SR 120 from Jamestown past Knights Ferry to pick up US 580 West.

YOSEMITE NATIONAL PARK

The Ice Age has left a legacy of rare beauty in the central ranges of the Sierra Nevada. When the first tourists entered 'the marvelous valley' in 1855, tears sprang unbidden to their eyes – 'it was sublimity materialised in granite', declared J M Hutchings, and 125 years later, though visited by more than two million sightseers annually, Yosemite National Park remains gloriously unsullied.

Yosemite Valley draws the greatest crowds. Here, between sheer granite walls that tower 4000 feet above the valley floor, is the park's greatest concentration of splendors – **El Capitan**, **Bridal Veil Falls**, **Yosemite Falls** (second highest in the world), and, dominating the upper valley, **Half Dome**, a magnificent granite loaf shorn in two by the force of moving ice over millennia. Here, too, is **Yosemite Village**, surrounded by campgrounds and hotels. The **Park Museum** houses natural history exhibits and relics of Yosemite's early days.

The best panoramic views of the Valley are from **Wawona Tunnel** just below Old Inspiration Point, and **Glacier Point**, up 3200 feet on the Valley's rim.

Wawona, amid the high meadows in the southwestern corner of the park, is the home of the Pioneer Yosemite History center which preserves a number of the park's oldest structures, moved here from other areas. Among them are a wagon shop, the Wells Fargo office, a jail and several old cabins. Nearby is the Wawona Hotel, constructed in 1885 and still open.

From Wawona the road runs southeast to **Mariposa Grove** with more than 200 of the tallest of all giant trees, *Sequoia Gigantea*. Possibly the oldest, certainly the best known tree in the grove is 'Old Grizzly', a 209-foot behemoth estimated to be more than 3000 years old.

The Tioga Rd (SR 120) running up from the Valley across the Sierra Nevada, provides access to the **High Country**, an untouched wilderness of crystalline lakes, streams and alpine meadows overshadowed by the peaks. From about mid-July, when the snows have cleared, to the fall, this is the domain of climbers, backpackers and anglers. Several hundred miles of trails radiate from **Tuolumne Meadows** into the remotest areas of the park and link with the 2400-mile Pacific Crest Trail from the Mexican to the Canadian border. There are several campgrounds in lovely settings close to the highway, and park concessionaires maintain five high country camps in the back country (see below). Even in midsummer nights are cold here: a warm parka and a sleeping bag with adequate range are wise investments.

Beyond Tuolumne Meadows the road negotiates the **Tioga Pass** (9941 feet), one of California's most spectacular drives. At times the highway seems merely notched in the granite canyon walls that drop away at awe-inspiring angles; your daring is rewarded with magnificent views of Mt Dana towering to the southeast, its dark red flanks rimed with snow, and Mono Lake glitters in the distance a mile below. Lake Tahoe, Bodie and Reno can all be reached quickly by US 395 at the bottom of the pass.

What's Available

Accommodation Year-round service at the *Ahwahnee Hotel, Yosemite Lodge* and *Curry Village* in Yosemite Valley; *cottages* and *Wawona Hotel* at Wawona (hotel closed in winter). High-altitude lodging at *Tuolumne Meadows* and *White Wolf Lodges* and five High Sierra trail camps which are open as seasonal weather permits (elevations from 7000 feet to 10,300 feet). For reservations, contact Yosemite Park & Curry Company,

Yosemite National Park, CA 95389; tel (209) 372-4671. Make them well in advance – six months is not too soon for summer.

Camping Three all-year and 16 seasonal campgrounds. Save for backcountry (permit required), restricted to designated campsites. Limits: seven days in Yosemite Valley and 14 days elsewhere in the park between 1 June and 15 September. Campground reservations may be made through Ticketron outlets.

Facilities Restaurants, cafeterias, stores, self-service laundry, filling stations in Yosemite Valley; food service, filling stations at Wawona.

Camping, cross-country and downhill skiing equipment rental. Ski instruction and chair lifts at Badger Pass. Ice skating equipment rental and instruction.

Activities Self-guiding nature trails; ranger-led hikes and evening special interest programs in summer. Horses and pack animals for hire in summer. Three to six-day High Country saddle trips (food and accommodation included); guide service. Downhill skiing, Nordic ski touring and outdoor ice skating.

Wildlife Plentiful, even in the valley which is haunted by mule, deer and black bears on the bum. Heed National Park Service advice and string up your food beyond the bears' reach; alas, the critters can climb too.

Getting There

Air Fresno has the nearest airport. Airground transportation tours from San Francisco and Los Angeles.

Bus *Greyhound* and *Continental Trailways* provide regular service to Merced, connecting with Yosemite Transportation System service to the park. Bus tours.

Train *Amtrak* service from Los Angeles and San Francisco to Merced, connecting with bus service to the park.

Information

For National Park Service maps, leaflets and wilderness permits, write to the Superintendent, Yosemite National Park, CA 95389 or Regional Headquarters in San Francisco.

BODIE

At the foot of the Sierra wall, the Tioga Rd joins US 395, which traverses a strangely beautiful region of volcanic tablelands and extinct volcanoes. The way to the notorious old ghost town of Bodie lies through Lee Vining, past Mono Lake, so alkaline that only a species of small brine shrimp can exist in it, and along a side road heading northeast across the desert.

Bodie's story began with the discovery of gold in the Mono region during the 1850s. Within a decade the town had earned such a reputation for lawlessness that a little girl whose family was moving there from nearby Aurora, concluded her prayers one night with a tearful 'Goodbye God, we're moving to Bodie'. Bodie reached the peak of its production in the late 1870s, but by 1885 all the mines except the Standard had closed down, and the town began its gentle deterioration into romantic ruin.

The California State Parks System maintains Bodie in a state of carefully arrested decay. Weathered boards, old paint, and sagging rooflines characterize the buildings which still stand, and it requires little effort to slip back into the days when Madame Moustache and Beautiful Doll reigned over the elegant bordellos of Virgin Alley and Maiden Lane.

Bodie is worth the most arduous effort to get there, particularly if you can arrive at dawn when a warm glow infuses the old timbers. The park has no visitor facilities – nearest accommodations are in Lee Vining some 15 miles away. Don't try a winter visit, for temperatures drop to 20 or 30° below and snow often piles so high that only rooftops are exposed.

SEQUOIA-KINGS CANYON NATIONAL PARK

Although these adjoining parks in the Sierra Nevada east of Fresno are as popular with visitors as Yosemite, they seem less affected by human use. No highway cuts through them, and at road's end, you are confronted by a pristine wilderness of peaks and canyons dominated by Mt Whitney, at 14,495 feet the second highest mountain in the United States.

The magnificent sequoia groves are the main attraction for those with little time to spare. To experience something of the largest surviving sequoia forest, follow the two-mile loop **Congress Trail** starting at Giant Forest Village park headquarters. It will take you to some of the more spectacular trees, including the President, the McKinley and the Chief *Sequoia* trees. The General Grant stands near Big Stump entrance: it's estimated to be more than 3000 years old, weighs around 2145 tons and towers 272 feet above the forest floor. **Moro Rock** is worth climbing for its superb views of the Great Western Divide, the Kaweah River canyons and the vast expanse of the San Joaquin Valley to the west.

But the parks, of course, are best explored on foot. Over a thousand miles of trails traverse the High Country, including a portion of the 225-mile **John Muir Trail** which begins in Yosemite. The **High Sierra Trail**, starting at Crescent Meadow, will take you to Mt Whitney 70 miles distant.

Climbing Mt Whitney is not as difficult as you might suppose; if you approach from the east it will take about three days. Start at the Whitney Portal Trail head, accessible by road from Lone Pine on US 395. You can make the summit round trip in a day on horseback – horses can be hired at Whitney Portal.

What's Available

Accommodation Cabins and motel rooms year-round at *Camp Kaweah* and *Wilsonia. Giant Forest, Stony Creek* and *Grant Grove Lodges* are open late May to October. *Bearpaw Meadow Camp* offers wood-platform tents and meals from late June to early September. For reservations, contact Sequoia and Kings Canyon Hospitality Service, Sequoia National Park, Three Rivers, CA 93271; tel (209) 565-3373. Reservations should be made well in advance – six months is not too soon for the summer vacation season.

Camping 20 developed campgrounds. Backcountry camping permits required. Fast food service at Giant Forest and Wilsonia. Campground reservations through Ticketron outlets.

Facilities Coffee shops at Grant Grove, Cedar Grove and Stony Creek; Giant Forest Lodge dining room – all open late May to October. Camper service stores. Cross-country and downhill skiing equipment rental. Ski instruction and chair lifts at Badger Pass. Ice skating equipment rental and instruction.

Activities Guided walks; year-round naturalist-led walks through the Big Trees; limited scheduled tours through Crystal Cave from May to September. Evening programs. Self-guiding nature trails. Horses and pack animals for hire during summer season.

Getting There

Air Fresno airport is served by four airlines. Connect with the park bus.

Bus *Greyhound* and *Continental Trailways* have regular service to Fresno. Sequoia and Kings Canyon Hospitality Service operates buses from the Fresno Greyhound depot into the park between mid-May and mid-September.

Information

Chief Ranger's office, Sequoia and Kings Canyon National Parks, Three Rivers, CA 93271; tel (209) 565-3306. Also from San Francisco regional office.

THE NORTHERN MINES

North of Auburn, the character of the landscape changes perceptibly, becoming more rugged, cooler and isolated in feeling. Beyond Nevada City communities lie a little farther apart than in the southern region, so it's wise to keep closer watch on your gasoline tank gauge. If you plan backroad safaris during the spring, check conditions locally first – side roads are usually unpaved and spring run-off often renders them impassable.

GRASS VALLEY

Grass Valley is a prosperous town which has risen above its origins at the foot of a grassy ravine to crown the heights of its surrounding hills. Placer deposits first drew the Argonauts to the tiny community settled by immigrants who came across the Truckee Pass in 1848, but it was the discovery of rich veins of quartz and the development of deep mining techniques that made Grass Valley the richest of the mining camps – more than \$400 million was taken out over the years. Mining continued well into the 1950s before high costs forced the shutdown of the famous North Star, Idaho-Maryland and Empire mines.

Although Grass Valley suffered a disastrous fire in 1858 that destroyed many of the original frame buildings, several historic structures remain. At 248 Mill St, west of SR 49, you'll find a small frame house associated with two of the 19th century's most glamorous entertainers. The **Lola Montez Home** was the scene of lavish parties and deliciously scandalous behavior when the legendary siren and her pet bear took up residence in Grass Valley in 1853. Born mere Eliza Gilbert in Ireland in 1818, Lola had parlayed her beauty and a talent for the theater into a sensational career that included a period as mistress to Ludwig of Bavaria.

During her stay, Lola befriended a little schoolgirl who came to call, teaching her some songs and dances. A year later the eight-year-old Lotta Crabtree was an immediate sensation at her first public appearance in the smithy of nearby Rough and Ready. Lotta went on to an immensely successful career which took her from the stages of the mining camps to vast wealth and international fame. Unlike her mentor Lola, who died impoverished in New York at the age of 43, Lotta lived happily ever after. She left the stage at an early age, ending her days in Boston in 1924 with a $4 million estate.

The **North Star Powerhouse Mining Museum** in Boston Ravine (at south end of Mill St) is considered the finest of its kind in the Gold Country. Displays illustrate gold mining techniques and include the Pelton wheel that was the largest in the world in 1896. It's open from 11 am to 5 pm daily, April to October; noon to 4 pm weekends rest of the year; tel (916) 273-9853.

Also of interest is the **Empire Mine State Historic Park** on Empire St east of the freeway where you can explore the grounds and view restoration of one of California's oldest and richest goldmines. The overseer's residence is a fine example of the Victorian baronial style. You can visit it any day from 9 am to sunset; tel (916) 273-8522.

Grass Valley is well endowed with lodgings and restaurants, and no doubt you'll spot a sign for Cornish pasties, a gastronomic legacy of the Cornish miners who settled here during the gold rush. From the first Friday after Thanksgiving to the Friday before Christmas the annual **Cornish Christmas Celebration** draws the crowds to Mill St with music, dance and song. A highlight are performances by the renowned Cornish Choir.

Places to Stay

The Grass Valley Chamber of Commerce, 151 Mill St, Grass Valley 95945 publishes useful accommodation, campground and restaurant lists. Write, drop by during normal office hours, or call (916) 273-4667.

The Purcell House (119 North Church St, Grass Valley 95945; tel (916) 272-5525). Handsomely renovated Victorian home next to the historic Holbrooke Hotel. Rates from $50 to $65 double include continental breakfast.

Places to Eat

Empire House Restaurant Historic gold mining photos decorate this popular family restaurant offering American and Mexican cuisine. (M/E)

Lunch, dinner. Open daily. 535 Mill St; tel (916) 273-3272.

Holbrooke Dining Room Quietly elegant restaurant is Grass Valley's famous old hotel; the Holkbrooke's bar has been in continuous operation since 1852. (M/E)

Lunch, dinner. 212 West Main St; tel (916) 272-1989.

NEVADA CITY

Nevada City is a wonderful place to abandon the car and walk slowly through the past. Its streets follow trails beaten out by the hooves of miners' pack mules more than a century ago, twisting up steep hills to striking Victorian residences set apart from the world by white picket fences and old shade trees. But for all its tranquil appearance today, Nevada City can look back on some vivid history. Fires virtually razed the town on seven occasions, perhaps stimulating the characteristic Gold Country architectural style of brick buildings with iron doors and shutters, certainly the establishment of three firehouses. The fire department still uses two; the third, Firehouse No 1, is the home of the **Nevada County Historical Society Museum,** open daily from 11 am to 4 pm summer; tel (916) 265-9941.

The **South Yuba Canal Building** at 130 Main St houses the Chamber of Commerce; armed with its visitors' map you'll have no trouble locating **James Ott's Assay Office,** where the first samples of the fabulously rich Comstock Lode were assayed, and the **National Hotel** on east Broad St which opened its doors in 1857. Furnished with period antiques, the hotel contains an historic tavern and a Victorian dining room. Two blocks west is the venerable **Nevada Theatre** (1865), California's oldest theater building, now restored as a community center.

Behind the theater at 325 Spring St is the **American Victorian Museum,** housed in a group of mid-19th century industrial buildings on the banks of Deer Creek. The first Pelton Wheel was manufactured here in 1878 and Andrew Halladie, inventor of San Francisco's cable cars worked in the foundry before going to the Bay Area. The museum offers a wealth of Victoriana and various entertainments in its Great Hall. On weekends the Old Stone Hall (1856) serves as the museum dining room and bar.

For program information, write to the American Museum, PO Box 328, Nevada City 95959 or call (916) 265-5804.

Also of interest are the **Artist's Gallery,** survivor of Nevada City's Chinatown; the gingerbread **Red Castle,** now operated as an inn; and the **Pioneer Cemetery** on West Broad St.

Places to Stay

Airway Motel (575 E Broadway, Nevada City 95959; tel (916) 265-4551). Budget travellers dream of finding motels like this quiet place in the lee of a hill, 10 minutes' saunter from the center of town. Rates from $21 double.

National Hotel (E Broad St, Nevada City 95959; tel (916) 265-4551). Landmark hotel tastefully furnished with Victorian antiques. Rates from $26 double (shared bath); $31 (private bath).

Piety Hill Inn (523 Sacramento St, Nevada City 95959; tel (916) 265-2245). Seven cabins high on the hill behind the American Museum comprise this attractive hostelry. Rates $38 and $48 double.

Places to Eat

Creeky Pete's Housed in the former Chinese jail, this pleasant restaurant offers a wide selection of American and Thai dishes. Drinks are served on a tree-shaded patio.

Lunch, dinner. Open daily. 302 Commercial St 265-6951.

Deer Creek Cafe and Bar Home cooking in the sunny cafe; drinks on the verandah poised above Deer Creek.

Breakfast, lunch, dinner. Open Monday to Saturday. 101 Broad St; tel 265-5808.

Selaya's Parlor & Diggins Fine Continental cuisine has earned Selaya's accolades with Gold Country gourmets.

Dinner Tuesday to Sunday. 320 Broad St; tel 265-5697.

MALAKOFF DIGGINS

If you like old mines you will find Malakoff Diggins State Historic Park well worth the occasionally difficult 50-mile roundtrip drive from Nevada City. Malakoff Diggins was the world's hydraulic gold mine; it is an awesome testament to the destructive power of water under high pressure. In their pursuit of gold-bearing gravels, the hydraulickers completely reshaped the mountain ridge, gouging deep ravines and a vast pit some 7000 feet long, 3000 feet wide and nearly 600 feet deep. So widespread was the damage to the environment caused by this technique that in 1884, after a 10-year battle in the courts, hydraulic mining was outlawed in California.

Tiny **North Bloomfield,** once the placer mining camp of Humbug, lies within the park and preserves several old pioneer structures on its single street. You'll find wagons used in the mining operations at **Ostrom's Livery Stable.** The **Park Museum,** housed in a former dance hall, focuses on the history of hydraulic mining, and is open daily in summer, rest of year, contact Park Ranger, tel (916) 265-2740.

To get to Malakoff Diggins, follow SR 49 for 12 miles east of Nevada City, then turn east on Tyler-Foote Crossing Rd which leads to the park via North Columbia.

DOWNIEVILLE

Beyond Nevada City, SR 49 winds through the magnificent scenery of Tahoe National Forest, following the course of the North Yuba River to the old placer mining camp of Downieville. The town's appearance has not changed much in a century or so and plank sidewalks still pave the way along its narrow streets.

Several old buildings are worth a browse. On the main street are the **Costa Store** (1852) with four-foot thick walls at the base, and the **Craycroft Building** of the same period, still with its huge iron doors. A few steps away is the **Sierra County Museum** with interesting relics from Downieville's early days.

The original **town gallows** erected in 1885 stand by the Courthouse, a poignant reminder of wilder days when Downieville achieved an infamous reputation throughout the state. Back in 1851 a Mexican dancehall girl named Juanita stabbed a miner to death. Downieville wasted little time rejecting her plea of self-defense and dangled Juanita from hastily-improvised gallows, assuring her a place in history as the first woman to be hanged in California. Juanita did not die in vain: news of her hanging so shocked the public that lynchings became rarer thereafter.

Beyond Downieville

From Downieville SR 49 continues eastward through the canyon of the North Yuba River, past the great massif of the Sierra Buttes and Sierra City to join SR 89 above Sierraville.

SR 89 North is the slow, lovely way up to Lassen Volcanic National Park traversing the eastern slopes of the Sierra Nevada, Plumas and Lassen National Forests and the shores of Lake Almanor.

There are many small towns with accommodation, but if you are travelling in summer, it is wise to phone ahead for reservations or make camp early in the day. The area is a very popular vacation center. SR 89 intersects I-5 just below Mt Shasta.

Follow SR 89 south through Sierraville and you come to Truckee straddling I-80 at the foot of Donner Pass. Turn east on I-80 for the bright lights and gambling casinos of Reno and Sparks, south for Lake Tahoe's resorts and the Stateline casinos.

LAKE TAHOE AREA

I-80 follows the old California Trail over the Sierra Nevada via the Donner Pass (7135 feet). The easy gradients of the new highway give no hint of the difficulties that ascent of the steep eastern face presented to the wagon trains of immigrants bound for California. Careful timing was essential: winter snows, which can last well into the spring, sealed the pass for several months.

The party led by George and Jacob Donner arrived late at the foot of the eastern slopes in October 1846 and unseasonably early snows trapped them in the pass. Supplies ran out after a few weeks and the starving immigrants resorted to cannibalism. In desperation a few set out on snow-shoes and reached Sutter's Fort early in 1847. But by the time help arrived, only 33 of the 81 were still alive. The story of the tragedy is recounted in displays at the Emigrant Trail Museum in **Donner Memorial State Park** east of the pass.

Lake Tahoe

Two miles short of Truckee, I-80 intersects with SR 89 running southward past California's Big Ski country and Squaw Valley (site of the 1960 Winter Olympics) to Lake Tahoe. The Indians' 'Lake of the Sky' lies at an elevation of 6225 feet, two-thirds in California, the rest in Nevada. Despite ever-encroaching developments, Tahoe is hauntingly beautiful, framed by tall pines and peaks that tower 4000 or more feet above ice-blue waters. For 72 miles of unparalled grandeur, simply follow SR 28-89 around the shoreline.

Like Janus, Tahoe has two faces. The lake is surrounded by some of the finest outdoor sports country in the United States, offering innumerable opportunities for backpacking, hunting, water and winter sports, fishing and mountaineering. At the same time, resorts, casinos and a star-spangled nightlife place Tahoe high on the list for those who prefer their recreation indoors. These two aspects can keep you going day and night; if you're not accustomed to living a mile high in the sky, proceed with caution for a while.

North Lake Tahoe The North Shore area from Carnelian Bay to Indian Village is comparatively quiet. Numerous small towns hug the shoreline and many of the best restaurants are to be found here. Most of the motels have their own private beaches. Best known of the ski areas here are Squaw Valley and Incline Village.

The state line passes through Brockway – and through the lobby of Cal-Neva Lodge; you'll find the gambling tables on the Nevada side! This famous old casino opened its doors in 1927, was rebuilt in 31 days after a fire in 1937, and was once owned by Frank Sinatra. Lodge facilities also include a disco, specialty shops and a large hotel.

Gambling casinos are also at the Crystal Bay Club, Hyatt Tahoe, Nevada Club and North Shore Club.

North Shore attractions include the **Ponderosa Ranch** of TV's 'Bonanza' fame. Park your car at the entrance near Incline Village, then hop the shuttle for a taste of the Old West as the Cartwright family knew it. There are guided tours of the ranch house, breakfast rides through the forest (plus all the victuals you can handle at the Cartwright wagon camp), and a stage coach to run you into the town for a browse in the curio shops and museum. Open daily from 10 am to 5 pm from May through October; spring and Fall schedule as announced. tel (702) 831-0691.

East Shore This is the least developed part of Tahoe. Its long beaches attract the summer crowds for the lake waters are shallower here – and consequently warmer. **Zephyr Cove** is home port for two lake cruise vessels, the windjammer *Woodwind* and the *M S Dixie*. The *Dixie* is a Mississippi paddlewheeler built in 1927 for hauling cotton; today it cruises the lake day and night between May and September. Call (702) 588-3508 for current times and prices.

South Shore Gambling is the raison d'etre for **South Lake Tahoe**, largest and busiest of the Tahoe resorts, located at the junction of US 50 and SR 89. That portion of the town in California is called South Lake Tahoe; there is no gambling here. That on the Nevada side is called Stateline and here the casino action never stops. Though the shows may not be so lavish as in Reno or Las Vegas, you'll find the big-name stars on stage in the show rooms and club lounges. There are eight to choose from, and they're all within walking distance of each other on the Nevada side.

There are beaches where you can sun yourself between bouts with the house odds. And if you want to rise above it all for a while, ride the **Heavenly Valley** tram which terminates at a restaurant 8300 feet above sea level. It operates between 9 am and midnight, costs $4, and there's no way to beat the splendor of its view unless you indulge in a little flightseeing from Lake Tahoe Airport. Call (916) 541-2110 for information.

West Shore Getting away from it all is perhaps easiest here. Most of the land along the western shoreline is under the jurisdiction of the U S Forest Service and the California State Park System and is set aside for recreational and watershed use. A network of trails has been blazed to the High Country where you will find the 'delicious solitude' that enraptured Mark Twain. The half dozen lakeside campgrounds between South Lake Tahoe and Tahoe City are very popular, so reservations (through Ticketron agencies) are recommended. For permits and information on Desolation Wilderness camping and hiking, go to the Visitor Center on SR 89 between Camp Richardson and Emerald Bay.

Emerald Bay is exquisite in every season. A one-mile trail from the Overlook leads down to **Vikingsholm**, a 1929 version of a 9th century Norse fortress built by Mrs Lora Knight. The 38-room castle is open daily from 9 am to 5 pm, July 1 through Labour Day. In a canyon nearby are **Eagle Falls**.

Fallen Leaf Lake, its surface about 100 feet higher than Tahoe, lies to the west of the highway. Worth the detour even for a quick look – photographers will appreciate the reflected images of the peaks.

Places to Stay

Visitor facilities in the Tahoe area are varied and plentiful. Resort hotels, motels and campgrounds line the lake – in the South Shore area alone more than 11,000 guest rooms are available year round. Nevertheless, reservations are recommended during the summer season. The South Lake Tahoe Visitors Bureau's Reservation service can help you find accommodation – in California, call 800-822-5922; in all other states call 800-824-5150. Before you set out, consult a travel agent about the many package plans available: you could save substantial sums. For detailed information on the area contact:

South Lake Tahoe Visitors Bureau
PO Box 15090
South Lake Tahoe CA 95702
(tel (916) 544-5050)

Getting There

Bus *Greyhound* and *Continental Trailways* stop at Truckee on their San Francisco-New York routes via the Donner Pass. Greyhound also serves South Lake Tahoe from San Francisco and Reno-Sparks. *Las Vegas Tonopah Stagelines* link South Lake Tahoe and Carson City.

Air Scheduled air service to South Shore Airport (commuter airlines only) and to Reno Airport where you can connect with Greyhound to South Lake Tahoe.

RENO-SPARKS

The former quickie-marriage-and-divorce capital of the US squats on the banks of the Truckee River between the Great Desert and the Sierra Peaks. Reno earns its living in much the same way as Las Vegas, but despite everything the city retains an Old West flavor. There are a number of sturdy brick buildings harking back to the days when Reno was just a rough and rowdy railroad town, the life style's definitely casual, and on Wild West Day in June, be sure you're dressed in your Western best.

Gaming The casinos cluster on and around North Virginia St in the center of the town, but the biggest little gambling complex in the world, the MGM Grand, lies about two miles east on Lewis St – catch the lavish 'Hello Hollywood' show if you can.

You'll find ballyhooed big name entertainment relatively cheap in the show rooms of the larger hotel casinos. Reservations are required, usually 30 days in advance, contact the Reno Convention and Visitors' Authority for reservations information and schedules. None are needed for the lounges and cabarets where, for as little as one or two-drink minimum, you can watch the up-and-coming talent.

There's more of the same three miles away in Sparks, also the location of **Harrah's Automobile Collection**. Among the 1100-plus vintage cars displayed is the Thomas Flyer which won the New York-Paris race in 1908. To get there, ride the complimentary shuttle from Harrah's Hotel in downtown Reno.

Places to Stay
Hard to go wrong in the Reno-Sparks area for the standard of accommodation is high and the cost reasonable in every category. The luxury headliners are *Harrah's*, the *MGM Grand, El Dorado, Sands* and *Sundowner;* prices here range from $35 to $70 double.

There's a wide choice of accommodation in the moderate and budget categories where you can still find a room for as little as $20 a night double. Reservations in advance are advised, especially at weekends.

Good, quick meals around the clock are a feature of the casinos. Three of them have six or more restaurants a piece. Prices on average are moderate, though you can pull out all the stops if you wish.

Planning ahead can stretch the budget nicely: package tours are plentiful. Check with a travel agent, or contact The Reno Convention & Visitors Authority, 4590 S Virginia St, PO Box 837, Reno, NV 89504; tel (702) 785-4800. The Authority's visitors center is open Monday to Saturday from 8 am to 5 pm.

Getting There
Nine major airlines are presently flying down to Reno. *Continental Trailways* and *Greyhound* provide frequent service. *Amtrak* also serves Reno.

PYRAMID LAKE
Brown hills stained with rose and purple are the setting of Pyramid Lake, a sparkling deep blue body of water about 30 miles long and 10 miles wide in the desert 33 miles northeast of Reno. It is the impressive remainder of Lake Lahontan that covered most of the northwestern Nevada in prehistoric times, and

an irresistible draw for fishermen who come for the cut-throat trout and the cui-ui, a prehistoric fish found nowhere else in the world. For ornithologists the fascination lies in one of the Tufa islands which rise sharply from the water – **Anahoe Island** is the largest white pelican rookery in the country. It's a National Wild Life Refuge and special permission must be obtained if you want to make a visit. The huge pyramid just to the north, which gave the lake its name, is also popular with the birds. According to the Paiutes, the rock is the home of the lake spirit which feasts on persons who dare swim in its waters. In fact, Pyramid can be dangerous in windy weather: storms come up with astonishing suddenness, so be sure to pay attention to the weather warnings if you want to go boating.

Warrior Point Park, nine miles north of Sutcliffe, has developed campsites and picnic facilities – a pleasant place to indulge in a little boating, swimming or fishing.

VIRGINIA CITY
About 24 miles southeast of Reno, Virginia City holds a scenic position on the barren Comstocks where, in 1859, two prospectors excavating a small reservoir happened upon the largest body of gold and silver the world has ever known. The wealth that streamed from the fabulous Comstock Lode in large measure financed the Union forces in the Civil War and rebuilt San Francisco after the 'quake; it also supported an extravagantly rich style still evident in the scattering of baronial homes and massive public buildings that front the worn boardwalks. Today Virginia City is merely a shadow of the town where no saloonkeeper was expected to give change for a $5 gold piece and one mine alone yielded $105 million in gold and silver.

The Visitors' Bureau on C St provides a useful background to civic history with a 15-minute audiovisual show, as well as directions to the major attractions. These conveniently cluster on C and B Sts – immediately opposite the Bureau is the *Territorial Enterprise* which hired the fledgling writer Mark Twain for $25 a week in the 1860s. In the same block are the celebrated **Crystal Bar** and **Bucket of Blood Saloon**. At the corner of Taylor St, you can take an underground tour of the **Best & Belcher Mine**, the Comstock's biggest producer – the entrance is in the Ponderosa Saloon.

B St's most notable sights are **Piper's Opera House** where stars such as Edwin Booth and Lola Montez performed, and **The Castle** and **A M Cole** mansions, two grandiose Victorian buildings open to public viewing. The Castle remains much as it was in the boom days, with its original Czechoslovakian crystal chandeliers, silver doorknobs and stair rods, and handblocked wallpaper from France. The **Cole Mansion** is as elaborately furnished. Other old places open to visitors are the **Savage**, **Chollar** and **Mackay** mansions, located at the south ends of C and D Sts.

St Mary's in the Mountains (1868), at the corner of E and Taylor Sts, is considered one of the loveliest Gothic church buildings in the country. Finely carved redwood columns and trusses support the ceiling, originally painted a delicate blue, with great effect. Close by is **St Paul's Episcopal Church**, rebuilt after the 1875 fire.

A block south of the churches is the **Virginia & Truckee Railroad Depot** where, between May 26 and September 30, you can catch a vintage steam train up to Gold Hill, a mining town which for a brief period rivaled Virginia City. The line follows its original 110-year-old right of way between some of the most famous of the Comstock mines.

Virginia City begins buckling down for the winter toward the end of October and attractions remain closed until spring – it depends a little on the weather. Everything is in full swing in the Summer.

Returning to California

If you're heading back to northern California, US 50 is an attractive alternative to I-80. It follows the Emmigrant Trail through the Nevada state capital, Carson City, to South Shore Lake Tahoe and Placerville in the Gold Country.

Yosemite National Park's entrance is roughly two hours' drive south of Reno via US 395. Turn west just beyond Lee Vining and follow the Tioga Pass Rd into the park – few sights equal the dramatic line of Sierra peaks rising sheer from the desert floor. As the pass often does not open until summer and may close as early as September, check road conditions first. In the vicinity of Lee Vining is the ghost town of Bodie.

CARSON CITY

When Mark Twain rode the stage coach into Nevada's capital, he found it a 'wooden' town, its population a bare two thousand souls, with board sidewalks inclined to rattle when walked upon and little white frame stores 'too high to sit down on, but not high enough for other purposes'. Carson City today is considerably larger, but it retains an easy-going, small-town charm.

The silver-domed **State Capitol** (1870), on Carson St between Second and Musser Sts, is open to visitors: it has a number of historical exhibits, including the original Nevada constitution. But the **Nevada State Museum** a little farther north on Carson St has a full-scale replica of a mine tunnel more than 300 feet long, furnished with equipment actually used in Nevada mines. Exhibits of ores, minerals and mining technology shed further light on the industry which is so important to the state's economy. Also of great interest are displays of Indian artefacts and culture. Open 8.30 am to 4.30 pm daily; free.

Carson City's numerous Victorian residences, built for nabobs of the Comstock years, are a delight to photographers and architecture buffs. The

Chamber of Commerce at 1191 S Carson St provides a map showing their location – many cluster on Curry, Nevada, Division and Minnesota, between Robinson and King Sts. A 10-mile drive north of Carson City takes you to an unusually handsome specimen, the **Bowers Mansion**. When Sandy Bowers struck it rich in the Comstock, he poured a large part of his fortune into building this home for his wife, Eilly. They furnished it lavishly – you'll find a wealth of cut crystal chand-eliers, mahogany and marble as you tour its 16 rooms – and lived in a manner impressive even in that fabulous era. But after Sandy died, the Bowers fortunes waned and Eilly was forced to take in lodgers, even tell fortunes, to make ends meet. In time she had to give up her dream and died in California in 1903. It's open May to October, 11 am to 4.30 pm; guided tours, admission charge; tel (702) 849-0201.

Northern California

Heading through Northern California to Oregon and the Pacific Northwest, there are three highways: the coast route (SR 1), the inland route (US 101) and the valley route (I-5). State highways interconnect them at various points, so it is possible to change from one to the other. SR 1 runs inland from Rockport to join US 101 at Leggett and from then on they become one highway, returning to the coast at Humboldt Bay and continuing as the coast road northward from there to loop around Washington's Olympic Peninsula.

The coast route takes longer to drive – it's a two-lane road winding around inlets, often climbing precipitous headlands only to plunge down again to sea level. But it is the most scenic drive, with grand seascapes, fishing villages, artists' colonies and numerous state beach parks to relax at.

US 101 runs up through the eastern foothills of the Coast Range, then crosses the range through majestic redwoods to the coast. It is largely a divided four-lane highway.

I-5, the West Coast's major north-south freeway, is the fastest route, being divided into four-lane highway much of the way. (To reach it, you have to take I-80 east from San Francisco to interchange I-505, after the Vacaville turnoff.) From the interchange, I-5 passes through rolling farmlands of the Sacramento Valley to Redding, where it begins to climb through the Siskiyou Mountains to Ashland in Oregon. I-5 takes you to the lakelands, Lassen Volcanic National Park, Mt Shasta, the Shasta Recreational area and wilderness areas of the Trinity Alps.

THE COAST ROUTE

Unlike Southern California, the Northern California coast remains relatively undeveloped. A contributing factor to its sparse settlement is the weather: summer fogs roll in in the early morning, burn off for a few hours, then return toward evening.

A further deterrent to development came in 1972 with the creation of the Coastal Zone Conservation Commission, with jurisdiction over building along the coastal strip. This means that the northern coast is not rimmed with resorts and oceanside motels. However, several towns offer a choice of accommodation, including some delightful restored country inns which recreate the atmosphere of a more genteel era.

There are numerous campgrounds, both privately run and in the state beach parks. Reservations for these in summer months are heavy as families from all over the country tour California in RVs (recreation vehicles) which, despite their gas-guzzling propensity, are still very popular here.

Although the Northern California coast was explored by Spanish navigators as early as 1602, settlement only began with the fur traders in the first decade of the 19th century. Hard on their heels came the lumbermen. Most coastal towns grew from the need to ship lumber from the interior forests to feed San Francisco's insatiable housing needs during the gold rush. Today, the area's major interests are lumber, fishing and ranching. This coast offers plentiful opportunities for fishing but the ocean is not good for swimming – it's cold and often dangerous. Beaches are popular for cookouts around drift wood fires and contemplative strolls rather than sunbaking.

North of the Golden Gate Bridge, the Marin hills, which form part of the Coastal Range, appear as softly rounded parallel chains, set apart by lush valleys cooled by the ocean fogs. Along the coast, where steep cliffs alternate with coves and long sandy beaches, there are several small fishing villages now weekend resorts for Bay Area residents and retreats for writers and artists. Inland, communities close to San Francisco are largely residential, but many retain hints of their former role as centers for the lumbering industry which exploited – and denuded – the great stands of coastal redwoods covering the valleys. Today, much of the region is devoted to dairy ranching and fruit farming and a drive along the narrow, twisting roads that thread the valleys reveals glimpses of fine old Victorian ranch houses set back behind screens of eucalyptus trees.

GOLDEN GATE NATIONAL RECREATION AREA

The GGNRA, set aside by President Nixon in 1972, extends from San Francisco deep into Marin County, adjoining Point Reyes National Sea Shore from Bolinas Lagoon to Olema. Within its boundaries you can escape to an unspoilt California over trails that run along the cliffs' edge hundreds of feet above the Pacific, dip into wooden glens, and traverse 35,000 acres of gorse-covered hills. It is an area of abundant wildlife which includes sea lions, deer, racoons, and an astonishing variety of birds. But beware of the poison oak in this park.

MARIN HEADLANDS

On San Francisco's doorstep are the Marin Headlands, a former Army reserve of open terrain, beaches and trails immediately north of the Golden Gate Bridge. GGT's buses passing through Sausalito stop at the entrance to Fort Baker; the MUNI provides weekend summer service to Fort Cronkhite.

A network of old Army roads permits leisurely exploration by car and access to Fort Baker's piers, Rodeo Beach and old coastal fortifications from pre-Civil War times to Nike missile sites. The WW II gun emplacements high above the Golden Gate's northern abutment offer splendid views. **Kirby Cove** is a particularly attractive picnic site tucked in the folds of the hills west of the Bridge, and at Rodeo Lagoon's **Marine Mammal Center** you can visit marine birds and mammals convalescing from injuries or illness – phone (415) 561-7284 to make sure the facilities are open to the public the day you go. For a GGNRA map, trail guides and advice on the best places to view the Headlands' water birds, stop by the Rodeo Lagoon ranger station. The AYH's Golden Gate Hostel is a mile or so to the southeast, housed in the former Officers' Headquarters (941 Fort Barry, Sausalito, CA 94965). Call ahead for reservations and the shuttle schedule, (415) 331-2777.

MUIR WOODS

A solemn grandeur invests Muir Woods grove of coastal redwoods towering majestically beside a small creek miles west of the Panoramic Highway. Here an easy two-mile loop trail (which takes about an hour to walk) leads between shade canyon ferns and some of the world's oldest and tallest trees in a cathedral-like calm. The admission fee includes a self-guiding leaflet to the quarter-mile nature trail, and there's a snack and gift shop where you can obtain light refreshments.

The grove is open daily from 8 am until sunset – it's very popular so you may encounter parking problems in summer and on sunny weekends. Many tour buses serve Muir Woods daily.

Follow Frank Valley Rd west of Muir Woods and you come to **Muir Beach**, a small cove that's ideal for picnicking and sunbathing. Like Muir Woods, it's popular and traffic can be bumper-to-bumper in good weather. To check conditions, call (415) 868-0942.

At the turn off to Muir Beach is the *Pelican Inn,* a reproduction of a West of England country hotel that serves authentic English pub food from 11.30 am to 9

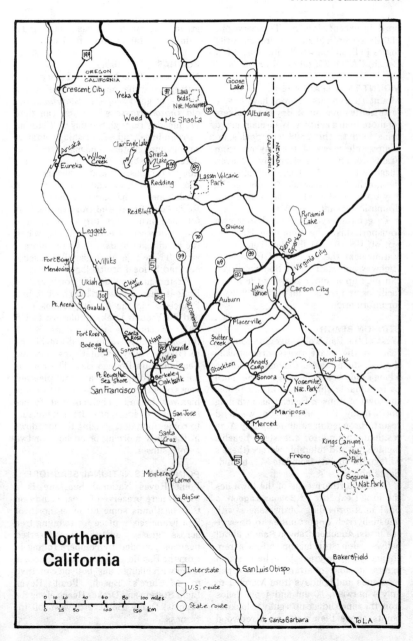

Northern California

pm daily except Mondays. To reserve one of the six overnight guest bedrooms, write to the Pelican Inn, 10 Pacific Way, Muir Beach, CA 94965; tel (415) 383-6000.

MOUNT TAMALPAIS AREA

Mount Tam and its environs have been a favorite destination of Bay area walkers for more than a century. Well-maintained trails lead to the 2608-foot peak's incomparable views of the Bay and San Francisco, and on a clear day it's even possible to see Mt Shasta 300 miles to the north. The **Mountain Theater** on the way up to East Peak is the setting of a dramatic pageant every May.

To get there you will need your own transport, take the Shoreline Highway exit off US 101. At the Pan Toll ranger station near the junction of Panoramic Highway and Ridgecrest Boulevard you can pick up a folder showing the area's facilities and trails. Call (415) 388-2070 for information.

STINSON BEACH

West of the Pan Toll ranger station, the road to the coast twists dramatically through steep ravines to come out above a long sandy beach sheltered at the south by formidable cliffs. Back in the 1800s, the town of Stinson Beach was a whaling port; today it's primarily a weekend resort, thronged in summer by Bay Area residents bound for the state beach's picnic sites and tolerable waters (there's a lifeguard on duty from late May to mid-September).

On the northern edge of the town lies the broad expanse of **Bolinas Lagoon**, a tidal inlet providing birdwatchers with unusually rich opportunities to observe sea birds. **Audubon Canyon Ranch**, about halfway along the lagoon, offers a rare chance to view great blue herons and egrets at close quarters. A trail, open weekends and holidays from March 1 to July 4 between 10 am and 4 pm, leads from the ranch house up a gully to lookout points above their nests in a redwood grove. The ranch also has a small museum, picnic tables and a bookstore.

BOLINAS

Northwest of the Lagoon, on a headland jutting into the ocean, Bolinas has a couple of good *seafood restaurants*, the old *Gibson House* where you can dine Wednesday through Sunday in Victorian surroundings, and a flourishing colony of writers and painters. The main attraction here is **Duxbury Reef**, a magnet for tidepool enthusiasts and rockhounds who come in search of agates and petrified whalebone. At the northern end of Mesa Rd is **Point Reyes Bird Observatory**, first full-time bird observatory established in the country, where early risers may watch the banding of birds. (Be there before 9 am.) There's also a small museum devoted to local ornithology.

At the junction at the north end of Bolinas Lagoon you can loop back to San Francisco via the Fairfax-Bolinas road and Sir Francis Drake Boulevard to US 101, or continue north along SR 1 through wooded valleys and ranchlands to Olema Valley, Point Reyes National Seashore and Bodega Bay. The road is narrow, winding, and has some pleasant views of old farmhouses set back from the highway behind lichen-covered fences and groves of eucalyptus. It is not unusual to come upon deer grazing the meadows in the early morning or an hour or two before sunset.

POINT REYES NATIONAL SEASHORE

Point Reyes National Seashore is a 67,000 acre preserve of great beauty on the coastlands some 60 miles north of San Francisco, a place for roaming free across grassy uplands to deserted beaches pounded by combers rolling in from the Pacific unrestrained. The area is laced with hiking trails, but you can drive to McClure's Beach, Point Reyes Light Station and Drakes Beach along Sir Francis Drake Boulevard west of Inverness.

Perhaps the most intriguing feature of the park is the ease of observing the processes which shaped the face of the land. You can walk a stretch of the 700-mile-long San Andreas Fault which caused the San Francisco earthquake by following **Earthquake Trail** from park headquarters on Bear Valley Rd just north of Olema. Plant life in the park goes back to the Tertiary age and includes six varieties that grow nowhere else in the world. As you drive, keep an eye peeled for the abundant wildlife; a herd of white deer roves the uplands.

No one knows if **Drakes Bay** is the lost harbor where Sir Francis Drake careened the *Golden Hind* and claimed the land for Queen Elizabeth on his voyage around the world in 1579, but the great white cliffs sheltering the beach are very like those at Dover. The bay is a popular picnicking spot with fine views of the Point Reyes Peninsula jutting into the Pacific. Snacks are available at the Visitor Center near the parking lot.

Point Reyes National Seashore can be reached by *GGT* bus (one trip each way daily). In San Francisco call (415) 332-6600 for times. There are walk-in campgrounds (and one drive-in campground) at the southern end of the park. For information, call Point Reyes National Seashore headquarters, (415) 663-1092. Also within the park, in a former ranch house one and a half miles from Limantour Beach, is the AYH's *Point Reyes Hostel.* Phone the hostel at (415) 669-9985 before 9.30 am for transport suggestions; for reservations write to PO Box 247, Point Reyes Station, CA 94956.

TOMALES BAY
Separating Point Reyes from the mainland is Tomales Bay, a long fjord-like stretch of water enclosed by golden hills to the east and wooded slopes to the west. The bay was first sighted by Juan Francisco de la Bodega in 1775, and though there is a scattering of villages on

its shores, it retains an untouched look.

Inverness is the largest community on the western shore, with a number of good antique stores, restaurants and two motels. To the east is **Point Reyes Station,** an arts-and-crafts center of no great visual appeal – but it's lively! At least two good restaurants here. Farther north is **Marshall,** where a dozen or so old houses stand on stilts in the bay. There's a good fish restaurant here where you can enjoy excellent views toward Point Reyes.

THE SONOMA COAST
Leaving the Point Reyes National Seashore, SR 1 veers inland around Tomales Bay, then heads west to rejoin the coast at Bodega Bay at the southern end of the Sonoma County coastline.

The 40-mile Sonoma Coast stretches from Bodega Bay to Gualala Point. This area has a milder climate than further north, with less fog. Much of the highway is switchback, following the contours of mountain slopes – plunging into forested ravines, cresting on bare wind-swept headlands and leveling on coastal terraces from time to time. During winter, frequent rainstorms can produce landslides, blocking the road, so it's best to check with the California Highway Patrol on road conditions after heavy rains.

BODEGA BAY
Bodega Bay is a small fishing village perched on the eastern edge of a natural harbor which provides the only protected small boat anchorage between San Francisco and Noyo on the Mendocino Coast. The lagoon is enclosed by a narrow sandy spit which curves toward the tip of Bodega Head, at the northern end of the bay. Both commercial and charter fishing thrive here, hunting salmon from May to October and bottom fishing the rest of the year.

Bodega Bay was discovered by Vizcaino in 1602 and named for Juan Francisco de la Bodega y Cauadra who sailed it in 1775. But it was inhabited only by Miwok Indians until the summer of 1809, when a party of Russian fur traders led by Ivan Alexander Kuskov headquartered here. In 1812, Kuskov returned to build a fort and the village of Kuskov, a few miles inland in the Salmon Creek Valley. Farmers planted wheat, barley and fresh produce. But declining catches of sea otter disaffected the Russians and in 1841 they abandoned the settlement, selling out to John Sutter. Nothing remains of Kuskov, save a cross commemorating the first baptism of Indians in Northern California, and a few old stones.

California's first steam-operated sawmill was built here in 1843 by Stephen Smith, who instituted the coastal lumber trade when he despatched the first ship laden with redwood south to San Francisco.

The village of **Bodega Bay** has attractive white-frame houses, seafood restaurants at the marina, and fine antique-hunting. A landmark is St Teresa Church, built in 1862.

Moviegoers will recognise some buildings from Alfred Hitchcock's thriller *The Birds,* which was filmed on location here and in **Bodega**, four miles inland in the Salmon Creek Valley. Bodega's Old Potter Schoolhouse, now converted to an art gallery and restaurant, evokes frightening memories; it was the schoolhouse in the film where the teacher fell under the birds' attack.

Places to Stay

Bodega Bay Lodge (Doran Beach Rd off SR 1 (Box 357), Bodega Bay CA 94923; tel (707) 875-3525). 40-unit motel with excellent rooms, some with kitchen, all with private patios. Views of ocean and lagoon. Rates from $58 double.
The Tides (SR 1 Bodega Bay (PO Box 186), Bodega Bay CA 94923; tel (707) 875-3553, 875-3595). 18-unit motel on marina, some kitchens. Dining room open 6 am to 10 pm. Fishing, party boats, market. Rates from $39.22 double.

Places to Eat

Dinucci's Family-style Italian dinners, good food. Local rancher hangout, old fashioned bar; recommended. (M)
Dinner daily. SRI Valley Ford (five miles east of Bodega Bay Lodge). Tel 876-3260.
Bodega Art Gallery & Restaurant Gourmet continental cuisine; sandwiches, salads and crepes. Beer and wine. Located in landmark Old Potter School. (B/M).
Lunch, Thursday to Sunday, dinner Wednesday to Sunday. 17125 Bodega Lane; tel 876-3257.

SONOMA COAST STATE BEACH

This is actually a string of beaches tucked in coves at the base of precipitous cliffs; access is by twisting trails from the road. Camping and picnicking facilities are available. Park headquarters are at Salmon Creek Lagoon, a mile north of Bodega Bay.

It's an easy drive along the Sonoma coast beaches as far as the village of **Jenner**. The road cuts into gently sloping shelf, giving fine views of the sea swirling around rocky islets in the coves. But once you cross the Russian River and pass by Jenner's weathered cottages perched above the river estuary, the terrain changes radically. Now the road winds tortuously up and down steep grades cut into sheer bluffs which seem to tumble one upon another into the whitecapped water below. Finally, some 13 awesome miles further on, you reach a wooded coastal terrace, dominated by the imposing redwood stockade, Fort Ross.

Places to Stay & Eat

Murphy's Jenner by the Sea (SR 1; PO Box 69, Jenner CA 95450; tel (707) 865-2377). Charming rooms in 1860s Stage Coach stop. Bed & breakfast in private homes also available. Rates from $40 double. Restaurant noted for seafood in congenial atmosphere. (B/M)
Breakfast weekends, lunch and dinner

daily (hours may differ October to March).

FORT ROSS

Kuskov selected the site for Fort Ross (*Rossiya* is an archaic term for Russian) because of its easy defense against attack from land or sea. The fort was built in 1812, the year Napoleon invaded Russia, and was subsequently armed with 40 French cannons left behind in the rout of his army. The original stockade consisted of nine buildings, including barracks, while some 60 more houses were scattered around outside. In the cove below, the settlers built their own ships. During the 1830s, Fort Ross was home to a princess; Commandant Alexander Rotcheff married Princess Helena de Gagarin, the czar's niece, who renounced her inheritance to become his wife.

The settlement of Russians at Bodega Bay and Fort Ross was viewed with some dismay by the Mexicans, Spanish and Americans in turn. When in 1823, US President James Monroe promulgated the Monroe Doctrine declaring American opposition to any attempt by European powers to 'extend their system to any portion of this hemisphere', the die was cast for Russian withdrawal. With the sea otter fur trade almost extinct, in 1840 Czar Nicholas I gave the order to leave California.

The state took over Fort Ross in 1906. It was severely damaged in the earthquake that year and has since suffered a number of disastrous fires, including several in the early 1970s. The complex has been painstakingly restored, with Russian aid, including the loan of the original plans found in the Kremlin, and closely resembles the original. It is now a National Monument. You can walk through the 356-acre park's buildings and a small museum in the Commander's House tells of life in days of Indian, Russian and American occupation. It's open daily from 10 am to 4.30 pm; admission charge. Parking lot north of park entrance.

Two miles up the coast, **Timber Cove** once served as a 'doghole port' for lumber schooners en route to San Francisco (as did most coves of any size). Timber Cove Inn on the point has been through hard times in recent years, but may see a renaissance under its new management (tel 707-847-3231). At any rate, it is worth walking around to the point behind it to view the late Beniamino Buffano's mammoth sculpted offering to peace.

SALT POINT STATE PARK

Midway between Jenner and Stewarts Point, Salt Point State Park encompasses about six miles of seashore and its 3500 acres stretch to the crest of the highlands, 1000 feet above sea level. As in each of the state parks up the coast, rangers are on hand to explain the natural history and marine life and there are facilities for picnicking and camping. Reservations for campsites should be made well in advance through Ticketron or State Department of Parks.

Kruse Rhododendron State Reserve

The 300-acre Kruse Rhododendron State Reserve, adjacent to Salt Point State Park, is at its most glorious April to June. Then you can wander paths between great rosy-bloomed bushes of *Rhododendron macrophyllum,* some as high as 20 feet. Follow the sign to the parking area, where you can pick up a map showing trails winding through the area, which is set aside to preserve this shrub, native to Pacific Coast forests up to British Columbia. To check on blooming season, phone (707) 865-2391.

SEA RANCH

This vacation home development stretches 14 miles north along the coast and reaches up into the wooded highlands. Many of the houses have won awards for their striking Bauhaus style architecture. Sea Ranch also has a restaurant, motel and a nine-hole golf course.

Places to Stay

Sea Ranch Lodge (SR 1 (Box 44), CA 95497; tel (707) 785-2371). 20 units, redwood walls, ocean-view windows, natural wood furnishings. No TV or telephones in rooms. Pool, golf. Rates $52 double.

Places to Eat

Sea Ranch Lodge Redwood-&-glass airy decor, seafood and Continental cuisine, reservations recommended. (B/M)

Breakfast, lunch, dinner daily. SR 1 between Stewarts Point and Gualala; tel 785-2371.

MENDOCINO COAST

Mendocino County's coast is 120 miles of magnificence: rugged cliffs, wind-twisted cypress clinging to their sides; salt-damp headlands protecting sandy coves; wooded gullies lush with ferns; wildlife-inhabited estuaries, landlocked behind sand bars until breached by winter storms; drifting fog; and 19th century mansions transformed into charming inns.

Spur roads off SR 1 offer opportunities to explore the Mendocino Highlands, forested in Bishop pine, western yew, Douglas fir, Sitka spruce, tan oak and redwoods, and Anderson Valley, sprinkled with dairy farms and apple orchards outlined by rickety fences. You share the roads with logging trucks from time to time, but the slow-going gives you a chance to appreciate the ever-changing scenery.

The local inhabitants are independent of mind – some citizens 'seceded' to form their own state in 1974, and a valley town has its own language. They welcome visitors with dignified warmth. Lumber, once the economic backbone of the country, is now joined by tourism and the arts as sources of revenue, since over the past 20 years the natural beauty and isolation have drawn many city-dwellers seeking an alternative lifestyle.

Gualala

First town across the county line, Gualala is an example of the changes. It was a lumber town from around 1860 into the 1960s; now it's a center for artists who display their work in the Dolphin, in back of the Post Office. (Open Tuesday to Sunday 11 am to 5 pm.) Their summer Art in the Redwoods show draws crowds each year.

Saturday night is a big night at the 1903 Gualala Hotel, where you can dine and dance with the locals. They've a few rooms, too.

The redwood-shaded Gualala River is popular with hardy winter fisherfolk searching for steelhead trout – this was one of Jack London's favorite streams.

St Orres

On a headland halfway between Gualala and Anchor Bay sits a fanciful redwood building, its towers topped by copper-covered onion domes. St Orres represents the fulfilment of a dream for designer Eric Black. The inn features hand-crafted wood-paneled rooms, stained glass doors and handmade quilted bedspreads. It took four years to be ready for its 1977 opening. Building is still going on to complete the 28-acre complex; the restaurant has already become popular with coast travelers.

Places to Stay

This section of coast offers numerous country inns in restored mansions and farmhouses, where you're personally hosted by the proprietors. Most of them are bed & breakfast, several offer other meals; most have share-bathrooms down the hall; some have a non-smoking policy. Since these are becoming better known, and most of them have only six to 10 rooms, reservations must be made well in advance – at least three months ahead and up to 12 months ahead for holiday weekends.

In addition, there are hotels and motels; again, in summer it is not wise to take a chance on finding accommodation without advance reservations.

Old Milano Hotel (Box 385, Gualala CA 95445; tel (707) 884-3256). Seven individually decorated Victorian rooms with double beds, in restored 1905 hotel perched on cliff with stunning views. Two communal bathrooms. Cottage and 'caboose' in gardens. Declared National Historic Landmark. Rates from $55 double includes Continental breakfast. Open April 1 to December 31 only.

St Orres (PO Box 523, Gualala CA 95445; tel (707) 884-3303). Eight handcrafted rooms each with double bed. Three bathrooms down the hall – His, Hers and Theirs! Two cottages with ocean view, fireplaces, queen-size beds, private bathrooms and sun deck. Rates from $50 double rooms, $75 cottages, includes Continental breakfast.

Places to Eat

Gualala Hotel Good Italian food. Cheerful local hangout, particularly Saturday night. Reservation advised. (B/M)

Breakfast, lunch, daily, dinner Wednesday to Monday. SR1 Gualala; tel 884-3441.

St Orres Superlative French haute cuisine using natural foods. Sunday brunch recommended. (E)

Dinner nightly, closed Tuesdays, Sunday brunch 11.30 am to 2.30 pm. SR1 between Gualala and Anchor Bay; tel 884-3303.

POINT ARENA

Point Arena has the distinction of being the closest mainland point to Hawaii. Here the highlands recede, leaving rolling pastureland where cattle graze above sandstone cliffs. It was once a whaling station; now activity is restricted to whale watching.

The 115-foot automated lighthouse replaced an original 1870 version, which had to be rebuilt after it was reported to have swung back and forth in the 1906 earthquake. (The San Andreas fault

enters the Pacific at Alder Creek, only a few miles from here.) The 'new' light-house's strong beacon has a 21-mile visibility and there have been no recurrences of the dreadful night of November 20, 1865, when 10 ships foundered on the rocks here.

Beyond Point Arena, cypress wind-breaks shelter communities of second homes such as Irish Beach, where houses can be rented from Irish Beach Rental, tel (707) 882-2467.

BOONVILLE

Turn inland on Mountain View Rd to Boonville, the town with its own language. It's in the Anderson Valley at the junction of SR 128. *Boontling,* the local lingo, evolved in the 1880s when the towns-people would gather to try and stump each other with a new *boont* word. Derivations of people's names and occupations were turned into descriptive nouns, always with underlying humor. The vocabulary of more than 1000 words has been handed down orally since then; only recently has the language been written down. So, if you ask a local for a *hairk,* he'll send you to the *hairk region –* where else would you get a hair-cut but at a barbershop? And if you go to church, the service is conducted by a *skipe –* derived of course, from sky pilot. You can buy a cookbook written in *Boontling,* with the appropriate translations included.

Apart from trying to interpret *Boontling* you can get into the valley's ranch life at Boonville, particularly during the Buck-a-roo Days rodeo in June and the July Woolgrowers' Meet, which features dog trials and sheep shearing contests, as well as a barbecue of local lamb.

Places to Eat

New Boonville Hotel Family-run enterprise featuring home-cooked food, using home-grown ingredients, in rooms decked with art and fresh flowers. (M)

Lunch, dinner daily. 14040 Hwy 128; tel 895-3478. No credit cards.

ELK

SR 128 connects US 101 with SR 1, returning to the coast just north of Elk.

The town of Elk straddles the coast road six miles south of the Navarro estuary. It has two of the Mendocino Coast's delightful inns, a smattering of time-worn stores and houses and a Catholic church gaily painted in buttercup yellow. The community overlooks Greenwood Cove's massive arched rock and craggy islets. In the early days of settlement the cove was a nightmare for navigators negotiating their steam schooners in to load lumber from a wire chute in the late 1880s.

Places to Stay

Harbor House (Elk, CA 95432; tel (707) 877-3203). Built as a lumber company guest house for VIPs, with a recreated Edwardian atmosphere. Five guest rooms in inn, four cottages. Breakfast and dinner included; dining room has sweeping view of Arched Rock. Rates from $95 double. Reservations necessary with $100 deposit.

Elk Cove Inn (PO Box 367, Elk, CA 95432; tel (707) 877-3321). 1880s lumber company house, converted to main house of inn; other rooms in 1920 Sandpiper House up road, which has redwood-beamed living room with fireplace – a congenial gathering place. Rates from $106 double at weekend include home-cooked breakfast and dinner. Midweek rates from $48 double, no meals. Reservations necessary.

ALBION

Rounding Navarro Head heading north again, you cross Salmon Creek and the graceful bridge arching the Albion River's bramble-choked gorge. Below the north end of the bridge is Albion Flat, which shelters a growing fleet of commercial and sport fishing boats, several resorts and camping for RVs. Just beyond Albion is one of the coast's most prestigious and historical inns.

The sod-roofed **Heritage House** was a farmhouse built in 1877 by the present innkeeper's grandfather, who operated a landing in the rugged cove below to ship redwood tiles and timbers to San Francisco. During Prohibition in the 1930s, the landing served bootleggers; Baby Face Nelson used the then-abandoned farmhouse as a hideout to escape federal agents. Today's luxurious resort sits on the clifftop above the pounding surf and attracts a regular coterie of fans.

LITTLE RIVER

Two miles further north in Little River are several other popular inns, including the rose-festooned 1853 mansion which now houses the Little River Inn.

Little River offers several diversions. **Van Damme State Park** encompasses a cove beach at the mouth of the Little River with surf gentle enough for swimming (for those hardy enough to brave the cold water), boating and good skin diving, often for abalone. Interesting is the **Pygmy Forest**, where twisted, lichen-encrusted cypress trees grow to a height of only a few feet in earth leached nearly white.

Van Damme offers the usual camping and ranger services, including campfire programs from July to Labor Day.

Places to Stay

Heritage House (Little River CA 95456; tel (707) 937-5885). 50 units. Cottages, some with fireplaces and antiques. Luxurious. Lovely setting. Breakfast, dinner included. Rates from $90 double. Reservations necessary with deposit. Open February to November only.

Little River Inn (SR 1, Little River CA 95456; tel (707) 937-5942). 1853 antique-filled mansion is core of complex; four rooms in mansion, balance in annex and two-bedroom cottages with private baths, some fireplaces and decks. Modern dining room and bar in old section. 9-hole golf course. Rates from $45 double.

SS Sea Foam Lodge (SR 1 (Box 475) Little River CA 95456; tel (707) 937-5516). Individual redwood units strung across top of rise overlooking cove, most with decks. Proprietor is friendly retired sea captain. No restaurant. Rates from $59 double.

Glendeven Inn (8221 N SR 1, Little River CA 95456; tel (707) 937-0083). Six rooms, two with private baths, in 19th century farmhouse. Each room, individually designed, has ocean view. Charming atmosphere, social parlor with fireplace. Rates from $50 double include breakfast, reservations necessary.

Places to Eat

Heritage House Elegant dining in plush setting of antique-filled 1877 farmhouse. Set menu, impressive wine list, traditional buffet Saturday nights. Jacket and tie required. (M/E)

Breakfast, dinner. Closed December to January. SR 1 Little River; tel 937-5885.

1882 Farmhouse, with fireplace, great ocean view. (M/E)

Dinner (two seatings: 6 pm and 8.20 pm), closed Sundays. SR 1 Little River; tel 937-0282.

Little River Inn Steak and seafood, with homemade breads and soup served in dining room with picture window onto floodlit fern and wildflower garden. (M/E).

Breakfast, lunch, dinner daily. SR 1 Little River; tel 937-5942.

MENDOCINO

From Little River, it's a three-mile drive to the town of Mendocino, sprawled across a cliff-bound tableland jutting into the Pacific. As you approach Big River Bridge, you see the village neatly spread before you, its distinctive skyline punctuated by square water towers.

Mendocino had its beginnings in the mid-19th century when a party of salvagers searching for a foundered Oriental silk ship returned to San Francisco with reports of the area's gigantic redwood trees. One Henry Meiggs responded by organising a company to set up a mill in July 1852, and for a short while the town was known as Meiggsville. After several false starts, the town grew and by 1870 was based along Main St, still the main thoroughfare.

However, as the lumber trade diminished in the late 1930s, so did the population. Discovery by artists in the 1950s triggered the town's revival; they were followed by 'beatniks' and, in the 1960s, 'flower children,' members of the counterculture and finally tourists. Real estate prices sky-rocketed.

The **Mendocino Headlands State Park** was created which excludes the village but protects the meadows and wave-sculpted cliffs of the promontory.

Mendocino's beauty and singularity have attracted film-makers over the years; the high-steepled 1868 Presbyterian Church, now a Historical Landmark, is preserved with earnings from *Johnny Belinda* and movie fans who remember the hilarious *The Russians are Coming, The Russians are Coming* will have a sense of *deja vu*. More recently *Summer of '42* was filmed here.

Midweek, when crowds are sparse, is the best time to wander and admire the New-England style architecture, legacy of the many State-of-Mainers among early settlers. Look for the elaborate embellishments on Carpenter's Gothic Victorian mansions, weathered salt boxes and roofs sharply sloped for snow that never falls. Atop the Masonic Hall on Lansing St is a tableau of Father Time braiding a maiden's hair, carved from a single piece of redwood in the 1870s.

Shoppers have a field day in Mendocino's boutiques. Main St's boardwalk leading to false-front stores is a good place to start. Pick up a *Mendocino Gallery and Shop Guide* at any store to know where you can buy antiques, clothing, handcrafted jewellery, books, gifts and such diverse articles as homebaked cookies, imported teas, black coral and second-hand classical records.

At the renowned **Mendocino Arts Center** on Little Lake Drive, you can watch painters, sculptors, printmakers and other creators at work, and sometimes join in events such as art fairs and wine tasting.

Heading west, Little Lake Drive becomes Heeser Drive which loops around the edge of the bluff, giving some of the best views of wave action on the Mendocino coast. Sunset is spectacular from this point.

Big River, which empties into the ocean on the south side of the Mendocino headland, is fine for trolling the elusive silver salmon and for canoeing upstream into the wilderness. However care must be taken at the river mouth, where there's a dangerous rip tide.

Catch-a-canoe rents canoes and paddleboats. SR 1 at Comptche Rd, open daily from 9 am to 6 pm; (707) 937-0273.

Places to Stay

MacCallum House (Albion St (PO Box 206) Mendocino CA 95460; tel (707) 937-0289). Honeymoon house for lumber magnate's daughter, built in 1882, with handsome furnishings intact. Refurbished bedrooms in house, baths down the hall. Barn apartment with private bath. Rates from $34.50 double rooms, $85 barn apartment. Dinner served in turn-of-century library (not included).

Mendocino Village Inn (Main St, Mendocino CA 95460; tel (707) 937-0246). 12 rooms in an 1882 mansion known as 'Doctor's House'. Rooms range from suites to cozy attics under sloping rafters, three rooms with private bathrooms. Double beds. Rates from $25 double.

Joshua Grindle Inn (44800 Little Lake Drive, Mendocino CA 95460; tel (707) 937-4143). Five rooms in 1879 mansion, each individually furnished in early American, private baths, some fireplaces. Gracious living and dining rooms. Full breakfast included. Rates from $50

double. Children discouraged.

Mendocino Hotel, (Main St (PO Box 587), Mendocino CA 95460; tel (707) 937-0511). 1878 hotel renovated in 1973 by fast-food king into pseudo-Victorian elegance with flocked wallpaper and Tiffany glass. Luxurious fittings include brass and four poster beds. Some private bathrooms. Rates from $45 double with Continental breakfast. Reservations necessary.

Sea Rock Cottages (SR 1 (PO Box 286) Mendocino CA 95460; tel (707) 937-5517). Cabins overlooking ocean and northern edge Mendocino headland. Private beach. Some two-bedroom, some kitchens. Friendly hospitality. Rates from $38 double.

Places to Eat

Mendocino Hotel Dining room decorated in lavish Victorian style with glassed-in section. Steak, seafood. Reservations recommended. (M)

Breakfast, lunch, dinner daily. Main St; tel 937-0511.

Cafe Beaujolais Excellent Continental cuisine using fresh local food. Delightful setting in an old Victorian building, with alfresco dining too. Beer and wine only. Reservations for groups of five up only. (M)

Breakfast, lunch from Monday to Saturday. Dinner, Friday to Sunday. Sunday brunch 9 am to 2 pm. Closed Tuesday. 961 Ukiah St; tel 937-5614.

The Sea Gull Popular restaurant rebuilt with aid of friends and neighbors after 1976 fire. Good food, featuring homebaked fresh fruit pies. Inn next door. (M)

Breakfast, lunch, dinner daily. Lansing St; tel 937-5204.

MacCallum House Romantic atmosphere in stately mansion living room/library. Fine Contintental cuisine plus homemade desserts make this exceptional choice. Reservations recommended. (M)

Dinner nightly, Albion St; tel 937-5763.

NOYO

From the high bridge spanning the fjord-like Noyo River, you can see on one side the ship channel to the ocean, and on the other, the provincial fishing village nestled on Noyo Flat. Noyo Harbor has become a center for sports fishing; salmon party boats operate from June to the beginning of October. On the docks, fuel bunkers, ice houses, and marine chandlers crowd popular seafood restaurants. Hour-long waits for a table can be spent over cocktails while gazing at the boat activity through wide windows. The Noyo River offers silver salmon runs in the fall.

Places to Stay

Harbor Lite Lodge (120 N Harbor Drive, Ft Bragg CA 95437; tel (707) 964-0221). New 50-unit motel; most rooms with private balconies overlooking Noyo fishing village and harbor. Queen-size beds, private baths. Sauna. Rates from $42 double.

Places to Eat

The Wharf Popular seafood and steak restaurant with wide-window views of harbor, fishing village. Entertainment Friday to Saturday 9 pm to 2 am. (M)

Lunch, dinner daily. Noyo Harbor; tel 964-4283.

El Mexicano Locally popular; good home-cooked Mexican dishes. Beer & wine. (B)

Lunch, dinner daily. 701 N Harbor Drive. tel 964-7164.

FORT BRAGG

Despite the profusion of motor lodges, trailer parks and vacation homes springing up from erstwhile sheep pastures, Fort Bragg is still palpably a lumber town, as stacked logs beside the road and drying yards remind the visitor. Tourism is on the increase but the town's economy is tied to the huge Georgia-Pacific sawmill – it's the only one of the Mendocino Coast towns where lumber is still king.

The original Fort Bragg was built in 1857 on the terrace north of the Noyo estuary to oversee the Mendocino Indian Reservation, a 24,000-acre area created in 1856 to house coastal Indians from as far south as Bodega. However, pressure from lumberworkers anxious to harvest the reservation's redwood forests prevailed; the Indians were moved and the fort was abandoned in 1864.

Development of the lumber industry in the 1890s by the Union Lumber Company led to the establishment of what today is Fort Bragg's main tourist attraction, the Skunk Railroad.

The Skunk Railroad

Chinese labor was used to build the railroad up the rugged Noyo canyon to Willits, 40 miles inland. In 1911, the completed railroad was connected to the Northwestern Pacific Railroad, thus linking Fort Bragg to San Francisco. In 1925, the first gasoline-motor cars replaced steam locomotives; their fumes immediately earned them the name 'Skunks'.

Today's Skunks are diesel electrics, except in summer when the Super Skunk, a refurbished century-old Mikado 2-8-2 locomotive, is pressed into service. The scenic trip winds up the river's edge, through towering redwoods into the highlands, along a spectacular route inaccessible by car. It stops frequently to drop off mail and passengers who occupy isolated summer cabins or camp out by the river (permit, obtainable at Fort Bragg depot, is necessary to camp out). The full-day round trips are very popular and reservations should be made in advance.

For current timetables and reservations, write to California Western Railroad, PO Box 907 Fort Bragg CA 95437; tel (707) 964-6371. Fares at writing are $12 adults, $6 children, round trip Fort Bragg to Willits or vice versa; $9 adults, $4 children, one way.

The Mendocino Historical Society and Georgia-Pacific have jointly developed a walking tour of historical Fort Bragg; you can pick up a free map from the Chamber of Commerce at 332 North Main St; tel 964-3153.

Fort Bragg's big festivity comes Labor Day weekend with celebration of *Paul Bunyan Days*, when their native son is feted with a carnival, gem show, logging show featuring axe throwing and pole climbing, and culminating with a Grand Parade on Monday morning.

Mendocino Coast Botanical Gardens
These privately-operated gardens are on the ocean side of SR 1, a few miles south of Fort Bragg. Stretching from the freeway to the sea, 47 acres of natural woods and meadows intersperse with an extravagant display of cultivated begonias, rhododendrons, fuchsias, gladioli, wild lilac and other seasonal blooms. The gardens have picnicking facilities, a coffee house, a Cliff House for ocean-viewing, local arts and crafts on display and Saturday afternoon concerts in summer. A two-mile network of hiking trails wind through fern grottoes and cross rustic bridges over trout-laden streams. The gardens are open daily from 8.30 am to 5 pm (8.30 am to 6 pm summer); admission charge; tel 964-4352.

Places to Stay
Fort Bragg offers a number of motels, mostly along SR 1, plus a charming inn; *The Gray Whale Inn* (615 N Main St (SR 1) Fort Bragg CA 95437; tel (707) 964-0640). 13 rooms in a transformed 1915 hospital charming individual decor, two penthouse rooms with sundecks overlooking Fort Bragg and the ocean. Most rooms have private bath. Rates from $35 double include Continental breakfast.

Places to Eat
Likewise there is a choice of dining opportunities, ranging from a fast food A&W on Main St to delis and fine dining houses, plus numerous seafood restaur-

ants at Noyo Harbor.

The Restaurant Home cooked food served in series of dining rooms decorated with fine paintings. Interesting, varied menu. Reservations recommended. (M)

Lunch, dinner, closed Wednesday. Sunday brunch. 418 N Main; tel 964-9800.

Mendocino Junction Menu features railroad terminology to describe dishes including chicken, juicy hamburgers etc. Children's menu. (B/M)

Lunch, dinner daily. 627 N Main; tel 964-7672.

Entertainment
Entertainment along the Mendocino Coast largely consists of socialising around a blazing log fire in your inn. However, Fort Bragg supports two seasonal theatre companies.

The *Gloriana Opera Company* presents Gilbert & Sullivan in the junior high school's Cotton Auditorium, Fir & Harold Sts, from early July to early September. Performances Friday, Saturday at 8 pm, Sunday 2 pm. (Program information and reservations, tel 964-7093 or 964-7125.)

The *Fort Bragg Footlighters* perform Gaslite Gaieties Saturday and Wednesday nights at 8 pm from Memorial Day weekend to Labor Day weekend at their Little Theater, 248 Laurel St. (For reservations, write to PO Box 575, Fort Bragg, CA 95437; tel 964-3806).

Getting to Fort Bragg
Greyhound Bus Lines schedule daily north/south service between Fort Bragg and San Francisco, via US 101, SR 128 and SR 1; tel (707) 963-2241.

Mendocino Transit Authority buses link Ukiah and Willits to Fort Bragg and Mendocino weekdays (tel (707) 468-4268).

WESTPORT
A side road from the former logging town of Cleone, a few miles up the coast from

Fort Bragg, leads to MacKerricher State Park.

From here, SR 1 passes through Westport, once a booming town and now virtually a ghost town of weatherbeaten houses, a general store and gas pump and a motel and delicatessen, all overlooking picturesque rock-pocked surf. A short way past almost-deserted Rockport on Cape Vizcaino, the road heads inland through the forest to join US 101 at Leggett.

Useful Addresses

Bodega Bay Area Chamber of Commerce (PO Box 146, Bodega Bay, CA 94923; tel (707) 875-3407.)
Fort Bragg-Mendocino Coast Chamber of Commerce (332 N Main St PO Box 1141, Fort Bragg, CA 95437; tel (707) 964-3153.)
Anderson Valley Chamber of Commerce (PO Box 275, Boonville, CA 95415.)

THE INLAND ROUTE

Leaving San Francisco, US 101 heads north across the Golden Gate Bridge, then runs through the rich farming valleys of Sonoma and Mendocino counties to Leggett, where it is joined by SR 1. Here it becomes the Redwood Highway, passing through one of the last natural habitats of the magnificent *Sequoia sempervirens,* the coast redwood.

En route, secondary highways branch off to give access to the Wine Country, Russian River's vacation resorts and the coast, the lake country, and further north, to the wilderness area of the Trinity Alps.

Non-drivers can ride the Greyhound Bus which operates daily service north, plus frequent service to Santa Rosa and other points off the freeway. Santa Rosa and surrounding area is also served by Golden Gate Transit, with daily schedule by US 101 and SR 116 from San Francisco (tel (707) 544-1323 in Santa Rosa, (415) 453-2100 in San Francisco.)

PETALUMA

Just 35 miles from downtown San Francisco, the ranching community of Petaluma was once known as the 'egg capital of the world'. With urban sprawl reaching well into the Sonoma Valley, ranchland is being encroached upon now by developers: it's only a 45-minute drive from San Francisco, well within commuting time. However this is still ranching and dairy country and there are plenty of back roads to explore, with handicrafts and roadway stands offering farm-fresh produce. Sonoma County Farm Trails, PO Box 6043, Santa Rosa CA 95406 issues a free map and guide on request; send a stamped, addressed envelope.

These days, Petaluma's claim to fame is that the world wrist-wrestling championship is held here each October. But there are some other attractions.

Petaluma Adobe State Historic Park, part of General Mariano Vallejo's ranch is one of the state's largest adobes still standing. It's best to allow two to three hours to explore the building and grounds; a specialist is on hand to answer questions on the 1846 building and its period furnishings. On Casa Grande Rd, 2.5 miles north of SR 116, follow signs. It's open daily 10 am to 5 pm, admission charge.

Marin French Cheese Co is a century-old cheesemaking company ('Rouge et Noir' label). Picnicking on their lawn overlooking the lake, on bread and cheese with wine, is popular with visitors after touring the cheese factory. At 7500 Red Hill Rd, nine miles west of Petaluma; tel 433-5545. There are free tours daily from 10 am to 4 pm; retail shop.

The Great Petaluma Mill – 1876 is a restoration development of restaurants, shops and a theater in the old Golden Eagle Feed Mill on the river's edge.

SANTA ROSA

Santa Rosa is the Sonoma County Seat (only, some say, because of the wild midnight ride in 1854, when Old Peg Leg Menefee stole the courthouse records from Sonoma and delivered them to the Santa Rosa town fathers!). It is the major center for the surrounding farmlands and orchards. But it, too, is transforming into a surburban residential area.

Santa Rosa's salubrious climate and fine soil induced Luther Burbank to settle here. He said of it: 'I firmly believe from all that I have seen that this is the chosen spot of all the earth as far as nature is concerned . . . .' and proceeded to prove it by spending 51 years developing his wondrous skills as a plant breeder. The resulting world-famed **Luther Burbank Memorial Garden** is a shrine drawing naturalists from around the globe. Burbank died in 1926 and is buried in the grounds beneath his beloved 118-foot Cedar of Lebanon. The gardens were renovated and dedicated to his memory in 1960; a Parks and Recreation representative is on hand to describe the various creations. On the corner of Santa Rosa Avenue, it's advisable to arrange weekday tours in advance; tel (707) 576-5115.

A block away is the Church of One Tree – the **Robert L Ripley Memorial Museum**, commemorating the native son of 'Believe-it-or-not' fame. The church which Ripley made famous was built in 1870 from a single redwood tree (grown near Guerneville). The museum contains the world traveler's memorabilia and some of his original cartoons. It's located at Juilliard Park on Sonoma Avenue and is open from 11 am to 4 pm daily mid-May to August, Thursday to Monday rest of year; closed December 6 to February 28; admission charge; tel (707) 778-4398 to arrange tour.

Places to Stay

El Rancho Tropicana (2200 Santa Rosa Avenue, Santa Rosa CA 95401; tel (707) 542-3655). 300 air-conditioned rooms set in 25 acres. Some kitchens, three pools, wading pool, whirlpool. Restaurant, bar,

entertainment. Rates from $49 double, extra persons under 18 free.

Best Western Hillside Inn (2901 4th St, Santa Rosa CA 95404; tel (707) 546-9353). 36 air-conditioned units, some balconies and patios, kitchens. Color TV. Pool. Coffeeshop. Beer and wine license. Rates from $37 double.

Motel 6 (2760 Cleveland Avenue, Santa Rosa CA 95401; tel (707) 546-9563). 100 air-conditioned rooms. Pool. Adjacent cafe. Rates from $19.95 double.

Places to Eat

The Marshall House distinctive luncheons served in 1876 Victorian mansion with original fixtures, including ceramic fireplaces, French-embossed paneling, crystal chandeliers. Wine only. (M)

Lunch, closed Sunday. 835 2nd St; tel 542-5305.

Highland House In former Santa Rosa Golf and Country Club, commanding view of Valley of the Moon. Renowned for Prime Rib. (M)

Lunch Sunday only, dinner nightly. Sonoma Highway and Los Alamos Rd; tel 539-0928.

RUSSIAN RIVER AREA

Healdsburg, some 20 miles north of Santa Rosa is gateway to the Russian River resort towns. Healdsburg itself sits in the bed where the river changes direction from north-south to east-west.

The Russian River resort area has long been a weekend favorite of San Franciscans – it is only an hour's drive from the Bay.

Once Pomo Indians lived along the river's banks, which the Russians explored but did not settle. The lumber barons came and started to work the forests in earnest in the 1850s. It was from here that the lumber came to rebuild San Francisco after the 1906 'quake.

The resort area comprises a string of towns tucked in redwoods along SR 116, which follows the river bank to Jenner on the coast. Vacation cottages, lodges and motels fill during the summer months.

Guerneville, the largest town, grows from some 4000 people midweek to 50,000 at weekends.

The season kicks off late May with Guerneville's **Russian River Rodeo and Stumptown Parade** and finishes at Labor Day weekend with the **Pageant of Fire**.

Monte Rio, a smalll town west of Guerneville, holds a small festival on July 4.

Near Monte Rio, a glade of majestic redwoods known as **Bohemian Grove** is a rustic retreat for celebrities, members of an exclusive San Francisco men's club. The Russian River is also popular for float trips. You can rent canoes in Healdsburg for one to five days; they'll pick you up downriver at a pre-arranged time and place. (For rates and reservations write Trowbridge Recreation, Inc, 20 Healdsburg Avenue, Healdsburg CA 95448; tel (707) 433-7427).

Russian River Wineries

Since the early 1970s, the Russian River valleys have gained respect as wine-producing areas. There are a dozen or so wineries off US 101 from Santa Rosa to Ukiah, among the more notable being:

Korbel Winery, in an attractive ivy-covered red brick building overlooking the river, is widely known for French style champagne and brandy. Open for tours and tasting at 13250 River Rd, Guerneville; tel 887-2294. Winery open from 9 am to 5.30 pm; tours every 45 minutes, 9.45 am to 3.45 pm summer, on the hour 10 am to 3 pm winter; retail wine shop.

Sonoma Vineyard which has a dramatic new building in Windsor. Apart from tasting, the winery puts on outdoor concerts and theatrical performances in summer and serves lunch and dinner by reservation from May to October. (Location: 11455 Old Redwood Highway, Windsor; tel (707) 433-6511, open 10 am to 5 pm daily.)

Chateau Souverain dominates a hillside with its stark contemporary building patterned on old hop barns. In addition to tours and tasting, continental lunches and dinner are available at its *Bacchus Restaurant*. (Location: Off US 101 between Healdsburg and Geyserville, follow signs; tel (707) 433-8281, open 10 am to 5 pm excluding holidays; restaurant lunch daily, dinner Wednesday through Sunday.)

Italian Swiss Colony at Asti is the main headquarters of this far-flung winery, established in 1887 as part of an agricultural commune founded by Italian Swiss migrants. (Location: off US 101 at Asti tel (707) 433-2333; open daily excluding holidays 9 am to 5 pm summer; 10 am to 5 pm winter. Tasting, movie and tours; retail gift shop; classic garden.)

At Geyserville SR 128 branches off from US 101 south-east through the Alexander Valley's vineyards to Calistoga and the Napa Valley. Just beyond Cloverdale it heads northwest to Boonville through the scenic Anderson Valley, then on through towering redwood forests to follow the Navarro River to the coast. From **Hopland**, in Mendocino County, SR 175 cuts across from US 101 to Clear Lake.

A pretty drive, particularly in springtime when blossoms turn apple orchards into a dazzling sight, is to loop from Guerneville south on SR 116 to Sebastopol west on SR 12 to Freestone, then north through **Occidental** and Monte Rio back to SR 116. This is also an opportunity to sample one of the family-style Italian restaurants for which Occidental is famed and to browse through the town's antique and 'collectable' stores.

Places to Stay

The Woods (16881 Armstrong Woods Rd, Guerneville, CA 95446; tel (707) 869-0111. Pleasant resort with 39 units, some kitchens, and cabins. Two pools, tennis. Dining room, coffee shop, cocktails. Rates from $60 double.

Northwood Lodge (Box 188 Monte Rio, CA 94562; tel (707) 865-2126). 25-unit motel, some kitchens. Cottages with fireplaces, bunk beds. Reservations, deposit required. Rates from $42 double.

Places to Eat
Fiori's Casual, family-style Italian multi-course dinners. (M)

Dinner nightly, lunch weekends; November 1 to May 1 closed Mondays. 3657 Main St, Occidental; tel 823-8188.
Union Hotel Mammoth Italian family-style five-course dinner featuring choice of three entrees. Setting is 1892 hotel. (M)

Lunch, dinner daily. Main St, Occidental; tel 874-3662.

UKIAH

Ukiah, county seat of Mendocino County, is a fast-growing city – it has more than doubled its population in the past 15 years. Its name is derived from the Pomo Indian words for 'deep valley', and it sits at the center of a fertile valley. Ukiah's **Lake Mendocino** is popular with campers.

Places to Stay
The Palace Hotel (272 State St, Ukiah, tel (707) 468-9291, toll free 800-862-4698). Restored 1891 landmark which has become popular as a weekend retreat for San Franciscans. Complimentary wine and continental breakfast come with the rooms. The dining room serves honest country food. Rates from $39 double weekdays, $44 weekends.

WILLITS

Willits is terminal point for two links with the coast: the Skunk Railroad through the Noyo River canyon and SR 20, which winds through sparsely inhabited mountains, heavily wooded with redwood and Douglas fir, to emerge at Noyo on the coast.

Willit's **Mendocino County Museum** chartered to 'preserve and interpret the total history of Mendocino County', is run by the County Historical Society. At 400 E Commercial St; tel 459-2736; it's open Wednesday to Sunday from 10 am to 4.30 pm; admission charge.

From Willits, US 101 curves around the Middle Fork of the Eel River, then runs northwest to pick up the Eel's South Fork at Leggett, gateway to the Redwoods.

THROUGH THE REDWOODS

The magnificent coast redwood, *Sequoia sempervirens,* truly merits use of the overworked description 'unique.' It is native only to the Californian coastal area and is amongst the tallest of the world's trees – the tallest known, Founders Tree, measured 367 feet, until storm damage reduced it to a mere 347 feet. The oldest known coast redwood was 2200 years when it was cut down in the 1930s – much younger than its inland relatives native to the Sierra Nevada, the *Sequoia dendron gigantea* which lives to 3200 years.

For more than a century, the coast redwood has been subject of an unending battle between the lumber industry and conservationists. Stands of the magnificent trees once covered a 30-mile-wide swathe from south of Monterey to Oregon. Now only small areas of primeval forests remain, concentrated mainly in the region from Leggett to Crescent City on the far north coast. Even much of this area is second-growth.

As early as the mid-19th century the 'Save the Redwoods' league was formed to fight for the tree's preservation. The League collected funds to donate to the state park system groves which today remain as virgin stands within second-growth forests. More recently, the Sierra Club led a fight to preserve the primeval giants within a national park. The joint efforts of many groups resulted in the Redwood Act, passed by Congress on March 27, 1978, which enlarged the existing Redwood National Park from 58,000 acres to 106,000 acres, with an additional 30,000-acre buffer zone (within which, at the discretion of the Secretary of the Interior, logging can be halted if it endangers the trees in the park). The national park covers a narrow coastal strip in Humboldt and Del Norte counties from the Redwood Creek south of Orick to the Smith River north of Crescent City (see below).

The Redwood Highway From Leggett to the coast, US 101, known at this point as the Redwood Highway, passes through giant redwood forests following the contours of the Eel River's South Fork toward the ocean. There are frequent opportunities for view stops and picnicking.

Richardson Grove State Park Though a small park, only 800 acres, Richardson Grove offers one of the best redwood nature displays in the area as well as camping, picnic areas and an Eel River beach. Just over the Humboldt County Line, Richardson Grove is a superb spot to 'stop the world and get off' for a while. Be sure to look at the interpretive display, located across US 101 from Richardson Grove lodge, for an excellent description of the coast redwoods and their environment. The park is open year-round and offers 169 campsites. You would be wise to make reservations through Ticketron, or Richardson Grove State Park, Garberville CA 95440; tel (707) 247-3318.

Places to Stay
Benbow Inn (2675 Benbow Drive, Garberville CA 95440; tel (707) 923-2124; on Eel River.) 54 rooms in Tudor-style inn, decorated in Art Nouveau. Golf, swimming, games in redwood-paneled lobby. Restaurant, cocktails. Rates from $50 double. Closed December 1 to March 27, except for Christmas week when it reopens from December 18 to January 2.
Hartsook Inn (Piercy CA 95467; tel (707) 247-3305.)
Rustic resort adjoining Richardson Grove State Park. Lodge and one to three

bedroom cottages. Swimming. dining room, gift shop. Rates from $32 for a double.

Places to Eat
Benbow Inn Continental Cuisine in attractive dining room or outdoor terrace. Fresh fish in season. (M)
Breakfast, lunch, dinner. Closes with hotel. Tel 923-2124.

Avenue of the Giants You should take the time to drive the Avenue of the Giants, which for 30 miles parallels and crisscrosses US 101 and the river. The entrance is at Sylvandale, about six miles beyond Garberville, and it rejoins US 101 some 30 miles south of Eureka.

. This two-lane scenic highway offers a more tactile experience of the rugged giants. Fern-tangled undergrowth, pierced here and there by the sun's rays, adds a fresh fragrance to the musky perfume of the ancient trees. Occasionally you will encounter a marked grove dedicated to a donor, testament to a concern for preservation.

Along the Avenue of the Giants are campgrounds and picnic sites, swimming holes and occasional towns. Turnouts and parking spots give access to trails winding into the eerie depths of the forest.

From June to September, tours are operated along the Avenue by open *Squirrel* bus, departing Garberville, tel (707) 986-7526 for information.

Humboldt Redwoods State Park The 43,000 acre Humboldt Redwoods State Park borders the Avenue of the Giants and the Eel River. Within its boundaries are more than 70 memorial groves and the Rockefeller Forest. Donated by the Rockefeller family, the forest has many trees over 350 feet tall and is considered one of the world's most valuable tracts of timber. Within the park, you will find three *campgrounds* situated in dense forests, picnic areas, more than 100 miles of hiking trails and river beaches. Nature programs are conducted in summer by park rangers. In winter, steelhead and salmon fishing are popular.

Camping reservations can be made through Ticketron or Area Manager, Humboldt Redwoods State Park, PO Box 100, Weott CA 95571; tel (707) 946-2311.

SCOTIA

At Scotia, a mill town built entirely of redwood lumber, you can tour the Pacific Lumber Company's mill – any week day – one of the world's largest, and follow the lumber process. Pick up a pass for a self-guided tour at the company museum.

Don't miss seeing the town's theater, built entirely of rough-finish redwood, elaborately detailed, it's well worth a look.

HUMBOLDT BAY

Beyond Scotia, US 101 emerges onto the coastal plain of the Eel River Delta, and skirts Humboldt Bay to enter Eureka.

Long and narrow Humboldt Bay is California's only bay area with miles of untouched shoreline. In 1971, acquisition of a 9350-acre preserve, including most of the South Bay and part of North Bay, was authorized for the **Humboldt Bay National Wildlife Refuge**. The mud flats, salt marshes and islands are feeding grounds for bird life, including snowy egrets whose rookery is on Indian Island where they mass like a white cloud on the tall cypresses.

A good way to view the bay and shoreline of Eureka is on a 75-minute narrated cruise aboard *The Madaket*, which sails from the foot of C St. It departs 1 pm, 2.30 pm, 4 pm daily between June and September, weekends only in May; admission charge; tel 442-3738 or 443-2741.

EUREKA

Eureka, Humboldt County seat, was founded in the 1850s as a shipping center, first for the Klamath mines then for lumber. The latter industry is responsible for the town's distinctive appearance, for lumber barons built their mansions here in the high Victorian style, embellishing them with sculptured eaves, gables and riotous ginger-bread.

Most notable, and a Californian landmark, is the **Carson Mansion**, built for William Carson in 1884. The redwood exterior is appointed in its original cream-and-spinach colours, which accent the fantasy of pitched gables, carved window frames and balustrades.Inside is out of bounds to visitors as it is now a private club, but the exterior is definitely worth viewing and possibly is photographed more than any other house in the country. Across the street is a small but delightful Victorian house built by Carson as a wedding gift for his son. You will find it on Second and M Sts.

After years of neglect, many of the city's Victorian homes have been restored. A free self-guided auto tour map showing the best of these handsome residences is available from the Chamber of Commerce, 2112 Broadway, tel 442-3738.

Old Town, centred on Second St, comprises restored 1800s buildings facing a brick-paved street, restaurants and shops, a fountain-splashed park and the nearby Clarke Museum. In summer, a five-hour Eureka Image Tour of the City's highlights is offered by reservation only; tel (707) 442-3738.

Clarke Memorial Museum, housed in a turn-of-the-century bank building, contains outstanding displays of Western Americana, Indian basketry and artefacts of Yurok, Hoopa, Karok, Pomo and Wiyot tribal life, as well as a considerable collection of bird specimens. On Third & E Sts, it's open Tuesday to Friday from 10 am to 4 pm; Saturday 10 am to noon, 1 to 4 pm; closed Sundays, Mondays, holidays and from late March to May; donations; tel 443-1947.

Fort Humboldt was built in 1853 to

protect settlers against retaliatory Indian attacks for encroachment of gold miners on tribal lands. Young Captain Ulysses S Grant, later to be general and president, served in the fort in 1854. Now a State Historic Park, Fort Humboldt is being restored. It offers a logging exhibit dating back to the 1850s, a small museum tucked behind park headquarters, a picnic area and fine views from atop its bluff overlooking the bay. At 3431 Fort Avenue; tel 443-7952; open daily in daylight hours.

A drive across the bridge to **Samoa** takes you over Woodley and Indian Islands, which lie between Humboldt and Arcata Bays. **Indian Island** was site of the 1860 massacre of Indians who had gathered on the island for a festive celebration. So enraged was Bret Harte, then a journalist on the Arcata *Northern Californian*, by their massacre that he wrote a scathing denunciation of the perpetrators, resulting in his enforced departure from the county. In Samoa, between the bay and the ocean, is the **Samoa Cookhouse**, last of the lumberjack cookhouses still operating in the West, where you can dine family style and inspect a museum of culinary relics and other momentos of early logging days.

Places to Stay

Eureka has a number of motels, mostly situated along Fourth St, which carries US 101 south through town. The Eureka Chamber of Commerce issues a pamphlet, *Where to Eat, Sleep and Camp in Eureka* which also covers areas south and north of the city. (Write: 2112 Broadway, Eureka CA 95501; tel (707) 442-3738. *The Eureka Inn* (7th & F Sts, Eureka CA 95501; tel (707) 442-6441). Recently refurbished English Tudor Inn. Pool, cable TV, restaurant, coffee shop. Rates from $48 double.

Places to Eat

Samoa Cookhouse Lumbercamp cookhouse food. Free museum of logging cookhouse relics. (B)
Breakfast, lunch, dinner. Samoa Boulevard, across bridge from Eureka; tel 442-1659.
Lazio's Seafood On Humboldt Bay, featuring dockside fresh seafood. (M)
Lunch, dinner. 4 C St; tel 442-2337.

MATTOLE VALLEY

An interesting side-trip from Eureka is through the pastoral Mattole Valley. You can choose a short loop from Loleta, 17 miles south of Eureka on US 101, through Ferndale and return; or a 73-mile loop which continues from Ferndale to Capetown, on to Petrolia, where California's first oil wells were drilled, out to Bull Creek and through Rockefeller Forest's redwoods to rejoin US 101 just north of Weott.

Highlight of the Mattole Valley is **Ferndale**, a jewel of Victorian elegance in the midst of rolling dairy pasturelands. Established by two English brothers in 1852, Ferndale became refuge for Danish immigrants fleeing the Schleswig-Holstein takeover in the 1860s. The soon prosperous dairy farmers apparently were inspired by neighboring Eureka when they built their Carpenter's Gothic mansions. But by the mid-20th century, the buildings along Francis St, the town's main street, were in disrepair. An influx of artistic escapees from big city life in the 1960s at first upset the townspeople. But when, in 1967, some started to restore one or two decaying Victorian houses, the locals rose to the challenge and soon a rash of refurbishing and repainting produced today's homage to Victoriana. Don't miss the **Golden Gate Mercantile** with its hodgepodge of antique furniture, old lace, stiff collars, pith helmets and old fashioned candy counter, a sharp contrast to the necessities and luxuries of contemporary living. Ferndale hosts an annual art festival in May, highlighted by the Great Ferndale Cross-Country Kinetic Sculpture Race, and the county fair in July/August.

ARCATA

Arcata, a few miles north of Arcata Bay, is known to readers of Bret Harte, for it provided many of the characters and settings for his stories. Incorporated as Uniontown in 1850, it is one of the pioneer cities of the Old West.

City center is the plaza, once terminus for mule trains supplying the Klamath and Trinity gold miners. You can pick up a free map guiding you on a scenic tour of Arcata, including reminders of the days of Bret Harte and gold mining, at the Chamber of Commerce, 780 7th St (Jacoby's Storehouse); tel 882-3619.

The major industry today is lumber. Also important is dairying, centered on the surrounding fertile lands of the Mad River Valley. The river was named for a heated discussion within the Josiah Gregg party, when their 1849 exploration reached this point, as to which direction they should take next.

The river, bay and ocean contribute bountifully to Arcata's restaurant tables; they are justly renowned for Humboldt crab, fresh salmon, sole, cod and shrimp. Anglers flock to the river for summer trout; after winter storms breach the sandbar, steelhead and king salmon draw them upriver.

Places to Stay

Fairwinds Motel (1674 G St Arcata CA 95521; tel (707) 822-4824). 27-unit motel opposite Humboldt State University. Color Cable TV. Rates from $20 double.

Arcata Youth Hostel (1390 I St Arcata CA 95521, PO Box 4958; tel (707) 822-9995. In old Victorian house, accommodations for family available.

Places to Eat

Youngberg's Spirited Dining Seafood and Italian food in terraced, oak paneled dining room. (M)

Lunch, dinner, closed Monday, 3rd floor, Jacoby's Storehouse, Arcata; tel 822-1712.

Bergie's Family-style version of the above, with pastas, Italian dishes, salads. (M).

Lunch, dinner daily. 1st floor, Jacoby's Storehouse; tel 822-7001.

Paradise Ridge Variable, interesting menu. Bright, airy atmosphere. Sunday brunch recommended. (M/E)

Breakfast, lunch, dinner daily. 942 G St; tel 667-3340.

The **Azalea State Reserve**, two miles east of Arcata off SR 299, is best seen in May when the 12-foot-high bushes are in riotous bloom.

SR 299 winds across the Trinity Alps and descends into the Sacramento Valley to join 1-5 at Redding. It is well traveled by lumber trucks and is slow going, but if your curiosity is aroused by tales of huge, elusive mountain men, follow it for 50 miles to **Willow Creek**, for this is the gateway to Bigfoot Country.

Bigfoot

Reported sightings of giant hirsute humanoids similar to the Himalaya's Abominable Snowman span a century in time and a geographic area from Alaska's Yakutat Bay to the northeastern wilderness of California. Perhaps seven to 14 feet in height and weighing from 300 to 800 lbs, the Bigfoot walk erect with a four to 10 foot stride, leaving behind only footprints as tangible evidence of their presence. They feature in old Indian tales – the Hoopa called them *Oh-Mah* and the Yurok *Toke-Mussi* – which describe them as 'shy men, who will do no harm.'

Sightings in recent years include two separate road crews working north of the Indian Hoopa Reservation in August, 1958, a couple on the Willits Rd, east of Fort Bragg, in January 1962, and campers in the Shasta-Trinity National Forest in 1970. Other reports include an 1884 incident in British Columbia, which detailed capture of a giant mountain man.

Labor Day weekend is chosen by

Willow Creek residents to celebrate their elusive neighbours with **Bigfoot Daze,** when you can compare your own footprint with the cast of a Bigfoot print. And, who knows . . . ?

HOOPA RESERVATION

You can visit the Hoopa reservation, 12 miles north of Willow Creek, where most of the surviving Klamath Indians – Yuroks and Hoopas – live in two settlements. The Trinity River running through the reservation provides splendid fishing and canoeing and you can buy Bigfoot casts and beautiful basketry, for which the Klamath Indians are known, at the village of Hoopa.

REDWOOD NATIONAL PARK

Back on the coast, US 101 is the freeway from Arcata to Patrick's Point, but numerous exits to the old road offer better views and side trips to seaside communities from Trinidad Head to Patrick Point State Park.

US 101 enters the Redwood National Park at Orick. The 106,000 acres of the national park encompass three long-established state parks: **Prairie Creek, Del Norte Coast** and **Jedediah Smith.** The latter is named for the famed fur trapper and mountain man who was the first white man to cross the Sierra Nevada in 1827, and who led the first expedition of whites from California to Oregon in 1828. Each of these parks is still administered by the state, while the overall park is run by National Park Service. Between them, the parks have 350 *campsites* and Orick offers a number of *motels;* all campsites except those in Del Norte Coast are booked out well in advance during the summer months.

From Memorial Day to Labor Day, buses shuttle from the National Park Information station in Orick every hour from 9 am to 4 pm taking visitors to within one mile of the tallest redwoods. A new park headquarters is planned for a site on US 101 just south of Orick. This Red-wood Information Center will have interpretive displays, NPS ranger activities, publications and it will become the starting point for the shuttle buses.

Take time to stop at the NPS wayside exhibits scattered along US 101 and US 199 within the park for insights into the nature and history of the magnificent sequoias. For details tel (707) 488-3461, the Redwood National Park Information Office, Orick.

Prairie Creek Redwoods has something of the feeling of the Northwest's rain forests. There are plenty of hiking trails, scenic Fern Canyon and you may be lucky enough to glimpse the herd of Roosevelt elk along Gold Bluff beach or even along US 101.

Northcoast Redwood Tours runs summertime tours of Redwood National Park and the northcoast. Tel (707) 677-3470 for information and schedules.

Klamath River At the park's northern tip, the highway crosses the Klamath River Bridge, crosses the Klamath River Bridge, guarded by two statues of golden bears as was the old bridge which was swept away by the Christmas flood of 1964. The deluge took with it several resort towns along the river, including old Klamath. New Klamath sits much further from the river's banks.

Klamath town hosts the annual **Salmon Festival** the last Sunday in June. Coast Indian ceremonial dances are performed in authentic costumes. Then an alfresco salmon bake is followed by boat races, logging contests and traditional Indian games.

The Klamath River lures anglers from all over the state for seasonal runs of king salmon, perch, sturgeon, flounder, steelhead and American shad. For information on seasons, write Klamath Chamber of Commerce, PO Box 476, Klamath CA 95548.

An exciting way to enjoy the Klamath River area is the **Jet-Boat Cruise** which speeds you 64 miles upriver through

Indian territory and wilderness inaccessible by car. The trip originates at the Requa Boat Dock, and picks up passengers at nine docks. It operates from June to September, departs 9 am, returns 3 pm, current rate $20 adults, $8 children, reservations advised; deposit necessary to hold reservations. *Klamath Jet-Boat Kruises*, PO Box 5, Klamath CA 95548; tel (707) 482-4191).

At Requa near the river's mouth is the 'Rekwoi' Yurok Indian House restored by the Del Norte County Historical Society from original material. Probably the oldest residence in California, the rectangular house was made from redwood slabs, hand-hewn with an elkhorn wedge. The Yurok town of Rekwoi had 24 family houses and 14 sweathouses, used by the men, before it was raided by Tolowa Indians from Crescent City in the 1870s. The Tolowas believed a Yurok shaman had cast a spell to prevent salmon from running up the Smith River. Turn left off US 101 on Requa Air Force Base Rd, then left, 0.6 of a mile past Requa Inn; open daylight hours.

A huge statue of Paul Bunyan marks the entrance to the Trees of Mystery Park up US 101. This privately-run park is rather commercial but still attracts many visitors. There's an American Indian museum, reached through the gift shop, walking trails through redwoods, and redwood carvings on display. It's open daily daylight hours; closed December and February and Thanksgiving; admission charge; tel (707) 482-5613.

CRESCENT CITY

Crescent City, Del Norte County seat, was founded in 1853 during the gold rush. It was named for its crescent-shaped harbor. Crescent City became famous on Good Friday 1964, when a Tsunami – a seismic tidal wave triggered by the Alaska earthquake – inundated the city. It destroyed a large portion of the downtown area, which is now a mall.

Coming out of the Del Norte Redwoods,

you see before you the sweep of Crescent Beach. During the gold rush fever of the 1850s, this beach was completely staked out with mining claims. Nearing Crescent City you will see townspeople fishing off Citizens Dock, which they built by co-operative effort. Commercial fishing boats bob in the bay and to the west. The catch is brought to table at restaurants around Citizens Dock.

Things to See & Do

You can view marine life at Undersea World. A stairway takes you below sea level; SCUBA show adds to the excitement.

Location: Anchor Way; tel 464-3522; open daily 9 am to 9 pm June to September, 9 am to 5 pm rest of year; admission charge.

A number of historical landmarks inform about early days in the area. The 1856 lighthouse housing the Battery Point Museum can only be reached at low tide when you walk across the ocean floor to the island on which this oldest California lighthouse was built. Open Wednesday to Sunday from May to October; admission charge.

The Del Norte County Historical Museum displays early pioneer relics and artefacts of Yurok and Tolawa Indian life. The Old County Jail is preserved on the 2nd floor. Located at 577 H St, tel 464-3922; open Friday to Sunday from 1 to 4 pm, closed two months during winter; admission charge.

Nearby, the McNulty Pioneer Museum depicts early pioneer life in a refurbished 1897 home on Seventh & H St, tel 464-3922; open Tuesday through Saturday from 1 to 4 pm, May to October; by appointment off season; admission charge.

The horrors of WW II are recalled by a plaque on the waterfront which marks the place where wreckage of the *SS Emidio* drifted into the harbor after it was sunk by Japanese torpedoes. Another tragedy at sea is witnessed by gravestones in the Brother Jonathan Cemetery. Many mark the graves of victims of the *Brother Jonathan,* wrecked on a reef off Crescent City on July 30, 1865. Only 19 survived of its 232 passengers and crew.

The **Redwood National Park** headquarters and information office is in Crescent City at Second and K Sts, (tel (707) 464-6101).

A few miles beyond Crescent City, the Redwood Highway splits. US 101 crosses the plain to the Smith River estuary, US 199 heads east into the Jedediah Smith Redwoods on its way to Grants Pass in Oregon.

Just outside the eastern entrance of Jedediah Smith Redwoods is the Redwood National Park's **Hiouchi Visitor Center,** with interpretive displays, publications and ranger activities in summer; tel (707) 459-3134 for information.

SMITH RIVER

The Smith River rivals the Klamath for fishing. Resorts clustered around the mouth of the river near Salmon Harbor are filled with anglers after steelhead king salmon, and sea-run cutthroat trout, for which the Smith is famed.

The town of **Smith River** is center for a flourishing Easter Lily industry: 90% of the world's bulbs grow here and in Oregon's neighbouring Curry County. An Easter Lily Festival celebrates harvesting of the blooms in July.

From the Smith River, US 101 passes the long, deserted stretch of Pelican State Beach to cross the border into Oregon.

Useful Addresses

Santa Rosa Chamber of Commerce (637 First St, Santa Rosa, CA 95404; tel (707) 545-1414).

Petaluma Chamber of Commerce (314 Western Avenue, Petaluma, CA 94952; tel (707) 762-2785).

Redwood National Park Headquarters (Second & K Sts, Crescent City, CA 95531; tel (707) 464-6101.) *Information*

Office (Highway 101, Orick CA 95555; tel (707) 488-3461.)

The Squirrel-Redwood Bus Tours (PO Box 353, Garberville, CA 95440; tel (707) 986-7526.)

Northcoast Redwood Tours (PO Box 177, Trinidad, CA 95570; tel (707) 677-0334, 677-3470.)

Eureka Chamber of Commerce (2112 Broadway, Eureka, CA 95501; tel (707) 442-3738.)

Del Norte County Chamber of Commerce (PO Box 246, Front & K Sts, Crescent City, CA 95531; tel (707) 464-3174.)

California State Automobile Association (AAA) (707 L St, Eureka, CA 95501; tel (707) 443-5087.)

Ukiah Chamber of Commerce (495 E Perkins, Ukiah, CA 95482; tel (707) 462-4705.)

California State Automobile Association (AAA) (415 S State St, Ukiah, CA 95482; tel (707) 462-3861.)

Willits Chamber of Commerce (15 S Main, Willits, CA 95490; tel (707) 459-4113.)

THE VALLEY ROUTE

The Sacramento Valley route north, I-5 appeals to two types of travelers: those seeking the fastest, most direct highway to the Pacific Northwest; and those with a predilection for bracing mountain air and cool, clear lakes rather than salt-damp coastal roads and imposing redwoods. For I-5 leads to the playgrounds of California's northern national parks and recreation areas in the Cascade Range and the Trinity Alps. Not without cause, local Chambers of Commerce boost the area as the 'Northern Wonderland'. Prominent amongst attractions are Lassen Volcanic National Park, the Whiskeytown-Shasta-Trinity National Recreation Area and majestic Mount Shasta.

The I-5 freeway cuts up the center of California, through the Southland's San Joaquin Valley, the Central Valley and the Sacramento Valley, into the Pacific Northwest. To reach it from the San

Francisco Bay Area, you take I-180 across the Bay bridge. Just past Vacaville is the I-505 interchange which jogs across to I-5.

The Sacremento Valley is a fertile agricultural basin. On each side of the road, pasturelands roll gently into the distance, where they meet the swell of the Coast Range on the west and the Sierra foothills to the east.

The few towns along the way are bypassed by the freeway. Well-marked interchanges lead off to them and to occasional wildlife refuges. Just past the Williams exit, Highway 20 cuts across to Lake County to the west and Marysville, Grass Valley and Nevada City to the east.

Some 95 miles from the junction of I-505 and I-5, you reach Red Bluff, gateway to the Northern Wonderland. Other ways to get there are by air or bus. Both Red Bluff and Redding have airports, with car rental agencies if you wish to hire one while there, or you can travel by *Greyhound* or *Continental Trailways*.

RED BLUFF

Red Bluff's situation, on the banks of the upper Sacramento River in proximity to the California-Oregon Trail, made it a natural supply center for miners en route to the Trinity diggings in the 1850s. Several features in and around town invite exploration.

Spawning salmon leaping up fish ladders provide a fascinating show during the fall and winter. You can watch from the **Public Television Salmon Viewing Plaza** while underwater cameras monitor the fish ladders. The plaza is on the corner of Williams and Gilmore Ave, off SR 36. Open daily from 8 am to 8 pm.

Some grand old Victorian buildings are sprinkled through the central district. A good place to start is at the 1880s period-furnished **Kelly-Griggs House Museum** at 311 Washington St. It includes Chinese and Indian artefacts and the Pendleton Gallery of Art and is open Thursday to Sunday 2 to 5 pm from June to 2 September; 2 to 4 pm balance of year, closed holidays. Donation.

You can buy a self-guided tour map of **Victorian Red Bluff** here, or from the Chamber of Commerce, 100 Main St, tel (527-6220).

The tour includes the cottage of Mrs John Brown, where the widow of the celebrated abolitionist came to live following her husband's hanging for the famous 1859 Harper's Ferry incident.

Near Red Bluff on the west bank of the Sacramento River is the **William B Ide Adobe State Historical Monument.** The shady park is a monument to the short-lived Bear Flag Party of which Ide became leader and, for a brief time, the first and only president of the California Republic. Take time here to browse the restored ranch buildings – a carriage house, smokehouse and corral – for a sense of ranch life in the 1850s. On SR 36 east of I-5; open daily 8 am to 5 pm; free.

Places to Stay
Red Bluff has several motels and tourists courts (1940s style cabins), among them:
Best Western Lamplighter Lodge (210 S Main St; tel (916) 527-1150). Rated 3-star by Mobil. 51 air-conditioned rooms, color TV, pool. 24-hour cafe. Rates from $34 double.
Motel 6 (20 Williams Avenue; tel (916) 527-8107). 61 air-conditioned rooms, pool. No restaurant. Rates from $19.95 double.

LASSEN VOLCANIC NATIONAL PARK

East of Red Bluff lie the spectacular contorted lava fields, hot springs and lakes of **Lassen Volcanic National Park**, dominated by towering Lassen Peak.

Situated about 45 miles to the east of I-5, midway between Red Bluff and Redding, the park can be reached from both by roads which actually form a loop – the Lassen Park Rd. Thus, you can take SR

36 from Red Bluff, and just beyond Mineral pick up SR 89 to enter the park's south-west entrance. SR 89 then loops through the park to the northeastern Manzanita Lake entrance, where it meets SR 44 heading west to Redding. This loop road is closed in winter, usually from the end of October to June. The only portions of the park accessible then are the ski area near the southwest entrance and the northwest entrance to Lake Manzanita. A spur road leads from Chester on SR 36, to Drakesbad, gateway to the Lassen wilderness (summer only). Concession bus service is available in season by arrangement from Redding to Manzanita Lake and from Mineral on SR 36, which can be reached by commercial daily bus service.

Best time to visit is September and October, when it is less crowded, fall colors are at their peak and Indian summer promises warm days and crisp nights.

Lassen Peak Lassen Peak itself has a turbulent history. Right up until the early 20th century it was known only as a landmark used by Danish Peter Lassen in his, some say, not-too-skilful guiding of emigrant parties over the mountains into the Sacramento Valley. (It has been said he confused Mount Shasta and Lassen Peak from time to time, using first one to fix his bearings, then switching to the other without realizing it.) Then on May 30, 1914, the dormant volcano awakened into a year-long spell of activity, erupting steam, gases, stones and ashes. One year later, on May 19, it spewed forth a column of molten lava, which cascaded down its northeastern flank, melting snow and sweeping huge boulders on a river of hot mud into the valleys below. But Lassen's fury was not yet assuaged. Three days later, on May 22, 1915, the mountain exploded. A fiery tower of steam and ashes shot 30,000 feet upward, spreading a carpet of ash as far away as Reno, 80

miles distant as the crow flies. The mountainside ripped apart from the blast of steam and hot gases and lava rushed down the northeastern flank devastating all in its path.

The volcano rumbled on with periodic eruptions, declining in fury, until 1917. Now it is the quiescent focal point of a park of awe-inspiring beauty.

Geologically, the 10,457-foot plug-dome volcano Lassen Peak is at the southern spur of the mighty Cascade Range of mountains, which stretch from Canada down into Northern California. Lassen Volcanic National Park created in August 1916, embraces 165 square miles of mountains, coniferous forests and 50 wilderness lakes, all surrounded by the Lassen National Forest.

Things to See & Do
Most accessible sights are along the Lassen Park Rd. You can buy a booklet, *Road Guide to Lassen Volcanic National Park*, keyed to markers along the 30-mile road, at the visitor center at each park entrance.

Starting at the southwest entrance, just past the winter sports area, is the **Sulphur Works** thermal area of hissing steam vents and bubbling mudpots. Remember when exploring this area, to stay on the trails and observe signs; apparently firm ground can be dangerously thin.

Bumpass Hell Basin, the park's largest and most spectacular thermal area, lies at the end of a trail just beyond Emerald Lake. Its boiling pools, fumaroles, lava fields like lakes of glass and rumbling steam vents testify to the fiery energy underlying the earth's crust.

Less than a mile beyond Lake Helen, the **Lassen Peak Trail** climbs to the summit of Lassen Peak, where in early summer you will find a sapphire crater pool. The dramatic panorama from the top embraces the peaks of the Sierra to the west, the Coast Range to the east and the icy cone of lofty Mount Shasta. You also get a clear view of the most recent volcanic devastation inflicted by the peak, already being softened by nature's touch as wild lupine push through the lava. The 2.2 mile trail which climbs 2000 feet can be comfortably hiked in a four to five-hour round trip (remember air is thinner at high altitudes and take it slowly).

A shorter hike from Kings Creek Meadows leads to the lovely **Kings Creek Falls**.

The road curves around from here past **Summit Lake**, where nightly campfire programs are held at the two campgrounds during summer months, to the **Devastated Area**, scene of the 1915 deluge of scorching mud, where natural reforestation is already taking place. Further on, the pink lava rockslides and jutting lava plugs of **Chaos Crags** and **Chaos Jumbles** have the appearance of a grotesque moonscape.

At **Manzanita Lake**, the park's main center, the Loomis Museum explains the park's volcanic history with a before-and-after diorama of Lassen Peak. Nearby you can view through a window a seismograph, recording with delicate instruments the earth's tremors.

Both Manzanita and Reflection lakes offer good swimming and fishing, and boating on Manzanita.

An interesting sight, which can only be reached by a spur road off SR 44, then trail, is **Cinder Cone**, a beautifully symmetric cone of ash and cinders which piled 700 feet high after a violent eruption in 1851.

Except for winter sports, activities are restricted to summer months. Most of them center around Manzanita Lake and include naturalist programs, featuring Indian basketmaking techniques, campfire talks and self-guided nature trail hikes. Indian lore programs, held twice daily, explore the history, customs and crafts of the Indian tribes who once made their summer camps here from spring to fall.

Of the four tribes – Atsugewi, Yana,

Yahi and Mountain Maidu – fewer than 70 descendants remain in the area. Much excitement was engendered among anthropologists when the last survivor of the Yahi was found in 1916. The man who called himself Ishi ('I am a man') was discovered emaciated and half starved, near Oroville. Anthropologist Dr Alfred L Kroeber took Ishi to the University of California at Berkeley campus, where he lived until his death five years later, contributing much to the knowledge about his people. His story is chronicled in *Ishi in Two Worlds,* published by the anthropologist's widow, Theodora Kroeber, in 1961.

Places to Stay

Accommodation within the park is limited to a *lodge* at Drakesbad, and eight *campgrounds* open only June to September, some modern, others undeveloped (there's a seven day limit in them). Campgrounds along Lassen Park Rd are at Manzanita Lake, Summit Lake, Kings Creek Meadows and the Sulphur Works. (Reservations can be made through Ticketron or Superintendent, Lassen Volcanic National Park, Mineral CA 96063).

Lodging is also available outside the park in Mineral, Chester and Childs Meadows, all on SR 36.

REDDING

Redding, located at the north of the Sacramento Valley where the river emerges from high country, was founded in 1872 when the California and Oregon Railroad selected the site as its northern terminal. It became the seat of Shasta County in 1884 and today is the hub of the Whiskeytown-Shasta-Trinity Recreation Area.

The **Redding Museum** in Caldwell Park on Rio Drive has a pre-Columbian exhibit, in addition to displays detailing Shasta County history, Indian artefacts and an art gallery. Open June to August daily except Monday, 10 am to 5 pm;

September to May, Tuesday to Friday noon to 5 pm, Saturday 10 to 5, Sunday noon to 5 pm; free.

Places to Stay

Redding's 'motel strip', Hilltop Drive, runs parallel to I-5; it has some excellent motels but choose your rooms carefully to be away from freeway noise. Other motels cluster on Pine St (business I-5). Below are some examples:

Red Lion Motor Inn (1830 Hilltop Drive, Redding CA 96001; tel (916) 221-8700). Large nicely furnished rooms around landscaped pool area, most with balconies. Airport transportation. Restaurant and coffee shop. Rates from $48 double.

The Shasta Inn (2180 Hilltop Drive, Redding CA 96001; tel (916) 221-8200). Attractive redwood three-story with 150 air-conditioned rooms. Pool, color TV. Restaurant with entertainment, dancing. Airport transportation. Rates from $48 double.

Motel 6 (1640 Hilltop Drive Redding CA 96001; tel (916) 243-8700). 81 air-conditioned rooms; pool; adjacent cafe; rates from $19.95 double.

Places to Eat

Wintoon Room Continental and American cuisine, homemade desserts. (M/E)

Dinner, Sunday brunch. Shasta Inn; tel 221-8200.

WHISKYTOWN-SHASTA-TRINITY NATIONAL RECREATION AREA

This 100,000 acres of national park and forest lands is the outcome of construction of dams on the Sacramento and Trinity Rivers as part of the Central Valley project, under which surplus Northern California water is carried to the arid south of the state. Created by the dams were the Whiskeytown, Shasta and Claire Engle (Trinity) Lakes.

Whiskeytown Lake

Closest to Redding is Whiskeytown Lake,

eight miles west on SR 299. The lakeshore Kennedy Memorial marks its dedication by President Kennedy in 1963. The lake is popular for fishing in the fall and early spring and in summer attracts swimmers, Scuba divers and waterskiers. The National Park Service Visitor Center is located on the east side of the lake off SR 299.

Shasta State Historical Park

Only six miles from Redding, before you reach Whiskeytown Lake, this park preserves the remains of the gold rush town of Shasta, which became a ghost town when hydraulic mining was stopped by law in 1884. Restored are the old courthouse, the jail – along with its gallows – and the Masonic Hall built in 1953. Rangers are on hand to describe life in the town during its heyday. Open daily from 10 am to 5 pm; admission charge.

Weaverville Joss House State Historic Park

Although this is 50 miles from Redding, it's worth the detour if you have time. At the height of Weaverville's gold rush, half of the town's population was Chinese. The park centers around the western hemisphere's finest remaining Taoist temple, the Joss House – dating back to 1873, when it replaced a previous temple destroyed by fire, it still serves a small congregation of Chinese elders. Its authentic interiors contain splendid gilded wooden scrollwork and priceless tapestries. There are daily guided tours every half-hour 10 am to 4.30 pm summer; hourly to 4 pm rest of year; admission charge.

SR 299 continues beyond Weaverville into the Shasta-Trinity National Forest and joins US 101 on the coast above Arcata.

Trinity Lake

Although the official name of this lake is Clair Engle, it is generally known as

Trinity Lake. The 16,500-acre catchment, along with Lewiston Lake downstream, forms the base of the Trinity National Recreation Area. Trinity Lake is reached by taking SR 3 from Weaverville for about 10 miles. The facilities are situated along the lake's west shore.

For further information, contact the District Ranger, US Forest Service, Weaverville CA 96093, or Shasta-Cascade Wonderland Association, PO Box 1988, Redding CA 96001; tel (916) 243-2643.

Shasta Lake

Heading north from Redding on I-5 the road starts climbing into the mountains. Oak and pine fringing the highway become thicker and you are aware of Mount Shasta looming in the distance. Entering Shasta-Trinity National Forest you come to Lake Shasta, largest of the northland's lakes. Covering an area of 30,000 acres, with 370 miles of shoreline, Lake Shasta reaches into the canyons of four waterways – the Sacramento, McCloud and Pit Rivers and Squaw Creek. Small lakeside resorts cluster along the route of I-5, *houseboats* can be rented, and there are numerous *campgrounds*. All of these fill quickly in summer, as Shasta is one of California's most popular holiday areas for swimming, fishing and boating (boats ranging from canoes to paddlewheelers are available by the hour or the day).

Things to See & Do

Shasta Dam, a massive structure 602 feet high and two-thirds of a mile across its crest, is California's second highest dam (Oroville tops it at 770 feet). A model and film at the Visitor Center explains its workings and you can take a guided tour of the dam and powerhouse. It is an impressive sight, backed by the vast lake with Mt Shasta in the distance.

Open Monday to Friday 7.45 am to 4.15 pm; free; tel 275-4463.

Lake Shasta Caverns comprise a series of limestone caves overlooking the lake's McCloud River finger. Fossil remains of ancient animals have been discovered in them and they are characterised by geological formations up to one million years old and multi-hued stone draped in huge folds and fluted in pillars, twisted crystalline stalactites and stalagmites and cascades of milky flowstone. A two-hour excursion includes a catamaran ride across the McCloud area of the lake, then bus up the precipitous limestone bluffs to the entrance 800 feet above. Guides lead you through well-lighted tunnels (this walk entails some climbing of stairs, so be in good shape; you'll also need a sweater for the cool interior temperatures).

Tours daily every hour from 9 am to 5 pm, May to September; tel (916) 238-2341 for schedule off-season; closed January. Admission charge.

Driving I-5 past Lake Shasta, each bend offers a different view. As the road winds towards Mt Shasta, from time to time you catch a glimpse of monolithic spires of granite rising above the forest. Suddenly as you round a bend, the full force of the grey crags thrusting skywards overwhelms you.

Castle Crags rise 4000 feet above the canyon in an impressive tangle of granite boulders and spires. They were the cruel setting for a bitter fight between Modoc Indians and white settlers in 1855, chronicled in an epic poem by the 'poet of the Sierras' Joaquin Miller, who claimed to have been hit by an arrow during the battle. The 3447-acre Castle Crags State Park, which straddles the highway and the river, offers swimming, fishing, hiking, camping and rock climbing.

Sixty miles above Redding, you reach the town of Mt Shasta, nestled at the foot of the mountain after which it is named.

Mount Shasta

Mighty Mt Shasta dominates the Northern Wonderland; it's visible for up to 100 miles in each direction. Actually two volcanic cones – Shasta, and smaller Shastina on its western flank – the sleeping giant has been dormant since ancient times, though experts do not agree as to whether it is a truly dormant volcano.

The titan is almost perenially snow-tipped and five glaciers inch across its flanks above the 10,000-foot mark. Below timberline are forests dense with white bark pines, and dotted with lakes framed with the famed Shasta lilies, and valleys.

Mt Shasta has long been a source of legend and lore. Its name comes from the Indian word *I-e-Ka* meaning 'white' perhaps for the snowcover, or for the paleness of the local Indians. To Indian tribes it is sacred, having seven points at which they once held devotional ceremonies. Indian legend told of a secret commonwealth, consisting of the Ilethelane and Yaktayvia people, who lived in two hidden cities within the mountain. They believed the Yaktayvia hollowed out the caverns by the ringing of great secret bells, whose high frequencies acted like laser beams burrowing through the mass, and whose vibrations were used to illuminate the cities. According to legend, when the wind strikes an invisible bell on the mountainside, its vibrations repel intruders, which some say explains the stalling of cars near the mountain.

The majestic mountain's mystique has been felt by many; a number of psychics, drawn by it, live in the town.

A road runs up to timberline. From there you can climb the summit, but it is a taxing ascent for the inexperienced. The Forest Service issues brochures showing the best routes; August is the most favorable time to climb. Equipment can be rented in town but climbers are asked to check in and out with the Mt Shasta City Police. For maps and information, contact the Chamber of Commerce, Box 201, Mt Shasta, CA 96067; tel (916) 926-4865.

The ski season normally lasts well into the spring and even into summer. The lodge offers a ski school, equipment rental, a cafeteria, and cocktail lounge, but there are no overnight accommodations on the mountain. Motels and restaurants are located in Mt Shasta City, Weed and Dunsmuir.

Beyond Mt Shasta, you pass Black Butte's imposing mass of ash and lava rock. At Weed, you've got a choice of two routes to Oregon: 1-5 continues through the Shasta Valley, while US 97 veers off to the east to Klamath Falls and Bend (see Through Oregon's Back Country).

From Weed, I-5 descends into a lush green valley, stippled by neat farm houses. At the head of the valley, **Yreka** presents an attractive facade to the bypassing freeway. Founded during the gold mining excitement of 1851, Yreka still boasts a few small working mines.

After crossing the high bridge over the Klamath River, the road climbs again into the scenic Siskiyou Mountains and through the Summit Pass into Oregon.

A less accessible but fascinating park lies in the northeastern part of California near the Oregon border – the Lava Beds National Monument.

LAVA BEDS NATIONAL MONUMENT

Seventy-two square miles of twisted lava beds, caves formed by pahoehoe lava tubes, historic petroglyphs and relics of California's only major Indian war are the attraction of this park.

The fields of contorted lava show volcanic activity over 15 centuries. Their outcroppings provided natural trenches and battlements for Kientepoos, known as Captain Jack, when he and a small band of Modoc warriors held off 500 troopers in the Modoc War of 1872-73. Finally betrayed by fellow tribespeople, he was captured and hanged and the last Indian resistance to white encroachment on their lands was ended. You can see **Captain Jack's Stronghold**, an almost impregnable fortress of lava, and other reminders of the war in the northeastern section of the park.

Over 300 lava caves have been found in the park, some holding rivers and waterfalls of ice which never melts. Conversely, **Fern Cave** contains a lush garden of ferns and moss as well as Indian pictographs. Lanterns are provided for self-guided cave exploration.

At the **Monument's Headquarters** in the southern section, a museum depicts the story of the park and in summer, talks on geology and campfire programs are scheduled. The Indian Wells *campground* is nearby.

The information desk is open daily from 8 am to 6 pm between mid-June and Labor Day; 8 am to 5 pm rest of year; tel (916) 667-2282. For information, write to Superintendent, Lava Beds National Monument, Box 867, Tulelake CA 96134.

Lodging and restaurants can be found in Tulelake and Newell on SR 139.

Getting There

You can reach Lava Beds Monument by taking US 97 from Weed to Klamath Falls in Oregon, then SR 139 back into California.

An alternative is to take SR 299 from Redding through the Pastoral Fall River Valley, connecting with SR 139 north.

This allows an opportunity to visit spectacularly lovely **Burney Falls,** twin streams which cascade down over 129-foot cliffs into a sparkling emerald pool below (on SR 89 a few miles north of its junction with SR 299).

Finally you can take SR 89 from Mt Shasta, heading south to join US 299 just past Burney Falls. This road takes you through the turn-of-the century gaslit town of **McCloud,** a small logging community in the wooded foothills of Mt Shasta. Look for the great old McCloud Hotel, built in 1918 to replace its fire-ravaged predecessor, and the town's emporium which sells anything and everything.

Useful Addresses

Shasta-Cascade Wonderland Association (S Market & Parkview Sts (PO Box 1988), Redding, CA 96001; tel (916) 2432643.)

Red Bluff Chamber of Commerce (100 Main St, Red Bluff, CA 96080; tel (916) 527-6220).

Redding Chamber of Commerce (1345 Liberty St (PO Box 1180), Redding, CA 96001; tel (916) 243-2541.)

California State Automobile Association (AAA) (1900 Court St, Redding, CA 96001; tel (916) 241-5625.)

Pacific Northwest

The states of Oregon and Washington are more closely akin than Northern and Southern California. They share geographic features and a common history – indeed, they were one territory until 1853.

The mighty Cascade Mountain range cleaves through the center of these states, separating the littoral rainbelt from the semi-arid plateaus to the east. This factor creates a natural division: coastal Oregon and Washington wherein are located the main cities and majority of the states' populations, sharing similar economies based on the vast forests and tourism; and eastern Oregon and Washington, agrarian-based communities more allied with the open-range lifestyle of the adjacent states than with the coastal portions of their own.

Since the eastern sections are less easily reached from California and do not offer much in appeal for travelers with limited time (even the remnants of the Old West here are poorly preserved in comparison to the Plains states or the Southwest), we are focusing our attention on the coastal portions of these states – with the exception of back country Oregon, on the eastern edge of the Cascades.

Facts

Oregon covers an area of 96,184 square miles, Washington an area of 66,570 square miles; the Columbia River forms most of the border between the two. Both states are roughly rectangular in shape; Oregon is bordered to the south by California and Nevada and in the north Washington butts onto the international border with Canada, while to the east, Idaho runs the full length of both states.

Oregon's population is 2,632,663; Washington, over 30% smaller in area, has a population of 4,130,163 (1980 census figures), reflecting its more labor intensive economy.

OREGON

Much of Oregon is mountainous. From the Siskiyou Range in the south-west corner, the Coast Range runs north to the Columbia, following the relatively uninterrupted 400-mile coastline. The Rogue and Umpqua River valleys cut through the southwestern mountains to the Pacific. Framed between the Coast Range and the Cascades is the Willamette (pronounced Wil-*am*-et) Valley, flanking the north-flowing Willamette River. This fertile valley, checkered with farmland and sheep ranches, holds eight of the state's 10 main cities including the capital, Salem, and at its head the major city, Portland.

Much of Oregon's land is forested in Douglas fir, pines and Sitka spruce. A great deal of it is protected in national and state forests, though you can still see heart-breaking evidence of rapacious logging in earlier times. Through the Cascades lakes abound, including the incomparable Crater Lake. The mountains' volcanic history is obvious in the desolate lava fields in the region of Bend. Oregon's highest peaks are the lofty Three Sisters, each towering over 10,000 feet, and Mt Jefferson (10,495 feet) in the central Cascades, and in the north, Mt Hood, rising to 11,245 feet.

WASHINGTON

Washington's coastline north of the Columbia mouth is deeply incised by Willapa Bay and Grays Harbor. In the north of the state, fjord-like 100-mile-long Puget Sound separates the mainland and the Olympic Peninsula. On the peninsula are the Olympic Mountains, detached like an imperial crown from the long line of the Coast Range. As in Oregon, the Cascades are heavily forested, though the original coastal forests are all but gone. Mightiest peaks of the Cascades in Washington are Mt Rainier (14,408 feet), Mt Adams (12,326 feet) and Mt Baker (10,750 feet). Most famous of the Cascade peaks in southern Washington these days is Mt St Helens which exploded into the news with its May 1980 eruption.

History

The States' early history is a tale of vying for dominion by English and American traders avid for pelts of the coast's sea otters and the forests' fur-bearing denizens.

Sir Francis Drake probably touched on the northern coast as early as 1578; certainly both Spanish and English navigators did in the latter years of the 16th century. In 1778 came Captain James Cook, continuing his search for the Northwest Passage; it was his accounts which turned fur traders' attention to the area. Americans entered the picture in 1788, when Captain Robert Gray explored the coast; in 1792, he was first to enter the Columbia River. Lewis and Clark's epic crossing of the American continent brought them to the Columbia in 1805 and their reports spurred eastern interests. In 1811, John Jacob Astor's Pacific Fur Company set up Oregon's first commercial outpost at Fort Astor, later Astoria. The British took over during the War of 1812 and the Hudson's Bay Company gained dominion over the fur trade, establishing their headquarters at Fort Vancouver on the Columbia River.

In 1818, the rival governments settled their quarrel by agreeing to joint rule, which lasted until 1846. Meanwhile the blazing of the Oregon Trail in the early 1840s brought an influx of emigrants from the Midwest, who came to settle and farm the Willamette Valley. Those seeking to make a quick fortune headed to the Californian goldfields. By 1844, the American cry was raised: 'Fifty-four Forty or Fight', demanding that the demarcation between British and American territory be set at latitude 54° 40'. (The following year an incident occurred which led to American settlement of Washington: a wagon train arrived in Oregon with a free-born, prosperous black among the party. Finding that the government excluded blacks in Oregon, the train headed north and settled on Puget Sound, at today's Tumwater.) Finally in 1846, agreement was reached setting the British-American border at the 49th parallel, now the Canadian border.

Changes came fast over the next few years: the Oregon Territory, established in 1848 to better protect citizens from Indian incursions, saw its own gold rush with the Rogue River Valley discoveries of 1851-52; Washington Territory came into being in 1853 and 10 years later was given its present borders with the establishment of Idaho Territory. Oregon achieved statehood on February 14, 1859; Washington followed on November 11, 1889.

With depletion of the Great Lakes forests in the early 1900s, the Pacific Northwest became the country's major lumber source, drawing lumberjacks from as far away as Scandinavia. To this day, lumber remains the backbone of Oregon's economy, abetted by agriculture and tourism. Washington has a more industrialised base; among its manufactures are aircraft, paper products and aluminium. Agriculture is important, too. The Columbia River wends its way southward from British Columbia through the eastern half of the state before it heads west to the ocean. Fishing ranks high for both states, particularly salmon which lures sports fishermen from all around the world to Pacific Northwest rivers.

Indian Culture Salmon fishing provided

the livelihood for the Coast Indians who greeted arriving settlers, usually with a friendly demeanor. Coastal Indians, who led a somewhat easier life than their inland counterparts with food and shelter always available, evolved a more materialistic culture than their inland brethren. Competition for prestige was their lodestar. They lavished the Pacific Northwest with decorative arts, handsome carved totem poles and the tradition of the potlatch – a huge party at which a leader gave away all his possessions, thereby gaining great esteem.

Fighting between whites and Indians, generally restricted to skirmishes rather than war, ceased by the 1870s but white diseases, especially smallpox, took massive toll. Today's small Indian populations live both on reservations and in outside communities. The most prosperous reservation, perhaps a portent for the future, is Oregon's Warm Springs, where the Confederated Tribes (incorporating Paiute, Wasco and Warm Springs Indians) have built a successful tourist resort. The profits are raising the educational and living standards of their peoples.

Oregon

The people of Oregon have earned the reputation of being the nation's leaders in conservation causes. The state is now relatively litter-free due to anti-litter ordinances enforced with heavy fines; air and water pollution have been greatly reduced; and public funds are used to better energy-conserving transportation.

Aware of their heritage, the people are actively involved in preserving the quality of life in their state. They are thoughtful of visitors, providing a wealth of information at centers marked by large blue-and-white signs. TravInfo Center gazebos placed in resort areas and highway rest stops explain local points of interest and facilities in exhibits; a coinless telephone allows you to make accommodations reservations. Clear road signs direct the way to lodgings and food.

For non-drivers, airlines serve most of the valley cities and several coastal cities as well as Redmond, a short distance from Bend.

Both Greyhound Bus and Continental Trailways roll along I-5, offering stops at most cities; Greyhound also serves the coast communities and Trailways operates on US 97 to Bend from the south.

Amtrak links San Francisco and Portland, crossing the Cascades on a scenic route from eastern Oregon to Eugene, then running through the Willamette Valley.

THE WILLAMETTE VALLEY ROUTE NORTH

ROGUE RIVER VALLEY
From the 4310-foot Siskiyou Summit Pass, I-5 descends into the picturesque Bear Creek Valley at the southern end of the Rogue River Valley. The freeway bypasses the valley's cities, carrying through traffic to the Willamette Valley and Portland.

The Rogue River Valley, though, is a place to dally, to tread byways imbued with history, amidst scenic splendor that in the 1850s convinced many weary emigrants they need seek no further for their new homeland.

Leave the freeway at the well-signed Information Center, then continue down that road to SR 99, the original road through the valley. This takes you into Ashland, home of the renowned annual Oregon Shakespearean Festival.

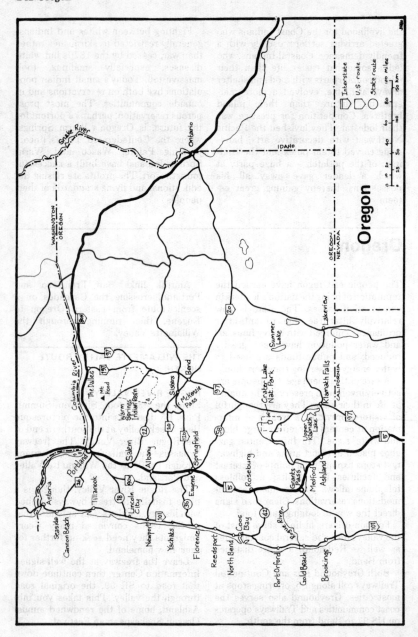

Oregon

IDAHO

OREGON
NEVADA

OREGON
CALIFORNIA

WASHINGTON
OREGON

Snake River

Ontario

20

Lakeview

Klamath Falls

Upper
Klamath
Lake

Summer
Lake

Crater Lake
Nat. Park

97

138

58

5

Grants
Pass

Medford

Ashland

Roseburg

Rogue River

Gold Beach

Brookings

Port Orford

North Bend

Coos Bay

Reedsport

Florence

Yachats

Newport

Lincoln
City

Tillamook

Cannon Beach

Seaside

Astoria

Portland

Salem

Albany

Eugene

Springfield

Sisters

Bend

McKenzie
Pass

Warm
Springs
Indian Rsn

Mt
Hood

The Dalles

Columbia River

101

18

99W

20

22

126

36

26

84

97

197

☐ Interstate
☐ U.S. route
○ State route

0 10 20 30 40 50 miles
0 15 40 80 120 km

ASHLAND

Ashland is an attractive city built on the western hills overlooking farmlands and orchards which spread across the valley floor. Its founders pitched their tents on the wooded banks of Ashland Creek back in January 1852. At the time, there were a few other whites scattered throughout the valley and an Indian village nearby. Fifteen miles away in Jacksonville the gold rush was in full swing following the strikes a year before. Those who came to Ashland elected to place their trust in lumber; they built a sawmill, then a flour mill and the settlement was on its way. In 1885, they laid out the nucleus for a permanent town site. At its heart was the Plaza, around which today's town thrives.

Things to See & Do

A block uphill is the start of **Lithia Park**, 99 acres of luxuriant lawns, picnic sites, duckponds, playgrounds and fountains dispensing rare mineral water from a nearby spring.

Taking pride of place in Lithia Park is the theater complex which houses the **Oregon Shakespearean Festival**. In 1935, a three-day festival billing itself as 'The First Annual Shakespearean Festival' played on a wooded hillside above town. It has been an annual attraction ever since, with the exception of a brief respite during WW II. By 1979, it had expanded into an ambitious nine-month season, occupying three theatres.

The Tudor-style facade of the Elizabethan stage stands at Lithia Park's entrance. The open-air stage follows the design dimensions of the original Fortune Theatre of Shakespeare's London, allowing for dynamic staging of the Shakespearean presentations. Adjacent is the 600-seat indoor **Angus Bowmer Theatre**, which shares major productions. Third theater in the complex is the **Black Swan**, an intimate house catering to experimental and new works.

The town decks itself in full Eliza-bethan regalia during the festival season, so popular that it draws around a quarter of a million visitors.

Merrymaking Elizabethan-style will greet you if you're there for The Feast of Will, marking the formal opening in June of the Elizabethan Stage season. Tudor Fair heralds each evening performance; it's a lively performance of Renaissance music and dances, held in the courtyard at 7.15 pm. Backstage operations are shown on tours, conducted by the performers and technicians, during the certain weeks of the season. Tours start at 10 am and reservations are necessary; admission charge.

For advance information on the festival's schedule and reservations, write Oregon Shakespearean Festival, Ashland, OR 97520; tel (503) 482-4331. During the season tickets are also on sale at Box Office locations at major stores in Oregon, California and Washington. There is also, an Information Booth open in Ashland Plaza from 8.30 am to 7 pm daily; they'll tell you about the Festival and other points of interest.

One of the town's special attributes is its collection of late 19th century architecture. The Ashland Heritage Committee has mapped a **self-guided walking tour** which takes in the most notable examples: pick up the map at the Information Booth for a modest donation.

Summertime picnics and winter skiing, enhanced by panoramic views, are the draw to **Mt Ashland**, in the Siskiyous just north of the California border. The lodge's ski shop rents equipment and offers ski lessons.

The valley has a number of lakes popular for fishing, boating and water skiing, as well as camping. The Ashland Chamber of Commerce issues a list describing them; pick it up at the Plaza Information Booth.

Hot-air ballooning allows a bird's-eye perspective of the Rogue Valley; flights are available May to September, weather permitting. Contact Above It All, 1257 Siskiyou Boulevard, #211, Ashland OR 97520; tel (503) 482-8301.

SR 99 parallels I-5 out of Ashland, linking the towns along Bear Creek, a meandering tributary of the Rogue River.

Places to Eat

Underground Gourmet Delicatessen Downstairs from Paddington Station; alternative entrance in rear alley. Deli with a British touch. (B)

Breakfast, lunch daily, early dinner Monday to Saturday. No credit cards. 125 East Main; tel 482-9111.

Banbury Cross Creperie Good crepes, using fresh ingredients. (B)

Breakfast, lunch early dinner daily June to September; no dinner balance of year. 55 N Main; tel 482-3644.

Chata Eastern European cuisine served in cottage on SR 99 in Talent, four miles north of Ashland Plaza. (M)

Dinner daily. 1212 Pacific Highway, Talent; tel 535-2572.

Mon Desir Dining Inn Steak and seafood in setting of 1910 country mansion. (M)

Dinner, closed Monday and holidays.. 4615 Hamrick Rd, Central Point (take exit 32 off I-5); tel 664-6661.

MEDFORD

Hub of the valley, and southern Oregon's largest town, is Medford, some 12 miles from Ashland. The city itself is not particularly interesting, except for some parklands along the banks of Bear Creek. But it has attractive surroundings, especially in April when the valley's pear orchards come into bloom. From Medford, you can reach two of the region's highlights: Crater Lake and historic Jacksonville. Medford's airport serves the entire Rogue River Valley.

Places to Stay

Between Medford and Ashland, there is a large selection of accommodation. Even so, during the festival space can be tight,

particularly on weekends. Should you have difficulty finding somewhere in Ashland, contact the Ashland Visitor and Convention Center, 110 E Main; tel (503) 482-3486. In Medford, the Visitors and Convention Bureau is at 304 S Central, tel (503) 772-6293. Some motels:

Places to Stay – Ashland

Ashland Hills Inn (2525 Ashland St, Ashland, OR 97520; tel (503) 482-8210; toll-free in Oregon 800-452-5315; outside Oregon 800-547-4747). Posh motor hotel with pool, tennis courts, executive suites, cable TV, lounge with entertainment, dining room. Rates from $64 double.

Knights Inn (2359 SR 66 (exit 14 from I-5); tel (503) 482-5111.) Air-conditioned units with king or queen-sized beds. Color TV, pool, restaurant, lounge, 10 minutes from theaters. Rates from $25.50 double.

Palm Motel (1065 Siskiyou Boulevard, Ashland OR 97520; tel (503) 482-2636). 17 air-conditioned units, pool, TV and kitchens. Two and three-bedroom cottages available June to September. Rates from $20 double.

Ashland Youth Hostel (150 N Main St. Ashland OR 97520; tel (503) 482-9217). Separate dorms and baths for men and women, commons and kitchen. Closed December. Rates $5.

Places to Stay – Medford

Red Lion Inn (200 N Riverside Avenue, Medford, OR 97501; tel (503) 779-5811). Large, well-run motor hotel; oversize beds, patios and balconies. Some non-smoker rooms. Cafe, dining room, entertainment. Pool. Free airport transportation. Rates from $44 double.

Cedar Lodge (518 N Riverside Ave, Medford, OR 97501; tel (503) 773-7361.) Family-style motel; color TV, free coffee in room. Some oversize beds; sundeck, pool. Cafe, bar, entertainment. Free airport transportation. Rates from $21 double.

Motel 6 (950 Alba Dr, Medford, OR 97501; tel (503) 779-6470.) Two-story, 168 air-conditioned rooms. Pool. No restaurant. Rates from $19.95 double.

CRATER LAKE

Some 6600 years ago, an icy monarch towered over the Rogue River Valley: Mt Mazama rose above the surrounding Cascade ridges to a height of around 12,000 feet. It lay dormant for perhaps millions of years, then exploded with tremendous force. Red-hot pumice spewed forth in rushing avalanches. Ash spread a pall as far distant as Canada.

The mountain's pent-up energy quickly spent itself. When the clouds cleared, a huge caldera, six miles across, was revealed. The sheared-off, gutted mountain had imploded on itself; its upper 5000 feet had disappeared. Over the centuries, the vast caldera gathered water from rain and snow melt.

Today all volcanic activity appears to have ceased. The nearest evidence of internal fires are the Klamath Falls hot springs 60 miles south. And Crater Lake has become the world's seventh deepest lake; sonic depth finders register 1932 feet at its deepest point. Light reflected from the sky on the water's surface and radiating from within its depths shades the lake an intense sapphire blue that is extraordinary to behold. Its tranquil surface mirrors the sloping ridged walls of the caldera. In winter, snow softens the outline of the cradling cliffs and mantles the pines, creating a vista of rare beauty.

You can admire the view from different perspectives at vantage points around the 33-mile **Rim Drive**, which circles the caldera's edge. The one-way clockwise drive is open only from early July through mid-October.

Cone-shaped **Wizard Island**, capped by its own crater, emerges from the water's surface. The **Phantom Ship** appears to be sailing across the water; it's actually a lava dyke remnant. Best place to view it is from the **Sun Notch** trail.

Most spur roads and trailheads lead off from Rim Drive to other attractions in the 250-square-mile National Park: the **Pinnacles**, striking spires of pumice rising 200 feet above Wheeler Creek Canyon, 8926-foot twin-peaked **Mount Scott** and the barren stretches of the **Pumice Desert** to the north.

Focal point of the park is **Rim Village**, which has the lodge, an Exhibit Building where you can buy maps and descriptive booklets, and the Sinnot Memorial Overlook buildings and from its broad terrace there is a magnificent view.

Things to See & Do

Ranger programs, bus and boat trips all operate only in summer. Rangers conduct campfire and naturalist programs; schedules are posted at Rim Village and campgrounds. Hourly talks on the lake's geologic origins are given from 9 am to 6 pm in the **Sinnot Memorial**. Bus trips around Rim Drive operate from the Lodge. From Cleetwood Cove, launches cruise the lake, stopping at **Wizard Island** where you can hike a trail to its 760-foot crater. The 1.1-mile switchback **Cleetwood Trail** from Rim Drive to the boat landing takes about a half-hour to hike down, three-quarters of an hour on the return trip.

No permit is needed to fish the park's streams or in the lake, but a permit is required for extended back-country hiking. No hunting is allowed. Use caution on trails and stay on them, particularly around the rim, as loose volcanic soil makes for poor footing.

Wildlife Most common are chipmunks and golden-mantled ground squirrels. Deer and bears can often be seen; less noticeable are the Cascade red fox, coyote, pine marten, porcupine, bobcat and elk. Very rarely, cougar are observed. Remember, these animals are wild and should not be approached. Bird life includes Clark's nutcrackers, gray and blue jays, eagles and hawks.

Places to Stay & Eat

Modest accommodation is available in Rim Village's rustic *Crater Lake Lodge,* plus some cottages and cabins, all open from mid-June to mid-September. For information and reservations, write to Crater Lake Lodge, Crater Lake, OR 97604; tel (503) 594-2511.

There are two *campgrounds,* one at Mazama and the other at Lost Creek. Each is open only from around mid-June to the end of September, depending on snowfall. Campsites cannot be reserved.

The dining room at *Crater Lake Lodge* opens from mid-June to mid-September. Rim Village's *cafeteria* serves food daily in summer; on weekends and holidays in winter, it serves light refreshments. Limited groceries can be bought at Rim Village. Gasoline is sold, in summer only, near park headquarters, located three miles south of Rim Village.

Getting There

The Rim Rd and most facilities are closed from around mid-October to late June or early July, depending on snow conditions. Winter views are quite lovely, but can only be enjoyed from the Rim Village area, which is open during the day throughout the winter months. Snow chains may be required. Winter sports are confined to cross-country skiing and snow-shoeing.

The south entrance, SR 62 from Klamath Falls, is open all year. The west entrance, SR 62 from Medford, usually closes in early December and reopens late March. Both the north entrance, which leads to SR 138 and US 97 to Bend, and the Rim Rd are closed from around mid-October to early July, depending on snowfall.

Both Klamath Falls and Medford have air service and Greyhound Bus service; Klamath Falls is also on the Amtrak route. Daily bus service is operated from Klamath Falls by Crater Lake Lodge from mid-June to mid-September.

Crater Lake National Park is also included on a number of summer tours of Oregon; typical is Discovery Tours of Portland's seven-day program which circles Oregon, visiting the major points of interest. Ask your travel agent about tour operators' programs.

For further information write to Superintendent, Crater Lake National Park, Box 7, Crater Lake, OR 97604; tel (503) 594-2211.

JACKSONVILLE

Gold in Oregon! The cry went out in the winter of 1851-52 when two mule train drivers passing through the valley discovered placer in Rich Gulch. Within weeks, Jacksonville was a booming town.

But along with fortune-hunting prospectors came people who settled on the fertile land. When the miners moved on around the turn of the century, they left behind no ghost town but a flourishing agricultural center. The lean depression years of the 1930s triggered a brief revival of backyard placer mining, with unfortunate consequences: in June, 1979, several streets caved in from that flurry of tunneling.

Since its gold lode became unproductive, Jacksonville has mined its historic aura. For in this small town nestled in wooded foothills, you step straight back into the past. Nineteenth century houses, taverns, stores and hotels, housing contemporary businesses, are restored as they were in the town's 1890s heyday. The railroad depot, once terminus for the privately-owned *Jacksonville Cannonball,* is now an information center; the original general store has taken on new life as an inn. So authentically has Jacksonville preserved its 19th century gold town appearance that it has been declared a National Landmark.

Things to See & Do

One of the nicest things to do here is to stroll the streets as it's quite likely you will meet up with an oldtimer who'll

happily share memories of more boisterous times before the placer ran low.
Even if you don't come across an old
prospector a short walk around town
imparts the feeling of life here at the turn
of the century. For a map and description
of the century. For a map and description
of its more than one hundred 19th century
Depot on Oregon and C Sts, from May to
September, home of the Chamber of
Commerce Information Center (tel 899-
8118). When the Chamber of Commerce
is closed, you can obtain maps from the
stores.

A good place to start your discovery is
at California and Third Sts. On the
northwest corner is **Beekman Bank**, which
opened its doors in 1863. Before it closed
down in 1912, over $31 million in gold
dust passed across the counters of this
Wells Fargo agency. It has been restored
with its original furnishings, and is open
every day.

As you cross the street to the **United
States Hotel**, relive the excitement of that
night of 28 September, 1880, when
President Rutherford B Hayes and his
party arrived to stay in the elegantly
decorated presidential suite. This was a
grand climax to the opening of the hotel
George Holt built to honor his courtship
promise to his wife, the oft-married Mme
Jeanne DeRoboam. Today its ground
floor houses a branch of the US National
Bank, re-created with furnishings of the
1840-50 period.

Next door, the **Lamplighter Gallery**
occupies the circa 1858 H Judge Harness
saddlery and harness shop. Adjacent to
that, the erstwhile Ryan and Morgan
General Store is now the **Jacksonville Inn**,
which offers eight antique-furnished
rooms and a restaurant. The building was
constructed in 1863, using locally
quarried sandstone and the walls of the
dining area and lounge have specks of
gold scattered through the mortar.

Jacksonville's first physician built the
fine house on the southwest corner of
California and Fifth Sts in 1861. His

family lived in the **McCully House** until
his daughter, Izzie, died in 1944. Only a
few dolls remain of the famed collection
housed here until recently, but the charm
of the Civil War period home attracts
many visitors.

(Open by appointment, call 899-1942;
admission charge.)

Opposite is the 1868 house of dentist
Dr Will Jackson who advertised that he
would 'visit Ashland in May and November and . . . Kirbyville 4th Monday in
October, each year'.

One of the more unusual homes you
can inspect is the **1893 Nunan Mansion**, a
rather eccentric version of Queen Anne
Victorian architecture set in five acres of
manicured lawns and formal gardens. It
was known as the Catalog House because
its owners selected components of the
design from eastern catalogs – A or B
porch, C or D chimney – which the builder
then integrated into the mansion. From
its grounds, you obtain fine views of the
Rogue River Valley. Situated at 635 N
Oregon St; tel 899-8118 for information;
admission charge.

You'll get an excellent picture of the
town's past in exhibits and memorabilia
on display at the **Jacksonville Museum**. It
occupies the old County Courthouse,
built of local brick and stone in 1883. On
5th St, between C and D; open Memorial
Day to Labor Day Monday to Saturday 9
am to 5 pm, Sunday noon to 5 pm; rest of
year Tuesday to Saturday 9 am to 5 pm,
Sunday noon to 5 pm, closed Monday;
free.

Reminders of eventful days are vivid,
too, in the **Jacksonville Cemetery**, where
inscriptions on gravestones tell of pioneer hardships, Indian raids and dreadful
epidemics. Follow the signs from the
junction of Oregon and E Sts. Open daily
8 am to 9 pm; free.

In 1859, seven covered wagons
rumbled over the old Oregon Trail from
Independence, Missouri, to Independence, Oregon, in celebration of Oregon's
centenary. One of those wagons was

driven by George McUne, founder of Jacksonville's Pioneer Village. He wanted to experience for himself the pioneer's tribulations, the better to interpret them for his visitors. **Pioneer Village** is a repository of early housing, transportation, including carriages and wagons used in filming *Gunsmoke,* and mining equipment, all illustrating pioneer lifestyles. There's a restaurant, and on summer weekend evenings, you can hiss the villains at performances of melodrama. On 725 N Fifth St; tel (503) 899-1683; open Monday to Tuesday 9.30 am to 5 pm, Wednesday to Sunday 9.30 am to 10 pm.

High on a landscaped hill overlooking Jacksonville and the valley beyond is an amphitheater, setting for the **Peter Britt Festival**, held under the stars each August. The festival draws professional musicians from across the United States to play concerts and recitals. It honors Britt, a Swiss photographer and horticulturalist, who recorded the Jacksonville of the mid to late-19th century on film. Indoor concerts are played at the United States Hotel. For schedule and rates, write The Peter Britt Gardens Music and Art Festival, PO Box 1124, Medford OR 97501; tel (503) 733-6077, 773-4051.

In mid-June, Jacksonville celebrates its past with a huge old-fashioned block party: **Pioneer Day** draws folks from miles around. Check with the Chamber of Commerce for date.

Places to Stay

Jacksonville Inn (175 E California (PO Box 359), Jacksonville, OR 97530; tel (503) 899-1900.) Eight air-conditioned rooms, furnished with antiques, in 1863 building. Rates from $32 double.

Places to Eat

Jacksonville Inn Dinner House Continental dinners in intimate basement dining room. Fresh seafood includes salmon and razor clams in season. (M)

Dinner nightly, 175 E California; tel 899-1900.
Pioneer House Seven-course dinner served in antique-furnished dining room. (M)

Lunch (summer only), dinner Wednesday to Sunday. Pioneer Village, 725 N Fifth; tel 899-1683.
Grandma's Kitchen Small, simple dining room seating 32 at tables of eight; set menu, five course dinner served family style. Hosts are gentle people, who serve fine home-cooked food, including an incredible choice of fresh fruit pies. Recommended. (B)

Breakfast, lunch, dinner. SR 238, Applegate (at Thompson Creek Rd); tel 846-6810.

GOLD HILL

From Jacksonville, you can take the Old Stage Road to Gold Hill, 10 miles north, where the **Old Oregon Museum** has relics of gold rush and stage coach days. The museum was built in 1865 with logs taken from an original stockade. It houses a collection of rare Indian artefacts, as well as antique guns and is on Sardine Creek Rd off SR 234; tel 855-1043; open daily March 15 to September 15, 10 am to 6 pm; admission charge.

Nearby a mysterious phenomenon will intrigue you in the **House of Mystery** at the Oregon Vortex. Once an assay office for a gold mining company, the house is the focus of magnetic forces which seem to prevent you from standing erect and distort your perspective in a weird fashion. On SR 234; open daily March 1 to October 14, 9 am to 5 pm; admission charge.

From Gold Hill, both I-5 and SR 99 follow the Rogue River to Grants Pass, gateway to Hellgate Canyon where the river cuts into the Coast Range. A detour from Rogue River nine miles up East Evans Creek Rd to Wimer will show you one of the surviving covered bridges.

GRANTS PASS & ROGUE RIVER
Water Trips

From its source in the mountains near Crater Lake, the Rogue River wends through pastoral valleys, meadowlands and rugged mountain canyons on its way to the Pacific Ocean. Sometimes calm and tranquil, sometimes wild and turbulent, the river offers extraordinary fishing and a wide range of boating opportunities, centered on two towns: Grants Pass for the upper Rogue, and Gold Beach on the coast for the lower stretches (see Oregon Coast Section).

A wide array of river experiences is available to you from Grants Pass. Take your choice of half-day and full-day jetboat excursions to the rapids of Hellgate Canyon, a narrow cleft through which the river passes into its wild and most scenic reaches within the Coast Range. Rates range from $12 for a two-hour trip to $30 for five hours. For information contact Hellgate Excursions, PO Box 982, Grants Pass OR 97526; tel (503) 479-7204.

You can rent a raft for half or full day and row yourself – no experience is necessary. Rates currently run $45. The same company operates guided day trips on a catamaran raft, which includes a whitewater stretch and lunch at Galice Resort for $30. Contact Galice Raft Trips, PO Box 638, Merlin OR 97532; tel (503) 476-3818. Other companies offer similar trips but they tend to come and go, so check around when you arrive for other options.

Trout – rainbow, cutthroat, German brown, brook, summer and winter steelhead; and salmon – chinook, Coho and kokanee – abound in the Rogue. You can fish from the riverbank or on a professionally guided fishing trip. Daily angling license costs $2.50 and a special vacationers license for 10 consecutive days costs $10, plus $2 for a salmon-steelhead tag.

For information on fishing guides and other river trips, write the Chamber of Commerce, PO Box 970, Grants Pass OR 97526; tel (503) 476-7717.

Places to Stay

Best Western Riverside Motel (971 SE 6th St, Grants Pass, OR 97526; tel (503) 476-6873.) 105 air-conditioned rooms at river's edge; sundecks, private patios and balconies, many overlooking river. Color cable TV, pool, whirlpool, some kitchens. Free airport transportation. Hellgate excursions (see Rogue River Trips). Rates from $36 double.

Redwood Motel (815 NE 6th, Grants Pass, OR 97526; tel (503) 476-0878.) 22 air-conditioned units, including some two-room. Color cable TV, pool, playground. Restaurant opposite. Rates from $26 double.

We-Ask-U-Inn (5560 Rogue River Highway, Grants Pass, OR 97526; tel (503) 479-2455.) Sportsmen's lodge six miles upriver from Grants Pass. Congenial hosts provide fishing and wildlife photography guides. Lodge has hosted such luminaries as Clark Gable, David Niven and Robert Taylor.

Places to Eat

R-Haus Popular restored lodge, filled with antiques and Americana, overlooking river. Large portions; steaks, chicken. (M)

Dinner, Sunday brunch. 2140 Rogue River Highway; tel 476-4287.

Riverside Motel Dining room and outdoor section overlook river. Steak and seafood, home baking. (M)

Breakfast, lunch, dinner. 971 SE 6th St; tel 476-6873.

OREGON CAVES NATIONAL MONUMENT

The popular Oregon Caves National Monument, 50 miles southwest, is an easy sidetrip from Grants Pass. Take US 199, the road to Crescent City, and turn off on SR 46 to Cave Junction, 20 miles away.

'The Marble Halls of Oregon', Joaquin

Miller called it after his 1907 visit. Two years later, President Taft proclaimed a 480-acre tract high in the Siskiyou Mountains the Oregon Caves National Monument, despite the fact that only a single cave has been found.

For millennia before hunter Elijah Davidson and his dog Bruno stumbled onto the cave in 1874, nature's forces had been shaping it. It started on the ocean's seabed some 200 million years ago with the formation of limestone. Uplifted by great force into the atmosphere, the limestone gradually recrystallized into marble, fractured by the intensity of its upheaval. Over eons, water seeped down into the fractured marble, layered under rock covering, and dissolved it into crevices, corridors and finally chambers. Elemental forces unceasingly continue to embellish and reshape what they have wrought.

Guides lead you through the maze of passages, pausing at softly lit chambers with romantic names: Paradise Lost, King's Palace, Neptune's Grotto, Niagara Falls.

The cave tour lasts about 75 minutes and entails much walking, occasionally in steep places. It is not recommended for anyone who is not in good physical condition. Since the going is slippery, shoes with nonslip soles are recommended; you'll need a warm sweater too. There are tours every hour from 8 am to 7 pm June 1 to September 10; the rest of the year at 10.30 am, 12.30, 2 and 3.30 pm; admission charge.

Things to Do
Campfire programs are held each summer evening except Sunday at dark. A number of nature trails connect with the adjoining Siskiyou National Forest. National Park Service rangers are on hand through the summer to help visitors.

Places to Stay
Available in the rustic *Oregon Caves*

Chateau from mid-June to early September. The lodge also has a dining room open from 7 am to 9 pm. Rates at the Chateau start at $36 double. Reservations: Oregon Caves Company, Oregon Caves, OR 97523.

There is no camping in the park, but the Forest Service operates two unimproved *campgrounds* off SR 46 in the Siskiyou National Forest from around the end of May to early September. Campsites are allocated on a first-come, first-served basis, they are rarely full.

Information
Superintendent, Oregon Caves National Monument, 19000 Caves Hwy, Cave Junction OR 97523.

THE WILLAMETTE VALLEY
From Grants Pass, I-5 heads north through low mountains to descend into the Willamette Valley. Along the way, several attractions tempt investigation.

Wolf Creek Tavern
In a forgotten backwater, just off the freeway some 20 miles north of Grants Pass is an inn which has been in continuous operation since the 1870s. **Wolf Creek Tavern** was a stagecoach way station, one of 60 on the 710-mile wagon route from Sacramento to Portland. This stagecoach trip was a tiring six-day journey, costing $60. The original tavern building, a fine example of 19th century Classical Revival style architecture, has been undergoing restoration since 1977. While a nod has been given to contemporary comfort with private bathrooms for guest rooms, as far as possible antiques and authentic reproductions are returning the inn to the way it looked in 1911 when Jack London completed *The End of the Story* here. Other honoured guests have included author Sinclair Lewis and film stars, Clark Gable and Mary Pickford. Today's travelers stop for their fresh strawberry shortcake with whipped cream, renowned far and wide.

Wildlife Safari

A curious camel or elephant might peer in your car window on a drive-through safari in this wildlife preserve at Winston in the Umpqua River Valley. Some 600 African and Asian animals freely roam its 600 acres of woods and rolling hills. Admission price includes taped commentary describing the animals – a help in identifying lesser known species – and two treks through the park. Special events include, in summer, an endangered birds-of-prey demonstration by such birds as eagles, hawks and owls. Off SR 42, a few miles west of I-5 Exit 119; tel (503) 679-6761, it's open daily daylight hours; admission charge.

SR 42 continues through the Umpqua Valley to join US 101 near Coos Bay on the coast. Eastward, it terminates at Roseburg, first of six major cities strung through the Willamette Valley between here and Portland. The freeway, I-5, bypasses each of them and there is little unique in any of them to invite a detour, except for the opportunity to observe life in communities representative of small-city America.

Of greater interest is Cottage Grove, just west of I-5 some 50 miles north.

Cottage Grove

Cottage Grove is set on the Coast Fork of the Willamette River at the southern end of the valley. It's starting point for a loop through the **Bohemia Mining District**, one of the Cascade's richest lodes of gold. A scenic 70-mile drive on a steep gravel road climbs into the Calapooya Mountains. Half-hidden mine shafts and weathered buildings mark the 1890s resurgence of mining, which lasted through WW I, and you can browse the ghost town of Bohemia City. The road is only open during summer and autumn; it's not an easy drive but the scenery is exceptionally beautiful.

You can obtain maps from the Cottage Grove Chamber of Commerce, PO Box 587, tel (503) 942-2411.

Covered bridges are a hallmark of this area – there are 21 of them throughout the country. Three of the weathered relics span Mosby Creek and two more bridge the Row (rhymes with cow) River within a few minutes drive of Cottage Grove.

An exciting way to sightsee the Row is chugging alongside it on *The Goose*, a genuine old-time hooting and whistling train. It's pulled by a steam engine weekends and a diesel weekdays, mid-June through Labor Day. The Goose, short for Galloping Goose, earned its name hauling logs in pre-WW I days. Now it carries tourists in air-conditioned luxury on a two-hour ride along the sparkling Row River, past Dorena Reservoir and neat farms nestled in secluded valleys in the Cascade foothills. A railroad museum adjacent to the depot is open all year.

(Depot is at the Village Green Motor Hotel; excursions depart mid-June to July 1, weekends only, 2 pm; July 1 through Labor Day weekdays 2 pm, weekends 10 am and 2 pm; admission charge; information: Oregon Pacific & Eastern Railroad, PO Box 565, Cottage Grove OR 97424; tel (503) 942-3368.)

An octagonal 1897 church houses the **Cottage Grove Historical Museum**, displaying artefacts of pioneer and Indian life in the area, as well as lumber and mining relics. It's on Birch Ave & H St; tel 942-8175; open mid-June to Labour Day, Wednesday to Sunday 1 to 5 pm, balance of year weekends only 1 to 4 pm; free.)

Places to Stay

The Village Green Motor Hotel (PO Box 277, Cottage Grove, OR 97424; tel (503) 942-2491.) Resort rated 4-star by AAA, set in spacious landscaped grounds. Some two and three-bedroom units, fireplaces, refrigerators. Air-conditioning, color TV, laundry. Pool, wading pool, par-3 golf, tennis. Rates from $54 double.

Places to Eat

Iron Maiden Dining Room (in Village Green Motor Hotel). Gourmet dining in attractively decorated room overlooking pool and grounds. Outdoor dining, too. Entertainment. Extensive wine list. Strict dress code. (M)

Dinner, Sunday brunch. Tel 942-2491.

Copper Rooster Coffee Shop (also in Village Green Motor Hotel – see above) Wide choice of menu, excellent food. (B)

Breakfast, lunch, dinner. Tel 942-2491.

EUGENE/SPRINGFIELD

About 20 miles north, the twin cities of Eugene and Springfield sit on either side of I-5.

The Eugene-Springfield area is devoted primarily to the products of the forests that cover the nearby mountains. Sawmills, plywood and paper plants have spawned corollary industries, such as pressed board.

Further north, though, the Willamette Valley is overwhelmingly agricultural. Its farmlands have prospered since the earliest settlers made good supplying the market created by the Californian goldfields.

The moods of the valley vary with the season. In spring, vast fields of undulating emerald emit the pungent fragrance of fresh-grown grass; from here comes much of the country's supply of northern-types lawn seeds. Explore rural roads in summer and you'll discover a cornucopia of crops, from wheat and flax to berries and orchards of cherries, peaches and walnuts. Increased activity across the landscape marks harvest time, when all hands turn to. A pall of smoke hangs over the valley in the late fall as fields of stubble are torched to ready them for next year's planting.

Wineries Viticulture is of growing importance in the valley. Wineries, which welcome guests, tend to be smaller and more informal than their Californian counterparts. Often the winemaker will show you around, then invite you to a tasting. Vineyards are mostly in the Forest Grove areas, west of Portland and around Roseburg, though others are scattered through the valley.

For information on Oregon wineries, contact the Travel Information Section, tel 800-547-9401 (inside Oregon, 378-6309).

With no detour, it's a 115-mile drive up I-5 from Eugene to Portland. Between them, a network of country roads lets you wander to your heart's content. You'll almost certainly encounter restored pioneer houses, churches and late 19th century structures wherever you roam in this historic valley.

Main reason for detouring into Eugene, the state's second largest city, is to explore the campus of century-old University of Oregon and the Butler Museum of American Indian Art.

The **University of Oregon** was founded in 1876. The original vine-covered buildings, including Deady Hall where the first classes were held, 1885 Villard Hall and 1893 Friendly Hall, are located in the northwest section on East 11th Avenue (take the Franklin Boulevard exit from I-5). On campus, there is a museum of natural history and an art museum boasting a noteworthy collection of Oriental art. (You can join a one-hour guided tour of the campus weekdays at 10.30 am and 2.30 pm, leaving from Oregon Hall at E 13th and Agate. The Information Booth here dispenses free campus maps.)

You'll find an exceptional collection of artefacts and art representing the culture of more than 100 North American Indian tribes at the **Butler Museum of Indian Art**. Guided tours and slide shows enhance their presentation. It's at 1155 W 1st Ave; open Tuesday to Saturday 10 am to 5 pm; closed holidays; admission charge.

The Eugene Chamber of Commerce Information Center is located 1401 Willamette; tel 484-5307. They have detailed maps of the city and county available.

McKenzie River

Eugene is gateway to leisure activities on the wild and beautiful McKenzie River. The boulder strewn river flows down from the Cascades, through dense stands of Douglas fir, providing exciting white water and stretches of tranquility.

Day-long **float trips** start with a scenic drive up the McKenzie Highway, SR 126, to Prince Helfrich Landing for transfer upstream to Blue River, where rafts await. You'll experience the exhilaration of shooting the roaring Martin Rapids, lunch on the riverbank amid splendid scenery and visit historic spots. These trips generally operate from May through October; for schedule and reservations, write River Expeditions, 1935 Hayes, Eugene OR 97440; tel (503) 342-3293.

Places to Stay

The Valley River Inn (PO Box 10088, Eugene, OR 97401; tel (503) 687-1023.) Located on the Willamette River adjacent to Valley River Center shopping complex. Rated 4-star by Mobil. Resort with air-conditioned, pleasant rooms, many with balconies overlooking the river. Color cable TV, pool, wading pool, whirlpool, sauna. Restaurant. Rates from $54 double.

Motel 6 (3690 Glenwood Dr, Eugene, OR 97403; tel (503) 342-6177.) 60 air-conditioned rooms. Pool. Restaurant adjacent. Rates from $19.95 double.

Chumaree Inn (1857 Franklin Blvd, Eugene OR 97403); tel (503) 342-4804.) 42 air-conditioned units, several suites, color cable TV, pool. Rates from $26 double.

Places to Eat

Coburg Inn Victorian atmosphere in gaslit 1877 former house. Continental and American cuisine with fish specialties. (M)

Lunch Monday to Friday, dinner daily. 109 Willamette St, Coburg; tel 484-0633.

SALEM

The state capital, Salem, was founded by Methodist missionaries in 1834. It became capital in 1860. Like many American cities, Salem is revitalizing its downtown area: its Victorian era Opera House, for example, now harbors specialty boutiques and restaurants. Refurbished pioneer-vintage homes are being collected into the **Mill Museum** at the Thomas Kay Historical Park near the capitol. On 260 12th St, SE; tel 585-7012; guided tours Wednesday to Sunday 1.30 to 4.30 pm June 1 to September 30, rest of year Wednesday and Sunday only; admission charge.

Main attraction in Salem is the **State Capitol**, a severe white marble structure topped by the gold-leaf Golden Pioneer statue. Marble engravings of the Lewis and Clark expedition and pioneers blazing the Oregon Trail flank the entrance, while inside are murals depicting events of Oregon's early years.

(Open Memorial Day to Labor Day; for tour schedule, tel (503) 378-4423).

Panoramic views including Mt Hood and Mt Jefferson await if you're prepared to climb the 121-step spiral staircase to the tower.

The other four modern Greek style buildings occupying the Capitol Mall are state buildings for Public Service, Transportation, Labor & Industry and the Library. From Salem a detour on SR 99E takes you to Oregon City, the birthplace of Oregon and the Pacific Northwest.

AURORA

En route, you pass through Aurora, where one of the West's earliest experiments in communal living, the **Aurora Colony**, thrived for almost a quarter of a century after its 1856 founding. Members of the colony, dedicated to living by the Golden Rule, involved themselves in philosophy and the arts. Colony-style pieces fashioned by skilled craftspeople such as furniture and household artefacts, are eagerly sought today by collectors.

You can see some of them at the **Ox Barn Museum**, part of the restoration of the circa 1860s colony buildings by the Aurora Colony Historical Society. Demonstrations of Colony crafts are staged for visitors and you can take a guided tour of the buildings Wednesday through Sunday from 1 to 5 pm (closed in January).

CANBY

At Canby up the road, take the opportunity to cross the Willamette River on the Lilliputian car ferry which fords it continuously in daylight hours. It's a chance to appreciate the beauty of the river, generally hidden from motorists' view by parkland.

OREGON CITY

The rushing waters of falls tumbling over horseshoe-shaped boulders some 26 miles above the Willamette's mouth would provide an excellent power source for a sawmill – so decided Dr John McLoughlin, the Hudson's Bay Company superintendent at Fort Vancouver, in 1828. In the next decade, Oregon City grew up around his sawmill at the base of the waterfalls. By the early 1840s, Americans who settled here were chafing at rule by the Hudson's Bay Company. In a historic meeting 20 miles upriver at Champoeg (pronounced Shamp-*poo*-eg) in 1843, they decided by a vote of 52 to 50 to draw up their own constitution. The provincial government at Oregon City became the first American government body west of the Rockies. Thus it was here that the plot charting the city of San Francisco was filed in 1850. You'll find the historic document framed in the County Clerk's office in Clackamas County Court House at Eighth and Main St.

Oregon City was capital of the vast Oregon Territory established in 1848 and only relinquished its importance with statehood in 1859; the following year the government seat moved to Salem. Dr McLoughlin, dubbed 'the father of Oregon,' switched his allegiance to the new government after the Champoeg vote. He resigned from the Hudson's Bay Company and lived in a white clapboard house in Oregon City from 1845 until his death in 1857. You can visit his home, which has been authentically restored with territorial period furnishings and some of his personal belongings. (Location: 713 Center St at 7th; open Tuesday to Sunday, 1 to 5 pm, closed January; admission charge.)

Next door is the historic home of Dr Forbes Barclay, a former Fort Vancouver surgeon who became a town leader from the mid to late 19th century.

Oregon City is uniquely terraced; the downtown business area edges the river while the residential district is built on two levels on a bluff overlooking the river. A free Municipal Elevator carries pedestrian traffic up the 90 feet from downtown to the lower residential terrace.

Across the river in West Linn, you can watch the century-old locks in action lifting river traffic around the falls. If you see numerous boats at the base of the falls you'll know the salmon are running.

The waters of glacial Missoula Flood which inundated this land some 8000 years ago left untouched a small area. The 22½-acre site on the basalt bluff high above West Linn contains more than 300 species of plants now rare in this part of the Pacific Northwest. If you visit the **Camassia Natural Area**, you'll probably meet students who come to study the meadow's plants and wildflowers. From Oregon City, it's a 12-mile drive to the center of Portland.

PORTLAND

Oregon's major city, Portland, lies at the head of the Willamette Valley, just south of the meeting of the Willamette and Columbia Rivers. This confluence provides a deep freshwater port, making Portland a major seaport although it is 110 miles inland from the ocean.

The Coast and Cascade Ranges girdle the city with green mountains. Strung across the metropolitan area are 160 parks and gardens covering 7500 acres. Forested hills sprinkled with fine old homes watch over downtown like brilliantly decked dowagers. There's a very human dimension to Portland, responsible perhaps for its being named as leader in 'quality of life' in a mid-1970s study of 243 American cities.

Among pioneers who wended their way across the Oregon Trail in the 1800s were two New Englanders – A J Lovejoy of Boston and Francis Pettygrove of Portland, Maine. The settlement which they laid out on the banks of the Willamette in the winter of 1844-45 would have been called Boston, Oregon, if the toss of the coin had gone the other way. From the beginning the town flourished, aided by its accessibility by steamboat. Today it is a thriving city of 366,960, the greater metropolitan area population exceeds one million.

Climate

Although Portland is on a more northern latitude than such cities as Minneapolis and Ottawa, Canada, it has a much milder climate due to the warming influence of the Japanese Current flowing south off the coast.

The months from June to September are most pleasant; highs rarely reach over the 90°F mark and most days are in the 70°s. In October, the rains start – and they can be constant and heavy; annual rainfall is 37 inches.

Orientation

Physically the city sprawls on either side of the Willamette – 11 bridges connect the two sides of the river. On the west bank, the grid-patterned downtown area is backed by wooded hills. The east bank is flatland, with industry along the foreshore, then residential districts spread north and east, following the Columbia's contours. Edging the Columbia on the Oregon side are parks, country clubs and Portland International Airport; across river is the city of Vancouver, Washington.

Portland is easy to find your way around because the city is divided into five sections – North, Northeast, Southeast, Southwest and Northwest. Addresses include the section designation; ie SE 60th Avenue and NE 60th Avenue.

THE WEST SIDE – DOWNTOWN

Despite it's rivers, lakes and parklands, Portland first appears to be a rather homely city. But once you see the downtown area that perception is changed. Thoughtful planning has resulted in complexes carefully designed not to overwhelm the natural surroundings. Touches of old-world charm soften the modernity – notice the cast iron light standards, occasional cast iron street clocks and the drinking fountains, donated during Prohibition to 'quench frustrated thirsts'.

Typical of the new office buildings catering to people's enjoyment as well as to commercial needs is the **Georgia-Pacific Building** at 900 SW Fifth Avenue. Look closely at the architecture of the 30-story building: there are no straight horizontal lines; they are all slightly curved. Stroll through the building's corridors, a gallery for over 450 works of Oregon's artists. On the concourse level is a **Logging Museum** with dioramas depicting oldtime and modern logging methods, historical artefacts and a movie. It's open Tuesday to Friday 10 am to 3 pm; free.

On SW Fifth, you come to **City Hall,** between Jefferson and Madison Sts. This imposing 1895 Italian Renaissance structure has its detractors. One critic described it as 'so ugly that it's cute'. If you'd like an opportunity to witness city government in action, city council meetings are open to the public Tuesdays through Thursdays, tel 248-3511.

The 40-story 1st Interstate Bank Tower at 1300 SW Fifth is overshadowed by the new 43-story US National Bank Tower at Fifth and Burnside. Neither of these, though, has elicited the storm of praise – and controversy – that has swirled around the **Portland building** on Fifth and Madison. A postmodernist design by architect Michael Graves, it leaves few people unmoved, either to praise or condemnation.

Nearby at SW Third & Clay is the popular Portland landmark, **Ira's Fountain.** It was designed by Lawrence Halprin to complement the rebuilt Civic Auditorium, which it fronts. Originally known as the Forecourt Fountain, its name was recently changed to commemorate the late Ira Keller, guiding force behind its construction in 1970. Ira's Fountain is a delightful series of waterfalls splashing over stepped concrete blocks into sparkling pools. Whatever its official name, it's invariably called the 'people's fountain' – summer months draw so many waders and splashers, there've been rumours about the city hiring a lifeguard!

The water runs from 9 am to 11 pm every day except Wednesday, recirculating 13,000 gallons per minute.

The **Civic Auditorium** is home to the Portland Opera, Oregon Symphony and Portland Junior Symphony. It holds 3000 people and is renowned for its fine acoustics. A vast glass wall extending the full three floors overlooks Ira's Fountain.

Typifying Portland's urban renewal projects is **Portland Center,** on Front and SW Fourth. The 80-acre complex, built in 1958, contains five apartment buildings with river views. Pedestrian malls connect them to plazas, shops and office buildings. Beautifully landscaped grounds are highlighted by Lawrence Halprin's exceptional Lovejoy Fountain, which he created after studying the flow of Sierra streams.

North on Jefferson is the **Oregon Historical Society.** The century-old society's exhibits are housed in a spacious modern building, allowing for comfortable viewing of displays detailing Indian and pioneer life, as well as models of historic ships which plied the Northwest coast. Look for the 1845 covered wagon which carried a family across the Oregon Trail – it makes you ponder the hardiness of the pioneers. The society's archives include a vast collection of historical manuscripts and almost a million photographs. A store sells books and other items pertaining to Oregon's history. At 1230 SW Park; tel 222-1741; free; open daily except Sunday 10 am to 5 pm.

Fronting the building is the green of **South Park Blocks,** which extend for 13 blocks along Park Avenue from the Portland State University campus to SW Salmon St. **North Park** – a six-block strip bounded by NW Glisan and SW Ankeny Sts, bordering Portland's 'Skid Rd' area – and South Park were set aside over a century ago. The plan was to lay a green belt around the entire downtown area, but unfortunately the intervening land was never acquired and the belt remains uncompleted.

Crossing Park Avenue, you come to the **Portland Art Museum.** The classically simple building, designed by famed architect Pietro Belluschi, houses an outstanding collection of Northwest Coast Indian art, as well as pre-Columbian, Cameroun West African, Asian and classical Greek art. European masters and 19th and 20th century American painting and sculpture are represented in permanent collections.

Contemporary Oregon artists exhibit in group shows and individually. An alfresco Sculpture Court is particularly delightful on summer afternoons. The Art Museum is not government supported; it is privately-owned and maintained. A museum shop sells excellent reproductions. Located at SW Park and Jefferson; tel 226-2811; free (donation welcomed); open daily excluding Monday, noon to 5 pm; Friday open until 10 pm.

Old Town Portland's surviving historical buildings are being preserved and refurbished. Many of them lie within the area known as Old Town, centered on the few blocks either side of Burnside St between the Willamette River and Fifth Avenue.

Outside this area, though, is the **Pioneer Courthouse,** which faces on SW Fifth between Morrison and Yamhill. Built in 1873, it was the Northwest's first federal building. The Italianate structure's interior has been restored to its former elegance and it now serves as judges' private chambers.

A good time to wander **Old Town** is any Saturday between May and December, when you'll find the street market in full swing under Burnside Bridge. You can browse stalls for handcrafted goods, and imported foods, perhaps enjoy an impromptu concert by street musicians. Open Saturdays and Sundays April to Christmas.

Near the waterfront is the handsome **Skidmore Fountain,** bequeathed by Stephen Skidmore in the late 1880s. Having prospered in the town, he wanted to be remembered by a fountain 'where horses, men, and dogs might drink'. It became a favorite turn-of-the-century gathering place and now, after restoration has overcome years of neglect, it is once again focal point of the area.

Old Town's shops and boutiques are popular for crafts, antiques, Indian jewellery and books.

Murder story addicts will want to visit the **Police Historical Museum.** Its collection of artefacts spans the period from 1870 to the present, and includes old murder weapons and turn-of-the century equipment. Present-day police manning this precinct wear 1890s uniforms. Location on 26 NW 2nd Ave (enter through alley); tel 223-5771 for hours; free.

Victoriana A revival of interest in Victoriana is catching on in the city's northwest section around 17th and 18th Avenues, NW Irving and NW Hoyt. Many of the existing Victorian houses have been renovated and a movement has started to relocate Victorian houses to vacant lots here from other city areas.

The Waterfront It is Portland's pride that before federal regulations required cleanup of America's rivers polluted by industrial effluents and sewage, the city's citizenry had raised an outcry which resulted in local legislation. The Willamette is now sufficiently pollution-free to encourage boating, water-skiing and salmon fishing.

Waterfront Park has opened up the riverside for the first time since the city's founding. The recently finished landscaped promenade stretches along Front St from the Burnside to the Hawthorne Bridge. Portland is looking ahead to projects opening up the entire waterfront.

The Port The Port Community Development Department arranges guided bus tours of the port Wednesday and Thursday afternoons during summer months, taking in facilities including container loading, floating dry docks and waterfront industries. Reservation necessary, tel 231-5000 ext 208; free.

You can watch container loading from an observation area in the administration building at John M Fulton Terminal 6. Tel 286-9671 to check when terminal is operating.

East Side

Across river, a pedestrian promenade stretching along the east bank between the Burnside and Hawthorne Bridges is a grand place for city skyline views, though the proximity of I-5 is a noisy irritation.

More peaceful and offering spectacular views is **Mt Tabor Park**, built around what is believed to be the country's only extinct volcano within city limits. On Yamhill and Division, east of SE 60th Avenue; free.

Portlanders flock in April and May to the **American Rhododendron Society's Test Gardens** for brilliant displays of azaleas and Rhododendron's. At Crystal Springs Lake Park, near SE 28th Avenue and Woodstock Boulevard; open daily 8 am to dusk; free (except on Mother's Day when annual show carries small admission fee.

Next door is prestigious **Reed College**, a private liberal arts campus which has more Rhodes Scholars to its credit than Harvard or Yale.

Parks

For nature-lovers, Portland's wealth of parks and gardens are big attractions. These include city blocks, such as **O'Bryant Square**, where brown-baggers enjoy the noonday sun around a three-tiered rose-shaped fountain, surrounded by 250 rose bushes.On SW-Stark and Washington Sts.

Washington Park Sovereign among them is Washington Park, part of a chain of contiguous forest parks which stretch for seven miles into the western heights above the Willamette. The 145-acre park is hub for Portlanders' outdoor activities. It has two of the city's loveliest gardens – the International Rose Test Gardens and the Japanese Gardens – as well as the zoo, OMSI (the Oregon Museum of Science and Industry) and the Western Forestry Center. The whimsically painted Tri-Met bus will take you there – call 231-3263 for information.

Portland is famed for its roses – in fact, it's dubbed 'The City of Roses'. June and September are best months to wander the **International Rose Test Garden**, which harbors hundreds of varieties, all identified. They are in bloom from late May into late November. An added pleasure is the panoramic view of the city and hills, backed by snow-capped Mount Hood.

The **Japanese Gardens** have five classic Oriental retreats, complete with stone lanterns, weeping willows, cherry trees and gentle streams. April is cherry blossom time.

Open daily 10 am to 6 pm mid-April to mid-September; 10 am to 4 pm rest of year; admission charge; tel 223-1321.

Both the gardens are reached from the park's main gate at the head of Park Place, south of W Burnside. The *Zooliner* diesel-powered train will carry you from the gardens through woodlands to the zoo on the other side of the park. It operates daily through spring and summer, weekends only in winter.

Washington Park Zoo has been open since 1887. Its 40 acres house the usual animals from around the world but it offers some unusual features. With animal 'teaching machines', you can try communicating with the denizens. Children can pet small animals and exhibits include Elephant Hill and Night Country, where nocturnal animals can be observed.

To reach the zoo directly: 4001 SW Canyon Rd north of US 26; open daily 9.30 am to dusk; admission charge (includes zoo railway); tel 226-1561 for information on railway schedules and special events.

Adjoining is **OMSI**. This collection of science and industry exhibits is a do-it-yourself delight. You can 'walk through' a human heart, study anatomy with the help of a transparent lady, command a ship's bridge, toy for hours with electronic devices, inspect aerospace vehicles and indulge in nostalgia inside a DC-3. Exhibits are constantly changing, and endlessly fascinating. Allow plenty of time for this one! Open daily from 9 am to 5 pm, later on summer evenings; admission charge; tel 222-2828.

Next door is the **Western Forestry Center**, which offers an intriguing look at Oregon's lifeblood, forestry, and its products. A handsome wooden building houses exhibits covering such areas as conservation, logging and recreation. At the push of a button a 70-foot 'talking' Douglas fir explains how it grows. A multimedia presentation documents the devastation of forest fires. It's open daily 10 am to 5 pm; admission charge; tel 228-1367.

Two other interesting attractions in Washington Park are the Hoyt Arboretum and the Pittock Mansion.

Hoyt Arboretum has an outstanding collection of native Northwest trees and other flora. Shady paths ramble through its wooded hills; numerous markers identify plants and trees. Pick up a trail map from the administration building; there are picnic facilities, too. On 400 SW Fairview Boulevard north of OMSI; open daily 5 am to midnight; guided tours Saturday to Sunday 2.30 pm; free; tel 228-8732.)

The **Pittock Mansion** took five years (1909-14) to build for Henry P Pittock, founder of *The Oregonian*. The imposing French Renaissance house, which sits some 1000 feet above the city, commands exceptional views of city and mountains. It has been restored and partially furnished in Edwardian period. At 3229 NW Pittock Drive, it's open Wednesday to Sunday 1 to 5 pm (later in summer); admission charge; tel 248-4469. Grounds open daily; free.

Around Portland

One of the most scenic drives in the West is the 169.5-mile **Mt Hood Loop**, which takes in the magnificent reaches of the Columbia River Gorge (see Columbia River section). You can pick up a loop guide at the Portland Convention &

Visitors' Association, at the corner of Front and Salmon; tel 222-2223.

Sauvie Island

A short drive north on US 30 takes you to the tranquil farmlands of Sauvie Island in the Columbia River. This pastoral retreat is popular with Portlanders who want to 'get away from it all' for some hiking, biking and fishing. On the island is the **Bybee Howell House**, a pre-Civil War farmhouse, restored and maintained by the Oregon Historical Society. It's open daily 10 am to 6 pm June to October; free (donations welcome).

If you're lucky enough to be there the last Saturday in September, you'll strike the 'Wintering In' picnic, when farmers sell their harvest goods – plus a few antiques.

Trojan Nuclear Power Plant

A little further north on US 30, near St Helens, this nuclear power plant's huge cooling tower dominates the Columbia River countryside. Visitor Center exhibits explain the workings of a nuclear power plant and trace its impact on the environment; a film in the unique Ecosphere describes the arrival of the Nuclear Age.

(Open Wednesday to Sunday 9 am to 5 pm; tours Thursday and Saturday 10 am to 3 pm on the hour.)

Places to Stay

Although there are a number of hotels and motels in the downtown area, the majority are across the river on the east side. There are plenty of motels to choose from, most in the $30 to $40 double a night range. An interesting and reasonably priced alternative is offered by *Northwest Bed & Breakfast*. Write them for details at 7707 SW Locust St, Tigard OR 97223; tel (503) 246-8366. *B&B International*, 1318 SW Troy St, Portland OR 97219; tel (503) 547-6316 also offer bed-and-breakfast throughout the West.

A sampling of Portland hotels and motels:

West Side – Top End
The Westin Benson (309 SW Broadway at Oak, Portland, OR 97205; tel (503) 228-9611.) Built in 1913 to be city's premier hotel and it remains so. Comfortable, bright, air-conditioned rooms, lower floors a bit noisy. Cable TV. Pay garage. Two fine restaurants, popular bar. Rates from $78 double.

Portland Hilton Hotel (921 SW 6th Avenue, Portland, OR 97204; tel (503) 226-1611.) Air-conditioned rooms, some refrigerators. Pool. Spa, sauna, whirlpool extra. Pay garage. Restaurants, coffee shop. Rates from $64 double.

West Side – Mid-range
Imperial Hotel(SW Broadway and Stark St, Portland, OR 97205; tel (503) 228-7221.) Conveniently located air-conditioned, color TV. Valet garage. Restaurant. Rates from $30 double.

Caravan Motor Hotel (2401 SW 4th Avenue, Portland, OR 97201; tel (503) 226-1121.) Air-conditioned, color cable TV. Pool. Restaurant. Rates from $26 double.

West Side – Bottom End
Lamplighter Motel (10207 SW Parkway, Portland OR 97225; Cedar Hills exit from US 26). 56-air-conditioned units, some two-bedroom, efficiencies. Cable TV. Rates from $22 double.

East Side – Top End
Red Lion Motor Inn-Jantzen Beach (919 N Hayden Island Dr, Portland, OR 97217; tel (503) 283-4466.) On Hayden Island in Columbia River. Large units, many with river view, balconies. Air-conditioned, color TV. Pool, wading pool, whirlpool, dock, tennis. Airport transport. Rates from $73 double.

East Side – Mid-Range
Hyatt Lodge (431 NE Multnomah St, Portland, OR 97232; tel (503) 233-5121. Air-conditioned, color TV. Pool. Restaurant across street. Rates from $39 double.

East Side – Bottom End
Cameo Motel(4111 NE 82nd St, Portland OR 97220; tel (503) 288-5981). 41-unit motel, most air-conditioned. Refrigerators, color TV. Restaurant across street. Rates from $25 double.

Places to Eat
London Grill In the Westin Benson. Award-winning, known nationwide for gourmet cuisine. Fine wine cellar. (E)

Breakfast, lunch, dinner daily. SW Broadway at Oak; tel 295-4110.

Sweet Tibbie Dunbar British pub atmosphere in former golf clubhouse. Steak and seafood. (M)

Lunch Monday to Friday, dinner daily. 718 NE 12th Avenue; tel 232-1801.

Hilaire's Encore Encore Seafood and steaks served in an atmosphere of European elegance. (M)

Breakfast, lunch daily, dinner Monday to Friday, closed Sunday. 622 SW Washington (off Broadway); tel 223-5192.

The River Queen Floating restaurant redolent of San Francisco gold rush days, serving good steak and seafood. Known for friendly service. (M) Lunch Monday to Saturday, Dinner nightly. 1300 NW Front St; tel 228-8633.

Mr C's Hippopotamus In Lloyd Center. Especially popular with families, with special children's dinners, omelettes served all day. (B)

Breakfast, lunch, dinner daily. 1103 Lloyd Center; tel 288-6153.

The Old Spaghetti Factory Fun restaurant in antique-filled room in historic section of town. (B)

Dinner nightly. SW 2nd at Pine; tel 222-5375.

Nightlife
Most of the major hotels feature en-

tertainment in dining rooms or cocktail bars, including occasional dinner theater shows. For listing of what's playing, check local daily press or the *Portland Guide,* published weekly, or obtain list from the Visitor Center at Front and Salmon.

Popular are the **Portland Opera,** which mounts four productions a year, the **Oregon Symphony Orchestra** and the **Portland Youth Philharmonic** all based at the Civic Auditorium. There are a number of theater groups, strongest of which is the **Portland Civic Theater** (1530 SW Yamhill; tel 226-3048).

Major events on Portlanders' calendar is the annual **Rose Festival,** held the first week in June since 1909. The celebration is multifaceted, culminating in selection of a Rose Queen and a parade.

Getting There & Getting Around

Air Portland International Airport, situated beside the Columbia River some nine miles northeast of the city, is served by major trunk as well as several commuter airlines.

Limousine service to downtown area takes about 25 minutes; at writing the fare is $3.75.

Bus *Greyhound Bus Lines* depot is at 509 SW Taylor, (tel (503) 243-2336; *Continental Trailways* at 1010 SW Sixth, tel (503) 228-8571.

Car The major car rental agencies maintain desks at the airport. Off-airport agencies are listed in the Yellow Pages. Driving downtown is easy – all streets are one-way, alternating direction (First Avenue heads west, Pine toward the river).

Taxis Taxis cannot be flagged down on the street; you must either phone or pick them up at ranks in front of the major hotels.

Public Transport The city bus system, *Tri-Met* operates from the downtown

Portland Mall. This brick-paved, tree-lined pedestrian mall on SW Fifth and Sixth Avenues runs from West Burnside to Madison St. Along it are European-style passenger kiosks, each equipped with color-coded maps which easily direct you to the bus you need for a particular destination. Overhead closed circuit TV in each lists timetable. It is one of the country's most up-to-date systems. Fare is 90c (exact change necessary – there are change machines in the kiosks.) However, the **Fareless Square** covers a 338-block area of downtown Portland bounded by the Willamette River, SW Market, NW Hoyt and I-405 (the Stadium Freeway): within that area, you ride free.

Tours

The Gray Line (921 SW Sixth Avenue; tel 226-6755) runs a daily three-hour city tour, as well as numerous other tours around the area.

Portland Walking Tours (PO Box 4322, Portland, OR 97208; tel 223-1017), offers two-hour guided walking tours of the city, as well as other pedestrian excursions.

Port tours are mentioned in the Port section.

Tours of Mt St Helens volcano are offered by *Gray Line* and flightseeing by *Aviation Enterprises*, tel (503) 667-1877.

Week-long **cruises** aboard the 83-passenger *Pacific Northwest Explorer* leave Portland Saturdays May to October to sail the Columbia and Snake Rivers. Information: *Exploration Cruise Lines*, 1500 Metropolitan Park Building, Seattle WA 98101; tel (206) 624-8551; toll-free 800-426-0600.

THE BACK COUNTRY ROUTE
Klamath Birdwatching

SR 97 from California enters Oregon as the birds fly – it is on the path of the Pacific Flyway. Millions of ducks and geese cloud the skies each spring and fall as they migrate from Arctic reaches south to the Mexican border. There are five national wildlife refuges within 50 miles of Klamath Falls, 12 miles north of the California border, where birdwatchers will be in their element. Not only ducks and geese, but pelicans, cormorants, terns, curlews, cranes, stilts and many, many more whirr and flutter overhead in long graceful V-formations. If you're a dedicated ornithologist, stop off at the **Tule Lake National Wildlife Refuge** across the border in California and pick up leaflets, maps and bird lists for the five refuges mentioned above (or write Klamath Basin National Wildlife Refuges, Route 1, Box 74, Tulelake, CA 96134).

Best times are spring and fall, but the Flyway remains active year-round. Dress warmly, for though days are clear and warm, mornings and noghts are cool.

KLAMATH FALLS

In spite of its name, Klamath Falls is heart of a lakeland, with more than 100 good fishing lakes nearby. Oregon's largest freshwater body, Upper Klamath Lake, runs north of town for 40 miles. In summertime, you'll see rare white pelicans, now protected, nesting here.

The Klamath River rises here in Lake Ewauna and flows across Northern California to the Pacific Ocean. When white settlers came to this area in the late 1860s, they were in constant conflict with local Indian tribes: the Modoc War of 1872-73 ended Indian resistance to the homesteaders. Today, Klamath Indians comprise the majority of the town's population. Indian lore and artefacts are well represented in local museums and over Memorial Day weekend, the town hosts **Pow Wow Days**, a festival highlighted by an all-Indian rodeo.

The **Favell Museum of Western Art and Indian Artefacts** displays an extensive collection of regional Indian arts, crafts and arrow heads, along with art and sculpture of contemporary western artists. There's also a miniature gun collection. At 125 Main St; tel 882-9996; open May 1 to December 31; Monday to Saturday 9.30 am to 5.30 pm; rest of year closed Mondays; admission charge.)

Klamath County history, including Indian history, is on display at **Klamath County Museum**. There's a particularly good representation on the Modoc War. Exhibits also detail geology and wildlife of the area. You will find it at 1451 Main St; open Tuesday to Saturday 9 am to 5 pm, Sunday 1 to 5 pm; free.

Presidents Theodore Roosevelt, William H Taft and Woodrow Wilson all stayed at the turn-of-the-century **Baldwin Hotel** in its heyday. Now restored as a museum, it contains many of its original furnishings. Be sure to look out for the fine leaded stained-glass panel over the entrance and the hand-crafted woodwork on doors and staircases. The address is 31 Main St; tel 882-2501, ext 207; open Tuesday to Saturday 9 am to 5 pm; closed holidays; admission.

Klamath Falls is in the vanguard of the alternative energy movement, putting to good use what geologists consider one of the earth's richest deposits of geothermal energy. A century ago, Klamath Indians tapped the hot springs for cooking and therapeutic uses; today many homes and businesses heat their buildings and draw hot water from subterranean wells. You may be walking on pavements de-iced by hot-water coils heated from the geothermal reservoir.

Klamath Falls is closest city to Crater Lake National Park (see Rogue River Valley chapter). At the north end of Upper Klamath Lake, SR 62 cuts off from US 97, loops up through Crater Lake National Park then down into the Rogue River Valley and Medford.

Two other roads link Klamath Falls and Medford: SR 66 through Ashland and SR 140 across the Rogue River National Forest. SR 58 provides a scenic route across the Deschutes National Forest, joining I-5 just below Eugene.

NORTH TO BEND

The direct route to Bend is on US 97 following the Deschutes River Valley, east of the Cascades. Some 11 miles north of upper Klamath Lake, a grassy oasis amidst the pine and sagebrush is the **Collier Memorial State Park**. You'll find early logging equipment housed in log buildings and rustic log cabins. Built by trappers, loggers and early home-steaders, these have been refurnished to show living styles of each in pioneer days. Cross sections of enormous logs give you some idea of the titans which have been logged from Oregon Forests.

DESCHUTES LAVA LANDS

Countless volcanic eruptions have be-queathed a dramatic landscape east of the Cascades, where cinder cones, buttes and buckled ridges project from flows of twisted lava.

Mt Newberry several eons back was one of the Cascade Ranges' mightiest mount-ains: 12,000 feet of fiery, restless energy, with a base some 25 miles in girth. But lava constantly draining through vents and fissures weakened the walls sup-porting the shield volcano's dome until finally it collapsed in on itself.

What remains is a huge crater with two lovely lakes, East Lake and Paulina (pronounced Paul-eye-na). To reach them, take Paulina Creek Rd east. You'll discover the lakes, waterfalls, and an interpretive trail through one of the country's most extensive fields of ob-sidian, volcanic glass released from Mt Newberry, which supplied generations of Indians with arrow heads. The view from the 7985-foot summit of Paulina Peak is magnificent.

A little farther north, you can see what happened when Mt Newberry's molten lava engulfed the pine forest around 6000 years ago. Lava encased the charred trees, which finally rotted away leaving behind a forest of stone trees rising above the lava fields. To reach the **Lava Cast Forest**, turn east off US 97 onto Forest Rd, opposite the Sunriver entrance, and take the cinder road which ends 10 miles in at a picnic area (no water available).

Sunriver is a luxury resort popular with the winter sports set who come here for cross-country skiing and downhill powder skiing on **Mt Bachelor**, Oregon's premier winter sports venue. In summer, golf, tennis, bicycling, horseback trail riding and canoeing on the Deschutes River are the attraction.

Places to Stay & Eat

Sunriver Lodge (Sunriver, OR 97702, tel (503) 593-1221.) 336 units in condom-iniums and resort homes. Fireplaces, porches, color cable TV, pool, saunas, dock, fishing. Transportation to Mt Bachelor ski area. Fee for boats, golf, tennis, bicycles, riding. Private airstrip. Dining room (moderate-expensive; open 7 am to 10.30 pm to public) and coffee shop. Packages available. Rates from $70 double.

Other restaurants in the area include *Casa de Ricardo* (Mexican), *Sunspot* (hamburgers) and *Trout House* (seafood).

The heart of the lava lands lies a little further up US 997: at **Lava Lands Visitor Center**, operated by the Forest Service as part of the Deschutes National Forest, automated displays and audio-visual presentations vividly describe the forces – natural and human – that have shaped this region. Trails outside lead you to witness for yourself the effects of volcanic rampages. Open daily 8.30 am to 6 pm May to September; Wednesday to Sunday 9 am to 4 pm October; by appointment rest of year; tel (503) 382-5668; free.

Drive up adjoining **Lava Butte** for good views of the countryside, including the 6000-acre magma flow streaming off to the northwest, disgorged by the Butte around 2000 years ago. You can walk a trail around the rim of the crater for different perspectives on the lava lands, sculptured peaks and forests.

Lava tubes and ice-filled caves occur throughout the area. One of the best examples is situated east of US 97 a mile or so south of Lava Butte: the **Lava River Caves State Park**, a mile-long subterranean tunnel through solid rock, created by a stream of molten lava pouring from Mt Newberry thousands of years ago. Its average 35-foot width opens in places to 50 feet and its ceiling reaches a height of 58 feet. You can explore the tube by the light of a rented lantern. Open daily 9 am to 4 pm May to September.

For information on where to find other lava caves, contact the Deschutes National Forest Service, 211 E Revere St, Bend, OR 97701; tel (503) 382-6922.

Oregon High Desert Museum, which opened in 1982, is an excellent opportunity to become acquainted with the region. Live animals are on display, and the 'living' history of Indians and early settlers is told in exhibitions.

On US 97 six miles south of Bend; open 9 am to 5 pm daily summer; closes 4 pm October to March; admission charge; tel (503) 382-4754.

CASCADES LAKES HIGHWAY

An alternative and very scenic route leaves US 97 at La Pine. The Cascades Lakes Highway (also called Century Drive) describes a 100-mile arc between La Pine and Bend, skirting eight lakes and reservoirs, all within a mile or two of the road, and offers spectacular vistas of the Cascades Peaks, particularly as it traverses the 6400-foot shoulder of Mt Bachelor.

If you have time, stop off at one or two of the sparkling lakes: you'll find exceptional fishing, boating and water skiing opportunities, rustic resorts and Forest Service campgrounds, trailheads for ventures into the forests and lava fields and pack and saddle trips you might join. In summer, wildflowers cover the alpine meadows and peep from rocky crevices.

Crane Prairie Reservoir is a refuge for ospreys which nest in rookeries atop the crags at its northwest end. There is an informative exhibit detailing efforts to save this endangered species and you might see these stunning birds power-diving for fish to feed their young.

Cascades Lakes Highway is generally open from late June or early July and remains open until the first heavy snowfall of the fall.

Crossing the Cascades

Yet another scenic route links Eugene-Springfield and Bend.

SR 126 from Springfield follows the McKenzie River into the Cascades to Belknap Springs, then heads north to join US 20, traversing high meadows to Bend.

The way is lovely no matter what the season. Springtime's dogwood blossoms, summer's rhododendrons and fall's brilliant golds and crimsons daub the green of virgin forests. On easy trails from wayside parking, you can reach waterfalls cascading down moss-covered rocks.

You come upon the dramatic sight of the vast lava fields, so like Hawaii's that the Hawaiian terms are used – *a'a* for the crumbly, jumbled lava and *pahoehoe* for the swirling, ropelike fields.

McKenzie Pass

Even more spectacular views of the lava beds are obtained by taking SR 242, the **McKenzie Pass Road**, from its junction with SR 126; it joins US 20 at Sisters This is a slower route, impassable in winter, but it's worth it for the top-of-the-world sight from the 5324-foot McKenzie Pass across Mt Washington and Three Sisters Wilderness Areas. At the summit, stop at **Dee Wright Observatory**, a tower of stone which has 11 windows, each framing one of the Cascades' peaks. To the north is the craggy outline of 7800-foot Mt Washington; south, the Three Sisters, each over 10,000 feet, dominate the skyline.

Signs along the half-mile Lava River Loop Trail from this point trace the volcanic evolution of this bizarre landscape, used by astronauts in training for moon walks.

The Pacific Crest Trail cuts across the Cascades here. If you're game for several hours' hiking, follow it north several miles to **Little Belknap Crater's** labyrinth of lava tubes and steam vents.

SISTERS
From the summit, SR 242 winds down through cool forests of evergreens to Sisters, a delightful country town that captures the period of the Old West, right down to hitching rails and false-front stores. From here to Bend, you cross rolling pastureland, passing occasional woodframe farmhouses which add to the attractiveness of the drive.

Places to Stay
Santiam Lodge Youth Hostel, Star Route, Sisters OR 97759; open May 1 to November 1, $3 single.

BEND
Hub of this central Oregon region is the delightful town of Bend, with a pop-

ulation of around 17,000. Set into a curve in the Deschutes River, it was originally called Farewell Bend by emigrants leaving this pleasant campsite behind as they headed their wagons northeast into sagebrush country.

US 97 passes through town, revealing only the commercial side of its personality. Head down toward the river and you'll find that Bend is a place to relax and take it easy amidst scenery that, particularly for city dwellers, imparts a sense of open space, with a great variety of vistas.

The clear, crisp atmosphere is exhilarating and many visitors find themselves staying longer than they had planned. There are scenic drives in every direction: visit the Bend Chamber of Commerce, located at 164 NW Hawthorne (tel 382-3221) and they'll be most helpful in pointing the way.

Bend is county seat, so the **Deschutes Historical Museum** is here; its exhibits include pioneer memorabilia and Indian artefacts, and it's at 129 NW Idaho; for hours, tel 389-1813; free.

Astronomers at the **University of Oregon Observatory** atop 6395-foot Pine Mountain welcome visitors and are happy to explain their work. A bonus is their panoramic view of mountains and desert. Thirty-five miles south-east of town: off SR 20E just beyond Millican; open Thursday to Sunday 2 to 5 pm, 7 pm until one hour after dusk; road closed in winter.

Places to Stay

Bend has many motels, as well as condominiums and resorts in the surrounding area. The Convention & Visitors' Bureau issues a complete list, including resorts and campgrounds: write to 164 NW Hawthorne, Bend, OR 97701; tel (503) 382-3221.

SR 97 is lined with motels but these can be noisy with constant traffic passing by, so we list a few off the highway as a guide.

In addition to Sunriver, another lodge caters to skiers who flock to Mt Bachelor:

The Inn of the Seventh Mountain (PO Box 1207, Bend, OR 97709; tel (503) 382-8711; toll-free Oregon only 800-452-6810.) Year-round resort on Century Drive, seven miles west of Bend. Offers all recreation facilities, including transportation to Mt Bachelor ski area. Lodge rooms, studio units and condominium apartments in mountain setting, furnished with Indian motif. Restaurant and lounge. Packages available. Rates from $46 double.

Bend Riverside Motel (PO Box 151, 1565 Hill St, Bend, OR 97701; tel (503) 382-3802.) Overlooking river. Some view units with balconies, suites, studios, cottages, kitchens, fireplaces available. Air-conditioning, color TV, free coffee. Indoor pool, sauna, whirlpool, tennis, picnic facilities, coin laundry. No restaurant. Rates from $24 double. Recommended.

Best Western Entrada Lodge (PO Box 975, Bend, OR 97701 (on Century Drive, four miles west of town); tel (503) 382-4080.) 25 air-conditioned units in secluded, wooded setting. Color cable TV,

pool, sauna. Breakfast only (7.30 to 9.30 am). Rates from $35 double.

Rainbow Motel (154 NE Franklin Avenue, Bend, OR 97701; tel (503) 382-1821.) 20 air-conditioned rooms, most with oversize beds. Some kitchens. Free coffee, color TV. No restaurant. Rates from $19 double.

Places to Eat

There are a number of them along US 97, mostly of the coffee shop variety. A few alternatives:

Le Bistro French restaurant in remodeled old church. Parisian decor with occasional entertainment, when former choir loft is opened for pastries and coffee, wine and cheese. (M)

Dinner, closed Monday. 1203 3rd St; tel 389-7274.

Pine Tavern Dining room, built around two 100-foot pine trees, with river view. Friendly atmosphere, good food including home baking. Very popular, so reservations advised. (M) Lunch, dinner Monday to Saturday; dinner Sunday. 967 NW Brooks St; tel 382-5581.

The Tumalo Emporium Western rococo decor, good steaks, seafood and casseroles. Traditional icecream desserts. Home baking. Reservations advised. (B/M)

Lunch, dinner, Sunday brunch. 64619 Highway 20; tel 382-2202.

Getting There

Apart from car, Bend is served by air through Roberts Field at Redmond, 17 miles northeast, and bus by *Pacific Trailways* daily from Portland. Car rental is available at the airport and locally.

BEND TO PORTLAND

Again you have a choice of routes. You can take US 97 and US 197 north to The Dalles on the Columbia River, then breeze along I-80, which follows the river's course down to Portland. You can drive US 20 west across the mountains to join I-5 heading north (see previous section: Crossing the Cascades). Or you could leave SR 97 at Madras and take US 26 into Portland, which crosses the Warm Springs Indian Reservation and the Mt Hood National Forest, passing by the foot of the mountain. Let's follow this latter route.

DESERT COUNTRY
The Deschutes River flows north through canyons outlined in jagged basalt into flat, sagebrush-covered farmland. Beyond Bend, it picks up the Metolius and Crooked Rivers. The lower stretches of the river are renowned for fine fishing and scenic splendor; beyond Pelton Dam, white water rafting has been introduced.

There's an awesome grandeur to this wide-open territory, especially when you've emerged from dense forests that obstruct the horizon. It's cowboy country, as you realize passing through the towns.

REDMOND
Redmond is known regionally for a reindeer farm and a unique rock garden, both southwest of town on SR 126. Just beyond it is a turnoff for **Smith Rock State Park**, embracing a sheer canyon carved by the Crooked River through multihued sedimentary rock. Rockhounds will have a field day here searching for agates and thundereggs, which abound in the area. In fact, Madras hosts a **Rockhound Pow Wow** each June, which draws enthusiasts from far afield. For exact dates, contact the Madras Chamber of Commerce, PO Box 770, Madras, OR 97741; tel (503) 475-2432.)

KAH-NEE-TA
From Madras, you take US 26 north to enter the **Warm Springs Indian Reservation**. The 627,916-acre reservation is owned by the Confederated Tribes, primarily Paiute, Wasco and Warm Springs Indians. It is an area of rolling, juniper-strewn hills, rushing streams, including the Warm Springs River, and strange rock formations.

Taking advantage of its warm, dry climate and mineral hot springs, the Indians have built a multimillion dollar tourist resort, **Kah-Nee-Ta**. To reach it, turn off at the village of Warm Springs and follow the signs.

You can rent a *Nee-sha* – a cottage with bedrooms, living and dining rooms, bath and kitchen – or if you're feeling adventurous, you might want to try one of the tepees, set up in an adjoining area to simulate an Indian encampment. Each tepee is built around a rock firepit set into a concrete floor – you must supply your own sleeping roll! Up on a hill a short distance away is a redwood-and-concrete lodge. Most of its skylit rooms, built around a central swimming pool, have views across the gently rolling hills. The lodge is attractively furnished in Indian motif, with wall murals depicting Indian lore and showcases displaying beautifully beaded Indian costumes. The dining room serves excellent food, featuring Indian specialties. The resort boasts an 18-hole PGA golf course and tennis and is quite luxurious. What you won't find is much exposure to Indian life, unless you visit the general store in the village of Warm Springs.

Places to Stay & Eat
Kah-Nee-Ta (Box K, Warm Springs, OR 97761; tel (503) 553-1112; toll-free Oregon only 800-452-1138.) 140-room air-conditioned lodge; one and two-bedroom cottages; tepees and camping. Golf, tennis, riding extra. Mineral spring hot pool and baths. Lodge pool. Indian crafts shop. Restaurants and snack bar, ranging from budget to expensive. Rates: from $67 double; cottages from $42 double; tepee $15.

The 100-mile drive from Kah-Nee-Ta to Portland takes you from arid plateaus with a smattering of junipers through a gradual transition of lightly wooded hills to mountains forested in giant pine. Before you looms the inescapable presence of Mt Hood.

MT HOOD

In an area of impressive pine-clad peaks, 11,245-foot Mt Hood is still exceptional. And being virtually in Portland's backyard, it is very popular with both skiers and sightseers. Not least of its attractions is the historic **Timber-line Lodge**, set at the 6000-foot level. The massive rustic lodge was built as part of President Franklin D Roosevelt's 1930s Works Progress Administration program and dedicated by the president himself in 1937. Its great timbered beams are hand-carved with figures of Northwest wildlife. Casement windows look out on the perenially snow-capped peak. As well as guest rooms, there are restaurants, snack bars and shops. A seemingly endless procession of skiers clomp through the halls; even when none is visible from the lodge, skiers can always find snow somewhere on the mountain. Don't let the bustle inside deter you from scrutinizing the furnishings and decor: each piece is hand-crafted, from the smallest lamp to the huge, hexagonal stone fireplace, testament to the talent and skills of those Depression-era artisans.

Places to Stay & Eat

Timberline Lodge (Timberline, OR 97028; tel (503) 272-3311; toll-free Oregon only 800-452-1335.) 58 rooms, some with fireplaces. TV, some color. Pool, sauna. Dining room.

Breakfast, lunch and dinner. Rates from $42 double.

From Mt Hood, it's a scenic 55-mile drive into downtown Portland on US 26.

THE OREGON COAST ROUTE

US 101 following the Oregon coastline from the California border to the mouth of the Columbia River is one of the country's most scenic and interesting drives. Mile after mile of pristine beaches scarcely know human footprints. Forested mountains encroach on the ocean, sometimes descending precipitously into the surf. Mountain streams trickle out onto the sands depositing a beachcomber's treasure trove in agate and jade rocks. Rolling sand dunes border a wooded lakeland where azaleas run rampant. Swift running rivers offer whitewater thrills.

Places to Stay

Oregon's enlightened policy of keeping the shoreline for all the people results in an unprecedented number of state parks and wayside picnic areas, all managed with great care.

Reservations are required for *campsites* in state parks; write the State Parks and Recreation Branch, Oregon State Highway Division, 525 Trade St, Salem, OR 97310; tel (503) 378-6305. For site availability, call toll-free (within Oregon) 800-452-6587; however, reservations cannot be made by telephone.

Some campgrounds operate on the honor system: you place the fee, along with the number of your site, in an envelope and leave it in a box provided for that purpose when you leave.

Most of the towns offer a good choice of motel accommodation, some with ocean views. However, those who like to smell and hear the ocean as well as seeing it from their room, be cautioned: many of the motels are air-conditioned and their windows do not open even a crack, so check first if you're a fresh-air fiend.

BROOKINGS

First town you reach is Brookings at the mouth of the Chetco River. The tang of salt in the air blends here with the fragrance of flowers for most of the year. In February and March, you'll find fields of daffodils; wild azaleas prompt the Memorial Day **Azalea Festival**; by July, acres of Easter lilies lend an alabaster glow. Watch for the increasingly rare Oregon Myrtle tree, its shiny foliage rounded so perfectly it looks like topiary work. Myrtlewood's deep grain and hardness make it a popular material for bowls, plaques, tables and other souvenirs, as you'll soon see in shops the length of the coast.

Beyond Brookings is some of the coast's most dramatic scenery. The road wends across bluffs above the rugged shoreline, dropping down to the sea at Pistol River, then climbing again to Cape Sebastian. Vista points afford views of offshore rocks sculpted into arches by the surf.

GOLD BEACH

Whitewater excitement awaits you at Gold Beach, embarkation point for lower Rogue River float trips. Several companies offer half-day, day-long and overnight 64-mile excursions up the Rogue by jetboat and raft. Trips are seasonal, lasting generally from April to November. From the open jetboat, you have a chance to appreciate the unsullied beauty of up-country forests. Keep a lookout for otters, deer and bears along the way.

On the 64-mile trip, you lunch generally at an Agness farmhouse-lodge; you've time to wander a little before they serve the sumptuous, home-cooked spread. The 104-mile trip takes you 20 miles further upriver into the section where the water turns turbulent, churning through solid rock gorges. Dress warmly – mornings are chilly on the river.

Reservations for trips should be made in advance; you can usually get space the night before. The major operators are:

Rogue Mail Boat Service, Inc (Box 1165, Gold Beach, OR 97444; tel (503) 247-6225.) Leaves from Mail Boat dock a quarter-mile upstream from north end of the Rogue River Bridge.

Court's White Water Trips (Box 1045, Gold Beach, OR 97444; tel (503) 247-6504 or 247-6676). Leaves from Jot's Resort, on ocean side of bridge across river from Gold Beach.

Jerry's Rogue River Jet Boats (PO Box 1011, Gold Beach, OR 97444; tel (503) 247-7601.) Leaves from Gold Beach side of river, west of bridge.

Gold Beach also offers excellent year-round fishing. Pickings are good for agates, driftwood and glass floats on the long stretch of white sand beach and you'll find numerous art galleries and boutiques to browse.

Places to Stay

Jot's Resort (PO Box 'J', Gold Beach, OR 97444; tel (503) 247-6676.) Located in twin town of Wedderburn at north end of the bridge. Spacious, well-furnished rooms with private balconies overlooking river mouth; queen-sized beds, color cable TV, some kitchens. Pool, gift shop. Rates from $36 double.

Places to Eat

Restaurants all the way up the coast tend to serve steak and seafood, except in towns like Lincoln City, where the choice is wider. However, Gold Beach does offer a fine dining experience:

Captain's Table Good cooking, served in pleasant atmosphere of converted house with an ocean view. Huge tossed salad precedes entree. Friendly people. (M)

Dinner nightly. On US 101 at South end town; tel 247-6308.

Rugged cliffs, dense green forest, sandy beaches and surf boiling around offshore seastacks mark the way from Gold Beach to Port Orford. Midway, you come to **Prehistoric Gardens**, where life-sized replicas of dinosaurs and other prehistoric animals are scattered through a lush rainforest. The gardens are open daily 8 am to dusk; admission charge; tel (503) 332-4463.

A short distance beyond, the highway veers inland around 1748-foot Humbug Mountain. Look up to see if the summit is clear – Indian legend holds that if so, the weather will be good; if the tip is lost in mist, you can expect a storm.

PORT ORFORD

Coming into Port Orford, you pass a solid rock promontory topped by a few wind-stripped pines jutting into the Pacific. On June 10, 1851, a band of nine white settlers held off an Indian attack on **Battle Rock** as it has been known ever since.

Port Orford today is a sportsman's center, but in the 1850s it was site of an army fort which became focal point of the military effort to quell Indian uprisings in southwestern Oregon. Nothing remains to remind of the fort's existence.

Fabulous Fifty Miles

Locals call the stretch from Port Orford to Bandon the 'Fabulous Fifty Miles Recreation Area'. Vacationers come here to fish and sail on the lakes west of the highway.

Just north of Port Orford, a road winds nine miles through pastoral Six River Valley to **Cape Blanco Lighthouse**. A coastguardsman will show you the beacon in this century-old brick lighthouse on Oregon's westernmost point. Open weekdays from 1 to 3 pm and weekends 1 to 4 pm when light is not in operation.

Deer Park Safari

Free-roaming animals nudging you to pet them might tempt you to remain longer here than you'd planned, if you're like most visitors to this walk-through safari park between Port Orford and Bandon. Animals include llamas, yaks, chimpanzees and lions like Elliot, who grew up sharing his quarters with Peter, a St Bernard – neither of them betraying any apparent regard for their difference in species. Open March 1 to October 31, daily 9 am to dusk; rest of year Monday to Friday, 9 am to dusk; admission; tel (503) 347-3106.

BANDON

South of Bandon, a beach loop road runs along the bluffs overlooking sandy beaches. There are a number of motels with access to the beach along this road, which leads you into Old Town. Bandon has the appearance of having been an important town; artists and craftspeople are spearheading a revival, opening galleries, boutiques and restaurants in the historical section.

Bandon is a dairy center, making cheddar cheese from predominantly Jersey milk, and a cranberry-growing area. A **Visitor Center** at Second, near the corner of Chicago Avenue, has information on visiting the dairy co-op and cranberry bogs.

Places to Stay

Sunset Motel (Box 373, Bandon, OR 97411; tel (503) 347-2453; on Beach Loop Rd; access to beach.) Rooms and housekeeping apartments. TV, some color, in-room coffee. Rates from $20 double.

Table Rock Motel (Box 236, Bandon, OR 97411; tel (503) 347-2700; on Beach Loop Rd.) One and two-bedroom units, some with ocean view. Some efficiencies and kitchens. TV, beach access. Rates from $18 double.

Sea Star Traveler's Youth Hostel (375 2nd St, Bandon OR 97411; tel (503) 347-9533). Open April to October. Rates $3.50.

Places to Eat

Andrea's Old Town Cafe Country cooking including home-made soups and breads; choice of two entrees nightly. Frequented by young local artists. Pleasant atmosphere, friendly service. Recommended. (B)

Lunch, dinner Tuesday to Saturday. 120 E Second at Alabama; tel (347-3022).

Seven Devils Coast Loop

From Bandon to Coos Bay, US 101 runs inland. A more interesting drive is the Seven Devils Coast Loop Rd which winds out to the cliffs of Cape Arago and three state parks. From the bluff in **Cape Arago State Park**, you can see sea lions romping offshore on Simpson's Reef (binoculars help). Steep trails descend to tidepools around the base of the cliffs.

Shore Acres State Park encompasses the former seaside retreat of a lumber magnate, whose formally landscaped gardens and Japanese garden provide a respite from rugged seascapes. A glassed-in observatory is a fine vantage point from which to watch winter storms at sea; you might even see whales spouting offshore.

Sunset Bay State Park's sheltered cove is one of the few places on the coast where the water is sometimes warm enough for a dip.

COOS BAY
The odor of fresh-cut timber wafts across the harbor as you enter Coos Bay. Fishing boats and ocean freighters share the waterfront piers. Great stacks of lumber and piles of chips by the roadside stress that this is a forestry town.

Just north of Coos Bay, also on the harbor, is North Bend. Its Simpson Park, jutting into the bay, provides an inviting venue for a picnic and you can browse the excellent **Coos-Curry Pioneer Museum**. Besides pioneer mementos and Indian artefacts, it boasts collections of flags and ammunition. (Open Tuesday to Saturday, 10 am to 4 pm, Sunday 1 to 4 pm; free.

Places to Stay
Thunderbird Motor Inn (1313 N Bayshore Drive, Coos Bay, OR 97420; tel (503) 267-4141.) On US 101. Spacious well-furnished units, many air-conditioned. Color cable TV, pool. Airport transportation. Dining room. Rates from $51 double.
Pony Village Motor Lodge (Virginia Avenue, Pony Village, OR 97459; tel (503) 756-3191.) In North Bend's Pony Village shopping center, distinctively built of local woods to affect a rustic appearance. 119 units. Color cable TV. Airport transportation. Dining room. Rates from $33 double.

Places to Eat
Manni's Hilltop House Intimate air-conditioned dining room with impressive views of Oregon dunes and bay. Local landmark for steak and seafood, Sunday brunch. Children's menu. (M)
Dinner nightly. 166 N Bay Drive; tel 756-6515.

From North Bend, mile-long McCullough Bridge crosses the harbor to totally different coastal vistas.

OREGON DUNES NATIONAL RECREATION AREA
For 48 miles from Coos Bay to Florence, great hillocks of sand intervene between the ocean and the highway. The dunes, unique in Oregon, comprise the 32,237-acre Oregon Dunes National Recreation Area, created in 1972. These mountains of golden sand patterned with swirling ripples bring out the child in many an adult visitor. You could be tempted to join those who throw themselves with abandon from atop a dune to roll downhill.

East of the highway is a chain of freshwater lakes, some edging the highway, others deep in the forest. Apart from the occasional roar of dune buggies, this area provides a peaceful retreat for vacationers. Across the dunes, isolated expanses of beach invite beachcombing. There are campgrounds and lodges, boating and fishing and, in summer, pleasant swimming in the more sheltered lakes. Above Winchester Bay, operators wait to rent dune buggies and horses.

There are motels at Winchester Bay and at Reedsport, a mill town set on the convergence of the Umpqua and Smith Rivers, where they flow into Winchester Bay. You'll find several in Dune City and still more in Florence.

FLORENCE

Florence is a small and friendly port at the mouth of the Siuslaw River. In May, coast rhododendrons flower alongside the road, setting field and hillside ablaze with brilliant pink blooms as far as the eye can see.

Head east off US 101 to explore Florence's downtown where old buildings, newly refurbished, make for delightful browsing. If you're lucky, your visit might coincide with the May Rhododendron Festival.

Indian Forest

Four miles north of Florence on US 101, a gift shop fronting the highway heralds Indian Forest, a privately-operated concern where you can see full-sized authentic replicas of North American Indian dwellings. Although this attraction appears to be suffering the ravages of time, it is interesting to compare the different types of housing used by Plains and Coast Indians. A rather rambunctuous herd of buffalo inhabit a corral similar to the type used by pioneers. The gift shop sells Indian arts and crafts as well as souvenirs.

(Open 9 am to 6 pm mid-May to September 30; admission charge; tel 997-3677).

Sea Lion Caves

Another commercial attraction up the road is Sea Lion Caves. In summer, the sea lions can be viewed from the cliff as they lounge on offshore rocks enjoying the sun. But in winter they seek refuge in a cave; an elevator ride down to a grotto opening onto this cave gives you a rare opportunity to observe them up close. (Open daily daylight hours, closed Christmas Day; admission charge; tel 547-3415.)

Heceta Lighthouse

On the tip of a jutting headland just above Sea Lion Caves is one of Oregon's most photographed sights: the 1894 lighthouse on Heceta Head, named for the early explorer Bruno de Heceta. The lighthouse is not open to visitors.

Places to Stay

Driftwood Shores Surfside Resort Inn (88416 First Avenue, Florence, OR 97439; tel (503) 997-8263.) Right on beach, with balconies facing ocean. One to three-bedroom units, some kitchens. Color cable TV, coin laundry, indoor pool, saunas, whirlpool. Dining room. Rates from $47 double.

Places to Eat

The Windward Inn Pleasant decor using natural woods highlight this good seafood restaurant. Dine by candlelight, accompanied by light classics played on the grand piano. Extensive wine list. Popular Sunday champagne brunch. (M)

Breakfast, lunch, dinner. Closed Monday. 3757 US 101 N; tel 997-8243.

CAPE PERPETUA

At Cape Perpetua, named by Captain Cook in 1778, turn off at the **Visitor Center** above the highway for some educational displays on forestry and the ecology of the area. The Forest Service personnel are friendly and informative and their 15-minute film provides interesting insight into the natural forces shaping the coastline. Signed trails lead to a blowhole, down to the beach and up to the peak; you can drive to the latter; if you'd prefer. The center is open summer, daily 9 am to 6 pm; mid-September to late May, Wednesday to Sunday 10 am to 4 pm.

From Cape Perpetua, the road descends onto a coastal plain, passing by the town of Yachats, a favorite with surf anglers. It skirts a string of beaches offering numerous wayside parks and picnic areas to reach Waldport on Alsea Bay, which is the broad estuary of the Alsea River. From here it's a 16-mile run into Newport, one of the most developed centers on the coast.

Places to Stay & Eat

The Adobe (Box 219, Yachats, OR 97498; tel (503) 547-3141.) Unprepossessing entrance leads to pleasant lobby and dining room with wall of glass overlooking ocean. Original rambling building of adobe brick, plus newish motel wing. Some fireplaces, two-bedroom housekeeping units. Color cable TV. Rates from $39 double. Dining room (moderate) serves breakfast and steak-and-seafood dinners.

NEWPORT

A few years back, Newport was a quiet seaside town with an occasional motel. Now it has exchanged its village atmosphere for that of a thriving seaside resort. You can explore the town, sprawled along bluffs on the north shore of Yaquina Bay, by following the seagull signs to beaches north of the Yaquina jetty. A forest of masts draws you down to the picturesque mile-long bay waterfront, where deep-sea trollers wait to take you sightseeing or fishing at your pleasure.

Life beneath the water is revealed at **Undersea Gardens** where over 100 large underwater windows allow you to observe marine plants and sea creatures going about their normal business. Scuba diving shows are performed at regular intervals. (At 267 SW Bay Boulevard it's open daily June 1 to Labor Day 9 am to 8 pm; rest of year 10 am to 5 pm; admission charge; tel 265-7541).

Standing sentinel above Yaquina Bay is the 1871 lighthouse. Its service was shortlived; in just three years, it was superseded by the more efficient beacon atop Yaquina Head. The old lighthouse has been restored in the period and style favored by lighthouse keepers of the 1870s and visitors are welcome. (Open Thursday to Monday 12.30 to 5 pm in summer; admission charge).

Take the marked road at the south end of Yaquina Bridge to reach Oregon State University's **Marine Science Center,** where research is conducted on oceanography, fisheries and water quality, among other subjects. There's a fascinating aquarium-museum and you might be able to tour one of the research vessels, which are open to the public from time to time. (Open daily mid-June to mid-September 10 am to 6 pm; rest of year 10 am to 4 pm; closed Christmas day; free; tel 867-3011).

If wax museums fascinate you, stop by the **Royal Pacific Wax Museum,** where wax figures by Josephine Tussaud herself recreate famous faces, past and present. (At 550 SW Coast Highway it's open daily during summer from 9 am to 8 pm, rest of year 10 am to 5 pm; admission charge; tel 265-2062).

An historical museum and an art center are numbered amongst other attractions in the resort town.

Places to Stay

Motels in Newport range from older, small units to large modern chain-operated motels fronting the ocean. Rooms are easy to find except in the height of the summer season. If you experience difficulty, contact the Chamber of Commerce, 555 SW Coast Highway; tel 265-8801. A sampling of what's available off the highway:

Newport Hilton (3019 N Coast Highway, Newport OR 97365; tel (503) 265-9411). 146 oceanfront units, many seaview. Pool, beach, whirlpool, color cable TV. Dining room (M), cocktails, entertainment. Rates from $50 double.

Best Western Windjammer Hallmark (744 SW Elizabeth St, Newport, OR 97365; tel (503) 265-8853). All 72 rooms have ocean view though non-opening windows. Some fireplaces, oversized beds. Color cable TV, free morning coffee. Airport and bus depot transportation. No restaurant. Rates from $49 double.

Dunes (536 SW Elizabeth St, Newport, OR 97365; tel (503) 265-7701.) 116 rooms, again with non-opening windows. Some kitchens, suites, oversized beds.

Color TV, indoor and outdoor pool, whirlpool. Cafe. Rates from $32 double May to mid-September, lower rest of year.

Bonnie View Motel (711 NW Coast St, Newport, OR 97365; tel (503) 265-5233.) Eight kitchen units, TV. Stairs to beach. Rates from $21 double.

Embarcadero Marina Resort (1000 SE Bay Boulevard, Newport, OR 97365; tel (503) 265-8521.) Rated 4 star by AAA, Mobil. Rooms, one and two-bedroom apartments, some with kitchen. Bay-view balconies, color cable TV, laundry. Indoor pool, saunas, whirlpool. Fishing facilities include outdoor fish and crab cooking pits. Private marina. Rates from $49 double.

Places to Eat

Seafood restaurants naturally take pride of place and their dishes include clams from the Yaquina tideflats and locally-caught Dungeness crabs.

Mo's Fish shack, first in chain hereabouts started by an Indian named Mohava Nimie; this one, according to critic David Brewster, is still best. Noisy, no decor to speak of, communal seating and exceptional fresh fish dishes, especially renowned chowder. No alcohol. No credit cards. (B)

Lunch, dinner daily. 622 SW Bay Boulevard; tel 265-2979.

Mo's Annex Specialises in fish casseroles in a quieter setting. (M)

Lunch. Open 11 am to 3 pm only. Diagonally opposite Mo's on Bay Boulevard.

Four Js Oceanfront restaurant, popular with families. Steak and seafood. (B/M)

Breakfast, lunch, dinner. 614 SW Elizabeth; tel 265-2562.

OTTER ROCK

Beyond Newport, the highway again traverses rugged cliffs above a windswept crescent of beach. The **Otter Crest Scenic Loop**, which runs from Otter Rock around Cape Foulweather to rejoin US 101 several miles south of Depoe Bay, has incomparable views of the spray-misted, indented coastline. At the Lookout, 500 feet above the surging waves, train the telescope on offshore rocks and you'll likely see white sea lions, sea turkeys and perhaps even Oregon penguins.

Places to Stay

Inn at Otter Crest (Box 50, Otter Rock, OR 97369; tel (503) 765-2111.) 264 units in fourplex and eightplex groupings set in woods on jutting headland. Ocean views, some fireplaces and refrigerators. Reputation does not live up to exalted setting. Pool, saunas, whirlpool, putting green, fee tennis. Dining room. Rates from $64 double.

Salishan Lodge

Rounding Cape Foulweather and crossing Depoe Bay's colourful vest-pocket fishing boat harbor, you come to one of Oregon's most celebrated resort developments, Salishan Lodge at Gleneden Beach. The resort is set amid acres of manicured lawns on a scenic promontory above Siletz Bay and draws sportsmen and conventioneers, many of whom fly in to the private landing strip. An 18-hole golf course spreads from the edge of the dense fir forest to grassy sand dunes on the beach side of the highway. A pause is recommended here for a refreshing drink or a meal, even if your schedule precludes staying a day or two.

Places to Stay & Eat

Salishan Lodge (Box 118, Gleneden Beach, OR 97388; tel (503) 764-2371.) Rated 5-star by AAA, Mobil. 150 luxuriously furnished rooms with fireplaces, king-sized beds, living room area, private balconies. Color cable TV, indoor pool, saunas, whirlpool, exercise rooms; fee tennis, golf. Beach access. Rates start from $74 to $84 double, depending on season.

Gourmet Room serves adventurous Continental-American cuisine; winner Holiday Magazine's 'Fine Dining Award' since 1973. Dinner. (E)

The Sun Room coffee shop is superior to the general run of resort coffee shops. Breakfast, lunch, dinner. (B/M)

Both in Salishan Lodge; tel 764-2371.

LINCOLN CITY

From Siletz Bay north, Lincoln City is a playground which the local Chamber of Commerce boasts as the '20 Miracle Miles.' Its clean beaches with rolling surf, beach parks, art galleries and good restaurants, and nearby Devil's Lake bolster their claim. The city, formed by the consolidation of five tourist towns spread along 7½ miles between mountains and sea, is relaxed and not over-commercialized. There's not a lot to do here; it's a place to dawdle; to beachcomb or explore musty secondhand furniture and antique shops.

Collections of dolls, several thousand of them, and antique guns, coins and musical instruments are on display at **Lacey's Dollhouse and Museum** at 3400 NE US 101; open daily 8 am to 5.30 pm; closed Thanksgiving and Christmas day.

Places to Stay

Lincoln City offers a wide selection of accommodation, from plush ocean-view establishments to on-highway motels and family-style apartment motels. Again, summertime brings an influx of vacationers so rooms are not as easy to find. For a complete list, write to Lincoln Chamber of Commerce, PO Box 787, 3939 NW Highway 101; tel 994-3070. Some samples:

The Inn at Spanish Head (4009 S US 101, Lincoln City, OR 97367; tel (503) 996-2161.) Plush inn set into cliff, overlooking ocean, at south end of town. Rooms, one and two-bedroom suites, efficiencies and kitchens available. Many rooms with balconies, ocean views. Color cable TV, pool, saunas, coin laundry. Valet parking. Dining room. Rates from $45 double.

The Coho Motel (1635 NW Harbor (at foot 17th St), Lincoln City, OR 97367; tel (503) 994-3684.) 50 spacious units, some two-bedroom, some kitchenettes, many fireplaces. Right on beach, with balconies overlooking ocean. Color cable TV. No restaurant. Friendly, helpful proprietors. Rates from $30 double. Recommended.

Surftides Beach Resort (2945 NW Jetty Avenue (Box 406), Lincoln City, OR 97367; tel (503) 994-2191.) 90-unit motel on beach. Some one and two-bedroom apartments, some fireplaces and refrigerators. Cable TV, mostly color. Coin laundry; indoor and outdoor pool, sauna, whirlpool. Dining room. Rates from $33.50 double.

Places to Eat

Pier 101 Natural wood decor accented with stained-glass windows, hanging plants. Possibly best hamburgers on coast, plus seafood dishes – try the seafood ragout; it's different and delicious. Recommended. (B/M)

Lunch, dinner. 415 SW US 101; tel 994-8840.

The Pixie Kitchen Popular family-oriented restaurant combining elements of amusement palace and good seafood kitchen. (B)

Lunch, dinner. 3519 US 101 N; tel 994-2175.

Henry Thiele's Restaurant Chef-owned coast spinoff from well-known Portland restaurant, popular in its own right. Tiered layout allows all tables ocean views. Seafood emphasized. (B/M)

Breakfast, lunch, dinner. In International Dunes, 1501 NW 40th; tel 994-5255.

La Plaza Restaurant In hotel set on cliff, commanding one of the coast's finest dining room views, particularly at sunset. Steak, seafood and continental specialties. (M)

Breakfast, lunch, dinner. In The Inn at Spanish Head; tel 996-2161.

TILLAMOOK VALLEY

From Lincoln City, US 101 follows the

coastline for some 20 miles then veers inland through the Tillamook Valley. Prosperous-looking farms and grazing cattle mark this fertile dairying enclave, from which comes the sharp cheddar cheese known throughout the country. Visit the **County Creamery** north of town to watch them making it.

Tillamook is also known, and justly so, for its **Pioneer Museum**, housed in the old County Courthouse. Pioneer and Indian artefacts, logging memorabilia and war relics graphically relate the history of the county. Outstanding natural history exhibits include a room devoted to birdlife. On Second and Pacific Avenue; tel 842-4553; open May to September, Monday to Saturday 9 am to 5 pm, Sunday 1 to 5 pm; closed Mondays rest of year; donation appreciated; tel 842-4553.

A scenic loop drive from Tillamook circles Cape Meares; alternatively, the **Three Capes Loop** leaves US 101 at Cloverdale, some 30 miles south of Tillamook, and links Capes Kiwanda, Lookout and Meares.

From Tillamook, SR 6 heads east to Portland while US 101 skirts the bay and follows the coast north.

The road climbs high around the shoulder of Neah-Kah-Nie Mountain, known to Indians as 'Place of the Fire Spirit', and along rugged coast to tunnel through the massive rock of Arch Cape. Doff your hat in homage as you pass Oswald West State Park, for it's named in honour of the maverick politician who, back in 1912, had the foresight to fight for preservation of the coastline so that you, and many thousands of others, could enjoy it.

A wide band of beach curves from Arch Cape to Tillamook Head, seven miles north. Halfway, marked by the famous Haystack Rock jutting 235 feet out of sand and sea, is Cannon Beach.

CANNON BEACH

This resort town of pretty cottages and grey-painted weathered wood buildings may be a little studied in its quaintness but it is attractive withal. There are boutiques and galleries, motels and numerous restaurants, and good beaches which draw children of all ages to enter an annual Sand Castle Building Contest. Portland State University drama students offer summer stock at the Coaster Theater Thursday through Sunday nights.

For information, contact the Chamber of Commerce, PO Box 64, Cannon Beach, OR 97110; tel (503) 436-2623.

Places to Stay

Tolovana Inn (Box 165, Tolovana Park, OR 97145; tel (503) 436-2211.) Off US 101 beach loop, two miles south of town. Beachfront motel; many efficiency units with fireplaces, two-room units, ocean views. Color cable TV, coin laundry, pool, sauna. Restaurant. Rates from $35 double.

Surfsand Best Western (Box 219, Cannon Beach, OR 97110; tel (503) 436-2274.) Beachfront motel on beach loop. Most units have private lanai or patio facing beach, fireplaces. Color cable TV, pool, whirlpool. Housekeeping apartments available. Rates from $44 double.

Places to Eat

Haystack House Shingle walls and stained-glass windows and lamps enhance pleasant atmosphere. Steak and seafood menu, homebaked bread. Champagne brunch on Sundays. Haystack House is center for social activities, too. (M)

Lunch, dinner. In Tolovana Inn; tel 436-2211.

SEASIDE

At Seaside you enter Lewis and Clark Country. These explorers, whose epic journey is described in the Columbia River following, halted here briefly in 1805. The salt cairn where they boiled sea water to extract salt for their return cross-country trek was located a few blocks south of the main street; it is reconstructed on Lewis and Clark Way. At the foot of Broadway, the **End of the Trail Monument** marks the turnaround point of the expedition.

Seaside has a fine beach, but it lacks the charm of Cannon Beach. A promenade fronts the ocean and it is definitely a tourist-oriented resort.

Places to Stay
There are over 40 motels and inns listed in the pamphlet on housing, restaurants and other tourist facilities put out by the Chamber of Commerce. To receive a copy, contact Seaside Chamber of Commerce & Boosters, 20 N Columbia, PO Box 7, Seaside, OR 97138, tel (503) 738-6391; for accommodation reservations, call toll-free within Oregon only 800-452-6740. A few samples:
Ebb Tide (300 N Promenade, Seaside, OR 97138; tel (503) 738-8371). Oceanfront motel; one and two-bedroom units, some fireplaces. Color cable TV, pool, saunas, whirlpool. Rates from $39 double.
Sand & Sea (475 S Promenade, Seaside, OR 97138; tel (503) 738-8441.) Six-story elevated building overlooking ocean. Some kitchen units, private balconies. Color TV, pool, sauna. No restaurant. Rates from $45 double.
City Center Motel (250 First Avenue, Seaside, OR 97138; tel (503) 738-6377. 33 one to three-bedroom units, some kitchens. Color TV, pool, sauna. Rates from $22 double.

Places to Eat
Crab Broiler Landmark restaurant set amidst Japanese garden; natural woods, stained-glass and antiques feature in decor; seafood on the menu. Steaks and chops served, too. Children's menu. (M)
Lunch, dinner. Closed early January. At junction of US 101 and SR 26; tel 738-5313.

FORT STEVENS STATE PARK

A few miles north, US 101 turns towards Astoria, but you can keep going up the coast to the south shore of the Columbia River. Here on a 15-mile stretch of wide, flat beach you come to Fort Stevens State Park. Apart from embracing several lakes, dozens of picnic sites and 600 campsites, the park contains the remains of the fort, built in 1864 to guard the Columbia from Confederate gunboats which never appeared. However, in 1942 the fort did come under attack – fired on by a lone Japanese submarine, making it the only mainland military installation to come under enemy fire in WW II, indeed since the War of 1812.

On the beach is reminder of a more tragic event: the storm-battered skeleton of the British schooner *Peter Iredale,* which ran aground in 1906.

From Fort Stevens, a short drive takes you to Astoria and the Columbia River.

COLUMBIA RIVER

Its source is a lake caught between two mountain ranges on the roof of the continent in British Columbia. From here it flows over 1200 miles, sometimes north, sometimes south, until finally, at the point where the Snake adds its water, it turns west, and separating the states of Washington and Oregon, flows the final 300 miles to join the Pacific Ocean. At times it is placid stillwater, more like lake than river; roaring, churning rapids mark its passage elsewhere.

History On the morning of May 11, 1792, the first American circumnavigator Captain Robert Gray sailed his ship across a foaming sandbar and so discovered the body of water men had dreamed of for two centuries. Though it was not the elusive Northwest Passage, it was the Great River of the West spoken of in Indian legend. Captain Gray, who named it for his ship *Columbia,* made claim on it for the fledgling American nation.

Five months later, an officer of Captain Vancouver's fleet sailed his ship inside the river's mouth, then in small boats continued upstream for a hundred miles. He claimed the land for the British Crown, thus starting a conflict of interest between the two nations which was not settled until 1846.

Lewis & Clark Expedition President Thomas Jefferson, who dreamed of an American nation from coast to coast, in 1804 despatched an expedition to cross the land. It was led by 29-year-old Captain Meriwether Lewis and 33-year-old Lieutenant William Clark. (Clark's captaincy actually was never approved by the War Department.) Their commission, apart from exploration, was to counsel Indian tribes along the way and to acquaint them with the terms of the Louisiana Purchase, which the year before had more than doubled the size of the new nation.

Laden with gifts for the Indians, the party set out on its epic journey on March 14, 1804, from east of St Louis, following the Missouri River all the way north. After a winter encampment near the present Bismark, North Dakota, they resumed their trek in April 1805. Crossing the Great Continental Divide at Idaho's Lemhi Pass, they finally reached the Snake River. On the night of October 16 they made camp at the junction of the Snake where it flowed into another great river. They had reached the Columbia.

For the next three weeks, as they found their way down the lower Columbia, they made friends with the many Indians they encountered; their enlightened attitude was to benefit future travelers, who were generally aided by Indians in negotiating the river's seething rapids.

'Ocian in view. O the joy!' wrote Clark on November 7 as early morning fog cleared to reveal the vista of 'this great Pacific Ocian which we have been so long anxious to see, and the roreing of noise made by the waves brakeing on the rockey shore . . .'

The expedition selected a site on the banks of a river off the estuary to build their winter encampment, consisting of a stockade and seven cabins. They remained at Fort Clatsop for five months, during which time they reported there were only five days when it did not rain. They used the time fruitfully to commit to their journals details of animals, plants, topography and reports on Indian tribes they had encountered on their odyssey – first report for the American people of what their land held.

In March of 1806, the expedition set off on its return journey, arriving in St Louis on September, 23, 1806. From word of their discoveries came the first clear incentive for Americans to push their frontier westward to the Pacific.

Fort Astoria John Jacob Astor took up the challenge. In 1810, he despatched two parties one by sea and one overland, to establish a branch of his American Fur Company on the Pacific. He had a simple plan: his Pacific Fur Company ships would carry pelts to China, reload there with spices for New York and complete the circle with supplies for Fort Astoria, as the settlement was to be named. On March 22, 1811, his 290-ton ship *Tonquin* broached the Columbia sandbar; his men selected a site on the south bank overlooking the river mouth and ran up the American flag.

Meanwhile the rival Northwest Company of Merchants of Canada, known as the Northwest Company or simply Nor'westers, had decided to chart the course of the Columbia River with a view to establishing British dominion over the region and its fur trade. Accordingly, David Thompson, an Englishman and the company's 'astronomer and geographer,' became the first known white man to gaze upon the river's source in Lake Columbia. He was first to travel its waters from source to mouth, paddling out of Lake Columbia on April 17, 1811. As he negotiated the final stretches three months later, his heart sank when he saw the fluttering American flag and realized he was too late to establish British supremacy. He had, though, mapped the course of the Columbia River.

British rule came to Fort Astoria a year later, anyway, with the War of 1812. Hearing that a British warship was en route, Astor's opportunistic factor sold out to the Nor'westers. In 1821, they were absorbed by the giant Hudson's Bay Company, who moved headquarters upriver to Fort Vancouver, on the north shore.

The Treaty of Ghent ending the war returned Astoria to the Americans but its fortunes declined until the year of the Great Migration, 1843. In 1847, one of the new arrivals in the barely existent village won a commission to open there the first Post Office west of the Rockies.

The California gold rush created an increased demand for timber and sawmills flourished. With the coming of the river traffic, riverboat pilots made Astoria their headquarters.

The first steamboat, *Beaver,* arrived at Fort Vancouver in 1836. And on July 3, 1850, Astoria launched the *Columbia,* first locally-built steamboat, thus beginning the romantic age when sternwheelers and side-wheelers plied the river. It lasted almost a century but the coming of railroads and then highways gradually squeezed river traffic out of competition. The steamboat era ended on March 20, 1947 when, with much fanfare and nostalgic ceremony, the *Georgie Burton* made her final run from Portland to The Dalles.

(Weeklong cruises up the Columbia and Snake Rivers are proving popular; for details see Portland Sightseeing.)

From the arrival of early pioneers, who were forced to endure the backbreaking effort of portage around the rapids of Celilo and the Cascades and floods which swept crops and whole towns out to sea, men dreamed of taming the arrogant Columbia.

The first attempt was Cascade Locks which in 1896 circumvented Lewis and Clark's 'Great Shute' with a 3000-foot canal and lifts.

Next came jetties to deepen and widen the channel at the river's mouth, adding a 30-foot depth over the sandbar dreaded by sailors since Captain Gray's crossing. To this day, though, currents at the mouth remain dangerous.

The Celilo Canal and locks carried shipping around the 80-foot falls above The Dalles. Then came the dams, built not only for navigation but to produce power and irrigation. The Bonneville Dam, which finally buried the Great Shute in a serene lake, started transmitting power in 1938. In 1942, the Grand Coolee Dam turned the sun-baked plateau of eastern Washington into a lush area producing wheat, fruit and vegetables. It supplied energy for 60% of America's aircraft production in WW II and powered the mysterious plant established downriver late in 1942, now known as the Hanford atomic works. Among numerous dams constructed more recently is the one at The Dalles, completed in 1961.

THE LOWER COLUMBIA – ASTORIA

Astoria today is a seaport with a distinctive character. In its heyday around the turn of the century, lumber magnates and sea captains built palatial homes on the slopes overlooking the river. Although a fire in 1922 destroyed much of the old town, some elegant Victorian buildings remain.

River pilot Captain George Flavel's mansion, built in 1883 of lumber brought around the Horn, houses the **Clatsop County Historical Museum**. As well as admiring the collection of shipwreck photos and Northwest lore, make sure you take a good look at the elaborate fireplaces, fashioned from imported woods and European and Asian tiles. The museum is on Eighth and Duane Sts; tel

325-2203; open May to September daily, 10 am to 5 pm; rest of year Tuesday to Sunday, noon to 5 pm; closed January 1, Thanksgiving and Christmas day; admission charge.)

A unique illustration of Astoria's history spirals the exterior of the 125-foot **Astoria Column**, erected in 1926 to commemorate events in the city's colorful past. An interior staircase of 166 steps leads to a platform from which you can view the river and ocean, wooded hills, Young's Bay and beyond, the Lewis and Clark River, where the expedition wintered. Try to time your visit for sunset, then watch as lights delineate the river's navigation system and the 4.1-mile toll bridge which crosses to Washington state. Signs mark the scenic drive up to Coxcomb Hill, setting of the Column. (Open daily 8 am to dark; free; information booth operates June 1 to Labor Day; tel 325-6311).

Astoria is very much a fishing port, catering to those interested in the sport and those in it for business; most of the commercial fleet is moored west of the bridge. The rough waters of the Columbia Bar hold a bonanza in tuna and salmon.

The annual **Astoria Regatta**, held each August since 1894, celebrates the safe return of the city's men from Alaskan waters and the fall bounty of salmon about to be reaped from the Columbia.

Its seafaring heritage is on show at the **Columbia River Maritime Museum**. You'll find exhibits on shipwrecks, whaling and fishing equipment, navigation of the Columbia and its tributaries and see figureheads and hardware from historic sailing ships. You may even board a seagoing vessel: the lightship *Columbia*, which marked the river mouth for half a century, was retired in 1961 and is now moored nearby as part of the museum. (1792 Marine Drive; open March to October daily 9.30 am to 5 pm, rest of year closed Monday; admission charge; tel 325-2323).

A block away, on Fifteenth and Exchange, is where it all began. Partially reconstructed walls and a marker are all that remain of America's first permanent outpost west of the Mississippi, **Fort Astoria**.

Lewis & Clark's Encampment

Lewis and Clark's historic winter encampment on the river bearing their name has been fully replicated. As you wander the buildings and grounds of **Fort Clatsop National Memorial**, reflect on the fact that some 50 men shared these cramped quarters through a terrible winter. During summer a Living History program recreates skills which enabled the expedition members to survive in demonstrations of handling of the flintlock rifle, with which they hunted elk, candle making, hide tanning and canoeing.

Off US 101 4½ miles southwest of Astoria, it's open daily mid-June to Labor Day 8 am to 8 pm; closes 5 pm rest of year. For further information, write Fort Clatsop National Memorial, Route 3, Box 504 F-C, Astoria, OR 97103; tel (503) 861-2471.

Places to Stay

Crest Motel (5366 Leif Erickson Drive, Astoria, OR 97103; tel (503) 325-3141.) 24 units set in landscaped grounds atop bluff overlooking the river. Pleasant rooms, some private lanais, refrigerators. Color cable TV. Rates from $26.50 double.

Thunderbird Motor Inn (400 Industry St, Astoria, OR 97103; tel (503) 325-7373.) At junction US 30 and US 101, overlooking marina. Rated 4-star by AAA. Suites available. Color cable TV. Airport transportation Rates from $44 double.

Dunes Motel (288 W Marine Drive, Astoria, OR 97103; tel (503) 325-7111.) Just east of interstate bridge. Many oversized beds, color TVs, free coffee in room. Rates from $28 double June to September 15, $20 double rest of year.

Places to Eat

Thunderbird Seafare Attractive restaurant with nautical decor, marina view. Steak and seafood menu. (M)

Breakfast, lunch, dinner. In Thunderbird Motor Inn; tel 325-3551.

Fiddler's Green (218 W Marine Drive, tel 325-4802; budget-moderate; open Tuesday to Saturday, 11 am to 10 pm; bar open until 1 am.) Chef-owned establishment with pub atmosphere. Features seafood, including cioppino specialty. Friday night Singalong. (B/M)

Lunch, dinner, Monday. 218 W Marine Drive; tel 325-4802.

Drop Anchor Restaurant Intimate atmosphere, set dinners and a la carte. (B)

Lunch, dinner, April to September, closed Tuesday. 11W Marine Drive; tel 325-3031.

ASTORIA TO PORTLAND

US 30 follows the Columbia River east to Portland, though for much of the way the river is hidden from view by stands of Douglas fir. As the road starts its climb into the Coast Range, stop at Clatsop Crest for a magnificent view of the island-studded river.

If you're heading north to Puget Sound and decide to bypass Portland, there's a ferry at Westport that will carry you and your car across river, around Puget Island, to Cathlamet. From there, Washington's SR 4 runs along the north shore to join I-5. Further upriver, a bridge links Rainier and Longview.

US 30 curves inland from Westport through farmlands and past river towns founded in the mid-19th century. Typical is **St Helens**, named for the snow-tipped Cascades volcano which erupted with devastating results on May 18, 1980. Detour here for a look at the landmark Columbia County Courthouse, which houses an historical museum, and the 1847 Knighton House.

Curving down past Sauvie Island (see Portland section), SR 30 enters the city of Portland.

THE COLUMBIA RIVER GORGE

One of the most spectacularly beautiful drives in the Pacific Northwest is the Columbia River Scenic Highway along the Columbia Gorge.

The gorge is a geological rarity in that the river plunges through the mountains instead of seeking the path of least resistance around them. The basaltic cliffs rising above the wide lake-like river are a palimpsest of the geology of the Cascade Range. Over their vertical heights, forest streams pour in sparkling cascades into pools hundreds of feet below. Many of these falls can be reached on short trails from the highway.

Columbia River Scenic Highway

I-80, the main east-west freeway, runs alongside the river. The Columbia River Scenic Highway branches off from it at Troutdale on the Sandy River to follow the clifftop. Much of the way lies through woodland, colored in spring by wildflowers and in fall by the blaze of gold and red of deciduous trees amongst the fir. A string of state parks offer picnic sites and hiking trails; campsites are available at Lewis and Clark and Ainsworth State Parks.

Beyond Corbett, the road forks; the road to the right ascends 4058-foot **Larch Mountain**, where there is a lookout point over the Columbia, Portland and the five main peaks of the Cascades.

Crown Point is first of the view points along the Scenic Highway. You catch a glimpse of **Latourell Falls** from the bridge below them. Then you pass Bridal Veil, Coopey and Mist cascades before reaching the famous **Multnomah Falls**, where Multnomah Creek makes its final leap over the vertical cliff to stream down 620 feet in two showers of rainbow-tinged mist. From the vista point below, a hiking path crosses the much-photographed footbridge and climbs beside Multnomah

Creek. Indian legends about the gorge, its geology and history are detailed in exhibits at the **Multnomah Falls Visitor Information Center**; they have maps of the hiking trails, too, including those leading to the lovely Oneonta Falls and Horseshoe Falls.

Beacon Rock, which you glimpse across the river from time to time, was a welcome landmark for Indians, fur trappers and pioneers, for it marks the beginning of tidal waters. Shortly after the road descends to river level, it reaches the Bonneville Dam.

Bonneville Dam

Bonneville Dam, completed in 1938, extends from both banks to Bradford Island, an ancient Indian burial ground. On the island is the **Visitor Center**, where you can peruse exhibits explaining the dam's operation and appreciate the complex allowances made for the migration of salmon. Near the head of each fish ladder you'll see the fish-counting station, always a source of fascination to visitors. You can watch the salmon through underwater observation windows and from paths by the fish ladders.

(Open daily 10 am to 6 pm summer, 9 am to 5 pm rest of year; free; tel (503) 374-8820.)

Upriver at the **Cascade Locks** you can see the cabless steam locomotive, the Pony Engine, used in portage around the Cascades rapids before the locks were completed in 1986. The history of sternwheelers which plied the river is told at the **Cascade Locks Park Visitor Center**; you can take a two-hour sightseeing cruise through the gorge yourself aboard the *Columbia Sightseer* tourboat if you visit in summertime. It departs Cascade Locks Marine Park from Memorial Day through the first weekend in October; daily 9 am, 11 am, 1 pm, 3 pm; fare at writing $7.50 adults; tel (503) 374-8474 or 427-8817.

Mt Hood Loop

The Bonneville Dam may have tamed the river but there is still a wild grandeur to the countryside from here to the Hood River, where another bridge spans the river.

Across in Washington is an unusual sight: a nine-mile **flume** carries logs from Willard down to Underwood, on the river west of the bridge. The rare flume is privately-owned and operated by the Broughton Lumber Co, often called the 'Lassie Lumber Co' because the flume featured in an episode of the canine star's television series.

HOOD RIVER VALLEY

Back in Oregon, Hood River is where you cut off to complete the loop to Mt Hood and back to Portland. SR 35 meanders through the scenic valley, which is orchard country, with acres of apples, pears and cherries stretching to the foot of Mt Hood. Don't neglect the Panorama Point turnoff a short way up SR 35, which gives sweeping views of the valley, particularly when springtime's blossoms transform it into an ocean of fragile whites and pinks.

The road curves around the shoulder of Mt Hood to join US 26 heading west to Portland (see Through Oregon's Back Country – Mt Hood).

Beyond the Cascades

Beyond Hood River, I-80 emerges from forest onto semi-arid plateau and follows the river to a deep bend on which is set The Dalles. For pioneers crossing the continent in the mid-19th century, this was the end of the Oregon Trail, though many continued on to the Willamette Valley.

Lewis and Clark camped here for several days, taking celestial observations from atop the rocks. They were visited by numerous Indians and remarked in their journals on the strange tribal custom of the Flatheads. These were Indians of the region who considered it fashionable to press their children's heads in a 'pressing machine' until the skulls achieved a flat shape.

The basaltic walls rising above the river show signs of even earlier visitors than Lewis and Clark: primitive photographs have been attributed to Bering Straits people who passed through here thousands of years ago.

THE DALLES

The Dalles (pronounced Dahls) today is a modern center for the wheatgrowing area around it. Much evidence remains though of its pioneer days and the 1860s when a gold rush in eastern Oregon turned it into a boom town. You can see the old courthouse, built in the late 1850s, several historic churches and a basalt marker showing the end of the Oregon Trail. An information center on West Second will point the way.

The only surviving building of the fort put up during the Yakima Indian wars of the late 1850s houses the **Fort Dalles Museum**, containing pioneer memorabilia, stage coaches and covered wagons. On Fifteenth and Garrison Sts it's open May to September, Tuesday to Friday 10.30 am to 5 pm; rest of year Wednesday to Friday noon to 4 pm Saturday to Sunday 10 am to 4 pm; free; tel (503) 296-4547.

The Dalles Dam

A gaily painted red, white and blue train will tansport you over the old portage tracks to the Dalles Dam during the summer months. The free passenger train departs Seufert Park every half-hour from 10 am to 4.30 pm daily, Memorial Day to Labor Day; tours by appointment rest of year; tel (503) 298-8732.

You can inspect the dam's powerhouse, fish ladders and counting station, and spillway, from which you'll see huge grain-laden barges passing through the 650-foot navigation lock. At the Visitor Center, exhibits cover the dam's operation and the Lewis and Clark expedition. Open daily, free; tel 296-6131.

The ancient fishing grounds where generations of Indians speared and netted salmon from precarious perches above the roaring rapids are marked by **Celilo Park**, 10 miles east of the dam. The turbulent wars which climaxed in the 80-foot drop of Celilo Falls are no more; The Dalles reservoir submerged them in 1961.

Before you leave the Columbia River take the bridge from Biggs across to Washington. Just downriver, standing grim and lonely on the cliff, is Maryhill castle, fulfillment of a man's dream.

Maryhill

James J Hill, the Empire Builder as he was called, was a railroad baron. In 1888, his daughter Mary married one Samuel Hill, whose daring and imagination matched his father-in-law's. Sam Hill had a vision of an imposing castle: while he was building it, from 1913 on, he variously explained its purpose would be a cultural center, an international museum, a universal school, even a fortress against invasion which he stated in 1920 would come from Japanese warships. He prevailed on his good friend, Queen Marie of Romania, to dedicate the still unfinished building in 1926.

After his death in 1931, Sam Hill's will revealed his wish that Maryhill become a museum. It opened as the **Maryhill Museum of Fine Arts** in 1940. Its collections are as eccentric as its progenitor, and include an excellent Indian collection, ancient books and manuscripts and the royal robes and other relics of the no longer existent Romanian monarchy. (Open March 15 to November 15 daily 9 am to 5 pm; admission charge.)

An even stranger figment of Sam Hill's fertile imagination stands five miles south on SR 14. You might not believe your eyes when you behold **Stonehenge** rising before you, but it is not a mirage. Sam Hill sent a team to England to make plaster casts of the original stones, which he then had duplicated in concrete, restoring in his version the stones missing from the original.

His engineers contrived to place the replica so that on the morning of the summer solstice, the rising sun aligns with the altar and the Hele stone, just as ancient builders, Druid or whomever, did with the original.

In the long and continuing saga of the Columbia, the Great River of the West, Sam Hill's remote, splendid chateau and mammoth replica of an ancient wonder remain two of the more interesting highlights.

Useful Addresses

Travel Information Section, Oregon State Highway Division, 101 Transportation Building, Salem OR 97310; tel (503) 378-6309; toll free 800-547-7842.

Greater Portland Convention & Visitors Association, 26 SW Salmon St, Portland OR 97204; tel (503) 222-2223.

State Parks & Recreation Branch, Oregon State Highway Division, 525 Trade St Salem OR 97310; tel (503) 378-6305; toll free within Oregon 800-452-6587.

National Forest Service, Pacific Northwest Region, 319 SW Pine St, PO Box 3623, Portland OR 97208; tel (503) 221-2877.

Oregon Department of Fish & Wildlife, 506 SW Mill St, Portland OR 97201.; tel (503) 229-5403.

Festivals & Events

January	*Mid-winter State Square Dance Festival* Lane County Fairgrounds, Eugene
February	*Oregon Shakespearean Festival*, Ashland (runs until October)
March	*Yachats Annual Arts & Crafts Fair*, Yachats
April	*Pear Blossom Festival*, Medford *Azalea Festival*, Brookings *Blossom Festival*, Hood River Valley
May	*Rhododendron Festival*, Florence *Pacific Northwest Championship All-Indian Rodeo*, Tygh Valley (north of Warm Springs Indian Reservation) *Fleet of Flowers Memorial Service*, Depoe Bay
June	*Portland Rose Festival*, Portland *Sisters Rodeo*, Sisters *Rogue River Rooster Crow*, Rogue River *All Rockhound Pow Wow*, Madras
July	*World Championship Timber Carnival*, Albany *Miss Oregon Pageant*, Seaside *Silver Smelt Fry*, Yachats *St Paul Rodeo*, St Paul *Bohemia Mining Days*, Cottage Grove
August	*Peter Britt Music & Arts Festival*, Jacksonville *Oregon State Fair*, Fairgrounds, Salem

September	*Indian Style Salmon Bake*, Depoe Bay
	Wintering-In Harvest Festival, Bybee-Howell House, Sauvie Island, Portland
	Oktober Fest, Mt Angel
October	*Yachats Kite Festival*, Yachats
November	*Emerald Empire Doll & Toy Festival*, Lane County Fairgrounds, Eugene
	Salem Wine Festival, Honeywood Winery
December	*Winter Solstice Wine Festival*, Amity Vineyards

Washington

The western part of Washington State is predominantly water-oriented. Most of its people live on or within easy reach of the Columbia River, the Pacific Ocean, Puget Sound, the Strait of Juan de Fuca connecting the latter two, or smaller waterways, such as the Olympic Peninsula's Hood Canal. People from Washington are outdoor types, preferring to ignore any weather-related inconvenience in the trust that it will go away. Naturally, they expect you will ignore it too. And, indeed, faced with so much natural beauty to see and enjoy, you'll find yourself doing just that.

Getting There
The major route north is I-5, which crosses the Columbia River at Portland, follows it downstream a ways then continues north to reach Puget Sound at Olympia. From here, it edges the Sound to the Canadian border, usually just out of sight of the water although there are frequent detours along the Sound.

At the Columbia's mouth, a toll bridge from Astoria carries US 101 across the river to circle the Olympic Peninsula.

Ferries These are a popular, and frequently the only, access to island and peninsula communities; they generally carry cars and provide splendid alternative routes to enhance sightseeing.

Air Seattle-Tacoma International Airport, known as Sea-Tac, is the major airport; most larger cities have air service at local municipal airports.

Bus *Greyhound* and *Continental Trailways* both operate along I-5. **Rail** *Amtrak* serves Olympia, Tacoma and Seattle.

TO PUGET SOUND

VANCOUVER
Crossing the Columbia River on I-5, you enter the State of Washington at Vancouver, which, for all it may appear today to be a suburb of Portland, has a historic past. Washington's oldest city was founded in 1824 as Fort Vancouver, a Hudson's Bay Company trading post, now reconstructed. As American claims to the Columbia prevailed, a US Army post was established here, facing downriver to meet any challenge. High on the slope where the officers lived, an 1849 house shelters a museum dedicated to one of the Post's most famous occupants: then Major Ulysses S Grant.

Stop at the freewayside information center just beyond Interstate Bridge for a self-guided walking tour map, which

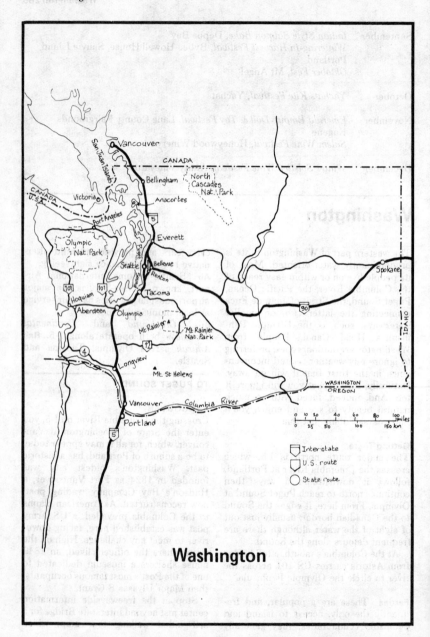

CANADA

San Juan Islands

Vancouver

Bellingham

North Cascades Nat. Park

CANADA
U.S.

Victoria

Anacortes

Port Angeles

5

Everett

Olympic Nat. Park

Seattle

Bellevue

Renton

Spokane

101

101

Hoquiam

Tacoma

Aberdeen

Olympia

90

IDAHO

Mt Rainier

Mt Rainier Nat. Park

4

12

Longview

Mt. St Helens

WASHINGTON
OREGON

Vancouver

Columbia River

Portland

5

0 10 20   40   60   80   100
                                                    miles
0   25   50   100   150 km

Inter-state

U.S. route

State route

Washington

takes in the reconstructed fort, Clark County Historical Museum and a wealthy pioneer's stately mansion, converted to a theater.

I-5 follows the old Lewis and Clark Trail alongside the Columbia until the river turns westward to the ocean.

ARIEL

At Woodland, a detour east on SR 503 takes you to Ariel, and **Lelooska's Northwest Carvings**. This is the home of woodcarver, Don Lelooska Smith, whose acclaimed carvings of masks, house posts and totem poles are brilliant and expensive. You'll also find here fine reconstructions of Northwest Coast Indian potlatch houses, superlative basketry and impressive Haida stonework. Look, too, for the superb silverwork of his sister Patty Fawn.

Lelooska, a Cherokee, was adopted by the Kwakiutl. He has devoted his life to bridging the cultural gap between white and native Americans. He and his family occasionally demonstrate traditional Indian dances, art forms and customs to interpret the culture of his people for the greater understanding of white visitors to his complex.

KELSO

At the twin cities of Longview and Kelso, the river turns west while I-5 heads north towards Puget Sound's cities, Olympia, Tacoma and Seattle. Longview is a milltown. Of interest in Kelso is a reconstructed log cabin, furnished in mid-19th century period and recreations of a pioneer country store and other buildings illustrating how the pioneers lived. You'll find them in the **Cowlitz County Museum**, near the county courthouse. Open Tuesday to Saturday 10.30 am to 4.30 pm, Sunday 2 to 5 pm; closed holidays; free.

MT ST HELEN'S NATIONAL VOLCANIC MONUMENT

At 8.32 am on Sunday, May 18, 1980, the long dormant volcano Mt St Helens exploded into eruption, spewing a vast mushroom of ash and pumice 12 miles into the air. The blast flattened giant trees like matchsticks and gigantic mudflows poured down the volcano's northern flank. About 1300 feet of the mountain's crest disappeared, opening a vast horseshoe-shaped crater some 3000 feet deep.

The volcano may remain intermittently active for years, and it will be some time before the mountain will be open for sightseers. However, on a clear day you can view the peak's misshapen crest as you drive north on I-5 from Portland.

There are a number of viewpoints from which to look out at the crater, some within the blast damage area and others outside it. Driving north on I-5, you can take Exit 21 at Woodland and follow SR 503 to Yale Park southwest of the mountain, where there is an interpretive display. The most thorough coverage of the volcano's history is at the Mt St Helens Visitor Center, run by the US Forest Service. Take Exit 68 from I-5, drive east on SR 12, then south on SR 505 following the clearly marked signs. In a one-hour visit to the center, you can see a 22-minute film and seven-minute video describing the mountain's eruption and view the breached crater by telescope. It's a worthwhile detour if you're interested in volcanic activity in the Cascade Range which forms the backdrop for your drive north. The center is open daily from 9 am to 7 pm summer, closes 5 pm winter; for information, tel (206) 864-6699; free.

There are flightseeing tours over the mountain from Portland operated by *Aviation Enterprises;* tel (503) 667-1877.

MT RAINIER NATIONAL PARK

SR 12 East is also access road to the magnificence of Mt Rainier. 'Takhoma' – 'the mountain that is God', the Indians call it, and indeed Mt Rainier's massive silhouette, visible from every quarter, is eloquent reminder of our significance in the cosmos.

'The Mountain' is a titan of fire and ice. Classified as extinct, yet it is capable of reawakening as Mt St Helens did. Two craters mark the eternally ice-capped 14,410-foot summit.

Mt Rainier National Park covers a 378-square-mile area, mostly encompassing the giant volcanic cone. A surrounding strip, five miles wide, is lushly forested in Douglas fir, western hemlock and red cedars soaring from fern-choked valley floors. It's easily explored on a network of roads and trails.

Visitors' activities center around four areas. **Longmire**, park headquarters, is one of the two open year-round. There is a visitor center and inn here. (The National Park Inn is open early May until mid-October). A network of trails originating at this point includes **The Trail of Shadows** self-guided nature walk.

Paradise draws most park visitors to its 5400-foot elevation for hiking trails which reward with spectacular vistas of glaciers, and mountain climbing. Rainier presents some rigorous ascents (Himalayan climbers have trained here) and climbing is regulated by the National Park Service. In summer, Rainier Mountaineering (201 St Helens, Tacoma WA 98402) conduct climbs; they rent equipment, too. The summit climb takes two days, plus determined effort and endurance. In winter, Paradise is restricted to day-use, open only on weekends for skiers and snow bunnies.

Ohanapecosh is situated on the forested banks of the Ohanapecosh River, at 1900 feet elevation. It lures fly fishermen after trout and woodsmen are attracted for its nearby 1000-year-old forest, the Grove of Patriarchs.

Highest point in the park accessible by road is **Sunrise**, set at tree line on the mountain's northeastern flank amid alpine meadows, flower-bright in springtime. From here you obtain perhaps the most striking views of the icy crest and glaciers. Easily hiked trails cross broad plateaus to viewpoints which overlook ridges enclosing secluded valleys.

Some strictures to bear in mind: glaciers have deep, hidden crevasses and rocks fall continuously from the snouts, so admire them from a distance. Snow-driving in winter may require snow chains or tires; always check ahead.

Things to Do & See

In the summer, park rangers conduct interpretive programs, nature walks and evening slide presentations at all centers: look for schedules at Visitors Centers and on campground bulletin boards. Visitors Centers at Longmire and Paradise are open all year; those at Ohanapecosh and Sunrise only in summer.

Wildlife is plentiful and easy to spot in the open subalpine landscape. Deer and mountain goats can be seen, and on the meadows just below tree line, marmots pose and burrow, and every now and then emit their high-pitched whistle – they're a photographer's joy.

Places to Stay

Lodgings at *National Park Inn* at Longmire (early May until mid-October) and at *Paradise Inn* (mid-June until Labor Day). For reservations and rates, write Mt Rainier Hospitality Service, 4820 S Washington, Tacoma, WA 98409; tel (206) 475-7755.

The National Park Service maintains five *campgrounds;* only one, at Sunshine Point near the Nisqually entrance, is open year-round. Campsites are available on a first-come, first-served basis, for 14 days only. Camping is allowed only in designated sites.

Places to Eat

The *Paradise Inn* dining room, a *snack bar* at Sunrise and *cafeterias* at Longmire and Paradise are open in summer only. Longmire's snack bar is open year-round, and the one at Paradise opens all summer and weekends and holidays during the winter. Limited groceries can be bought at Longmire and Sunrise in summer. Gasoline is available year-round at Longmire and during summer only at Sunrise.

Getting There

Mt Rainier is the most accessible of mountains. US 12 cuts off from I-5 at Exit 68 south of Chehalis, and joins SR 123 to Ohanapecosh. SR 123 heads north on the eastern side of the park and joins SR 410; off this is the spur road through the White River entrance to Sunrise. Longmire lies 70 miles southeast of Seattle. SR 706 from Tacoma runs to the Nisqually park entrance for Longmire and Paradise. For information on mountain road conditions, tel (206) 455-7700 or 624-6424.

Bus *Gray Line Tours* operates a nine hour trip, departing Seattle's Olympic Hotel at 8 am and spending two hours at Paradise, from May through October; tel (206) 682-1234 for information and rates.

Information

Superintendent, Mt Rainier National Park, Ashford, WA 98304; tel (206) 569-2211.

OLYMPIA

I-5 bypasses the twin cities of Chehalis and Centralia and reaches Puget Sound at Olympia, the state capital.

Olympia, incorporated in 1859, is one of the state's oldest and most attractive cities. Its lures for visitors are the State Capitol set amid landscaped grounds – and some of the most succulent oysters you could wish.

The **State Capitol** complex is decked out in its finest array in spring, when cherry blossoms grace the spacious grounds. During summer, the sunken rose garden and great masses of rhododendrons bloom. Gardeners should take time to go through the **greenhouse**, across the grounds near the Eleventh Avenue entrance.

Dominant is the legislature's domed Roman-Doric building, reminiscent of the nation's Capitol building in Washington DC. From its interior hangs a vast 185-foot-high brass Tiffany chandelier. When the legislature is not in session, an organist plays lunchtime recitals in the domed antechamber on weekdays at 1.30 pm. (You can join a narrated tour of the building Monday to Friday, 8.30 am to 4.15 pm, plus weekends 1.30 to 4.15 pm, mid-June to mid-September; closed state holidays; free.)

A block away, the **State Capitol Museum**, housed in a handsome Spanish-style mansion, displays Northwest artists and geological descriptions of the state, as well as some pioneer artefacts. (On 211 W 21st St; open Tuesday to Friday, 10 am to 4 pm, Saturday to Sunday, noon to 4 pm; closed January 1, July 4, Thanksgiving and Christmas Day; free.)

Most of the town's restaurants feature fresh oysters from nearby Oyster Bay. Of course, they suggest you accompany them with a draught of Olympia beer, which is actually brewed in neighbouring Tumwater. On weekdays, you can tour-and-taste from 8 am to 4.30 pm at the **Olympia Brewing Company's** plant. It's located off I-5's Exit 104, adjacent to Tumwater Falls Park, a great place for a picnic.

Olympia is gateway to the **Olympic Peninsula** and a starting point for the US 101 loop drive around the peninsula's periphery (see below).

Places to Stay

Governor House (621 S Capitol Way, Olympia, WA 98501; tel (206) 352-7700.) Downtown 118-unit motel, air-conditioned, color cable TV, some refrigerators. Pool. Dining room, coffee shop, entertainment. Rates from $35 double.

Carriage Inn Motel (1211 S Quince, Olympia, WA 98501; tel (206) 943-4710.) Air-conditioned, color cable TV. Pool. Restaurant adjacent. Rates from $34 double.

Golden Gavel Motor Hotel (909 Capitol Way, Olympia, WA 98501; tel (206) 352-8533.) 27-unit motel, some two room units. Rates from $26 double.

Places to Eat

Craig's Olympia Oyster House Waterfront restaurant serving oysters, of course, plus other seafood, steaks and prime rib. Children's menu. (M)

Lunch, dinner daily. 320 W 4th St; tel 943-8020.

Northwest Trek

Elk, bison, deer, moose, caribou, mountain goats and bighorn mountain sheep, mink, raccoons, wolves and black bears roaming free in a wilderness environment are the attraction at Northwest Trek. Located between Olympia and Tacoma, east of I-5, the 600-acre wildlife park describes itself as a 'biotic community'. You can tour it on a 5½ mile Trek Tram ride, accompanied by a naturalist guide, or on foot. Special self-guided trails for the visually handicapped and meandering trails for visitors in wheel chairs have been incorporated into the park. Near Eatonville on SR 161; take SR 510 just past Olympia and SR 702; or just past Tacoma follow SR 161 from I-5; open mid-February through October, November 26 to 28 and December 26 to 30 10 am to 5 pm, closed rest of year; admission charge; tel (206) 832-6116 to confirm scheduled opening times.)

TACOMA

The city of Tacoma on Puget Sound between Olympia and Seattle sprawls out toward each of them, making an almost continuous urban chain along the Sound. Though Tacoma is basically a mill town and port, it does present some historic sights in and around its renascent center.

The 1893 **Old City Hall** at Seventh and Commerce has been converted into shops and restaurants; you can dine in what were once the jail cells. Free guided

tours of the 2½-ton clockworks in the tower leave hourly on weekends from Daley's Jewelry on the building's 4th floor.

The **Union Passenger Station** at 1713 Pacific Avenue is a good example of modified Beaux-Arts Classical architecture of the 1885-1902 period. The Chamber of Commerce maintains an information center here in tourist season; their permanent office is at 752 Broadway; tel 627-2175.

Point Defiance Park contains several historic attractions. **Old Fort Nisqually** is a reconstruction of the 1833 Hudson's Bay Company outpost. It includes the state's oldest existing building, an 1843 granary. A typical logging camp of the 1880-1900 period is recreated at the **Camp Six Logging Museum**. Exhibits include a steam-powered Shea locomotive that runs weekend rides at a nominal charge. Tacoma's first home, built in 1865 for Job Carr is also in the park.

Places to Stay

Doric Tacoma Motor Hotel (4th St & St Helens Ave, Tacoma, WA 98402; tel (206) 572-9572.) Downtown location, 140 units, some air-conditioned. Color TV. Some two-room units, suites. Pool, parking. Rates from $36 double.

Motel 6 (5201 20th St, E Tacoma, WA 98424; tel (206) 922-2612.) 120 air-conditioned rooms. Adjacent cafe. Rates from $19.95 double.

Calico Cat Motel (8821 Pacific Avenue, Tacoma WA 98444; tel (206) 535-2440). 17 units, most air-conditioned, and including some two-bedroom and kitchens (extra). Color TV, coin laundry. Restaurant opposite. Rates from $21 double.

Places to Eat

Cliff House Steak and seafood house, excellent views Mt Rainier and Commencement Bay; background music, piano bar. (M)

Lunch, Monday to Friday, Sunday,

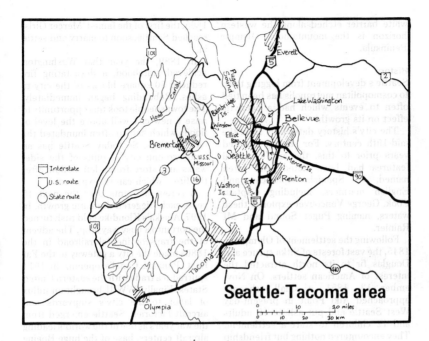

Seattle-Tacoma area

dinner nightly. 6300 Marine View Drive, tel 927-0400.

Old Spaghetti Factory (1735 Jefferson St; tel 383-2214; budget; open 5 to 9.30 pm (Friday and Saturday until 11 pm), Sunday 4 to 9 pm; closed November 22, December 24 and 25. Decor has an emphasis on nostalgia; menu consists of a variety of spaghetti dishes. Children's menu. (B)

Dinner nightly. 1735 Jefferson 5; tel 383-2214.

PUYALLUP

At Puyallup, in an area east of Tacoma that is covered in springtime by golden daffodils, is pioneer Ezra Pound's home. It is maintained as a museum commemorating his efforts in retracing the Oregon Trail, driving an ox team, in 1906-07. It's at East Pioneer Avenue and is open on Sunday from 1 to 5 pm.

VASHON ISLAND

Instead of driving I-5 the 30 miles north to Seattle, you could take a less conventional approach: ferry from Point Defiance to the south end of Vashon Island, then drive through this quiet backwater to its northern end. From here another ferry will take you to West Seattle. To check schedules, tel toll-free 1-800-542-0810.)

SEATTLE

Seattle is the Emerald City of the Pacific Northwest. It is an exceptionally attractive city, nestled in hills and ridges carpeted by lush greenery, bounded on the west by fjord-like Puget Sound, formed during the last Ice Age, and on the east by expansive Lake Washington. Fifty miles inland, the verdant spine of the Cascade Mountains is capped by Mt Rainier. Across Puget Sound, a blue-white barrier etched along the western horizon is the mountainous Olympic Peninsula.

History

Seattle's development from logging town to cosmopolitan metropolis has been tied often to events which had a catalytic effect on its growth.

The city's history dates only from the mid-19th century. For several hundred years prior to this, the area's coastal features had been noted, and often named, by Spanish, American and English mariners, including Captain Cook. George Vancouver explored these waters, naming Puget Sound and Mt Rainier.

Following the settlement of Olympia in 1845, the vast forests of Sitka spruce and Douglas fir to its north attracted the interest of American settlers. On November 13, 1851, a small schooner approached Alki Point in present-day West Seattle and put ashore 12 adults and 12 children to start a settlement. They encountered nothing but friendship from the coast Indians, whose great Duwamish leader, Chief Sealth, is honoured in the city's name.

The small band soon found the Alki Point site too exposed and the harbour too shallow for San Franciscan ships calling for lumber. In February of 1852, they abandoned it and moved around the point to the edge of sheltered Elliot Bay, in the area that is now Pioneer Square. Here Henry Yesler built his sawmill. Logs were eased to the mill down a log-stepped road: thus 'Skid Road' was born. In later years, the name would become synonymous with seediness, as this became the old, neglected part of town until restoration revitalized it.

The rich forests quickly lured settlers and Seattle flourished. But by the 1860s a dire need was being felt; it was a town of men without women. So Asa Mercer, founder of the Territorial University, headed east to rectify the situation and in

1865, the first of the famed 'Mercer Girls' reached Seattle, soon to marry and settle in.

In 1889, the year that Washington achieved statehood, a devastating fire reduced 50 square blocks of the city to ashes. Rebuilding began immediately. The townspeople took this opportunity to raise a new city well above the level of floods which had so often inundated the old buildings. So today Seattle has an 'underground city' – ruins of the sidewalks and store fronts left hollow after the fire – which can be explored.

A series of events over the next 45 years each triggered dramatic growth. In 1897, Alaska's Klondike gold rush turned the port into a busy way stop. The advent of the transcontinental railroad in the 1880s made the city a gateway to the Far East. Panama Canal's opening in 1914 spurred sea trade with the eastern United States. Finally, WW II brought an influx of labor to the city's shipyards and aircraft factories. Seattle emerged from the war years as one of the world's leading aircraft centers, base of the huge Boeing Company. This led to some anguish in the early 1970s when a recession in the aerospace industry led to a high rate of unemployment in the Seattle area, a situation now much improved, with Boeing currently experiencing a backlog on orders.

The most recent event to make its mark was the 1962 Century 21 Exposition, more commonly known as the Seattle World's Fair. This was a gamble which paid off; it gave Seattle a sense of cohesive civic pride – plus a legacy of artwork and buildings, most notably in the Seattle Center.

Climate

Much has been written about Seattle's heavy rainfall but in fact the annual rainfall is only 34.1 inches. The rain is not heavy, merely constant from November through May. Natives seldom even use umbrellas, preferring to deal with the

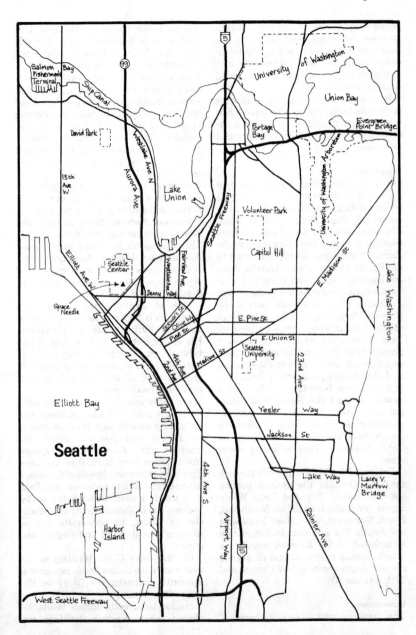

gently weeping skies protected only by a raincoat. We recommend rainboots, too. Best time to visit is July through October; summer days are usually in the 70°s, with cool nights – the one and only recorded century was in 1893!

Winter daytime temperatures average in the mid to high 40°s. Although storms bring snow to the higher elevations in the Cascades, Seattle itself is seldom coated with white.

Orientation

Seattle is a sprawling city and getting a 'fix' on it is difficult at first. A key is understanding its relationship to its waterways: Puget Sound and the lakes. The island-studded Sound extends from Olympia for some 100 miles north to the Juan de Fuca Strait, which connects it to the Pacific Ocean. On its eastern shore are Tacoma, Seattle and Everett. To the west is the ragged coastline of the Kitsap Peninsula, which is actually part of the Olympic Peninsula, with the Hood Canal driving a deep wedge between the two. Lake Washington Ship Canal carves a passage from Salmon Bay on the Sound east through Lake Union to the expanse of Lake Washington, which forms the entire eastern boundary of the city of Seattle. Along Lake Washington's eastern shore are the suburban bedroom communities. Thus, many of Seattle's people have the pleasure of living on lushly foliaged slopes affording water views.

Freeway I-5 runs south-north through the city. Outside the central portion between Elliott Bay and Lake Washington, areas are divided into Northwest, North, Northeast, West, East, Southwest and South. The appropriate designation is included in the address, which is a street running east-west and an avenue running south-north; ie NW 65th St and 27th Avenue NW.

Downtown

The financial and shopping heart of Seattle is the downtown Business District, an area bounded by the Freeway Park and Third Avenue, Madison and Stewart Sts. Within the area are not only Seattle's leading hotels, major department stores and fine restaurants, but some stunning architecture and works of art. A fine pamphlet to guide your viewing is *Art and the Urban Experience,* obtainable from the Downtown Seattle Development Association, 1318 Joseph Vance Building, on the corner of Third and Union. It maps a walking tour, describing architectural highlights and fountains, statues and other artworks in plazas, and buildings along the way.

Freeway Park at Sixth Avenue and Seneca serves as a land bridge across I-5. This imaginative five-acre park, designed by Lawrence Halprin Associates, conceals the freeway with landscaping and a series of cascading waterfalls similar to Portland's Ira's Fountain.

One of Seattle's most impressive structures is Minoru Yamasaki's **Rainier Tower** on Fifth Avenue and University. His design features 30 stories of offices balanced on a slender 12-story pedestal. This opens the plaza for a sense of spaciousness, allowing glimpses of more traditional buildings.

On Fifth and Seneca is Yamasaki's earlier arched-based **IBM Building,** with its underground plaza, and across from it, on Fourth and Seneca, stands the gracious 1924 *Four Seasons Olympic Hotel.* Taken over in 1980 by the prestigious Four Seasons Hotels of Canada, it has been restored to its former grandeur. It is worth a stroll through the lobby, perhaps a refreshment in the sumptuous Garden Court, to appreciate one of America's most grand and elegant hostelries.

On the older Cobb Building to the west, notice the Indian heads mounted as decoration between the floors on this 1910 office structure.

Similar terra cotta Indian heads, retrieved when another building was demolished, are now on display at the **Seattle-First Bank** on Fourth and Madison. Pause a while in the bank's plaza to view Henry Moore's giant *Vertebrae in Three Pieces – 1968* 'floating' on a sheet of water. Then walk around the base of the towering bronze-colored building, designed by Seattle's Naramore Bain Brady & Johanson, to admire the graceful George Tsutakawa fountains and Guy Anderson's paving mural. Entitled *Sea Marks,* the mural expresses the designer's sense of the elements at work in the Northwest, interpreted with Indian design components. From Mirabeau's bar on the 46th floor (50-floor Sea-First is Seattle's tallest skyscraper), you'll enjoy a fine panorama on a clear day.

Below, the showers of sculptural lights draped in fountains were created by Harry Bertoia as an experimental form in 1969-70.

A block east, the **Seattle Public Library's** strong vertical lines are offset by numerous works of art. Among them, the bronze leaping figures of Ray Jensen's *Pursuit of Knowledge* and George Tsutakawa's *Fountain of Wisdom* each symbolize man's search for knowledge and wisdom. James Wegner's *Alice,* interpreting Lewis Carrol's heroine, is carved from California sugar pine.

Places to Eat

Shuckers Fresh coastal seafood dispensed in an elegant 'chop house' that is an old Seattle tradition. (M)

Lunch Monday to Friday, dinner nightly. In Four Seasons Olympic Arcade, 4th Avenue, tel 621-1700.

Mirabeau Formal restaurant atop Sea-First Building commands spectacular panoramic views. Continental cuisine, children's menu. Reservations advised. (E)

Lunch, dinner, closed Sunday. 46th floor, Seattle First National Bank Building, 1001 4th Avenue; tel 624-4550.

Shopping

Seattle's three major department stores – Bon Marche, Frederick & Nelson and Nordstrom – are situated within a few blocks of each other. A bronze marquee welcomes you to **'The Bon,'** a handsome, mammoth building on Fourth Avenue and Pine, housing anything and everything you could possibly want. **Frederick & Nelson,** up the block at Fifth and Pine, is a division of Chicago's famed Marshall Field, and is rather more grand, catering to the carriage trade. Diagonally opposite is **Nordstrom,** the mod fashion center; it offers a particularly fine collection of shoes. A branch of San Francisco's fashionable **I Magnin** is a block away on Sixth.

Boutiques line the sidewalks of the downtown blocks, too, making for fine browsing, especially for clothing and jewelry.

On Fourth between Pine and Pike, you come to **Westlake Mall.** Flower stalls, food vendors and pigeons fluttering around benches that accommodate the foot-weary and just plain people-watchers enliven this tiny plaza of Parisian flair. This is the starting point for the Seattle Center, site of the 1962 World's Fair; your carriage is the Monorail.

Things to Do & See
The Monorail

This was designed to carry World's Fair visitors from the heart of the city to the fairgrounds; it remained to become a popular feature of the city. In 95 seconds, the comfortable car whisks you above Fifth Avenue to the Seattle Center, 1.2 miles north, affording good city views during your brief ride. It operates daily from 10 am to midnight, until 12.30 am on Fridays and Saturdays and 10 pm on Sundays; fare 20c one-way, purchased at the gate before boarding.

Seattle Center

This 74-acre complex lies at the northern end of downtown on what was one Indian ceremonial ground. Its selection as site of the 1962 World Fair turned a sometime carnival area, with a few buildings such as the then armory and civic auditorium, into Seattle's answer to Copenhagen's Tivoli. It now draws 8,500,000 million visitors each year.

Immediately recognizable is the 607-foot **Space Needle**, symbol of Seattle's surge into the front ranks of US cities. A glass-walled elevator will take you to the top in just 43 seconds (the $1.50 charge keeps the Space Needle profitable) to dine (expensively), or sip a cocktail in the revolving restaurant while the whole of Seatttle passes below you. On a clear day, the panoramic sweep takes in the far-off Cascade and Olympic ranges.

Highlight of the complex is the **Pacific Science Center**. Beneath its towering white arches lies a grand collection of scientific gadgets for you to play with and learn from. You can become an astronaut at the controls of a Gemini spacecraft mockup, visit a Kwakiutl longhouse, create energy, solve mind-boggling puzzles and enjoy the dazzling play of lights across a 78-foot dome in Boeing's Laserium show. Near the Space Needle at 200 Second Avenue N; tel 622-4210; admission charge; open daily 10 am to 6 pm closes 4 pm weekdays September to May.

Nearby is the Seattle Art Museum's **Modern Art Pavilion**, exhibiting contemporary art from the 1920s to today. Painters and sculptors of the Northwest are represented and fine touring shows are offered – this was home to the fabulous *Treasures of Tutankhamen* show in 1978. It's open from Tuesday to Sunday between 11 am and 6 pm, Thursday evening from 6 to 8 pm, closed Monday; tours conducted Thursday, Saturday and Sunday 2 pm; tel 447-4710, 447-4795; admission charge except Thursday free.

The old armory is now **Center House**, featuring restaurants offering international cuisines on the court level, with international shops and galleries on the balcony and fountain levels. Center House Court is open daily 10 am to 9 pm summer; closes 7 pm balance of year.

Other attractions include Paul Thiry's striking **Coliseum**, the Seattle Repertory Theater **Playhouse** and the 3100-seat **Opera House**, converted from the original Civic Auditorium, where the western hemisphere's only annual performances of Wagner's *Ring* cycle in English and German are performed.

Scattered throughout the complex are some extraordinary fountains, notably the International Fountain executed for the fair by Japanese artists – its 217 nozzles in the shape of a sunflower are programmed electonically with colored lights and classical music and James Fitzgerald's bronze Fountain of the Northwest in the Playhouse's courtyard.

People of all ages enjoy the rides in the Center's **Fun Forest**, particularly the overview from Sky Ride's gondolas.

Places to Eat

Jake O'Shaughnessey's Irish-style restaurant and bar popular with young, affluent locals. Convivial atmosphere, good food including alder-roasted fresh salmon. (M)

Dinner nightly. 100 Mercer St; tel 285-1898.

Two other recommendations for inexpensive snacks if you're in the Seattle Center (both are opposite, on Mercer St): *Block's Cafeteria* and *Harry's Hamburgers* – try the mud pie for dessert.

The Waterfront

For an overview of the city explore the waterfront, an area stretching from Pier 48 below Pioneer Square to Pier 70 at the foot of Broad St, which borders the Seattle Center. The waterfront is a place to wander around and browse through the international bazaars and smart specialty shops along the piers that no longer know the activity of arriving ships (they dock now at Harbor Island). There are restaurants, too, but locals often prefer to pick up fish and chips, or an alderbark-smoked salmon sandwich, and eat at an outside table.

A streetcar service, using vintage Australian trolleys, operates along waterfront Alaskan Way between Pioneer Square and Pier 70. Starting at the south end, Pier 48 is *Alaska Ferries,* as the Alaskan totem pole in the park before it implies. Souvenir-crammed **Ye Olde Curiosity Shop** has good Alaskan and Indian Artifacts and shares pier 51 with the Polynesia restaurant, which has great views of ferries plying to and fro.

Pier 52 is terminal for *Washington State Ferries.* Take the ferry here for a jaunt to **Bremerton** or **Bainbridge Island** (see Puget Sound Tours).

You might see fireboats going through pumping drill off Pier 53, for this is locale of Firehouse 5; there's a small **museum** devoted to local firefighting, too. One of Seattle's 'characters', Ivar Haglund, is host at Acres of Clams on Pier 54, while a genuine ship's **chandlery** is the attraction on Pier 55.

Pier 56, home of *Seattle Harbor Tour* boats, is embarkation point for the daily excursion to Blake Island's **Tillicum Village,** described in Puget Sound Tours.

At Pier 57 is **Waterfront Park.** Pick up a snack at The Galley fishstand and relax at one of the outdoor picnic tables to savor it, while you watch others catching their dinner through holes cut in the deck.

At Pier 59 is the **Seattle Aquarium.** Opened in 1977, it is considered one of the country's finest. The signed route through it is designed to introduce you to the environment of the Sound and the life it harbors. You may have to wait in line to get in, but it's worth it. Open daily May 1 to September 30, 10 am to 9 pm; balance of year 10 am to 5 pm; admission charge; tel 625-5030.

Working piers occupy the intervening space to Pier 69, where the venerable *Princess Marguerite* plies back and forth

to Victoria, British Columbia, departing at 8 am on a summer morning and returning that evening, gaily lighted, to dock at 8.45 pm. These trips go from mid-May to early October; *British Columbia Ferry System,* tel 623-5560; fare at writing $19 adults round trip.

Pier 70 has been transformed into a complex of restaurants and shops, mostly devoted to arts and crafts.

Finally, just north of Pier 70 is **Myrtle Edwards Park** offering several miles walking, biking, jogging and roller skating paths.

Metered parking adjoins this pier, and is spotted along the waterfront under the Alaskan Way Viaduct; however, it's easy to reach the waterfront from the Pike Place Market by the Hillclimb Corridor stairs or elevator, which open onto a walkway to Waterfront Park.

Pike Place Market

The Pike Place Market is a great place to browse for foodstuffs as diverse as little-known vegetables, hot-buttered crumpets and international delicacies. It's also a chance to talk with market gardeners and craftspeople. The Market has changed greatly since its founding in 1907 as a collection of market garden stalls. Now the seven-acre complex, which recently underwent extensive restoration, has evolved into a flea-market-cum-shopping bazaar, while preserving its authentic flavor as a produce market dispensing vine-fresh fruits and vegetables. On the corner of First Avenue and Pike St it's open Monday to Saturday 9 am to 6 pm.

Places to Eat

Labuznik Fine Czech and Hungarian cooking in two-level dining room; on sunny days, spills onto sidewalk cafe. (M/E)

Lunch, dinner; closed Sunday, Monday. 1924 First Avenue; tel 682-1624.

Athenian Inn Vast, boisterous cafe overlooking bay. Serves seafood, and

Greek/American specialties. (B)

Breakfast, lunch, dinner; closed Sunday. In Pike Place Market; tel 624-7166.

Old Spaghetti Factory Family-style spaghetti house. Children's menu. (B)

Dinner nightly. 2801 Elliott Avenue; tel 623-3520.

Pioneer Square

Imaginative restoration has revived the site of Seattle's beginnings: Skid Rd is now the eminently attractive – and tourist-attracting – Pioneer Square.

Listed on the National Register of Historical Places, the quarter is a wonderful place for strolling along shaded sidewalks, studying the ornate older buildings. Many of them were designed by one architect, Elmer Fisher, after the Great Fire of 1889. He loved to treat windows in different fashions and had a penchant for hiding faces within facade ornamentations – see if you can locate some of them.

It is fitting that the square is once again a center for entertainment; the great Pantages vaudeville circuit was born here during the 1890s gold rush. The area harbors an abundance of boutiques, antique shops, restaurants and pubs. You can pick up a map locating members of the Pioneer Square Association at almost any shop.

For an unusual view of Seattle's past, take the 1½-hour **Underground Tour**, which leads you through musty subterranean passages, sidewalks of the original town. A guide entertains with anecdotes about life in the early settlement. (This is a walking tour over uneven terrain, and involves climbing stairs; a flashlight is advantageous.) It starts at Doc Maynard's Public House, 610 First Avenue; tel 682-4646; daily tours run at 11 am, 1, 3, 5, and 7 pm; reservations a must; admission charge.)

Places to Eat

Brasserie Pittsbourg French provincial cuisine in vintage 1893 cafe. Buffet lunch, more formal dinners. (M/E)

Lunch, dinner daily, closed Sunday. 602 First Avenue, Pioneer Square; tel 623-4167.

International District

Just a short distance away is the 48-square-block area known as the International District. Roughly bordered by Fourth and Eighth Avenues, S Main and Lane Sts, the district is predominantly Japanese and Chinese. Proximity to Kingdome stadium makes it popular with pre-game diners; the daytime stroller finds cultural museums tucked between shops, pocket parks and a profusion of oriental restaurants.

A good introduction is the **Chinatown Walking Tour**. It starts at the Center for Asian Arts and takes in a Japanese cookie factory, a narrated slide show, museum, and a one-time gambling den among its stops. The tour ends at the bustling Asian market in Hing Hay Park; lunch or dinner can be included if you wish. For necessary reservations, tel 624-6342; at writing, fee for the tour is $2, lunch included $7, dinner included $11 adults, less for children.

Places to Eat

The Mikado Japanese restaurant rated as 'the very best' by critic David Brewster. Sushi bar. Tatami rooms for parties of four or more. (M)

Dinner nightly, closed Sunday. 514 S Jackson St; tel 622-5206.

The Kingdome

The King County Domed Stadium, known as the Kingdome, is home to the Supersonics basketball, Seahawks football, Sounders soccer and Mariners baseball teams in their respective seasons, when it can draw a capacity crowd of 60,000.

When it's not in use, you can take a 45-minute guided tour of the impressive stadium, which includes a look at what is claimed to be the world's largest video screen and sports museum. Call 628-3331 for tour times; admission charge.

Lake Washington Ship Canal

Much of Seattle's leisure life centers around the lakes, particularly Lake Washington.

The eight-mile long Lake Washington Ship Canal links saltwater Shilshole Bay on Puget Sound with freshwater Salmon Bay, Lake Union and Lake Washington. It was started in 1860 when Harvey Pike single-handedly shoveled a shallow canal between Lakes Washington and Union. The completed project, including the locks, was dedicated on July 4, 1917. The **Chittenden Locks** are 825 feet long by 80 feet wide, with a maximum lift of 26 feet. They handle an astounding 78,000 vessels each year. A fascinating sight any Sunday is the collection of boats of every size, shape and purpose which the lockkeepers pack in to lift up or down. Watch it from paths on either side or walkways atop the locks themselves. A Visitor Center, housed in a former blacksmith shop, explains the operation in interpretive displays and tours. To get there take NW Market St to parking lot entrance; open daily June 15 to September 15, 11 am to 8 pm; rest of year closes 5 pm; free; tel 783-7059.

A seven-acre park near the parking lot which is open daily from 7 am to 9 pm, is worth seeing for its Asian exotics amongst its well-labeled gardens.

Across the canal, an observation room lets you view salmon leaping up the fish ladder. Scenic **Shilshole Bay** has good salmon fishing. For charter boats, contact *Bendixen's*, 373 Nickerson; tel 283-3963. For sailboat tours, including sunset and inter-island sails, try *Wind Works Sailing School & Charters*, 7001 Seaview Avenue NW; tel 784-9386.

In **Discovery Park** on the bay's south head, you'll find the contemporary Daybreak Star Art Indian Cultural Center, designed to emphasize the homogeneity of Northwest tribal groups. An Indian Art Mart, held here on the second Saturday of each month, displays the works of local Indian artists. It's open weekdays 9 am to 5 pm; weekends 10 am to 5 pm; for schedule and times of Art Mart, tel 285-4425.)

Salmon Bay

The Salmon Bay **Fishermen's Terminal** at the south end of Ballard Bridge is a photographer's delight. You can wander out on docks where the fishing fleet of local trollers, Bering Sea crab boats and the huge Alaska halibut and salmon fleet tie up.

To delve into a corner of Scandinavia, take time to explore **Ballard**, a turn-of-the-century enclave of fishermen and Scandinavians who hold themselves somewhat aloof from mainstream Seattle. Food shops stock Norwegian and Danish specialities and at times you are completely engulfed in conversations in Norwegian.

Places to Eat

The Wharf Famous for its clam chowder and fresh seafood served in dining room overlooking fishing fleet at dock. Children's menu. (E)

Breakfast Monday to Saturday; lunch, dinner daily. Fishermen's Terminal, Salmon Bay; tel 283-6600.

Vaersgo Seattle's Danish restaurant serving Danish cuisine and beers in Scandinavian atmosphere. (M)

Lunch, dinner daily. 2200 NW Market St; tel 782-8286.

Lake Union

Vantage point to watch sailboats skimming across Lake Union is the offbeat Lake Union Park on its north shore. It's better known as **Gas Works Park**, for that's what it was until this innovative reclamation turned the prime 20-acre site back to the people. Now you can picnic among remains of the gas manufacturing plant. Check out the time of day at artists

Chuck Greening and Kim Lazare's giant 28-foot sundial: stand in its center and your shadow tells the time.

For a **flightseeing jaunt** over the city by seaplane, contact *Lake Union Air Service* (tel 284-0300) or *Kurtzer Flying Service* (tel 284-1234); both operate from Lake Union.

Places to Eat

Canlis View of Lake Union highlights fine seafood and American cuisine. Popular, reservations necessary. Elegant bar for waiting. (E)

Dinner, closed Sunday. 2576 Aurora Avenue; tel 283-3313.

The America's Cup Trendy decor with exposed pipes, skylight and windows plus mirrors open to exceptional vistas of the lake, hills and city. Seafood and international specialties, soup and salad included. (M)

Lunch Monday to Saturday, dinner nightly. 1900 Northlake Way; tel 633-0161.

Lake Washington

Seventeen-mile-long Lake Washington is the playground of Seattle including sailing, bike paths, walking trails through its six parks, swimming beaches, tennis courts, and hydroplane racing. Two floating bridges cross the lake; one – Evergreen Point – is the world's longest pontoon-supported bridge. The other, the Lacey V Murrow Bridge, gives access to **Mercer Island's** attractive residential suburb. Heading south from Washington Park, a lakeside drive to Seward Park allows views of some fine old mansions on the hillside above and glimpses of contemporary houses blending into the woods on the ridges of Mercer Island.

On the eastern shore, in **Kirkland's Waterfront Park**, you can go aboard three historic ships; *Wawona*, a 136-foot three-masted schooner, the ancient tug *Arthur Foss* and lightship *Relief*. Open June to September, noon to 5 pm weekdays, later weekends; admission charge.

University of Washington Campus

The sprawling campus occupies the land separating Portage Bay and Union Bay, opening onto Lake Washington, and is bounded inland by NE 45th St and 15th Avenue NE. Its enrollment of some 35,000 students makes it one of the country's largest. You can obtain campus maps at each entrance, or at the Visitor Information Center at University and NE 40th St. **Thomas Burke Memorial-Washington State Museum,** at the 45th St entrance, focuses on the geology, anthropology and zoology of humans and animals inhabiting the Pacific Rim. Open Tuesday to Saturday 10 am to 4.30 pm; Sunday 1 to 4.30 pm; free; tel 543-5590.

At the nearby **Ethnic Cultural Center and Theater,** displays tell you about American Indians, Asian Americans, Chicanos and blacks in contemporary America.

At the **Henry Art Gallery,** a collection of 19th century paintings and works of contemporary artists and artisans is highlighted by tactile arts designed for the blind. Open Tuesday to Friday 10 am to 5 pm, Saturday to Sunday 1 to 5 pm, Thursday evening 7 to 9 pm, free; tel 543-2280.

Architecturally interesting is modernistic **Red Square,** which the designers, Kirk-Wallace-McKinley of Seattle, based on Sienna's grand town square. **Suzzalo Library's** handsome gothic facade is at its best in the evening when the glow illuminates its stained glass windows.

The campus also has four theaters (tel 543-5636 for show information) and a **Waterfront Activities Center** (tel 543-2217) where you can rent canoes and rowboats if you've a mind to go boating on Lake Washington.

An unusual garden lies between Frosh Pond and the Medical School; an English tea hedge bounds two acres of pharmaceutical plants. The air is heady with the fragrance of jasmine and lavendar, but the garden also harbors such plants as periwinkle, cascara and horehound.

Cross the Montlake Bridge and take Lake Washington Boulevard to reach the university's **Arboretum** in Washington Park. Its 160 acres shelter 5000 labeled varieties of plants. A more scenic drive is on Arboretum Drive, but this is open only during daylight hours. Pathways wend between rhododendrons, dogwoods, magnolias, tree peonies and crabapples. For a break, you can take tea in the Japanese Garden's authentic tea house, particularly lovely when the flowering cherry and quince trees are in bloom.

Maps are available at Arboretum office, north end of Arboretum Dr E; greenhouse open Monday to Friday, 7.30 am to 4 pm; Japanese garden open spring-fall, 10 am to sunset; modest admission fee.

Off-campus, 'the Ave' (University Avenue) and its cross streets are nucleus of the collection of trendy clothing shops, bookstores, coffee houses and pubs invariably attendant on a university.

Also in Washington Park, at 2161 E Hamlin St, is the **Museum of History and Industry**. Here you can view such reminders of Seattle's past as early Boeing planes, an old fire engine, and one of the zoo's favorite gorillas, now stuffed. (Open Tuesday to Saturday, 10 am to 5 pm; Sunday noon to 5 pm; closed New Years Day, Memorial Day, Thanksgiving and Christmas day; free; tel 324-1125.)

Capitol Hill

Not far from here is Capitol Hill, named at the time when Seattle hoped to situate the State Capitol on this lovely hill rising above Lake Union to the east and Lake Washington to the west. The Capitol did not eventuate but what did is a cosmopolitan residential neighborhood, Seattle's answer to Greenwich Village and San Francisco's Union St. At its heart is **Broadway St**, where the affluent shop, dine and pass their time in elegant watering holes.

Places to Eat

Surrogate Hostess French country cuisine, served cafeteria-style. Firm no smoking rule. (B)

Breakfast, lunch, dinner daily. 746 19th Avenue East; tel 324-1944.

Volunteer Park

Off E Tenth St, a continuation of Broadway, is a jewel of a park. Volunteer Park was laid out by the renowned 19th century landscape designers, New York's Olmsted Brothers. Manicured lawns, spreading trees and gracious gardens form the setting for the Seattle Art Museum, a conservatory and a lofty water tower. If you climb its winding stairs, you'll see all of Seattle and its environs at your feet. On the viewing platform, a plaque identifies principal peaks in the Cascade and Olympic ranges.

The **Seattle Art Museum's** small building holds a wealth of Asian art, including a priceless jade collection, as well as Islamic, Persian, pre-Columbian and early European art – two of America's Tiepolo ceilings are here. In addition, Northwest painters are represented, including Mark Tobey and members of the school known as the Northwest Mystics. Open from Tuesday to Saturday 10 am to 5 pm; Thursday evenings 7 to 9 pm; Sunday noon to 5 pm; tours daily 2 pm; admission charge (except Thursday free); tel 447-4710.

Green Lake

Seattle's third lake is set in lush **Woodland Park**, another romantic effort from the Olmsted Brothers. The locals come here for swimming, tennis, bicycling, picnicking, lawn bowling and boating (rentals are available). Major attraction for visitors is **Woodland Park Zoo**, where older cages are being replaced gradually by a more natural habitat. Featured are a children's petting zoo, nocturnal house, African Savannah and Gorilla exhibits.

It's on Phinney Avenue between N 50th and N 59th Sts; open daily 8.30 am to sunset; admission charge; parking charge.

Places to Stay

Seattle offers a plethora of hotel rooms in all price ranges. However, be warned that in the summer season, from Memorial Day to Labor Day, they become difficult to obtain. Indeed, only in the off-season, from November to March, can you reasonably expect to just drop in and get a room easily.

A number of bed-and-breakfast operations function in Seattle. Acting as a clearing house is *West Coast B & B Club* 11304, 20 Pl, SW, Seattle, WA 98146; tel (206) 246-2650. Others include *Travellers' Bed & Breakfast,* PO Box 492, Mercer Island WA 98040; tel (206) 232-2345; *Vashon B&B,* Rt 2, Box 304, Vashon WA 98070; tel (206) 463-9425. Rates at writing in these run from $25 to $35.

The youth hostel is called *Sea Haven Youth Hostel,* 1431 Minor Avenue, Seattle WA 98101; tel (206) 382-4170; reservations are suggested June to September.

Hotels and motels cluster downtown, around Sea-Tac Airport (which can be noisy), and some around the lakes. A few samples:

Top End

Four Seasons Olympic (411 University St, Seattle WA 98101; tel (206) 621-1700). Distinguished hotel with large, tastefully furnished rooms and a truly gracious atmosphere. Fine dining in the Georgian. Valet parking. Rates from $115 double.
Westin Seattle Hotel (Fifth Avenue and Westlake, Seattle WA 98801; tel (206) 624-7400). Flagship of the prestigious Westin chain. Handy downtown shopping, monorail. **Luxurious rooms in twin towers.** Pay parking. Rates from $105 double.
Park & Seattle Hiltons, Sixth Avenue and Seneca; Sixth and University, Seattle WA 98101; tel (206) 464-1980 (Park),

and (206) 624-0500 (Seattle). Both centrally located – Park on Freeway Park and Seattle one block away – with deluxe rooms, all amenities. Pay parking. Rates from $93 double Park, $83 double Seattle.

Mid-Range

Edgewater Inn (Pier 67, 2411 Alaskan Way, Seattle WA 98121; tel (206) 624-7000). Seattle's only waterfront hotel. Some rooms with balconies overlook Elliott Bay, others a parking lot. Rates from $46 double.
The College Inn (4000 University Way NE, Seattle WA 98105; tel (206) 633-4441). 27 antique-filled rooms in restored historic Tudor mansion next to university. Shared bathrooms, complimentary breakfast. Rates from $36 double.
Best Western Continental Plaza Motel (2500 Aurora Avenue, Seattle WA 98109; tel (206) 284-1900. 88 units, most with view of Lake Union and Mountains. Most air-conditioned. Color TV, pool. Some suites, kitchens, refrigerators. Rates from $49 double.

Bottom End

Georgian Motel (8801 Aurora Avenue, N, Seattle WA 9 103; tel (206) 524-1004). 18 units, some two-bedroom, kitchens, refrigerators. Color cable TV. Rates from $24 double.
Park Plaza Motel (4401 Aurora Avenue N, Seattle WA 98103; tel (206) 632-2101). 14-unit motel, color TV. Restaurant opposite. Rates from $25 double.
Sandstone Town & Country Inn (19225 Pacific Highway S, Seattle WA 98188; tel (206) 824-1350). 98-unit motel near Sea-Tac Airport. Some suites, kitchens. Rates from $28 double.

Places to Eat

The Seattle dining scene continues to grow more sophisticated as ethnic restaurants proliferate. Naturally two elements which are relatively easy to find are good seafood houses and view restaurants. In addition to restaurants described above you'll find a considerable choice listed in *Pacific Northwest*, available at newsstands.

Nightlife

National, and worldwide, opera lovers' attention focuses on **Seattle's Opera Company** in July, during their Wagner Festival, when they present in consecutive performances the entire four operas of the *Ring Cycle*, in German and English. The company also presents its normal season repertoire of five operas each year in the opera's native language and again in English. For schedules and reservations, tel 447-4711.

The **Seattle Symphony**, in operation since 1903, has seasons of concerts, which run October to April. Telephone the box office, 447-4736, for current information.

Seattle also has several resident dance companies, including **Pacific Northwest Dance** (447-4655) which performs a short subscription season at the Opera House. For drama, the **Seattle Repertory Theater** is in residence at the Seattle Center Playhouse from November through mid-May (tel 447-4764). **A Contemporary Theater**, ACT, (no connection with San Francisco's American Conservatory Theatre) performs mid-May to late October in their small, 800-seat theater (schedule and information, tel 285-5110).

Washington State liquor laws mean that taverns serve beer and wine only. They are a good opportunity to meet and mix with convivial Seattlites – try 'red beer', with a shot of tomato juice added for piquancy. Many of the taverns serve pizza, hamburgers and other light fare.

More sophisticated restaurants, particularly in the major hostelries, have entertainment and dancing into the early morning.

Getting There

Air Sea-Tac International Airport is situated between I-5 and Puget Sound, 13 miles south of Seattle and 20 miles north of Tacoma. It is one of the country's best designed airport facilities; their proud boast is that no one need walk more than 600 feet.

Basis of the layout is a Main Terminal with four concourses, each accommodating gates for two or three airlines, plus two satellite terminals, reached from the Main Terminal by a subterranean automated people-moving system.

In addition to domestic service, Sea-Tac is a gateway to the Orient and Europe, as well as Canada and Mexico. At writing, 21 major airlines service Sea-Tac on international and domestic routes, along with several commuter airlines.

International flights arrive at the South Satellite Terminal, where Customs, Health, Immigration, and Agriculture are cleared. After clearing Customs you step across the visitor reception room into the subway, which whisks you to the Main Terminal. Representatives of the Seattle-King County Convention & Visitors Bureau meet all international flights as part of their 'Operation Welcome'. Should you miss them and need information, they have a desk in the Main Terminal, opposite Continental's baggage claim area.

Other arrivals are into the Main Terminal, except for United which uses the North Satellite Terminal.

Both satellite terminals have cocktail lounge, coffee shop, duty-free shop, newsstand and restrooms; the Main Terminal also has a restaurant, (*The Carvery* – fine for plane-watching and good food), bank (open Monday to Saturday 8 am to 5 pm), nursery and shops. On its second floor are an observation deck, auditorium, TV area, police and Lost and Found department, plus a Meditation Room. Original artworks, funded by airline fees and concession revenues, decorate the terminals.

Car Rentals All the major agencies have desks on the ground floor of the Main Terminal, opposite baggage claim areas; cars are picked up and returned on the 3rd floor of the parking terminal, which fronts the Main Terminal and is connected to it by skyway paths. The Control Center, with a bank of TV monitors watching the subway system and corridors, is on the 4th floor of the garage between the skybridges – you can watch them watching through a window.

Getting Downtown

Airport taxis, limousines and the Hustlebus and city bus are found directly in front of the baggage claim area of the Main Terminal.

The *Hustlebus*, (682-5950), departs once every 20 minutes from 4.15 am to midnight, stopping at major hotels en route to the Olympic Hotel garage; fare is $4.75. Downtown-to-airport trips also depart every 20 minutes, from 4.30 to 12.20 am.

Metro, bus 174, (see below) runs a 36-minute trip between Sea-Tac and Second and Pike once an hour; fare 75c during non-peak hours, 90c during peak-hours. The bus departs downtown 10 minutes before the hour, the airport 42 minutes after the hour.

Taxis from Sea-Tac to downtown currently cost around $20 to $25 with tip. Look for 'taxi call-up' buttons.

The limousine holding area is at the northern end of the drive outside arrivals. They can carry 10 to 12 passengers; cost depends on the number of people and destination. The limousines also carry passengers to Bellevue, Tacoma, and Olympia on request.

Bus *Greyhound Bus* terminal is at Eighth and Stewart (tel 628-5510). *Continental Trailways* is located at 1936 Westlake (tel 624-5330).

Rail *Amtrak* connects Seattle with Vancouver, Canada, and Portland, San Francisco, Los Angeles and Salt Lake City. Eastbound trains head for Spokane in eastern Washington and thence to Chicago. The depot, King St Station, is at Third and S Jackson; tel 524-0593 for local ticket office; toll-free 1-800-421-8320 for schedule information and reservations.

Getting Around

Public Transportation The Metro bus system operates around 100 routes here; most of them pass through downtown. A 'Magic Carpet' zone bounded by the waterfront and Sixth Avenue, S Jackson and Bell, is free. Beyond that, you pay, in exact change 50¢ single-zone, 75¢ two-zone in non-peak hours; 60¢ and 90¢ in peak hours. Single-zone monthly passes for $23, and two-zone passes for $34 allow unlimited travel and senior citizen and handicapped passes are available at Metro Customer Assistance Office, 1214 Third Avenue; tel 447-4800 (24-hour service) for schedule and route information.

Taxis There are insufficient taxis to meet peak needs, so telephone well ahead at such times as Friday afternoon. Cab stands are located near major hotels and several downtown spots. Technically, cabs cannot stop if you flag them, but some do. Basic rates are $1 flag fall, plus $1.20 per mile. Major companies are *Farwest* (tel 622-1717) and *Yellow Cab* (tel 622-6500).

Ferries have already been described earlier in this chapter. For schedule information, tel 464-6400; outside Seattle from 8 am to 6 pm toll-free 1-800-542-0810.

Tours

A number of tour operators run sightseeing tours; predominant among them is *Gray Line Tours*, which offers several city tours, an excursion to Mt Rainier (see Mt Rainier – Getting There), a North Cascades tour in summer and a water tour from Lake Washington through the locks into Puget Sound. Tel 343-2000 for information.

Other operators include *American Sightseeing* (tel 624-5815) and *Seattle Harbor Tours* (tel 623-1445).

Puget Sound Opportunities to cruise Puget Sound range from regular harbor tours to charter sails (see Lake Washington Ship Canal – Shilshole Bay) and island cruises.

Harbor Cruises An hour-long narrated harbor tour around Elliott Bay shows you the city's waterfront, shipyards and working dock areas. These tours leave from Pier 56 daily summer 11 am, 12.15, 1.45, 3.15 and 4.30 pm; check for other times; tel 623-1445; fare $3.50 adult.

Ferries provide a great opportunity for checking out Kitsap Peninsula and island towns. (For information on ferry schedules, tel 464-6400; from outside Seattle, toll free 800-541-9274 from 8 am to 6 pm.)

A one-hour ferry ride from Pier 52 takes you across to **Bremerton** on the Kitsap Peninsula, where you can visit the battleship *USS Missouri* and see the exact spot where General Douglas McArthur received the Japanese surrender ending WW II.

Visiting hours in summer are from 10 am to 8 pm daily; rest of year weekdays noon to 4 pm.

A naval museum is on the upper floor of the ferry terminal.

Bainbridge Island ferry, which also **departs from Pier 52,** provides a fine roundtrip luncheon or sunset cruise; it is a 30-minute run each way.

The Tillicum Village half-day outing is one of Seattle's most popular excursions. Departing from Pier 56, you cruise the Sound past Alki Point, where Seattle began, and cross to Blake Island, said to be the birthplace of Chief Sealth. Today Blake is a Marine State Park, its pristine beaches and forests untouched by settlement save for the cedar longhouse tucked in the woods at the water's edge where you can have a baked salmon dinner, followed by traditional native American dances. There are nature trails to stroll and handicrafts to shop for before boarding the ferry to return to Seattle.

For information and schedule, contact your hotel desk or *Tillicum Tours Service,* 2366 Eastlake Avenue E, Seattle, WA 98109; tel (206) 329-5700; at writing it costs $22 adults; duration of tour four hours (five hours Sunday afternoon).

You can indulge in even more leisurely cruising on the *Pacific Northwest Explorer,* which operates four-night and five-night cruises out of Seattle, through the Sound, San Juan Islands and into Canadian waters. Turn-around point for the return is Princess Louisa Outlet; cruises depart regularly throughout the summer. For information contact *Exploration Cruise Lines,* 1500 Metropolitan Park Buildings, Seattle WA 98101; tel (206) 624-8551, toll-free 800-426-0600.

Industrial Tours A large number of businesses and industries welcome visitors to tour their offices and plants in and around Seattle. The Seattle-King County Convention & Visitors Bureau will supply you with a current list. Among the most popular: **Rainier Brewery** offers 40-minute tours every weekday afternoon; a good chance to see the beer-brewing process and do a little tasting. (Location 3100 Airport Way S; tel 622-2600; Monday to Friday 1 to 6 pm; free; reservations not necessary.)

A unique experience is touring **Boeing's 747 plant** in the world's largest building at nearby Everett. The tour lasts 1¼ hours and is absorbing and informative. (To get there take 1-5 north to exit #189, follow SR 526 to 20th Avenue exit; hours Monday to Friday at 8.30 and 9.30 am, 12.30 and 1.30 pm; arrive early; no children under 12; free; tel 342-4801).

THE OLYMPIC PENINSULA
The peninsula divides naturally into several areas: the Hood Canal shore; the northern coast on the Strait of Juan de Fuca; the Pacific coast, mostly wilderness inaccessible by road except for brief sections; the shores of Grays Harbor in the southwest; and, most importantly, the Olympic National Park.

HOOD CANAL SHORE
For Washingtonians, and even some out-of-staters, this is a summer playground. Sheltered in woods along US 101 are small communities and summer cottages, though a number of folk have the fortune to live here year-round, too. Beach parks and tidelands on the canal side yield choice oysters, clams and crabs; boaters, water-skiers and anglers share the sparkling waters and occasional resorts sit at water's edge. The inland side of the highway attracts mountain lovers. Backpackers, fishermen and hikers flock to the woods, lakes and rivers interspersed along the way.

The only sizeable towns along this 85-mile stretch are Shelton and Hoodsport, but you'll encounter restaurants and motels enough to care for your needs. Keep a watchful eye for signs pointing to side-road facilities. Typical is Discovery Bay Lodge: just where US 101 starts to turn west, a small sign by the road leads down to the water's edge. Here you find a good motel and restaurant. Brunch is delicious here.

Take a detour east around Discovery Bay on SR 30 for a look at **Port Townsend's** eccentric gingerbread Victorians. Pick up a free map from the Tourist Information Center pinpointing highlights in this once-glittering city, which in its heyday in the last decades of the 19th century was an important western port.

ALONG THE STRAITS
Heading inland from Discovery Bay, US 101 comes to **Sequim** (pronounced 'Skwim'), a small town which benefits by being in the direct rain shadow of Mt Olympia as it gets annual rainfall of only 16 inches. A few miles north off US 101 on a windswept point of coast is **Dungeness**, which gives the tables of America the sweet-tasting crab bearing its name. Between the two is the **Olympic Game Farm**, breeding ground and research station for endangered species such as the Siberian tiger. It's also a haven for 'resting' animal movie stars. Drive through it, and you might catch animals in training for their next movies. It's open during summer from 9 am to 7 pm; rest of year 10 am to 3 pm; admission charge.

Places to Eat
Dupuis Seafood Inn Somewhat inconsistent but venerable institution; try the Hood Canal oysters and cracked crab. (M)

Lunch, dinner daily. US 101 seven miles east of Port Angeles; tel 457-8033.

Three Crabs Specialises, naturally, in fresh crab (in season October to March) plus other seafood. You can dig for your own geoduck clams on their private beach if the time is right. (M)

Lunch, dinner daily (closed 7 pm Sunday. Dungeness Spit; tel 683-4264.)

PORT ANGELES
Focal point of the north coast is Port Angeles, gateway to Canada's Vancouver Island across the straits and to the Olympic National Park to the south. As a starting point for visitors going in either direction, Port Angeles has grown from a fishing village to a busy tourist center with numerous motels and restaurants. A daily year-round ferry plies the 18 miles between the port and Victoria, making it possible to drive up the northern coast of Washington, ferry through the San Juans to Vancouver Island, then head south again through the Olympic Peninsula (see San Juan Islands below).

If you didn't come into Port Angeles by ferry, drive out to **Ediz Hook** sandbar forming the town's natural harbor to look back at the stunning view of the Olympic mountain range framing the coast. From Port Angeles, a short drive up SR 111 puts you in the Olympic National Park.

Places to Stay

Red Lion Bayshore Inn (221 N Lincoln St, Port Angeles, WA 98362; tel (206) 452-9215). Waterfront setting, many rooms with view of harbor and straits, some balconies. Chain noted for excellent rooms, service. Color cable TV, pool. Restaurant. Rates from $47 double.

Royal Victorian Motel (521 E First St, Port Angeles, WA 98362; tel (206) 452-2316.) On US 101, 11-room motel, some two-room, some efficiencies. Color cable TV. Rates from $25 double.

Uptown Motel (Second and Laurel, Port Angeles, WA 98362; tel 9206) 457-9434.) Deluxe units on bluff, many with marine view. Others in older section; some two-room efficiencies. Color cable TV. Friendly proprietor. Rates from $28 double.

Places to Eat

Haguewood's Steak and seafood in pleasant setting overlooking waterfront. (B/E)

Breakfast, lunch, dinner daily. At Red Lion Bayshore Inn, 221 N Lincoln, Port Angeles; tel 457-0424.

OLYMPIC NATIONAL PARK

The Olympic National Park is 915,426 acres of unspoilt grandeur. The park's main area lies in the central northern portion of the peninsula, plus a narrow coastal strip on the Pacific Ocean running between the Makah Indian Reservation on the north tip to the Quinault Indian Reservation, 50 miles south.

Overpowering is the Olympic Mountain Range capped by 7965-foot Mt Olympia. The peaks are relatively young, only 70 million years old, and as yet not much altered by the elements, though nature's cycle is in progress. As moisture-bearing clouds from the Pacific encounter the Olympian heights, they shed their pentup load in driving snow and rain. Thus the mountains mold the elements into the very weather that over eons will subdue them.

Geological Background

The mountains of the Olympic Range were squeezed upward by the meeting of the Juan de Fuca oceanic plate with the North American plate. Inching forward at the rate of two inches a year, the oceanic crust slid under the continental plate, forcing its upper layers to separate and pile upward. The Olympic Range was born. Its vernacular material is ocean floor sediments. Evidence of lava, which welled up through fissures in the earth's crust to be cooled by the sea, can be seen in rounded outcroppings on the eastern edge of the mountains and in the jagged peaks of The Needles.

Glaciers heading seaward and rushing rivers sculpted deep valleys and indented the Pacific shoreline. Glacier melt created lakes in valley bowls, while some flow caught high in the mountains, produced tarns, glacial ponds.

All this is only an hour's drive from Port Angeles on the peninsula's northern coast edging the Strait of Juan de Fuca.

Climate

The action of the Olympic Range on moisture-bearing clouds produces a wide-ranging weather pattern on the peninsula: Mt Olympus, with 200 inches of rain annually, is the continent's wettest spot. Just 40 miles east, outside the park, Sequim with 16 inches is the driest spot in the coastal Northwest. From October to March, drenching rains fall; three-quarters of the total precipitation occurs in these months. Some 40 feet of snowfall blankets the high country each year, the greatest amount in the contiguous states.

Temperatures range from 70°s in the summer to 40°s in winter on lower elevations; the high country is closed by snow from early fall until May or June.

You should be prepared for sudden, extreme changes in winter.

Things to See & Do

Hurricane Ridge is a 20-mile drive up a seven percent grade on SR 111 from Port Angeles at sea level to a 5200-foot altitude. This is the vantage point for the most spectacular views of glaciated mountains you could imagine. Mammoth forested ridges tower above you; above them, snow-capped peaks disappear into the clouds. *Hurricane Ridge Lodge* is open only for day-use. During ski-season, ski rentals and tow service are available when weather permits.

You can enter the centuries-old rain forests – of Sitka spruce, western red-cedar and Douglas fir, wrapped in lush moss and lichen-draped – in the valleys of the Quinault, Queets and Hoh Rivers.

The **Hoh Rain Forest**, off US 101 on the west, has a Visitor's Center explaining the forest's growth in exhibits. A nature walk elaborates with explanatory markers. During the summer, a naturalist is on duty to answer questions, too.

Quinault Lake in the south is the most developed rain forest area. The lake is jointly administered by the National Park Service, Forest Service and the Quinault Indian Reservation, since it is actually on the Reservation. The lake's northern shore and the Quinault River form the border of the park. Concessionaire campgrounds and lodges ring the lake, including *Quinault Lodge*. Rain forest edges the north and south shores and continues into the high country. The northernmost campgrounds are departure points for high-country hikes across the Olympics peaks. Willaby and Fall Creek have swimming beaches and boating.

Things to See & Do

Ranger-naturalists conduct illustrated talks, campfire programs and guided nature walks in summer.

Back-country hiking (permit required for overnight treks) and mountaineering can be hazardous; parties are asked to register with park rangers, who can supply maps and advise on conditions. Fishing licenses are not required, but a state punchcard is necessary for steelhead and salmon; get a copy of the regulations at a Visitor Center or ranger station. If hiking on beaches, watch out for incoming tides which can trap you quickly against the cliffs.

Pack horse trips are available in summer. A list of stables and packers is available from the park superintendent, or at visitor centers.

There is plenty of wildlife around, including deer. Marmots colonize the slope near Hurricane Ridge Lodge and black bear are drawn to campgrounds, so keep food and packs off the ground and inaccessible to the tree-climbing marauders. Groups of Roosevelt elk roam the high country and occasionally mountain goats are sighted. Along rivers, otters and raccoons are found; at the ocean, harbor seals and shorebirds. In spring and fall, you might even sight migrating gray whales.

Places to Stay

Privately-operated cabins, lodges and trailer parks are located within the park's boundaries at Lake Crescent and Sol Duc, and La Push (on a spur road off US 101), and Kalaloch on the coast; outside the park at Port Angeles and Quinault.

Campgrounds Within the park are 17 *campgrounds* with a total of 992 sites and there are numerous private campgrounds nearby. For information and reservations in the park, write the Superintendent, Olympic National Park, 600 E Park Avenue, Port Angeles, WA 98362. Outside the park, address the Olympic Peninsula Resort and Hotel Association, Colman Ferry Terminal, Seattle, WA 98104.

Facilities Visitor Centers at Port Angeles and Hoh Rain Forest are open all year; at Lake Crescent, the Storm King Center is open summer only. All centers have exhibits, publications and maps detailing roads and self-guiding nature trails throughout the park. Be cautioned that vehicles are not allowed off established public automobile roads, and some roads cannot take trailers.

Snacks are obtainable at **Hurricane Ridge**. **Fairholm on Lake Crescent, Sol Duc, La Push and Kalaloch.**

Information

Olympic National Park Visitor Center and Historical Museum, 600 East Park Avenue, Port Angeles, WA 98362.

Places to Eat

Lake Quinault Lodge Spectacular view of lake and mountains. Steak and seafood menu; home baking. (M)

Breakfast, lunch, dinner daily. Lake Quinault; tel 288-2571.

West of Quinalt, the **Queets River** rain forest is less developed. From US 101, an unpaved road meanders along river's edge to a park campground, where trails lead off into the high country.

Sparkling **Lake Crescent**, 642 feet deep, is reached by paved road from US 101 in the north. Cradled in the foothills, it provides a tranquil haven for vacationers in cottages and resorts around the lake's edge. Waterfowl and beaver abound and trout can be fished without a license. Ranger naturalist programs are conducted in summer at the Storm King Visitor Center, and there are campgrounds and boat rentals. A paved road from the lake's western point climbs alongside the Sol Duc River to a park campground and high-country trailhead; you can swim in the **Sol Duc Hot Springs**.

Getting There

Access to the interior main part of the park is by car from US 101, which circles the peninsula and the park, running through a portion of the park's coastal strip. Numerous spur roads off US 101 lead to the rain forest valleys, higher country and the coastal area. There are no roads through the heart of the park. Gateway cities are Seattle, then ferry from Keystone on Whidbey Island to Port Townsend; Port Angeles by ferry from Victoria, British Columbia; or road through Olympia to US 101.

THE NORTH COAST

From Port Angeles west, the straits coastline is marked by salmon fishing ports backed by the forested mountains. The Makah Indian Reservation occupies the northwest corner of the peninsula, on Cape Flattery. SR 112 runs along the coast to the reservation, linking Port Angeles with the fishing resorts of Clallam Bay, Sekiu and Neah Bay, the latter within the reservation.

THE PACIFIC COASTLINE

The peninsula's western ocean coast is a string of storm-tossed wilderness beaches and barren windswept headlands, bounded by a narrow strip of the Olympic National Park. US 101 runs inland most of the way, except for a short stretch between Ruby Beach and the start of the Quinault Indian Reservation, edged by the highway as it moves inland again. **Kalaloch**, on US 101 below Ruby Beach, is a resort town with a *lodge* and *campgrounds*. Six miles of sandy beaches flanking it invite strolling and surf casting, since they are easily accessible.

Occasionally, side roads lead off from US 101 to touch the coast, and to the south SR 115 edges the shore from Grays Harbor to the Quinault Reservation. The Quinaults, discouraged by the actions of graffiti experts and other vandals, prefer not to have tourists on their sands.

Head for the Grays Harbor area to sunbathe and enjoy the shore.

GRAYS HARBOUR

Since the early 1960s when Hollywood money started investing in resort property development at **Ocean Shores**, on the beach side of Grays Harbor, this formerly sleepy area has become a lot livelier, although it is still no Southern California. What it does have to offer is some pleasant resorts and sandy beaches (rich with razor clams) from Ocean Shores to Pacific Beach. Though the Hollywood venture didn't prosper, Ocean Shores bears the legacy in some attractive lodges and restaurants tucked into the trees, an 18-hole golf course and a 112-acre park embracing the sand dunes.

ABERDEEN/HOQUIAM

At the end of the sheltered harbor are twin cities, Aberdeen and Hoquiam. **Aberdeen** is a fishing and logging center, with lighthouses and canneries marking its shoreline. **Hoquiam** is more industrial; a highlight here is Hoquiam's Castle, restored 1897 mansion of a lumber baron, who showed an obvious penchant for castles in his turreted residence. Elegant furnishings include chandeliers and antique pieces. At 515 Chenault Avenue it's open daily 11 am to 5 pm mid-June through Labor Day; Saturday to Sunday only balance of year; 11 am to 5 pm; admission charge; tel 533-2005).

From Hoquiam, US 12, a four-lane freeway most of the way, completes the loop back to Olympia.

Places to Eat

The Bridges Highly rated steakhouse with good salad bar. (M)

Lunch, dinner daily. 112 N G St Aberdeen; tel 532-6563.

SOUTH TO THE COLUMBIA MOUTH

Alternatively, you can take US 101 south, edging Willapa Bay to the Columbia's mouth at Ilwaco, then follow the river to the toll bridge across to Astoria in Oregon.

A detour on SR 105 follows Grays Harbor out to **Westport** on the southern headland. A sleepy fishing village which boomed into a roistering sportfishing resort, it now has a waterfront area where motels, restaurants and charter fishing agencies crowd each other on land as do fishing craft offshore. SR 105 continues a scenic route around the north shore of Willapa Bay to join US 101 at Raymond. The road skirts oyster-producing beds from here to Cape Disappointment, on the tip of North Beach Peninsula, which guards the Columbia estuary.

NORTH BEACH PENINSULA

This long finger of hard-packed basalt sand beaches rarely rises higher than 40 feet above sea level. Beach cottages and lodges in the resorts of Long Beach, Seaview and Ocean Park reveal nostalgic reminders of the time, in the Gay 90s, when the inhabitants of Oregon flocked to the seaside here. 1970s additions prove the area's still popular, particularly with berry pickers and clammers; the razor clam population is rife here and cranberry bogs abound. At the northern end of the peninsula, the oyster is still king. Nahcotta's canneries and smokehouses are open to visitors in late fall and early winter.

At Cape Dissapointment where Lewis and Clark finished their epic cross-country odyssey in 1805, you can recapture some of their experiences in an interpretive center, set among the old gun emplacements, which impressively depicts incidents from that journey. **Fort Canby State Park**, situated between the center and North Head on the ocean side, offers camping, fishing and vantage points from which to thrill to the elements when winter storms rage.

Wending east along the river, you come to **Fort Columbia State Park's** Spanish-American War buildings and batteries needlessly protecting the river's mouth. Now the park provides a fine place for a picnic and you can even splash in the Columbia on the only river swimming beach west of Vancouver.

The drive across the high toll bridge to Oregon provides unique views of Astoria's distinctive Victorian buildings.

NORTH TO THE BORDER

From Seattle, I-5 runs inland from the coast, crossing the border into Canada through Blaine's Peace Arch Gate, 100 miles north. Along the way are opportunities for side trips and detours if time allows. Not to be missed, if possible, are the San Juan Islands because of their exceptional beauty. Clustered in the northern Puget Sound between the mainland and British Columbia's Vancouver Island, they can be reached by ferry from Anacortes. Drive to Anacortes by taking US 20 west off I-5, or you can detour from Everett through Whidbey Island.

EVERETT

If you choose the Whidbey Island route, head out through Everett on SR 526, passing the huge Boeing plant (tel 342-4801 for information on tour) and crossing Paine Field, the site of the Northwest Air Fair held each July.

WHIDBEY ISLAND

A few miles before Mukilteo, SR 525 leads you to the ferry for Columbia Beach on Whidbey Island (one-way fare $1.50 for car and 50c each passenger). At Freeland, SR 20 takes you up the island through tranquil pastoral scenery. In **Fort Casey State Park**, you'll see late 19th century fortifications and old gun emplacements intact. The Lighthouse Interpretive Center explains the Puget Sound Defense System in existence from 1900 to the beginning of WW II. It's north on Engle Rd just past Keystone; and is open from Wednesday to Sunday between 10 am and 6 pm from April through September, tel 678-4519.)

COUPEVILLE

A little further on, you come to one of Washington's oldest towns, Coupeville. Artists and craftspeople have brought new life to the shoreside original village, just east of the new town straddling SR 20. Several old block houses are to be seen in and near the town. The Chamber of Commerce maintains an Information Center at 6th and N Main, open Tuesday through Sunday noon to 5 pm.

Giant oaks point the way to Oak Harbor, selected as location of the Whidbey Naval Air Station because of its weather, favorable for flying 96% of the time. The Station opens to visitors on Navy Day, October 27, and Armed Forces Day, the third Saturday in May.

ANACORTES

Deception Pass State Park's overhanging cliffs and quiet beaches lead to the Deception Pass Bridge over the turbulent narrows separating Whidbey from **Fidalgo Island**, on which Anacortes is situated. For a panoramic view of Puget Sound, the San Juan Islands and the mainland's Skagit Valley, take the spur road at the north end of Lake Campbell to the 1300-foot summit of Mt Erie.

Three miles down the road lies Anacortes and the San Juan ferry. Anacortes is a curious mixture of serenity and industry. Its wooded outskirts, secluded beaches and marinas crowded with bobbing pleasurecraft juxtapose with the activity of busy oil refineries.

Fans of Rodia's Watts Towers and Gaudi's works in Barcelona should drop by **Causland Park** to check out its unusual rock walls.

Places to Stay

Anacortes Inn (3006 Commercial Avenue, Anacortes, WA 98221; tel (206) 293-3153.) Pleasant comfortable units, color cable TV. Some kitchens. Pool. No restaurant. Rates from $30 double. Recommended.

Ship Harbor Inn (5316 Ferry Terminal

Rd, Anacortes, WA 98221; tel (206) 293-5177.) Overlooking ferry terminal, harbor views, balconies and lanais. Color cable TV. Coin laundry. Transportation to ferry. Some kitchens, suites. Cottages available. Rates from $25 double.

Places to Eat
Charlie's Restaurant (Ferry Terminal Rd; 293-7377; moderate; open Monday to Saturday 6 am to 10 pm; Sunday 7 am to 10 pm). Uphill from ferry terminal, overlooking marina. Pleasant atmosphere, straightforward dishes. Can be crowded in summer, so reserve. (M)

Breakfast, lunch Monday to Saturday, dinner nightly. Ferry Terminal Rd; tel 293-7377.

THE SAN JUAN ISLANDS
Few sights could be lovelier than these pine-clad islands spread across a deep green sea. Some are little more than emerald slivers above the waterline. The four most inhabited – Lopez, Shaw, Orcas and San Juan – are still havens of serenity, with country roads wending through virgin woods and meadows to isolated beaches strewn with driftwood. The lifestyle seems a thousand years removed from big-city Seattle, less than 100 miles away.

History
The story of the San Juan Islands begins with the earliest Spanish explorers, such as Juan de Fuca who gave his name to the straits (in actual fact, he was a Greek and his real name was Apostolos Valerianos!) and Francisco Eliza who, in 1790, charted and named the islands.

After the Revolutionary War, the British, determined to expand their fur trade in the Northwest, sent the intrepid Captain George Vancouver to explore, as places named for his crew members attest – Puget, Whidbey, Ballard, Baker. Fur trading with island Indians led to the granting of a commercial monopoly on the islands to the Hudson's Bay Com-

pany by the British Crown in 1850. In 1853, the Company set up a farm on San Juan Island; sheep were imported and Hawaiian Islanders were brought in as sheep herders.

But the Oregon Treaty of 1846 between the British and the Americans setting the Northwest boundaries had left the demarcation of this vicinity rather ambiguous. Meanwhile, a number of Americans had settled in the islands. The stage was set for a Gilbert and Sullivan incident which almost triggered a new war between Britain and America: the 'Pig War' of 1859.

An American settler killed a British pig on San Juan Island. That's how it started and before too long the affair burgeoned to the point where a British force of five of Her Majesty's ships and 2000 men were poised in Griffin Bay against an American force of 461 men, sworn to hold the islands for the United States. Luckily, cooler heads prevailed and a joint occupancy was arranged while a Boundary Commission arbitrated the dispute. A British camp set up at the north end of the island, the Americans at the south end (under command of Captain George Pickett, who four years later was to lead the charge on Cemetery Hill during the Civil War Battle of Gettysburg). Finally, after 12 years of fruitless deliberation by the Boundary Commission, Kaiser Wilhelm I was asked to arbitrate. On November 25, 1872, he established the boundary as we know it today, vindicating the American position.

San Juan Island
Friday Harbor is the county seat and administrative center of the San Juan group. It boasts five of the island's nine resorts and a nine-hole golf course.

A **Whale Museum**, located in one of the island's earliest buildings, tells the story of the whales in exhibits, carvings, scale models and art. On 62 First St; open June to September, 10 am to 5.30 pm daily; rest of year Wednesday to Monday, 10 am to 5 pm; admission charge; tel 378-4710.

San Juan National Historical Park commemorates the 'Pig War'. The blockhouse, commissary and barracks of English Camp at Garrison Bay, 10 miles from Friday Harbor, have been restored. Vestiges of the American defenses can still be seen at American Camp on the island's southeastern tip, five miles from Friday Harbor. East of camp is the site of Old San Juan town, destroyed by fire in 1890. The park has beaches and trails, as well as picnic sites. Rangers are present in the summer. (Park grounds open year-round sunrise to sunset; buildings open summer only. Information: Superintendent, San Juan National Historical Park, Box 549, Friday Harbor, WA 98250; tel (206) 442-2240).

Orcas Island

Orcas, biggest of the four main islands, is site of their largest park, **Moran State Park**. It offers three lakes, all with trout fishing, and one, Cascade, has rental rowboats and a swimming beach. From the stoneblock observation tower atop its 2454-foot Mt Constitution, you obtain a splendid view of all 174 islands in the Archipelago.

Lopez Island

Lopez's Spencer Spit offers one of the group's few swimming beaches, as well as a resort and several camping parks.

Shaw Island

Sleepiest of all, Shaw has no public facilities but is well worth a day's exploration. By the ferry landing several stores include a general store and the post office. Beyond that lie apple orchards, forests, rocky meadows and isolated beaches – a delightful place to poke around by bicycle, which you can carry across on the ferry.

Part of the joy of a visit to the San Juan's is the ferry experience itself. The nautical esprit of bearded crew members, who look like descendants of the Vikings, handling arrival and departure at small island docks draws admiring passengers to the bow at each stop.

Places to Stay

There are resorts and motels on each of the main islands with the exception of Shaw Island. Summer bookings are heavy. For list of accommodations and current rates, write Chamber of Commerce , Friday Harbor, WA 98250; tel (206) 378-4600. There are restaurants on San Juan, Orca and Lopez; on Shaw, it's picnic time.

Getting There

Ferry The Anacortes ferry terminal lies west of town. Washington State ferries make seven trips a day in each direction in winter, more in summer. One a day continues on to Sidney on Vancouver Island, British Columbia. Ferries stop at each of the above islands; on occasional trips the outbound ferry picks up inbound passengers. It's about a 1¾ hour cruise to Friday Harbor; fare at writing runs about $6.80 one way for car with one passenger; with a special rate for foot passengers with limited time ashore. There's a restaurant aboard. For schedules and rates, write Washington State Department of Transportation, Colman Dock, Seattle, WA 98104; tel 464-6400 in Seattle; toll free 800-541-9274 from out-of-area 8 am to 6 pm.

An alternative to returning to Anacortes is to overnight in the San Juans, next morning take the ferry on to Vancouver Island and spend a day or two in Victoria (be sure you have the correct visas to enter and leave Canada) and take Black Ball Transport's ferry from Victoria to Port Angeles on the Olympic Peninsula. For schedule and rates, write 814 Wharf St, Victoria, BC, V8W ITS; tel (604) 386-2202.

Air Scheduled flights on San Juan Airlines link Friday Harbor with Sea-Tac in Seattle and Bellingham.

BACK ON THE MAINLAND

From Anacortes up to the border, several scenic detours beckon you away from I-5. Don't miss **La Conner**, south of SR 20 West, between Anacortes and I-5. This picturesque fishing village presents a melange of rickety piers and canneries, galleries featuring the works of painters, potters and weavers newly settled in town and charming Victorian houses. Best of these is the imposing 22-room **Gaches Mansion**.

NORTH CASCADES NATIONAL PARK

SR 20 East follows the course of the Skagit River through the Ross Lake National Recreation Area dividing the two parts of the North Cascades National Park, then continues across state. The road, only completed in 1972, is an engineering achievement, cutting as it does through some of the most rugged and forbidding territory in the state. Here granite peaks soar vertically above spectacular canyons sheltering fjord-like lakes. Snow closes SR 20 in the mountains for as long as early October to late June.

The **Skagit Valley** is reminiscent of Holland. Cows browse contentedly in lush meadowlands and in season fields of waving tulips daub the landscape with splashes of vivid color. Standing sentinel over the peaceful scene, snow-capped Mt Baker hints at the majesty of the hinterland mountain ranges to come.

North Cascades National Park, established in 1968, is undeveloped in comparison to other parklands. This is the wilderness experience, pure and untrammeled. The most dramatic overview of its alpine splendor is obtained by flightseeing charter from Bellingham airport.

Activities on the ground are limited to experienced mountaineers and back-country travelers; the only facilities are primitive campsites. The iciness of lake waters confine acquatic activities to boating and fishing even in mid-summer. Skiing facilities do not exist, though cross-country skiing is gaining popularity. The nearest accommodation is in towns several hours' drive-away.

If you only have limited time this is an area you can only get a taste of on a day's drive to the Ross Lake overview. Apart from the spectacular views, keep your eyes open for America's symbol, the bald eagle, wheeling overhead: the road between Rockport and Marblemount passes through a 1500-acre sanctuary for the once endangered species.

BELLINGHAM

From Burlington to Bellingham, you've two choices of scenic routes other than I-5. SR 9 takes you up the lovely Skagit Valley, passing through neat farming communities. Alternatively, SR 11 follows the coastline along the Samish and Chuckanut Bays, offering superb seascapes. A fiery sunset over the San Juans is incomparable.

The city of Bellingham is beautifully situated on Puget Sound within view of the San Juans, the Olympic and Cascade mountain ranges, with the snow cone of Mt Baker seeming to hover overhead. Its major attraction, apart from the mid-May Blossomtime Festival when the tulips are at their peak, is the eye-poppingly ornate 1892 former City Hall, which now houses the excellent **Whatcom Museum of History and Art**. Works primarily by Northwest painters such as Mark Tobey and Kenneth Callahan fill the ground floor; above, historical exhibits describe Indian life and logging in the area. At 121 Prospect St, it's open Tuesday to Sunday noon to 5 pm, free; tel 676-6981.

Bellingham also has several fine parks and a number of hotels and motels, concentrated along Samish Way – take Exit 252 from the freeway.

Stunning views of the Cascades, including the northwest corner of the Cascades National Park are yours by driving SR 542 northwest following the Nooksack River. Turn up to **Mt Baker**

Lodge & Ski Area, then follow the winding road to 4700-foot Austin Pass. On summer weekends, you can ride the chairlift to Panorama Dome where you look out over the 'top of the world'. Mt Baker's ski-fields are scene on July 4 of the Slush Cup downhill run: contestants are sometimes described as a touch daft.

If you happen to be in Bellingham in June, check the date of the **Lummi Stommish,** an Indian festival held at Marietta on the nearby Lummi Indian Reservation. It's a chance to see Indian dances and canoe races and to take part in a salmon bake.

Between Bellingham and Blaine, turn off I-5 at **Ferndale** (Exit 262) for a look at a typical family farm of this region, maintained in the Hovander County Park. You can wander through the 1903 farmhouse and the old barn, housing vintage farm equipment and friendly animals. Open Wednesday to Sunday 10 am to 6 pm Memorial Day-Labor Day; admission charge; tel 384-3444.

THE BORDER

Although the great white arch straddling the border in Blaine's Peace Arch State Park marks the beginning of Canadian territory, there is still a piece of American soil which you can only reach by driving

north! The tip of Point Roberts on the Strait of Georgia was forgotten when the mapping party drew their straight line across the 49th Parallel. So now at the end of a Canadian promontory sits a US village, a 60-mile roundtrip drive away from their fellow Americans.

Useful Adresses

Tourism Promotion & Development Division, (Department of Commerce & Economic Development, General Administration Building, Olympia, WA 98504; tel (206) 753-5600.)

Seattle-King County Convention & Visitors Bureau (1815 Seventh Avenue, Seattle, WA 98101; tel (206) 447-7273.)

Washington State Parks & Recreation Commission (PO Box 1128, Olympia, WA 98504; tel (206) 753-5755.)

Department of Fisheries (115 General Administration Building, Olympia, WA 98504; tel (206) 753-6600.)

Regional Forester, US Forest Service (310 SW Pine, Portland, OR 97208; tel (503) 221-2877.)

National Park Service, Northwest Regional Office (Fourth and Pike Building, Seattle, WA 98174; tel (206) 442-1144.)

Sierra Club, Pacific Northwest Chapter (4534½ University Way NE, Seattle, WA

Festivals & Events

January	*Seattle Boat Show*
February	*Fog Festival*, Ocean Shores *Discovery Bay Fire Dept, Annual Fish Derby* *Fat Tuesday (Mardi Gras)*, Seattle
March	*Daffodil Festival Coronation*, Tacoma
April	*Puyallup Valley Daffodil Festival,* Tacoma *Saltwater Festival & Blessing of the Fleet*, Westport *Seattle Art Museum's Annual Architecture Tour*
May	*Rhododendron Festival*, Port Townsend *Viking Festival and Arts & Crafts Show*, Poulsbo, Kitsap Peninsula

June	*Lummi Stommish*, Gooseberry Point (near Bellingham)
July	*Pacific Northwest Festival* (Der Ring Des Nivelungen), Seattle
	Capital Lakefair, Olympia
	Pacific Northwest Arts & Crafts Fair, Bellevue
	Seafair, Seattle (into early August)
September	*Vancouver Sausage Festival*, Vancouver
November	*Harvest Festival*, Seattle
December	*Christmas Around the World*, Seattle
	Christmas Cruise, Lake Washington

The Southwest

ARIZONA AND NEW MEXICO

The Southwest, as you will quickly discover, is fascinating.

It is a vast region embracing, in broad historical and cultural terms, all of the country south of a line drawn from Santa Barbara on the Pacific coast to the Gulf of Mexico – sun-drenched country of overwhelming beauty and a distinctive heritage blended from three cultures, the Indian, the Spanish and the Anglo-American. Arizona and New Mexico are the heart of it.

Much of their fascination has to do with the grandeur of the landscape with the intense colors of the earth that shade from tans to ochre and fiery reds, with spectacular stone monuments and mesas that rise sheer out of sandy wastes, and with a boundless sense of space. Dominating the north are mountain massifs with peaks reaching the 13,000-foot elevation, extensions of the Rocky Mountains and the Continental Divide, and the high Colorado Plateau. This is untouched country, raw, rugged, slashed by deep canyons, where you will find extensive forests as well as arid wildernesses of rock. Then the land falls away to shimmering deserts that sweep up from Chihuahua and Sonora in Mexico to fan out across southern Arizona into California and Texas. This land of very little rain is characterized by broad plains broken by short, barren mountain ranges. Bringing life to the whole region are two major rivers, the Colorado and the Rio Grande, both traversing Colorado's mountains to flow southwest respectively for hundreds of miles.

While Arizona and New Mexico are magnificent outdoor adventure country, they exert a further fascination for the traveler; nowhere are there more intriguing imprints of man's long occupation of the US, from the pit and cave dwellings of early man and the towering apartment houses of Pueblo Indians to old towns and lonely mission outposts founded by the Spanish, many within a short distance of large cities established just a century or so ago. The juxtaposition of the Southwest's three cultures are clear in language, customs, folklore, religious beliefs and a unique indigenous architecture – in fact it is the only part of the country that *has* any indigenous architecture. And nowhere else will you so strongly feel the strength of the Indian presence or so easily observe the impact of two centuries of Spanish occupation.

History

The first to come were the ancestors of the Indians, bands of nomadic hunters who crossed the Bering Straits from Asia perhaps 37,000 years ago, slowly settling the western hemisphere from Alaska to Tierra Del Fuego. In Sandia, New Mexico there are traces of occupation dating back 25,000 years. By 1000 AD sophisticated agricultural civilisations were to be found throughout the region – the Anasazi in the Four Corners area where Arizona, New Mexico, Colorado and Utah meet; the Mogollon from Alamogordo to Arizona; and the Hohokam who farmed the Gila and Salt River valleys of southern Arizona. The Anasazi have left dramatic evidence of their culture in the cliff dwellings of Mesa Verde and Keet Seel and the pueblos of Chaco Canyon.

In the 13th century the Anasazi abandoned their classic homelands, possibly because of drought, and moved south and east, settling in the canyons of the Pajarito Plateau and later on the banks of the Rio Grande north of Albuquerque. Of the several pueblos they established which are still inhabited, Taos Pueblo is the most famous. During the same period the ancestors of the Hopi

Indians established themselves at Old Oraibi on Black Mesa in Arizona. By the end of the century the Mogollon peoples had also moved into the Rio Grande Valley.

The written history of the Southwest began when the Spanish conquerors of Mexico sent exploratory parties north through the Sonora Desert in search of the legendary Seven Cities of Cibola. These mythical golden cities were as important an influence on Spanish expansion as the legend of *El Dorado,* the gilded man, that inspired the conquest of Peru. It was a Franciscan friar, Father Marcos de Niza, and his companions who first entered Arizona and New Mexico, penetrating the region as far as the Zuni pueblo of Hawiku, not far from modern Gallup. His imagination construed the sight of the pueblo as a great city of tall buildings behind whose walls were riches in gold and silver. The news he brought back to Mexico inspired the first major expedition into the area.

Francisco Vasquez de Coronado and his conquistadores journeyed for two years, between 1540 and 1542. Though the quest for Cibola proved fruitless, Coronado opened up a region that embraced Arizona, New Mexico, all the pueblos of the Rio Grande, and parts of Texas, Oklahoma and Kansas. Over 50 years later Don Juan de Onate established the first Spanish colony at San Gabriel on the Rio Grande near San Juan Pueblo in 1598. In 1610 the city of Santa Fe was founded.

Spanish exploration and settlement of Arizona came about more slowly, in large measure the result of the explorations and missionary work of Padre Eusebio Kino between 1691 and 1711. Kino's parish extended from Magdalena in Mexico to the Gila River and from San Pedro to the Colorado.

Although the Pueblo Indians drove the Spanish into temporary exile in Texas from 1680 until 1692, Spain and Mexico governed the Southwest for two centuries without challenge to their authorities from outsiders. Not until the Mexican regime did American traders enter the region in substantial numbers, following the Santa Fe trail blazed by William Bechnell in 1821. During the 1846 war with Mexico the Americans invaded New Mexico, requiring most of it under the Treaty of Guadalupe Hidalgo in 1848 and a portion of Mexican Sonora by the Gadsden Purchase of 1853.

American dominion did not come easily. The Comanches, Apaches and Navajos were not subdued and herded off onto reservations by the US Army for at least 20 years, until the brilliant Apache warleader Geronimo surrendered in 1888. But throughout the period, Americans were moving west to seek their fortunes. Great deposits of gold, silver and copper were discovered in Arizona, copper and rare minerals in New Mexico, drawing a stream of prospectors. Others saw their future in ranching and agriculture. It was a turbulent era that has given rise to the mystique of the Old West – the era of Billy the Kid, of range wars between the cattlemen and sheepmen over land and water rights, of Doc Holliday, the Earps and Bat Masterson.

In July 1945, a mushroom cloud rising above the desert near Alamogordo, New Mexico, ushered in the Nuclear Age and a new period of development in the Southwest. While the traditional industries of the pioneers and Indians are still important, Arizona and New Mexico are deeply involved in the development of space age technology and solar energy: Paolo Soleri's experimental community of Arcosanti near Phoenix and the atomic city of Los Alamos point the way of the future. These contrasts are part of the fascination of traveling in the Southwest.

Climate

The overworked phrase 'year-round vacation land' is appropriate in Arizona and New Mexico where climate depends on elevation as much as on season. Clear skies, low humidity and sunshine are the norm. In late fall, winter and spring, Southern Arizona's low-lying desert lands lure sun lovers with a pleasantly warm, sunny climate. Daytime temperatures average 67°F, but the mercury often falls 20° or more at night.

Much of that period is winter sports time in the uplands over the 6000-foot

elevation whree the range is between 14° and 44°F. Summer here is refreshing, varying from 44° to 78°. Air-conditioning has tempered the effect of desert temperatures which hover round the century mark and shoot over 110° in some places. Throughout the region expect thunder and rain storms during July and August; in the desert these can cause flash floods.

Arizona

THE VALLEY OF THE SUN

Phoenix arose from the desert, embraced Scottsdale, and they begat the Valley of the Sun – prosperous, resort-studded, and the favourite winter training grounds of Big League baseball – rimmed by the Superstition and Mazatzal Mountains to the east. In spite of urban sprawl and a network of freeways rivaling Los Angeles', the Valley is a comfortable, friendly place with a relaxed style that manages to combine urban sophistication and an old-fashioned simplicity harking back to the days when Phoenix and Scottsdale were small centers of a cattle ranching and mining area.

For the visitor in search of complete relaxation with all the amenities, the twin cities are the place. Weather is fine year-round (it may get a little too hot for some in the summer months when the mercury hovers around 100°F, but the humidity is low). Tennis, golf, horseback riding, gliding, hiking and rock climbing are readily enjoyed. Nightlife centers on the clubs and resort lounges where big name entertainers perform. 'Little Theater' supplements the Phoenix Symphony orchestra and Scottsdale's Chamber Opera and Musical Comedy Theater, and a crowded events calendar includes the annual **Rodeo of Rodeos** in Phoenix in March and the February **Parada del Sol** in Scottsdale. Dial 956-6200 for a 24-hour

recording of what's happening in the area.

Some of America's most famous resorts are here, including the legendary Marriott's Camelback Inn, The Registry Resort, and Del Webb's Mountain Shadows. There are, of course, accommodations for the budget-minded and substantial discounts (up to 50%) can be obtained if you visit off-season between mid-May and mid-September. There are package plans, too, which reduce high season costs. For information, write to the Phoenix & Valley of the Sun Convention and Visitors' Bureau, 2701 E Camelback Rd, Suite 200H, Phoenix, AZ 85016, or call (602) 957-0070.

PHOENIX

The Arizona state capital stands on the site of Hohokam settlements more than a thousand years old, but was only founded in 1860. It was named by an English adventurer with a penchant for the classics, 'Lord' John Duppa, who also christened nearby Tempe. Downtown, highrises cluster around **Civic Plaza,** an ultra-modern, six-block complex of spacious piazzas with a handsome concert hall and convention center. Phoenix's excellent museums are the main sightseeing attractions, however.

The **Heard Museum** at 22 E Monte Vista Rd has one of the most important

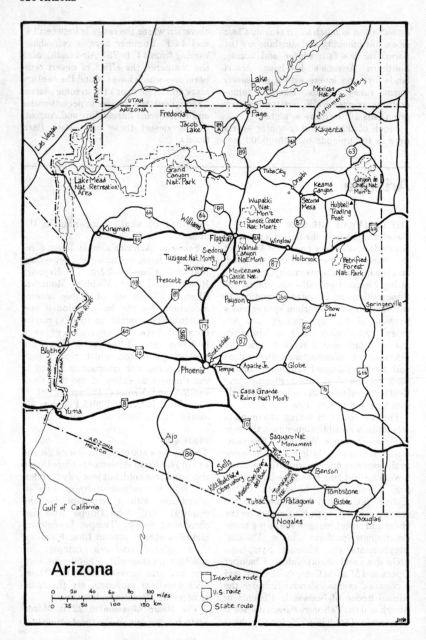

Arizona

⬡	Interstate route
▢	U.S. route
◯	State route

collections of American Indian Art in the Southwest, including an unusually fine display of Hopi and Zuni Kachina dolls. Indian craftspeople from several tribes foregather here each spring for the annual Indian Fair which features the dances, rituals and music of Arizona's Indians as well as their arts. In fall the museum hosts the Indian Arts and Crafts Exhibit where all the items entered for competition are for sale. Open Monday to Saturday, 10 am to 5 pm; Sunday 1 to 5 pm; admission $1.50; tel 252-8848.

Nearby, the **Phoenix Art Museum**, 1625 North Central Avenue, focuses on Western American, contemporary and Oriental art, and has a particularly attractive collection of 18th century French paintings. Open Tuesday to Saturday 10 am to 5 pm; (Wednesday till 9 pm) Sunday 1 to 5 pm; admission free; tel 257-1222.

Pueblo Grande, located at 4619 E Washington, is an excavated 13th century village of the Hohokam Indians who populated the Valley of the Sun some 3000 years ago. They were among the first peoples in the world to develop irrigation canals – so efficiently that modern engineers followed their courses for the canals which irrigate the desert today. Displays in the **museum** explain their lifestyle. Open Monday to Friday, 9 am to 5 pm; Sunday 1 to 5 pm; closed Saturday; admission charge; tel 275-3542.

The essence of Victorian Phoenix is preserved in **Heritage Square**, an attractive agglomeration of restored homes, specialty shops and restaurants occupying a full block at 6th St and Monroe. **Rosson House** (1894) has been furnished with turn-of-the-century antiques, and there's also a museum and a display area.

Open Wednesday to Saturday, 10 am to 4 pm; Sunday noon to 4 pm; tel 262-6711.

Arizona is the leading copper producer in the country and you can follow the history of mining in the state in the

Mineral Museum, located in the southwest corner of the Arizona State Fairgrounds at the intersection of Grand Avenue and West McDowell Rd. One of the world's largest quartz crystals is displayed in the mineral collections. Open Monday to Friday, 8 am to 5 pm; admission free; tel 255-3791.

Shopping & Entertainment Centers

With their flower-filled squares and varied architectural styles, restaurants and entertainments, local shopping centers have a powerful attraction for visitors and locals alike. Most are located north of Civic Plaza and east of I-17. Among the famous names are **Biltmore Fashion Park** on Camelback Rd at 24th St; **Chris-Town Shopping Center**, Bethany Home Rd between 15th and 19th Avenues, contains some 200 stores, movie-houses and restaurants; and **Metrocenter** on Black Canyon Freeway between Dunlop and Peoria. The **Sundome Center for the Performing Arts** at 19403 RH Johnson Boulevard in Sun City West is the Valley's main location for Broadway shows, concerts, ballet and other entertainments.

Phoenix is blessed with several parks; if time is short, visit **Papago Park**, with its Desert Botanical Garden containing a vast array of native and exotic cacti, succulents and native trees. It's open daily from 9 am until sunset (small entrance fee). There are excellent views of the Gila and Salt River Valleys from vista points in **South Mountain Park**.

SCOTTSDALE

Scottsdale lies at the foot of Camelback Mountain, merging imperceptibly with Phoenix. It's a lively resort and retirement center for the wealthy, with stylish homes, a handsome Civic Center, and 15 golf courses. Shopping is a popular sport here, pursued in elegant stores on **Scottsdale Mall**, between Civic Center and Brown Avenue, **Fifth Avenue**, where perfumed fountain plays in Kiva Plaza, and in **Old Town**, Scottsdale's link to the Old West. Here, on streets lined with pioneer-era buildings and hitching rails, you can pick out the best in western apparel, Indian art and turquoise and silver jewelry. Western art is prominent in the galleries.

Things to See & Do

The **Cosanti Foundation** at 6433 Doubletree Rd is a showcase for the avant-garde ideas of Paolo Soleri. On exhibit are models of future housing, and sculptures and those famous bells are for sale in the display areas. You can also take a look at the workshops. The studios are open daily 9 am to 5 pm; tel 948-6145.

Scottsdale's attractions draw heavily on the Old West myth. In the foothills to the north, **Rawhide's** amusements include some good museums of western artefacts, horseback riding, a shoot-out, and seven sheep that have the freedom of the town's one street. Its old buildings are authentic ghost town relics, brought down from the hills, and the Golden Belle is straight out of a shoot-em-up, right down to its burnished brass rails. Open Monday to Friday; 5 pm to midnight; weekend, noon to midnight; admission free; tel 992-6111.

Pinnacle Peak Patio and **Reata Pass** on Pinnacle Peak Rd, and the little towns of **Carefree** and **Cave Creek**, nestling amid the saguaro cactus east of US 17, offer more of the same. Cave Creek features **Frontier Town**, with melodrama at Pierre's Playhouse; the big draws at Pinnacle Peak are the re-enactments of an old-fashioned hanging and outsize steaks.

For contrast, visit the western campus of Frank Lloyd Wright's renowned architectural school, **Taliesin** on E Shea Boulevard. Here Wright's ideas are expressed in both the buildings and landscaping. Open daily 10 am to 4 pm (noon to 4 pm Sundays); admission $3; opening times are occasionally altered; for information call 948-6670.

Between mid-March and the end of September, the wave-making machines of **Big Surf**, at 1500 North Hayden Rd in Tempe are in action. In addition to swimming and surfing, you can scoot down a 300-foot twisting surf-slide. Open daily March 6 to end of September; admission free; tel 947-2478.

In a 15-acre park 30 miles south of Phoenix on I-10 (and accessible by public transportation) is a recreated Indian village; **Gila River Arts & Crafts Center**, illustrating the lifestyle and culture of the Hohokam, Pima, Papago and Apache peoples. Indian built and Indian staffed, the Center's attractions include demonstrations of basketry and pottery making, tribal dances, and a small museum with a gift shop. The restaurant in the main building has Indian meals, featuring several different ways of consuming fry bread, a staple of Southwest Indian fare. Try it with honey or with a taco filling. Open daily, 9 am to 5 pm; admission fee; tel (602) 562-3411.

The Lost Dutchman Mine

Of all the mysteries that color the history of the West, none has captured public imagination more than the legend of the Lost Dutchman Gold Mine in the Superstition Mountains 40 miles east of Phoenix. Facts are few. The one certainty is that the mine is named for Jacob Waltz, a German prospector who came out of the Superstitions in the 1870s boasting of a fabulous strike, with bags of gold nuggets as solid verification. According to some, the mine was first discovered at the turn of the 19th century by members of the Peralta family of Chihuahua, Mexico. Waltz reportedly encountered three Mexican peons who showed him the mine – and were murdered for their naivety.

The old prospector took the secret of its exact location to his grave, bequeathing only a number of conflicting clues. The key is a stripped palo verde tree pointing away from Weaver's Needle, a peak long used as a landmark on the Apache Trail and visible from any part of the Superstitions. Nevertheless, for nearly a century now, undeterred by tales of mysterious deaths and even murder, thousands of treasure-hunters have tried to follow Waltz's faint trail into the peaks. Treasure maps and horseback tours of the Superstitions are offered for the adventurous in Apache Junction (see Phoenix Sightseeing Services).

Places to Stay – Phoenix

Of all the famous names, we list only a few in order to give you some idea of your options and the cost. If you're planning a resort vacation in the Valley of the Sun, do write well ahead to the Valley of the Sun Convention and Visitors Bureau requesting individual brochures. If you're just passing through, remember their free hotel-resort reservations number: 800-528-6149. The Grand Canyon's South Rim hotels are on the system. Prices quoted are for high season.

Arizona Biltmore (24th St and Missouri, Phoenix 85004; tel (602) 955-6600; 800-228-3000). Famous resort hotel with bungalows amid beautiful gardens. Heated pool, tennis, golf, social programs and entertainment are just some of the amenities. Golf and tennis package plans. Reservation deposit required. Airport transportation. Rates from $155 double.

Civic Plaza TraveLodge (965 E Van Buren, Phoenix 85006; tel (602) 252-6823). Within walking distance of Civic Plaza and bus terminals. Heated pool, air-conditioning, color TV, complimentary coffee. Reservation deposit required in season. Rates from $38 double.

Desert Sun Hotel (1325 Grand Avenue, Phoenix 85007; tel (602) 258-8971). Close to Encanto Park, in pleasant grounds. Heated pool, color TV, air-conditioning and a sidewalk cafe. Rates from $22 double.

Portland House (506 E Portland St, Phoenix 85004; tel (602) 252-6344). AYH hostel approximately a mile from the bus station. Rates: $5.25 (members).

Valley of the Sun International Hostel (1026 N 9th St Phoenix 85006; tel (602) 262-9439). This AYH hostel is close to the park, museums and theater. Rates from $5.25 member; $7.25 non-member.

Dunes Motor Hotel (2935 E Van Buren, Phoenix 85008; tel (602) 275-4491.) Heated pool, most rooms air-conditioned. but some air-cooled. Color TV. Some kitchen units. Weekly rates available. Reservation deposit required. Rates from $20 double.

Hyatt Regency (122 N 2nd St, Phoenix 85004; tel (602) 257-1110 or 800-228-9000.) A really good hotel, overlooking Civic Plaza. Heated pool, air-conditioning, color TV, entertainment, plus two fine restaurants and a coffee shop. Rates from $79 double.

Motel Six Four locations in the Phoenix-Scottsdale area, each with heated pool. Most conveniently located are: 5315 E Van Buren, Phoenix 85008; tel (602) 267-8553. (Airport bus service.)

2323 E Van Buren, Phoenix 85008; tel (602) 267-1397.

6848 E Camelback Rd, Scottsdale 85018; tel (602) 947-7321.

Each has heated pool. TV available. Rates from $19.95 double.

Places to Stay – Scottsdale

Marriott's Mountain Shadows Resort (5641 E Lincoln Drive, Scottsdale 85253; tel (602) 948-7111 or 800-228-9290). They've held a 5-star rating for 15 years. Spacious grounds, two pools, health club, tennis, golf and entertainment are some of the attractions. Airport transportation. Rates $145 double.

Marriott's Camelback Inn (5402 E Lincoln Drive, Scottsdale 85252; tel (602) 948-1700 or 800-228-9290.) One of America's most famous resorts, also rated 5-star (for 10 years). Landscaped ground with two pools, tennis, golf and entertainment.•Some suites with kitchens, fireplaces and private pool. Reserve deposit required. Airport transportation. Rates from $155 double.

Sunburst Hotel (4925 N Scottsdale Rd, Scottsdale 85251; tel (602) 945-7666 or 800-528-7867.) Spacious grounds, heated pool, putting green, tennis. Some kitchen units. Air-conditioning, color TV, and a free newspaper every weekday. Airport transportation. Rates from $95 double.

Places to Eat – Phoenix
There was a time, and not so long ago either, observed a local critic, when dining in the Valley of the Sun meant dried jerkie and refried beans. Not so today! The Valley abounds in fine restaurants, and while the barbecued steak occupies a hallowed niche, you will find a wide variety of international cuisines offered. A good resource tool is Boye De Mente's *Insider's Guide: Phoenix, Scottsdale, Tempe, Mesa, Tucson*. Your options include:

Golden Eagle Restaurant Award winning Continental cuisine (and a chance to sample buffalo steak) in this elegant restaurant with sweeping views of the Valley. Entertainment in the cocktail lounge. Reservations recommended. (E)

Lunch weekdays, daily. 201 N Central, 37th floor; tel 257-7700.

Hyatt Regency Hotel Three good bets here. *The Compass* is a revolving rooftop restaurant offering Continental and American cuisine for lunch and dinner daily, from 11.30 am (Sundays from 6 pm). *Hugo's* elegant restaurant, popular with local celebs, also features Continental dishes. Open for lunch and dinner daily (Sunday from 6 pm). The *Coffeeshop* is a haven for the price conscious with a hankering for good food at budget prices. Open from 6.30 to 11 pm.

122 N 2nd St; tel 257-1110.

Navarre's One of Phoenix's most popular eateries with a wide ranging menu of Continental and American dishes. Sandwiches at noon, too. (M)

Lunch, dinner. Open daily. 52 E Camelback Rd; tel 264-5355.

Organ Stop Pizza Rated the best pizza joint in town, with imaginative sandwiches and calorie-unconscious desserts on the menu, too. Informal setting and music by the mighty Wurlitzer. (B)

Lunch, dinner. Open daily. 5330 N 7th St; tel 263-0716.

Places to Eat – Scottsdale
Cafe Casino Turn-of-the-century Parisian decor and a dedication to fine French fare at low cost. Self-service cafeteria with take-out counter. (B)

Open daily, 11 am to 10 pm. 1312 Scottsdale Rd; tel 947-1987.

Ianuzzi Restaurant Scores high locally for tasty Northern Italian dishes and pleasant atmosphere. Art gallery adjoins the cocktail lounge. Reservations recommended. (E)

Dinner daily. 7340 Shoeman Lane; tel 949-0290.

Trader Vic's Award-winning scion of the Trader Vic Bergeron family of Polynesian restaurants. American, Continental and oriental cooking. Reservations recommended. (E)

Lunch weekdays; dinner daily. 7111 Fifth Avenue; tel 945-6341.

Getting There
Air Sky Harbor International Airport is approximately five miles from downtown Phoenix. Airport Transportation Company and the Phoenix Transit System (see above) will get you into town if you're not planning to rent a car.

Bus *Continental Trailways,* 5005 North Black Canyon Highway (about six miles from downtown Phoenix) (tel 257-0257) and *Greyhound* 525 E Washington (tel 248-4040). Both terminals about half a mile from Civic Plaza.

Rail *Amtrak's* passenger terminal is located at 401 W Harrison St. For information, call 1-800-421-8320 or 253-0121.

Getting Around
Bus *Phoenix Transit System* with a central terminal and information booth at

First and Adams Sts in downtown Phoenix (near the Adams Hotel) operates local (air-conditioned) bus service in Phoenix, Scottsdale and Glendale. Fares begin at 50c in Phoenix, 60c in Scottsdale. Discounted ticket books available. For information call 257-8426.

Taxi Rates in the Valley of the Sun are based on 70c for the first fifth of a mile, plus 20c for each additional fifth of a mile. Fare between Sky Harbor Airport and local motel row, Van Buren Way, costs approximately $5, between airport and downtown hotels, $8. Call *Yellow Cab Co,* in Phoenix; *Village Cab Co,* 994-1616 or 945-8241 in Scottsdale.

Limousine Service *Airport Transportation Company,* Sky Harbor International Airport, serves downtown Phoenix hotels, resorts, Sun City, Tempe, Mesa and Chandler. Current charge downtown is approximately $3.50. Call 273-1241. *Gray Line of Phoenix Inc,* 100 E Jefferson (tel 248-6030) and *Rolls Royce Chauffeur Driven Service,* 4902 E Acoma Drive (tel 996-7280), both in Phoenix, also offer limousine service.

Tours
Bus As you might expect in a resort area, Phoenix and Scottsdale have many sightseeing enterprises. Space does not permit more than a few examples: *Gray Line of Phoenix* (600 E Jefferson, Phoenix; tel (602) 248-6030). Three of this company's tours give a good sense of the area: a half-day tour of Phoenix and the Valley of the Sun ($7.75); a full day Oak Creek Canyon tour including Jerome, Sedona and Montezuma Castle National Monument ($23), and a day in Tucson and Old Tucson ($39). Check out short package tours.
The Dons (201 N Central Avenue (Box 3), Phoenix 85002; tel 258-6016. This is not a commercial touring company but a non-profit civic club of business and professional people dedicated to preserving

the legends and folklore of the Southwest. Definitely worth writing well ahead for information on its Travelcades which may include treks to the Superstition Mountains-Los Dutchman Mine (one day/$22); Colorado High Mountains (four days $282) or a tour following the trail of Fray Marcos de Niza (two nights $109).
OK Corral Stables (Apache Junction 85220; tel 982-4040.) Custom-packed trips into the Goldfield and Superstition Mountains and a program of guided trail rides – sample: $12.50 for a breakfast ride, $20 for a day trip.
Superstition Stables (Apache Junction 85220; tel 982-1380 or 986-0751.) Similarly offer day trips (with lunch, $20) and custom pack trips.
Chuck Hall Outfitters (1650 N Mesa Mesa; tel 964-8253.) Their Superstition horseback adventure and steak cookout lunch costs $45 per person. Two to seven-day overnight trips run $75 per person per day.

Flightseeing Several Phoenix airline outfits offer flightseeing tours of the Grand Canyon, with and without a stopover in the park. Among them:
Grand Canyon Airlines (PO Box 3038, Grand Canyon 86023; tel 638-2463). They offer a five-hour roundtrip tour from Scottsdale between December 1 and April 30, which includes a 20-minute canyon flight, a meal and ground transportation to and from the South Rim.
Southwest Airlines, Inc (15000 N Airport, Scottsdale; tel 948-2400). Features scenic charter flights throughout Arizona with full day Grand Canyon tours that allow time to visit the park.

Useful Addresses
Phoenix and Valley of the Sun Convention and Visitors Bureau (2701 E Camelback Rd, Suite 200H, Phoenix 85016; tel (602) 957-0070). As well as providing up-to-the-minute information, maps and brochures, the Bureau offers a free *hotel-resort*

reservations service – just call 800-528-6149. For recorded events, dial 956-6200. Open Monday to Friday, 8.30 am to 5 pm. The Bureau also has branches at Terminals 2 and 3, Skyharbor International Airport.

Meeting the Americans
Sierra Club (2331 E Virginia Avenue Phoenix; tel 267-1649).

NORTHERN ARIZONA

The shortest, fastest route from Phoenix to Flagstaff and the Grand Canyon Country is US 17, the 'Black Canyon Highway' which traverses the northern Sonora Desert and the pine-clad uplands of the Mogollan Plateau. Driving time to Flagstaff a distance of some 140 miles, is just under three hours. But on both sides of the highway are vast stretches of wild and beautiful country, veined with deep gorges of red sandstone, and if time is not the essence, it is preferable to leave US 17 at Cordes Junction to follow US 69 through Prescott and approach Flagstaff by way of US 89A. This scenic highway takes you 7000 feet up the slopes of Mingus Mountain to the old copper mining town of Jerome, then drops down into the Verde Valley to run through dramatic Oak Creek Canyon, second only to the Grand Canyon in its splendor. The area is rich in old mining towns and prehistoric monuments; its national forests are ideal for camping, hunting or fishing vacations.

Pioneer Arizona Museum
About 25 miles north of Phoenix on US 17 is the largest open-air 'living history' museum west of the Mississipi. Here you can browse through old buildings brought together to illustrate the settlement of the Southwest and watch costumed guides re-enact the pioneer lifestyle. Open Tuesday to Sunday, 9 am to 5 pm; admission charge; tel (602) 993-0210.

ARCOSANTI
Cordes Junction, 38 miles further north, is the turn-off point for a visit to the 21st century. Paolo Soleri's Arcosanti is the prototype of a city built on the principle of living in harmony with nature. When completed, the single structure will provide homes and work space for 5000 people. Solar energy is used extensively and a huge terraced greenhouse provides food. To get there, follow a well-signed dirt road for roughly two miles northeast of Cordes Junction. It's open daily; 9 am to 5 pm; guided tours hourly; admission charge; tel (602) 632-7135.

PRESCOTT
A mile high above sea level and surrounded by peaks and vast pine forests, Prescott lies 34 miles northwest of Cordes Junction via US 69. The former capital of Arizona Territory began in 1864 as a center for ranching and mining; today it's a resort town with an exceptionally fine climate and pure clear air. The feeling of the Old West is strong here, and Prescott's citizens celebrate the past with a four-day Frontier Days fiesta each Fourth of July. In August, the Smoki – an organisation of business and professional people – perform the dances and ceremonials of Southwestern Indian tribes.

The Sharlott Hall Museum on Gurley St contains the collections of a remarkable woman who came to Arizona Territory by covered wagon in the 1880s. Sharlott Hall's fascination with the lore and history of the state led to the establishment of this evocative museum of pioneer life. Its buildings include the Old Governor's Mansion (1864); the first schoolhouse; Bashford House (1878); and Fort Misery, Prescott's first house. Open Tuesday to Saturday, 9 am to 5 pm; Sunday 1 to 5 pm; admission free; tel (602) 445-3122.

Also of interest is the **Smoki Museum** on Arizona Avenue at Willis St with its fine collection of Indian artefacts in a building modeled on early pueblo structures. It's open Tuesday through Saturday, 9 am to 5 pm between June 1 and August 31; admission free.

JEROME

North of Prescott, US 89A begins a serpentine ascent of Mingus Mountain to the former copper mining town of Jerome, founded a century ago to exploit the high-grade ores of Cleopatra Mountain. When the last mine closed in the 1950s, the town's population had dwindled to 200 from the 15,000 of its heyday; it's up to 400 today, mining a rich vein of tourists who come to wander around the abandoned buildings and antique and crafts stores. The **Douglas Mansion** in Jerome State Historic Park displays machinery used in the mines, as does the **Mine Museum** on Main St.

Tuzigoot National Monument

The Sinagua Indians built the impressive hilltop pueblo of Tuzigoot, two miles east of Clarkdale, during the 12th century. By 1450 they had abandoned it to the mercy of the winds and the sun; it was not until the 1930s that archeologists of the University of Arizona began to bring Tuzigoot's history to light. Bracelets made of shells from the Gulf of California indicate that the Sinagua engaged in commerce far afield. Intricate mosaic jewelry has also been found, and in the museum, among the immense ollas and fine basketry of woven grasses, bark and yucca, there is a necklace consisting of 3295 tiny beads. A self-guiding trail leads through the ridgetop dwellings. Open daily 8 am to 7 pm, from June to Labor Day; 8 am to 5 pm, rest of year; admission charge; tel (602) 634-5564.

OAK CREEK CANYON & SEDONA

Arizona's second most popular scenic attraction, Oak Creek Canyon, is on the southern edge of the high plateau that encompasses the Grand Canyon, shaded by dark green oaks that counterpoint the brilliant reds, yellows and browns of the canyon walls and pinnacles. Multi-spired **Cathedral Rock** is the most famous of the unusual rock formations that tower on each side of the highway as you approach from the south.

Marvellously weathered buttes form the setting for Sedona (and for a number of Westerns) at the south end of the canyon. Sedona's small-town charm is rigorously preserved by residents who number among them several of the Southwest's leading exponents of naturalistic painting. There's good browsing at the **Arts Center** and **Tlaquepaque's** galleries and crafts boutiques, set in a grove of giant sycamores.

The **Chapel of the Holy Cross**, rising dramatically from a niche in the red sandstone cliffs, is a famous landmark. It was built in 1956 as a family memorial and is open to the public daily. For excellent views of the great rocks, follow Schnebley Hill Rd which runs eastward from Sedona to US 17.

Sedona is also the gateway to the wilderness country of Kaibab and Coconino National Forests – for information on jeep tours, hiking trails and camping, as well as Sedona's motels and rental cabins, drop by the Sedona-Oak Creek Chamber of Commerce, or write to Chamber at PO Box 478, Sedona, AZ 86336; tel (602) 282-7722.

Montezuma Castle National Monument

Should you elect to take US 17 all the way from Phoenix to Flagstaff, it's well worth visiting Montezuma Castle, one of the best preserved cliff dwellings in the country, two miles north of the Camp Verde turnoff. The Sinagua Indians of the 12th century took advantage of a vertical cliff some 46 feet above the slope to erect a five-story apartment dwelling that was inaccessible save by ladders. Its hand-fitted stone walls and sycamore beams remain largely as the Indians fashioned them.

Because of the dangerous condition of

the structures, visitors are no longer permitted to tour the castle. Nearby, however, the ruins of another pueblo may be toured.

Montezuma's Well, seven miles northeast and detached from the monument, is a vast limestone sinkhole 470 feet broad and 55 feet deep which supplied the Sinaguas with water for their fields. You can still see sections of the irrigation system they constructed. The well is surrounded by numerous ruins of pueblos and cliff dwellings. It's open daily 8 am to 7 pm in summer; 8 am to 5 pm, rest of the year; admission charge; tel (602) 567-3322.

FLAGSTAFF

Though overshadowed by its role as gateway city for the Grand Canyon, Flagstaff has sufficient attractions of its own and in the immediate vicinity to warrant stopping over. The astronauts trained here for the first moon walk; there are important cliff dwellings in the vicinity; and in winter, ski bunnies are only 15 miles from the popular Arizona Snow Bowl in the San Francisco Peaks. The Chamber of Commerce, 101 W Santa Fe, has brochures, maps and guidebooks on the attractions and can help you find accommodation.

Things to See & Do

The **USGS Center for Astrogeology** at 2255 N Gemini Drive, stands in a lunar landscape where the astronauts studied before going to the moon. Among the interesting exhibits are a geologic mapping of the moon and research on volcanic craters . Open weekdays 9 am to 5 pm; admission free tel (602) 779 3311.

Lowell Observatory, astronomers explore the universe from a mountain-top retreat about a mile west of Flagstaff via Santa Fe Avenue. Here, in 1930, the planet Pluto was discovered. You may view the observatory's 24-inch refractor telescope on a one-hour guided tour offered Monday to Friday at 1.30 pm.

During summer, weather permitting, there's stargazing and a slide lecture each Friday evening; free tickets are available at the Chamber of Commerce.

For a look at Flagstaff's early days, browse through collections of the **Pioneers' Historical Museum**, two miles north of town on US 180. Works by local artists are displayed in the 'Art Barn' near the main building. It's open Monday through Saturday, 9 am to 5 pm; Sunday 1.30 to 5 pm; admission free; tel (602) 774-6272.

The **Museum of Northern Arizona** stands amid a pine forest three miles northwest of Flagstaff on US 180. It houses an important collection of Navajo and Hopi arts and crafts along with exhibits explaining the natural history, geology and archeology of the area. You can also purchase authentic Indian arts and crafts in the museum shop – and if you're passing through Flagstaff in July, check the date of the Hopi Crafts Show held at the museum; demonstrations of Indian craft techniques add understanding to the displays. Open Monday to Saturday 1.30 to 5 pm; tel (602) 774-

Walnut Canyon National Monument

More than 300 Sinagua cliff dwellings are preserved in Walnut Canyon National Monument some seven miles east of Flagstaff via US 40. The Sinaguas probably occupied the canyon around 1000 AD; the cliff dwellings you see date from the 12th century and were abandoned a century later. A self-guiding trail enables you to see a number of their homes at close quarters, and you get good views of the dwellings honeycombing the cliffs opposite. Open daily 8 am to 7 pm, Memorial Day to Labor Day; 8 am to 5 pm; rest of the year; admission charge; tel (602) 526-3367.

Meteor Crater

Some 22,000 years ago a giant meteorite slammed into the Arizona desert east of Walnut Canyon, forming a crater 600 feet deep and 4150 feet from rim to rim with almost vertical walls. This awesome depression in the earth's surface is regarded by scientists as one of the best preserved meteoric craters on earth and NASA used it as a training ground for astronauts. Actual space suits and equipment can be seen in the **Astronauts Hall of Fame** in the visitor centre. There's a museum of astrogeology there, too, and a continuous audiovisual presentation tells you everything you need to know about meteors and meteorites.

Meteor Crater is 19 miles west of Winslow, six miles south of I-40. Open daily 6 am to 6 pm mid-May-mid-September; 7 am to 5 pm rest of year; Admission charge. Tel (602) 774-8350.

Petrified Forest National Park

This 93,500-acre desert park lies on either side of US 66 some 87 miles east of Flagstaff and 25 miles northeast of Holbrook, preserving one of the world's largest concentrations of petrified wood. The process of transforming dead logs into rainbow-colored stone began 180 million years ago as volcanic ash, sand and mud covered the fallen trees before they could decay. Silica-bearing water, stained with iron oxide and other minerals, seeped down and, cell by cell, turned them into stone. Later upheavals of the land and erosion exposed large numbers of the trees. Fossilized plants and bones have also been discovered.

Best place to see these petrified trees is the southern sector of the park, near the Rainbow Forest Visitor Centre. To get there, follow US 180 to the entrance 18 miles east of Holbrook. The park road runs due north for 27 miles, past **Crystal Forest, Jasper Forest,** and **Puerco Indian Ruins,** an Anasazi pueblo, to the **Painted Desert.** Several picnic sites here, with wonderful views across the brilliantly-tinted sands. You can, of course, enter the park from the northern, US 66, entrance.

There's a visitor center with a museum, restaurant and gas station at both entrances to the park. No overnight accommodation, however, and camping is only permitted for hikers in the Rainbow Forest and Painted Desert wilderness areas (a backcountry permit is required). Open daily, sunrise-sunset; admission charge; tel (602) 524-6228.

Places to Stay

Branding Iron Motel (1121 E Santa Fe Avenue, Flagstaff 86001; tel (602) 774-6651.) Cable TV. Restaurant next door. Rates from $24 double.

Little America (2515 E Butler Avenue, Flagstaff 86001; tel (602) 779-2741.) Air-conditioning, color TV, heated pool, entertainment. Rates from $49 double.

Saga Motel (820 W Highway 66, Flagstaff 86001; tel (602) 779-3631.) Air-conditioning, color TV and a heated pool. Restaurant nearby. Rates from $26 double.

TraveLodge of Flagstaff-East (2285 Butler Avenue, Flagstaff 86001; tel 800-255-3050 (602) 774-1821.) Heated pool, saunas, air-conditioning and color TV. Some rooms with balconies or patios. Rates from $50 double.

Motel Six (2010 E Butler Avenue, Flagstaff 86001; tel (602) 774-3535.) The super-budget chain has opened a new link in Flagstaff. Rates from $19.95 double.

Weatherford Hotel (23 N Leroux, Flagstaff 86001; tel (602) 774-2731). This AYH hostel operates a courtesy bus from the Greyhound depot during daylight hours. Rates from $7.28 members; $9.36 non-members.

Places to Eat

Granny's Closet Steaks and seafood house, plus some Italian dishes. Attractive turn-of-the-century decor. Entertainment. (M)

Lunch, weekdays, dinner daily and weekends. 218 S Sitgreaves; tel 779-4133.

Western Gold Dining Room Wide range of continental and American dishes, plus entertainment and dancing. (E)

Lunch weekdays, dinner daily and weekends. In Little America Hotel, 2515 E Butler Avenue; tel 779-2741.

Cottage Place, 126 W Cottage and *Finley's Restaurant Mercantile,* 17 N San Francisco have been recommended to us for good fare at moderate prices.

Getting There

Air Flagstaff Airport is presently served by *Cochise, Desert Air* and *Sky West,* connecting with major airlines at Phoenix.

Bus Both *Continental Trailways* and *Greyhound* serve Flagstaff. Greyhound's depot is at 399 Malpais Lane (tel (602) 774-4573), Trailways at 114 W Santa Fe Avenue (tel (602) 774-3356).

Rail *Amtrak* service. For information and reservation services, call toll free 1-800-421-8320.

Getting Around

Bus *Gray Line of Flagstaff* (Nava-Hopi Tours Inc, Box 339, Flagstaff 86002; tel(602) 774-5003.) Visit Museum of Northern Arizona, Sunset Crater, Wupatki National Monument and Walnut Canyon ($15); Montezuma Castle National Monument ($23). Half-day tours include Oak Creek Canyon ($12) and Sunset Crater-Wupatki National Monument ($10). There's also a full-day tour of the Navajo and Hopi Indian Reservations for $26.50 and daily bus service to the Grand Canyon.

Flightseeing *Northland Aviation Inc* (PO Box 956, Flagstaff 86002; tel (1-602) 779-4118). 35 and 50 minute tours of Flagstaff area sights. Call for current prices. A 1½ hour tour over the Grand Canyon area costs $50 per person.

Back Country, Camping, Float Trips *Canyoneers Inc* (PO Box 2997, Flagstaff 86003; tel (602) 526-0924.) Package tours by coach and jeep, guided camping trips, treks and combination hiking trips. Write well ahead of departure date for current information cn costs and reservations. Also offered are motorized and rowboat float trips through the Grand Canyon. Sample per person costs: seven day motorized trip, $850; 14 day rowboat trip, $850.

Useful Addresses

Flagstaff Chamber of Commerce (101 W Santa Fe, Flagstaff 86001; tel (602) 774-4505.) Brochures, maps, guide books and information on accommodation. Open Monday to Friday, 8 am to 5 pm.

ROUTE TO THE GRAND CANYON

US 180 is a 79-mile scenic route from Flagstaff to the South Rim of the Grand Canyon which skirts the dramatic San Francisco Peaks. About 15 miles north of Flagstaff is the **Arizona Snow Bowl**, the state's most famous winter recreation area, with slopes to suit skiers of all grades. In summer, from Memorial Day to mid-October, you can ride the 6800-foot chairlift up to the 11,600 foot level of Mt Agassiz for a magnificent view of five states that includes the rim of the Grand Canyon 60 miles away. Nearby is Arizona's highest mountain, Humphreys Peak: its 12,670 feet is a fitting challenge for ambitious hikers.

But take the longer route to the Canyon, US 89-SR 64, and you can include two of Northern Arizona's sights along the way. The distance from Flagstaff via Cameron is 117 miles.

Sunset Crater National Monument

This flamboyantly colored cone was formed less than a thousand years ago in a series of violent eruptions which scattered volcanic ash and lava over 800 square miles and created a rich topsoil farmed by the Sinagua, Hohokam, Anasazi and Cohonina Indians for 200 years. But the winds which created this fertile area also destroyed it and today you see a bare, lunar landscape which was used as a training ground by the Apollo astronauts for their moon walk. Exhibits at the visitor center, two miles east of US 89, graphically portray the geologic history of the area. Visitor center open daily 8 am to 7 pm in summer; 8 am to 5 pm; rest of year; tel (602) 526-0586.

Wupatki National Monument
The fertile soil created by Sunset Crater's eruptions created something of a land rush in the 11th century; scattered across Wupatki's plain, you'll find some 800 Indian dwellings inhabited between 1100 and about 1225. Some of the red sandstone structures rise two to three stories high and contain nearly a hundred rooms. Most impressive is **Wupatki** ('Tall House in the Hopi language) which housed 300 people. Nearby is an oval ball court very similar to those of Mexico and Central America – archeologists conjecture that Arizona's prehistoric Indians may have played a similar ritual basketball, or perhaps a game like the Algonquin Indians' lacrosse. A number of hard rubbered spheres have been unearthed on the site. Also of great interest are the ruins of **Wukoki, Lomaki** and the **Citadel**. The center is open daily 8 am to 7 pm summer; 8 am to 5 pm rest of the year; tel (602) 774-7000.

COLORADO RIVER COUNTRY
From Moab, Utah to Parker, Arizona much of the land along the Colorado River has been set aside as a national playground embracing no fewer than three national parks and two vast recreation areas. This is high adventure country with something for everyone. Confined by narrow gorges the river offers white-knuckle excitement for rafting enthusiasts; backed up behind great dams, it opens out into huge lakes that provide endless opportunities for boating, fishing, water-skiing and diving. The Colorado's backcountry is mountain wilderness at its most rugged, some only partially surveyed even today – ideal for the hiker who wants to experience the vermilion and sage solitudes of the high desert. Backcountry roads reward the auto-explorer with marvellous sights, ghost towns and long-abandoned mines. Traveling here calls for some planning however. Summer temperatures often zoom close to the century mark, settlements are far apart; it's wise to take adequate supplies of gasoline and water and a good map at very least. Hikers and boaters would do well to leave word with someone about where they're going and when they plan to return. Never travel alone.

Las Vegas, Nevada, Boulder City, Kingman, Flagstaff and Page, Arizona are major gateways to the northern Colorado River Country; Lake Havasu City and Kingman (again) to the southern. You can get to all of them by public transportation but to make the most of the recreation areas, there's no substitute for your own car.

GLEN CANYON NATIONAL RECREATION AREA
Extending from Utah's Canyonlands (which lie outside the scope of this guide) to the northernmost limits of the Grand Canyon, Glen Canyon National Recreation Area contains Lake Powell and a substantial wilderness hinterland to the north. The 186-mile-long lake, formed by the impounding of the Colorado River by Glen Canyon Dam, is a year-round water sports center that offers an outstanding boating experience with its sinuous shoreline, fjordlike inlets and broad, sheltered bays overshadowed by vermilion cliffs. With a fishing license you may go after the abundant rainbow trout, bass and crappie. Not the least of the area's attractions is the opportunity to combine boating with a little rough canyon country hiking, enhanced in spring by brilliant displays of wildflowers on the mesas.

While sightseeing is more properly nature-seeing in Glen Canyon, a visit to Glen Canyon Dam, near Page, at the southern end of Lake Powell, is worthwhile. This concrete arch dam towers 583 feet above the river bed. Hydroelectric power generated here is used by cities and industries throughout the West. Self-guided tours of the dam begin at the visitor center adjoining Glen Canyon Bridge on US 89. It's open daily, 8.30 am to 4 pm; admission fee; tel (602) 645-2471.

Page is the hub of commerce at this end of the lake. You can arrange flightseeing jaunts over Lake Powell at the airport, learn much about the Colorado River and its explorer Major John W Powell at the museum named after him on 7th Avenue at Navajo Drive, and arrange for rafting trips and accommodation with information provided by the Chamber of Commerce. The Chamber's mailing address is Box 727, Page, AZ 86040; tel (602) 645-2741.

Lees Ferry, a few miles downstream from Glen Canyon Dam as the river flows, but some 40 miles from Page via SR 80, is a historic river crossing established in 1879 by John D Lee. This little place has a pioneer fort, a trading post, campground, ranger station and a launching ramp. Marble Canyon, 3½ miles away, has the nearest restaurant, store and service station.

Places to Stay

There are four resort marinas within the recreation area, at *Wahweap*, Arizona and *Bullfrog*, Halls Crossing and *Hite* in Utah. All feature small-boat rental facilities, lodging and stores. For information about their resorts, tours and package vacations write to Reservations, Del Webb Recreational Properties, Box 299040, Phoenix, AZ 85038; tel 800-528-6154. The Superintendent, Glen Canyon National Recreation Area, Box 1507, Page, AZ 86040; tel (602) 645-2471 can provide general information on National Park Service and other concessionaire-operated facilities.

Getting There

Nearest airport is at Page, Arizona. Car rental facilities are available at the airport, or in Page. *Continental Trailways* provides bus service.

THE GRAND CANYON

The Colorado River carved out this most famous of canyons – 277 miles long, a mile in depth and as much as 18 miles wide. It is overwhelmingly beautiful, with sheer precipices and weathered forms glowing red, gold, green, pink, mauve and countless gradations of colour as the light shifts across the strata of rocks forming the canyon walls. These strata reveal the history of the earth over 20 million years – and within the inner gorge geologists have found the oldest rocks so far exposed on this planet, two billion years old.

Viewing the Grand Canyon

Open all year, the **South Rim** is well developed and drives provide a succession of magnificent views. **West Rim Drive** (closed from May to September) has superb observation points at Hopi, Mohave and Pima Points. **East Rim Drive** passes Mather (where most visitors get their first look at the canyon), Yaki, Grandview, Moran and Lipan Points – about three miles east of Yaki Point is the Duck-on-the-Rock formation so popular with photographers, which may be reached by a trail down the slope. **Desert View** has a 70-foot watchtower with a glassed-in observatory giving views north to the junction of the Colorado and Little Colorado rivers and across the Painted Desert and Kaibab National Forest. Along the way, stop in at **Tusayan Ruins and Museum**. Here a cluster of low stone walls among the trees outlines an 800-year-old pueblo and kiva. The museum houses artefacts recovered from the pueblo and provides descriptions of the culture. Open daily 8 am to 5 pm; admission free.

The **Visitor Center** near the South Rim entrance also contains a museum where a ranger-naturalist is on duty to explain exhibits of the geological history of the canyon. Original river-running craft are on display; you may also catch a demonstration of Navajo rug weaving. It's open daily 7 am to 7 pm in summer; 8 am to 5 pm rest of year; admission free.

There is a third museum on East Rim Drive, at Yavapai Point, which focuses on the geology, flora and fauna of the canyon and is open daily from 8 am to 7 pm in summer; 9 am to 5 pm rest of the year; admission free.

Inner Canyon The best way to follow the history of the Grand Canyon is to descend to the canyon floor, either on foot or on mule back. If you plan to hike, consider this: Bright Angel Trail (which starts west of Bright Angel Lodge) is 11 miles down to the Colorado River; Kaibab Trail (starting from Yaki Point) is 6½ miles to the Colorado River suspension bridge. Both are rated arduous by the Park Service and should only be undertaken by experienced hikers in top condition. No water is available on the trails so you would have to carry your own (one gallon per person per day is recommended). There are emergency telephones on both trails (rescue services are expensive).

Overnight accommodation is available at *Phantom Lodge* and in the five public *campgrounds* on the valley floor. Reservations and a backcountry camping permit are essential. (See Camping, Inner Canyon.)

Far easier on your physique is riding one of the famous mule trains in and out of the depths (see Mule Trips). The only hazard is acrophobia: these trips are not for those who fear heights – at many ponts the trail skirts sheer drops of several hundred feet.

North Rim This offers an entirely different sense of the canyon. It is higher in elevation, cooler, less crowded and comparatively undeveloped. It is also only open from mid-May until the end of October. But you will probably feel closer to nature here, especially in the Tuweep area in the northwest corner which can be reached only by unimproved road from Fredonia, Arizona or St George, Utah. Here, at Toroweap Point, the canyon is less than a mile wide and 3000 feet deep. Improved roads from the North Rim entrance lead to **Point Imperial** where the Colorado emerges from Marble Canyon and enters the Grand Canyon, and **Cape Royal** overlooking the Painted Desert; **Point Sublime** is worth the 17-mile primative road, for you will see the narrowest portion of the canyon.

The distance from South Rim to North Rim is some 214 miles by road. During summer air transportation is available from Grand Canyon Airport to De Motte airstrip where ground transportation to the North Rim may be picked up.

Places to Stay and Eat – South Rim Year round service at *Bright Angel Lodge, El Tovar Hotel, Kachina Lodge, The Motor Lodge, Mushwhip Lodge* and *Thunderbird Lodge* in Grand Canyon Village, and at *Yavapai Lodge* opposite the Visitor Center. Reservations must be made through Grand Canyon National Park Lodges, Grand Canyon, AZ 86023; tel (602) 638-2401. South Rim Hotel reservations may also be made via the Valley of the Sun Convention and Visitor Bureau's toll-free resort reservations number, 800-528-6149.

Outside the park there are motels in Tusayan (eight miles south of Grand Canyon Village); Cameron (32 miles east of Desert View); Gray Mountain (nine miles south of Cameron), Flagstaff (84 miles south-east of Grand Canyon Village); and Williams (61 miles south of Grand Canyon Village).

Two South Rim *campgrounds: Mather Campground,* open year-round, makes unreserved campsites available on a first-come, first-served basis. Reservations may be made at Ticketron outlets. There is also a year-round *trailer village* near the

Visitor Center. Limit of seven days.

Outside the park there is a *Ten X Campground* 10 miles south of Grand Canyon Village, without water, but open year-round. Also, private campgrounds at Valle (31 miles south of Grand Canyon Village) and private and public campgrounds near Flagstaff and Williams.

Restaurants, cafeterias and a *delicatessen* are located in Grand Canyon Village (some are closed in winter). Tusayan has restaurants and there is a snack bar at Desert View.

Facilities General and camping supplies, service station, post office, telephone, telegraph and laundry facilities located in Grand Canyon Village are open year-round. Both Tusayan and Desert View have a general store and service station, but Desert View facilities are closed in winter.

Places to Stay and Eat – North Rim
North Rim has only *Grand Canyon Lodge*, open between mid-May and mid-October. For reservations, write TWA Services, Box TWA, Cedar City, UT 84720; tel (801) 586-7686.

Outside the park there are motels at *Kaibab Lodge* (18½ miles north of North Rim Entrance Station) and *Jacob Lake* (32 miles north of North Rim Entrance Station). Accommodation is also available at Fredonia, Marble Canyon and Page, Arizona and at Kanab, Utah.

One *campground* on the North Rim, open in summer only, plus *USFS campgrounds* at DeMotte and Jacob Lake outside the park. All are operated on a first-come, first-served basis. Limit within park is seven days.

Grand Canyon Lodge provides meals and refreshments.

Facilities General store, post office, showers, laundry and gasoline at North Rim Campground.

Places to Stay and Eat – Inner Canyon
Phantom Ranch, on the canyon floor, provides lodge and dormitory accommodation and meals. Reservations must be made in advance through the Reservation Department, Grand Canyon National Park Lodges, Grand Canyon, AZ 86023; tel (602) 638-2401.

Overnight hiking reservations and permits are required for use of Indian Gardens, Bright Angel, Cottonwood and Roaring Springs *campgrounds*. Reservations are accepted three months in advance of the month requested. Contact Back-Country Reservations Office, Grand Canyon National Park, Grand Canyon, AZ 86023; tel (602) 638-2474.

Getting There
Air Commuter airlines provide scheduled service to Grand Canyon Airport. Ground transportation is available from the airport to the park. (See also Flightseeing Tours.)

Bus *Navajo-Hopi Tours,* a division of Greyhound, operates scheduled bus services from Flagstaff to Grand Canyon Village. Both Continental Trailways and Greyhound serve Flagstaff.

Rail *Amtrak* trains stop in Flagstaff where you may pick up the bus or hire a car.

Getting Around
Bicycles may be hired in summer at Maricopa Point and Hermit's Rest on the South Rim. You'll need a driver's license or major credit card as a security deposit.

Bus Free *shuttle buses* operate from May to September between Grand Canyon Village lodges, shops and villages and Mather Campground, and along West Rim Drive.

Car Car hire may be arranged through South Rim hotels and at Grand Canyon Airlines from Grand Canyon Airport (South Rim) to De Motte Park airstrip where you can pick up ground transportation to the North Rim.

Tours
Bus and Limousine Tours operate from Grand Canyon Village to Hermit's Rest,

Desert View and Cameron on the Navajo Reservation (summer only). Bus trips every afternoon in summer from Grand Canyon Lodge (North Rim) to Point Imperial and Cape Royal, with geology talks included.

Flightseeing Tours by *Grand Canyon Airlines* leave from Grand Canyon Airport daily in summer. Phone (602) 638-2463 for information and current rates. Grand Canyon Helicopters offers helicopter tours out of Tusayan.

Flightseeing tours also originate in Flagstaff, Page, Phoenix, Scottsdale and Williams in Arizona, and from Los Vegas, Nevada.

Guided Hikes and Vehicle Tours are offered in summer only by *Grand Canyon Trail Guides,* Santa Fe Railroad Depot, Grand Canyon Village. You can also rent backpacking equipment – again, in summer ony. Trail Guides is a division of Canyoneers Inc, PO Box 2997, Flagstaff, AZ 86003.

Mule Trips into the depths of the Grand Canyon are very, very popular, so make your reservations well in advance! South Rim trips operate year-round, weather permitting, to Plateau Point (one day) and Phantom Ranch (two days). Contact the Reservations Department, Grand Canyon National Park Lodges, Grand Canyon, AZ 86023; (602) 638-2401.

North Rim trips descend the North Kaibab trail to Roaring Springs, a nine mile round trip. For reservations, write to Grand Canyon Scenic Rides, Kanab, UT 84741, or inquire at the Transportation Desk, Grand Canyon Lodge.

If you weigh more than 200 lbs, start slimming now. You must weigh less, be physically fit, and over 12 years of age to ride the mules. Also required: long trousers and rugged shoes. Wide-brimmed hats and long-sleeved shirts, *de rigeur* in warm weather, can be rented from the Transportation Desk, Grand Canyon Lodge.

River Trips A float trip along the Colorado River through the Grand Canyon is the quintessence of adventure. Trips are aboard oar or motor-powered craft and vary in length from three to 18 days. (You can get a taste of it on a five-hour, smooth water trip from Glen Canyon Dam to Lees Ferry. Enquire at the Transportation Desk, Grand Canyon Lodge.) For a list of river-running concessionaires, write to the Park Superintendent, Grand Canyon National Park, AZ 86023. Hurry: some trips are sold out more than a year in advance.

HAVASUPAI INDIAN RESERVATION

There is a Shangri-La to the west of the Grand Canyon's main park area, a remote, narrow canyon where turquoise-blue waterfalls spill from the heights and peach orchards stand out in sharp relief against crimson cliffs. **Havasu Canyon** is the home of the Supai Indians who have overnight accommodation in *guest lodges* and *campgrounds* for those prepared to make the arduous 2000-foot, six-mile descent to the canyon floor; it is another two miles to Supai village. If you'd rather not walk, you can arrange for horses to meet you at Hualapai Hilltop parking lot (where you must leave your car). Reservations are required for accommodations, the campgrounds and saddle horses. To make arrangements and obtain more information, write to the Havasupai Tourist Enterprise, Supai AZ 86435, or call (602) 448-2121.

Lake Mead National Recreation Area

Below the Grand Canyon the Colorado has been twice dammed to provide flood control and hydroelectric power for the West and the man-made lakes behind them comprise the river's second great year-round water playground. Soaking and sunning, backcountry hiking, fishing and wildlife watching are the attractions here.

Lake Mead is impounded by one of the highest dams ever built. Rising an awesome 726 feet from the river bed, the **Hoover Dam** plugs the Black Canyon of the Colorado like a massive concrete wedge. You can cross the canyon via the dam's 45-foot wide crest and take an elevator down some 500 feet for a guided tour of the power plant below. The **Exhibit Building** at the west end of the dam contains a topographical model of the whole Colorado River Basin. Flightsee the dam locally or from nearby Las Vegas.

Open daily, 7.30 am to 7.30 pm, Memorial Day to Labor Day; 8.30 am to 4.15 pm, rest of year; admission charge. Tel (602) 293-8367.

The recreation area also includes **Lake Mohave**, a slim lake compared with sprawling Lake Mead, confined by the Eldorado and Black Mountains, it extends 67 miles south of Hoover Dam to Davis Dam.

What to See and Do

Lake Mead's main recreational centers are at Temple Bar, Arizona, on the south shore; Boulder Beach, Las Vegas Wash, Callville Bay, Echo Bay and Overton Beach. On **Lake Mohave** are Willow Beach, Katherine Landing and Cottonwood Cove. Write to Play Mate Resort Marinas' Central Reservation Office, 767 South Cypress, La Habra, CA 90631; tel (213) 691-2235 or (714) 871-1476 for information on resort marinas at Boulder Beach Temple Bar, Overton and Katherine Landing. Del Webb Recreational Properties operates the resorts at Cottonwood Cove and Callville Bay. Call toll-free at 800-528-6154 or write Reservations, Del Webb Recreational Properties, Box 29040, Phoenix, AZ 85038. (Note that there's no lodging at Callville Bay.)

All developed areas have ranger stations, marinas with ramps, boat rentals and supplies, restaurants and stores amongst their facilities and all except Willow Beach have campgrounds. For general information on National Park Service facilities contact the Superintendent, Lake Mead National Recreation area, 601 Nevada Highway, Boulder City, NV 89005; tel (602) 293-4041.

Getting There

The nearest airport is at Las Vegas, Nevada; cars may be rented there. Las Vegas is also served by *Amtrak. Greyhound* will bus you to Bullhead City and to Las Vegas where you can connect with Las Vegas, *Tonopah & Reno Stagelines* service to Boulder City.

LAKE HAVASU CITY (LONDON BRIDGE)

'London Bridge is falling down, falling down, falling down . . .' And who but an American entrepreneur would have thought of transporting it block by block from England to the Arizona desert to serve as the showpiece of a resort city built in 1964? The bridge, the Colorado River and the Chemehuevi Mountains blend surprisingly well together, contributing with the climate to Lake Havasu City's rapid growth as a major recreational center. There are equestrian and watersports facilities, Colorado River tours, attractive beaches, championship golf courses, tennis courts and a 26-acre Elizabethan village with two pubs which have barmaids dressed in period costume. Nearby are Havasu Wildlife Refuge, its Topock Marsh unit home to the the rare birds, ghost towns, and 33 miles downstream, the old Indian trading center of **Parker** with its important **Colorado River Indian Tribes Museum** and **Library**. Write to Lake Havasu Area Chamber of Commerce, 2074 McCulloch Boulevard, Lake Havasu City, AZ 86403 for comprehensive information on the area's resorts and recreational facilities, or call (602) 855-4115.

NORTHEASTERN ARIZONA

Northeastern Arizona (and contiguous portions of Utah, Colorado and New Mexico) encompasses the traditional homelands of the Navajo and Hopi nations. The land is utterly unspoilt, high desert country, sculpted by the elements to an awesome grandeur over millions of years. Winter brings snow to the land; spring thaws turn the dirt roads into quagmires and fires the valleys with brilliantly colored wildflowers; and in summer, the temperatures hover in the high 90°s F. You can expect short, violent thunderstorms between mid-June and September. Fall is the ideal time for touring for the days are comfortably warm and sunny, and nights are cool.

You will need a car. Buses serve major cities, but most attractions are far from the highways, gas pumps and accommodation. Before you venture into the backcountry, do check conditions with the local office of the AAA, NAC or Highway Patrol, and pick up a few hints on safe driving in the desert. A good map and water are basics.

Phoenix and Flagstaff are the main gateways for touring the area. From Phoenix, follow SR 87 across the Mogollon Plateau, a magnificent region of forests and valleys that Zane Grey made famous in his novels, to Winslow; Second Mesa and Old Oraibi in the heart of the Hopi country are some 60 miles due north. Canyon de Chelly lies east of the Hopi country, in the vast Navajo reservation. To reach the area from Flagstaff, take I-40 east to Winslow and pick up SR 87.

HOPI RESERVATION

The Hopi, the People of Peace, have occupied the three bare mesas rising abruptly from the desert northeast of Flagstaff for at least 1500 years. Their traditions speak of a mythical underworld and a mysterious Red City to the south as their original home, and of a time of wandering. Certainly they are of diverse origins; many descend from the Anasazi, they speak a Shoshonean language, and are related culturally to the Pueblo Indians of northern New Mexico.

The Hopi entered recorded history in 1540 when a detachment of Coronado's expedition searching for the Seven Cities of Cibola rode into the easternmost villages of what is now called the Jadito Valley. Franciscan missionaries followed in 1629. When the Pueblo Revolt broke out along the upper Rio Grande in 1680, the Hopi were wholehearted participants – only the cattle and sheep of the Spanish were spared. From that time they have succeeded in remaining apart, preserving a spiritual and cultural independence. Even today most of the Hopi nation continue to practise the old ways.

These ways are based on a complex system of religious beliefs expressed in colorful ceremonies. Best known is the Snake Dance, climaxing many days of rituals during August, in which participants dance with live snakes in their mouths. Kachinas, supernatural beings from the underworld heaven, believed to dwell in the San Francisco Peaks, visit their villages between December and July. The Kachina doll so popular with collectors of Indian art are representations of these beings.

Visiting Hopi Villages Before visiting any of the Hopi villages you *must* obtain permission of the village leaders and notify the superintendent at the village to that effect. Permission to photograph, sketch or paint is also necessary. And do respect posted signs. For information and assistance, contact Hopi Tribal Headquarters, New Oraibi (tel (602) 834-2440); the Hopi Cultural Center, Second Mesa (tel (602) 734-2401); or the Hopi Indian Agency, Keams Canyon (tel (602) 738-2221).

Should you be fortunate enough to attend any of the Hopi dances (which are never publicised), please remember that these are religious ceremonials. Photographing and taping are absolutely forbidden.

First Mesa

First Mesa, most easterly of three mesas, containing three villages. At Polacca, a small community at the foot of the mesa, a side road leads up through Hano and Sichomovi to Walpi at the top of the ridge. This is not the pueblo sighted by the Spanish, which stood at the foot of the cliff, but its successor, founded between 1660 and 1700. The Snake Dance is performed here during odd numbered years. *Hano* is inhabited by descendants of Tewa refugees who fled the Rio Grande Valley after the Pueblo Revolt of 1680. The pottery and Kachina dolls of these villages are highly esteemed.

Second Mesa

Second Mesa towers above the junction of SR 87/264. Beside the highway you will find the **Hopi Cultural Center** complex, built in a style reminiscent of Pueblo architecture, which provides an excellent introduction to Hopi culture with its museum and arts and crafts shops. You can put up for the night at the Center's modern motel for $33 double high season (April to September). For reservations (essential during the summer season), phone (602) 734-2401. The motel's restaurant is open daily. Tours of the villages may be arranged at the reception desk.

The villages of Shongopovi, Shipolovi and Mishongnovi all date from around 1700. The Snake Dance is performed at Mishongnovi in odd-numbered years, at Shongopovi in even-numbered years.

Third Mesa

Crowning Third Mesa is **Old Oraibi**, a leading contender for the title of oldest continually inhabited community in the country. This dramatically situated village, blending so perfectly with the rock, dates from at least 1150. To the north are the ruins of a mission built by the Franciscans in 1629. Old Oraibi is seldom open to visitors.

New Oraibi, at the foot of the mesa, contains the headquarters of the Tribal Council. **Bacobi** and **Hotevilla**, three miles west, were founded in the early years of the 20th century. Craftworkers of these villages are well known for their basketry, Kachina dolls and sashes; dances are particularly colorful here.

Public campgrounds are located at Oraibi Wash, one mile east of Oraibi on SR 264, and near the Hopi Cultural Center. Both are open all year. There are motels and an all-year campground at **Keams Canyon**, 11.4 miles east of Polacca. The Hopi Indian Agency is also located here.

NAVAJO RESERVATION

The vast homelands of the Navajo nation cover more than 25,000 square miles of northeastern Arizona and portions of southeastern Utah and northwestern New Mexico, completely surrounding the Hopi Reservation. Within the reservation boundaries are three of the Southwest's most famous attractions, the **Canyon de Chelly**, **Monument Valley** and **Navajo National Monument**, spaced far apart but immensely rewarding for their natural beauty and antiquities.

The Navajo, who call themselves simply the *Dine* (the people) in their own tongue are descended from nomadic hunters and gatherers related to the Athabascan-speaking peoples of northwest Canada and to the Apaches. They first appeared in the Southwest around 1000 AD and were greatly influenced in the development of their culture by both the Pueblo Indians and by the Spanish – both of whom were a rich source of plunder for them. Neither Spain nor Mexico ever succeeded in dominating the Navajo and it took the Americans 17 years to do so, from 1846 until 1863 when the scorched-earth tactics employed by Colonel Christopher 'Kit' Carson destroyed the Navajo economy. Many Navajos retreated into wilderness fastnesses, such as the Canyon de Chelly; others surrendered to the Americans and endured the 'Long Walk' to Fort Sumner in New Mexico where they were held captive for four years. In 1868 they were permitted to return to a portion of their homelands in Arizona.

Today the Navajo are the most economically progressive and populous of the Indian tribes – uranium, gas, oil, and coal royalties supplement their traditional source of income, sheep and cattle herds. Tourism plays an important role in their economy and you will find yourself welcome among them. There are, of course, proprieties to observe: should you attend a ceremonial gathering, maintain a discreetly low profile and do not ask for explanations. Behave as you would in your own place of worship. Request permission before taking photographs of anyone at any time (a small gratuity is proper), and do not enter a *hogan,* the Navajo dwelling, without invitation. Before hiking or mountain climbing, do make certain you are not intruding on a sacred place for the Navajo regard the locations where legendary events took place as holy ground.

Canyon de Chelly

Drive east on SR 264 and north on SR 63 a distance of 87.5 miles from Second Mesa, to visit one of the grandest monuments of Anasazi culture in Arizona. The Navajos have lived in Canyon de Chelly (d'Shay) and its tributary canyons Del Muerto and Black Rock for 300 years, but long before then the prehistoric Basketmakers constructed circular pit dwellings at the base of the stupendous red sandstone cliffs, which in places rise a sheer 1000 feet above the canyon floor. The monument contains hundreds of ruins of apartment-style dwellings built by their descendants between 1100 and 1300 in caves and crevices of the rock. There is evidence of sporadic occupation by the Hopis after 1300, and pictographs on the canyon walls date from the earliest period until Navajo times. Today, descendants of the

Navajos who came here in the 17th century use the canyon as summer range for their livestock and for farming.

Most spectacular of the Anasazi cliff dwellings is the **White House,** about five miles east of the visitor center. Tree ring dating shows it was occupied between 1060 and 1275. It is the only ruin which you may enter on your own, for under the terms of the treaty by which the US government leased the monument lands from the Navajo nation, visitors are not allowed in the canyons unless accompanied by an authorized guide. Good views of **Sliding Rock, Antelope House** and **Mummy Cave** ruins are obtained from the monument roads; park rangers at the visitor center will help you arrange for a guide and the necessary permits to tour the canyon floor. Justin's Thunderbird Lodge, near monument headquarters, offers jeep tours of the canyons between April 1 and October 31. Half-day tours presently cost $18; full-day tours with lunch included are $30.

Places to Stay & Eat

Camping is permitted only in the *Cottonwood Campground* near the visitor center. *Justin's Thunderbird Lodge* offers meals and lodging (double rooms in the lodge or motel units range from $36 (summer), and you should have a reservation. Write to Thunderbird Lodge, box 548, Chinle, AZ 86503, or call (602) 674-5443 or 674-5265.

Canyon de Chelly Motel (PO Box 295, Chinle, AZ 86503; tel (602) 674-5288). Off SR 63, near entrance to the monument. Air-conditioned rooms, TV and restaurant. Rates from $42 double (summer).

Accommodation and meals are also available at nearby Chinle.

For further information on monument visitor services, write to the Superintendent, Canyon de Chelly National Monument, Box 588, Chinle, AZ 86503; tel (602) 674-5436.

Hubbel Trading Post

Back in 1876, a young man from Pajarito, New Mexico, opened a trading post in the low stone building that stands beside the highway about a mile west of Ganado on SR 264. 'Don Lorenzo' Hubbell's establishment is still doing business in the traditional way and offers a fascinating glimpse of the life of an Indian trader's family a century ago. Navajos foregather here to exchange news and meet old friends as much as to trade their beautifully handcrafted rugs and jewelry for supplies stacked on shelves behind the massive counters.

The trading post and Hubbell home have been a National Historic Site since 1967 and park rangers conduct tours through the Hubbell house daily. Open daily 8 am to 6 pm, May 1 to September 30; 8 am to 5 pm rest of the year; closed New Year's, Thanksgiving and Christmas days; tel (602) 755-3254.

Monument Valley

This vast region lies some 73 miles northwest of the Canyon de Chelly as the crow flies (but 128 miles by road via Mexican Water and Kayenta). Within it is the most famous section of the Navajo Reservation, **Monument Valley Navajo Tribal Park**, containing an astonishing array of red sandstone spires and buttes, weathered over millions of years to fantastic shapes which the play of light continually transforms. Their great beauty has long made the valley a favorite location with western moviemakers and you will no doubt have a sense of *deja vu* if you saw John Ford's classic *Stagecoach* or *How the West was Won.*

Begin your visit to Monument Valley at the **Visitor Centre** four miles southeast of US 163. There are good views of some of the rock formations from its observatory, and you can purchase Navajo arts and crafts in the sales room. There is a 14-mile loop drive around the valley that you can make in your own vehicle; for jeep trips into the rugged back country, enquire at the visitor center or get in touch with Gouldings Lodge and Trading Post, tel (801) 727-3231. There is a primitive campground at the visitor center.

Visitor center open 8 am to 6 pm in summer, 8 am to 5 pm rest of the year; admission charge; (602) 725-3287.

Navajo National Monument

About 30 miles from Kayenta an important group of 13th century cliff dwellings – Betatakin, Keet Seel and Inscription House – is preserved amid the rugged country of Navajo National Monument. The visitor center is at Monument Headquarters in **Betatakin** – to get there, turn off US 160 at Black Mesa onto SR 564 and travel north for nine miles. Here a steep 1½-mile trail leads to the ancient apartment dwelling built in a great cave in the canyon wall. Several of the original roofs are still in place. You may explore the ruins only on a three-hour tour conducted by park rangers daily in summer at 8.30 am and 1.30 pm. There is a 20-person limit per tour. You can obtain a good view from Betatakin Point a short distance from the visitor center.

Visiting **Keet Seel**, Arizona's largest and best preserved cliff dwellings, is something of an adventure. The eight-mile trail is difficult, and only 20 persons a day are permitted access between April and September (closed the rest of the year). You may hike in (be prepared to ford the stream) or take a Navajo guided horseback trip which leaves from the visitor center at 8.30 am. To do either, you must register with Monument headquarters by 4 pm on the preceding day. For information, hiking permits, or to reserve horses, get in touch with the Superintendent, Navajo National Monument, Tonalea, AZ 86044; tel (602) 672-2366.

Inscription House, 25 miles northwest of Monument headquarters, may not be open to visitors. If it is, there is a 10-person limit. Check with the park rangers. At the visitor centre you will find a Navajo arts and crafts shop; camping facilities are nearby.

Open daily, 8 am to 6 pm June 1 to August 31; 8 am to 5 pm rest of the year; tel (602) 672-2366.

Places to Stay
Accommodation in the Monument Valley-Navajo National Monument area is far apart. Reservations are advised.
Gouldings Lodge and Trading Post (PO Box 1-AAA, Monument Valley, UT 84536; tel (801) 727-3231). Closest to Monument Valley Navajo Tribal Park, two miles west of US 163. Air-conditioned rooms, restaurant. KOA campground adjoins. Rates from $38 double.
Holiday Inn (PO Box 307, Kayenta, AZ 86033; tel (602) 697-3221). One mile south of US 160 at junction with US 163, large, elegant, with all the conveniences, including a pool, air-conditioning and TV. Restaurant. Rates from $48 double.
Navajo Campground (Navajo National Monument, Tonalca, AZ 86044; tel (602) 672-2366). 20 miles south of Kayenta, off US 160 and SR 564. Managed by National Park Service. Open mid-May to mid-October.
Wetherill Inn Motel (PO Box 175, Kayenta, AZ 86033; tel (602) 697-3231). Located about a mile north of junction of US 160 on US 163. Air-conditioning, color TV. Reservation deposit required in summer. Cafe nearby. Rates $38 double.

SOUTHERN ARIZONA
Between Phoenix and the Mexican border extends a vast tract of the Sonoran Desert given perspective by the sudden upthrusting of volcanic peaks. Irrigation has turned much of it into rich agricultural land near Phoenix; further, the desert comes into its own again. For all its harshness, people have managed to live here from prehistoric times – or earlier perhaps. Prehistoric remains indicate that the ancestors of the Pima and Papago Indians settled here over 10,000 years ago. In the 17th century the Spanish established dominion with a scattering of missions and presidios, of which Tucson was the most important. The Americans gained a footing in the early decades of the 19th century; by the Gadsden Purchase of 1854, the region became part of Arizona Territory.

Cattle ranching and mining traditionally were the economic staples. Today, tourism dominates. Southern Arizona, with Tucson still its capital, is a popular refuge for winter and spring vacationers with a yen for the sun and a taste of the Old West with all the trimmings. On your way to the perfect tan, you can explore a very different land where Spanish is spoken as often as English and evidence of a rich history is everywhere at hand.

Casa Grande Ruins National Monument
I-10 is the direct route from Phoenix to Tucson, a distance of 125 miles. About 40 miles south you will see signs pointing the way to Casa Grande, a four-story adobe apartment building and watchtower built by the Hohokam Indian farmers of the Gila Valley six centuries ago. The detour is worthwhile: in addition to the tower (which still bears the imprints of the hands of its makers), there are remains of a pueblo and two circular ball-courts similar to those of Mexico and of Wupatki, near Flagstaff. The Visitor Center **museum** contains artefacts taken from the complex and is open daily 8 am to 6 pm. Self-guiding tour; ranger-conducted talks; admission charge; tel (602) 723-3172.

TUCSON
Arizona Territory's former capital, Tucson, lies on a broad, flat plain, ringed by six mountain ranges. It's had a colorful history, whether you begin with the prehistoric Indian village of **Chuk Son**, located at the base of what is now a

mountain, or with the founding of a presidio here by the Spanish in 1776. Early American travelers sprinkled their descriptions with comparisons to Sodom and Gomorrah. Every man went armed to the teeth, it seemed, and street fights were daily occurrences. Time was measured in drinks – 'first drink time', 'second drink time', and so on – and most of the businesses conducted by the Americans were either saloons, dance halls, or gambling saloons. It was not the kind of place even the most intrepid tourist should consider.

A very pleasant modern resort city now stands on the site of this den of iniquity. The **Tucson Community Center** at Main and Congress Sts downtown symbolizes the city's new look. Completed in 1971, it includes a large convention hall, a theater and a music hall, interconnected with landscaped patios. **La Placita's** collection of boutiques, art galleries and restaurants, surrounding a charming old bandstand left over from Territorial Days, offer good browsing and refuge from the desert sun. At the southern end, at 151 S Granada Avenue, is the **Casa del Gubernador (Fremont House Museum)** (1858), rented in the 1880's by Arizona's fifth governor, John C. Fremont. This adobe is now a museum, furnished with period antiques.

Open Wednesday to Saturday, 10 am to 4 pm; tel 622-0956.

Things to See & Do
El Presidio Park
A pedestrian bridge over Congress St leads to El Presidio Park, situated in the southern portion of the presidio founded by the Spanish in 1776. Here you will find the **Kino Memorial**, a monument to Father Eusebio Francisco Kino, the Jesuit missionary-explorer who opened up so much of Sonora and Baja California for Spain in the alte 17th century. Kino is an extraordinary figure in the history of the Southwest. Born in the tiny mountain town of Segno in the Italian Tyrol in 1645,

he entered the Society of Jesuits and was sent to Mexico in 1678 where his talents as explorer, cartographer and administrator were brilliantly deployed. In a remarkable career he founded 29 missions, baptised more than 4000 converts, and explored much of the vast Sonoran Desert from the San Pedro River to the Colorado. Kino died in 1711. For two centuries the exact whereabouts of his grave was unknown; then in 1966, after three years of spellbinding detective work, archeologists discovered the remains of The Padre on Horseback in Magdalena, not far from Nogales, Mexico.

Tucson Museum of Art
Follow Meyer Avenue half a block north from the Alameda St intersection and you come to the Tucson Museum of Art, housing pre-Columbian artefacts, Spanish Colonial furnishings and paintings, and objects recalling Tucson's multi-cultural heritage. In the grounds are three historic adobes dating from the last years of the 19th century, the **Fish House** (1868), the **Hiram Sanford Stevens Home** and the **Leonardo Romero House** (c 1868). A fourth adobe, **La Casa Cordova**, is believed to be one of Tucson's oldest surviving buildings. It has been restored as a Mexican heritage museum and retains its unplastered walls and earth floor. Open from Tuesday through Saturday, 1 to 5 pm; Sunday, 10 am to 5 pm; admission free; tel 624-2333.

University of Arizona Campus
A mile or so northeast of the downtown area is the University of Arizona campus, attractively planted with more than 150 different varieties of trees and shrubs. A self-guiding tour pamphlet is available at the Student Union information desk or from the **Arizona State Museum** at Park Avenue and University Boulevard. The museum's collections of Southwestern archeology are outstanding ranging from early Stone Age cultures of 10,000

years ago to those of the modern Indian. Open Monday to Saturday, 9 am to 5 pm; Sunday 2 to 5 pm; closed holidays; admission free; tel 626-1604.

At the **Grace H Flandreau Planetarium** you'll find a 16 inch telescope available for night viewing and more than 30 exhibits. An hour-long planetarium show is held three times a week.

Exhibit areas open Tuesday through Sunday, 1 to 6 pm and 7 to 10 pm; admission free; planetarium shows $2; tel 626-4515.

Arizona Pioneers Historical Society

Across Park Avenue from the campus, at 848 E 2nd St, is the Arizona Pioneers' Historical Society's collection of pioneer artefacts and research library. Open Monday to Friday, 9 am to 5 pm; Saturday 9 am to 1 pm; Sunday 1 to 5 pm; admission free; 628-5774.

Fort Lowell Museum & Park

Also of interest is Fort Lowell Museum, dating back to the Apache wars when the fort served as base for cavalry and infantry. The reconstructed Commanding Officer Quarters contain four rooms furnished as they were in 1885; military equipment is also displayed.

Open Tuesday to Saturday, 10 am to 4 pm; admission free; tel 885-3832.

The grounds of the fort are a charming haven, with a swimming pool and shaded picnic tables among the amenities.

Barrio Historico

Take time to visit the Barrio Historico south of the Community Center (Cushing St marks the dividing line) which contains at least 150 adobes and is being restored by private individuals to its late 19th century splendor. Notable are the **Montijo House**, one of Tucson's grand old homes, and **El Fronterizo**, printing of a Spanish language newspaper founded in 1878.

On the 300 to 400 block of Main Avenue is **El Tiradito Shrine** (The Cast-away), known locally as the 'Wishing Shrine'. Here, according to popular belief, the young herder Juan Oliveras was killed in a dispute over the favors of a lovely senorita. Pious townsfolk, concerned that Juan was buried in unconsecrated ground, prayed for his soul and lit candles at the spot. Lighted candles are still placed here at night in the belief that your wish comes true if your candle remains burning until morning.

Places to Stay

Tucson is well provided with accommodation in the budget and moderate price brackets as well as with resort hotels and guest ranches. Local motel rows are Miracle Mile and the Tucson Benson Freeway. Check with the Metropolitan Tucson Convention & Visitors Bureau at (602) 624-1817 for help. Prices quoted below are for the winter season – substantial discounts can often be obtained in summer.

American Six Motel (3688 S Park Avenue, Tucson 85713; tel (602) 294-4492). Located some 3½ miles south of downtown area. Heated pool, air-conditioning, color TV. Restaurant next door. Rates from $22 double.

Budget Host American Star (810 E Benson Highway, Tucson 85713; tel (602) 884-5800. Amenities include a heated pool, air-conditioning and TV. Restaurant nearby. Rates: from $28.95.

Ghost Ranch Lodge (801 W Miracle Mile (Box 50166), Tucson 85703; tel (602) 791-7565, 800-352-1222 (in Arizona), 800-528-1234 (outside Arizona). In eight acres of grounds, 3½ miles north of downtown area. Two heated pools, putting green, air-conditioning, color TV, restaurant. Eight cottages with kitchens and private patios, too. Rates from $38 double.

Marriott Hotel (180 W Broadway, Tucson 85701; tel (602) 624-8711). Close to La Placita shops. Pleasant atmosphere with patios, swimming pool, air-conditioning, color TV. Rates from $65 double.

Motel Six (960 S Freeway, Tucson 85705; tel (602) 624-6345. Also 1031 E Benson Highway, Tucson 85705; tel 884-8107). Heated pool, of course, and TV available. Rates from $19.95 double.

Guest Ranches

Hacienda del Sol (Hacienda del Sol Rd, Tucson 85718; tel (602) 299-1501.) In the desert, nine miles east of Tucson. Heated pool, exercise room, tennis courts. Not all rooms air-conditioned. Airport transportation. Rates from $125 double.

Sundancer Saddle & Surry Resort (4110 Sweetwater Drive, Tucson 85705; tel (602) 743-0411.) Surrounded by 100,000 acre game sanctuary. Facilities include pool, tennis courts, putting green. Riding, hunting in season. Not all rooms air-conditioned. TV (some color). Airport transportation. Rates from $188 double.

Places to Eat

Bobby McGee's Conglomeration Costumed employees, salad bar in a bathtub, tiffany lamps, packing crate booths . . . and disco dancing. Reservations recommended for this informal, amusing place. (M)

Dinner daily 6424 E Tanque Verde Rd; tel 886-5551.

El Adobe Housed in the 'Old Adobe' (1868) in the Community Center Complex. Dine indoors or on the patio on Mexican cuisine. (M)

Lunch, dinner. Open daily except Sundays. 40 W Broadway; tel 791-7548.

Organ Stop Pizza Satisfying slices of pizza, great sandwiches and a cheerful atmosphere. Organ music every evening.

Open daily, 6350 E Tanque Verde Rd; tel 885-6733.

The Tack Room The informally elegant Tack Room has won Mobil's coveted 5-star rating and Travel-Holiday's award for its cuisine that features continental dishes. Wonderful views of the desert, too. (E)

Dinner daily (closed Mondays in summer). At Rancho del Rio, 2800 N Sabino Canyon; tel 298-2351.

Triple C Chuckwagon Fifteen miles north of Tucson, but you'll probably agree the authentic chuck wagon fare and after-dinner show are worth the drive. Reservations required. (B)

One-sitting dinner. Open Tuesday through Saturday, November to mid-May. 8900 W Bopp Rd; tel 883-2333.

Nightlife & Entertainment

Professional theater in Tucson is performed by the Arizona Civic Theater. Performances are held in the Community Center's Little Theater. The Tucson Symphony Orchestra dominates the music scene with a 12-performance season from October to April. The University of Arizona may also be counted on, offering a six-month artists and celebrity series and concerts and dramas presented by the Drama Department and Musical College. There's also some well-supported community theater.

Nightlife centers on the lounges, dinner theaters and a handful of Country and Western clubs. For who's playing where, consult the free *Tucson Visitor*.

Getting There

Air Tucson International Airport is served by major national and international airlines. Tucson Transit buses and Arizona Stage Coach limousines provide transportation into town.

Bus *Greyhound's* depot is at E Broadway and 4th Avenue; Information: tel 792-0972. *Continental Trailways* are nearby, at 201 E Broadway. Information tel 882-0005.

Citizen Auto Stage, the bus line with daily trips to Nogales, Mexico, operates out of the Greyhound bus depot. Information: tel 792-0972.

Getting Around

Public Transportation *Sun Tran,* 315 S Plummer Avenue, operates the buses. Ask for route map and time schedule. Information: tel 792-9222.

Taxis *Tucson Yellow Cab Co,* 625 N Stone Avenue (tel 624-6611). Current rates are 70c for the first quarter mile, 70c for each mile thereafter.

Airport Limousine *Arizona Stage Coach,* serving all major hotels. Fare to downtown Tucson runs around $4.25. For information call 889-9681.

Limousine *Gray Line* of Tucson (see above); tel 622-8811.

Tours

Bus *Gray Line of Tucson* (PO Box 1991, Tucson 85701; tel (602) 622-8811.) Several tours year-round. Among them: Old Tucson or Arizona-Sonora Desert Museum with Mission San Xavier del Bac, $12.95; Nogales, Mexico, $12.30; Tombstone and Boot Hill, $13.70. Also offered are two and three-night trips.

Ghost Town Excursions (PO Box 18412, Tucson 85701; tel (602) 884-0777.) One-day Prospector's Tour (weekends only) of Tombstone and south-east Arizona's ghost towns, $38.50 – three days advance reservation required. There's also a two day/one night tour of the mining country for $132 (single), $119.50 (double).

Useful Addresses

Metropolitan Tucson Convention & Visitors Bureau (120 West Broadway Boulevard, PO Box 3028, Tucson 85702; tel (602) 624-1817). Maps, brochures and accommodation information. Open Monday to Friday, 8 am to 5 pm.

AAA-Arizona Automobile Association (228 W Drachman, Tucson 85705; tel (602) 623-5871.) Open Monday to Friday, 8.30 am to 5 pm.

Mexican Border Office is at 941 N Grand Avenue, Nogales 85621; tel (602) 287-2749 – open Monday to Saturday, 8 am to 5 pm.

Meeting the Americans

Sierra Club (tel (602) 887-2078.)

AROUND TUCSON

Old Tucson

Old Tucson is Tucson's most popular attraction, set amid the saguaro covered range of Tucson Mountain Park 12 miles west of the city. You've probably been there before, courtesy of Hollywood's filmmakers, who have expanded Columbia Pictures' 1939 replica of Tucson in the 1860s (created for the epic *Arizona)* into a 320-acre combination of theme park and movie studio. *Wagon Train, Gunsmoke* and *The Rifleman* are just a few of the famous shows filmed here – and it may well be that your favorite stars are on location when you visit.

If walking where John Wayne hath trod is not enough, you can ride a stage coach, antique car, frontier train and an ore car (through the Iron Door Mine), watch gunslingers blaze away on Front St, or gallop along desert trails on a rented horse. There's a guided tour behind scenes at the sound studio which shows some of the tricks of movie making, and the Arizona Theater shows a film tracing the history of Old Tucson. It's open daily from 9 am to 6 pm; 9.30 am to 5.30 pm all inclusive admission $5.95; tel (602) 883-0100.

Pima Air Museum

For antique aircraft buffs, Pima Air Museum is a must. Located on Davis Monthan Air Force Base, the museum displays a fine collection of nearly 100 vintage aircraft, some of them on loan from the Smithsonian Institution in Washington. Open daily, 10 am to 4.30 pm; weekends and holidays until 6 pm; tel (602) 889-0462.

Arizona-Sonora Desert Museum

If you would like to understand the desert that surrounds you, pay a visit to the Arizona-Sonora Desert Museum, 14 miles west of Tucson via the Speedway at

Kinney Rd. Picked as one of the world's most oustanding zoos by the BBC, it's ingenious layout combines the best aspects of indoor museum, outdoor zoo and botanical gardens. In the zoo area you will find almost all the desert creatures – ocelot, bobcat, jaguarundi and margay, as well as jaguar, wolves, bear, coyote, bighorn sheep, beaver and otter. There is a fine display of desert plant life too, and the **Congden Earth Sciences Center** features a walk through the history of the earth by means of a simulated limestone cave and explanatory disaplays. Open daily from 7 am to sundown, June 1 to Labor Day; 8.30 am to sundown rest of year; admission $5; tel (602) 883-1380.

Saguaro National Monument

Divided into two sections, Saguaro National Monument preserves great stands of towering saguaro cacti in the Rincon and Tucson Mountains north of Tucson. These cacti, which have a lifespan of 150 to 200 years and can attain a height of 50 feet, grow only in southern Arizona and Sonora, Mexico. They bloom in May and June, and the tart red berries which ripen in July come to table locally as jams, jellies and beverages.

Nearest is **Tucson Mountain Unit**, 15 miles northwest of Tucson via Speedway Boulevard. Here a nine-mile scenic loop road and hiking trails lead through young saguaro. **Rincon Mountain Unit**, 17 miles east of town via East Broadway, contains much older specimens. There is a nine-mile loop drive here, too, and in winter park rangers conduct nature walks. Enquire about them at the visitor center.

Rincon Mountain visitor center is open daily 8 am to 5 pm; drive 8 am to sunset; admission charge; Tucson Mountain Unit open daily, 8 am to 5 pm; admission free; tel (602) 296-8576.

Kitt Peak National Observatory

Located in the Quinlan Mountains on the Papago Indian Reservation about 40 miles east of Tucson is one of the most important centers of ground-based optical astronomy in the country. Kitt Peak National Observatory is not only the site of the largest solar collection of astronomical instruments but also of the largest solar telescope, the McMath, 500 feet in length, with three-fifths of it underground. At the visitor's center you can actually operate a solar telescope as well as browse through exhibits featuring models of telescopes and research programs under way at the observatory. Films are shown on weekends and holidays.

You can follow the self-guiding trail or take one of the guided tours conducted at 10.30 am and 1.30 pm every Saturday, Sunday and holidays – not least of the attractions is the view from the observation deck of the Moyall telescope which extends over 100 miles in any direction on most days.

Open daily; 10 am to 4 pm, save Christmas Day; picnic sites but no food facilities. admission free; tel (602) 325-9200.

SOUTH TO THE BORDER

In Tucson you are only 65 miles from the Mexican border and the twin cities of Nogales-Arizona and Nogales-New Mexico. This easy day trip can be made by tour bus or aboard Citizen Auto Stage buses (see Getting There, Tucson), but preferably by car for I-19 follows the lovely and historic Santa Cruz River Valley much of the way.

Mission San Xavier Del Bac

Perhaps the finest example of Spanish mission architecture in the country lies nine miles southwest of Tucson in the Papago Indian Reservation (just off the freeway). The 'White Dove of the Desert', Mission San Xavier del Bac traces its origins to the mission established by the legendary Father Eusebio Kino in 1700.

Kino's church at Bac was the first of three, possibly four, to occupy the site; the present magnificent structure was begun in 1783 and completed in 1797. It is a blend of the Byzantine, Moorish and late Mexican Renaissance styles, laid out in the form of a Greek cross. Ornamentation is unusually rich, with barely any part of the interior left plain – the reredos is a particularly impressive example of the Churrigueresque. The two lion-like figures on either side of the communion rail represent the 'Lions of Castille' who reigned over Spain in the last decades of the 18th century. To the left of the altar you will find a reclining figure of St Francis Xavier, still the object of pilgrimage.

Open daily except Sundays, 9 am to 6 pm; taped 15-minute lectures hourly, 9.30 am to 4.30 pm; no admission charge but donations accepted; tel (602) 294-2628.

TUBAC

The old Spanish garrison town of Tubac, 32 miles farther on, is the first European settlement in Arizona. Founded in 1752 to protect the Jesuit missions, Tubac was for 10 years under the command of Juan Bautista de Anza who, in 1775 set out from the presidio with a small company of soldiers and 136 men, women and children to begin the settlement of San Francisco Bay. Later the town flourished as the commercial center for silver mining in the area. Today, you will find a vigorous artists' and retirement colony, with a number of craft shops, studios and an excellent restaurant. Tubac's annual **Festival of the Arts**, held in February, is a highlight of Southern Arizona's events calendar.

Tubac Presidio State Historic Park carefully preserves the fragments of the old presidio. Its museum contains artefacts of the Spanish Colonial period and is open daily, 8 am to 5.30 pm; closed Christmas day; admission charge; tel (602) 398-2252.

Tumacacori National Monument

On the lonely desert, two miles south of Tubac, stands the impressive shell of **Mission San Jose de Tumacacori**, founded by Father Kino on the abandoned site of a Pima village about 1691. The Romanesque buildings which stand today have their roots in the late 18th century when the Franciscans began construction of a mission church they hoped would rival the splendor of San Xavier del Bac. For five years that hope seemed realized, until the expulsion of the Franciscans and the firing of the mission by hostile Apaches in the 1820s initiated a century of neglect and pillage. Not until Tumacacori was declared a National Monument in 1908 was any attempt made to preserve the ruins. At the visitor center museum, exhibits relate their history and use.

Tumacacori is the focus of many legends of the days of the padres. You will probably hear that before the missionaries left, they buried vast quantities of gold and built an underground passage from the mission to be used in case of attack. Alas for romanticism, no trace of either has ever been found. It's open daily, 8 am to 6 pm; admission charge; tel (602) 398-2341.

NOGALES

Both Nogales, Arizona and Nogales, Mexico are of considerable historic interest, but crossing the border to take advantage of duty-free shopping on the Mexican side is the main attraction. No car permit is required to drive across the border; you may prefer to park on the US side and walk, bus or taxi into Mexico. If you are not an American citizen, be sure to carry your passport (properly visa-ed for Mexico and for re-entry to the US) as it will be inspected by US officials on your return.

Nogales' markets and stores brim with

Mexican handicrafts – silver, and glass items, leather goods, pottery and basketry are good buys. You will also find Japanese cameras and optical products, French perfumes and silk, German cutlery and cameras among the many imports from around the world. Two things to remember: compare prices before you buy for they vary considerably (bargaining is *de rigeur,* of course) and anticipate paying duty on some items when you re-enter the US. You may only bring back one quart of liquor into Arizona per adult per month.

On your way back to Tucson, try state routes 82 and 83 as an alternative to I-19. You'll get a glimpse of the lovely ranch country around Patagonia and Sonoita and add only a few miles to the drive.

TOMBSTONE

No visit to the Tucson area would be complete without a look at the 'Town Too Tough To Die'. Tombstone, epitome of the Old West of fact, folklore and TV, traces its history back to 1877 when Edward Schieffelin set out into Apache hill country in search of silver despite warnings that all he would find would be his grave. Instead he found rich ledges of silver and, tongue lodged firmly in his cheek, named his claim 'The Tombstone'.

The boom town which sprang up in the rush that followed attracted some of the Old West's most famous personalities – Wyatt Earp and his brothers, 'Doc' Holliday, Bat Masterson, Luke Short, the Clanton Brothers and the McLaurys, spawning a raft of legends that Tombstone has worked effectively since the decline of the silver mines. The **OK Corral** where the Earp Brothers and Doc Holliday shot it out with the Clantons and the McLaurys on October 27, 1881, stands between Third and Fourth on Allen St. Re-enactments each Sunday at 2 pm; admission charge; tel 457-2227.

Next to the entrance to the Corral is 'Historama', a multimedia presentation recounting Tombstone's history. Shows are presented on the hour daily between 9 am and 5 pm and there is a small admission charge.

A stroll around Tombstone's museums throws light on those explosive days. The **Wells Fargo Museum and General Store,** 511 Allen St, and the **Territorial Courthouse** display interesting memorabilia. Particularly evocative is the **Bird Cage Theater** (1881), once a notorious night spot where the waitresses warbled prettily as they sold the miners drinks. The original furnishings, fixtures and interior remain intact. The theater is open daily from 9 am to 5 pm; small admission fee. Also of interest is **Schieffelin Hall** at 4th and Fremont Sts, one of the largest adobe buildings in the West.

A refreshing reminder that Tombstone was not merely an arena for violence is the **world's largest rose tree,** shading the patio of the Rose Tree Inn Museum at Fourth and Toughnut Sts. This botanical wonder has a trunk eight feet in circumference and extends over 6000 square feet. The original cutting came from Scotland in 1884. Also on display is antique furniture brought to Tombstone by covered wagon in 1880. Open daily, 9 am to 5 pm; admission charge; 457-3326.

Don't leave Tombstone without visiting **Boothill Graveyard,** where weathered headboards record the manner of a citizen's transition, to wit: 'John Blair, died of smallpox. Cowboy throwed Rope over Feet & Dragged Him to his Grave.' Open daily, 8 am to 6 pm; donation.

For light refreshment, drop by the *Oriental Saloon,* where Bat Masterson and Luke Short used to deal faro; the management pushes a fine line in sandwiches today. The famous Crystal Palace Saloon is still operating at its old stand on Allen St.

Tombstone attracts a large number of visitors and accommodation is limited – reservations should be made well ahead if you want to stop over, especially during the annual **Helldorado Days** festival in October.

Festivals & Events

Arizona's multi-cultural heritage is reflected most colorfully in a year-round calendar of events and festivals. Those listed below are only the more famous of those held in the area covered by this guide.

January
: *Annual Square Dance Festival*, Tucson
Lost Dutchman's Days Celebration Parade and Rodeo, Apache Junction
Hopi Arts & Crafts Guild Show, Phoenix

February
: *La Fiesta de Los Vaqueros* – rodeos, parades and carnival entertainment, Tucson
Parada del Sol and 'all star' rodeo, Scottsdale
Gold Rush Days, Wickenburg

March
: *Rodeo of Rodeos* featuring 'world class' cowboys, Phoenix
Pima Indians Mu-Cha-Tha, celebration with rodeos, bazaar – Sacaton

March or April
: *Yaqui Indian Holy Week Ceremonials*, New Pascua Village

April
: *Tucson Festival Week*, Tucson
Heard Museum Indian Fair, Phoenix

July
: *Annual Frontier Days, Independence Day*, Prescott

August
: *Annual Ceremonial Dances* (not always open to the public),Hopi Indian Reservation

September
: *Navajo Tribal Fair*, Window Rock

October
: *Feast of St Francis of Assisi*, with candlelight procession, Mission San Xavier del Bac, Tucson
Helldorado Days, Tombstone

November
: *Papago Indian Fair*, Sells
Arizona State Fair (the State's biggest show), Phoenix

December
: *San Xavier Fiesta* with fireworks and Indian dances, Mission San Xavier del Bac, Tucson

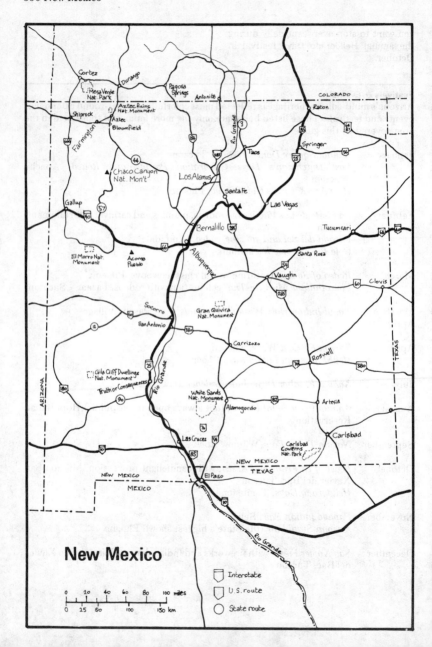

New Mexico

	Interstate
	U.S. route
	State route

0   20   40   60   80   100 miles
0   15   50   100   150 km

New Mexico

ALBUQUERQUE

Albuquerque lies astride the Rio Grande, sprawling across the valley floor toward the Sandia Mountains that raise a formidable wall of peaks to the northwest. At first sight New Mexico's largest town seems to have little to offer the tourist other than the convenience of an international airport and a number of good hotels in which to pass the night before moving on to Santa Fe. But for all the immediacy of Albuquerque's ugliness, there are half a dozen excellent reasons for stopping over a few hours.

Albuquerque can trace its beginnings to 1706 when Governor Francisco Cuervo y Valdas moved 12 Spanish families from Bernalillo to a new site on the river 17 miles south, naming it for his patron, the Duke of Alburquerque. The atmosphere of those early days lingers pleasantly in **Old Town**, the center of the old community lying off Central Avenue to the west of the modern downtown area. Here a number of older adobe buildings fronting the plaza have been attractively refurbished to form the nucleus of a shopping and dining complex.

On the northside of the plaza is the **Church of San Felipe Neri** (1706), the first structure completed by the Spanish settlers. Its rather plain interior may not detain you long, but before you pop into the little museum next door to browse through an astonishing collection of ecclesiastical bric-a-brac, note the height of the windows, set 20 feet above ground – the church was also a fortress in times of strife.

The **Indian Pueblo Center** at 2401 12th St NW is an excellent introduction to the arts and crafts of the Pueblo peoples. Outstanding examples of traditional and contemporary jewelry and pottery are for sale here, and the museum's interpretive displays provide insight into the forces that inspired them. A 'living arts' program complements the exhibits with programs of dance, film and drama; tours of Pueblo villages may be available. There's also a restaurant featuring typical Pueblo meals, which is open daily from 9 am to 5 pm; Sunday, noon to 5 pm; tel 843-7270.

The **University of New Mexico** campus is worth visiting for its architecture alone, a harmonious modern interpretation of old Pueblo forms that reflect the state's multicultural heritage, traditions and landscapes. The mile-high campus covers some 600 acres bounded by Central **Avenue entrance. The Information Office phone number is 277-5813.**

The **Maxwell Museum of Anthropology** is a high point for those interested in the complexity of Indian culture. Displays include pottery by Maria, San Ildefonso's renowned potter, Hopi Kachina dolls, basketry and jewelry, as well as costumes from around the world. Open from Monday to Friday, 9 am to 4 pm; Saturday, 10 am to 4 pm; Sunday 1.30 to 5 pm; tel 277-4404.

Student life centers around the plaza at noon; for a pleasant alfresco luncheon spot, you can't beat the shores of the small lake nearby, surrounded by flowering trees. Also of interest: the **Institute of Meteorites** and the **University Art Museum** and its rotating exhibits of modern art.

If you are interested in nuclear energy, the **National Atomic Museum** on Kirtland Air Force base offers much of interest. Here you'll find a collection of nuclear weapons, including examples of the first two atomic bombs, 'Little Boy' and 'Fat Man'. The base is located next to Albuquerque International Airport on Gibson Boulevard.

Open daily, 9 am to 5 pm; tel 844-8443.

Sandia Peak

We recommend a visit to Sandia Peak early in the morning or at the turn of the afternoon into evening to enjoy the colors of the landscape to their fullest, though the view from the top is spectacular at any hour. The country's longest aerial tramway (2.7 miles) will drop you off at the 10,378 feet level overlooking the Rio Grande Valley; on a clear day your eye can travel over 11,000 square miles. Easy-going trails wind through the pines of Cibola National Forest which surrounds you. For refreshments there are two good restaurants, one at the lower tramway terminal, the other two miles up.

Sandia Peak Tramway is accessible from either US 40 or US 25 approximately four miles from downtown Albuquerque.

Open daily, 9 am to 10 pm (except 10.30 am to 10 pm Memorial-Labor day); admission $6.75; $5.50 senior citizens; $5 students and children; tel 298-8518.

Places to Stay

Plenty of motels to choose between in the outskirts of the city on US 40 and US 25. In Albuquerque try:

AMFAC Hotel (2910 Yale SE, Albuquerque; tel (505) 843-7000). Large luxury hotel with heated swimming pool, tennis courts, dining room, cocktails and entertainment. Air-conditioning and color TV. Rates from $63.

The Regent of Albuquerque (3rd and Marquette NW, Albuquerque; tel (505) 247-3344. In the heart of the downtown area. Color TV, sauna, whirlpool, dining room, coffee shop and cocktail lounge.

Lorlodge Motel West (1020 Central Avenue SW, Albuquerque 87101; tel (505) 247-4023.) Comfortable with air-conditioning, TV (some color) and small heated pool. If they're full up, try *Lorlodge Motel East* at 801 Central Avenue NE. Rates from $18 double.

Sheraton Old Town Inn (800 Rio Grande NW, Albuquerque 87102; tel (505) 843-6300.) New addition to the chain, a short walk from Old Town's boutiques and restaurants.

Places to Eat

Indian Pueblo Cultural Center Restaurant Pueblo and American style dishes. Informal atmosphere. Perhaps your only opportunity to sample authentic Indian food. (B)

Lunch, dinner. Open daily. 2401 12th St NW; tel 843-7270.

La Crepe Michel Attractive small restaurant specialising in crepes, soups and quiches. (B)

Lunch daily; dinner Tuesday to Sunday. 400 San Felipe NW, Old Town; tel 243-4174.

La Esquina Authoritative Southwestern cuisine in Albuquerque's centrally located Galeria. Patio dining by a waterfall. (B/M)

Lunch, Monday to Wednesday; dinner Friday. First Plaza Galeria, Second and Tijeras; 242-3432.

La Placita Housed in the 18th century Casa del Armijo, this elegant restaurant serves New Mexican and American dishes. (M)

Lunch, dinner. Open daily. Old Town Plaza; tel 247-2204.

Tinnie's Maria Teresa Steaks and seafood in a beautifully restored mid-19th century hacienda. Reservations recommended. (E)

Dinner. Open daily. 618 Rio Grande NW: 242-3900.

Getting There

Air Albuquerque International Airport, approximately five miles from downtown Albuquerque, is served by major national carriers as well as by several commuter airlines.

Bus *Greyhound* and *Continental Trailways* services. Both use the bus depot at 300 2nd St SW. For information, call Greyhound at (505) 243-4435 and Continental Trailways at (505) 842-5511.

Rail *Amtrak* service. Phone toll free 1-800-252-0001 for information and reservations.

Useful Addresses

Albuquerque Chamber of Commerce (Convention Center, 401 2nd St NW (basement level), Albuquerque 87102; tel (505) 842-0220). Free pamphlets on dining, accommodation, sightseeing. Small charge for street map. Open Monday to Friday, 8.30 am to 5 pm.

AAA-New Mexico Division (2201 San Pedro Boulevard NE, Building 3, Albuquerque 87110; tel (505) 265-7611.) Members only services. Open Monday to Friday, 8 am to 5 pm.

ACOMA

Acoma is the stuff of which dreams are made. The ancient 'City of the Sky' clings to the crest of a vast outcropping soaring a sheer 357 feet above the desert floor, as isolated in place and spirit from other pueblos today as it was in 1539 when Father Marcos learned of a 'great city built on the rock' west of the Rio Grande. Allow a day for your excursion; the distance is approximately 130 miles round trip from Albuquerque via US 66 west and a side road, SR 23, that turns off to the south at Paraje.

This road passes close to **Katzimo**, the 'Enchanted Mesa', which the Acoma Indians regard as their ancestral home. Here, according to tradition, their forefathers lived until one day a fearful storm arose, sweeping away the ladder trail that was their only means of ascending Katzimo's perpendicular cliffs. Most of the Indians had been harvesting crops on the plain below, but three women who had remained on the mesa were stranded. One jumped and was buried where she fell. The cries of the two who starved to death may still be heard as the night grows long and the winter winds swirl around the great rock. Archaeologists have found some signs of human occupation on Katzimo but the evidence for a settlement is not conclusive.

Three miles farther you come to Acoma, blending so well with the rock that it is difficult to make out the buildings. Parking is provided at the base and in the plaza atop the mesa.

The top of the mesa extends about 70 acres, almost cut in two by a deep gorge. To the north are three parallel rows of stone and hand moulded adobe dwellings, rising three terraced stories in the characteristic pueblo style and separated from each other by *calles* or streets. The calle between the middle and south rows was built wider than the others to provide a ceremonial plaza.

The exact age of the buildings is not known. It's possible that the Acomas came from Mesa Verde in Colorado which was abandoned at the end of the 13th century, giving the pueblo a solid claim to the title of the oldest continuously inhabited town in the country. As you pass between the dazzling white buildings, take a look at their finely carved doors and corbels that probably date from the Spanish period. The beehive shaped structures outside the houses are ovens, still in use today.

Captain Hernando de Alvarado and his detachment of Spanish soldiers from Coronado's expedition were the first Europeans to visit Acoma in February, 1540; later that year Coronado himself stopped there on his march to Tiguex. Relations with the Indians were cordial at first but in 1598 the Acomas massacred 12 members of a later expedition, an act which was summarily avenged in a brief war which destroyed much of the pueblo.

Thirty years later Father Juan Ramirez came to Acoma as the first permanent missionary with no defence, according to the legend, save his breviary and his crucifix. Miraculously, the hail of arrows which greeted his arrival left him unharmed. As he climbed the steep trail leading to the village, a little girl accidentally fell from the summit to the rocks below. The friar's prayers initiated her equally miraculous revival, so impressing the hostile Indians that they soon became his disciples. You'll find his route, El Camino del Padre, on the northwest side of the mesa, a challenging ascent to this day.

Father Ramirez remained for 20 years. Under his supervision the Indians built the great mission church of **San Estevan Rey** which still stands at the south end of the plaza. It is a testament to his powers of persuasion, for all the materials – soil and water for the adobe, stone and timber – had to be brought up from the valley. The beams were logged in the Cebolleta mountains 30 miles away and carried on the shoulders of relays of Indians, who, it

is said, never permitted them to touch the earth until they were set in place. The old, dim painting of San Jose (St Joseph) is said to be the gift of Charles II of Spain; it is reputed to work miracles.

Admission $3; parking fee 50c; $8 a person photo fee; tel (505) 552-6606.

LAGUNA

As you return to Albuquerque, watch for the sign LAGUNA, just off US 66, about five miles from Paraje. This is the only pueblo founded under Spanish rule by order of Governor Piedro Rodriguez Cubero in 1699, and one of the largest. Spanish and Indian architecture blend interestingly here, but the chief attraction is the **Church of San Jose de Laguna**, completed in 1706. The interior is considered one of the handsomest in New Mexico, with a ceiling of brightly painted saplings laid in a herringbone pattern, and an unusually ornate chancel. The chancel ceiling is richly decorated with Indian symbols of the sun, moon, stars and a rainbow. The side walls of the church are covered with murals. For information, tel (505) 552-6651.

ISLETA

Formerly on an island in the Rio Grande which has altered its course and left it high and dry, the ancient pueblo of Isleta lies 13 miles south of Albuquerque. Although the date of its foundation is unknown, tradition holds that the ancestors of the Isleta Indians came from the north, possibly because of the great drought in the last quarter of the 13th century.

Its plaza is dominated by the heavily buttressed **Mission San Augustin de Isla**, erected between 1621 and 1630 by Father Juan de Salas. The church was fired during the 1680 Pueblo Rebellion and is much restored. Despite this it's a striking Gothic-style building with twin towers and a gabled clapboard front. There is a photo fee; tel (505) 869-3111.

SANTA FE

La Villa Real de la Santa Fe de San Francisco, better known as Santa Fe looks out over the majestic ranges of the Sangre de Cristo and Jemez Mountains from a high plateau some 7000 feet above sea level. For all its prominence as the capital of New Mexico and a center of the arts, its atmosphere is essentially (and charmingly) small-town Spain. So, too, is the tempo: you can – you must, unless you rent a car – walk or flag a tour bus to the sights for Santa Fe has no local public transportation.

But this is no deterrent. Most of the historic buildings are located within a few minutes' walk of the old plaza, and strolling best reveals the pleasures of the narrow streets.

The Spanish laid out the city in 1610 when Don Pedro de Peralta decided to move the capital from San Gabriel on the Rio Grande to a site more centrally located among the pueblos. Spanish law dictated the plan precisely. There was to be a large plaza at the center of the new villa, a church set sufficiently apart that it might be seen from all sides and venerated, and Casa Reales, the administrative center between the plaza and the church at a proper distance so as not to interfere with or obstruct the view of the church.

Things to See & Do

The first church has gone, but the **plaza** is still the center of civic life. A good place to watch the action is the Ore House lounge where you'll encounter locals doing exactly the same thing, though gyrating skateboarders are less colorful than the mule trains which unload their cargos here after the long journey from Mexico City along the Camino Real. The plaza has been the setting for numerous fiestas, cockfights and military drills – even, for a time in 1844, the pageantry of the bullring. The summer fairs now held here each year are no less picturesque – particularly the Indian and Spanish

markets and the Fiesta de Santa Fe, oldest non-Indian celebration in the country. It celebrates the peaceful reconquest of New Mexico in 1692 by Don Diego De Vargas with three days of parades, street dancing, an arts and crafts fair, and most spectacularly, the burning of Zozobra (Old Man Gloom).

On the north side of the plaza is the **Palace of the Governors**, diminished in size from its heyday when the walled area extended two blocks to the north, but still an impressive reminder of Spanish authority. Built in 1610, the Palace has served as the office and residence of New Mexico's governors under Spain, Mexico and the United States until a new capitol was completed in 1886. Lew Wallace wrote much of *Ben Hur* here during his tenure as governor, and that quintessential juvenile delinquent of southwestern history, Billy the Kid cooled his heels for a while in the palace jail.

The palace now houses the history division of the Museum of New Mexico, recapturing the flavor of early New Mexico life with re-creations of period rooms, including a chapel with an early 19th century reredos and santos, interpretive displays and a collection of early colonial paintings. Regional arts and crafts are for sale in the museum shop and outside on the portal you can deal directly with Pueblo Indian vendors of jewelry and crafts. Try bargaining. Open daily, 9 am to 4.45 pm; admission free.

The **Museum of Fine Arts** stand a block away on Palace Avenue at Lincoln St. Rotating exhibitions display an extensive collection of works by New Mexico and southwest Indian artists. The building itself is a classic example of the southwestern architectural style, enclosing a charming patio garden where fountains play. It's open daily, 9 am to 4.45 pm; admission free; tel 827-2437.

Just across the street is the **Delago House** (closed to the public), a good example of late 19th century local adobe

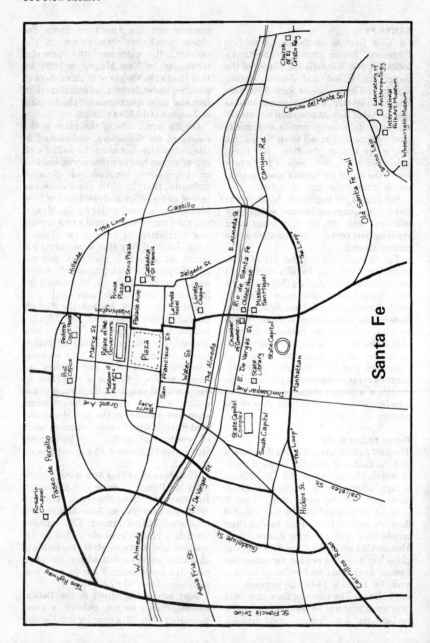

Santa Fe

Church of El Cristo Rey

Laboratory of Anthropology
International Folk Art Museum
Wheelwright Museum

Camino del Monte Sol

Camino Lejo

Canyon Rd.

Old Santa Fe Trail

Castillo

"The Loop"

Hillside

E. Almeda St.

Rio de Santa Fe

"The Loop"

Sena Plaza

Cathedral of St. Francis

Delgado St.

Prince Plaza

Palace Ave

Loretto Chapel

La Fonda Hotel

Oldest House

Mission San Miguel

Federal Court House

Washington

Marcy St.

Palace of the Governors

San Francisco St.

Water St.

The Almeda

Chamber of Commerce

E. De Vargas St.

State Capitol

Post Office

Museum of Fine Arts

Plaza

State Library

State Capitol Complex

Manhattan

Grant Ave

Burro Alley

Don Gaspar Ave

South Capitol

Paseo de Peralta

Rosario Chapel

Galisteo St.

"The Loop"

W. De Vargas St.

Hickox St.

W. Almeda

Guadalupe St.

Taos Highway

Agua Fria St.

St. Francis Drive

Cerrillos Road

construction built by the wealthy merchant-trader Don Felipe Delgado in 1890.

A walk around the plaza's arts and crafts galleries will bring you opposite the palace once again, but rather than follow the perimeter exactly, turn down **Burro Alley** which parallels the west side of the square. A century ago you would have had to pick your way through the strings of patient pack animals which gave the street its name.

La Fonda, the Inn at the End of the Trail, stands just off the plaza, at the intersection of San Francisco St and the Old Santa Fe Trail. This historic hotel traces its origins to the adobe inn which stood on the site from the early 17th century until 1919 when it was demolished to make way for the present building.

East of the Palace of the Governors, the low adobe buildings of **Prince** and **Sena Plazas** stand in a contiguous huddle on Palace Avenue. The windows of their little specialty shops are so attractive that it's all too easy to miss the opening to one of Santa Fe's most appealing courtyards – a narrow passage beside the bookshop. It leads to the patio of Jose Desiderio Sena's 33-room 19th-century hacienda. This is a pleasant place to relax as it's tree-shaded and planted with a profusion of flowers. The upper story is a later addition and the buildings where Don Jose's 23 children resided have been converted into a complex of boutiques. Between 1943 and 1963, the Manhattan Project (now the Atomic Energy Commission) occupied some of these buildings.

On Palace Avenue, again, the massive bulk of **Cathedral of St Francis** looms behind a screen of trees. (The entrance is to the south, on Cathedral Place.) The present building is the third to stand on the site, superseding the 18th century adobe building which had replaced the simple chapel put up between 1626 and 1629. The Romanesque architecture, somewhat at odds with the prevailing Spanish-style, reflects the influence of Archbishop Jean Baptiste Lamy, protagonist of Willa Cather's novel, *Death Comes to the Archbishop.*

Lamy came to Santa Fe from the Auvergne in 1851 and set about replacing the old adobe church with the cathedral in 1869. To accommodate the congregation during construction, the shell of the new cathedral was erected around the adobe church which was subsequently dismantled and removed piecemeal – all that remains of it is the Chapel of La Conquistadora, housing the oldest representation of the Madonna in the country. The richly dressed image has a dramatic history; brought to Santa Fe by a Franciscan missionary in 1625, it was rescued during the 1680 Indian Revolt when the Spanish were forced to abandon the city and remain with the colonists during their 13-year exile in El Paso, Texas. On the reconquest of New Mexico by Don Diego De Vargas in 1692, the Virgin led the procession back to Santa Fe. In commemoration, 'La Conquistadora' is borne in state through the city streets each June, to be lodged for a week in the Rosario Chapel, believed to have been built by De Vargas to celebrate his victory.

Around on the corner on Water St is the Gothic **Chapel of Our Lady of Light**, built in the 1870s by the Sisters of Loretto, to the model of the Sainte-Chapelle in Paris. It is the unusual spiral staircase leading to the organ loft that compels attention. According to the legend, on completion of the chapel it was discovered that a stairway leading to the organ loft had been omitted from the plans and the Sisters were faced with a choice between using a ladder or rebuilding the loft. A conventional staircase was not feasible because it would take up too much room. So they prayed to St Joseph for a solution. On the last day of the novena, a gray-haired man with a carpenter's tool chest and a donkey mysteriously appeared and asked if he could help the sisters build a stairway. Using only a saw, T-square and a hammer he constructed the singularly beautiful staircase, then left as suddenly and mysteriously as he had come. In the minds of many, St Joseph himself had answered the Sisters' prayers.

The design is as miraculous as the story for in the opinion of some experts, the stairway should have collapsed the first time it was used. Alas, the legend has not stood the test of time quite so well. In 1970, a local journal revealed the identity of the builder as being Yahon Hadwiger, a master carpenter from Germany.

The city's second oldest settlement, the **Barrio de Analco** is reached by the old Santa Fe Trail across the Rio de Santa Fe. The Barrio was settled before 1620 by Tlaxcalan Indians from Mexico who had accompanied the Franciscan missionaries to New Mexico. Several buildings put up pre-1776 still stand in the Barrio but the district's great treasure is **Mission San Miguel** on the corner of the Santa Fe Trail and De Vargas St. The exact foundation date of the sturdy adobe is not known, but it was certainly before 1628, so it is probably the oldest church in the United States. The bell tower has suffered many changes over the centuries but the interior has been faithfully restored to the original simplicity of the Spanish Colonial period. In front of the altar peep holes allow a view of the original mud floor and two broad adobe steps leading to the sanctuary. Among the church's treasures is a bell which rang out over the plains of Andalusia six centuries ago. Tradition relates that it was brought to Mexico in 1712 and that a century later a lady of the Ortiz family obtained it for her chapel in Santa Fe.

Across De Vargas St from the Mission is Santa Fe's **Oldest House**, believed to have been built by Indians more than 800 years ago. Rude, simple and constructed of puddled adobe (poured mud), it's the sole survivor of the Barrio de Analco's early buildings.

By contrast, a little farther up the Old Santa Fe Trail is the **New Mexico State Capitol**, dedicated in 1966. The design of the building incorporates the form of the Zia, an Indian sun symbol signifying friendship, composed of four groups of four sun rays around an inner circle. Guided tours are conducted through the capitol year-round and during the legislative session these include the State House and Senate Chambers.

Follow De Vargas St two blocks east of the Oldest House, crossing the Paseo de Peralta; you'll come to **Canyon Rd**, center of Santa Fe's renowned art colony. Canyon Rd is lined with galleries offering the best in southwestern art and crafts. Several restaurants provide comfortable way stations for the weary browser. About a mile from the Canyon Rd-Paseo de Peralta intersection, you'll find the modern **Church of El Cristo Rey** preserving an ornate 18th century stone reredos.

Three important museums cluster on the Camino Lejo at the southeastern edge of town (just off the Old Santa Fe Trail), about 1½ miles from the plaza. The **Laboratory of Anthropology**, a research and study center of the Museum of New Mexico, houses important collections of basketry, silverwork, pottery and textiles, some of which are displayed in interpretive exhibit galleries. It's open Monday to Friday, 9 am to 4.45 pm; admission free; tel 827-4321.

Nearby, on a mesa offering a sweeping view of the Jemez Mountains, is the **Museum of International Folk Art**. Don't pass up this opportunity to view an astonishing collection of folk art from more than 1000 nations including the 106,000-piece collection donated by Alexander Girard in 1978. The museum has, of course, a strong collection of Spanish Colonial and Latin American arts, but its displays illustrating the fantasy and humour of the folk artists around the world are particularly appealing. Open daily 9 am to 4.45 pm; admission free; tel 827-2544.

The **Wheelwright Museum** across the compound is a showcase of Navajo ceremonial art and silverwork. In the basement you will find a replica of an old style trading post offering a wide selection of choice Indian crafts at moderate prices. Open Monday to Saturday, 10 am to 5 pm; Sunday 1 to 5 pm; admission free; tel 982-4636.

South of Santa Fe at the Municipal Airport, roughly nine miles from the plaza, is the **Wings of Yesterday Flying Air Museum** – a 'must' for vintage airplane buffs. For not only do its collections range from a 1918 Fokker V-V11 to an F-100 'Super Sabre', but, weather permitting, you can fly in antique aircraft too. The current charge per person for 15 minutes aloft is $30. Make your reservation at least a day ahead by calling (505) 471-0368. Other exhibits illustrate the history of aviation from Icarus to man's first visit to the moon. Open daily in summer, five days a week in winter, 9 am to 4.30 pm.

Although **Old Cienega Village Museum** at Rancho Las Golondrinas is presently open only on the first Sunday of each summer month and for gala fiestas in spring and autumn, it's well worth knowing about. Plans are afoot to increase the number of visiting days. The historic, 200-acre rancho, established by a Manuel Vega y Coca in the 1650s was well known to travelers over the centuries as they worked their way up the Camino Real from Mexico to Santa Fe. Here they could count on a tradition of hospitality that guaranteed 'a full stomach and a contented heart'. Las Golondrinas is now a living museum of the Spanish Colonial era. Its original structures have been augmented by buildings brought from all parts of New Mexico and furnished with original tools, furniture and artefacts. On festival days you can watch craft demonstrations, folk dancing and a folk play.

Allow half a day to take full measure of this museum and wear suitable shoes to negotiate the hilly trails. For information, call (505) 471-2261 on weekdays, between 8.30 am and 4.30 pm. To get there from Santa Fe, take US 85 south and turn right at the Race Track exit (approximately 10 miles). Near the race track grandstand, turn right again and follow the dirt road some three miles to the rancho entrance.

Places to Stay

Garrett's Desert Inn, 311 Old Santa Fe Trail, Santa Fe 87501; tel (505) 982-1851. Three blocks from the plaza with air conditioning, color TV and heated swimming pool. Restaurant. Rates from $56 double.

The Inn at Loretto, Old Santa Fe Trail & Alameda, Santa Fe 87501; tel (505) 933-5531. Striking pueblo-style architecture. Air-cooled, color TV, heated pool. Some fireplace units. Restaurant, coffee shop, entertainment. Rates from $83 double.

Inn of the Governors, 234 Don Gaspar, Santa Fe 87501; tel (505) 982-4333. Two-plus blocks from the plaza. Color TV, heated pool, some rooms with fireplaces. Restaurant; entertainment. Rates from $55 double.

Motel 6 3007 Cerrillos Rd, Santa Fe 87501; (505) 471-2442. Close to Santa Fe Opera. Pool, air-conditioning. Rates from $19.95.

Sheraton-Santa Fe Inn, 750 St Francis Drive, PO Box 2347, Santa Fe 87501; tel (505) 982-5591. In the outskirts of Santa Fe, near the Santa Fe Opera. Heated pool, color TV, air-conditioning. Dining room, entertainment. Airport transportation. Rates from $66 double (peak season); $46 double (off season).

Places to Eat

The Bull Ring Continental and Mexican cuisine in a charming old adobe, with courtyard dining in summer. Informal. Nightly entertainment and dancing. (B/M)

Lunch, Monday to Friday; dinner only Saturday. 414 Old Santa Fe Trail; tel 983-3328.

The Compound Award winning restaurant housed in a tree-shaded hacienda. Continental cuisine. Reservations recommended. (M/E)

Lunch, dinner Tuesday to Sunday. 653 Canyon Rd; tel 982-4353).

Guadalupe Cafe Informal, and very popular with aficionados of New Mexican cooking. (B)

Lunch, dinner Monday to Friday. 135 Guadalupe; tel 982-9762.

La Paloma Pleasant, informal restaurant with patio dining in summer. The breakfast specials are rib stickers. (B)

Breakfast, lunch, dinner. Open daily. 225 E De Vargas; tel 982-8182.

La Querencia Classical music accompanies your meal in this pleasant, informal little place. Breakfasts are mouthwatering here. A wide array of sandwiches, soups, quiches and crepes for luncheon. (B)

Breakfast, lunch daily; suppers Friday to Sunday. 227 Don Gaspar; tel 982-1438.

La Tertulia One of Santa Fe's most popular restaurants for an evening out, housed in an adobe hacienda. The cuisine is New Mexican and American, the setting charming, and the clientele rather dressy. Reservations recommended. (E)

Lunch, dinner Tuesday to Sunday. 416 Agua Fria; tel 988-2769.

El Nido Informally elegant, with continental and Mexican cooking. Flamenco dancing a part of the summer entertainment – Thursday to Saturday. (M/E)

Open for dinner. Near Santa Fe Opera; tel (505) 983-9073.

El Paragua Famous Mexican restaurant, with American dishes, too. Informal, relaxing atmosphere with lots of greenery. (M)

Open daily from 11 am for lunch and dinner. One block east of Taos Highway on SR 76, Espanolo; tel 753-3211.

Rancho de Chimayo One of New Mexico's most famous restaurants featuring Mexican cuisine in a restored Spanish Colonial building. Patio dining and strolling musicians in summer. Reservations recommended. (E)

Open for lunch and dinner daily, noon to 9 pm, June to August; opening hours variable at other times. (505) 351-4444 or 351-4375 for information. Closed January 2 to 30. (Chimayo, 30 minute drive north of Santa Fe.)

Tinnie's Legal Tender Elegant steak and seafood restaurant in restored turn-of-the-century mansion. Reservations recommended. (E)

Open daily 5 pm to 11 pm. Lamy (20 minute-drive from Santa Fe); tel (505) 982-8425.

Getting There

Air Nearest airport is Albuquerque International, served by national and commuter airlines. Bus and limousine service to Santa Fe.

Bus *Greyhound* and *Continental Trailways* service to Albuquerque, connecting with the local service to Santa Fe. Santa Fe bus depot is located at West Water St. For information call 982-8564.

Rail *Amtrak* trains stop at Albuquerque and Lamy. While Lamy is the traditional stop for Santa Fe (15 miles distant), unless you arrange for transportation to meet you there, it is better to get off in Albuquerque and take the bus.

Getting Around

Public Transportation None at the time of writing.

Airport Limousine *Shuttlejack Inc* (PO Box 5793, Santa Fe 87501; tel (505) 982-4311. Operates scheduled limousine service between Santa Fe and Albuquerque International Airport. Reservation required from Santa Fe, requested from Albuquerque. Driving time 70 minutes. Fare is $12 one-way.

Taxi Call 982-9990 or 982-6172.

Tours

Bus *Gray Line of Santa Fe Enchanted Tours* (125 W Water St (bus depot), Santa Fe 87501; tel (505) 982-8564.) Three basic tours of Santa Fe and its environs offered. The Santa Fe city tour costs $7. A full day to Taos via the high Rd, including the Santuario at Chimayo and the Rio Grande Gorge, is $19. $14 will get you to Bandelier, Los Alamos and San Ildefonso Pueblo.

Gray Line also offers chauffered limousine service.

Santa Fe Tours Inc (126-133 Water St; tel 982-8564.) Three tour program includes seven hour tours of Taos, Chimayo and Truchas ($22.90) and Los Alamos-Bandelier ($16.45); Santa Fe City Drive (1½ hours, $5).

Float Trips Between May and September, depending on the Spring runoff and dam releases, you can float the Rio Grande, the Rio Bravo and the Rio Chama. It's pure adventure amid spectacular scenery and you can choose between half and whole day runs or arrange for longer trips.

Rio Bravo Tours (PO Box 400, Santa Fe 87501; tel (505) 988-1153.)

Rio Grande Rapid Transit (Box A, Pilar 87571; tel (505) 758-9700).

Southwest Safaris (PO Box 945, Santa Fe 87501; tel (505) 988-4246.)

Rail You don't have to be a steam railroad buff to enjoy trips offered by *The Cumbres & Toltec Scenic Railroad* through some of New Mexico and Colorado's grandest scenery. Vintage steam powered trains chug through the 10,000-foot Cumbres Pass and Toltec Gorge from Chama, New Mexico and Antonito, Colorado repectively to Osier, Colorado where there's time to purchase a hot lunch or picnic while the trains exchange engines and crews for the return trip.

The C&TSR operates Friday to Tuesday in June, daily July to October. Both round trips cost $24. In season reservations may be made by mail, telephone or in person at C&TSR depots, PO Box 789, Chama, NM 87520 (tel (505) 756-2151) and PO Box 668, Antonito, CO 81120 (tel (303) 376-5483). The nearest terminal to Santa Fe or Albuquerque is Chama, New Mexico, just south of the Colorado border.

Useful Addresses

Santa Fe Chamber of Commerce 330 Old Santa Fe Trail, (PO Box 1928), Santa Fe 87501; tel (505) 983-7317. Free pamphlets, maps, brochures and information on Santa Fe sightseeing, dining and accommodation.

New Mexico Tourism and Travel Division, Bataan Memorial Building, Santa Fe 87503. Tel (505) 827-5571; 800-545-2040 outside New Mexico. State-wide information and brochures on New Mexico sightseeing and activities.

AAA-New Mexico Division 811 Cerrillos Rd, Santa Fe 87501; tel (505) 982-4633. Members-only services. Open Monday to Friday 8.30 am to 5.30 pm.

Meeting The Americans

The Santa Fe Council of International Relations, La Posada Inn, Room 180, 330 E Palace Avenue, Santa Fe 87501; tel (505) 982-4931. Local COSERV affiliate helps with accommodation and tours.

Sierra Club, 1709 Paseo de Peralta, Santa Fe, NM 87501; tel (505) 983-2703.

NORTH OF SANTA FE

The fastest route from Santa Fe to Taos is US 285/68 which runs beside the Rio Grande from Espanola to Pilar before veering northeast to Ranchos de Taos and Taos (some 140 miles roundtrip). You can make a scenic loop day trip by following the High Rd (SR 76) from Espanola to Taos through centuries-old Spanish villages and pueblos tucked in the valleys of the Sangre de Cristos Mountains and return from Taos by way of SR 68.

As you head north from Santa Fe on US 285, the forested slopes of the Sangre de Cristos rise steeply to the east, forming a great bowl stippled with snow well into the summer months. The area provides excellent skiing facilities, with poma lifts, a chairlift to one of the highest peaks in the range, two lodges and runs suited to every level of skill. US 285 keeps to the valley floor, passing Tesuque Pueblo, Pojoaque and Nambe Pueblo toward Espanola – no compelling reasons to turn aside here unless you wish to purchase the local pottery on the spot, though Tesuque does retain two-story pueblo structures clustered around it's plaza.

The High Rd begins at Espanola, 25 miles north of Santa Fe. There follow the signs to Chimayo. You'll probably want to pause in **Santa Cruz De La Canada** for a look at the massive church (1733) dominating the plaza. It is one of the largest mission churches in the area, containing many old paintings and religious ornaments.

CHIMAYO

Nestling in a secluded valley eight miles farther is *Chimayo,* one of the most interesting communities in the state. For here is the **Santuario de Chimayo,** a shrine for the miraculous healing of disease under the patronage of Our Lord of Esquipulas in Guatemala. Within the simple adobe church, in a small room to the left of the altar, is a pit of sacred earth which, when dissolved in water and imbibed, is believed to effect a cure. When or how the virtues of the earth were discovered is not known; the site of the Santuario was held sacred by the Indians for its curative properties centuries before the Spanish came to Chimayo. It's probably that the cult of the miraculous Image of Our Lord of Esquipulas was introduced in 1805 and grafted onto the older tradition. It is certain that in 1814 Don Bernardo Abeyta and others of the community were given permission to build the church which was completed around 1816. Since that time Chimayo has become the Lourdes of the southwest and the walls of the side chapel are hung with braces, crutches and votive offerings of those who were miraculously cured.

The Santuario is a treasury of early 19th century art by native craftspeople, illuminating the dim interior with glowing color. The *bulto* of Santo Iago on horseback is particularly appealing. Also of interest is the figure of Santo Nino, housed in a rough shelter in the chapel. This richly dressed figure of the Christ Child is also credited with healing powers and requires new shoes daily, for Santo Nino walks the countryside by night to make sure that all is well.

Chimayo's finest horsemen don medieval armor each July for performances of 'Los Moros y Christianos', a folk play celebrating a Spanish victory over the Moors in the 15th century. It was first performed in New Mexico in 1598, making it the first European play to be enacted in the United States.

The town is also famous as a center of fine handweaving by descendants of the Spanish settlers. You'll find excellent examples at El Chimayo Trading Post and Ortega's Weaving Shop near the intersection of Highway 76. Here, too, is one of New Mexico's famous restaurants *Rancho de Chimayo* housed in an attractive old hacienda.

CORDOVA

Cordova, the home of woodcarvers, lies four miles north, just off the highway. So narrow are its unpaved streets that wooden biers are used at funerals there's no room for a modern hearse. Here you can purchase sculptures of animals, birds and santos, executed with considerable skill.

TRUCHAS

The High Rd now climbs up to Truchas, presenting a remarkable view of the upper Rio Grande from a ridge 8600 feet above the valley; behind you soar the Trampas and Truchas peaks, the highest reaching 13,102 feet. Icy winters have modified the prevailing architectural style here and you will come across log houses with steeply pitched roofs more reminiscent of Scandinavia than New Mexico.

LAS TRAMPAS

Eight miles beyond Truchas is Las Trampas, a lovely old village where the inhabitants retain many customs handed down unchanged over three centuries. The adobe church of **Santo Tomas del Rio de Las Trampas** on the plaza, built in the 1760s, has a finely carved pulpit, a number of old paintings and a bell named Gracia, said to contain a quantity of silver and gold. The reredos is believed to have come from Spain by way of Mexico.

Las Trampas is a center of the **Penitentes**, a religious brotherhood of men of Spanish descent and the Roman Catholic faith. Because their beliefs are secret and public rites emphasize dramatic re-enactments of Christ's passion at Easter (including flagellation and a simulated crucifixion), you may hear some rather vivid accounts of their activities. We suggest you refer to Marta Weigle's *The Penitentes of the Southwest* for a deeper understanding.

PICURIS

At Penasco, it's worthwhile turning left off the High Rd and following SR 75 about one mile west to visit Picuris Pueblo. Here, in a valley surrounded by pine forests, you can take a good look at the old and new ways of Pueblo Indian life. The excellent little museum portrays the story of the Picuris Indian with exhibits that include a replica of an 800-year-old kiva; contemporary Indian arts and crafts are for sale in the museum shop. Picuris pottery, typically with a sparling micaceous wash, is the preferred cooking ware around Santa Fe.

Northwest of the Catholic Church are the remains of the old pueblo dating from the 13th century. One of the kivas, with well preserved original paintings, is open to the public.

After returning to Penasco, the High Rd to Taos is marked first SR 75, and then becomes SR 3. There's a long climb up US Hill, rewarded at the crest by a view of New Mexico's highest peak, Mt Wheeler, thrusting its 13,161 feet above the line of the northern Sangre de Cristos. Continue north through the aspens and conifers of Carson National Forest, past Pot Creek and Talpa where, on the northern limits of the town (to your left) you may discern one of the last of the *torreones,* defensive round towers put up by the Spanish against Indian attack.

RANCHOS DE TAOS

Ranchos de Taos, not to be confused with Taos proper, lies astride the intersection of Highway 68. Its massive 18th century **Church of San Francisco de Asis** (1772) dominates a broad plaza. Inside you will find some notable early santos, and a large carved reredos. The church's famous mystery painting, *The Shadow of The Cross,* by the Canadian artist Henri Ault has been moved to the rectory. By day or under artificial light the figure of Jesus stands on the shore of the Sea of Galilee. In complete darkness the background takes on a luminous glow and the figure of Jesus alters – a cross appears on the left shoulder and a halo is visible above the head. You can witness the phenomenon between 10 am and noon and 1 and 4 pm Monday to Saturday and on Sunday, from 2 to 4 pm.

TAOS

Taos is well rooted in the past, retaining much of the form and flavor of the 18th century village established by Spanish settlers who had come to the valley before 1615. Then, as now, life centered around the plaza, originally roughly circular in form, its buildings abutting to form a continuous wall of defense against raiding Indians. The pueblo-style architecture of the boutiques, restaurants and galleries which line the perimeter today are an aesthetic link to the past for Taos, destroyed in the Indian Rebellion of 1680 and rebuilt entirely around 1710, has few buildings from its early period. Look out for 'Old Glory' fluttering above the square; Taos was until recently the only place in the country permitted to fly the national flag at night. The custom commemorated the gesture of Kit Carson and Smith Simpson, loyal Unionists in the Civil War, who nailed the Stars and Stripes to a pole and stood guard day and night against Confederate assaults.

Things to See & Do

The **Kit Carson Home and Museum** stands roughly a block east of the plaza, set back from Old Kit Carson Rd in an attractive patio. It's open to the public daily and the $1 fee admits you to an excellent example of an early frontier home, complete with bell-shaped adobe fireplaces and smoke-darkened *vigas*. Carson, the West's most famous scout, and his wife Josefa Jaramillo lived here for 24 years – one room is devoted entirely to memorabilia of his colorful career. Their graves are in the Old Spanish cemetery nearby. (To get to the cemetery from the museum, walk 200 yards or so east along Old Kit Carson Rd and turn left on the dirt road just before the bridge. Alternatively, you can follow the path from Kit Carson State Park on North Pueblo Rd.)

The brutalities of frontier life are sharply underscored at the **Governor Bent House, Museum and Gallery**. In this simple old building on Bent, one block north and half a block west of the plaza, Charles Bent, New Mexico Territory's first governor under US rule, lost his life while covering his family's escape during the 1847 uprising of the Taos Indians. The museum's interesting collections focus on the history of the Southwest. It's open daily, 9 am to 5 pm; admission charge; tel (505) 758-2376.

On SR 240, about two miles west of the plaza, is a third historic house taking you back to Taos' early days. The **Don Antonio Severino Hacienda**, built between 1800-27, was a fortress more than a home. It is being carefully restored and refurnished to period. Open daily, 9 am to 5 pm; closed Thanksgiving, Christmas and New Year's Days.

Tao's considerable reputation as an art center can be traced to the 1885 visit of a young American painter, J H Sharp. His paintings of the Taos region inspired two art students, Ernest L Blumenschein and Bert G Phillips to embark on a sketching trip through New Mexico in 1898. As the story goes, damage to their wagon enforced a stay in Taos; so enchanted were they by the beauty and spirit of the place, they journeyed no further. Their works in turn attracted others, resulting in a community where art is a staple of the economy.

Paintings by these early artists are often displayed at the **Harwood Foundation Museum and Library** on Le Doux St. This beautiful old building with fine antique Spanish furniture and crafts in its collection, is sufficient attraction in itself. Open Monday to Friday; 10 am to 5 pm; Saturday 10 am to 4 pm; admission free.

Also on LeDoux St you'll find the home of Ernest Blumenschein, now a registered National Historic Landmark. The house is open to the public daily.

Taos also attracted the wealthy, spirited and by the standards of the time highly unconventional socialite Mabel Dodge Stern who raised eyebrows by divorcing her second husband to marry a Taos Pueblo Indian, Tony Lujan. Her home on Lujan St knew many famous literati, not the least of whom was D H Lawrence. Lawrence and his wife Frieda were guests for several months, eventually purchasing a small ranch 15 miles north of Taos which is now used by writers in residence at the University of New Mexico.

Taos Pueblo

Taos Pueblo, that extraordinary evocation of the Pueblo Indian world before the white man came to the southwest, lies amid well watered farmlands, three miles north of Taos. The Cubistic forms of its two great five-story structures stand out in bold relief against the brooding mass of Mt Wheeler, separated from each other by the Taos river that cuts through the centre of the plaza. Archeologists believe the pueblo has been continuously inhabited for at least 800 years and that portions of the buildings still in use were standing when a detachment of Coronado's expedition visited Taos in 1540. With more poetry, Indian legend tells of its founding long ago by a great chief who followed an eagle to a stream at the foot of the mountains. Two plumes dropped from the bird, one settling on either side of the stream, and here he led his people to build their homes.

All the buildings are made of puddled adobe, a method of shaping mud into long broad walls used by the Indians long before the Spanish introduced the technique of making adobe bricks. Originally there were no doors or windows on the ground floor; for security's sake the only way to enter was by means of ladders to the first terrace. These are still used. The log structures that look like unfinished archways scattered around the plaza and the streets are *ramadas;* hay stored on top creates sheltered areas for livestock.

West of the pueblo entrance are the stubs of twin towers and ruined walls, all that remains of the 18th century mission destroyed by the Americans during the Mexican War of 1846. To the east is the church which replaced it, an unassuming little place, rendered more dashing by zebra stripes of white and terracotta painted on the enclosing wall.

Taos Pueblo is open to visitors from 8 am to 6 pm daily. If you wish to take photographs, you must pay a fee of $5 in addition to the entry charge. For information, tel (505) 758-8626.

D H Lawrence Ranch & Shrine

At the urging of Mabel Dodge Lujan who hoped he would interpret 'this mysterious land' of New Mexico, the English novelist D H Lawrence and his wife Frieda lived in Taos for three periods between 1922 and 1925. Here Lawrence wrote or revised several works, and though he used little of his Taos experience directly, his philosophy crystallised during this period. Lawrence died in France in 1930 and his ashes were later brought to Taos and placed in a chapel built at the ranch where he had lived. Frieda Lawrence's grave is in front of the chapel. The chapel and shrine are open to the public. To get there, take SR 3 north from Taos Plaza for about nine miles, then turn right at the sign. The ranch is about six miles farther; it is not open to the public.

Rio Grande Gorge

At the junction with SR 50, SR 64 turns due west across the plain towards the Jemez Mountains. After six miles you come upon the Rio Grande Gorge with dramatic suddenness.

Parking is provided for those who would view the Rio Grande 650 feet below.

Millicent A Rogers foundation

Returning to Taos by the same route, turn right on the side road signed for the Millicent A Rogers Foundation. This museum houses important collections of Indian art of the plains and the southwest and Spanish-Colonial folk art. Open Tuesday to Sunday 10 am to 4 pm (winter); daily 9 am to 5 pm (summer); closed major holidays; admission $2; tel (505) 758-2462.

SR 68 runs due south from Taos to Santa Fe, following the east bank of the Rio Grande between Pilar and Velarde. Here the river, running swiftly between steep hills, is a popular venue for white water canoeists and the rafting set. At Pilar there is a bridge leading to Rio Grande Gorge State Park.

San Juan Pueblo

Five miles short of Espanola is San Juan where the first Spanish settlement was established in 1598. Today it's noted for performances of **Los Matachines**, a Mexican-Indian dance, and the local pottery. You can also pick up wood carvings, embroidery, leatherwork and beadwork.

Places to Stay

El Monte Lodge US 64 (PO Box 22) Taos 87571; tel (505) 758-3171. Near Plaza, with some kitchen units and fireplaces. Rates from $30 double.

Sagebrush Inn, South Santa Fe Rd (PO Box 1566), Taos, 87571; tel (505) 758-2254. Renowned Pueblo Mission style hotel furnished with rare antiques located two miles south of Taos. Restaurant, pool, tennis courts. Rates from $40 double.

Places to Eat

Apple Tree American and international cuisine in old adobe house near the plaza. Garden dining. (B/M)

Breakfast, lunch, dinner. Open daily. 26 Bent St; tel 758-1900.

La Dona Luz The building dates back to 1802; the chefs feature continental and Mexican dishes. (M)

Lunch, dinner. Closed Sunday. E Kit Carson Drive; tel 758-3332.

Useful Addresses

The *Taos County Chamber of Commerce,* located on the Plaza, provide pamphlets on restaurants, accommodation, activities and sightseeing in the area. Write to the Chamber at Drawer 1, Taos, New Mexico 87571, or phone (505) 758-3873.

WEST OF SANTA FE

The peaks of the Jemez Mountains rise west of Santa Fe, running from Bernalillo in the south to the Colorado border. The area is rich in archeological sites and historic pueblos, linked by mountain roads that enable you to have several leisurely days of exploration. The circle route may be driven in a day, starting either in Albuquerque or Santa Fe.

SANTA CLARA & PUYE CLIFF DWELLINGS

With Santa Fe as your base, drive 25 miles north to Espanola, then follow SR 5 to Santa Clara, renowned through the southwest as the home of gifted potters and painters. Around the plaza tree-shaded adobes invite you in with signs advertising the sale of pottery. Characteristically, it is black, highly polished and incised with strong, simple designs, but you'll find red and polychrome ware too, and charming figurines of animals and birds.

The ancestors of the Santa Clara Indians made their homes in the cliffs of the Pajarito Plateau. To reach Puye, follow SR 5 south, then turn right on the steep curving road signed for the Puye Cliff Dwellings and Santa Clara Canyon. These impressive ruins were built between 1450 and 1475 and abandoned toward the end of the 16th century. Easy trails lead from the Visitors Center to the first level of dwellings; for the athletic, ladders and toe holes cut in the vertical cliff face provide access to the ruins of the pueblo crowning the mesa; there is also a dirt road enabling you to drive to the plaza. In late July each year, the plaza comes alive again as the Santa Clara Indians hold a brilliant festival of arts and crafts, enhanced by performances of their traditional dances. Open daily 8 am to 6 pm (April to October 31); $2; photo fee; tel (505) 753-7326.

SAN ILDEFONSO PUEBLO

San Ildefonso Pueblo, home of the celebrated potter Maria Martinez, lies due south of Santa Clara as the crow flies, but you will have to follow SR 5 and 30, turn east on SR 4, cross the Rio Grande at Otowi Bridge, and take either the first or second road left through the pueblo lands. The adobe buildings clustering around San Ildefonso's vast plaza include two rectangular ceremonial chambers and a circular kiva, but here perhaps the greatest attraction is the superb pottery produced not only by Maria but by other famous artists. Many sell their work from home. You'll find a wide-ranging selection of ceramics, rugs, jewelry and paintings in the Popovi Da Studio of Indian Arts near the Hollywood Gate.

LOS ALAMOS

To reach Los Alamos, retrace your route across the Rio Grande and follow SR 4 up into the heights of the Jemez Range. Los Alamos, of course, ushered in the Atomic Age. Before 1942 only a boys' school stood in the secluded valley until the government chose it as a research center of the Manhattan Project. Now a town of some 15,000 inhabitants, Los Alamos is still devoted to research on nuclear and thermonuclear weapons and the laboratories are definitely off limits. You can tour **Bradbury Science Hall** (closed at weekends) where exhibits explain nuclear chain reaction and ballistic cases for the 'Little Boy' and 'Fat Man' bombs are displayed.

BANDALIER NATIONAL MONUMENT

By backtracking to the intersection where SR4 turns due south and following the signs to White Rock and Frijoles, you come to the entrance to Bandelier National monument where some of New Mexico's finest cliff dwellings and pueblo ruins are preserved. The monument extends over 46 square miles of the rugged Pajarito Plateau, formed about a million years ago when the Jemez crater erupted for the last time. About 1200 AD the area was settled by peoples from Mesa Verda and Chaco Canyon to the north, driven from their homelands by a drought. By 1540 their descendants had moved again, to the Rio Grande Valley building, the pueblos in which their descendants live today. It's worth taking a half hour or so to study the exhibits at

the Visitor Center **Museum** before setting out on a journey into prehistory along the Frijoles Canyon trail.

Two miles of cliff dwelling pockmark the north face of the canyon. On the way you will pass the excavated ruins of **Tyuony,** a nearly circular pueblo, probably occupied between the 13th and the 16th centuries. Some 60 miles of trails lead to other points of interest such as the Stone Lions Shrine, Painted Cave and the pueblo ruins of San Miguel and Yapashi.

The monument is open year-round. There's a campground near the entrance station (open March 15 to September 29) with sites available on a first-come first-served basis. Snack bar food service is available at the Visitor Center in summer. For information, tel (505) 672-3861.

VALLE GRANDE & JEMEZ RIVER VALLEY

From Bandelier the road leads west across the immense green meadow of **El Valle Grande,** the caldera of the Jemez volcanoes. Trees outline its rim, enclosing an area of some 176 square miles.

Near La Cueva, amid lofty peaks that soar well above the 10,000 foot level, SR 4 turns south through the San Antonio gorge and San Diego canyon. About a mile before you reach Giusewa is **Soda Dam,** a large natural dam built up by thermal springs on Jemez Creek. It's about 400 feet long and 50 feet high. At the top of the hill across the road is the entrance to **Jemez Cave,** where in 1934 archeologists found a 13th century mummy of a child, now in the museum of New Mexico.

Jemez Springs is a small spa with mineral hot springs, known to the Indians long before the Spanish came. You can try their healing properties at the village bath-house (closed Mondays).

Opposite the monastery of Villa Codi on the northern edge of town is **Jemez State Monument,** preserving the crumbling ruins of an early 17th century Franciscan mission and a 13th century pueblo.

Hemmed between steep mountain walls 12 miles south of Jemez Hot Springs is **Jemez Pueblo**, inhabited by Indians believed to be the descendants of the Pecos (see Pecos National Monument). The Pecos Bull Dance is performed here on August 2. Stores around the plaza offer some attractive pottery and handloomed textiles. Baskets woven of yucca are particularly appealing souvenirs.

Journey on through Jemez Canyon between cliffs tinted grey, yellow and buff and you come to San Ysidro near the junction with US 44. Turn east along the highway for the entrance to **Zia Pueblo**, perched on a rocky knoll north of Jemez Creek. This ancient pueblo, established about 1300, is renowned for its handsome pottery and is the birthplace of several well known painters. The Zia sun symbol was incorporated into the design of New Mexico's state flag and the State Capitol in Santa Fe.

CORONADO STATE MONUMENT

The fascination of Coronado State Monument lies not so much in the fact that Coronado may have wintered here on his exploration of New Mexico, but in the carefully preserved ruins of 13th century **Kuaua Peublo**. Within the two larger plazas are five sacred kivas, one of which, the 'Painted Kiva' has been restored, enabling you to see where the men of Kuaua spoke with their gods five centuries ago. Artifacts and reproductions of kiva murals exhibited in the museum offer insight into their lives.

To get to the monument, turn left off US 44 just before you come to Bernalillo, a small town settled by descendants of Bernal Diaz del Castillo, the historian-soldier who accompanied Cortez on his conquest of Mexico. Open 9 am to 5 pm Thursday to Monday; closed state holidays. Tel (505) 867-5351.

EAST OF SANTA FE

For a day in the peaks of the Sangre de Cristos east of Santa Fe and a visit to the ruins of the first pueblo known to the Spanish, drive south to pick up I-25 and then turn east for Pecos National Monument. You should leave I-25 at the Glorieta interchange and follow the signs. At Pecos SR 63 runs deep into Santa Fe National Forest, following the valley of the Pecos River to an area rich in recreational opportunities. Along the way you will pass several small Spanish villages, some of which date from the 18th century. SR 63 deadends in Cowles, gateway to the Pecos Wilderness, a 167,416 acre tract of some of the grandest scenery in the state. Forest roads provide access.

PECOS NATIONAL MONUMENT

Pecos National Monument has impressive ruins of a 14th century pueblo and an 17th century Spanish *convento*. It was here in 1541 that Francisco Vasquez de Coronado abandoned his search for the legendary Seven Cities of Cibola and their riches, to return to Mexico and disgrace. A century later the Franciscans successfully founded the **Mission de Nuestra Senora de Los Angeles de Porciuncula**. The splendid *convento* and church with 'walls so wide that services were held in their thickness' was burned to the ground in the Pueblo Rebellion of 1680. Though re-established 12 years later, the mission never regained its former magnificence. By 1838 both the mission and the pueblo were abandoned, due, it was believed to witchcraft in the village and nearby town.

At its peak in the middle of the 15th century **Pecos Pueblo** was one of the largest in the area, with a population of 2500 living in a 660 room multi-storied dwelling. Archaeologists have restored two kivas which you may enter; nearby you can trace the ruts made by wagon wheels on the historic Santa Fe Trail.

The monument has a small museum

and picnic facilities. Camping is not permitted – plenty of campsites in the upper Pecos Valley and national forest, however. It's open daily, 8 am to 5 pm; closed Christmas, New Years Day; tel (505) 757-6414.

THREE GREAT MONUMENTS

Three of the southwest's most important centers of Indian culture lie within a day's drive of each other in northwestern New Mexico and southwestern Colorado. Chaco Canyon, Aztec Ruins and Mesa Verde are monuments to the Anasazi – the 'Old Ones' in Navajo – a word now used to describe prehistoric cultures of the region where Arizona, New Mexico, Colorado and Utah meet. Ideally, allow a day in each to gain a sense of the richness of the cultures these communities once supported. If you propose to make a circle trip from Santa Fe, the longest runs are from Santa Fe to Chaco Canyon (201 miles) and from Mesa Verde back to the New Mexican capital, which takes approximately seven hours via Durango, Pagosa Springs and Tierra Amarilla without allowing time for stops. If you're travelling around the West by public transport, we suggest temporary investment in a set of wheels – only Mesa Verde is near a bus route; between mid-October and mid-May there is no bus service into the park.

Chaco Canyon National Monument

Chaco Canyon lies 201 miles west of Santa Fe via US 84, SR 96, SR 44 and SR 57, a route which takes you through the northern Jemez Mountains, past Abique, home of the great painter Georgia O'Keefe, into the high desert country of the Jicarillo Apaches. A gravel road (Indian Rd 45/SR 57) turns south from SR 44 at Naqeezi, running 23 miles through the desert to the monument's north entrance. The visitor center is seven miles further. Driving this gravel road is *slow*, and you'll be very isolated. Be sure you have sufficient gasoline for

there is none available in the canyon.

For all its present aridity, Chaco Canyon a thousand years ago must have been a fertile place. There is evidence of irrigation systems and Navajo lore tells of a living stream within the memory of their immediate ancestors. Agriculture, the basis of life for the southwest's prehistoric peoples, was on a scale to support an estimated population of 10,000 inhabitants who engaged in commerce with Mexico, built a complex networks of roads far into the desert, and developed a highly organised social life in which religion played an important part. The most impressive evidence of their high culture is the buildings, massive structures of exquisitely fitted sandstone blocks, fashioned without benefit of metal tools.

The monument preserves more than 400 sites, the largest of which are Pueblo Bonito, Chettro Kettle, Pueblo Arroyo and Casa Rinconada. **Pueblo Bonito**, 3½ miles northwest of the visitor center, is the most imposing. Construction here probably began around 1000 AD; by the middle of the 12th century the D-shaped complex had grown to over 800 rooms, rising at least four stories high. The original timber ceilings are still in place in some of the chambers. Within the courtyard are the ruins of 35 Great Kivas measuring 50 feet in diameter.

Chettro Kettle, **Pueblo Arroyo** and **Casa Rinconada** are only a short distance away, the last particularly noteworthy for its Great Kiva, 64 feet in diameter. At Chettro Kettle a striking banded effect was achieved in the masonry by alternating layers of large stones with smaller ones.

The museum at the visitor center provides a good background for understanding the history of the Anasazi in Chaco Canyon. During summer, park rangers conduct tours of Pueblo Bonito and other ruins daily – enquire at the visitor center for the current schedule. There is one campground (closed in winter) in the monument, operated on a first-come, first-served basis. Camping is limited to 14 days. No food service, however, nor gasoline, repair services or lodging. You'll find accommodation in Farmington, Bloomfield and the City of Aztec. Nearest services are in Blanco Trading Post and Nageezi (30 miles north) and Crownpoint (40 miles south). For information, tel (505) 786-5384.

If you plan to do a little back country hiking or visit the outlying sites, you must obtain a back country permit. Wildlife includes prairie rattlesnakes, which are rarely seen. If you do encounter one, maintain a discreet distance and don't harm the blighter; the monument is also a wildlife refuge.

Aztec Ruins National Monument

The name of Aztec Ruins National Monument implies a connection with the Valley of Mexico that archeological truth belies. This impressive pueblo, standing in the outskirts of the City of Aztec, is about halfway between Chaco Canyon and Mesa Verde, and shows the influence of both cultures. It was built between 1100 and 1121 by a people whose techniques were similar to those of the Chacos. Within a century they were gone, and the village was re-occupied by others with characteristics of the Mesa Verde culture. By the end of the 13th century Aztec, like all the others, was completely abandoned. Exactly where the people went is still not known. Possibly the fertile Rio Grande Valley was the lure.

The pueblo ruins which still stand on the banks of the Animas River contain 500 rooms and about 20 kivas, grouped around a courtyard. The **Great Kiva**, more than 40 feet in diameter at the floor, is the main attraction. It was restored in 1934, and you can view an interior that re-creates the ceremonial settings of the 12th century.

Exhibits and artefacts in the visitor center provide a useful background to your explorations and park rangers are on hand to answer questions. No camping or food service in the monument; the nearest campground, operated by the City of Aztec, is only a mile away, however. Accommodation is to be found in the City of Aztec and Farmington. For information tel (505) 334-6174.

To reach the monument from Chaco Canyon, return to US 44 via SR 57. Aztec lies 35 miles due north of Blanco Trading Post.

Mesa Verde National Park

Perhaps the most famous of all the prehistoric pueblo sites is Mesa Verde, located on a forested plateau 7000 feet above sea level in the extreme southwestern corner of Colorado. Here you can trace the development of Anasazi culture over seven centuries, from the pit dwellings dug by the first inhabitants to the dramatic cliff dwellings so mysteriously abandoned in the 13th century.

Archeologists believe Mesa Verde was settled by Indians from the Four Corners area about 1300 years ago; these people displayed a considerable skill in basketry, cultivated beans, corn and squash, and domesticated dogs and turkeys. By the middle of the 8th century their descendants were building homes above ground, and within two centuries stone apartment buildings were replacing these. No-one knows what caused the Anasazi to abandon the mesa tops for fortress-like villages set into the cliffs; quite possibly it was for protection from enemy attack. And by the end of the 13th century these, too, were abandoned and Mesa Verde stood silent until its rediscovery in 1874. The prevailing theory is that repeated drought and crop failures set off migrations to the valleys of the Rio Grande and its tributaries.

The most spectacular ruins – **Square Tower House, Spruce Tree House, Sun Temple, Balcony House** and **Cliff Palace** – are on Chapin Mesa, 21 miles from the park entrance. Vantage points on **Ruins**

Rd, which divides into self-guiding loops near Spruce Tree House, give good views of the cliff dwellings. You may tour the mesa top ruins on your own but must join a guided tour conducted by a park ranger to enter the cliff dwellings. For the current schedule, check at **Far View Visitor Center** (open 8 am to 5 pm summer only) or **Chapin Mesa Museum** (open 8 am to 6.30 pm in summer; 8 am to 5 pm the rest of the year). In winter, tours are conducted through Spruce Tree House only, depending on weather and trail conditions. You can also pick up concessionaire-operated commercial bus tours to Chapin Mesa at the visitor center.

Wetherill Mesa is off-limits to private vehicles – to visit Long House and Step House ruins, catch the free park mini-bus at the visitor center and be prepared for a short hike to the sites.

When you're visiting Mesa Verde, it's important to remember that you are a mile above sea level and that visiting a cliff dwelling is strenuous, requiring the climbing of steps and ladders. Appropriate footwear is definitely recommended, too. In summer, daytime temperatures range between 85 to 100°F, dropping 55 to 60° in the evening. Winter lows can reach -25°F with plenty of snow to go with it.

Places to Stay

Camping in Mesa Verde is allowed only in designated campsites at *Morfield Campground,* 3.7 miles from the park entrance (open May 1 to October 31). You can put up at the *Far View Lodge* between mid-May and mid-October. For reservations, write the Mesa Verde Co, PO Box 277, Mancos, CO 81328. Call toll free (out-of-state) 800-525-6421; (Colorado only) 800-332-5797. The Lodge has a *cafeteria* as well as a *restaurant.*

Getting There

To reach Mesa Verde by car from Aztec Ruins National Monument, follow US 550 north to Durango, then turn east on SR 789-US 160. The park entrance lies some six miles east of Mancos.

Getting there by public transportation is possible in summer. From mid-May to mid-October, buses run into the park from Cortez, which is on the Continental Trailways route. Nearest airports with scheduled flights are Durango and Cortez; *Amtrak* serves Grand Junction, Colorado and Gallup, New Mexico, with bus service to Cortez from those points.

Carlsbad Caverns National Park

For speleologists and bat freaks Carlsbad Caverns National Park can never be too far off the itinerary for a visit. Located in the Guadaloupe Mountains of southeastern New Mexico, this Stygian world of delicate stone formations, canyons, and caves large enough to accommodate the national Capitol, has been 250 million years in the making, formed by the action of mountain building forces and rainwater on a massive limestone reef built up during Permian times.

Humans came late to the caverns. Prehistoric Indians camped near the entrance a thousand years ago, but for millennia before them the famous bats had used one cave as a summer home. Huge quantities of guano laid down under their roosts have been profitably exploited as fertiliser since the middle of the 19th century. But not until James Larkin White, a foreman of the guano mines, began his exploration in 1903 was the full extent and beauty of this underground realm known.

More than 50 caves are preserved in this 46,753-acre park. Above ground you can explore a harsh land of rugged mountains separated by winding canyons. Wildlife abounds and more than 200 different species of birds, including the golden eagle, have been identified. Hikers require back country permits for overnight camping.

Underground tours begin at the visitor center near the cavern entrance, seven miles west of US 62-180, at the end of SR 7. You have a choice between walking in through the natural entrance on a three-mile round trip or descending by elevator for a 1¼ mile tour of the **Big Room**. On both tours you return to the surface by elevator. As downhill trails in the caves are damp and slippery, wear suitable shoes; the temperature is a steady 56°F and you may need a light jacket.

For the energetic there are primitive lantern trips to **New Cave** near the entrance to Slaughter Canyon; these require strenuous climbs. And most dramatically, in summer you can watch the bat flights at sunset, when as many as 5000 bats a minute stream out of the cavern. Exact times are posted daily at the visitor center.

You can reach Carlsbad Caverns by public transportation from either Carlsbad, New Mexico (20 miles northeast) or El Paso, Texas (150 miles west). Both cities are served by scheduled airlines and buses and you can pick up a bus to the park. No overnight accommodation or camping in the monument, but there are several motels, hotels and campgrounds nearby. Lunch and refreshments are available underground as well as at the restaurant next to the visitor center. Open daily, 8 am to 5 pm; admission $3 per vehicle or $1 commercial bus passenger; tel (505) 885-8884.

FESTIVALS & EVENTS

Few states can match New Mexico in the number, variety and color of its public festivals – someone, somewhere, is celebrating something almost every week of the year. The New Mexico Travel Division's *Que Pasa?*, available free of charge at any chamber of commerce, contains a state-wide listing. Here are some of the best known.

All year	**Pueblos** – Ceremonials, celebrations, dances
Easter	**Taos** – Penitente service in various moradas **Chimayo** – Pilgramages to El Santuario
June	**Gallup** – Annual Indian Capital Amateur Rodeo **Albuquerque** – New Mexico Arts & Crafts Fair
July	**Santa Fe** – Annual Independence Day Celebration and Los Compadres Street Breakfast in the plaza **Santa Fe** – Annual Rodeo de Santa Fe; Spanish Market; Santa Fe opera season beigns **Taos** – Annual Fiesta de Taos
August	**Lincoln** – Billy the Kid Pageant **Santa Fe** – Annual Indian Market **Gallup** – Intertribal Indian Ceremonial
September	**Albuquerque** – Annual New Mexico State Fair and Rodeo **Santa Fe** – Annual Fiesta de Santa Fe (oldest in the southwest); annual festival of the arts begins

October	**Taos** – Annual Festival of the Arts
	Albuquerque – Annual International Hot air balloon Fiesta
December	**Taos** – Annual Our Lady of Guadalupe Candlelight Procession
	Taos-Santa Fe – 'Las Posadas' Spanish folk drama
Christmas	Lighting of Luminaries

The Hawaiian Islands

Polynesia, Japan, China, Korea, the Philippines and Europe – part of the culture and beauty of each came with the settlers and migrants to their new homeland of Hawaii. The islands themselves contributed a near perfect climate and plentiful food and shelter.

Hawaii's appeals are legion: beaches washed by a warm ocean; perenially green mountains; the thriving city of Honolulu and relaxed country towns; a cultural blend which some sociologists term the 21st century society and an easy-going, ebullient lifestyle embodied in that all embracing concept, the aloha spirit.

Geography

If the waters of the Pacific ocean were drained, the islands of the State of Hawaii would be revealed as a massive mountain range strung some 1600 miles across the mid-Pacific. Countless volcanic upheavals have raised the peaks above the ocean to form 124 islands and islets.

The eight High Islands at the eastern end of the chain are those commonly thought of as the Hawaiian Islands: Oahu, Kauai, Niihau, Maui, Molokai, Lanai, Kahoolawe and Hawaii. The closest island to the US mainland, Hawaii, lies 2100 miles off the West Coast. The rest of the islands are mostly uninhabited coral atolls and lava shoals, known as the Leeward Islands.

Kauai is oldest of the High Islands. Hawaii, the younger, is still growing. It has two active volcanoes which erupt from time to time; when a stream of molten lava flows down to meet the sea, the steaming impact results in accretion of new acreage for the island. Hawaii is already nearly twice as large as the rest of the High Islands combined. Hence it is known as the Big Island to differentiate it from the state name.

History

The first Polynesians came to the Hawaiian Islands aboard great twin canoes lashed together. On platforms straddling the hulls rode families, animals, plants even huts. They came from the Marquesas and Society Islands to the south in waves of migration lasting from around the 8th century to the 12th or 14th century. The era of the 'long voyages' is thought to have finished some 600 to 800 years ago.

With them the Polynesians also brought their social structure and religion based on the complex *kapu* (tabu) system, which provided rules for fishing, planting and harvesting, arts and crafts, social intercourse – in short, rules for living.

The earliest arrivals found lush empty islands, though several showed signs of earlier occupants, believed to be the Menehunes. These tiny people, thought by many to be merely mythical characters, actually lived on the islands perhaps a thousand years ago. Their origin and the cause and place of their disappearance are lost in legend.

The Polynesian pantheon of deities included four major gods: Kane, Ku, Lono and Kanaloa. When Captain James Cook sailed into the Islands in 1778, the Hawaiians welcomed him as the god Lono, returning from a legendary trip to Kahiki. Though Cook himself was killed on the beach at Hawaii's Kealakekua Bay during a tragic confrontation over a stolen cutter, the logs of his ships *Resolution* and *Discovery* acquainted Europeans with the Sandwich Islands, as he named them.

Traders from France, Russia, Germany, England and America were soon using Honolulu and Lahaina as ports in pursuit of the fur and sandalwood trade with China.

In 1782, the young chief Kamehameha

of the island of Hawaii embarked on an ambitious venture to defeat the numerous kings ruling the islands and unify all under his sovereignty. By 1795 only Kauai remained undefeated and in 1810, Kaumualii of Kauai acknowledged Kamehameha's suzerainty. At last the islands were joined into one kingdom under the rule of Kamehameha I, the progenitor of a dynasty that lasted for 62 years, through the rule of his two sons and two grandsons. Matching Kamehameha the Great in stature was Kaahumanu, favourite amongst his wives, who ruled as regent or *Kahina-nui* during the reign of both Kamehameha II and III, until her death on June 5, 1832.

In 1819, Hawaii's year of change, four events occured which affected the Islands future course. Kamehameha the Great died. His son, Kamehameha II, encouraged by Kaahumanu and his mother, Queen Keopuolani, abolished the *kapu* system. Protestant missionaries sailed aboard the *Thaddeus* from Boston to carry the gospel to Hawaii, arriving in perfect time to fill the religious void. The missionaries not only spread the gospel of Jehovah, they brought education to the Hawaiians, giving written form to the Hawaiian language in order to teach. In October of that year, whalers from New England sailed into the Islands, forerunners of the great whaling fleets which descended on the Islands each spring and fall for the next four decades, spurring commerce and the growth of Honolulu and Lahaina. In the inevitable conflict between the staunch uprightness of the missionaries and the carousing sailors, the fun-loving Hawaiians definitely leaned to the seamen's point of view. The Polynesians' guileless attitude toward life and love was to cause no little grief to the missionaries and their ladies.

Toward Statehood

Kamehameha V was followed on the throne by elected scions of other chiefly families: King Lunalilo, King David Kalakaua and the last monarch, Queen Liliuokalani, who was deposed by a group of *haole* (white) businessmen and planters, mostly of American origin.

The economics of sugar, which by the time of the coup in 1893 had become linchpin of Hawaiian commerce, dictated close ties to the United States. When the businessmen-revolutionaries proclaimed Hawaii a republic with Sanford R Dole as president on July 4, 1894, they had one goal in mind: American annexation.

A comic-opera recurrence of insurrections and conspiracies in Honolulu over the previous five years was frightening off foreign investment, needed if they were to prosper. They had virtually lost their American sugar market as a result of the McKinley Act, which allowed importation of tariff-free raw sugar from all countries (heretofore only they had enjoyed that privilege under reciprocity treaties which ceded Pearl Harbor to America as a naval base) and paid a bounty to domestic producers. Annexation was vital to their self-interest.

They achieved their goal in 1898; the American flag was hoisted in Honolulu on August 12. Hawaii had taken the first step toward statehood.

Almost 60 years after it achieved territorial status, Hawaii finally became the 50th state in the union on August 21, 1959.

In today's Hawaii, sugar has given way to tourism and military spending in the economic pecking order, while pineapple plantations are all but disappearing except on Oahu and Lanai. Elaborate tourist resorts are rising where a decade ago spiky grey-green pineapple rows stood out against the red soil.

Language

The Hawaiian alphabet has only 12 letters – a, e, i, o, u, h, k, l, m, n, p and w. What appears to be a bewildering repetition of letters within a word becomes more simple if you remember that every letter is pronounced each time it appears; thus *a'a* is not drawn out 'aaahhh' but 'ah-ah.' You can also train your eye to break a word into syllables; 'Kamehameha' may look daunting until you learn to recognize 'Ka-meha-meha.'

You'll find many Hawaiian words woven into everyday speech, most notably *aloha*, one of those marvellous multiple-meaning words which can be used for welcome, hello, love, greetings, farewell. Others you'll encounter frequently are: *kamaaina*, local person; *malihini*, outsider; *alii*, chief; *kahuna*, ancient priest; *mauka*, inland or upland; *makai*, toward the sea; *kapu*, sacred or forbidden; *kane*, male or husband; *wahine*, female or wife; *luau*, feast; *pali*, cliffs; *haole*, originally any foreigner, now generally used for Caucasian. You'll also hear pidgin, these days used more in fun than serious speech, such as 'da kine' and 'hey, bruddah'.

Food

Tourists will rarely see Hawaiian food except at a *luau*, when a pig is wrapped in leaves and baked over hot rocks in an *imu*, an underground pit. Other foods which might accompany the *kalua*, as the pork is called, are *lomi salmon*, salted salmon marinated with onion and tomato; *opihi*, limpets; *laulau*, pork, butterfish and beef steamed in taro leaf; and the ubiquitous *poi*, a paste made from pounded taro root, which is definitely an acquired taste.

Fresh fruits abound in the Islands, of course, most notably delicious papaya (pawpaw), mango, bananas, guava and pineapple.

Hawaii's multicultural society shows in its restaurants, with fine Japanese and Chinese cuisine readily available. A Hawaiian specialty is *saimin*, an adaptation of the Japanese fish and noodle soup. Gourmets will find more than enough Continental Restaurants, too, both in the Waikiki and on the Neighbor Islands, as the other islands are known.

Climate

Much is made from the fact that ancient Hawaiians had no word for weather in their language. It is true that the Islands enjoy a good two-season climate. Summer, from May into October, brings temperatures in the 80s; nights are about 10° cooler. When it does rain, showers are brief – just wait awhile and the sun will soon shine through again.

Winter temperatures range from the 60s at night up to the 70s and even low 80s. Rain is more frequent and heavier in winter months, even so things dry off very fast.

The climate can vary considerably from one side of an island to the other: Waikiki is dryer than northern Oahu; Kailua-Kona receives a great deal less rain than Hilo (although the folks at Hilo insist that most of their rain conveniently falls at night).

One thing to watch out for is when you plan to go up the mountains: temperatures can vary 40° from sea level to the summit of Haleakala on Maui or snow-capped Mauna Kea on Hawaii.

Choosing Your Island

Oahu and each of the Neighbor Islands is distinctive, so you can choose what appeals to you particularly. Most first-time visitors to the Islands do visit **Oahu** for Waikiki – and so they should. Despite the oft-written criticism that it is over-built and crowded, Waikiki still has a great deal to offer in good beaches, shopping and plenty to do and see. **Maui** is the beach island, where resorts and condominiums proliferate. **Kauai** is the lush, nature-lover's place. **Molokai** is for hunters, and those who want to get away from it all; **Lanai**, even more so. **Hawaii** is wide-open spaces attracting sportspeople and fishing enthusiasts, and is the island of history. **Niihau** and **Kahoolawe** cannot be visited: the former is privately-owned and the latter is a bombing target for the military.

Getting to and Around the Islands

Visitors to Hawaii these days invariably arrive by plane, except for those in the few ships that call at the Islands once or twice a year.

Airlines flying into Honolulu International Airport currently include all the transpacific airlines, foreign and domestic, plus major US carriers serving domestic routes. Several carriers are now flying from the US mainland directly to Kahului, Maui and Kailua-Kona on the Big Island. The entry of low-cost carriers on the West Coast-Hawaii route has triggered another fare war – a frequent occurrence on hotly contested routes in these days of uncertainty for the airline industry. However, the resulting budget fares may be short-lived.

Interisland Travel

Air Scheduled air service to the Neighbor Islands is provided by *Hawaiian Air, Aloha* and *Mid Pacific* using jet aircraft, and *Royal Hawaiian Air Service* and *Princeville Airways* by propeller planes. Further details on these services are given under the Getting There section for each island.

The three main inter-island airlines are also competing with discounted fares. As these are constantly changing, bargain hunters would be wise to make careful enquiry through a travel agent for up-to-date special promotional fares.

Air Tours People scheduled to stay on just Oahu, who haven't time to visit the other islands but would like to see them, can take advantage of one-day air tours offered by several companies. These include stops and sightseeing at several of the islands. Among the firms offering these tours are *Hawaiian Airlines,* 1164 Bishop St, Honolulu (tel (808) 537-5100); and *Panorama Air Tours,* 214 Lagoon Drive, Honolulu 96819 (tel (808) 836-2122). Tariffs are running around $180 to $200 per person, including hotel transfers and lunch.

Cruises *American Hawaii Cruises* introduced interisland cruises aboard the *Oceanic Independence,* formerly American Export Lines' *Independence,* in June 1980. The 750-passenger liner, now renamed *SS Independence,* is based in Honolulu and features seven-day cruises sailing each Saturday at 10 pm. The ship calls at Hilo and Kona on the Big Island, Kahului on Maui and Nawiliwili on Kauai. In June 1982, the *SS Constitution,* joined the run, which sails from Honolulu on Saturdays at 10.30 pm, following the same route in reverse.

The major difference between the two, apart from the direction in which they sail, is that the *Independence* spends two days on Maui and the *Constitution* spends two days on Kauai.

Cruise rates at writing are from $895 to $2295 per person, double occupancy. Pre-cruise packages are a good buy.

According to present planning, each of the ships is to make one transpacific cruise per year to the West coast, stopping at Los Angeles and San Francisco before the return cruise. Transpacific fares are ranging from $795 to $3696 per person.

For information and reservations: American Hawaii Cruises, 3 Embarcadero Center, San Francisco CA 94111; tel (415) 392-9400; toll free (in California) 800-622-0666, (nationwide) 800-227-3666.

Yacht Charters Finally, you can choose to cruise the islands on a chartered yacht, either bareboat or with a skipper. Several companies based in Honolulu's Kewalo Basin offer a variety of craft; one being *Hawaiiana Yacht Charters,* PO Box 8231, Honolulu, HI 96815 (tel (808) 521-6305).

Car Rental This is a highly competitive business in the Islands, which can lead to offers of all kinds of special deals during off-peak periods – and the disappearance of these deals in peak months (August, December, February) when it may be difficult to rent a car at all. Look over all charges carefully – a cheap daily rate might include a mileage minimum which could raise the charge to that offered by other companies.

Companies sometimes refuse to rent to persons under 25 years of age. Many require a deposit unless you are using a credit card. Always check out the car before you drive away; they are sometimes in less than tip-top condition if rented from a 'cheapie' lot.

Rental of a jeep or four-wheel drive vehicle is recommended only on Lanai, except for those people who want to explore the unpaved offbeat roads on Maui or Molokai.

The major car rental agencies – Hertz, Avis, National and Budget – are all represented on most islands. However, Hawaiian chains offer reliable service, often at cheaper rates. Included among them are Tropical Rent-a-Car (tel (808) 922-2385), Roberts Hawaii Rent-a-Car (tel (808) 947-3939) and Dollar Rent-a-Car (tel (808) 922-6415). On a recent trip, we found Tropical to be amongst the least expensive – $19.95 daily or $107.95 per week for Compact Stick Shift, with no mileage; $21.95 daily for Compact Automatic. Most companies offer island-hopping rates too, so ask about them.

Another money-saver can be the Fly/Drive programs offered by some of the car rental companies in conjunction with airlines and tour operators. Check with your travel agent or the airline offices. These packages often include accommodation and admission to attractions.

Most car rentals include island maps and you can get very good road maps from the Hawaii Visitors' Bureau offices on each island. A help in locating major attractions are the Hawaii Visitors' Bureau Warrior markers which point the way.

Oahu

Oahu, third largest of the main Hawaiian Islands, is where three-quarters of Hawaii's population lives. The Islands' capital, Honolulu, and tourism center, Waikiki, are on the leeward coast.

The Koolau Range and Waianae Mountains – their volcanic activity produced Oahu – now provide a dramatic backdrop to the populated coastal areas. The major area embracing both Waikiki and Honolulu stretches from Diamond Head along the southern coast to Pearl Harbor and Ewa beach in the west.

This geographic layout provides *kamaainas* (locals) with their own direction-finding language: ask the way and you will be directed not north, south, east or west, but 'so many blocks diamondhead' or 'so many blocks ewa' and, throughout the Islands, *mauka*, meaning inland, or *makai*, toward the ocean.

HISTORIC HONOLULU

Ancient Hawaiians favored the beach areas for living and left the Plains of Kou, where Honolulu now stands, bare. But this is the only protected deepwater harbor in the Islands and the advent of sailing ships needing safe anchorage soon promoted the growth of Honolulu.

After his victory at the Battle of Nuuanu in 1795, Kamehameha the Great remained on Oahu. In 1810, he moved his residence from the traditional royal grounds at Waikiki to Honolulu to be nearer his enterprises, including ships plying the sandalwood trade routes to China.

Liholiho, Kamehameha II, started his reign in 1819 at Kailua on the Big Island, but six months later he moved the court to Honolulu where it remained until he died of measles during a state visit to England in 1824.

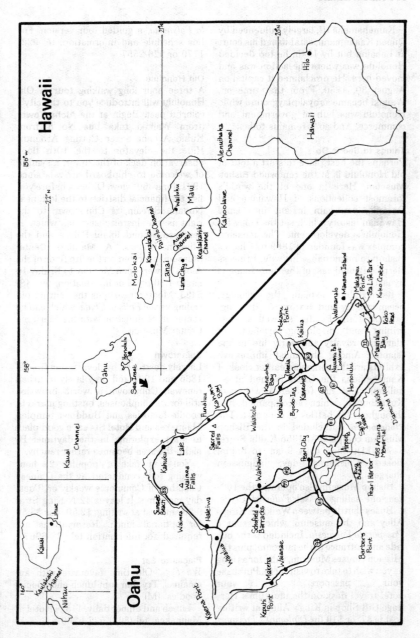

Kamehameha III, largely influenced by Queen Kaahumanu, established his court at Lahaina but by 1845, he too decided Honolulu was where the action was and moved here. He proclaimed it capital on August 30, 1850. From that time on, Waikiki became a royal playground while Honolulu was hub of government and commerce. And so it remains today.

Things to See & Do

Perhaps the best place to start a tour of old Honolulu is at the renowned **Bishop Museum**. Here in one of the world's foremost collections of Hawaiana and Oceania, you gain insight into early Hawaiian history which set the stage for Honolulu's development. The museum complex was founded in 1889 by Charles Bishop to memorialise his wife, Princess Bernice Pauahi, last of the Kamehameha dynasty.

Its exhibits explain the geology, oceanography and history of the migrations of the Pacific, as well as describing and displaying artefacts of Hawaiian royalty and early life in the Islands. Among the most impressive exhibits are the gorgeous feather cloak of Kamehameha the Great (valued at $1 million), and his feathered war god, Kukailimoku, which accompanied him throughout his battles of conquest. The **Planetarium** is included in the Bishop Museum complex. At 1355 Kalihi St (tel 847-3511); open daily 9 am to 5 pm; closed Christmas day; admission charge.

Bishop Museum also operates the 100-year-old sailing vessel *Falls of Clyde*.

Buses shuttle between Waikiki's King's Alley and the museum, which issues a *Passport to Polynesia*. Included is the bus ride and entrance to the museum, plus the Mission Houses Museum, valid for as long as you wish to take to visit them. Purchase your passport at your hotel travel desk on the museum's Heritage Gift Shop in King's Alley; at writing cost is $7, or $10 for *Diplomat's Passport to Polynesia,* a guided tour version. For bus schedule and information, tel 922-1770 or 926-2557.

Old Honolulu

A three hour long walking tour of Old Honolulu will introduce you to the city's colorful past. Begin at the **Aloha Tower** (from Waikiki take bus No 8 from Kuhio Avenue – see Getting Around). Ride the elevator to the 10th floor observation deck of the tower, a symbol of welcome to shipboard arrivals since 1921, for a 360° view. Directly before you lies the financial district; to the left, near Nuuanu Stream, is Chinatown; to the right is the historic section, which is centered around Iolani Palace and the Mission Houses. A **Maritime Center Museum** is located on the 9th floor of the Aloha Tower; open Monday to Friday 10 am to 4.30 pm. For information, tel 548-5433. Moored nearby is the century-old sailing vessel *Falls of Clyde*, which can be visited in conjunction with the Maritime Center Museum.

Chinatown

Largely destroyed by devastating fires in 1886 and 1900 and prey lately to urban renewal, Chinatown is worth browsing still for its shophouses, bustling markets, noodle factories and Buddhist temples, Maunakea and Hotel Sts are a good place to start exploring, in the daytime. By night, the area becomes rather rauchy.

You can take a popular 2½-hour walking tour conducted by the Chinese Chamber of Commerce weekly on Tuesday mornings. It leaves 42 N King St at 9.30 am; cost at writing, $2.50 plus $3.50 for optional lunch. Reservations are required; for information tel 533-6967.

Places to Eat

Wo Fat Old time favourite with ka-maainas. Try dim sum lunch and special noodles. (M)

Lunch and dinner daily. 115 N Hotel at Maunakea; tel (808) 537-6260.

Financial District

Fort St Mall, a pedestrian and shopping mall, stands on the site of the original fort which protected the fledgling city from 1816 to 1846. Parallel to it is **Bishop St**, heart of Hawaiian commerce for it is on this and adjoining streets that the Big Five companies are headquartered. These companies – C Brewer & Co, Theo H Davies & Co, Amfac (American Factors), Castle & Cooke and Alexander & Baldwin – were all formed by men who traced their lineage back to the missionaries from New England. Through the first half of the 20th century, their power was paramount in Hawaiian trade. They remain eminent, particularly in development of the tourist industry.

Places to Eat

If hunger pangs assail you here, try: *Michael's Cafeteria* – unpretentious decor but heaped helpings of good, honest food (Chinese and Western) at rock bottom prices. (B)

Breakfast, lunch and early supper; closed Sunday. Amfac Center, 745 Fort St; tel (808) 521-5602.

A stroll of the few blocks along Queen and Merchant Sts bounded by Bishop and Nuuanu reveals some architectural gems. Look out for the 1929 Italian renaissance **Dillingham Transportation Building** at the foot of Bishop; Brewer's distinctive 'missionary style' stone **headquarters** secluded in a walled garden on Fort St Mall and Queen; and the gracious Edwardian **Stangenwald** at 119 Merchant, Honolulu's first 'skyscraper' built in 1901.

Places to Eat

Around Merchant Square, the historic blocks bordering Chinatown and the Financial District, restored late 19th century edifices now house a cluster of eateries offering pub-style food in turn-of-the-century ambience: *Jamesons Irish Coffee House* and *Matteo's Royal Tavern*

are on Merchant St near Nuuanu St; *Merchant Square Oyster Bar* is around the corner on Nuuanu. All are budget-moderate and open for lunch and dinner Monday to Friday only.

Old Town

This is the area of government buildings imbued with memories of royalty, and missionary Honolulu.

Most visitors will immediately recognise one building: **Iolani Palace** is known to television viewers around the world as headquarters of *Hawaii-Five-O*. In actual fact it was the royal residence, built for King David Kalakaua in 1882, the only royal palace in the United States. It was here that Queen Liliuokalani was held under house arrest after a January 1895 abortive attempt against the republic by pro-royalists failed to restore her to the throne. After the revolution established the republic, Iolani served as capitol building first for the republic, then the territory and finally for the 50th state, until 1969 when the new State Capitol was built.

Tour buses are allowed only to pause and look at Iolani Palace for a moment. If you want to go through its refurbished chambers, tours are available, but you'll need to make reservations at S King and Richards Sts (tel 536-2474); tours Wednesday to Saturday 9 am to 2.15 pm; admission charge, (no children under 5 admitted).

In the palace grounds you'll find the **Royal Bandstand**, built for Kalakaua's coronation on February 12, 1883; free concerts are given here each Friday at 12.15 pm. The **Iolani Barracks**, originally built in 1870 to house the Royal Household Guard, were moved here in 1965 to make way for the new State Capitol.

Facing Iolani Palace on South King St is a statue of **King Kamehameha I** dressed in his royal feathered cloak and helmet, his arms raised as though in welcome to the Aliiolani Hale behind him. On May 1,

Lei Day, and June 11, Kamehameha Day, he all but disappears under a multiflorous draping of leis. This statue is actually a replica of the original which was lost at sea en route from Florence. Later recovered, the original now stands at Kapaau on the Big Island, near Kamehameha's birthplace.

The **Aliiolani Hale** (Judiciary Building), designed by an Australian architect, was started as a palace for Kalakaua but was modified before its completion in 1874 when the government decided official chambers were needed more than a royal residence. Kalakaua, whose gregariousness led to his nickname the Merry Monarch, persuaded them it could be double duty, so by day it housed the courts and parliament while in the evening he hosted lavish receptions and balls in its halls.

More solemn royal occasions were held in **Kawaiahao Church,** a block east on South King St. Designed by missionary leader, Hiram Bingham, in 1837 and dedicated in 1842, it was originally known as the King's Chapel. Here royalty was christened, married, inaugurated and given last rites. It was used as a meeting house too; Hawaii's first constitutional convention took place in it. Kawaiahao still sustains a Hawaiian congregation and services are conducted in both Hawaiian and English. If you attend the Sunday 10.30 am service, you will hear the choir, famous for its singing of *himeni,* Hawaiian versions of Christian hymns. In the Kawaiahao grounds are an **Adobe School House** built in 1835, the **Lunalilo Mausoleum,** where the first elected king insisted on being buried close to his subjects, and a **missionary cemetery.** The headstones here are a litany in stone to early missionary families whose names now resound in Hawaiian commerce. The church is open Monday to Saturday, 8.30 am to 4 pm.

Shades of the God-fearing missionaries hover as you stroll through the **Mission Houses Museum.** The 1821 Frame House, Hawaii's oldest wooden house built of timbers brought around the Horn, was home to Hiram Bingham, Gerrit Judd and Elisha Loomis. A well-versed volunteer will tell you about missionary days as you wander through the buildings. On S King St a block east of Kawaiahao; open daily 9 am to 4 pm; closed January 1, Thanksgiving, Christmas day; admission charge.

A museum volunteer guide, usually descended from a missionary family, brings history to life on **Historic Honolulu,** a 2½-hour walking tour of the Capitol area, Kawaiahao Church and the Mission Houses. It leaves Monday through Friday at 9.30 am; reservations necessary (tel 531-0481); charge currently $5.

At the **State Capitol,** across the mall behind Iolani Palace, observe how the architecture was designed to symbolize the islands: the two legislative chambers are cone-shaped to resemble volcanoes, its slender pillars represent palm trees and the surrounding pools, the ocean. When it is illuminated at night, it is a striking sight.

The grounds of **Washington Place,** behind the Capitol on Beretania are a picture of tranquility in the warm sun. But they were the scene of high drama when Queen Liliuokalani was living here following her overthrow. A cache of firearms retrieved from the flower gardens at the time of the attempted counter-revolution led to her imprisonment in Iolani Palace for nine months. Upon her release, she returned to Washington Place and lived quietly here until her death in 1917. Now it is the governor's mansion, not open to visitors.

About half a mile east on Beretania, you come to a handsome example of Hawaiian-style architecture, the **Honolulu Academy of Arts.** Its halls display a rare collection of Oriental Art and fine local works, as well as European and American masterpieces. If you time your visit at either 11.45 am or 1 pm from Tuesday through Friday, you can indulge in a gourmet luncheon served by members of the Academy Volunteers Council in their Garden Cafe; proceeds go toward new acquisitions. (They also serve supper at 6.30 pm on Thursday evenings.) The academy is open Tuesday, Wednesday, Friday, Saturday from 10 am to 4.30 pm; Thursday 11 am to 4.30 pm, 7 to 9 pm; Sunday 2 to 5 pm; free. Luncheon and supper reservations required (tel 531-8865 Monday 9 am to noon; Tuesday to Friday 9 am to 2 pm).

An adjunct of the Academy which appeals to art lovers and horticulturalists alike is the **Alice Cooke-Spalding House**. Both house and gardens are a subtle blend of Orient and Occident; collections include Asian decorative arts, *ukiyo-e* prints and James Michener's Japanese prints dating from the 17th century. At 2411 Makiki Heights Drive; open Tuesday to Sunday 1 to 4.30 pm, closed Monday; admission charge, except Tuesday free.

A delightful park opposite the main Academy building reminds of one of those brief quirks so prevalent in Hawaii's past. **Thomas Square** honors British Rear Admiral Richard Thomas who was instrumental in restoring the independence of the Hawaiian kingdom five months after Kamehameha III had been forced to cede it to Great Britain in 1843. The park's great banyans provide a shady path to stroll from Beretania to South King, where the **Blaisdell Center** convention and exhibition complex is, set amidst attractively landscaped grounds. The theater-concert hall, home to the Honolulu Symphony, features an exhibit of bronze and copper sculptures in its foyer.

WAIKIKI

Hard to believe now that Waikiki was once an area of taro patches and swamps. Royalty and *alii* (chiefs) built their homes in coconut groves along the water's edge. With annexation came fame to the area known locally simply as 'The Beach'. In 1901 the first hotel, the *Moana,* opened;

Waikiki was on its way as a popular playground.

But the name Waikiki means 'spouting water' and indeed floods frequently threatened it, so in the early 1920s a massive reclamation project dredged the Ala Wai Canal, filled the swampland and duck ponds with coral and channeled the mountain streams away, transforming Waikiki into a dry, attractive area ripe for development.

'Waikiki Beach' describes a two-mile stretch from the Outrigger Canoe Club just beyond Sans Souci Beach to the Kahanamoku lagoon near Ala Wai Yachting Marina. The beaches, protected by an offshore reef, are relatively coral-free, excellent for swimming and snorkelling. They are usually safe for beginners in the ancient art of surfing, once enjoyed here by Kamehameha I and Kaahumanu who were often seen riding the waves on their koa boards.

Along Waikiki's main artery, Kalakaua Avenue, activity seems to be orchestrated in allegro tempo. At the eastern end of Waikiki, however, the pace quietens as the Avenue enters the quiet haven of Kapiolani Park.

Kapiolani Park

Dedicated in 1877 during Kalakaua's reign and named for his wife, the park is a favorite of both *kamaainas* (locals) and *malihinis* (visitors) alike. It's best known to visitors as site of the **Kodak Hula Show,** when dancers perform the hula and other Polynesian dances from Tuesday through Friday, 10 am; free.

A collection of rare Hawaiian birds and the Islands' only snakes (two non-poisonous males, a requirement imposed by a legislative act!) in addition to the usual menagerie are the draw to the **Honolulu Zoo,** which you'll find at the park's entrance. Open daily 8.30 am to 4.15 pm,; Wednesday nights until 7.30 pm June to August; admission charge.

A popular **Art Mart** decorates the zoo's fence with local artists' works weekends from 10 am to 4 pm.

Waikiki Aquarium, one of the world's first, contains an interesting display of tropical species and is open daily 10 am to 5 pm; closed holidays; nominal admission charge.

Garden lovers will enjoy the park's hibiscus-bordered **Rose Garden** and the brilliant spring and summer displays of shower trees and monkeypods in bloom. You can see them between 8 am and 3 pm daily.

Places to Eat

Two restaurants worth checking out here in the cluster of hotels by Sans Souci Beach, one award-winning and expensive, the other a favorite with locals for its setting:

Michel's Classical French cuisine exquisitely presented in elegant room; highly acclaimed Sunday champagne brunch. (E)

Breakfast Monday to Friday, lunch Monday to Saturday, dinner daily. In Colony Surf Hotel, 2895 Kalakaua; tel 923-6552 (reservations necessary).

Hau Tree Lanai Enjoy good steak and seafood dishes served in a delightful setting under hau trees on terrace overlooking sand. (M)

Breakfast, lunch and dinner daily. In New Otani Kaimana Beach Hotel, 2863 Kalakaua; tel 923-1555.

Things to See & Do
Kalakaua Avenue

Walking west from the park, you come to Kuhio Beach Park, originally part of Prince Kuhio's property which he opened to the public in 1918. The beloved prince was Hawaii's first representative to the US Congress in 1902. He served until 1922 and was father of the Homestead Act of 1920 which gave Hawaiians of more than half native blood the right to a 99-year lease on a lot of land – today's homesteads, which you'll see clustered throughout the Islands.

Water sports are catered for at the **Waikiki Beach Center** at the west end of Kuhio Beach Park. Here you can arrange surfing lessons and outrigger canoe rides, as well as renting surfboards. Behind the Beach Center, look for the four **Healing Stones** set in the sand near the sea wall. Legend tells that four *kahunas* (priests), each posessing great wisdom and powers of healing, visited from a distant land. When they departed, each endowed a stone with his *Mana* (spirit) making them a source of healing.

From Kuhio Beach Park to Ala Moana Boulevard, Kalakaua Avenue and the blocks each side of it are lined with luxury hotels, more modest apartment-hotels, restaurants, shopping complexes and souvenir shops. For a look at the Waikiki that was, wander up the side streets between Kuhio and Ala Wai. You'll see weather-worn cottages tucked amongst the high rises, survivors of the era when the blocks from Ala Wai to the beachfront were filled with similar houses. Skyrocketing real estate prices preclude the luxury of such low density housing now, but strolling these blocks you'll find that even the towering hotels and apartment blocks are softened in appearance by lush tropical foliage.

If you're shopping bent, try **King's Alley**, it's stores are designed to re-create the 19th century period of the monarchy. You can witness the Changing of the Guards ceremony here each evening at 6.15 pm. The always popular **International Market Place**, occupying a former royal estate, has stalls selling beach clothes, shell jewelry and souvenirs, and restaurants and nightclubs dispense victuals and entertainment. Newer to the scene are the **Waikiki Shopping Plaza**, the **Royal Hawaiian Center** fronting the Royal Hawaiian Hotel and the adjacent **Rainbow Promenade**, all harboring restaurants from elegant to interesting budget fast-food. There's good, budget-priced eating available at Woolworths, on the other side of Kalakaua – it's popular for breakfast. Lunch and dinner are served, too.

Several hotels along Kalakaua Avenue are worth exploring, no matter where you are staying. The **Hyatt Regency** centers around an atrium which is highlighted by a waterfall. The **Moana**, evocative of colonial days, is popular for its Banyan Court – although remodelling has reduced its charm, the view from beneath the banyan's awning is still great. A short walk along the sands from here is the **Royal Hawaiian Hotel**, one of the Grand Old Ladies of the Pacific, affectionately known as the 'Pink Palace'. The original building, opened in 1927 on the site King Kamehameha V chose for his summer palace in the 1870s, still reflects the regal elegance of its heyday in the chandeliered entrance lobby and ornately-decorated halls. It has been named an Historical Landmark. To see what Waikiki looked like in the 'good old days', take the escalator in the **Sheraton Waikiki** to its convention rooms floor and follow the signs to the 'Historical Room', where a photographic exhibition illustrates events in Waikiki's past. Much further

down the beach, **Hilton Hawaiian Village's** international shopping area, the Rainbow Bazaar, is fun to browse.

The Hilton edges Fort deRussy, which the US Army maintains in park-like condition. Military uniforms, hardware and artillery are on display at the **museum**, which is open Tuesday through Sunday 10 am to 4.30 pm; closed Christmas Day and New Year's Day; free.

Backing Fort DeRussy is one of Waikiki's best beaches, which seldom is as crowded as the others.

Beyond the Hilton on Ala Moana Boulevard is the **Ilikai Hotel** where you can watch a torchlighting ceremony and Hawaiian entertainment free any evening at 6.30 pm.

Places to Eat

Tahitian Lanai Polynesian dining in genuine island setting. Piano bar popular with locals. (M)

Breakfast, lunch, dinner. Waikikian Hotel, 1811 Ala Moana Boulevard; tel 946-6541.

In the *TraveLodge* opposite there's an all-you-can-eat restaurant – at $6.95 it's a good buy! Further along, *Victoria Station* offers ribs, all-you-can-eat, for $11.95 at dinnertime.

In Discovery Bay, the more expensive *Bon Appetit* serves excellent French dinners.

ALA MOANA

Not strictly speaking in Waikiki but adjoining it is the vast **Ala Moana Center**, definitely worth investigating. It's not only a place to shop, but it's great for people watching and observing crafts-

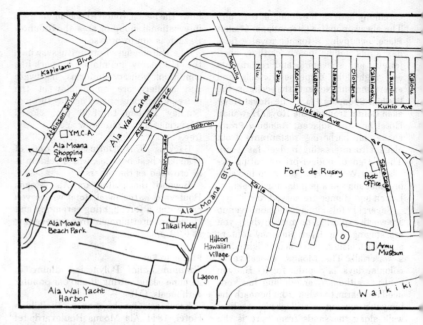

people at work. The malls are decorated with sculptures by Hawaiian artists and provide the setting for a free hula show by young folk every Sunday at 9.30 am. Stores of every variety from Sears to quick food counters are geared more to *kamaaina* (local) than *malahini* (visitor) and their ethnic mix is a striking reminder of Hawaii's pluralistic society.

Photographers who want to get a sweeping shot of Waikiki Beach should wander across to **Ala Moana Park**, where a jutting peninsula called Magic Island offers the perfect opportunity. The park, a great favorite with locals on weekends, stretches from the Ala Wai Boat Harbor to Kewalo Basin, where you go for charter fishing boats and cruise sailings (see Cruises). Popular with families is *Fisherman's Wharf*, a budget to moderate seafood restaurant at Kewalo Basin.

Shoppers might also check out Ward Center, west on Ala Moana Boulevard, which includes a *Spaghetti Factory* and other restaurants.

PEARL HARBOR

Pearl Harbor, or Puuloa as it was known then, was in ancient times the traditional home of Ka'ahupahau, the Shark Queen. Sharks were revered by Hawaiians of old as protective gods. Special food offerings were prepared for them, so the sharks would guard the coast and assure munificent fishing grounds. When Pearl Harbor was ceded to the US government in 1887 and the navy began construction of its base, Hawaiian warnings not to offend Ka'ahupahau went unheeded. Soon afterward, dredging machinery was destroyed in a storm and a huge drydock collapsed as it neared completion. Draw your own conclusion as to whether the unhappy history of Pearl Harbor, culminating on December 7, 1941 with the devastating attack on the United States' largest naval base, might have been written differently had the Shark Queen

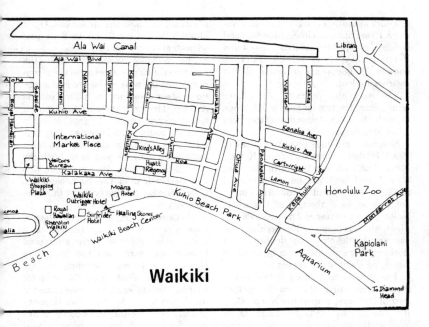

Waikiki

been appeased!

Pearl Harbor actually consists of three lochs in cloverleaf shape: East Loch and Middle Loch are separated by Ford Island, off which lies the USS *Arizona* Memorial. The main portion of the US Naval Base sits on the jutting spit of land between them and West Loch.

The *USS Arizona* Memorial, enshrining the watery tomb of 1102 crewmen, lures more visitors than almost any other tourist attraction in Hawaii. You've a choice of how you visit it.

USS Arizona

To actually set foot on the memorial, you must take the navy boat from the **Arizona Memorial Visitor Center** at Halawa Gate. You can reach this by taking bus no 20 from Waikiki or a tour bus with pickups at hotels. (For a shuttle running every half-hour at a cost of $4 round trip, contact USS Arizona Memorial Shuttle, 2370 Kuhio Avenue, tel 926-1938; it is approx-

imately a one-hour bus trip from Waikiki to the Halawa Gate.)

On arrival at the Visitor Center, operated by friendly and informative National Park Service members, you are given a ticket and number for the boat, which runs every 15 minutes from 8.15 am to 3 pm. Then you enter a theater for a navy film about Pearl Harbor and the attack, after which you can wander around the WW II museum until your number is called to board the boat.

Once on the memorial, you look down on the superstructure of the battleship a few feet below the water's surface, wander the shrine room bearing the engraved names of the 1177 men killed and see the ship's bell.

It is best to arrive early in the day if possible as the wait gets longer with each hour. Since the Memorial is closed Mondays, Tuesday is the busiest day and there can be a very long wait with little chance of getting a ticket after 1 pm.

Tours operate Tuesday through Sunday 8.15 am to 3 pm; closed Mondays and holidays except Memorial day, July 4 and Veterans day; free; tel 422-2771 to enquire if boats are running should weather be bad.

The navy also operates a one-hour cruise from Halawa landing which stops at both the *USS Arizona* and the *USS Utah* Memorials.

Several companies operate cruises of Pearl Harbor, which sail from Kewalo Basin. These obviate the waiting line but they cannot land you on the memorial itself; you simply cruise around it. You do get a good look, though, at the whole facility, nerve center of America's Pacific Fleet, which is home to 60 warships. You can see battleships and destroyers at dock, perhaps a nuclear submarine or two. (See Cruises for details.)

The submariners' story is told in the **Pacific Submarine Museum** in another part of the base; stop at the Nimitz Gate for visitor pass and directions. Open Wednesday to Sunday, 10 am to 5 pm; free.

NUUANA VALLEY

You'll find a number of attractions, historic and contemporary, in the Nuuanu Valley above downtown Honolulu.

A century or so ago, a Dr William Hillebrand was sent off to search the Americas and Asia for labor needed to work the sugar plantations. He brought back not only field hands but cuttings from which has sprung one of the most renowned gardens in the Pacific. In the idyllic setting of **Foster Botanic Garden**, you'll become acquainted with many of Hawaii's plants and flowers. It's at 180 N Vineyard Boulevard; open daily 9 am to 4 pm; free.

Another outstanding garden you can tour is the six-acre estate known as the *Walker Gardens*, at 2616 Pali Highway (SR 61). Rare old trees, a profusion of orchids and an area of native Hawaiian plants are amongst the attractions. Open Monday to Friday 9 am to 3.15 pm; admission charge; tel 595-7565.

The reigning monarchs, with the exception of Kamehameha the Great and King Lunalilo, were all laid to rest at the **Royal Mausoleum**, up the hill on Nuuana Avenue. The royal remains were moved to family crypts within the grounds and in 1922 the mausoleum became a chapel. A state parks folder points the way for a self-guided tour or you may be lucky enough to encounter the custodian, who is a descendant of the Kamehamehas. Open Monday to Friday 8 am to 4 pm; Saturday 8 am to noon; free.

At **Queen Emma's Summer Palace**, country retreat of Kamehemeha IV's strong-willed widow who twice attempted to become monarch, you'll see many rare Hawaiian artefacts, including an exquisite handcrafted *kapa*, the quilt for which Hawaiian women became famed in missionary days. At 2913 Pali Highway (SR 61); open Monday to Friday 9 am to 4 pm; Saturday 9 am to noon; closed Sunday and holidays; admission charge; tel 595-3167.

Detour on Nuuanu Pali Drive, off Pali Highway, for a drive through tranquil forest en route to the climax of your exploration, the **Pali Lookout**. From here you get a panoramic view of the valley framing Kaneohe Bay, and as you lean into the always gusty wind, remember that on the very place where you stand, on a day in 1795 warriors fought a desperate battle which changed Hawaii's history. Kamehameha the Great had driven the forces of Kalanikupule from Waikiki up the Nuuanu Valley to their final stand. Defeated overwhelmingly, many Oahu warriors leapt to their death on the rocks below. Kamehameha had won the final battle in his quest to unify the islands.

PUNCHBOWL

Warriors of more recent wars rest in the **National Memorial Cemetery of the Pacific**, cradled in Punchbowl crater. The extinct volcano was once called Puowaina, the Hill of Sacrifice, for the *heiau* (temple) which stood atop the hill. Today the cemetery harbors the dead of three wars: WW II, Korea and Vietnam. On Memorial Day, each grave is draped with a flower lei made by school children.

If you wish to seek out a particular grave, stop at the office; they'll look up the number of the plot and give you a map indicating the area in which you can find it. Open daily from 8 am to 5 pm; free.

From Punchbowl, you cab take the Tantalus-Round top loop drive, which circles the shoulders of these two lofty hills. The hairpin-curve drive affords vistas of the Waianae Mountains and the ocean and, from Round Top, Manoa Valley. The road wends through an exclusive residential area and sweet-smelling tropical forests, ablaze in summer with scarlet mountain apple and exotic tiger's claw. You can even pick guava ripe from the tree when they're in season. The lookout in pocket-sized **Ualakaa Park** puts the whole of Oahu's south coast, from Koko Head to the Waianaes, at your feet.

MANOA VALLEY

Main attraction in this well-populated valley is the 300-acre **University of Hawaii Campus**, which does not offer much of architectural interest but contains many exotic trees and plants. You can take a tour of the internationally-oriented **East West Center** weekday afternoons from Jefferson Hall and the whole campus from Bachman Hall (tel 948-8856 for information).

One of the world's largest free-flight aviaries inhabited by many species of brightly-plumed birds draws bird lovers to **Paradise Park**. Trained birds perform at intervals throughout the day.

Open daily 9.30 am to 5 pm; closed Christmas and New Year's days; admission charge.

Half-day tours are operated, with pickup at Waikiki hotels; current rate is $7.50

adults; reservation required, tel 988-2141.

AROUND THE ISLAND

It took Queen Emma two weeks to circle the island on horseback but you can do it in a day's driving, though many people prefer to overnight, perhaps at the *Turtle Bay Hilton and Country Club* on the North Shore. Or you can take the 'short loop' around the eastern tip only.

THE EASTERN LOOP (Short Loop)

Beyond Kapiolani Park, Kalakaua Avenue becomes Diamond Head Rd, running around the base of the famed landmark. The extinct crater of **Diamond Head** once the home of Pele, Goddess of Fire, is part of a military reservation. You can drive into the crater through a tunnel between 7 am and 5 pm daily, or view its interior from either Wilhelmina Rise or Maunalani Heights.

The road ends at the **Kahala Hilton**, which you can explore on a self-guided walking tour – pick up a folder at the front desk. Worth noting: the lobby chandeliers containing 28,000 pieces of glass! If you're there around 10.30 am, 12.30 pm or 2.30 pm, you can watch the feeding of porpoises, turtles and fish in the lagoon.

HANAUMA BEACH

From Kahala, you drive the Kalinianaole Highway, SR 72, around the southeast coast. One of the Islands' finest beaches is on **Hanauma Bay**, a lagoon-filled crater; swimming and snorkelling in the coral gardens off its crescent-shaped beach are particularly fine.

KOKO HEAD

At the **Halona Blowhole Lookout,** you not only see incoming waves spewing water out through a submerged lava vent, but on a clear day you can make out the island of Molokai across the Kaiwi Channel. Above, **Koko Crater,** Pele's last attempt to find a home on Oahu, cradles a 200-acre botanic garden of cactus, succulents and other dry land plants.

MAKAPUU POINT

The beaches from here to Makapuu Point are favorites with local surfers but definitely are not for novices. Makapuu Point gives you a clear view of the northeastern shore. The lighthouse on the point was built in 1906, after the liner *Manchuria* had foundered on a nearby reef. Makapuu Beach has long been one of the most popular for bodysurfing; it's the venue for world championships.

Lately a new sport has entered the picture here: look up and you might see hang-gliders wafting on the air currents below the cliffs.

Sea Life Park

Beyond the beach is Sea Life Park. Stroll down the spiral ramp around the 300,000-gallon Hawaiian Reef Tank to view marine life to a depth of three fathoms. You can observe the training of porpoises and penguins in the Ocean Science Theater and watch small whales showing off their tricks in the Whaler's Cove. The skeleton of a 36-foot Humpback whale is centerpiece of the Whaling Museum, which displays whaling artefacts and examples of scrimshaw. It's open daily 9 am to 5 pm; last show 3.15 plm; closed Christmas day; admission charge; tel 259-7933; museum closes at 4.30 pm; free.

The larger island you see offshore is Manana, Rabbit Island, where royalist counter-revolutionaries hid arms and ammunition for their desperate and abortive attempt to reinstate Queen Liliuokalani in 1894. The other one, Kaohikaipu, Turtle Island, is a bird sanctuary.

PALI HIGHWAY

Passing through the Waimanalo area, where many of Oahu's vegetables and flowers including the wax-like anthurium are grown, the road terminates at its junction with SR 61, the Pali Highway. To the right lie Kailua and Lanikai, known as the bedroom communities of Honolulu, both of which offer good swimming on quiet beaches. North of Kailua, the land juts out into the Mokapu Peninsula, mostly occupied by a Marine Corps Air Station. Once much favored as a royal resort, the peninsula had the dubious distinction of receiving the first bombs on December 7, 1941 from Japanese bombers on their way to Pearl Harbor.

SR 61 leads across the Koolau Range back to Honolulu, eight miles away – take this road to complete the 'short loop'.

THE NORTH SHORE LOOP
Kaneohe Bay

If you're continuing on, a few miles inland you'll come to SR 83, the Kamehameha Highway, your route around the North Shore. From the Heeia Kea Boat Harbor, you can take the Coral Gardens Glass Bottom Boat out on Kaneohe Bay to view the coral reefs, sadly depleted by pollution these days. You'll get a fine view of the shoreline against the backdrop of the Koolau Range, and the Heeia Fishpond, one of the few surviving old Hawaiian ponds used for storing and fattening fish.

The tour lasts an hour and you will need to make reservations; tel 247-0375; rate currently $5.

Two popular attractions inland from Kaneohe Bay lie in the shelter of a secluded valley. Haiku Gardens was formerly a private estate; now it is a restaurant set in lushly tropical grounds, featuring bamboo thickets, orchids and ferns, and a water lily pond.

Byodo-In Temple replicates the famous classic Japanese temple on the outskirts of Kyoto; it was built in 1968 to commemorate the centennial of Japanese migration into Hawaii. Framed by the fluted verdant pali and reflected in its carp-filled lake, the temple presents a picture of serenity. To reach it, follow the Valley of the Temples signs off Kahekili

Highway west of Haiku Rd. It's open daily 9 am to 5 pm; admission charge.

Kahkili and Kamehameha Highways emerge at Kahaluu, passing through groves of bananas and papayas and skirting beach parks shaded by kamani and ironwoods. Offshore is **Mokolii Island**, better known as Chinaman's Hat. Legend tells that the isle represents the tail of the dragon-like lizard Mo'o, which one of the Pele's sisters slew and threw into the ocean.

KAHANA BAY

You pass a poi factory at Waiahole, where you can stop for a demonstration of how the paste is made from the taro plant, the ruins of Dr Judd's **old sugar mill**, which closed in 1871 and, at Kahana Bay, an overgrown stone wall marking **Huilua**, Oahu's oldest fishpond and now a National Historical Landmark.

Above looms the rock formation called the **Crouching Lion**; by legend this is a Tahitian demigod who was turned to stone and doomed to rest eternally in this crouching position. In its lee is one of this area's better-known restaurants.

If you're in the mood for a gruelling but rewarding 3-mile hike, pull off at the sign for the **Sacred Falls**. From the fee parking lot, a rocky trail through the verdant gorge brings you to a shaded pool fed by the 87-foot cascade. You can take a refreshing dip while admiring the peaks towering overhead. Don't attempt this hike in bad weather and you may protect yourself from slipping by placating the pig-god Kamapuaa, to whom this area is sacred. All you need do is place a stone on a pile of leaves in his honor!

En route to Laie you pass through **Hauula**, named for the once abundant hau trees whose profuse blossoms bloom bright yellow in the early morning, then change with the day's passage to a red-gold by sunset and finally dark red at night, when they fall to the ground. Early Hawaiians used the hau for medicine, nets, tapa and lashings. Only a few trees remain in the area, but you can still see them changing color in July and August.

LAIE

In 1850 the American-based Church of Jesus Christ of the Latter Day Saints, the Mormon Church, sent missionaries out into the Pacific to colonize in Hawaii and the Samoa. Their headquarters established at Laie in 1864 grew into today's 6000-acre development. It embraces the Mormon Temple, an impressive structure set in formal gardens, which was completed on Thanksgiving day, 1919; a campus of **Brigham Young University**; a lodge and restaurant; and one of Hawaii's foremost tourist attractions, the Polynesian Cultural Center.

Polynesian Cultural Center The center serves a dual purpose, preserving and displaying arts and crafts of Pacific peoples while providing jobs for Brigham Young students. By foot, tram or canoe you can visit villages of the Marquesas and Tahiti (French Polynesia), Maori New Zealand, Samoa, Fiji, Tonga and old Hawaii, clustered around waterways and a lagoon. Traditional double-hulled canoes bear singing and dancing villagers through the lagoons in the *Pageant of the Long Canoes* at 3 pm. Lunch and dinner are served in a restaurant and two snack bars – being Mormon, no alcohol is allowed.

The day is climaxed by the extravaganza *Invitation to Paradise*, featuring music and dance of the cultures including ancient chants and hulas. Open Monday to Saturday 10 am to 7 pm; closed holidays. Show Monday to Saturday 7.30 pm; reservations a must, as early as possible; tel (808) 293-3333, toll-free 800-367-7060. The full-day package including dinner and the evening show is currently $34; admission only $14; buffet dinner $13 and evening show only $15 (prices may change from time to time).

Free tram tours from the Cultural

Center will take you to the Mormon Temple and Brigham Young University.

KUILIMA

Near the northern tip of Oahu on Kawela Bay sits the *Turtle Bay Hilton and Country Club*, the first major hotel development on the North Shore. It offers swimming, tennis and golf, as well as attractive restaurants and watering holes, so you may elect to stay over to break the Circle Island drive; facilities are described in the Places to Stay section.

SURFING BEACHES

The North Shore is where you find the fabled surfing beaches. These are strictly for experts and novices should restrict their interest to watching only – particularly in winter, when waves turn into walls of water 35 feet high!

Good vantage points from which to watch surfing action are **Sunset Beach**, the **Velzyland** surfing break on Kaunala Beach just past Sunset Point, and the famed **Banzai Pipeline**, best seen from Ehukai Beach Park.

You'll have a panoramic view extending from Waimea Bay to Kaena Point at the island's western tip from Oahu's largest ancient *heiau* (temple) **Puu O Mahuka** – look for the HVB Warrior sign at Pupukea Rd (you may find the road too rough for driving after a storm). It was at this *heiau* that a *kahuna* (priest) predicted the overrunning of the Islands by white strangers from a far-off land.

WAIMEA VALLEY

The history of a once thriving rural community wiped out by floods in 1864 is told on the tram ride into **Waimea Falls Park**, where you'll see rare Hawaiian birds and plants. You can buy picnic fixings at the remodeled turn-of-the-century Country Store and enjoy the falls-fed swimming hole. Cook's ships stopped here for water in 1779 on the way home after his death; visitors still appreciate the valley's natural beauty. Open daily 10

am to 5.30 pm; admission charge; tel 923-8448 or 638-8511.

HALEIWA

Haleiwa still shows signs of it's turn-of-the-century heyday when the railroad terminated here and it was a fashionable resort. Its somewhat Bohemian atmosphere is sparking a revival and it is popular with sports fishermen. You can rent boats in the harbor under the arched Anahulu Stream bridge. Look for the 1861 Protestant Church, sometimes called **Liliuokalani Church** because in 1890 the queen presented the clock with hours marked by the letters of her name. Notable are the 15-stained glass windows by contemporary artist, Erica Karawina, and the graveyard with headstones dating back to the 1830s.

From Haleiwa, Kamehameha Highway (SR 99) heads toward Pearl Harbor or you can take the more scenic but slower Kaukonahua Rd (SR 803). From Wahiawa, freeway H-2 will take you to Pearl City, where you pick up H-1 back to Honolulu.

MOKULEIA

You can drive along the coast from Haleiwa toward Kaena Point but the paved road deadends short of the point. On Sunday afternoons from March through September, you can catch a **polo** match at Mokuleia. It starts at 2 pm and there is an admission charge.

If you'd like a bird's-eye view of the ocean with its coral reefs and sugar and pineapple plantation fields edged by the volcanic Waianaes, take a glider ride from **Dillingham Air Field**, beyond Mokuleia, between 10 am and 5.30 pm; tel 623-6711.

THE INNER ISLAND ROUTE

The Inner Island route cuts across the fertile Leilehua Plateau, which sits between the Waianae and Koolau Ranges 1000 feet above sea level. This is pineapple country, with precisely contoured rows forming geometric patterns across the plateau's 18,000 acres. The pineapple industry was started in the Islands in the late 19th century; today Hawaii grows half the world's pineapples.

WAHIEWA

You can learn about the industry's history at the **Dole Pineapple Pavilion** (pick up some travel-pack cartons here, too) and the **Del Monte Pineapple Variety Garden** on the way to Wahiawa. Wahiawa is center for pineapple workers and service families from nearby **Schofield Barracks** and Wheeler Air Force Base.

Home of the 25th Infantry Division, Schofield until WW II was the army's largest installation, familiar to those who remember *From Here to Eternity*. Ask directions to the **Tropic Lightning Museum**, a well-displayed collection which traces the post's history. Open Wednesday through Friday between 10 am and 4 pm; Saturday and Sunday noon to 4 pm; free.

Watch for the statue of the Golden Dragon, made by two soldiers using kitchen tools to honor the 14th Infantry's assault on Peking during the 1900 Boxer Rebellion.

PEARL CITY

This route passes through forested hills and over deep Kipapa Gulch, named for the warriors who were trapped and fell 'one on top of the other' when invading forces were repelled here in a 14th century battle. Above Pearl Harbor, you pass through Pearl City with its landmark *Pearl City Tavern*, popular for an extensive menu of Japanese and seafood dishes, its Monkey Bar, bonsai gardens and weekend alfresco art shows.

ALOHA STADIUM

Nearing Pearl Harbor, you can see the 40,000-seat Aloha Stadium, home of the Islanders baseball team and the University of Hawaii football games, as well as the prestigious annual Hula Bowl game. Built in 1975 at a cost of $32 million, the stadium's revolutionary design allows conversion from football to baseball configuration by remote control.

MOANALUA GARDENS

Kamehameha V's summer cottage and an old Chinese entertainment hall are set in Moanalua Gardens. The 26-acre private park is noted for its huge monkeypod trees and white mahogany tree. Visitors are welcome to picnic, even fish in the meandering stream. On Puuloa Rd (SR 66) off H-1; open daily.

CASTLE PARK HAWAII

Castle Park Hawaii is a fun park designed more for locals than visitors. Families enjoy its slides, bumper boats, mini-racing cars and mini-golf. Focal point of the park is a moated castle restaurant. If you go, remember to take swim suits and towels; dressing rooms are available. At 4561 Salt Lake Boulevard; tel 367-5670; open daily 9.30 am to 10.30 pm; admission charge.

THE LEEWARD COAST ROUTE

Leeward signifies the portion of coast away from the prevailing winds, basically the south and southwestern coast of Oahu. Farrington Highway skirts Pearl Harbor, then dips south to pass around the tip of the Waianae Range before running up the Waianae Coast, stopping just short of Kaena Point.

WAIANAE COAST

This coastal strip is rich in legend and little developed, except for the area around Makaha. The highway passes between sparkling beaches and Hawaiian Homestead land tucked on the arid coastal shelf in the lee of the Waianaes. The nine-mile stretch from Kahe Point to Makaha has some of the island's best swimming beaches (use caution though, for the rip can be heavy), picnic and camping facilities and good fishing.

Roads lead back into valleys where truck farming, mango orchards and taro patches flourish.

Many Samoans have recently settled in this area and on a Sunday in their churches, you can hear them singing *a capella* – it's a thrilling experience.

POKAI BAY

You'll find sport-fishing boats for charter in scenic Pokai Bay and its breakwater makes for safe swimming. Legend says that a great ancient chief named Pokai planted Hawaii's first coconut tree here and that a few trees remain of the famous grove as **Ka Ulu Niu o Pokai**.

Kaneilio Point, which separates Lualualei Beach Park and Pokai Bay, was the site of a famed temple of learning, **Kuilioloa Heiau**, where Kamehameha the Great is reputed to have attended services before setting out on his first attempt to conquer Kauai. The *heiau* ruins make a fine vantage point for views of the towering Waianae Range and the coastline.

MAKAHA

Makaha Beach is known primarily as setting for the **International Surfing Championships**, which have drawn aficionados of the sport to watch the best in action each year since 1952; they're held in late December, usually.

Makaha is rapidly developing as a resort area, with the *Sheraton Makaha Resort and Country Club* a mile up the valley, and a growing number of condominiums both in the valley and along the beach.

North of Makaha, the road passes several good, sparsely populated beaches; the beauty of these is that you'll probably be sharing them with Hawaiian families rather than other tourists!

KAENA

Just past the now silent Barking Sands, you come to **Kaena Cave**, legendary domain of Kane, ancient god of creation. Often called Makua Cave, the 450-foot-long cavern is also reputed to have sheltered the legendary Nanaue, half-shark and half-man, who carried his victims into the back of the cave. Finally, his duality discovered, he was himself slain.

Makua Beach had a moment of glory in 1965 when Hollywood reconstructed 19th century Lahaina here to use for location filming of *Hawaii*.

Kaena Point

Just beyond, the paved road ends; the coral and gravel track around the end of Kaena Point is difficult even for four-wheel drive vehicles. However, you should view the sunset from here before turning back; it touches the waters of the Kauai Channel with a fiery incandescence.

Things to Do

Cruises & Water Sports Cruises from Waikiki and Honolulu are easy to find; along Fisherman's Wharf at Kewalo Basin, docks are lined with sailboats and cruisers ready to charter for sightseeing or deep sea fishing. Regularly scheduled cruises tend to change frequently so the examples below are given only for guidance. Check with your hotel tour desk for current schedules and prices, or wander down to Kewalo Basin.

Very popular are the narrated cruises which leave Kewalo morning and afternoon, usually at 9.30 am and 1.30 pm, for a 2½-hour cruise to **Pearl Harbor**. Amongst current trips are Hawaiian Cruises' *Adventure* (tel 923-2061) and Paradise Cruises' *Pearl Kai* (tel 536-3641). Costs are ranging from $6 to $10. Hilton's catamaran *Rainbow 1* departs from behind the Hilton and costs $14.50, (tel 955-3348). Remember, on these cruises, you cannot disembark at the *USS Arizona* Memorial, though you do view both this and the *USS Utah* Memorial.

The Sheraton-Waikiki's 42-foot catamaran *Leahi* makes six daily trips off the hotel's beach to cruise off Diamond Head at $8, plus a sunset cruise with open bar for $15 (tel 922-5665).

Coral viewing is offered aboard the *Ani Ani* which sails from Kewalo Basin daily at 9.30, 10.30 and 11.30 am and 1.30, 2.30 and 3.30 pm and costs $7. For information on hotel pickup, tel 923-2061.

Numerous sunset and dinner cruises are available, ranging from a picnic-style dinner, such as Hilton's *Rainbow I* to a sit-down affair aboard Windjammer Cruises' *Rella Mae,* a 1000-passenger replica of a Yankee Clipper (tel 521-0036; toll free 800-367-5000). Other possibilities: *Aikane Catamarans* (tel 538-3680) has a sunset and a moonlight dinner sail; Paradise's 110-foot cruiser *Pearl Kai* (tel 536-3641) and Hawaii Surf Sails catamaran *Hula Kai* (tel 524-1800) offer dinner sails. Dinner costs range from $20 to $34.

The catamaran *Hokunani* has a 'brown bag' lunch cruise on Fridays – bring your own lunch and it's $1.50, or you can buy a box lunch aboard for an additional $4; reservations are a must (tel 926-0681).

Other cruises include various picnic sails, champagne cruises and charter sails; the companies mentioned above can give you information on these.

Scuba and **snorkeling** shops abound and they cater to beginners and experts. Rates for introductory excursions are running around $45 for a half-day for Scuba and $20 for a half-day for snorkelling, including gear and instruction. Most Dive Shops offer free hotel pickup; check the Yellow pages for listings.

You can take **windsurfing** lessons at Kailua Beach; two hours cost around $22. Check the Yellow Pages for listings of operators. Several concessions along Waikiki's beaches offer **surfing** lessons for around $7 per hour, and you can usually rent boards for about $3 once you've learned to ride the waves.

Deep sea fishing charters operate out of Kewalo Basin; usual charter is from 7 am to 3.30 pm. Charter rates for six persons

run $285 to $416. Individual bookings run from $75 for full day, from $55 for half-day. Check yellow pages for charters.

Tours

Flightseeing operations on Oahu fall into several categories. There are air taxi and air charter companies which operate tours of the Neighbor Islands, as well as offering charter sightseeing flights over Oahu.

Principal amongst these are *Hawaiian Air's Island in the Sky* Scenic Air Tours (tel 836-0044) and *Panorama Air Tours* (tel 836-2122). *Brandt Air* (tel 847-2321) in addition to offering tours flies some scheduled runs into Kaluapapa and Molokai Airport.

Several helicopter companies fly tours over Waikiki and Diamond Head, Pearl Harbor, the Windward Coast and they will fly you around the island. Basic tours are starting at approximately $90. Each flies out of the Ala Wai Heliport behind the Ilikai Hotel; for information and rates contact *Hawaii Pacific Helicopters* (Cloud 9) tel 836-1566), *Royal Helicopters* (tel 836-2869 or 941-4683), and *Paradise Helicopters* (tel 955-7861).

Incidentally, another excellent opportunity for sightseeing from the air if you are flying interisland is to take one leg of your trip on Royal Hawaiian Air Service's Cessna; the obliging pilots make excellent tour guides, pointing out interesting features as you swing over them.

Sightseeing These are available on air-conditioned motorcoach, five-passenger limousine, private car, and van by a number of companies. Major tour operator is *Gray Line Hawaii* (tel 836-1883); several others are listed in the yellow pages. Basic tours tend to be the same with all operators and costs are similar; among them: *Circle Island* (nine hours, including a 3½ hour stop at Polynesian Cultural Centre) $26.50 by motorcoach; (eight hours without Polynesian Cultural Centre but including North Shore beaches), $21.50 by bus, *Small Loop* (including Sea Life Park, five hours) $14 by bus, $15.25 by limousine. *Honolulu, Manoa Valley* and *Punchbowl* (four hours), $8 by bus. *Pearl Harbor* (three hours, including transfers and boat cruise from Kewalo Basin around Pearl Harbor) $10.

Several companies offer hiking and nature tours, which take you off the beaten track. Check with the *Sierra Club* (tel 533-7606) to see what hiking or camping trips they have planned.

Industrial Several factory tours are very popular with visitors: those at the **Dole Pineapple Cannery** and Honolulu Fashion Center.

Dole offers a free film tour explaining the canning process for pineapple in this, the world's largest fruit cannery, which at peak operation processes a quarter of a million pineapples every hour. During the canning season, you can also take the optional $2 walking tour through the plant.

Location: 650 Iwilei Rd; take TheBus No 8; open weekdays 8.30 am to 2.30 pm; free.

At the **Honolulu Fashion Center,** you're greeted with a lei and refreshments, then you see the actual making of *aloha* wear in the bright, floral patterns. Afterwards you can browse and buy at less than retail prices in their 20,000-garment show-room.

Location: 440 Kuwill St, one block from Dole Pineapple Cannery; open daily 8 am to 4.30 pm; free.

You can combine these two on the *Free Hawaii Attractions Tour:* start at the Kodak Hula Show (Tuesday to Friday 10 am in Kapiolani Park); then a free FunBus will take you on to the Cannery and the Fashion Center before returning you to your hotel (tel 538-3662).

Places to Stay

The *Hawaii Visitors Bureau Member Hotel Guide* for 1984 lists 122 hotels, apartment-hotels, condominiums and villas on Oahu, 99 of them located within Waikiki. And more are opening all the time. So it becomes a choice of the type of accommodation you want and the location.

Most of Waikiki's resort hotels lie along Kalakaua Avenue or within a few blocks of it; their rates vary from $26 to $30 double at the Reef to $65 to $140 double at the Hyatt Regency. However, in the side streets between Kalakaua Avenue and Ala Wai Canal, within easy walking distance of the beach, you can find apartment hotels with kitchen facilities with rates running as low as $18 double.

It is possible to rent homes and condominiums on Oahu, some with a car. A mansion in the Kahala or Diamond Head residential areas might cost around $1000 a week but it will usually accommodate up to eight easily. Houses on the Windward Coast can cost as little as $350 per week. The Hawaii Visitors Bureau will supply a list of rental agents handling homes and condos; write them at 2270, Kalakaua Avenue, Honolulu, HI 96815. You can pick up a copy of their *Hotel Guide* at any HVB office. Information is also available from Hawaiian Rental Homes, PO Box 867, Makaha HI 96792.

As a guide, we list below some of the Waikiki resorts and apartment hotels, plus several accommodations outside the Waikiki area.

Waikiki – Top End

Ilikai Hotel (1777 Ala Moana, Honolulu, HI 96815; tel (808) 949-3811; toll-free 800-228-1212.) Luxurious hotel on beach; many units have kitchens. Specialises in tennis. Restaurants and disco. Excellent service. Rates from $50 double.

Royal Hawaiian Hotel (2259 Kalakaua Avenue, Honolulu, HI 96815; tel (808) 923-7311; toll-free 800-325-3535.)

Grand old hotel, plus new wing, on beach in center of Waikiki. Rates from $90 double.

Mid-Range

Moana Hotel (2365 Kalakaua Avenue, Honolulu, HI 96815; tel (808) 922-3111; toll-free 800-325-3535.) Original hotel, recently refurbished. Right on beach. Rates from $49 double.

Island Colony Hotel (445 Seaside Avenue, Honolulu HI 96815; tel (808) 923-2345) Apartment-hotel with studio and one-bedroom units, kitchens, pool. A few minutes walk to beach. Rates from $40 double.

Holiday Isle (270 Lewers, at Kalakaua, Honolulu HI 96815; tel (808) 923-0777) 285 rooms, pool, restaurant, cocktail lounge. Rates from $42 double.

Bottom End

Waikiki Holiday Apartment Hotel (450 Lewers St, Honolulu, HI 96815; tel (808) 923-0245.) Overlooking Ala Wai Canal, 10 minutes walk from beach. Units with kitchen from $28 double.

Waikiki Surfside (2452 Kalakaua Avenue, Honolulu, HI 96815; tel (808) 923-0266) Across from Waikiki Beach. 80-unit hotel. Rates from $26 double.

Honolulu International Youth Hostel (2323A Sea View Avenue, Honolulu HI 96822; tel (808) 946-0591). New University campus at Manoa. Rates $4.

Outside Waikiki

Turtle Bay Hilton and Country Club (Kahuku, Oahu, HI 96731; tel (808) 293-8811) Resort on North Shore; pool, tennis, golf, horse riding extra. Rates from $70 double. *Sheraton, Makaha Resort and Country Club* (PO Box 896, Waianae, Oahu, HI 96792; tel (808) 695-9511, toll-free 800-325-3535) Resort in Makaha Valley one mile from beach. Golf, tennis, pool. Rates from $65 double.

Pat's at Punaluu (53-567 Kamehameha Highway, Hauula, Oahu, HI 96717; tel (808) 293-8111) Condominiums, studio to three-bedroom penthouse, on Windward Coast beach. Pool, restaurant. Rates from $40 double.

Camping

Camping is possible at many of the beach parks. Permits for a maximum stay of one week can be obtained from 650 S King St, Honolulu, HI 96813; tel (808) 523-4525; permits are free.

If the price of gasoline doesn't frighten you off gas-guzzlers, you can rent a camper. *Beach Boy Campers* offers fully equipped campers on Oahu, Kauai, Maui and Hawaii from $45 plus mileage per night. Contact them at 1720 Ala Moana Boulevard, Honolulu, HI 96814 (tel (808) 955-6381).

Sea Trek Hawaii offers camping and sailing adventures, including treks, plus natural history tours. Contact PO Box 1585, Kaneohe HI 96744; tel (808) 235-6614.

Places to Eat

The Oahu dining scene is almost as sophisticated as you might expect to find in San Francisco. Cuisines of all nationalities are represented, some in award-winning restaurants. Dining out here is often expensive, but there are also some good moderately-priced and inexpensive places. And there is a wide variety of fast food outlets serving such delicacies as sushi and dim sum as well as the inevitable hamburgers and chicken.

A number of publications will help you choose: Honolulu Magazine's *Annual All-Island Restaurant Guide*, which covers 275 noteworthy restaurants; Hawaii Visitors' Bureau issues a free *Member Restaurant Guide* on request and the numerous complimentary tourist publications, such as *This Week on Oahu*, list many restaurants.

Luaus

The best opportunity most visitors have to sample Hawaiian food is at a luau, usually one featured at one of the resort hotels which schedule them on different nights. However, the most inexpensive and genuine luau can be found by watching the newspaper for a church luau, to which the public is invited. These also provide a good opportunity to meet local people who make you feel warmly welcome.

At writing, the following luaus are regularly scheduled: Royal Hawaiian Hotel Sunday and Monday nights, $30.50 (tel 923-7311); Sea Life Park Wednesdays, $29 including transportation (tel 923-1531, 259-7933); Chuck Machado's luau at the Outrigger Waikiki, $19.50 including transportation (tel 836-0249); Germaine's luau on the beach near Barbers Point nightly except Friday, $34 including transportation (tel 941-3338); Paradise Cove luau at Campbell Estate, nightly except Thursday, $34 including transportation (tel 922-4635 for schedule); and the Waikiki Beach Luau, Tuesday, Friday and Sunday nights at the Waikiki Outrigger Hotel, $16.50 tel 944-8833.

Entertainment

Hawaiian entertainers and lavish Polynesian revues rate high with visitors to the Islands and Waikiki offers numerous opportunities to enjoy both. The Polynesian shows usually embrace a mixture of Tahitian, Samoan, Maori and even Fijian music and dance. Hawaiian hulas, banned in the 19th century by missionaries as lascivious, are actually intricate dances interpreting traditional and sometimes comic themes.

Perenially favorite Hawaiian entertainer *Don Ho* is currently headlining the show in the Hilton Hawaiian Village Dome. *Tihati's South Seas Spectacular* is at the Bora Bora Room of the Waikiki Beachcomber Hotel.

Discos are still attracting both visitors and locals to such popular spots as the Ilikai's *Annabelle's at the Top of the I*, which features disco by Juliana's of London from 4.30 pm to 2 am and *Spats* at the Hyatt Regency. The big band sound is in the Royal Hawaiian's Tea Dance, Saturday 3 to 6 pm. Jazz reigns in various lounges, including the Hyatt Regency's *Trappers*, where the beat is New Orleans.

Again, check the free publications such as *This Week on Oahu* and *Waikiki Beach Press*, which you'll find in hotels and streetcorner dispensers, for entertainment listings.

Getting There

Air Most arrivals are into *Honolulu International Airport*, which is located between Pearl Harbor and Honolulu, some 10 miles west of Waikiki.

Like most major city airports, Honolulu International seems to be in a permanent state of expansion and reconstruction. It is a sprawling complex, yet easy to find your way through.

The main building is Y-shaped, with gates down the length of both sides of the 'Y' and attractive gardens in the center. Long passages lead out to the Ewa Concourse, where international carriers berth, and the Diamond Head Concourse, where domestic flights dock. Since the distances to the gates at the extremes of these two concourses is quite far, articulated buses known as Wiki-Wikis shuttle back and forth to the main building.

International arrivals take the Wiki-Wiki to the Immigration and Customs Halls, from which you emerge onto street level at the western end of the terminal. Here you'll find courtesy telephones for certain hotels, car rental agencies and information.

Passengers arriving from the mainland find the baggage claim areas on street level; television screens clearly indicate at which area your particular flight's baggage is collectible.

The interisland terminal for *Hawaiian Air, Aloha* and *Mid Pacific* is located west of the main terminal, at right angles to it. commuter airlines, *Royal Hawaiian Air*

Service and *Princeville Airways* are located in a small terminal north of the Diamond Head Concourse. A shuttle bus connects the terminals, with service every 20 minutes from 7 am to 10 pm, cost 25c.

Air taxis and flightseeing charters are based in a separate part of the airport, mostly at the foot of Lagoon Drive.

Honolulu International terminals boast a large number of shops, mostly on the expensive side, restaurants and coffee shops.

An unusual service is offered by *The Shower Tree*, where you can shower, shampoo, shave and even sleep a while. There are bunk beds, bathrooms fully outfitted, down to hair dryers and toothbrushes. It's a pleasant place to spend an hour or two on layover. Cost is $7.50 for shower facilities and $3 per hour for a bed.

Airport Transfers If you intend to rent a car on Oahu, you will no doubt pick it up at the airport and drive to your hotel. Courtesy phones at the airport terminal connect you to most car rental agencies who will pick you up. It's a 25-30 minute drive to Waikiki; when you exit the airport onto Nimitz Freeway, head to the right. Nimitz leads into Ala Moana Boulevard which takes you to Kalakaua Avenue. Traffic flows around the airport terminals from Nimitz Freeway in a counterclockwise direction. To return a rental car, bear left as you enter the airport – signs are very clear.

Gray Line operates the *Airporter* bus on an hourly schedule from 8 am to 10 pm, with dropoff at most major hotels. Cost is $5 one way, $8 round trip. You'll find their courtesy telephone near the baggage collection area.

An excellent alternative which provides door-to-door service by reservation is *Waikiki Express*. Their charge is $4.50 going to the airport; to reserve, write Waikiki Express, PO Box 30447, Honolulu, HI 96820 (or tel (808) 942-2177). *Aloha Paradise's Airporter* from Waikiki hotels costs $4.50; tel 945-3522.

Getting Around
Car Rental Features of car rental agencies are discussed in the introduction to this chapter. *Hertz, Avis, Dollar* and *Budget*

have booths in the airport terminal; the rest are easily reached by courtesy telephone or, in the case of the smaller, and even cheaper companies, through the yellow pages.

However, should you be planning to stay in Waikiki and spend most of your time on the beach you might consider not even renting a car. Public transportation on Oahu is good and many tour buses visit the major points of interest. With a rented car, you are faced with high gasoline charges and parking fees, as well as the daily rate plus $6 a day insurance if you take comprehensive coverage. (On the Neighbor Islands, a car is more necessary.)

Mopeds and Bicycles Mopeds are highly popular in Hawaii as they are eminently suited to sightseeing excursions and reaching uncrowded beaches. Rates run around $21 for 24 hours; bicycles cost $10 for eight hours.

Taxis Taxis are metered; current rates are $1.40 flagfall and 20c for each 1/6 of a mile. They are supposed not to cruise but wait at designated taxi stands; however, you can sometimes hail them. You can also telephone one of the many companies listed in the yellow pages. An unusual one is *Handicabs of the Pacific* (tel 524-3866), which takes wheelchair visitors shopping and nightclubbing.

Pedicabs A recent addition to the Waikiki scene, pedicabs are also ideal for sightseeing at a leisurely pace. For around $10 per hour, two people can sit back in comfort while a bronzed young man or woman peddles you around on a sightseeing tour.

Bus Honolulu and all of Oahu is served by a good bus operation, commonly known as *TheBus* as it is painted on the side of the vehicles. TheBus routes cover the city and circle the island. Fare, even for the four-hour circle-island trip, is a flat 50c and exact change is required. Senior citizens (65 or over) may apply for a special pass allowing them free travel, but this takes several weeks to come through making it unavailable to short-term visitors. Call 531-1611 for information and schedules. You can also pick up bus guides for $1.70 at most newsstands.

Useful Addresses

Hawaii Visitors' Bureau (2285 Kalakaua Avenue, Honolulu, HI 96815; tel (808) 923-1811).

Chamber of Commerce of Hawaii (735 Bishop St, Honolulu, HI 96813; tel (808) 531-1411).

Automobile Club of Hawaii (150 Kaiulani Avenue, Outrigger East Hotel lobby; tel 923-7345 – emergency 24-hour service tel 537-5544).

Sierra Club (PO Box 22897, Honolulu, HI 96822; tel 533-7606).

National Park Service (300 Ala Moana Boulevard, Honolulu, HI 96850; tel 546-7684).

Division of Fish & Game, State of Hawaii Department of Land & Natural Resources (State Office Building, Punchbowl St, Honolulu, HI 96813; tel (808) 548-4002).

Hawaiian Trail & Mountain Club (PO Box 2238, Honolulu, HI 96804).

Emergency *Ambulance, Police, Fire* (tel 911 – no coin needed from public telephone.)

TheBus Information (tel 531-1611)

Interisland Airlines *Aloha Airlines* 836-1111; *Mid Pacific* 836-3313; *Princeville Airways* 836-3505; *Hawaiian Air* 537-5100; *Royal Hawaiian* 836-2200.

Visitor Information *Honolulu Airport* (836-6413 daily, 6.30 am to 11.30 pm)

Kauai

Kauai is the first born of the main islands in the Hawaiian chain. Its genesis some five million years ago through volcanic upheavals raised from the ocean the bulk of Mt Kawaikini and Mt Waialeale, which is 5243 feet and 5148 feet dominate the island. Mt Waialeale holds great spiritual significance for Kauaians. The wettest spot on earth, with an annual rainfall of over 450 inches, it is source for seven rivers, making much of Kauai a lush wilderness and earning it the sobriquet 'The Garden Isle.'

Volcanic activity on Kauai ceased some 40,000 years ago, as the Fire Goddess Madame Pele moved on to seek a home on other islands. The collapse of a vast volcanic caldera created the 30-square-mile lush Alakai Swamp on Kokee Plateau atop the island. Eons of torrential rains and wind eroded deep gorges and sculpted fluted pali and secluded valleys, which today make Kauai a favorite for naturalists.

Kauai was home to the *Menehune,* legendary dwarfs who worked only by night and who, because of their great strength, energy and sheer number, were able to perform prodigious tasks of stonemasonry in a single night. Their disappearance is shrouded in the mists of legend. It is said that one night they all left Haena on a magic floating island, never to be seen again. There are those, though, who claim Menehunes still live in the island's hidden valleys.

Menehune are not to be confused with the *Mu,* tiny hirsute rascals who can steal food from a cooking pot in the wink of an eye. Oldtimers say there are still Mu around Wainiha, where things have a habit of disappearing mysteriously.

Kauai also saw the advent of the *haole:* Captain Cook made his first landfall at Waimea in January 1778. Because of its 95-mile distance north-west of Oahu,

Kauai was spared bloodshed in the wars of the 18th and 19th centuries which culminated in Kamehameha's victory. It was when King Kaumualii of Kauai swore allegiance to Kamehameha in 1810 that the unification of the Islands was complete.

Sugar has long been the mainstay of Kauai; Hawaii's first plantation was started on the island at Koloa in 1835. Nowadays, though, tourism has become number one, and resorts and condominiums are springing up around the island.

LIHUE

The sleepy town of Lihue, the island's main center, grew up around the Lihue sugar plantation which began operation in the mid-19th century.

The story of Kauai from volcanic birth to annexation is told in the **Kauai Museum.** Handicrafts in the Hawaiiana display include some from Niihau, the 'Forbidden Island'. At 4428 Rice St; tel 245-6931; open Monday to Friday 9.30 am to 4.30 pm; Saturday 9 am to 1 pm; admission charge.

Grove Farm Museum allows a glimpse of gracious 19th century plantation life. Unhurried tours with no more than six people at a time show the grounds and home, which has a feeling of time suspended since its last occupancy. Off SR 58 (Nawiliwili Rd); tel 245-3202. Open for tours by reservation only Monday, Wednesday and Thursday 10 am and 1.15 pm; admission charge.

NAWILIWILI HARBOR

At the foot of Lihue's SR 51 is Nawiliwili Harbor, the island's main port, and the Kauai surf resort on **Kalapaki Beach.** The harbor is base for sailing cruises, and occasionally you see the sparkling white interisland cruise ships docked here.

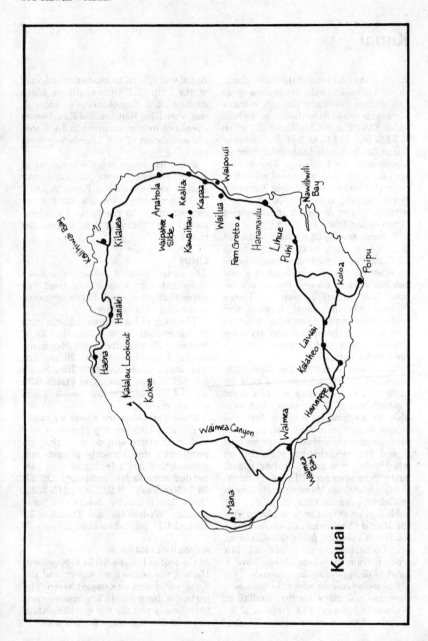

Kauai

The Menehunes are attributed with building the **Alakoko Fishpond** at the mouth of Huleia River. According to legend, they agreed to build it for a prince and his sister on condition that they could work unobserved. The pair agreed. But curiosity overcame them and they peeked, whereupon the Menehunes turned them into pillars of stone, which to this day stand on the mountainside above the pond. However, the interruption prevented the Menehunes from finishing the task in the one night; it was left to Chinese fishermen to finish it in the 1880s. To view the fishpond, take SR 58 from Nawiliwili Harbor to the top of the hill, where from an unmarked turnoff you can look down on it.

Places to Eat

Tip Top Cafe & Bakery Renowned for bakery goods. Wide menu of American and Chinese dishes – try the specialty, Chinese-style oxtail soup. (B)

Open daily. Breakfast, lunch, dinner. 3173 Akahi St, Lihue; tel 245-2333.

Club Jetty Local institution serving Cantonese and steak and seafood; food usually good, atmosphere always fun. Entertainment. (B)

Open every night except Tuesday for dinner. Nawiliwili wharf; tel 245-4970.

AROUND KAUAI

Sightseeing is done on two basic trips, using Lihue as base. It's best to allow a full day for each trip as there's a lot to see along the way.

One direction is around the southern shore on Kaumualii Highway (SR 50) to Waimea Canyon and the Kokee Plateau. The other follows the Kuhio Highway (SR 56) north to Haena. Since the Na Pali cliffs have defied efforts to construct a road (some say Pele would not allow it), you cannot drive completely around Kauai.

True to its title 'The Garden Island', Kauai has such varied botanical offerings, we describe them separately under the section Gardens of Kauai at the end of the chapter.

THE WESTERN ROUTE

Take SR 50 out of Lihue to head toward Waimea Canyon. About 10 miles west, turn left on SR 520 for Poipu, one of the island's main resort areas. Heading coastwards, you skirt the **Hoary Head mountains,** where the mokihana berry is gathered in the rainforest. Native only to Kauai, the mokihana entwined with maile leaves is symbol of Kauai. A procession of stately eucalypts, somewhat denuded by Hurricane Iwa, form a leafy canopy over the road to Koloa.

KOLOA

Koloa was a thriving plantation town from 1840 to 1879. You'll see the ruins of Hawaii's first sugar mill, established in 1835, on the right as you enter town. Missionaries came to Koloa in 1835 too; you'll find the old mission buildings clustered beyond the Poipu Rd intersection. Koloa is worth a stroll to admire its weathered wooden buildings and several small Japanese temples.

POIPU

It's dry climate tempered with soft trade winds has made Poipu a popular area from Kauai's earliest days. Whalers wintered at **Koloa Landing;** now condominium resorts line the shore.

Poipu's beaches offer good swimming and snorkeling: **Poipu Beach** lies between the Sheraton and Waiohai hotels. **Brennecke's Beach,** formerly a popular surfing spot, and **Shipwreck Beach** are further east toward **Makahuena Point**. Beyond Makahuena Point lies the rocky private beach of **Mahaulepu,** where Kauaians claim they defeated the remnants of Kamehameha's fleet of war canoes in 1795; most of the fleet had been turned back by a storm and returned to Honolulu, and historians recorded the rest were lost at sea, but Kauaians disagree.

Lawai Rd along the coast to the west, past Prince Kuhio Park to Kukuiula Harbor and the **Spouting Horn** blowhole. As water spurts up through the lava vent tube, listen for the moan of Mo'o, the legendary lizard, mourning his lost sisters who were turned to stone on the south shore of Niihau.

Prince Kuhio Park commemorates the birthplace of Prince Jonah Kuhio Kalanianaole, born here in 1871.

Places to Eat

Plantation Gardens Setting is restored 19th century plantation home, decorated with pieces of old Hawaiiana. Cuisine is basically seafood.

Open daily lunch, dinner. Poipu Rd, in Kiahuna complex; tel 742-1695.

Koloa Broiler Down-to-earth steak and hamburger grill, where you cook your own over charcoal. (B)

Open daily lunch, dinner. Koloa town; tel 742-9122.

Tamarind Room Elegant dining room with very fine, sometimes exotic cuisine. Specialties include Thai and Indonesian dishes, as well as fresh Kauai seafood. (E)

Open dinner nightly except Sunday. Waiohai Hotel, Poipu Rd; tel 742-9511. (The resort's Terrace is famed for Sunday brunch).

LAWAI

Backtracking to Koloa, you can take SR 530 through bucolic Lawai Valley to Lawai's 175-acre **Pacific Tropical Botanical Garden** (see Gardens). As you rejoin SR 50, uphill are 88 tiny shrines. They cover sacred soil from Japan's 88 Holy Places of Kobo Daishi, an ancient Buddhist teacher.

KALAHEO

You obtain a grand view across the Lawai Valley to the ocean from Kalaheo's **Kukuiolono Park**. Once a private estate, the park has a 9-hole golf course and Japanese garden, as well as a group of legendary Hawaiian boulders, including the anchor stone which held Kauai and Niihau together. (Tel 332-9151.)

A sign marks the **Olu Pua Gardens** just beyond Kalaheo (see Gardens).

HANAPEPE

Hanapepe Valley Lookout offers a different view: red cliffs and mist-tipped hills frame a lush valley.

Across the highway in what is now a sugar cane field, Kauai's last battle was fought on August 18, 1824, when insurgent George Humehume, son of King Kaumualii, was defeated by Kamehameha II's forces.

Modern buildings lining the highway greet you at Hanapepe, but don't pass on by. Explore the old part of town (take the first exit), where quaint wooden shops and riverside Chinese stores present a picturesque tableau.

An interesting side trip is to the bayside **Salt Pond Park**. In the nearby ponds in spring and summer, you might find members of the *Hui Hana Paakai O Hanapepe* (syndicate of Hawaiian saltmakers) carrying on the ancient art of making salt by evaporating sea water as Hawaiians have done for centuries. Hawaiians were unique among Pacific Islanders in olden times, being the only ones who preserved fish and meat with salt.

Places to Eat

Green Garden Family-managed since 1948, this restaurant serves generous portions of very good food in a cheerful, garden atmosphere. (B)

Open lunch daily, dinner nightly excluding Tuesday. Off SR 50 in Hanapepe; tel 335-5422.

WAIMEA

Waimea Bay played a significant role in the sweepstakes in which various European nations vied for Hawaii. It saw the first contact with England, when Captain Cook made landfall here in January 1778 and named the islands the Sandwich Islands for the sponsor of his Pacific expeditions. A plaque on the beach marks his landing spot.

In 1817, a German employee of the Russian Fur Company of Alaska built **Fort Elizabeth** on the bluff, thus as he hoped laying claim to the Islands for the Czar. The Czar, however, was not interested. The fort was occupied by Hawaiians on order of Kamehameha I; in 1853, it was abandoned. The ruined walls of the six-pointed fort overlooking the river, overgrown now with vines and ferns, can be reached by a path from the signed parking lot.

Waimea, a former Polynesian capital, was a center of the sandalwood trade and by 1850 many foreign ships were sailing in and out of its port. Kauai's first mission was built here in 1820. Take Makele Avenue to the 1853 coral and sandstone church and you can wander around a mission graveyard by its side; on the other side is an Oriental cemetery.

Along the river road you can view ruins of one of the Menehunes' finest efforts. The **Menehune Ditch** was built in ancient days for King Ola. The king's *kahuna* (priest), Pi, arranged a huge pile of equal-sized stones then called the Menehunes to work. They toiled all night, fitting the stones so perfectly, without benefit of mortar, that not a drop of water escaped from the great aqueduct. It's quite a drive up the riverside though, with little left to see to reward the effort.

Also in Waimea is a **Shingon temple** similar to Lawai's, with 88 shrines dedicated to soldiers killed in WW II.

MANA

The road ends at Mana, though an unpaved road continues to Polihale State Park, which offers camping and swimming – visitors should use caution indulging in the latter. Beyond Polihale stretch the jagged folds of the **Na Pali** coast, whose hidden valleys and beaches remain inaccessible except by helicopter,

boat or, for the more adventurous, an 11-mile strenuous hike (see North Shore section).

NIIHAU

From here you get a clear view of privately-owned Niihau across the Kumakihi Channel. The island has been a private ranch since 1864. Its 280 or so ranch hands are mostly full-blooded Hawaiians, who retain their Hawaiian language and customs and have little contact with the world outside. Access to Niihau is prohibited.

Waimea Canyon

'The Grand Canyon of the Pacific', Mark Twain called the great gorge at heart of the 1866-acre **Waimea Canyon State Park**. While it is not as large as Arizona's canyon, Waimea Canyon presents a spectacular sight. The gorge started as a fault or rift, then water action slowly eroded it into its present dimensions of one mile wide, 10 miles long and up to 4000 feet deep. Three tributary gorges run into it.

You obtain the best views from the lookout, 3657 feet above its floor, where you gain the full impact of the ever-changing play of light on earth tones tinged with tropical greens and yellows. You see the Waimea stream wending across the canyon floor, **Waipo Falls** tumbling over an 800-foot cliff and dominating cinder cone **Puu Ka Pele** from which, according to legend, the Fire Goddess leapt across to Oahu in search of a home.

You can hike down to the canyon floor on the **Kukui Trail**, a 2000-foot descent over 2½ miles; look for the sign about 1½ miles inside the park entrance. An easier walk is the quarter-mile **Iliau Loop** nature walk, named for a native flower similar to Maui's silversword which blooms in June and July. The path allows fine views of the canyon and distant **Waialae Falls**. Another trail follows the rim of the canyon.

KOKEE STATE PARK

Kokee State Park several miles up the road is a popular holiday place for *kamaainas*, with a lodge, cabins and camping. For the latter, pick up a free permit, valid for seven consecutive days, from the State Parks Division, 3060 Eiwa St, Lihue (tel 245-4444). The park is laced with 45 miles of hiking trails and streams attract trout fishermen. From mid-June to early August, families drive up to pick their limit of 10 pounds of luscious Kokee plums.

Stop by the **Kokee Museum** near the lodge for exhibits describing the geology and natural history of the parks and Alakai Swamp region. It's open from 10 am to 4 pm; donations appreciated; tel 335-9975.

Kokee Lodge is a popular spot for weekend dining, as well as for budget-priced accommodation.

KALALAU VALLEY

Continue up the road past the Kokee **Tracking Station**, part of the worldwide system of satellite tracking installations, to the **Kalalau Lookout** for a view of the secluded lush Kalalau Valley 4000 feet below. Adequate words to describe this vista elude most writers. We concur.

In olden days peacocks strutted between taro patches and the valley's people lived the good life. But the last Hawaiians left in 1920 and the valley became known for the sad tale, chronicled by Jack London, of *Koolau, the Leper*. He killed all intruders who tried to move him and his family to Kalaupapa and died of the disease still in his beloved valley. There are no trails down into the valley and the only access to the beach is by boat, helicopter, or hiking the trail around the Na Pali coast from Haena.

Since the valley is frequently enshrouded with mist which is more likely to clear in the morning, we suggest you visit the Kalalau Valley Lookout first, and do your sightseeing on the return journey. Do remember to take a sweater with you for though it might be warm when you leave the coast, the breezes at Waimea and Kokee can be cool.

THE NORTH SHORE ROUTE

From Lihue to Haena at the end of SR 56 is roughly 40 miles. The road passes some of the island's loveliest beaches, often almost deserted, so take a swimsuit. Walking shoes are advisable, too, so you can explore the trails from Haena along the Na Pali a little.

Wailua Falls

The first detour comes soon after you leave Lihue. Turn inland on SR 583 at Kapaia to head through the canefields to Wailua Falls. Wailua means 'twin waters'; two cascades drop over an 80-foot cliff into a pool ringed by flowering hala trees. After a heavy rain, the falls become an awesome torrent pouring over the full width of the cliff. In olden days, it is said, courageous *alii* (chiefs) would dive over the rushing falls to impress their womenfolk.

HANAMAULU

The village of Hanamaulu back on the main road is part of the giant Lihue Plantation and has become a low-cost residential area for plantation workers. You can get good buys in carved bowls and trays at Hanamaulu's Hardwood Factory and some claim the *Hanamaulu Cafe* serves the best Oriental food on the island.

A side road leads to **Hanamaulu Beach Park**, where a coconut grove, lilypond and shady ironwoods line the bay shore.

Between Hanamaulu and Wailua the road is backed by the **Kalepa Ridge**, whose slopes were once covered in sandalwood and from which watch was kept for invasion from Oahu.

WAILUA

The 18-hole **Wailua Golf Course** – in its clubhouse is a restaurant with an ocean view – and **Lydgate State Park** mark the beginning of the Wailua River area.

Wailua holds great historical and religious significance for Kauaians and for all Hawaiians: some claim it was here that the first Polynesians landed. Any child of royal blood had to be born here to be recognized as a true high chief. The most sacred *heiaus* (temples) were located along the Wailua River. Kuamoo Rd along the river's north shore follows the old **King's Highway** over which Kauai's rulers were carried so that their sacred feet should not touch the ground. The ruins of a **Temple of Refuge** can be seen in a coconut grove where the Wailua River empties into the ocean and **petroglyphs** are revealed when the tide cleans the sand from lava rocks on the ocean side of the bridge.

The King's Highway

Follow Kuamoo Rd, between the river and Coco Palms, to the restored **Holo-Holo-Ku Heiau**, one of Kauai's oldest temples, where human sacrifices were made. Atop the hill, stone walls overgrown with grass and trees mark **Poliahu Heiau**; here the king's house and private temple stood, commanding sweeping views of the river, mountains and sea. A trail leads down to the **Bell Stone**, which was sounded with a rock to herald that a royal birth had taken place at **Pohaku-Ho-Hanau**, the sacred royal birthing stone which you pass near Wailua State Park downhill. Across the road you can see **Opaekaa Falls** plunging over a cliff into a pool from a lookout.

The road continues to elegant residential **Wailua Heights** and on into the **Homesteads**, a more pastoral region.

Things to See & Do
Fern Grotto

One of Kauai's most popular excursions is the boat trip up the Wailua River to Fern Grotto. On the scenic ride upriver, a guide gives you the history and lore of the area and the friendly crew entertains with Hawaiian songs. A short walk brings you to the grotto, festooned with dewy ferns. From a leafy glade, the crew serenades you with the oft-repeated yet still haunting Hawaiian Wedding song – and both companies operating the tours are doing a roaring trade in arranging Fern Grotto weddings.

They also run Luau cruises and other special evening jaunts. Boats leave Wailua River Marin daily every half-hour from 9 am to 4 pm for the 1½-hour long trip. The fare is $7. Contact Smith's Motor Boat Service (tel 822-4111); Waialeale Boat Tours (tel 822-4908).

Coco Palms

At the foot of Kuamoo Rd, the Coco Palms resort is built around a lagoon in a coconut grove where kings once held court. The spirit of old Hawaii is evoked each evening at dusk when to the accompaniment of conch shells and drums, malo-clad runners bearing flaming torches perform the torchlighting ceremony. The resort's Chapel in the Palms, originally built for the Rita Hayworth movie *Sadie Thompson* which was filmed on the grounds, stands where the beloved queen Deborah Kapule built a church for *alii* in 1838. Commoners would stand outside and join in the singing and chanting. The resort also has a zoo and library and museum, appointed with pieces of the monarchy period and containing a collection of rare books on Hawaii. Nonguests are invited to visit it. For hotel facilities, see Places to Stay. The museum is open daily from 8 am to 4 pm, and offers free guided tours of the property every day at 1 pm.

Coconut Plantation

A mile north of Coco Palms, is Coconut Plantation. The complex embraces several hotels, including the *Sheraton Coconut Beach Hotel*, *Kauai Sands* and *Plantation Hale* condominiums, restaurants and the Market Place. Here you can browse dozens of specialty shops in an atmosphere reminiscent of a sugar plantation; the decor is highlighted by brightly painted equipment from an old mill.

Kapaa

The town of Kapaa retains its old-world charm, combining new businesses and 19th century false-front shops.

If you like ocean swimming, take the spur road to **Anahola Bay** where on a weekday you'll find blessed solitude. **Moloaa** also harbors a hideaway beach. As you enter Kapaa, see if you can distinguish the mountain known as the **Sleeping Giant**, supposedly the giant Puni who the Menehunes inadvertently killed when they tried to wake him by throwing rocks at him.

Places to Eat

Kountry Kitchen Concentration here is on hearty meals, rather than decor. Polynesian omelet and beef kabob are specialties. (B)

Open breakfast, lunch, dinner daily. Wine and beer. 1485 Kuhio Highway, Kapaa; tel 822-3511.

Aloha Diner Authentic Hawaiian food served in small diner by charming owner. Special dinners or a la carte. (B)

Lunch, dinner daily except Sunday. In Waiuopuli Shopping Complex, about half a mile past Coconut Plantation.

KILAUEA

Kilauea has two churches worth inspecting: craggy-facaded tiny **Christ Memorial Church**, with its luminous stained-glass windows, and **St Sylvester's** Catholic church-in-the-round, which boasts frescoes by Jean Charlot.

The **Kilauea Lighthouse**, atop the jutting peninsula which is the state's northernmost point, was automated in 1976. It's worth the detour for the view from the bluff overlooking the tempestuous sea, and for the sight of the red-footed booby birds and other birds inhabiting the wildlife refuge. The refuge is interesting and instructive, with

plaques describing birds and sea mammals. A small building beside the lighthouse houses an amusing 'goony bird' exhibit and a map showing all the leeward islands. Open Sunday to Friday, noon to 4 pm; free.

KALIHIWAI BAY

One of the island's most attractive views is from Kalihiwai Bay, about a mile beyond Kilauea. The tiny settlement that appears so tranquil has seen disaster twice in recent decades. A tsunami roared in on April 1, 1946, and another on March 3, 1957, carrying everything with them. You might be lucky enough to happen by during a *hukilau,* when everyone helps to haul in a huge net full of fish and is rewarded with part of the catch. **Aninini Beach** across the bay is a favourite spot for torch fishing; it's a good swimming beach. Visitors are cautioned not to swim in Kalihiwai Bay, which can be very dangerous.

HANALEI

Back on the main road, you come to **Princeville at Hanalei,** a burgeoning resort community centered around a 27-hole golf course, sometime site of the World Cup. It's worth a detour to *Hanalei Bay Resort,* popular with the tennis crowd for its 11 tennis courts and elegant condominiums. Dining at the resort's *Bali Ha'i* or cocktails at its *Happy Talk* lounge afford a stunning view across Hanalei Bay.

Back on the main road, at **Hanalei Valley Lookout,** you'll enjoy one of the island's most favourite panoramas. Shimmering taro patches carpet the broad valley framed by waterfall-laced mountains; through the valley, the Hanalei River meanders toward the ocean. Descending into the valley, the scene is just as lovely. The occasional willows you see grew from slips taken from Napoleon's tomb on St Helena and carried around The Horn on an early ship.

Things to See & Do

The town of Hanalei retains its missionary-era flavor. Behind the 1912 **Waioli Hui'ia Church** you'll find the 1836 **Waioli Mission House**. It has been restored with some original furniture by descendants of the Mission family; the caretakers will take you through it if you happen upon them and it is open for viewing Sunday mornings, following the Church service.

Hanalei's social life centers on the **Waioli Social Hall**, the original mission church which was built in 1841 following the lines of the old thatched building it replaced.

At **Hanalei Museum** you can inspect a private collection of turn-of-the-century agricultural tools and artefacts. The museum does not open regular hours, so just take a chance and see if someone's around; a nominal donation is requested.

Beyond Hanalei Bay you come to possibly one of the world's most photographed beaches. **Lumahai Beach** was the nurses' beach in *South Pacific,* where Nellie Forbush 'Washed That Man Right Out of Her Hair.' Follow the trail down the pandanus-covered cliff to the pristine beach, where by raking the sand you might find small olivines. You shouldn't swim, though, unless the water is really calm and even then be very careful, for there's a strong undertow and tricky currents.

Places to Eat

Bali Ha'i Attractive restaurant with spectacular view and friendly service. Reservations recommended for dinner. (M)

Open daily, breakfast, lunch and dinner. Hanalei Bay Resort, Princeville; tel 826-6522.

HAENA

Haena beach is also too dangerous for swimming. Instead you can explore the area, which is rich in legend. Its mist-veiled, jagged mountains and palm-fringed beaches have long attracted writers and artists. *South Pacific's* exotic Bali Ha'i was created at the beach near the Dry Cave.

Maniniholo Dry Cave was dug by the Menehunes seeking an *akua* (evil spirit) who had stolen their fish. **Waikapalae** and **Waikanaloa Wet Caves** were excavated by Pele in her endless search for a home. Some say that Mo'o lives in the upper cave; that his body may be seen in the water and from time to time you can hear him moan.

Dominating Haena is **Makana,** the Fire Cliff, from which specially trained young men would hurl blazing hau wood logs, which were light enough for the wind to carry out to sea trailing their sparks. People from all over Kauai and Niihau would come in canoes to watch the spectacle.

The road ends at the beginning of the Na Pali cliffs. Walk down to the northern end of **Ke'e Beach** and you can see the spectacular coastline stretching all the way to Mana. Near the road's end was one of the most celebrated *Hula Halau,* or hula temples, of ancient times. Young people from all over the islands came to learn the great traditions, chants and dances of their people's past.

Na Pali

The Kalalau Trail from Ke'e Beach along the Na Pali is one of the state's best known hikes. It's a rather rigorous but rewarding trek over the cliffs and down into rainforested valleys framing tiny, pristine beaches. Waterfalls provide swimming holes and there's fruit in abundance. If the 11-mile hike into the Kalalau Valley sounds too strenuous, you can opt for the two-mile trail into **Hanakapiai Valley,** from which two loop trails branch off. Even this is a rugged hike over a trail that requires caution. For details on hiking trails and camping and maps, contact the office of Economic Development or Department of Land and Natural Resources, Kauai Forest Reserve Trails, in the State Building, Lihue (PO Box 1671, Lihue), Kauai, HI 96766.

A helicopter ride over the Na Pali is a splendid way to sightsee the hidden valleys and fluted ridges of the coastline. For information, see below.

Things to See and Do

Gardens Menehune Gardens is a privately-owned garden in which these days seem to open only intermittently. The guided tour (sometimes by Mr or Mrs Kailikea) explains Hawaiian food and medicinal plants and includes demonstrations of customs and musical instruments, if you're fortunate. To get there take the SR 58 at Nawiliwili; tel 245-2660; admission charge.

Plantation Gardens embraces famed Moir cactus gardens, plus tropical plants and trees and old Hawaiian herbs. Part of Kiahuna Plantation condominium complex; tours held daily; tel 742-6411 for information.

Olu Pua Botanical Garden is a former pineapple plantation manager's estate which includes eight gardens: native and orchid, hibiscus, Oriental, palm, sunken, succulent, blue and *kau kau* (food). On SR 50 at Kalaheo; tel 332-8182; open daily 8.30 am to 5 pm; admission charge.

Pacific Tropical Garden is a center for botanical and horticultural research; it incorporates Robert Allerton's famed Lawai-Kai estate. Tours of the garden are conducted by reservation only Tuesdays at 9 and 10.15 am. On SR 53 Lawai Valley; reservations write PO Box 340, Lawai, Kauai, HI 95765; tel 332-8131; admission charge.

Cruises & Water Sports Apart from the Fern Grotto boat trip, Kauai offers several opportunities for cruising offshore and for indulging in other water sports.

A good one-stop service for information and reservations, not only for water sports but all activities and tours, is provided by Paradise Activities, tel (808) 245-7156 or 245-3631. On the north shore, try Princeville Activities, tel 826-9691.

Cruise operators tend to come and go, but among the more reliable are:

Kalapaki Kai II, a 45-foot catamaran; sails from the Kauai Surf on hour-long afternoon cruise (currently $12.50 plus tax) and a sunset cruise ($20 plus tax). Tel 245-3631, ext 7666.

The *Lady Ann,* 32-foot sport fisher offers fishing charters from $70 for half-day share to $500 for full day exclusive, maximum six passengers. Contact Lady Ann Charters, PO Box 3422, Lihue HI 96766; tel (808) 245-5218.

Sailing Adventures offers catamaran rides from Poipu Beach, in front of Kiahuna Plantation, for $15 per person for a half hour.

In summer when seas are calm, *Na Pali Zodiac* will take you along the Na Pali coast in motor-powered zodiac; prices currently are $40 to $70 roundtrip; contact them at PO Box 456, Hanalei, Kauai, HI 96714 (tel 826-9371).

You can take a three-hour kayak trip up the Huleia River to its source for $26, including box lunch; tel 245-7156 or book through the Kauai Surf.

Scuba diving and **snorkeling** classes and rental are offered by a number of shops, chief among them **Fathom Five** (tel 742-6991), and **Kauai Divers** (tel 742-1580), both based in Koloa and **Sea Sage Diving Center** (tel 822-3841) of Kapaa. Rates for scuba at writing are running from $55 half-day introductory lesson, to $275 full certification course; outings from $35 for one-tank shore dive, and rentals $23 for complete package. Snorkeling lessons including tour are $20; rental of gear $7. A bonus on off-shore excursions is the sight of whales cavorting in season.

Windsurfing at Nawiliwila costs $30 for a two-hour lesson, $10 to $15 board rental (tel 245-9290). Windsurfing is popular at Hanalei Bay, too (tel 826-6441).

Water skiing on the Wailua River currently costs around $40 hour of accumulated time, $20 for half-hour; tel 822-3574.

Hobie Cats and **Toppers** can be rented at the Kauai Surf (tel 245-9290) and **Pedal'n Paddle** (tel 826-9069) in Hanalei rent boats and boards.

Trail Riding Stables at two different parts of the island have riding facilities, including lessons, regular rides and guided beach and mountain trail rides, some with picnic and swimming. *Highgates' Ranch* (tel 822-3182) is in the Wailua area; *Pooku Stables* (tel 826-6777, 826-6484) is at Princeville. Current rates run from $13 hour to $35 for a waterfall picnic ride. Pooku also mounts seasonal rodeos, which are grand fun.

Tours

Flightseeing by **helicopter** allows you to really appreciate the Na Pali coastline with its hidden valleys and Waimea Canyon. Typical rate runs from $70 to $100 per person to hover over the Na Pali and Waimea Canyon. For information, contact *Papillon Helicopters* (Princeville Airport, tel 826-6591); *Kenai Helicopters* (tel 245-8591), *Jack Harter Helicopters* (tel 245-3774), *Island Helicopters Kauai* (tel 245-8588), *Menehune Helicopters* (tel 245-7705), and *South Sea Helicopters,* whom we can recommend (tel 245-7781).

Sightseeing A number of tour operators offer sightseeing tours around Kauai, including the basic tours; Wailua River-Waimea Canyon; Wailua River-Hanalei Valley; Poipu-Wailua River Hanalei Valley. These currently run around $14.50 to $17 half-day and $21 to $53 full-day, by coach or limousine. Tour companies tend to come and go, but perpetual are *Gray Line Kauai* (tel 245-3344), *Holo Holo Tours* (tel 245-9134) and *Niele Tours* (tel 245-8673).

Places to Stay

Generally accommodation ranges from motels in Lihue for as little as $16 double up to the luxury resorts such as the Waohai, Coco Palms, two Sheratons and the Kauai Surf.

There are a large number of condominimums, such as Hanalei Bay Resort at Princeville and Kiahuna at Poipu, which run around $60 and up, double, and offer full resort facilities, including golf, tennis, water sports, restaurants and entertainment either on property or nearby.

Hotels and condominiums are mostly clustered around Lihue, Poipu, Wailua/Coconut Plantation and Princeville/Hanalei. Below are samples to give you an idea of your choices:

Top End

Waohai Resort (RR1, Box 174, Poipu Beach HI 96756; tel (808) 742-9511). Luxurious beachfront hotel with 460 units, several dining rooms and bars, three swimming pools, tennis, water sports, fitness center, golf close by. Rates from $87 double.

Kauai Surf Resort (Nawiliwili Harbor, PO Box 1729, Kauai HI 96766; tel (808) 245-3631) Kauai's largest resort with 552 rooms set in landscaped grounds at the edge of Kalapaki Bay. Good beach, 18-hole golf course and tennis (both fee), pool. Numerous restaurants and cocktail lounges. Rates from $69 double.

Coco Palms Resort Hotel (opposite Wailua Beach, Box 631 Lihue HI 96766; tel (808) 822-4921.) Elegant resort in historical setting; decor is Old Hawaii. Some cottages by lagoon; three pools, museum, small zoo; fee tennis. Four restaurants, cocktails, entertainment. Rates from $65 double.

Sheraton Coconut Beach Hotel (Coconut Plantation Kapaa HI 96746; tel (808) 822-3455.) 311 units on beach; (Sheraton-Kauai is on Poipu Beach). Pools, restaurants and cocktail lounges, tennis. Center for entertainment. Market Place nearby. Rates from $65 double.

Hanalei Bay Resort (at Princeville, PO Box 220, Hanalei HI 96714; tel (808) 826-6522.) 280 units, including hotel rooms, studio, one, two and 3-bedroom units with kitchens. Eleven tennis courts, beach, pools, saunas. Championship golf course and adjoining. Rates from $60 double.

Mid-Range

Kauai Resort Hotel (3-5920 Kuhio Highway, Kapaa HI 96746; tel (808) 245-3931.) 242 unit hotel near Wailua Beach; Pool, restaurant and cocktails, shops. Rates from $41 double.

Coral Reef Motel (1516 Kuhio Highway, Kapaa HI 96746; tel (808) 822-4481). Spartan but clean hotel with 16 beach-front units; refrigerators but no cooking; near Coconut Plantation. Rates from $28 double.

Bottom End

Ocean View Motel (3445 Wilcox Rd, Nawiliwili HI 96766; tel (808) 245-6345). Attractive 21-room motel opposite Nawiliwili Harbor, two miles from downtown Lihue. Refrigerators, shopping center and restaurants nearby. Rates from $18 double.

Tip Top Motel 3173 Akahi St, Lihue, PO Box 1231, HI 96766; tel (808) 245-2333). 34-room motel in heart of Lihue. Popular bakery/cafe downstairs. Rates from $24 double.

Ahana Motel-Apartments (Akahi St, Lihue, PO Box 892, HI 96766; tel (808) 245-2206). Studios and one-bedroom apartments with kitchens, garden, down street from Tip Top Motel in central Lihue. Rates from $16 double, $22 with kitchenettes.

Camping

Permits are required for camping in county parks, on which there is a four-day limit; and in state parks, which carry a seven-day limit. Obtain county permits from Kauai War Memorial Convention Hall, 4191 Hardy St, Lihue (tel 245-4982) or from the Kauai Police Department, 3060 Umi St, Lihue (tel 245-6721). Reservations and permits for state parks are obtained from the Division of State Parks, 3060 Eiwa St, Lihue HI 96766 (tel (808) 245-4444).

Campers sleeping from two to six persons can be rented from Beach Boy Campers, 2951 Kalena, Lihue HI 96766 (tel (808) 245-3866). Rates start around $30 a day including mileage, but not gas.

Cabins and tents are rented at **Kahili Mountain Park**, PO Box 298, Koloa, Kauai, HI 96756 (tel (808) 742-9921). Facilities include centralized bath and shower, kitchenettes, a swimming lake, and furo (Japanese hot bath). Rates for cabins run $15 to $50 double.

Places to Eat

Culinary possibilities run the gamut on Kauai. Apart from those we have included above, there are numerous good restaurants both in the hotels and outside, and modest cafes, often with fairly good food, along the highways. You'll find a large selection of restaurants and dining rooms listed in *This Week on Kauai,* free in your hotel.

Nightlife

Most of the nightlife for visitors centers on the hotels which feature local and imported talent in dinner shows and in the cocktail lounges. Boogie fans should check out the *Club Jetty,* which follows a 9.30 pm Polynesian Show with dancing to live groups until 4 am (closed Tuesdays), or the *Hale Kai Boogie Palace Bar* in the Kauai BeachBoy Hotel at Coconut Plantation. The nearby *Spindrifter Restaurant* entertains at a lower decibel-level with a piano bar. In Hanalei, try the *Tahiti Nui,* long a favorite watering spot popular for spontaneous local entertainment.

Luaus are offered by the *Sheraton-Kauai* (tel 742-1661), *Sheraton Coconut Beach Hotel* (tel 822-3455) and *Kauai*

Resort Hotel (tel 245-3931). Contact them for information on schedules, costs and reservations.

The *Sheraton Coconut Beach* also has a popular dinner theater show, currently twice weekly on Mondays and Thursdays at a cost of $22.50; reservations tel 822-3455.

Getting There & Getting Around

Most visitors arrive at Lihue Airport aboard *Hawaiian Air, Aloha* or *Mid-Pacific Jets. Princeville Airways* flies directly into Princeville, where a shuttle bus can be summoned by courtesy phone to take you to your condominium.

There is no ground transportation from Lihue Airport; taxis into Lihue cost around $4 to $5; to Poipu Bach around $20; to Wailua-Coconut Plantation $10, and to Hanalei $40. Large suitcases will cost 25¢ each extra.

Tour operators run shuttle transfers to the hotels from Lihue Airport for around $4 to $8.

Car Rental However, most people who plan to spend a few days on the island prefer to rent a car; there are a large number of car rental desks across the road from the terminal building, including all the major agencies and several local ones. In most instances, you'll probably do better to negotiate a flat rate, if possible, instead of a mileage charge. You can also rent a car at the Princeville airstrip.

Older cars (dating back to 1968) can be rented from Rent-a-Jeep for $10 to $20 a day; tel (808) 245-9622 for reservation and airport pickup.

Bus The only public transportation at the moment is the somewhat unpredictable *Aloha Bus,* which runs hourly service between the Kauai Surf and Coconut Plantation between 9.25 am and 11.55 pm. Fare is $2 each way for information, tel 822-9532.

Other Rentals You can *Rent-A-Jeep* at 3174 Oihana, Lihue (tel 245-9622) or mopeds and bikes at *Hanalei's Peddle'n* ⟨ *Paddle* (tel 826-9069). (they also rent surf and windsurfing boards, canoes, motorised river craft and Hobie Cats). However, roads are good enough not to really need a four-wheel drive and mopeds are almost as costly as cars to rent, so there's not much advantage to either.

Useful Addresses

Hawaii Visitors Bureau (Suite 207, Lihue Plaza Building, 3016 Umi St, Lihue, HI 96766; tel 245-3971.)

Division of State Parks (State Building, Lihue; tel 245-4444). Trail maps, camping permits.

Paradise Activities 322 Kuhio Highway, Suite 2, Lihue HI 96766; tel (808) 245-7156.

Interisland Airlines Aloha Airlines 245-3691; Hawaiian Air 245-3671, Mid Pacific Air 245-7775, Princeville Airways, 245-8982.

Visitor Information (Lihue Airport) (245-8183 daily, 6.30 am to 9 pm.)

Maui

Though Maui has been the scene of many historical events through the days of royalty, missionary and whaler, it is very much the island of today – the beach island, with resorts proliferating at beaches from Lahaina to Kapalua on west Maui and at Kihei, Wailua and Makena on the east side of the island.

Maui, the geologists tell us, was originally two volcanic islands which over

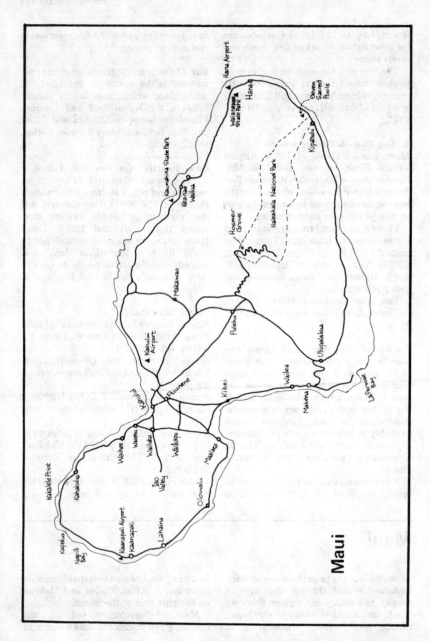

Maui

eons became joined by the narrow isthmus which runs from Wailuku to Maalaea. But to hear the *kamaainas* (locals) tell it, it's still two islands: residents of both West and East Maui tend to refer to their opposite with a slightly patronizing 'the other side'.

The island is named for the demigod responsible for the other theory of its origin: legend attributes the existence of all the Hawaiian Islands to Maui who, with his great hook, fished them up out of the ocean's depths. Then he snared the sun to slow it down, so days on Maui are long and sunny.

As well as beaches, Maui's 728 square miles encompass the magnificence of Haleakala, the world's largest dormant volcano. Its flanks at lower reaches are an enchantment of jungle-choked gorges dappled with bright color by mountain apple, hau, African tulips and pungent wild ginger. Above yawns its crater, so great it could swallow the island of Manhattan.

Small wonder, then, that Maui counts well over one million visitors a year, including people from the other islands who vacation by its beaches.

Though Maui's resort facilities are celebrated, there is another side to its pleasures: rural towns, populated by *paniolos*, Hawaii's cowboys, and seaside villages where the ways are those of old Hawaii, unaffected by the visitors who descend by the planeload on its shores.

History

It was often the custom for Hawaiian kings and queens to marry within their own families, even a brother or a sister, since it was considered no other person held equal rank. Polygamy and polyandry were practised to such an extent that by the 18th century the warring *alii* (chiefs) were closely interrelated, especially those of Maui and Hawaii.

Maui's powerful King Kahekili was probably Kamehameha the Great's father. Before Kamehameha's successful endeavor, Kahekili came close to controlling all the islands. He defeated the chief of Oahu, which gave him sovereignty over Maui, Molokai, Lanai and Oahu. He reached an agreement with King Kaeo of Kauai, who was his half-brother. Only the chiefs of Hawaii stood in his path when he took up residence in Waikiki, leaving his son Kalanikupule to rule on Maui.

Kamehameha conquered Maui in 1790 and Kalanikupule fled to Oahu where, several months after his father's death in 1794, he defeated and killed Kaeo. Kaumualii became king of Kauai; in 1810, he peacefully accepted Kamehameha's rule over all the Islands.

Kamehameha I had 21 wives. In addition to Maui-born Kaahumanu, whose father was half-brother to Kahekili, he married Keopuolani, whose grandmother was Kahekili's sister. Keopuolani ranked as the Island's highest noblewomen and Kamehameha determined she should be mother of his heirs. She bore him Liholiho, **Kamehameha II,** and Kauikeaouli, **Kamehameha III.**

Following Kamehameha's death, Queen Keopuolani married Hoapili, the chief responsible for concealing the late king's remains in a secret burial cave according to tradition, who became governor of Maui. An early convert to Christianity, Keopuolani persuaded the Reverend William Richards to establish Maui's first mission in Lahaina in 1823, the year of her death.

Maui's golden years came in the reign of Kamehameha III, who ruled from Lahaina for 20 years before moving his court to Honolulu in 1845.

Getting Around

The best way to tour Maui is by car. But there are a few things to remember. A road does go all the way round both West and East Maui; however the section around the northwest from Honokohau to Waihee is unpaved gravel and dirt, recommended for four-wheel drive only. Car rental agencies stipulate Nakalele Point as the turn-around point. Similarly, in the east SR 31 is rough dirt for a section between Kipahulu and Ulupalakua, forbidden to rental cars and recommended only for four-wheel drive. This section is often closed because of winter storm damage.

Mileages can be misleading on Maui, particularly for those accustomed to freeway driving. The distance between Kahului and Hana is only 53 miles, but it's a good two-and-a-half to three-hour drive, considering there are some 600 or more curves and a myriad of things to stop and admire.

Finally, you can encounter considerable temperature change in one day's driving. Leaving Kahului, it could be 85°F, whereas if you wait for the sunset at the summit of Mount Haleakala a parka might be more than welcome!

We'll look at Maui in four segments: Central Maui, West Maui, East Maui and upcountry to Mt Haleakala.

CENTRAL MAUI
Kahului
Kahului is relatively new and the center of commerce. It has little to offer tourists in the way of sightseeing, except for the **Kanaha Pond** near the airport. Once an ancient fishpond, it is now a bird refuge, particularly for the Hawaiian Stilt and other migratory shorebirds.

Places to Eat
Apple Annie's Omelets, burgers and Mexican dishes served up in rustic setting. Salads of Kula greens for vegetarians. (B)

Breakfast, lunch, dinner daily. Kaahumanu Center, Kahului; tel 877-3107.

Wailuku
Wailuku, a few miles away, is worth exploring. The historic district lies on the west side of High St.

Hale Hokeike, the Maui Historical Society's museum housed in an 1834 home, provides a good introduction to the island's history through ancient Hawaiian artefacts, historical paintings and missionary era furnishings.

At 2375 Main St; tel 244-3326, it's open Monday through Saturday 9 am to 3.30 pm; admission charge.

Nearby is Maui's oldest church, **Kaahumanu Congregational Church,** built in 1837 on the site of King Kahekili's temple. It is named for Kamehameha the Great's favorite wife, born in Hana, who played such an important role in the history both of her island and of the kingdom.

There's a fine collection of Hawaiiana in the **Wailuku Library** just across the street. It's open from Monday to Saturday between 8 am and 4 pm.

History of a different kind comes to mind in the old quarter of **Happy Valley** at the lower end of Market St. Its weathered wooden buildings are redolent of a more boisterous time when ladies of the night entertained here.

Iao Valley
Highlight of Wailuku is the Iao Valley which Mark Twain, with his penchant for comparisons, described as 'Yosemite of the Pacific'. Forested cliffs tower over the ravine. This peaceful valley was once the Sacred Valley of the Kings, where until 1736 Maui royalty was laid to rest. It's tranquility was shattered in 1790 by the roar of cannon as Kamehameha, trapped the army of Kalanikupule. It was the first use of cannon in the islands; the carnage was so great that bodies choked the stream, causing the decisive battle to be known as Kepaniwai ('the damming of the waters'). Kalanikupule, son and heir of King Kahekili, escaped across the ridge to Lahaina and made his way to Oahu. Here he again faced Kamehameha in the battle of Nuuanu, where he was finally captured and killed.

In Kepaniwai Park, near the entrance to the valley, the Heritage Gardens are a tribute to the cultural mix of Maui's population. You'll encounter *kamaaina* families spending leisure hours at pavilions honoring the Hawaiians, Chinese, Japanese, Filipinos, Portuguese and Koreans.

The road climbs to **Iao Valley State Park** at the base of the basaltic cliffs, most famous of which is the dramatic **Iao Needle**, jutting 1200 feet above you. A trail from the park lookout is a two-mile hike ascending 500 feet to the top of the ridge; vistas from this point and from a detour loop are more than adequate reward for the climb.

Leaving the valley on SR 32, locals are fond of pointing out the rock which resembles a profile of John F Kennedy.

Across the Isthmus

Sugar cane fields cover the isthmus from Kahului to Maalaea. Heading for West Maui, you take SR 38 from the Kahului Airport which cuts across the isthmus to join SR 30, the main artery from Wailuku which circles around West Maui. If Kihei or Wailea is your destination, you follow the signs for SR 35.

WEST MAUI

West Maui is shaped like a head, the isthmus being the neck joining it to the body, East Maui. Responsible for forging it and dominating its geography are the sheer West Maui mountains, peaked by 5700-foot Puu Kukui in their center which is reputedly the second wettest spot on earth with over 400 inches of rain annually. From high in this range, radiating like the spokes of a wheel, flow dozens of streams. In their headlong rush to the sea, they have carved out gorges, overgrown with forests of wild fern and kau, kukui and pine. On the coastal shelf, these streams nurture taro, pineapple and the fields of waving sugar cane which blanket much of the west side. At their mouths, pandanus and fern meet sand in sheltered coves favored by locals for swimming and snorkelling.

Maalaea

When *Seaflite* was running, its passengers disembarked in this village on Maalaea Bay. Now it has reverted to its former languor, except for the condominiums which sprang up along the bay. Maalaea Bay provides harbor for the deep sea fishing fleet.

For the regular visitor, crossing from East to West Maui there is a moment approaching Maalaea which never fails to thrill with its visual impact. It is the moment when you first sight the south shore. Above it, the green mass of Haleakala sweeps gently up into the clouds. To the right, Kealaikahiki Channel between Kahoolawe and Lanai points the way to Tahiti, as it did for the intrepid Polynesian navigators. On the horizon sit Molokini and Kahoolawe. To absorb this scene, stop at the **Scenic Point** above McGregor Point; between December and March, you might be lucky enough to see whales spouting offshore.

Olowalu

SR 30 continues along the water's edge to Lahaina. At one stage you pass through a tunnel – notice the thoughtful road sign 'Tunnel' just as you're about to enter it! You might almost miss Olowalu, reduced now to a couple of weatherbeaten shops, one of which harbors a fine French restaurant, *Chez Paul.*

Excellent examples of petroglyphs, some 200 to 300 years old, adorn the rocks off a dirt road which heads inland here. However, these have been closed to the public because of vandalism. Nearby, at the **Kaiwaloa Heiau**, it is whispered the spirits walk at night. In a lighter vein, Olowalu beach offers good beachcombing for shells and 'Maui diamonds', tiny quartz stones which resemble the real thing. There are several beach parks along this shore.

This stretch of coast was the scene of tragedy in February 1790, when men of the American ship *Eleanora,* in retaliation for the killing of a sailor, massacred over 100 Hawaiians who were gathered around the ship in their canoes. Aboard the *Eleanora* was John Young, soon to be captured on Hawaii by Kamehameha. He remained in the islands for the rest of his life as a royal adviser, attaining *alii* rank.

Places to Eat

Chez Paul Vest-pocket room serving fine French cuisine. Popular – reservations are a must. (E)

Dinner nightly except Monday. Honoapiilani Highway, (SR 30), Olowalu; tel 661-3843.

Lahaina

More than any other place in the Hawaiian Islands, Lahaina is a living repository of its history, a history intertwined with royalty, whaler and missionary and the great changes they wrought one on the other. Within a few short blocks, easily covered on a walking tour, are reminders of the fateful half century following Kamehameha's victory in the Iao Valley.

Kaahamanu loved Lahaina. In 1802, she persuaded Kamehameha I to build a summer palace here for her; they remained here one year. One story about the cannons now pointing silently out to sea from Wharf St is that they were retrieved by Kamehameha's divers from a sunken British ship and brought to guard his palace. You can see remnants of the Brick Palace, built by two ex-convicts from Botany Bay, *in situ* adjacent to the library on Front St.

Lahaina's historic buildings reflect the conflict that ensued in the years following Kamehameha the Great's death. It was here that the events of 1819, which brought whalers and missionaries to Hawaii and a new monarch to the throne, culminated in confrontation. The puritanical missionaries were faced with roistering whalers, whose credo was 'No God west of the Horn', being welcomed by the Hawaiians, whose Polynesian mores were considered libertine by standards even less rigid than those of the New England Calvinists. **The missionaries could do little to influence whalers on shore leave but, with the approval of Queen Keopuolani, they could and did manage to subdue the conduct of the Hawaiians.** This was not achieved without incident; at one stage a whaling ship, whose crew was enraged by a *kapu* (tabu) forbidding *wahines* (women) to visit the ship, lobbed cannon balls at a mission home, fortunately without inflicting much damage.

Thus the characters and mood of the times, as chronicled by James Michener in his fictional *Hawaii*, to illuminate your exploration of old Lahaina.

Things to See & Do

To locate the scenes where this drama was played out, pick up a map for a self-guided walking tour from the Lahaina Restoration Foundation in the Master's Reading Room, Maui's oldest existing building, built in 1834, which you'll find next door to the Baldwin House on Front St.

Start your tour at the **banyan tree**, planted by the sheriff of Lahaina on April 24, 1873, to celebrate the 50th anniversary of the missionaries' arrival in Lahaina. Behind it is the **Court House**, built in 1859 using stones taken from the **Hale Piula**, Kamehameha III's unfinished palace at the foot of Shaw St which was destroyed by a great wind in 1858. The Court House was used as Customs House and government building during the years that Lahaina was the Island's capital; now it is the Lahaina district courthouse.

Those crumbled walls nearby are the remains of the **Waterfront Fort**, which Hoapili ordered erected as a show of force to the unruly whalers. Since the fort could not be reconstructed without removing the banyan tree, an unthinkable possibility, this corner was restored as an indication of the fort's existence.

The **Lahaina Roadstead**, that stretch of water between you and Lanai, sheltered the vast whaling fleets each winter. In 1846, up to a 100 ships at a time anchored here and it was said you could walk a mile on wooden decks without touching water. You can relive those days aboard *The Brig Carthaginian*, which is a floating whaling museum.

It's open daily 8.30 am to 4.30 pm; closed Christmas and New Year's days; admission charge.

Opposite it is the **Pioneer Inn**, dating back to 1901. Its posted original House Rules, including *'women is not allow in you room'*, *'You are not allow to give you bed to you friend'* and *'you are not allow in the down stears in the seating room or in the dinering room or in the kitchen when you are drunk'* give an idea of the tenor of the times! Its Old Whalers Grog Shop is a popular watering hole.

Across Front St, the **Baldwin House** shows you life in missionary days as the pious Dr Baldwin and his fecund wife lived it there from 1838 to 1871. It was next door that in 1827 the Reverend William Richards and his family cowered in the cellar as cannon balls from the whaling ship whistled overhead. Open daily from 9.30 am to 5 pm; admission charge; tel 661-3262.

Sailors whose carousing become excessive were 'cooled off' in **Hale Paahao** prison, built in 1852-54 with blocks of coral stone from the old fort. They often shared the honor with Hawaiians, whose fondness for rum plagued the missionaries. You'll find the reconstructed jail on Prison St, a few blocks inland from Front St.

It was near here that Maui's first Christian service was conducted by missionaries at the invitation of Queen Keopuolani in 1823. The oft-rebuilt **Waiola Church** stands today where the original church, then called Wainee, was built to mark the site. Do take the time to wander around the **Waiola Cemetery**. Under ancient palms and fragrant plum-eria, you'll find gravestones marking the final resting place of Kamehameha's queen, Keopuolani (an early convert to Christianity) and Hoapili, as well as Kauai's King Kaumualii, who the imperious Kaahumanu took for husband, Princess Nahienaena, beloved sister of Kamehameha III, and the influential royal advisor, Reverend William Richards.

Walter Murray Gibson, flamboyant advisor to King Kalakaua in the 1880s, is reputedly buried in the **Episcopal Cemetary** behind the Hale Aloha along Wainee St. The Hale was built in 1858 to commemorate Lahaina's deliverence from a smallpox epidemic through the determined efforts of Dr Baldwin and it served as a Christian meeting place.

Lahainaluna

You'll obtain an outstanding view from Lahaina's public school, Lahainaluna, which sits on the hill above the town. The school was built by missionary students in 1831, making it the oldest American school west of the Rocky Mountains. In its grounds is the **Hale Pa'i** printing museum. The first newspaper west of the Rockies, *Ka Lama Hawaii*, was published in 1834 and the current printing press went into service in 1837.

Below Lahainaluna, the **Pioneer Sugar Mill** has been in operation since 1860. The sugar industry's creation of a polyglot society while fulfilling its labor needs is evidenced in Lahaina by the **Chee Kung Tong Society Building** on Front St and the **Jodo Mission**, a half-mile north of town. Here you see the largest image of Buddha outside Japan, erected in 1968 to mark the centennial of Japanese immigration.

On Front St north of Papalaua, you pass the restored **Seamen's Hospital** where stricken sailors were cared for from 1844 to 1862.

Places to Eat

Bluemax Decor draws fans of flying, with models and pictures of aviation history, and food appeals to lovers of Provencale cuisine. Entertainment until 2 am. (E)

Lunch, dinner, daily. Sunday brunch. 730 Front St, Lahaina; tel 661-8202.

Moose McGillicuddy's Wide range of Mexican dishes and unusual hamburgers. Happy hour. (B/M)

Breakfast, lunch, dinner, daily. Open to 2 am. 844 Front St, Lahaina; tel 667-7758.

Kaanapali

Continuing on the loop of West Maui, SR 30 skirts the 150-year-old Royal Coconut Grove and Sandbox Beach (Waihikulu State Park), where you're likely to meet *kamaainas* sunning and swimming.

Three miles from Lahaina, you reach the **Kaanapali Beach** area, an Amfac development of luxury hotels and condominiums built around two superior golf courses.

Gazing down on Kaanapali, try to imagine grass huts instead of hotels, taro patches instead of golf fairways and outrigger canoes on the beach instead of sailing boats and volley ball courts. That was the scene a few hundred years ago, when an ancient village and the royal gardens of Maui's early kings occupied the site where the Royal Lahaina Hotel's beach cottages sit. Puu Kekaa, the Sheraton Maui's **Black Rock,** was the sacred 'Spirit Rock' from which the souls of warriors jumped into the great beyond after death. Now their descendants climax the Sheraton's evening torch-lighting ceremony with a spine-tingling dive into the surf from that same point.

At the development's center, **Whalers Village** is a unique combination of alfresco whaling museum and a shopping plaza, including several restaurants.

The only living reminders of the boisterous whaling era are the whales themselves. Hunting them has been replaced by the delight of watching them cavort offshore during their November to March migration; good vantage points are Napili, Kaanapali and on party boats that put out regularly from Lahaina.

Toward the hills, fields of waving sugar cane are often arched by a vivid rainbow, symbol of royalty in olden times. You can recapture the setting of the turn-of-the-century riding the **Lahaina Kaanapali & Pacific Railroad,** which carries passengers between Kaanapali and Lahaina on the narrow gauge railway over which sugar cane was hauled from 1890 to 1910. The 25-minute run affords vistas of canefields and ocean while period-costumed conductors entertain. Buses shuttle between Lahaina depot and major points of interest in town and the Kaanapali depot and Kaanapali Beach resort. The LK & PRR features in a variety of sightseeing packages (see Sightseeing Tours). The train operates daily departing Puukolii, above the Royal Lahaina, 9.35 am to 3.05 pm; fare currently $4 one-way, $6 round-trip; tel 661-0089.

North of Kaanapali Beach, set amidst fields of cane, is the **Kaanapali Airstrip,** used by Royal Hawaiian Air Service. **Plans have called for a new airport; when this is accomplished, the site of the present airstrip will be developed under** Amfac's 20-year-plan, which includes construction of **Hawaiian Sea Village.** Visitors will tour this attraction, which will encompass thatched-roof buildings housing arts and crafts demonstrations, along waterways by double-hulled canoes.

Above the highway just beyond the airstrip is the **Hawaiian Transportation Center,** where you can rent cars, jeeps and mopeds. There's also a Hawaiian Air ticket service.

Places to Eat

El Crab Catcher Oceanfront restaurant with superlative view, particularly at sunset, and good seafood. Mexican specialties, too. (M/E)

Lunch, dinner daily. Whalers Village; tel 661-4423.

Kapalua

From Kaanapali to Kapalua, condominiums and apartment hotels vie for space with neat cottages and beach parks along the coast road. A section of the new highway which will bypass this built-up section is open at writing from Honokowai to just beyond Kahana, where it jogs down to join the coast road. Beyond Napili, the prestigious new Kapalua Bay Hotel and several condominium villages border two golf courses and attractive crescents of beach on Kapalua Bay. Public access remains to these beaches, as it must to all beaches by Hawaiian law.

Places to Eat

Pineapple Hill Venerable restaurant in former plantation house, which sits at the head of a Norfolk pine-lined drive on a hill above Kapalua. Specialties include fresh fish, chicken Pineapple Hill. (M)

Open for dinner daily. Kapalua Bay; tel 661-0964.

AROUND THE NORTHWEST COAST

Beyond here, you leave the tourist area behind and come to secluded beach coves favored by local swimmers and surfers. (If you see a sudden flurry of activity in Lahaina, followed by disappearance of most of the young bloods, you can guess word has spread that the surf is up!)

As you head around the northern shore, pineapple fields give way to banana trees, barren cliffs and taro patches farmed by people for whom life is little different than it was for their parents.

Kahakuloa

If you decide to brave the road all the way around to Wailuku, look for the little known blowhole in the rocks beyond Lipoa Point. Descending into Kahakuloa Valley, where people still cultivate and fish in the manner of their ancestors, a Bell Stone marks the approach to the village of Kahakuloa. This was a favorite place for King Kahekili, who enjoyed the sport of *lelekawa*, diving from a high point into the sea, off Puu Koae. If you go by Kahakuloa on a Sunday, do visit the church to hear the local choir singing old Hawaiian hymns.

The road is dirt until a few miles before **Waihee**, and you're likely to encounter *paniolos* (cowboys) droving cattle down it which calls for a little patience. At **Waiehu**, the municipal golf course is on the site where Kamehameha and Keopuoloni were betrothed. A little further on, watch for the sign indicating the hilltop on which sit **Halekii** and **Pihana Heiaus**, commanding a panoramic view over central Maui and Kahului Harbor. It was at Pihana, consecrated in 1779, that Kamehameha made sacrifice to celebrate his victory in the battle of Kepaniwai.

From this point you can drive through Wailuku's Happy Valley and Main Street to return to West Maui, or continue on to Kahului.

EAST MAUI

It is more difficult and time-consuming to complete the loop around East Maui, and it should only be attempted in a four-wheel drive vehicle.

Kihei

Kihei lies almost directly south of Kahului across the isthmus. From Kihei, SR 31 (Piilani highway) bypasses the Kihei area en route to Wailea, while SR 31 (Kihei Rd) runs along the coast.

This southwestern shore has long been popular with Canadian visitors and is now the fastest developing condominium resort area on the island. This was the traditional shore for invading war canoes and you may occasionally come across weed-covered WW II blockhouses along the road and remains of cement tank traps on the beaches, defence against an invasion which fortunately never came. The coast is noted for superb sunsets framed by the islet of **Molokini** and **Kahoolawe Island**, the uninhabited military bombing range. Public access lanes lead to beaches, where you can frequently retrieve 'Maui diamonds' from the sand.

The *Maui Lu Hotel,* long popular with Canadians, is a social center for this coast. Its weekly Thursday *Aloha Mele* luncheon draws *kamaainas* and *malihinis* alike to eat Hawaiian (or other) dishes and enjoy a Hawaiian show. Visiting performers from all the islands join in and the lunch sometimes becomes a celebration where well-known artists gather to pay homage to one of their own, and the feeling of *ohana* (family) reigns. Call 879-5858 for reservations.

Watch for the HVB Warrior marker for the **Trinity Church by the Sea**. It's worth the detour a few blocks to see this Congregationalist church, built in 1853 by native son David Malo and reactivated in 1976. Set in a grove of kiawe trees, its stone walls rise only to pew height, encompassing pews and altar open to the sky. Telephone 879-6554 for information on services.

Approaching Kihei Village, look for the totem pole monument, which marks the spot where Captain George Vancouver, England's far-ranging navigator, landed in the early 1800s.

Places to Eat

La Familia Waterfront restaurant, great at sunset. Dishes for all the family. Margaritas a happy hour specialty. (B)

Breakfast, lunch, dinner daily. Kamaole II Beach Park, Kai Nani Village; tel 879-8824 (also in Wailuku).

Wailea

On the other side of the village, you enter the **Wailea Resort** area developed by Alexander & Baldwin, one of the Big Five, who thoughtfully have built mini parks at each of the five beaches within the resort area for public use. The resort community encompasses several luxury hotels and condominium villages built around an award-winning town center, plus all the requisite activities such as golf, water sports and tennis, including Hawaii's first public lawn courts.

Makena

From Polo Beach to Makena Beach, you, encounter rough roads and great beaches; in the early 1970s these were popular with bathers who enjoyed their sunbaking *au naturel,* but this practise is being discouraged by police nowadays except at Little Makena beach. Makena is the latest area to be developed; an 18-hole championship golf course opened in 1981 and Makena Surf condominium resort is under construction at writing.

From Makena, a gravel road winds upland through the kiawe forest to meet SR 31 – the narrow, rugged road which runs around the southeastern tip of the island to Hana – at Ulupalakua, where it joins SR 37 leading to Kula and Haleakala National Park (see Upcountry to Haleakala).

La Perouse Bay

You can continue south from Makena in a four-wheel drive vehicle, but use extreme caution as the road conditions worsens. The road traverses the 1790 lava flow yielded by Haleakala's final upheaval; reaching the sea, the lava formed **Cape Kinau** (Nukuele Point) at the south end of Ahihi Bay. The **Ahihi-Kinau Natural Area Reserve,** extending over 1238 acres of land and 807 acres of adjoining ocean, offers fascinating exploration of tidepools and coral reefs. The road, such as it is, ends at **La Perouse Bay,** named for the French navigator, who anchored here in 1786 before sailing away to disappear at sea.

From here a hiking trail, the **King's Highway Coastal Trail,** follows an old Hawaiian path across the lava fields past ancient house sites and burial caves to Kanaloa Point, thence through private land to join SR 31 where it heads inland from the coast. If you're interested in hiking this or other Maui trails, check with the **Sierra Club** (tel 946-8494 in Oahu) for information.

The Road to Hana

The drive to Hana is a very special experience. Seen from a bird's eye view, the road is a narrow ribbon etched into the precipitous flanks of Haleakala just above the ocean, hugging cliffsides and plunging into ravines. On the ground, each of its hundreds of turns is a revelation of beauty.

Color dazzles the eye as a profusion of foliage – koa, ohi, pandanus, bamboo, breadfruit and fern, highlighted by pale green kukui – spills into the cobalt sea. The sound of water is pervasive: splashing down rocky gorges; dripping from tree to fern to flower; crashing on lava rocks.

Although SR 36 from Kahului to Hana is just over a 50-mile-drive, you'll want to allow a full day for the trip. It takes a good three hours driving each way with more than 600 curves and 50 bridges, many single lane, and you should leave plenty of time to enjoy the town, known far and wide as 'Heavenly Hana'.

Pick up a picnic lunch, perhaps in the plantation town of **Lower Paia**, known for its Buddhist temples and the popular *Mama's Fish House* and fill the tank with gas – there are no such mundane things as restaurants and gas stations along the way. Don't forget your swimsuit for numerous waterfall pools will tempt you.

You'll find the first waterfalls about 20 miles from Kahului. A mile or so beyond **Kakipi Gulch**, follow the marked trail to **Twin Falls** for a dip in a mountain stream fringed by moss-covered hau and giant ape leaves.

Further on, pause at **Kaumahina State Park** above the road to see its exotic haleconia blooms. The park provides a vantage point to contemplate jewel-like Kaenae Peninsula far below.

Places to Eat

Mama's Fish House Simple pleasant atmosphere, fresh fish daily. Specialty is Polynesian lobster, sauteed and served with sweet-and-sour sauce and smothered in macadamia nuts. (M)

Dinner daily. Kuau Cove, Paia; tel 579-9672.

Keanae

Detouring down into Keanae village is like entering a time warp. Villagers still tend their taro patches, pound the taro into poi and launch their skiffs into the surf to fish as their ancestors did when Captain Cook anchored off the lava-edged shore. It was on this shore that invaders from Hawaii landed in the 14th century to capture the district of Hana. Keanae marked the start of the ancient *aina alii*, the royal land of Hana, which extended to Kipahulu on the south shore.

At **Koolau Gap Lookout**, you can look down on the geometric pattern of terraced taro patches around the secluded fishing village of Wailua, and up through the Koolau Gap to the rim of Haleakala.

Wailua

Take the spur road down to Wailua village, past cottages shielded by ti plants and crotons, to visit quaint **St Gabriel's Church** adorned with twin red hearts. Villagers call it the Miracle Church because when their ancestors decided to build it in 1860, overnight the sea washed up the needed coral and sand. Drive through the banana groves and taro patches to the end of the road, and you'll likely find small boys surfing in the narrow cove at the mouth of a mountain stream.

At **Puaa Kaa State Park**, a series of fern-rimmed waterfall fed pools offer another chance for a dip. Or you can take the spur to **Ulaino** for a stream-fed freshwater pool right at ocean's edge.

Nearby is Hawaii's largest discovered

heiau (temple), *Piilanihale*, built by the great 16th century King of Maui, Pi'ilani. The *heiau* and adjoining gardens are now part of a 120-acre site being developed by the Pacific Tropical Botanical Garden to show the foods, fibers and medicines used by early Hawaiians. Hana Gardenland ships plants too.

Waianapanapa State Park

Just past Hana Airport, a turnoff leads to Waianapanapa State Park on Pailoa Bay. The park has cabins and camping, picnic areas, a black sand beach, a natural rock arch and a blowhole. A short walk through tropical groundcover and flowering periwinkle bushes takes you to the Waianapanapa and Waiomao caves, filled with icy water which only the hardy will brave to plunge in. Legend tells that the jealous husband of a princess who had taken refuge in Waianapanapa Cave slew her here one April many moons ago; now each spring the water turns red with her blood.

You can hike from Waianapanapa to Hana along the old stone-paved shoreline trail, once part of *Ka Alaloa O Maui,* the highway around East Maui built by King Pi'ilani in the 16th century.

HANA

Lovely Hana is one of the island's most historic towns. This pastoral haven is populated mostly by Hawaiians and part-Hawaiians who work on the 15,000-acre Hana Ranch and its offshoot, the famed Hotel Hana-Maui. White-faced Herefords graze emerald pastures and peaceful Hana Bay shows little sign of its stormy history of invasion by successive fleets of war canoes from Hawaii across the Alenuihaha Channel.

Things to See & Do

Puu Kauiki, the fortress-like cliff standing sentinel over the bay, saw the pitched slingshot battle in which a youthful Kamehameha fought. It was while he was resting here following that battle that he

first saw and fell in love with the 11-year-old Kaahamanu and swore he would make her his wife. He did several years later, after her family fled to the Big Island to escape the endless warfare at Hana.

It was also from Hana that Kamehameha first beheld the strange sight of Captain Cook's ships riding at anchorage in 1778.

Walk along the base of Kauiki on the ocean side and you'll find a plaque marking the cave which was Kaahumanu's birthplace.

Wananalua Church up the hill was built by hand from lava rock over a 20-year period in the early 19th century. Sunday services are conducted in English and Hawaiian.

Nearby **Hasegawa General Store**, acclaimed in a once-popular song, still sells a little of everything.

Beyond Hana, you pass **Muolea Point**, where the stone ruins of royal summer homes poke up through the weeds on a meadow above the ocean and come to Wailua Gulch (not to be confused with Wailua village further back). Here you'll see the impressive twin cascades of **Wailua waterfalls** which splash down the slopes of Haleakala into a grove of gnarled kukui trees, remnants of a sacred grove. The concrete cross above the road commemorates Helio Kawaloa, an 1840s Catholic convert who proselytized thousands of his countrymen. Further on, notice the lei-draped shrine containing a marble statue from Italy. The **Virgin by the Roadside** is objective of an annual pilgrimage by Hana's faithful.

Kipahulu

Ten miles from Hana, you arrive at the **Seven Pools of Kipahulu**, known as Seven Sacred Pools, which is part of Haleakala National Park. Once forbidden to all but royalty, the waters of the terraced pools are an irresistible invitation to swim.

Kipahulu was site of twin heiaus on either side of the road called **Heiau Kane**

Kauila, which Kamehameha I rededicated in the early 1800s; their ruins are still visible.

The beauty and tranquility of Kipahulu so moved Charles Lindbergh, who made his home on Maui, that he chose it for his final resting place. His grave, marked by a simple marble stone, is in the churchyard of the 1850 **Kipahulu Hawaiian Church**. To Lindbergh, Maui's motto 'Maui no ka oi' – Maui is the best – was no idle claim.

UPCOUNTRY TO HALEAKALA

The upcountry slopes of Mt Haleakala present another world from the tropical environment below. Tree-shaded roads bordered with colorful jacaranda and wildflowers traverse fields of vegetables.

The Kula region is the market garden of Maui. In the late 1840s (coincident with the Irish potato famine), potato growing boomed as orders poured in from the Californian goldfields. Demand today is for the distinctive Maui potato chips and sweet Kula onions, though the major cash crop for Maui now is probably marijuana, the popular 'Maui Wowie'.

To reach Haleakala, take SR 37 from Kahului to Pukalani, then SR 377 and SR 378 to the summit. There are a few worthwhile detours along the way.

MAKAWAO

Turn left at Pukalani and a few miles down the road you enter Makawao, a wonderful mix of Hawaii and Old West. *Paniolos* lounge on boardwalks under storefront awnings of weathered wood. Trendy ateliers and momma-and-poppa saimin shops stand side-by-side, and the pace of life slows to a crawl – except on July 4, when the **Makawao Rodeo** attracts visitors from all over and excitement reaches fever pitch.

Continuing on SR 37 past Pukalani, look for the octagonal **Church of the Holy Ghost**, perched on a grassy knoll above the highway. Built in 1897, its original parishioners were Portuguese farmers.

Haleakala National Park

The 23,000-acre park, created in 1961, is almost wholly occupied by the dormant volcano's vast crater. The caldera, one of the largest on earth, is seven miles long, two miles wide and 21 miles in circumference; the cone-studded floor lies 3000 feet below its rim. Park boundaries extend in an eight-mile strip down the Kipahulu Valley to the eastern shore, taking in the Seven Sacred Pools. This valley is an ecological reservation of rare native plants and birdlife in a tangled rain forest almost undisturbed by man.

Just inside the park entrance, a turnoff leads to **Hosmer Grove**. This spot at the 7000-foot level is ideal for picnicking and camping. A nature walk winds through groves of trees from many lands, including mainland American pine, cedar, juniper and spruce, Indian deodar, Japanese cryptomeria and the ubiquitous Australian eucalyptus.

You'll find **park headquarters** a mile inside the park, where rangers supply map-guides and information. They'll also help in planning crater hiking and camping trips.

Viewpoints on the road to the summit occur at the head of the **Halemauu Trail** at 8000 feet and, at 8800 feet, the **Leleiwi Overlook**. Here in the late afternoon you might experience the strange effect known as the 'Specter of the Brocken' – your own shadow projected against the clouds, encircled by a rainbow. At the 9324-foot **Kalahuka Overlook** you'll see the famous silverwood, as well as exhibits explaining the craters cones and lava flows. The unique silversword, a member of the sunflower family, takes between four and 20 years to grow its rounded mass of stiletto-shaped leaves prior to its moment of glory. A stalk bearing a mass of feathery purple blossoms bursts forth, blooms briefly then dies, leaving behind seeds to start a new cycle. You might also catch sight of a **nene**, the rare goose which is Hawaii's State bird.

The geology, archeology and ecology of the park are described in exhibits at the **Haleakala Visitor Center** at the 9745-foot level – it's one of the few buildings in the Islands where you'll find central heating, and be glad of it.

Finally, at 10,023 feet, you reach the summit and gaze down into the awesome crater. Changing light imbues the desolate earth and symmetrical cinder cones rising from its floor with glowing shades of orange, pink and purple, creating an almost mystical pattern of light and shade. At times, though, the crater disappears in a veil of mist and clouds. It's best to check with the Park Service (tel 572-7749 or 572-9306) before driving up.

If the day is clear, climb to the **Puu Ulaula Visitor Center** for views of the other islands except Kauai and Niihau.

Things to See & Do

The National Park Service maintains a network of 32 miles of hiking and horseback trails within the crater. Cabins can be reserved overnight through the park rangers and you should register with them before embarking on a hike. Trails are rugged in parts. Park rangers conduct free guided hiking tours in summer; reserve well in advance (tel 572-7749), see address below.

Holo Holo Maui Tours operates sunrise, and when possible midday tours (see Sightseeing Tours), and helicopter tours include Haleakala (see Flightseeing).

Experienced bicyclists can join the Haleakala Downhill tour for the thrill of coasting over 38 miles down the mountainside. Cost is $70; tel 667-7717.

Sunrise and sunset are popular viewing hours because the crater is usually clear of mist. However, do remember it will be cool at these hours. From January through March, you might encounter light snow or ice at the summit. Check ahead on the weather so you can dress appropriately. Late afternoon provides the best light for photographing the crater.

Places to Stay

There is no accommodation nor a restaurant in the park (except for hikers' cabins within the crater), nor is gasoline available. Two crater campgrounds, each for 25 persons, are limited to two-night permits. Camping is permitted (limit of three nights per month) in an undeveloped meadow campground near Oheo stream at Seven-Pools.

Information *Haleakala National Park* (Box 369 Makawao, Maui, HI 96768; tel (808) 572-7749).

Kula

On leaving the park, turn left on SR 377, Kekaulike Highway, for **Kula Botanical Garden**. It has more than 700 tropical, subtropical and temperate climate plants, including a kapu garden of poisonous species. Open daily 9 am to 4 pm; admission charge; tel 878-1715.

Kula is center, too, for the burgeoning industry of **protea cultivation**. The flower, native of Australia, is fast becoming as identified with the Islands as the anthurium. The different species of protea are on display, and sale at Tedeschi's in Ulupalakua.

Places to Eat

Kula Lodge Spectacular vistas over isthmus and West Maui mountains from flank of Haleakala. Good food, friendly place. (B/M)

Open for breakfast, lunch, dinner. Kekaulike Highway (SR 377); tel 878-1535.

Ulupalakua

SR 37 leads to parkline Ulupalakua, where it meets SR 31 from Hana and the winding road to Makena, described earlier

Ulupalakua Ranch, originally established in the 19th century by Captain James Makee, now the setting for Maui's first winery. You can sample Emil Tedeschi's Maui Blanc in the wine tasting room located in Makee's 1857 lava-and-plaster jailhouse. You'll find the Maui Blanc pineapple wine surprisingly dry; the first wine-grape crop is just becoming available for tasting. It's open for wine-tasting Monday through Friday between 9 am and 5 pm, weekends 10 am to 5 pm; free. The Tedeschi Winery is on several tour itineraries.

Things to See & Do

Cruises Maui is the aquatic sports mecca. Beaches are expansive and provide good beachcombing, swimming, snorkeling, and surfing. Snorkeling is particularly good in the coral gardens off Napili, at Honolua Bay and near the rocks bordering Kamaole III on the Kihei coast. Novice surfers will do well at Napili. For the more experienced, body surfing is good at Little Makena (Small Beach) and Wailea; board surfers head for Honolua and locally popular Fleming Beach.

The proximity of the islands of Lanai and Molokai adds to the scenic pleasure cruising off West Maui and the Wailea area. Such a plethora of cruises is offered out of Wailea, Lahaina, Kaanapali and Kapalua, it is impossible to list them all. You've a choice of cruises for coral viewing, sunset, dinner, picnic lunch and snorkeling, scuba diving and fishing, as well as sport fishing charters. Some samples: the *Wailea Kea*, a 65-foot catamaran, sails from Wailea to Molokini islet, offering snorkeling instructions and a picnic for $40 per person, scuba and lunch for $60 (Contact Ocean Activities Center, Wailea, Maui, HI 96753; tel 879-4485.) Also on offer are sunset sails and sport fishing charters.

Aloha Activity Center in Lahaina has cruises ranging from a 1¼ hour coral viewing jaunt aboard the *Lin Wa* glass-bottom junk for $9.50 to a certification open-ocean scuba course for $225. For example a luncheon/snorkeling trip aboard the Ketch *Viajero* costs $32. Scuba cruises run $45 for an introductory course, with gear; $35 to $45 for a two-tank cruise for certified divers and a five-day certification course costs $225. Sunset dinner cruises cost around $32 and cocktail cruises around $22.

Charter fishing rates are currently $400 full day and $250 half-day, or $60 a half day and $90 a full day share boat, trolling for manimahi, ono and tuna in the waters between Maui, Molokai and Lanai.

The Hotel Inter-Continental Maui has a 55-foot powerboat, the *Sea Sport.* Kihei Sea Sports is operating snorkeling cruises morning and afternoons aboard it, as well as sunset cruises and it is available for charter by groups. Rate for snorkeling cruise, including instruction, is $35 per person (whale-watching cruise is substituted in season); cocktail sunset cruise costs $22 per person. Contact **Kihei Sea Sports in the Kihei Town Center** (tel 879-7734).

At Kaanapali, the Hyatt Regency's *Kiele V* yacht has snorkeling cruises for $45 and cocktail cruises for $25.

A six-night cruise aboard the 90-foot three masted schooner *Resolution* sails Saturdays from Kihei for a cost of $695 double occupancy at writing. Contact Paradise Fruit Maui, PO Box 1086, Kihei HI 96753; tel (808) 879-4337 or 879-9322.

Water Sports Snorkeling, diving, windsurfing and sailing are readily available at all resort areas, sometimes offered to hotel guests on a complimentary basis. There are more than 10 dive firms operating on Maui; one of them, American Dive Shop also offers *parasailing* from the Hyatt Regency beach at Kaanapali, and on the bay south of there is *jet skiing.*

Water skiing charters and classes are offered by *Maui Sailing Center* in Kibei; tel 879-5935. Professional surfing champion Nancy Emerson conducts group and private **surfing** lessons; contact her at 244-3728 or through Aloha Activities Center.

Horseback Riding Stables offering riding and trail rides are located at Napili (Kapalua), Kaanapali, Hana and Kula. Cost runs around $30 for up to two hours; check telephone directory or Aloha Activities for reservations.

Two concessionaires are authorized to offer trail rides and pack trips into Haleakala; Charley's (contact Charles Aki, c/o Kaupo Store, Kaupo HI 96713; tel (808) 248-8209) or Herbert Feliciano, PO Box 8, Kula HI 96790; tel (808) 878-6855.

Whale Watching From late December to early April, these great mammals are in abundance off Maui's shores as they migrate south to mate and calve. Cruises provide a marvellous opportunity for a closeup view as they broach and dive. Most cruise companies offer special whale watching trips, as well as being on the lookout for whales on regular outings. Whale watching cruises run around $15 to $20.

Lanai & Molokai Cruises Half-day and day cruises to these islands, many including beach picnics, snorkeling and sightseeing tours, are becoming very popular. Highly recommended is the Coon family's Lanai cruise aboard the trimaran *Trilogy* or the *Kailani,* which includes a renowned continental breakfast aboard, tour of Lanai, snorkeling and beach picnic for $80 (tel 661-4743). Seabird Cruises' ketch *Viajero* offers the Lanai cruises for $59, plus $10 for the optional land tour; and an interesting Molokai sail/picnic excursion on catamaran *Onomana* for $59 plus optional sightseeing on Molokai (tel 661-3643). Windjammer Cruises' *Spirit of Windjammer* day cruise to Lanai costs $58.50 weekdays, $32.50 weekends when the beach cannot be used; tel 667-6834. Unicorn Tours combines the Lanai and Molokai excursions on its powerboats for $80, or offers them as half-day outings for $60 Lanai and $56 Molokai; Unicorn also

has sunset cocktail and whale watching cruises (tel 879-6333).

Cruise offerings change constantly. The most convenient way to make your choice and reservations is through one of the activities centers: Aloha Activities Center is at Building C, 2435 Kaanapali Parkway, Lahaina HI 96761; tel (808) 667-9564. There is also an office at Whalers Village at Kaanapali and a desk in front of Lahaina's Wharf Shopping Center.

Tours

Flightseeing Helicopter tours include Haleakala crater overflight, circle island and flights over Molokai's Pali and Kalaupapa. *Kenai, Maui Helicopters* and *Papillon* fly from Wailea. *Papillon* and *South Sea Helicopters* fly from Pineapple Hill above Kapalua. Rates run from $90 to $215. For information and reservations: *Papillon Helicopters* (tel 669-4884), *South Sea Helicopters* (tel 244-7572), *Kenai Air Helicopters* (tel 661-4426), *Maui Helicopters* (tel 879-1601).

Sightseeing Day tours to Hana and to Haleakala crater and Iao Valley are offered by *Gray Line* (tel 877-5507), and *Holo Holo Maui Tours* (tel 661-4858). Typical rates for the full-day tour to Hana range from $50 to $58.

Holo Holo Maui Tours runs two daily tours to Haleakala to the **Sunrise Spectacle,** from 3 to 10.30 am, $33 per person, including Continental breakfast; and the **Midday Marvel,** from 7.30 am to 3.30 pm, $36 per person, including Continental breakfast and lunch.

The *Lahaina-Kaanapali & Pacific Rail Road* has three tours which include the Sugar Train ride: **Passport to Lahaina,** 4¼ hours including the train ride, coral viewing aboard the *Coral See* and lunch at the Pioneer Inn for $15; **Tour A,** 3½ hours combining the train ride and *Coral See* cruise for $11; **Tour B,** 3 hours, is their Historic Lahaina experience which in addition to the train trip, visits Baldwin

House and *The Brig Carthaginian* for $7.50.

Places to Stay

Maui's main resort areas are along the beaches between Lahaina and Kapalua on West Maui and Kihei-Wailea on East Maui's south shore. Other hotels are in the Kahului central area, upcountry in Kula and in the village of Hana on the island's eastern tip.

Currently Maui has approximately 6500 hotel rooms and about 8000 rental condominium units, including a dozen or so full-scale resorts with all the facilities and activities for a complete vacation. Obviously we cannot list them all but perhaps a few comments and some samples will help you choose. Lahaina and Kaanapali have long been favorite with regular visitors (remember Lahaina does not have a beach). Kaanapali offers the advantage of a planned resort area within easy reach of Lahaina. The condominiums between Kaanapali and Napili have attractive settings on the coast, some with superb views of Lanai and Molokai. They are not all on beaches, though there's usually one close by. It helps to have a rental car if you select one of these; often the package includes a car with the condo.

Kihei's resorts tend to be informal and popular with families; condominiums line the Kihei shore. Wailea's hotels and condominiums are set in the newly-developed residential-resort community, which offers everything the vacationer could want in a self-contained area. Maalaea's condominiums are close to the deep-sea fishing fleet.

Accommodations on Kahului Bay do not have a beach but they are in the center of the business community. Hana is a hideaway with limited offerings; its legion of regulars love its seclusion and would stay nowhere else.

Condominium and apartment-hotel rates range from $35 to $150 double per night with most in the $35 to $75 bracket; many have a two or three-night minimum stay. Since there are so many variables applicable to these, we suggest you pick up a Hotel Guide from the Hawaii Visitors Bureau nearest you or consult your travel agent. Many packages are offered by the airlines in conjunction with a rental car agency and accommodation so your travel agent can best advise what meets your individual requirements.

Maui 800 provides a free reservations service for hotel and condominium accommodations, ground transportation, sightseeing, fishing and other activities. Contact them at PO Box 1506, Kahului, Maui, HI 96732 (tel (808) 877-2748).

Some hotel examples:

Top End

Kapalua Bay Hotel (One Bay Drive, Kapalua, Maui 96761; tel (808) 669-5656; toll-free 800-545-4000). Prestigious hotel and condominium villas set above Kapalua Bay in former pineapple plantation. All water sports, golf, tennis, shopping complex. Rates from $120 double in hotel; villas from $75.

Napili Kai Beach Club (Napili Bay, Maui 96761; tel (808) 669-6271; toll-free 800-367-5030). Studios, one and two-bedroom units set in spacious grounds on excellent white sand beach. Pool, tennis, putting greens, shops. Hawaiian entertainment. Rates from $100 double.

Sheraton-Maui Hotel (Kaanapali Beach, Lahaina, Maui 96761; tel (808) 661-0031.) Hotel rooms and cottages on beach and set into cliff; Pleasant rooms. All water sports, tennis, golf nearby, tour desk. Rates from $95 double.

Hyatt Regency Maui (Kaanapali Beach, Lahaina Maui 96761; tel (808) 667-7474; toll-free (worldwide) 800-228-9000.) **Kaanapali's grandest resort set in 20 landscaped acres on the Lahaina end of the beach. Water sports, tennis, health spa; golf nearby. World's largest swimming pool. Tours daily of tropical and Oriental gardens. Rates from $125 double.**

The Whaler on Kaanapali Beach (2481 Kaanapali Parkway, Lahaina, HI 96761; tel (808) 661-4861; toll-free 800-367-7052). Condominium resort on beachfront, next to Whalers Village. Studio, one and two-bedroom units with kitchens fully equipped. Rates from $79 double.

Stouffer's Wailea Beach (3550 Wailea Alanui St, Wailea, Maui 96753; tel (808) 879-4900; toll-free 800-228-3000). Beachfront hotel set in 15 acres; rated 5-star by AAA. Tennis, golf, shopping, all water sports. Rates from $115 double.

Lahaina Shores Hotel (475 Front St Lahaina, Maui 96761; tel (808) 661-4835; toll-free 800-367-2973). Studios and one-bedroom apartments, all with kitchens, lanais with ocean or mountain views. Beach, therapy pool. Rates from $72 double. No restaurant.

Hotel Hana-Maui (Hana, Maui 96713; tel (808) 536-7522, 248-8211). Luxurious hotel set in gardens; pool, tennis, croquet, pitch-and-putt golf. Adjunct of Hana Ranch. Shuttle bus to private beach. Fee transfer from Hana airport. Rates from $180 double including all meals.

Mid-range

Maui Palms Hotel (Kahului, Maui 96732; tel (808) 538-6817). 103-room hotel on Kahului Bay. Pool. Rates from $29 double.

Kula Lodge (RR 1, Box 475, Kula, Maui 96790; tel 878-1535.) On Haleakala at 3200 feet, 16 miles from Kahului. Five chalet units; some fireplaces. Dining room. Rates from $38 double.

Kauakea Kottages (PO Box 266, Hana, Maui 96713; tel (808) 248-8391.) Six studio cottages, fully equipped. Horseback riding available. No restaurant. Rates from $31.20 double.

Bottom End

Pioneer Inn (658 Wharf St, Lahaina, Maui 96761; tel (808) 661-3636.) On waterfront facing yacht marina. 1901 hostelry in center of town; pool, shops. Nautically atmospheric. Recommended. Original

building rates from $21 double.

Lahainaluna Hotel (127 Lahainaluna Rd, Lahaina, Maui 96761; tel (808) 661-0577.) Half a block from Lahaina Bay. Spartan rooms; higher-priced rooms boast lanais with mountain or ocean view. Minimum two-night stay. Rates from $21 double.

Nani Kai Hale (73 N Kihei Rd, Kihei HI 96753; tel (808) 879-9120; toll-free 800-367-6032.) Studio, one and two-bedroom apartments on beach; no maid service; pool, TV. Minimum three to seven days dependent on season. Rates from $22 double.

Camping Permits for a maximum of one week are available for state camping grounds at Haleakala's Hosmer Grove, and Kaumahina State Wayside and Waianapanapa State Park (cabins and campsites) on the Hana Rd. Write Department of Land and Natural Resources, Division of State Parks, PO Box 1049, Wailuku, Maui 96793 (tel (808) 244-4352.)

County park permits can be obtained through the Division of Forestry, PO Box 1015, Wailuku, Maui 96793 (tel (808) 244-7750). Permits are good for three nights and cost $1 per person per night.

Fully-equipped campers can be rented from Beach Boy Campers, 535 Haleakala Rd, Kahului, Maui 96732 (tel (808) 877-5225). Prices at writing run from $34 per day.

Places to Eat

The gastronomic gamut is almost as broad as the accommodation choice. The resort hotels usually feature several restaurants, often with ethnic cuisine. In West Maui, the Wailea area and Wailuku-Kahului, the selection ranges from snacks and icecream parlors to gourmet dining. Hana is fairly much limited to the Hotel Hana-Maui dining room, which offers haute cuisine at corresponding prices.

Luaus

Each of the three major resort areas has its share of luaus, all with Hawaiian entertainment. One of the longest-running is the Aloha luau at Kaanapali on the Sheraton's grounds. Current luau offerings: Kapalua Bay Hotel, Tuesday, $37.50 (tel 669-5656); Sheraton Maui, Sunday, Tuesday, Thursday, $32 (tel 667-9564); Kaanapali Beach Hotel, Wednesday, Friday, $22.50 (tel 661-0011); Royal Lahaina Hotel, nightly except Monday, $31 (tel 661-3611); Maui Lu, Monday, Wednesday, Friday, $26 (tel 879-5881); Intercontinental-Maui Hotel, Thursday $23 (tel 879-1922); Stouffer's Wailea Beach, Tuesday, $29.50, (tel 879-4900).

Nightlife & Entertainment

Most of the hotels feature live entertainment and often Hawaiian and Polynesian revues in lounges and restaurants. Do try to catch *Auntie Emma Sharpe's* show wherever it is scheduled (check *This Week on Maui*). She is co-host of Maui Lu's Aloha Mele lunch.

The *Wet Noodle* and *Foxy Lady* discos swing into action from 9 pm until 2.30 am at Kaanapali. Country/Western music for dancing is popular at the *Stouffer's Wailea*, 9 pm to 1 am.

You're likely to find a celebrity sitting in with the local rock or jazz group at the *Bluemax,* starting from 10 pm nightly.

There are many other options – check out the schedule in *This Week on Maui* which you'll find in your hotel.

Getting There & Getting Around

Air Maui's main airport is located at Kahului; there are airstrips currently used by commuter airlines at Kaanapali and Hana. However, the Kaanapali airstrip will be deactivated when a planned new West Maui airport is established.

Kahului Airport is served by *Hawaiian Air, Aloha* Jets, plus the commuter airlines *Royal Hawaiian* and *Princeville*. All of these link Maui with the other islands. Sometimes you can island-hop from Oahu, stopping off in Molokai and Lanai without extra charge, so check out that possibility if you are interested. *United Airlines* flies direct mainland-Maui service from Los Angeles and San Francisco and Seattle.

Kahului Airport is often crowded and noisy, added to by cacophonous birdsong emanating from the banyan tree at the heart of the terminal building. It has a restaurant, snack bar, cocktail bar, shops and an Information Desk (tel 877-6431). Near this, you'll find a bank of courtesy phones for some hotels and off-airport car rental agencies. Baggage carousels are both inside and outside the building; there are no lockers. Gray Line's desk is located inside the terminal to the left facing the street. Other car rental agencies' desks are outside the building to the left. Taxi fares to West Maui run around $30, so renting a car is more feasible (see below).

Kaanapali Airstrip (tel 661-3132) is located immediately north of the resort area. It is served by *Royal Hawaiian* only (plus occasional charters). The small terminal building houses a Royal Hawaiian ticket desk, several car rental desks located outside the building, and a cocktail bar at the top of a spiral staircase.

Hawaiian Air checks in passengers at the Kaanapali Transportation Center above the highway for flights departing Kahului. They issue boarding passes and baggage tags, but passengers are responsible for getting themselves and their baggage to the airport; the advantage is in avoiding check-in lines at the airport.

Hana Airstrip (tel 248-8208) is served by Royal Hawaiian during daylight hours only; arrangements for transfers are made with your hotel.

Airport Transfers *Gray Line* operates six shuttles daily from *Kahului Airport* to Wailea, cost $6 per person and eight shuttles daily to Kaanapali for $8 per person. At other times, they have limousine service available. For information, check at their airport desk or telephone 877-5507.

Car Rental Most visitors to Maui rent a car and drive to their hotel. The rental scene on the island seems to be in a constant state of flux, with companies and rates frequently changing. However, the companies with booths at the airport (near the exterior baggage carousel) and courtesy phones for pickup are reliable; again remember with companies represented on all islands, you can negotiate an all-island deal if you are island-hopping. A word of warning: in high season (June to August, December to Easter), it is wise to reserve your car in advance either before you leave your hometown or from Oahu. And if you plan to drive the winding road to Hana, you would do well to rent an automatic drive.

Other Rentals Those who would do some exploring off the beaten track might consider renting a jeep. *Rent-A-Jeep* currently offers four-wheel drive vehicles from $65 to $70 per day; you can contact them by courtesy telephone from the baggage area at Kahului Airport or by telephoning (808) 877-6626. There are several other companies offering jeeps; check the yellow pages.

Bicycles and mopeds can be rented at shops in Kahului and at Go Go in Kaanapali (tel 661-3063). Rental rates for mopeds at *Go-Go Bikes* are $5 per hour and $30 for 24 hours. Bikes are $10 for a day, $12 for 24 hours.

Useful Addresses

Maui County Visitors Association (PO Box 1738-02TW, Kahului, HI 96732; tel (808) 877-7822.)

Aloha Activities Center (building C, 2435 Kaanapali Parkway, Lahaina HI 96761; tel (808) 667-9564).

Ocean Activities Center (Wailea Shopping Center, Wailea HI 96753; tel (808) 879-4485).

Maui 800 (PO Box 1506, Kahului, HI 96732; tel (808) 877-2748; toll-free 800-367-5224).

Haleakala National Park (Box 369, Makawao, Maui, HI 96768; tel (808) 572-7749.)

Interisland Airlines: *Aloha Airlines* 244-9071; *Hawaiian Air* 244-9111; *Royal Hawaiian Air* 244-3977; *Mid-Pacific Air* 242-4906; *Princeville Airways* 871-9431.

Visitor Information (Kahului Airport) tel 877-6481 daily, 6 am to 9 pm.

Lanai

A sign at Lanai Airport welcomes you to 'the world's largest pineapple plantation' but only one-fifth of the island's 90,000 acres is developed in this way. The rest is an undiscovered, undeveloped playground of isolated beaches and a wild, wooded hinterland.

The island of Lanai, 17 miles long and 13 miles wide, is actually a single extinct volcano. Its crater, Palawai Basin, is overshadowed by 3370-foot Mt Lanai-hale. From here, the ridge slopes to a high coastal plateau atop rugged cliffs along the west coast. Its eastern flank is etched with rain-forested gulches, dropping down to a hospitable coastal shelf.

History

Long after the other islands were settled, Polynesians gave Lanai a wide berth. Evil spirits dwelled here, they believed, and so they dared not land. Then a West Maui king, harassed by his mischievous son Kaululaau exiled him across the Auau Channel to Lanai. Kaululaau fought the spirits and drove them from the island. At last Hawaiians were able to live here.

It was a favorite haven for Kamehameha the Great after he had consolidated his kingdom.

The most noted of Lanai's settlers, though was not Hawaiian. Flamboyant American-born Walter Murray Gibson came to Lanai in a self-appointed crusade to put new life into a languishing Mormon colony. The native City of St Joseph had been established on Lanai by the Mormons in the early 1850s. But in 1857, Brigham Young ordered the missionaries to return home for the duration of the church's struggle against the US government. Gibson proclaimed himself 'Chief President' of Hawaii's Mormons and solicited donations to buy the valley of Palawai for the church's Hawaiian headquarters. He acquired the land but the title was registered in his name not that of the church. Eventually he was excommunicated but he retained the land and the Mormons moved to Oahu, where they established themselves at Laie.

Undaunted, Gibson went on to win election from Lahaina to the national legislature in 1878. He became the influential premier and foreign affairs advisor to King David Kalakaua from 1882 to 1887, when he was edged out of power by the Reformers who finally overthrew the monarchy.

Gibson's daughter inherited the Lanai property but lost it when her sugar plantation failed at the turn of the century.

The Dole Pineapple Company purchased the island from Maui's Baldwin family for $1.1 million in 1922. Dole has since been acquired by Big Five company, Castle & Cooke.

Getting Around

Many of the roads on Lanai are unpaved, making a jeep or Land Cruiser the best way to explore. Do be careful to check directions with locals because through roads can be confused easily with the many pineapple roads.

LANAI CITY

Focal point for life on Lanai is the company-owned town of Lanai City, a village set amid Norfolk pines on a central plateau 1600 feet above the sea. Its predominantly Filipino population live in pastel-colored frame cottages surrounded by gardens. Untouched by tourist developments, the town has an aura of 1930s Hawaii.

Three paved roads radiate out from Lanai City to the coast. SR 44 heads to the northeast coast, where a dirt road runs the length of the northeast shore from Shipwreck Beach to Naha. On the other side of Lanai City, SR 44 drops down past the airport to Kaumalapau Harbor. SR 441 heads to the south shore beaches of twin bays, Hulopoe and Manele. Dirt roads connect all of these. In addition, a rough dirt road heads northwest to Polihua Beach.

Always check on weather conditions before you set off on these dirt roads, which become virtually impassable after heavy rain.

WESTERN SHORE

SR 44 heading southwest traverses endless fields of pineapple. In goggles and gloves field workers bend over rows of spiky fruit pushing from the plastic-covered earth. In this age of mechanism, harvesting must be done by hand still as the fruit does not ripen uniformly and it takes the skilled eye and hand to pick each at the right moment.

From the plateau, the road winds down to busy **Kaumalapau Harbor**, seven miles from Lanai City. Here at the company's 400-foot pier, cranes load as many as 1.3 million pineapples a day onto barges which carry them to the cannery on Oahu.

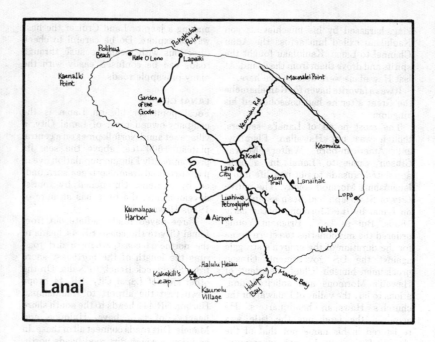

Lanai

Along the coast in either direction, sheer *pali* (cliffs) reach up from the ocean to the plateau 1000 feet above. Further south lie some of the most comprehensive ruins of an old Hawaiian village to be found in the Islands. **Kaunolu** was a favorite retreat for Kamehameha, who came here to relax and fish. You can wander through ruins of many houses spread over the ledge above the sea, cliffside burial caves and caves where ancient petroglyphs have been discovered. Nearby are **Halulu Heiau** and **Kahekili's Leap,** where warriors' mettle was tested: they had to leap from the 60-foot high ledge, under which hangs a 15-foot outcropping of rock, into the surf below. To reach Kaunolu, detour off SR 44 just beyond the airport, then follow the jeep track to the coast.

SOUTH SHORE

SR 441, Manele Rd, runs south from Lanai City to two fine beaches edging adjoining inlets. The cliff-bound inlet at Manele Bay is destination for the day excursions from Maui (see Maui cruises). You'll also come across sailing craft from all over the Pacific anchored here.

At **Hulopoe Bay** you'll find a beach park with a stretch of golden sand, coves and lava-impounded wading pools. Kiawe groves shelter picnic sites, with grills (and color-coded picnic tables: yellow for visitors, green for residents) as well as showers and rest rooms. A few campsites are clustered at the end of the beach (see Camping). Swimming, surfing, snorkeling and surf-casting are all good here.

Mt Lanaihale

From the lookout atop 3370-foot Mt Lanaihale, the island's highest point, you get brilliant views across the wooded ridges and deep canyons of the eastern part of the island to Maui and beyond, the

Big Island. Turn around and in front of you are Molokai and Oahu.

You can reach Lanaihale from Koele on SR 44 north of Lanai City, where the **Munro Trail** jogs off and climbs through dense rain forest to the summit. From here it swings south through Waiakeakua to meet Hoike Rd, which runs into Manele Rd. The seven-mile dirt Munro Trail is named after one of Lanai's most productive visitors, New Zealand naturalist George Munro, who introduced the moisture-gathering Norfolk pine to the island. He also planted seedlings and plants from his native land, which surprise and delight exploring New Zealanders.

Several miles up the road from SR 44, look for the notches carved into Hookio Ridge above Maunalei Gulch, reminders of defenses in an unsuccessful attempt to repel an invasion from Hawaii in 1778. Stop at **Hauola Gulch** and follow the path for a view into the lush 2000-foot ravine.

Heading back to join SR 441, take a detour through the pineapple fields to locate the **Luahiwa petroglyphs**, which are among the best preserved ancient rock drawings in all the Islands. Ask in Lanai City for explicit directions because they are not easy to find, but it's well worth the effort to see these centuries-old rock carvings relating ancient epics.

NORTHEAST SHORE

From Lanai City, SR 44 north cuts through rolling grasslands and winds down to the arid shelf along the windward coast. Some eight miles from town, turn north on unpaved Poaiwa Rd, which leads you under a canopy of feathery kiawe branches to **Shipwreck Beach**. Dozens of ships have met their doom on the offshore reef here over the past few hundred years; you'll see the remains of a WW II Liberty ship on the beach. Washed up debris has been recycled into the squatters' shacks you pass. The wind-swept beach offers good pickings for beachcombers; follow the white arrows painted on rocks to more petroglyphs.

A rugged dirt road follows the shore south for 12 miles, with views of Molokai, Maui and Kahoolawe. The beaches are better for beachcombing, snorkeling and fishing than they are for swimming.

Six miles down the road, ruins of an old church mark the former village of **Keamuku**, abandoned when the Maunalei Sugar Company collapsed in 1901. Old-timers lay the blame for the company's demise on the fact that the sugar people stole sacred stones from nearby **Kahea Heiau** to build their railroad. Soon afterwards, the mill's sweet water turned brackish. There are some more petroglyphs in the area of the *heiau*, (temple) which you'll find inland from the old water tower.

The road ends a few miles further on where the ancient village of Naha once stood.

NORTH TO POLIHUA BEACH

Kanepuu Highway, a dirt road, runs northwest from Lanai City through pineapple fields then out into open country heading for the coast. This region of the island has changed little over the centuries. Today it is popular with hunters.

The road skirts the dramatic **Garden of the Gods**, a canyon with bizarre lava rock formations rising from the red earth which are dappled with rainbow hues by the changing light. Sunrise and sunset are best viewing times.

At Pohakuloa Point, you reach **Polihua Beach's** expanse of untramelled sands. It can be windy here, but locals say the fishing is the best on the island. Swimming and snorkeling are fine, too, but do use caution.

The adventurous can explore rough spur roads to Lanai's largest *heiau* at **Kaenaiki** and **Kaena Point**, where for a brief period in 1837, adulterous women were banished to live in exile.

Things to Do

Many visitors come to Lanai to hunt and fish. The people at Hotel Lanai will put you in contact with guides. Charter fishing boats usually have to come over from Maui, which should be pre-arranged (see Maui cruises). The scuba and snorkeling guide most often recomm-nded is Ronald McOmber (tel 565-071).

There's a nine-hole golf course and tennis courts at the school, but you'll need your own clubs, rackets and balls.

Tours

Half-day tours by limousine and bus are operated as concessions by Oshiro's and Nishimuras.

Places to Stay & Eat

You have one choice: the 10-room *Hotel Lanai* is the island's only lodging! And in it is the main restaurant.

Hotel Lanai PO Box A-119, Lanai HI 96763; tel (808) 565-6605. Friendly establishment; modest rooms with private baths. Rates from $45 double. Reservations are a must.

The restaurant serves budget-priced home-cooked meals from 7 to 9.30 am, 11 am to 1 pm, and 5.30 to 8 pm.

Camping Camping is forbidden on the island everywhere except for the six sites at Hulopoe Bay. For these, a permit is necessary which costs $5 plus $3 a day for a seven-day maximum. Reservations must be made well in advance. Contact: Lanai Company, PO Box 486, Lanai City, Lanai 96763 (tel (808) 565-7115).

Nightlife

Take a good book or two with you. Hotel Lanai's restaurant and lounge swings until around 9 or 10 pm. That's it.

Getting There & Getting Around

Air Lanai Airport (tel 565-2685) is a swath cut through pineapple fields, naturally. It is served once a day by *Hawaiian Air's* jets and by flights of *Royal Hawaiian* Cessnas. The small terminal building has no facilities and opens only for flights.

Transportation to Lanai City four miles away is provided by either Hotel Lanai, on request, or by one of the service stations from whom you are renting a vehicle. A taxi from the airport to the hotel costs $5; it is there until 5.30 pm only and not on Sunday (it can be reserved ahead on Sundays.) There is no public transportation on the island.

Car/Jeep Rental Cars – or more practically jeeps – are rented from either of Lanai City's service stations: *Oshiro's* (tel 565-2515) and *Nishimura's* (tel 565-6780) each offers jeeps or Toyota Land Cruisers. Rates vary, running from $55 per day, no mileage.

Molokai

Molokai has rightly been dubbed the 'Friendly Isle'. Once a refuge for persecuted natives since the power of its *kahunas* (priests) was respected throughout the Islands, Molokai today offers a tranquil respite for island-hoppers. The gentle rhythm of old Hawaiian life prevails and every turn is rich in folklore.

Geographically, Molokai is 38 miles long and 10 miles wide at its extreme, with 100 miles of coastline. Volcanic mountains form the distinctive eastern and western sections of the island, which are separated by the gully-ribbed plain of Hoolehua. West Molokai is the 'dry' side: rolling brown hills slope down from 1380-

foot Maunoloa to deserted beaches west and south. Steep *pali* (cliffs) rim its northern coast. Much of the land is occupied by the 67,000-acre Molokai Ranch, originally established by Kamehameha V.

A jungle-clad spine of mountains dissects 'wet' East Molokai. Stream erosion and the northeastern trade winds have incised their flanks into sawtoothed ridges, deep narrow gulches and fertile valleys. One of the Islands' most awesome sights is to fly low along the northern coast to view the cliffs reaching from ocean into cloud. Sunlight glints from innumerable ribbons of water plunging down their faces. In the distance, Kalaupapa's peninsula seems to float like an emerald jewel, it's extraordinary beauty belying it's tragic past.

History

For several centuries before unification of the Islands, Molokai was coveted by, and alternately conquered by, chiefs of Maui and Oahu. Molokai's chiefs were of Hawaiian royal blood, being descendants of the Big Island's great king Keawe. Keawe's 'Molokai wife' Kanealai later married the Maui king Kekaulike, father of Kahekili. When Kahekili became king of Maui, he wanted for himself Molokai's great walled fishponds and land rich in water and taro patches. He asked for and received Halawa but this did not satisfy him and he finally conquered the island in the mid-1780s, on his way to capturing Oahu. Kamehameha the Great's victory on Maui in 1790 gave him dominance over Molokai. Kamehameha spent some months here at that time; then he lost Molokai, reconquering it finally in 1795.

Years later his grandson Kamehameha V chose Molokai as his retreat from kingly cares. He established his vacation home, Malama, on the beach at Kaunakakai and planted the coconut grove called Kapuiawa, remains of which are seen today.

It was in Kamehameha V's reign that the drama of Kalaupapa began. It is a story of tragedy and inspiration. In 1866, with the dread disease of leprosy spreading in Honolulu, the first group of afflicted were dumped on the Makanalua peninsula – or more truly, off the peninsula. There was no landing space so the people were tossed overboard and forced to swim ashore. The site had been well chosen. A 2000-foot insurmountable cliff face isolates the peninsula from contact with the rest of the island and the world outside. The community of lepers (it later came to be known as Hansen's Disease) was destined to live in isolation; any children born in the village were immediately removed and sent back to Honolulu. The discovery of sulfone drugs in 1946 led to control of the disease and ended the need for segregation of its sufferers. Today's victims are treated at a hospital near Honolulu. However, several hundred people elected not to leave their homes at Kalaupapa and remain there today.

During the bleak years of their exile, few came to the peninsula to minister to the victims. A quiet 33-year-old Belgian priest named Joseph de Veuster arrived in 1873. He cared for the sick physically and spiritually for the next 16 years. In 1889, the man the world came to know as Father Damien himself died of the disease at Kalaupapa. In 1977, Pope Paul VI proclaimed him Venerable Father Damien.

Getting Around

Exploration of Molokai takes three directions: east along SR 45 to the Halawa Valley; northwest on SR 46 to Maunaloa and Kepuhi Cove; and north to the Palaau State Park and Kalaupapa.

KAUNAKAKAI

Molokai's urban center, if a sleepy town which could be a Hollywood set for a period Western might thus be described, is Kaunakakai. Extolled by Hilo Hattie in

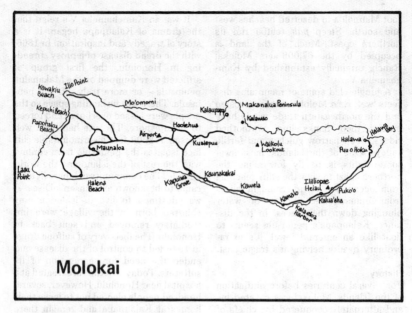

Molokai

the popular song of the 'thirties, 'The Cockeyed Mayor of Kaunakakai', it has probably changed little in the intervening years, except for fashions in cars and clothing. It is at Kaunakakai that the roads converge.

MAKANALUA PENINSULA
Kalaupapa
Since the tragedy of Kalaupapa pervades Molokai, most visitors put this first on their agenda. In the more than 100 years since the first afflicted struggled ashore, patient toil has transformed the once inhospitable windswept tableland into a place of beauty. It is awe-inspiring to confront the spirit of people who built a life out of desolation, a spirit perhaps personified by the pidgin-English graffiti painted on a rock near the Damien Monument: 'Smile – it no break your face'.

All visitors to the Makanalua Peninsula must take one of the tours (see tours). You are taken to visit the ruins of the original settlement of Kalawao, where Father Damien ministered from his St Philomena Church. He was originally interred in the church grounds, but in 1936 his remains were sent to Belgium. Next door to 'Father Damien's Church' is the Siloama Protestant Church.

From **Kalawao Park**, a view of the furious ocean battering against unsurmountable cliffs conveys the sense of isolation experienced by the exiles.

Eventually they moved across the plateau and built the settlement of Kalaupapa on the warmer side, where today's residents greet visitors. It is a village of neat cottages, gardens and a hospital and community hall.

Permission to enter Kalaupapa must be obtained from the State Department of Health: in Honolulu, tel 548-2211, in Molokai, tel 567-6613. However, if you are taking one of the tours, permission will be arranged for you automatically. Since it has been found that children are more susceptible to the disease, no one under 16 years of age may visit the settlement.

Getting There

The most adventurous pilgrimage to Kalaupapa is by mule down the precipitous 2000-foot cliff (see Tours). Hikers can venture down the path trodden by the sure-footed mules. It is recommended, however, that you be in excellent shape, and be experienced because the going is tough.

Otherwise, you fly in by small plane. *Royal Hawaiian's* Cessnas fly in from 'topside' as do *Air Molokai* and *Polynesia Air*. We recommend Royal Hawaiian's excellent service; you can also fly with them directly from Honolulu. Once there you cannot explore solo but must take a guided tour.

Kalaupapa Overlook

An alternative to touring the Makanalua Peninsula is to view it from the overlook in Palauu State Park atop the cliff. SR 47 from Kaunakakai takes you past the Kaulapuu Resorvoir, the world's largest rubber lined water cache. Although it is a more impressive sight from the air (obliging Royal Hawaiian pilots will swing over it on request), the reservoir is undeniably a remarkable engineering feat. A huge underground aqueduct carries up to 25 million gallons of water a day from the wet side of the island to be used on the dry side, solving a long term problem for the people of Molokai.

Palauu State Park

Passing through the Del Monte company town of Kualapuu, the road traverses rolling hills to end in a wilderness of cypress, ironwoods (known locally as 'Australian pine') and paperbark trees in Palauu State Park. Two trains branch off from the parking lot. The path to the north wends through an ironwood grove to the **Kalaupapa Lookout**. From here you obtain spectacular views of the colony and the dramatic pali coastline.

A 10-minute climb up the second trail through a cool forest of pine brings you to the Phallic Rock, *Kauleonanahoa* in Hawaiian, where in olden times women came to ask the blessing of fertility. Legend tells of a god who looked at another woman, whereupon his wife set upon him in a jealous rage. During the struggle, the wife toppled from the cliff; in retribution, the god was turned into a six-foot high stone in the form of a phallus. Nearby is a female counterpart rock.

WEST MOLOKAI

Heading west on SR 46 from Kaunakakai towards Maunaloa, you pass the foundations of Kamahamaha V's Summer Home Molokaians are proud of their connection to the Kamehameha dynasty. Many claim that Kamehameha the Great was raised on their island (his sacred taro patch and royal bathtub reputedly are hidden high in the mountains).

A few miles west of Kaunakakai, you see hundreds of coconut palms, all that remain of the 1000 trees Kamehameha V planted in the 10-acre **Kapuaiwa Grove** in the 1860s. Opposite the grove, the profusion of churches on what is known as **church row** is explained by the fact that any church with Hawaiian parishioners is granted land to build on by the Hawaiian Homes Commission. Sundays can produce a veritable traffic jam on this stretch of highway!

A short way past the Molokai Airport, climb 1381-foot **Puu Nana** ('Viewing Hill'). You can see as far as Oahu on a clear day.

Continuing on SR 46, the road takes you through stretches of barren brown land, rutted in evidence of the pineapples which were Molokai's major crop until the past decade, when Dole closed down the operation on this island. Still, acres of shimmering grey-green in geometric pattern against the red clay mark Del Monte's pineapple fields. Numerous other crops are being experimented with, including corn grown for seed which is then sent back to the Midwest for cultivation. About six miles past the airport, a sign says laconically 'beach'. Take the cutoff and you'll come to **Kawakiu Beach**, tucked on an inlet on the island's northwest point at the end of a bumpy dusty drive (Molokaians are noted for always seeming to wear a layer of red dust). Kawakiu cove is good for beachcombing, swimming and picnicking. Molokai Ranch allows camping here at weekends, though there are no improvements. In the evening when it's clear, you can see the glitter of lights from Waikiki.

The subsequent turnoff from SR 46 takes you to the Kalua Koi development of condominiums and the Sheraton Molokai fronting Kepuhi Beach. Continue on past the hotel for **Papohaku Beach**, a treasure trove for puka shells and driftwood.

Molokai Ranch Wildlife Park

A mile from the Sheraton Molokai is Hawaii's first exotic animal preserve. In the Molokai Ranch Wildlife Park, more than 250 African and Asian animals roam over 500 acres of grassy, kiawe-shaded hills and gullies which resemble the African veldt of Kenya and Tanzania. Hour-long camera safaris offer a chance to encounter giraffes, eland, sable antelope, ostriches and rhea, and other captivating wildlife. The tours operate from the Sheraton Hotel, daily except Sunday.

For schedule and rates, contact the Sheraton Molokai tour desk or the Molokai Ranch, PO Box 8, Kaunakakai, Molokai HI 96748; tel (808) 553-5115 or 552-2757; admission charge.

Maunaloa

SR 46 ends at Maunaloa, a plantation town when Dole was still active on Molokai. Maunaloa, set in a grove of Norfolk pines, is a good example of a Hawaiian plantation community. The nicer houses on the hill belonged to plantation managers.

Sandalwood Measuring Pit

Another detour worth following if the weather is dry is to take the gravel-and-dirt road off SR 46 (just south of its junction with SR 47) to the Sandalwood Measuring Pit, *Lua Moku Iliahi*. Molokai's hills were once clad in pungent sandalwood until the island was finally stripped of it about a century ago.

Continue on the same road a few miles to the **Waikolu Valley Lookout** for a stunning vista of the 3000-foot gorge.

EAST MOLOKAI

Turning eastward, SR 45 from Kaunakakai to the Halawa Valley 32 miles away hugs the southeast coast, allowing constantly changing views over the Kalohi and Pailolo Channels to Lanai and Maui. It is wise to take a picnic lunch and make sure you have plenty of gas for this excursion as there's no fill-up station along the way, either for the car or you.

In a short while you come to the first fishpond, one of 56 reputedly built by Menehunes of coral and basalt rocks, some weighing up to half a ton. The fishponds were used to fatten and keep the fish, ready for harvesting on order of the *alii* (chiefs). Inland, the steeply rising mountains are green with a tangle of kiawe and monkeypod, banana and coconut trees, highlighted by morning glory and lantana. The mountain range is peaked by 4970-foot **Kamakou**.

Kawela

At Kawela, a marker denotes an inaccessible city of refuge. This area was the site of a fierce battle during Kamehameha the Great's campaign to dominate the islands. It is said that his canoes lined the beaches here for four miles and slingshot stones may still be found around Kawela, which translates as 'heat of battle'. Nowadays it is the scene of a new development.

Kamalo

In a more peaceful vein, St Joseph Church

at Kamalo was built by Father Damien in 1876 and has been restored in recent years by parishioners. It now boasts the statue of Father Damien which a parishioner of Our Lady of Sorrows Church carved from a single monkeypod, a tree originally planted by the Belgian priest in 1874.

A short distance away, a small roadside **monument** marks the rather unexpected end of the first civilian transpacific flight in 1927. Ernest Smith and Emory Bronte crash-landed in a thicket of kiawe trees at this spot, luckily without injury. Further on, **Kaluaaha Church**, built by the first Protestant missionaries to come to Molokai in 1834 is being restored, complete with its 1844 bell.

This area is rich in legend and history. According to historian Samuel M Kamakau, Kamehameha I declared Kaluaaha sacred ground, making it a place of refuge, because it was land belonging to Kaahumanu.

Mapulehu Valley

Above the road in the Mapulehu Valley lies one of the largest and most impressive *heiaus* (temples) in the Islands. Set between two forks of the Mapulehu Stream, Iliiliopae Heiau was originally built in the 13th century by Menehunes, supposedly on the same night they constructed the Punalula fishpond at Pukoo. Stones for the terraced, platform-type *heiau,* which was inspired by a *kahuna's* dream, had to be carried one by one from the Wailau Valley. The original heiau, which was reputedly 920 feet long, was used as a sacrificial temple. But a man named Umoekekua, who had lost nine of his 10 sons on the altar, appealed to the shark god Kauhuhu for help. Kauhuhu sent a great flood down the valley, which destroyed the heiau and washed the priests to sea where they were devoured by sharks at Pukoo harbor. The present heiau, now 268 feet long, was rebuilt from stones of the original.

Pukoo

At Pukoo, stop by **Our Lady of Sorrows Church** set in a palm grove, which Father Damien built in 1874.

On this drive, you see many local people who live along the road's edge, fishing and toiling in taro patches. Once at Pukoo we met a woman trudging back from the sea with a pail of fish over her shoulder. She and her husband, now in their 80s, had raised and educated 12 children on the earnings from their fishing nets, she told us. She went on with quiet pride to say that one son was in the state legislature and another with a government agency. But the parents lived as they had always done and the children were returning one by one, to the tranquility of Molokai.

Puu-O-Hoku Ranch

Near the eastern tip of the island, the road starts to climb away from the sea until, at 750 feet, you enter the Puu-O-Hoku ranchlands. Note the magnificent view from here of Mokuhoomiki islet and Maui across the channel.

Near here is a cutoff to **Tooth Rock**, a place where Hawaiians came to seek relief from toothache.

Close to the ranchhouse, a **kukui grove** planted by the great *kahuna* Lanikaula shelters the grave of this revered ancient prophet. You may enter the grove, considered one of the most sacred places in the Islands, but you should touch neither trees nor stones.

Halawa Valley

From there, the road climbs, snaking through cool pines and scented eucalyptus, wispy ferns and bright colored lantana. Suddenly you round a curve and there, far below, lies the lovely Halawa Valley. The curving beach looks so peaceful, with no hint of the fury with which, on April 1, 1946, a seismic wave swept in from Alaska. It destroyed homes, taro patches and the whole community, which had numbered hundreds of residents. Now the valley is empty, except for scattered buildings. The broad, grassy plain is hemmed by jungle-covered mountains, down which cascade **Moaula** and **Hipiapua Falls.**

The three-mile descent into Halawa Valley is rough and bumpy, but worth it for the pleasure of beachcombing and exploring the valley. It's a 45-minute hike on a trail winding through tangled vines and wild fruit-laden trees, across tumbling streams, to the pool at the foot of Moalua Falls.

Legend says that Mo'o the lizard lives in an underwater cave here and you must ask his permission before you swim. Drop a ti leaf on the water. If it floats, dive in and enjoy it. But if the leaf should sink, Mo'o is in an angry mood and perhaps you'd better swim elsewhere.

Things to See & Do

As Lanai, Molokai attracts hunters and fishermen. The Penguin Bank off the island's southwest coast is renowned for sports fishing. Charters are offered by *Sportfishing Molokai* (tel 567-6571) on their 27-foot *Maikai, Fish & Dive Corporation* offers fishing charters, as well as snorkeling and diving. Contact them at PO Box 576, Kaunakakai, Molokai HI 96748; tel 553-5926. *Molokai Charters* operates fishing and cruises aboard their 42-foot sloop *Satan's Doll*; telephone them at 553-5045 for details.

Tennis and **golf** are available at the Sheraton-Molokai to guests and non-guests (the latter must pay a fee).

There are several wilderness **hiking trails** on Molokai, mostly recommended only for experienced hikers. For trail information and maps, write Maui District Forester, 54 High St, Wailuku, Maui 96793 (tel (808) 244-4352) or in Kaunakakai, contact the Department of Land & Natural Resources in the State Offices (tel 553-5019).

Tours

Most notable of the guided tours are those to Kalaupapa. Visitors can choose a route into Kalaupapa which is a thrilling experience in itself. You can ride a mule down the 2000-foot cliff face by a switchback trail named for Jack London, who preceded you. *Rare Adventures* operate a seven-hour excursion. It's not for the faint-hearted since the sure-footed animals pick their way down the one-mule wide trail bounded on one side by bushy cliff and on the other by a sheer drop. But it's completely safe, so while the mule-drivers goad the mules down the path, you can sit back and savor one of the Islands' most spectacular views. The tour costs $50, which includes a tour of the Makanalua Peninsula by mini-bus and a picnic lunch.

Reservations must be made in advance; contact Molokai Mule Ride, 1188 Bishop St, Suite 1601, Honolulu HI 96813; tel (808) 526-0888.

Damien Tours, run by Mr and Mrs Richard Marks, residents of Kalaupapa, offers a four-hour tour of the peninsula but you must make your own flight arrangements. Damien Tours can be contacted at Box 1, Kalaupapa, Molokai, HI 96742 (tel 567-6171).

Gray Line runs a five-hour **Grand Tour** of Molokai for about $25 to $32. The tour takes in the view from the Kalaupapa Overlook and of Halawa Valley from above. For information and reservations (tel 567-6177).

4x4 Mountain Adventures runs wilderness half day and day tours, ranging in price from $30 to $50, as well as overnight and 5-night camping trips (including meals and sleeping bags). Contact them at Box 335, Kaunakakai, HI 96748; tel (808) 553-5936.

Places to Stay

The accommodation picture on Molokai is limited. The only major resort is the Sheraton-Molokai on the western shore. Other resorts are scheduled to be built on that coast over the next few years. There are also several condominium complexes, the *Hotel Molokai* and a small hotel on the shore at Kaunakakai.

Sheraton-Molokai (Kepuhi Beach, Molokai, HI 96770; tel (808) 552-2555). Resort hotel fronting fine beach; Polynesian style buildings surrounding golf course. Twin rooms, studios, one-bedroom suites and eight cottages. Rates from $80 double.

Hotel Molokai (PO Box 546, Kaunakakai, Molokai, HI 96748; tel (808) 553-5347.) Polynesian style buildings in garden setting overlooking lagoon near Kaunakakai. Pool, tour desk. Restaurant and cocktails on shorefront. Rates from $39 double.

Pau Hana Inn (Kaunakakai, Molokai, HI 96748; tel (808) 553-5342; toll-free 800-367-5072). Molokai's original hotel; cottages and hotel wing in lush green on waterfront, with view across Kalohi Channel to Lanai. Within walking distance of town center. Rooms range from modest standard to newer deluxe. Pool; restaurant and popular bar. Rates from $25 double.

Wavecrest (Star Route, Molokai, HI 96748; tel (808) 558-8101; toll-free 800-367-2980. One and two-bedroom condominium appartments on southeast shore, 12 miles from Kaunakakai. Color TV, pool, tennis courts (nightlighted) and store. No restaurant. Small white sand beach. Rates from $35 double (minimum 2-day stay).

Molokai Shores (Star Route, Kaunakakai, Molokai HI 96748; tel (808) 553-5954; toll-free 800-367-7042). One and two-bedroom condominium apartments on shore one mile east of Kaunakakai. Color TV, pool, no restaurant. Small white sand beach. Rates from $50 double.

Camping Camping is permitted in the interior forested state park at Palauu for seven days; obtain permit free from Department of Land & Natural Resources in the State Offices at Kaunakakai (tel 553-5415). For camping in country parks, contact the County Parks and Recreation office in Kaunakakai (tel 553-5141). Camping is permitted without permit on some beaches owned by the Molokai Ranch; for information, write Molokai Ranch, PO Box 8, Kaunakakai, Molokai 96748; tel (808) 553-5115).

You cannot rent campers on Molokai but camping equipment can be bought or rented from Fish & Dive Corporation in Kaunakakai (tel 553-5926).

Places to Eat

The only gourmet dining you'll find is in the hotels, with the exception of an Italian place in Maunaloa. Some budget-priced cafes line Kaunakakai's main drag, Ala Malama St; try the *Hop Inn* for Chinese and *Oviedo's* or *Rabang's* for Filipino food. A Molokai institution is *Kanemitsu's Bakery*, and their oatmeal and macadamia nut cookies, home-baked rolls and bread; they also serve a delicious breakfast.

For gourmet dining try:

The Ohia Lounge Handsome multi-level restaurant with view of ocean. Salads, steak and seafood, featuring *mahimahi* dishes. (B/M)

Open daily. Breakfast, lunch, dinner. Sheraton-Molokai; tel 552-2555.

Pau Hana Inn Perhaps not gourmet but generous helpings of good, basic food in attractive seaside. (B)

Open lunch, dinner daily. Kaunakakai; tel 553-5342.

Nightlife & Entertainment

Nightlife is limited to hotels for the most part. *Pau Hana Inn's* piano bar and alfresco terrace around a century-old banyan tree are popular with locals.

Kaunakakai caters to the younger set with live rock going loud and strong weekends at the *Hele On* (tel 553-9978). You probably won't need directions to find it – just follow your ears! However, if that fails, locals will be glad to direct you.

Getting There & Getting Around

Air Molokai Airport is located on the Hoolenua plain, eight miles west of Kaunakakai. The tiny airport is busy: *Hawaiian Air* has daily flights, connecting Molokai with Honolulu and the other Islands. *Royal Hawaiian, Princeville, Air Molokai, Reeves Air* and *Paradise Air* provide commuter flights each day.

Royal Hawaiian also flies direct service from Honolulu into Kalaupapa Airport.

Hourly shuttles transfer guests to the Sheraton-Molokai from the airport. In addition, *Gray Line* has three daily shuttles to the Sheraton-Molokai for $6 per person; transfers to other hotels can be arranged (tel 567-6177). Airport taxis are available. There is no public transport on the island.

Car/Jeep Rental Molokai has several rental companies; of the big names, only *Avis* is represented. *Tropical Rent-a-Car* and *Molokai Island U-Drive* maintain desks at the airport.

Jeeps can be rented for around $45 a day from *Fish & Dive Corporation* (tel 553-5926), (tel 553-3866).

Other Rentals You can rent bicycles from the Hotel Molokai and Pau Hana Inn for around $3 per day; they're fine to browse the flat central plain and southern shoreline. The Sheraton Molokai has mopeds.

Information

For tourist information on either Lanai or Molokai, contact *Maui County Visitors Association* (PO Box 1738-02TW, HI 96732; tel (808) 877-7822).

Hawaii – The Big Island

When another name was needed to distinguish island from state, a natural choice was the Big Island. The island of Hawaii is big, almost twice as large as the others, even islands combined.

It offers scenic grandeur of very diverse qualities, from the fire of Volcanoes National Park to the icy snow-fields atop Mauna Kea. There are the sweeping green ranchlands of Kohala, Ka'u's wild and craggy coastline, Hamakua's acres of sugar cane riven by jungle-choked gorges and Kona's flower-bright forested lava slopes.

It is the island of history. The Big Island offers fascinating insight into Hawaii's past. The arrival of the Polynesians; the saga of Kamehameha the Great's birth and growth to his eventual domination of the Islands, and of his death; Captain Cook's visits and his untimely death; dissolution of the trad-

itional *kapu* (tabu) system and the coming of the missionaries with a new religion: evidence of all these events remains. Even the genesis of the islands themselves is evoked in volcanic activity, which can be viewed without peril.

To rush your visit to the Big Island is to cheat yourself. We recommend a stay of at least two days in Hilo, base for exploration of the windward side including Volcanoes National Park. Allow two to three days on the other side in order to have time to investigate the Kona coast and Kohala and to indulge in the activities available.

Geography

The Big Island covers 4038 square miles, a figure which grows with each major eruption when lava flows into the ocean, adding acreage to the coastline. It lies 2100 miles off the mainland coast, on a parallel with central Mexico. Thus, its southern tip, KaLae, is the southernmost point of the United States.

Looming over the island are the five volcanoes which gave it birth. Mauna Kean, dormant for some 4500 years, rises 13,796 feet above sea level. Measured from subterrainean base to summit, it is probably the planet's highest mountain. Kohala Volcano in the north has been extinct long enough for streams to carve huge high-walled canyons into its northeastern slope. On the western side, Hualalai last poured forth lava in 1801. Still active are a 4090-foot Kilauea and the mighty shield volcano, Mauna Loa, at 13,680 feet above sea level.

Since ancient times, the Big Island has been divided into six districts: Hilo, Puna, Ka'u, Kona, Kohala and Hamakua. Modern administration has broken these down to North and South Hilo, North and South Kona and North and South Kohala. Good roads around the island give easy access to each of these areas. The usual bases for sightseeing the island are Hilo on the windward side and Keauhou and Kailua on the leeward coast. The Hilo area, which receives greater rainfall, is lush with rain forest, orchids and anthurium. The drier Kona coast is the sunny playground, rich in history and legend.

SR 11 from Hilo to Kona around the south coast is 127 miles. While it takes only 3½ hours approximately to drive it straight through, you'll find a full day barely enough as there are so many points of interest compelling you to stop and explore. The northern route, SR 19 along the Hamakua coast to Waimea, then following Queen Kaahumanu Drive from Kawaihae to Kailua-Kona is 98 miles. Again, many diversions and detours generally make progress slow.

SR 20, the Saddle Rd, is a scenic but rough road passing between Mauna Kea and Mauna Loa. It is frequently hidden in clouds and is forbidden for rental cars.

History

It was at KaLae (South Point) that the first wave of Polynesians is thought to have made landfall in the middle of the 8th century. From these beginnings many *alii* (chiefly) families became powerful in different regions of the island during the thousand years that Hawaii remained isolated from the rest of the world.

By the mid-18th century, the paramount chief on the island was Kalaniopuu, a grandson of the great chief Keawe. He ruled not only the island of Hawaii, but also the districts of Hana and Kipahulu on Maui, which he had annexed from Kahekili. Late in his 29-year reign, he called his chiefs together to Waipio and named his son Kiwalao as his rightful heir. At the same time, significantly, he passed on his feathered war god Kukailimoku to his nephew, Kamehameha. This young chief from Kohala had gained a reputation as a fierce and fearless warrior. From that moment on, Kamehameha's followers encouraged his ambition to unite Hawaii, and all the Islands, under his rule.

In January 1782 Kalaniopuu became ill and died. Kiwalao ceremoniously placed his father's remains alongside those of former chiefs in the Hale-o-Keawe at Honaunau. Then followed a bitter struggle, engendered by the division of land, between the followers of Kiwalao allied with his uncle Keawemauhili, Kamehameha, and Keoua, Kiwalao's half-brother. Kiwalao was killed in battle and Keawemauhili gained power over Hilo and part of Hamakua, while Kamehameha ruled Kona, Kohala and the rest of Hamakua and Keoua became chief of Puna and Ka'u.

Despite frequent battles between their forces, this balance of power remained unchanged for the next decade. In 1790, Keawemauhili aided Kamehameha in his conquest of Maui at Kepaniwai. In retaliation, Keoua fought and killed Keawemauhili. Immediately Kamehameha returned from Molokai and the two chiefs met in an indecisive battle in Hamakua. Keoua retired to Ka'u to regroup, losing some of his forces en route when a volcanic eruption overtook them.

Heeding a *kahuna's* (priest's) prophecy that he should build a great *heiau* (temple) for his god Kukailimoku and he would henceforth rule all the Islands, Kamehameha personally led the construction of Puukohala Heiau. Then he sent emissaries to Keoua, inviting him to the dedication. Convinced he was going to his death, Keoua nevertheless set forth in his double-hulled canoe, accompanied by high ranking friends. As he sailed into the cove below the great *heiau*, he was set upon by the followers of Kamehameha and killed. At long last Kamehameha ruled this island; soon he was king of all the islands. The kahuna's prophecy was finally fulfilled.

Although Kamehameha the Great ruled from Honolulu, towards the end of his life he returned to his own island where he died at Kailua in 1819. His son Kamehameha II succeeded to the throne and it was in Kailua that, encouraged by the two dowager queens, Keopuolani and Kaahumanu, he ordered the *kapu* system abolished. *Heiaus* were desecrated, idols demolished, but the people were left without a religion. Into this void came the missionaries. The *Thaddeus,* bearing the first company of Congregational missionaries from New England, anchored at Kawaihae on March 30, 1820. So persuasive were they and so open-hearted the Hawaiians' acceptance of their teaching, that within two decades Hawaii was a Christian nation. Many old churches, including the 1837 Mokuaikaua Church in Kailua, testify to their zeal.

Thus you will find as you move around the Big Island you are constantly treading the path of history.

HILO

The attractive town of Hilo, spread around its sheltered bay, appeals to those who like friendly, low-key places. Its people welcome visitors warmly but they have not turned their city into a tourist trap. Rather it has the feeling of the Hawaii of an earlier time.

The city rises up from Hilo Bay, climbing the wooded lower slope of Mauna Kea. Cloud cover which generally hangs low over the mountain clears occasionally to reveal its majestic summit, capped in winter months with sparkling snow. On the north end of town, the Wailuku River spills down the gulch it has carved to empty into the bay. Beyond, houses are scattered through fields of sugar cane covering the slope.

In the center of town, a large open area is perpetual memorial to the devastating tsunami (seismic wave) which swept in on May 22, 1960, destroying this section. The older part of downtown between here and the Wailuku River is lined with woodframe stores where merchants still take time to gossip leisurely. Hilo is the ideal opportunity to mingle with local people and observe ordinary Hawaiian life.

Downtown Hilo

A fascinating look at island living in olden days is provided at the **Lyman Mission House and Museum**. The Reverend David Belden Lyman and his new wife, Sarah Joiner Lyman, arrived in Hilo with the Fifth Company of missionaries in July 1832. They remained to open a boys' school and raise a family of eight. In 1839 they built their first home, across the street from the present site: soon it became a gathering place for Hawaiians of all ranks. Each monarch from Kamehameha III to Queen Liliuokalani crossed its threshhold.

In 1932, the centenary of the Lymans' arrival in Hilo was marked by the opening of their house as a museum. Their granddaughter, Emma Lyman Wilcox, raised the funds to move the house and refurnish it with original and donated period pieces. A guided tour of its rooms

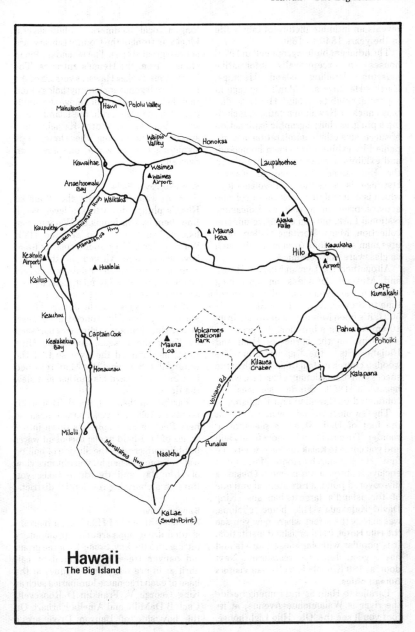

Hawaii
The Big Island

reveals an intimate picture of family life in the years 1840 to 1880.

The adjacent building, opened in 1973, houses an exceptionally informative museum detailing Island Heritage, Earth's Heritage and Man's Heritage in separate exhibits. Island Heritage displays ancient Hawaiian artefacts, including a pili grass hut; a graphic explanation of successive ethnic immigration, accompanied by exhibits from each homeland; and exhibits detailing missionary life on the Big Island. Included in Earth's Heritage is a section on volcanology which is a useful introduction to volcano activity prior to a visit to Volcanoes National Park, plus an extensive mineral collection. Man's Heritage Gallery features man's creations from minerals, such as glassware and ceramics.

Altogether, the Lyman Mission House and Museum provides an absorbing experience and you should allow plenty of time to browse. At 276 Haili St; tel 935-5021; it's open Monday to Saturday from 10 am to 4 pm; admission charge.

Nearby, on the corner of Haili and Ululani Sts, the apricot-and-white wooden church is **Haili Church**, fifth in the succession of missionary churches, which began in 1859. Sunday services are conducted in Hawaiian and English.

The few blocks of old downtown Hilo at the foot of Haili St are a pleasure to wander. Turn right on Kinoole from Haili and you come to **Kalakaua Park**, where the first Haili Church stood. The quiet enclave features a war memorial beside a lily-covered pond, a rare sundial and one of the island's largest banyans. King David Kalakaua's Hilo home, Niolopa, was across the street where now you see the **Hilo Hotel**, itself an island institution. It is popular with Japanese tourists and has a good Japanese restaurant. Next door, at 180 Kinoole is an **Hawaii Visitors Bureau** office.

Parallel to Haili St and running beside the river is Waianuenue Avenue; at its foot you'll see the 'Ole' Hilo Lighthouse, long a local landmark. Uphill several blocks, in front of the County Library, are set two great stones. The legendary **Pinao** stone is from the Heiau's entrance. The Naha stone evokes Hawaii's version of the Excalibur legend: ancient mythology held that the person who could move the 5000-pound stone would rule the Islands. It is said that as a youth Kamehameha succeeded in turning the stone, thus signifying that he would one day reign over all.

Wailuku River Falls

Several waterfalls mark the Wailuku River's plunge down to sea level; you'll find them by continuing up Waianuenue, bearing right until you see the HVB Warrior signs. Most spectacular is **Rainbow Falls**, best viewed in the early morning hours, when a rainbow is clearly visible in the cascades' mist. Look closely and you'll see a cave at the base of the cliff. Legend says that the demigod Maui and his mother Hina onced lived here. When Maui was away, Hina was harassed by Kuna the Dragon, and while Hina slept, he dammed the river so that the water filled her cave. But Maui returned just in time to save his mother and slew the dragon.

Farther up the road, the HVB Warrior points to **Boiling Pots**, so named because here Peepee Falls splashes down into a series of lava-held pools; turbulent water bubbling up creates the illusion of boiling water. From this height, you obtain a view of Hilo Bay and the drive takes you through a charming residential district.

Banyan Drive

At the south end of Hilo Bay, a banyan-shaded drive loops around a promontory jutting into the bay. Some 46 of the grand old banyan trees were planted by celebrities in pre-war years. Plaques at the base of each tree name luminaries such as King George V, Franklin D Roosevelt, Cecil B DeMille and Amelia Earhart. On the bay side of Banyan Drive are a number of restaurants and hotels, including the popular Naniloa Surf.

At its south end, **Liliuokalani Gardens** provides a pleasant stroll. The 30-acre park replicates traditional Japanese gardens, with arching bridges, pagodas and a ceremonial teahouse. A pedestrian bridge leads to **Coconut Island**, where pavilions provide an inviting spot to picnic while you gaze across Hilo Bay at the town framed by Mauna Kea. The promontory and island were sacred places of refuge in ancient times.

A relatively recent addition to the park is **Bicentennial Park**, created by an artisan from Kyoto, Hilo's sister city, and dedicated on July 4, 1976 in honor of the country's 200th birthday.

Early risers can enjoy one of Hilo's most fascinating experiences at the **Suisan Fish Market**. Located near the mouth of the Wailoa River adjacent to Liliuokalani Gardens, the market comes alive at 8 each morning, when a tumultuous multilingual auction sells off the morning's catch. It's open from Monday to Saturday.

Across Kamehameha Avenue, the Wailoa River forms Waiakea Pond in **Wailoa River State Park**, scene of the devastation caused by the 1960 tsunami. The octagonal Visitor Center features exhibits describing the island's culture and history. Nearby you might see canoe clubs practising the ancient sport of outrigger canoe racing.

Mauna Kea

Mauna Kea is a boon to the study of the universe: the dry, cloud-free atmosphere of its summit assures an exceptionally clear perception of the observable planets. In 1979, astronomers completed three major observatories atop the mountain.

Skifields

While astronomers probe celestial reaches from the slopes of Mauna Kea, others use them to enjoy the novel experience of skiing on a tropical Pacific island. Mauna Kea gets skiable snow from early January to April or May. The unmaintained ski runs, which are around the 13,000-foot level, vary from beginner to expert. *Ski Shop Hawaii* rents gear and provides transportation and guide service to the skifields. Get in touch c/o General Delivery, Kamuela, HI 96734; tel (808) 885-4188 in season; rest of year at 830 Ala Moana Blvd, Honolulu HI 96813, tel (808) 537-4065 (office open 12.30 to 4 pm).

Kaumana Cave

A few historic sites lie up SR 20, the Saddle Rd (Kaumana Drive), which leads to Mauna Kea's summit. In 1880, Mauna Loa erupted and sent tongues of lava inching down toward Hilo. These stopped only a few miles short of town. Testifying to how close Hilo came to devastation, just 4½ miles uphill from the center of town are the Kaumana Caves, lava tubes formed in that eruption. Those interested can explore a half-mile section of one cavern; the other is dangerous so make enquiries for directions first.

SOUTH OF HILO

Along SR 11, which leads south from the far end of Banyan Drive past the airport and toward Volcanoes National Park, are a number of interesting places. You can encompass them in a day's touring or you could combine them with a visit to the Volcanoes National Park. However, we strongly recommend against the latter course, if possible, since you would not have time to enjoy them fully and to cover all the points of interest in the park.

Hale Manu Crafts

Several miles south on SR 11, an HVB sign to the right points the way to this crafts shop, located in the Panaewa Forest. Here you can watch craftspeople weaving *lauhala* in the time-honored way from leaves of the pandanus tree, often called the 'walking tree' because of its exposed root system. The friendly people explain the process and how it was used in olden days and you can buy crafts and souvenirs at relatively uninflated prices.

Open 8.30 am to 4.30 pm Monday to Friday, and Saturday until 4 pm, closed Sunday, free; tel 959-7412.

Nani Mau Gardens

Hilo's plentiful rainfall makes the area a huge natural hothouse, where orchids, anthuriums and other blooms proliferate. A number of orchid farms, which export all over the world, welcome visitors; the Hawaii Visitors Bureau suplies a list on request. One of the loveliest and most relaxing ways to admire Hilo's flora is through the dream of one man, 'Mac' Nitahara. Over the past 10 years, he has built his 20-acre **Nani Mau ('Forever Beautiful') Gardens** into a Xanadu. Over 2000 varieties of orchid, as well as fern groves carpeted in anthuriums, beds of pungent red ginger and a host of other flowers and plants fill the gardens. In addition, there are orchards of tropical fruits, which Mac hastens to tell the visitor are to be picked and eaten at will.

You will find it at 421 Malalika St; tel 959-9442; open daily 8 am to 5 pm; admission charge; guided tours available.

Panaewa Zoo

A little further along SR 11, a county sign marks the turnoff to Panaewa Zoo, deep in the rainforest. Opened only in 1978, the evolving zoo exemplifies the 'natural environment' concept. Species indigenous to rainforest mingle in free-form enclosures blending into the land's contours. Freely roaming peacocks preen and strut the paths as though guiding you to visit tigers, gibbons, brilliantly plumed parrots and Hawaiian nenes.

Open daily 9 am to 4.15 pm; admission charge; tel 959-7224.

Macadamia Nut Orchards

Back in the 1880s, the first macadamias were introduced from Australia. Now the Big Island is famed for macadamia orchards and products. At **Mauna Loa Company's** orchard and mill off SR 11 about five miles south of Hilo, an audio-visual explains the process of growth from ground clearing to canning (it takes seven years for a tree to become productive). You view the processing through windows onto the mill floor and then have an opportunity to indulge in a little tasting and buying.

It's three miles east of SR 11 at HVB Warrior sign; tel 966-9301; open Monday to Friday from 8 am to 4.30 pm.

Places to Eat

JD's Banyan Broiler Steak and seafood house with good salad bar, pleasant atmosphere. (M)

Dinner nightly. 111 Banyan Drive; tel 961-5802.

Reuben's Far-from-fancy decor but good Mexican food, margaritas. (B)

Lunch, Monday to Saturday, dinner nightly. 336 Kamehameha Avenue; tel 961-2522.

KK Tei Japanese and American cuisine; popular restaurant in traditional garden setting. Reservations needed for their tatami rooms and Yakiniku House. (B/M)

Lunch, Monday to Saturday, dinner nightly. 1550 Kamehameha Avenue; tel 961-3791.

Volcano House Good food in dramatic setting overlooking crater. Extensive buffet luncheon; steak and seafood dinner. (M)

Breakfast, lunch, dinner daily. Hawaii Volcanoes National Park; tel 967-7321.

HAWAII VOLCANOES NATIONAL PARK

Thirty miles south of Hilo is the major attraction of the Big Island, and for some, of all the islands: Hawaii Volcanoes National Park. Here, when the Fire Goddess, Madame Pele, is in the throes of tempestuous activity, you witness the awesome grandeur of the elements which created these islands. Few sights on earth could be more breathtaking than watching a lake of 1500°F liquid lava rolling and crashing like ocean waves against the walls of a crater. Even when Pele is in repose, you will see impressive expanses of lava and yawning craters.

Volcanoes National Park focuses on Kilauea Caldera, the vast crater of active Kilauea volcano. Park boundaries also reach northwest to include the summit of Mauna Loa and southeast in a wedge-shaped section down to the coast.

Mauna Loa's gently sloping silhouette is deceptive. The mountain's bulk, 10,000 cubic miles, is greater than the entire Sierra Nevada. From sea floor to summit, the colossus rises 2000 feet higher than Mt Everest. Only Mauna Kea is loftier. Mauna Loa last erupted in 1975, after a 25-year period of inactivity, but the flow lasted only one day.

Kilauea, on the other hand, is frequently active, though rarely are its eruptions violent. The 'non-explosive' classification of its activity has drawn volcanologists to use it as a living laboratory. When lava swells up inside the mountain to burst out through the summit caldera or through one of its two fault rifts, its spectacular pyrotechnics attract thousands of spectators, earning it the description 'drive-in volcano'. Over recent years, eruptions have sent fountains of fire hundreds of feet into the air. Curtains of molten lava have cascaded over the inland *pali* and covered the coastal plain, forming rugged cliffs above the ocean and adding acreage to the island. Yet there has been virtually no injury to any person.

Madame Pele Few who enter her domain can deny the aura of Pele's presence. Ancient Polynesian mythology recounts that she came to the Hawaiian Islands fleeing her cruel sister, Na Maka o Kahai, Goddess of the Sea. Many sites throughout the other islands are tied in legend to Pele's odyssey in search of a home. When she reached Kilauea, the Fire Goddess' search was ended. She found refuge from Na Maka deep in Halemaumau firepit, where from time to time she sends rivers of lava down the *pali* (cliffs) to pour into her sister's domain.

Pele is an imperious goddess. She wreaks havoc on those who scorn her and spares others: a lava flow from Hualalai destroyed all in its path except for a village where, it is said, Pele had been given food. Throughout the highlands, forests of ohia are constant reminder of the effects of her wrath. It is legend that Ohia was a young man much loved by Pele. But he loved the beautiful Lehua. In a jealous rage, Pele transformed Ohia into a twisted tree. Other gods took pity on the lovers and turned Lehua into the delicate crimson blossom which adorns the ohia lehua tree today. Hence it is said that if you pick the lehua blossom it will rain, for Lehua weeps at being parted from her love.

One person who successfully defied Pele was Chiefess Kapiolani, who converted to Christianity. In December 1824, she stood at the brink of Kilauea and cried out to Pele that Jehovah was all-powerful. By this she demonstrated to her followers that, since no eruption occured, the Christian God must indeed be supreme.

Pele is reputed to appear in human form, sometimes as a beautiful woman, but more often as an old crone – in the district of Puna where the park is located, few would ignore a hitchhiking old lady. Traditionally the people pick berries of the ohelo, which grows high in the park, to offer in homage to Pele. Others satisfy her predilection for gin. To the people of the Big Island, the Fire Goddess is demanding, but not evil. As one man is reported to have explained: 'If she comes, she comes. Maybe she takes my place. I do not think she will hurt *me* '

Even scientists are not immune to Pele's mystique. During the 1975 eruption of Mauna Loa, two volcanologists flying over the summit reported clearly seeing two men and a woman who were in imminent danger. When a helicopter went to their rescue, the pilot found only two men who said there had never been a woman with them.

Visitors are cautioned not to souvenir Pele's lava. The mail frequently brings boxes of lava back to the Big Island from anonymous persons who apparently rue the day they removed them.

Things to See & Do

Start your sightseeing at **Kilauea Visitor Center,** which is park headquarters, where you can pick up a brochure and map detailing the points of interest, trails and picnic and camping sites. A 10-minute film explaining volcanic activity is shown every hour on the hour from 9 am to 4 pm. The Museum is open daily 7.30 am to 5 pm; free.

Nearby **Volcano House,** an historic hotel, perches on the rim of the caldera. From its dining rooms and cocktail lounge, you look out at the crater. Steam rising from vents in the surrounding ohia forest reminds that beneath the earth's crust is molten lava; the steam rises as groundwater seeps onto the hot rocks through vents in the forest floor.

From the Visitor Center, 11-mile **Crater Rim Drive** circles Kilauea Caldera and the adjacent pit crater, Kilauea Iki. Numerous overlooks allow differing perspectives of dense rain forest slashed by ribbons of lava, expanses of ropy *pahoehoe* and chunky *a'a* lava and *puus* hills built by cinder and pumice. Trails allow you to hike in for closer views. A hiking trail also circles the Crater Rim.

It was in **Kilauea Iki** in November 1959 that Hawaii's highest ever lava fountain was recorded: 1900 feet, which spread a carpet of pumice five feet thick over a half-mile area and built a 150-foot conical hill, Puu Puai. You can walk **Devastation Trail** from the Kilauea Iki lookout across this desolate field of ash toward the *puu.* Step off the wooden trail and you'll

understand why astronauts trained here for moonwalking! The colors and shapes of this bizarre landscape textured with gaunt ohia trees are a delight for photographers.

Across Kilauea Caldera is **Halemaumau** firepit, Pele's home, which is a collapsed crater about 3200 feet wide within the main caldera. Much of Kilauea's eruptive activity has originated here. For many years in the late 19th and early 20th centuries, Halemaumau was a lake of liquid lava. A trail from Volcano House leads through the forest and across the caldera floor, skirting Halemaumau; you can hike it in approximately two hours, each way.

Further around Crater Rim Rd, you come to the **Hawaiian Volcano Observatory,** where scientists are studying the volcano's activity. You are welcome to visit; you'll find the view of Halemaumau spectacular.

Chain of Craters Rd descends the steep pali to the southeast coast section of the park. It follows the line of craters which mark the east rift, some dating from prehistoric times. Others are of more recent vintage, including the parasitic shield cone Mauna Ulu which was created during the 1969 series of eruptions that closed the old Chain of Craters Rd. Signs at the frequent lookouts indicate the history of craters and lava flows and the road allows stunning vistas of the lava-strewn coastal plain. At the coast, a sign marks the trail leading to the Puu Loa petroglyphs, considered one of the finest concentrations of petroglyphs in the Islands.

Here Chain of Craters Rd meets SR 13 which leads out of the park to Kalapana. Near this park entrance, 28 miles from Kilaueau Visitor Center, is the impressive **Waha'ula Heiau.** This most sacred temple was built by the Tahitian *kahuna nui* (high priest) Paao, who arrived in Hawaii with the 13th century wave of Polynesians. Paao, whose story has been passed down in chants from generation to generation, is attributed with introducing the *kapu* laws and human sacrifice to Hawaii at Waha'ula Heiau. Self-guided walking tours explain the structure of the restored temple and point out indigenous plants along a dramatically scenic nature trail. Pick up the map from the Visitor Center. Open daily 8.30 am to 5 pm; free.

In summer months, interpretive programs include talks, nature walks and other activities; you can obtain a schedule from either Kilauea or Waha'ula Visitor Center or by writing park headquarters (see below).

The **Volcano Art Center,** housed in the original 1877 Volcano House, includes a gallery and offers crafts seminars and evening concerts in an intimate atmosphere. Telephone 967-7511 for a schedule.

Maps of Kilauea summit and Mauna Loa summit hiking trails are available from Visitor Centers. Registration at park headquarters is required for overnight hikes.

Places to Stay & Eat
The only hotel is *Volcano House,* which offers 37 rooms, some with crater view. The Sheraton-managed lodge has been renovated recently, with dining facilities enlarged to accommodate up to 400. Restaurant is open from 7 am to 9 pm and features a buffet luncheon from 10.30 am to 2.30 pm. Rates run from $37 double and reservations are necessary. Write directly to Volcano House, Hawaii Volcanoes National Park, Hawaii, HI 96718; tel (808) 967-7321 or through Sheraton's toll-free number (800) 325-3535; from Honolulu 800-922-4777.

There are five drive-in *campgrounds* with a limit of seven days per campground, no reservation or fee required. Cabins at Namakani Paio are operated by the Volcano House. Shelters and cabins are available for hikers; you must register with park headquarters.

Groceries, gasoline and camping supplies are available at the nearby town of Volcano, one mile north of the park on SR 11, and food at Kalapana, four miles east of the coast entrance to the park on SR 13. (For a taste treat, stop by Mountain View Bakery in the small plantation town of the same name for unique cookies, baked for sale in the afternoon only. Take N Lauko Drive off SR 11 just past the 14-mile marker to the grey-and-white frame building; if it's not open, just knock at the side door!)

Getting There
All the major tour operators offer tours to Hawaii Volcanoes National Park from Hilo (full day, rates range from $20 to $26) and the park is included on Hilo-Kona and reverse tours.

Volcanoes National Park is open year-round. At the higher altitudes, it can be cool and rain can fall at any time of the year so be prepared. In winter, snow might extend down to the 10,000-foot level on Mauna Loa.

Information
Hawaii Volcanoes National Park, HI 96718 (tel (808) 967-7311). A hotline gives recorded information around the clock on eruption activity (tel 967-7977).

THE PUNA-KA'U ROUTE TO KONA
This route follows SR 11 from Hilo south through Volcanoes National Park to Ka'u and on to Kona. However, we highly recommend that you detour on SR 130 at Keaau, which veers off southeast through sleepy towns to the tropical Puna coastline, crossing gigantic lava flows. Then you swing up the Chain of Craters Rd through Volcanoes National Park to rejoin SR 11, which takes you across Ka'u back to the coast and around the southern tip of the island to South Kona.

PUNA
The district of Puna is particularly fertile. Fields of sugar cane greet you as you

cross the district line.

Soon after entering Puna, you take SR 130 toward Kalapana. This is a good road, which cuts through small communities where life revolves around 'main street'. Take the time to pause and get the feeling of a bygone era. At Keaau, turn left at the first corner and you'll come to a classic example of a Hongwanji Buddhist temple.

Sugar cane gives way to roadside anthurium farms, where the exquisite blooms are grown under plastic tents. Forests of ohia harbor thousands of wild orchids and occasionally you pass a Christmas tree farm, where young Norfolk pines are sprouting.

Pahoa

The town of Pahoa, center of the anthurium industry, show signs of revival as more and more young people seeking a relaxed lifestyle settle here and in other towns like this. Visitors are welcome to stop by the anthurium nurseries, incidentally. Check with the Hawaii Visitors Bureau for a current list and opening hours.

Lava Tree Park

A little further on the road forks; SR 130 continues to the coast at Kaimu Black Sand Beach. However, if you follow SR 132, you can visit Lava Tree Park, where you'll see lava in unusual sculpted forms. This was caused when molten lava engulfed ohia trees in the 1790 eruption, burning out the trees within the hardened lava and leaving rigid tree-shaped shells as a perpetual reminder of the forest. Be careful when wandering here, or anywhere in volcano country, not to venture off the path for the earth could be unstable and have dangerous cracks.

Kapoho

Continuing on SR 132, you drive through rain forest under a canopy of monkeypod branches. Delicate pinks and purples show through the trees from a carpet of wildflowers. Suddenly the rain forest stops, obliterated by lava flows from Kilauea's east rift. Vanda orchids and papaya are growing again now and only an HVB marker and graphic display remain where the village of Kapoho stood. On January 14, 1960 lava broke through a vent on the east rift and poured eastward toward the ocean, forming a fan-shaped flow which destroyed the buildings of Kapoho. Fortunately, its inhabitants had time to evacuate. At the end of the road, you see another of Pele's caprices. The lava stopped a few feet short of Kumakahi Lighthouse, then circled its base and pushed on down to the ocean where it added another 500 acres to the Big Island.

Returning to the intersection, turn left on SR 137, the shore road which takes you to Kalapana. Soon the barren desolation of lava is replaced by tropical growth along the ocean's edge.

At Pohoiki Bay, you'll doubtless see keikis (children) surfing in the cove; this is the first of several beach parks where you can picnic, swim (with caution) and sometimes camp (to enquire about the latter, telephone the Department of Parks & Recreation at 961-8311).

From here, the road passes through ohia and ironwood forests and emerges onto more lava flow. From the road you can clearly see where lava poured into the sea and threw up the fantastic rock formations which mark the Puna coast. Where the lava was spewn back in tiny particles, it formed black sand beaches such as Kaimu and the famous Kalapana beach. These palm-fringed beaches are beautiful to stroll but dangerous to swim because of heavy undertow.

Half-way to Kalapana, you cross the east rift of Kilauea, delineated by steam vents and a line of spatter cones, through which the lava poared over Kapoho and into the ocean.

Kalapana

Beyond Kaimu Beach, SR 137 joins SR

130 heading for Kalapana. Soon you reach the **Harry K Brown Park**, largest and best-equipped of the beach parks. Swimming and shore fishing are safe here, except when a high surf is running. On the shore across from the park is the **Star of the Sea Painted Church**. A Belgian priest painted the brilliantly colored pictures and murals which cover the interior of this small Catholic church, built in the 1920s. Behind the church you'll see a canoe ramp, still in use, which dates back to the Stone Age. Kalapana and the Painted Church almost shared the fate of Kapoho in October, 1977, but the lava flow stopped abruptly one-quarter of a mile from its outskirts.

The **drive-in** across from the church is one of the few places where you can eat Hawaiian snacks, such as *laulau* (beef and fish steamed in taro leaf), *lomi salmon* (salted salmon marinated with onion and tomato) and *poi*. It also has a wide menu of more regular fare.

About 2½ miles down the road, look for the trail to **Queen's Bath**; you can take a refreshing dip in this freshwater pool where once queens bathed.

From here, you enter Volcanoes National Park. SR 130 joins the Chain of Craters Rd which takes you to SR 11 and on to Ka'u. Highlights of the park are described earlier in this chapter.

Ka'u

Traversing the park on Chain of Craters Rd, take Crater Rim Drive to the left to join SR 11 northwest of park headquarters. Heading out of the park, you'll see a trail marker on the ocean side of SR 11 for **Footprints Trail**. It's a half-day roundtrip trek to where the ill-fated soldiers of Keoua's army, caught in the volcanic eruption of 1790, left the imprint of their bare feet permanently embedded in hardened volcanic ash.

As you head south out of the park, on the ocean side of the road stretches the barren, volcanic Ka'u Desert. Upland, though, the slopes of Mauna Loa are green with lush ranchlands. From an elevation of 3500 feet, you descend now toward the southern coast.

Punalu'u

Near sea level, follow the turnoff for Punaluu toward the ocean. You'll pass between hedges of multihued bougainvillea, plumeria (frangipani) and poinciana to reach one of the island's loveliest and most popular spots.

Turn off at the first parking lot for Black Sand Beach Park, a wide black sand beach and palm-shaded lagoon. This is an excellent swimming beach; restrooms and a pavilion nearby cater to picnickers and campers.

The Ka'u Coast is a special, sacred place for Hawaiians. It was a landing site for the earliest Polynesians. Later, a triangle of *heiaus* was dedicated: one on the point here, a second on the promontory down the beach at Ninole and the third inland. You can view the ruins of **Kanaelele Heiau** by climbing around the point to the left of the beach. Concrete slab blocks are all that remain of a sugar cane loading pier destroyed by a 19th century tidal wave. Ka'u was Keoua's base while he withstood Kamehameha; it was from here that he sailed to his betrayal and death in Kohala.

An Easter Sunday sunrise service is held here to commemorate Punalu'u native son Henry Opukahaia, who traveled to New England in the early 19th century and inspired the first Christian missionaries to come to Hawaii.

Ninole

Drive on around the bay and you come to the golf course and condominiums of **SeaMountain Colony**, first resort on this coast. You can hike out onto the point to explore extensive ruins of a *heiau* and ancient school. On a small cove beach on the far side, you might find some of the extraordinary 'mother' stones inside which, it is said, are 'baby' stones which multiply.

From Ninole, you can rejoin SR 11 and head towards South point. En route you pass through the villages of **Na'alehu**, southernmost town in the United States, and **Waiohinu**, known for the monkeypod tree planted by Mark Twain. A high wind blew it down in 1957, but the roots have taken hold again and the tree is flourishing. Ka'u's only tourist accommodation apart from SeaMountain condominiums is Waiohinu's *Shirakawa Motel,* tucked in a garden setting back from the road.

KaLae (South Point)
The turnoff for the 12-mile drive out to the southernmost tip of the United States is about three miles west of Waiohinu. KaLae's cape is a windswept tableland bounded by rugged cliffs. Atop the plateau are remains of three *heiaus,* remnants of a settlement dating back to 750 AD, **Makalea Cave**, used for shelter by the early settlers, and **Palahemo Well**, rimmed with petroglyphs. The forces of Keoua and Kamehameha battled here and military relics of a more recent vintage remain, including a row of cairns set to guide WW II pilots. It would take several hours to thoroughly explore this historic plateau. But it is worth the drive simply to stand at cliffs' edge and watch the waves roar in with a power unchecked by land for thousands of miles. Below are ancient canoe moorings carved into the lava rock and wooden platforms used by fishermen to land their catch from the outstanding offshore fishing grounds.

Two miles from the road is a green sand beach, which can be reached only by four-wheel drive or on foot.

Back on SR 11, as you head northwest, after rounding the tip, the countryside changes. Ohia and eucalyptus cover the slopes of Mauna Loa. Below, the land drops sharply towards the ocean.

Further along, barren lava flows are being graded for development as home sites. Soon you leave Ka'u and start up the Kona coast.

THE KONA COAST
Many visitors to the leeward coast are confused about what the name 'Kona' actually applies to. Strictly speaking, the 'Kona coast' describes the western slopes of Mauna Loa and Hualalai, divided into the North Kona and South Kona districts. South Kona covers the area from Ka'u to Kealakekua; North Kona includes the summit of Mauna Loa and continues to Kohala. Main center of North Kona and of the leeward coast is Kailua, often called Kailua-Kona to differentiate it from Kailua on Oahu. However, locals confuse the issue further by simply referring to the resort area embracing Kailua and Keauhou as Kona.

South Kona
This area is fast becoming known as the 'Gold Coast' because of the amount of real estate development and sky-rocketing land costs. Much of this land is being reclaimed from fields of jagged lava which flowed down from Mauna Loa's Great Fissure in 1950.

Milolii
A turn-off sign points to this old fishing village; the drive is a long, rough five miles. Once spoken of quietly by *kamaainas* (locals) as a fragile oasis in the fast-changing Kona area, the village today sadly is losing its charm as development encroaches on its isolation. If you have limited time we recommend that you forego this detour to allow more time for the City of Refuge.

Pu'uhonua O Honaunau (City of Refuge)
In ancient days, defeated warriors, breakers of the *kapu* and other fugitives were absolved if they could reach a place of refuge. Historically the most important in the Islands, **Pu'uhonua O Honaunau National Historical Park** is also a delightful sanctuary from 20th century bustle. At the Visitor Center, a push-button audio system explains the concept of this place of refuge. Then you enter a

quiet area of stately palms and sandy paths around Keone'ele Cove, sheltered by the Great Wall which separated the pu'uhonua (place of refuge) from the royal residence, also included in the park. On the cove shore stands the re-created **Hale-o-Keawe Heiau**, which housed the bones of 23 chiefs, from the great 16th-century chief Keawe to a son of Kamehameha I. Several other *heiaus* on the ocean side of the Great Wall are being restored by the Bishop Museum. There are carved images, ancient games, koa wood canoes and legendary stones – a self-guided walking tour map from the Visitor Center explains the significance of each item.

The park is open daily 7.30 am to 5.30 pm; free; guided tours 10, 10.30, 11 am and 2.30, 3 and 3.30 pm; tel 328-2288.

Honaunau

Above the park, on Middle Keei Rd off SR 160, is **St Benedict's Catholic Church**. Known as the Painted Church of Honaunau, its interior is decorated with folk art paintings on pillars, walls and ceilings, the work of Belgian priest Father John Berchmans Velghe. He was the teacher of the artist-priest who painted the Star of the Sea at Kalapana.

Kealakekua Bay

From the City of Refuge, you can drive a narrow and rough coastal road across the plain of Keei, where Kamehameha's forces defeated and killed the rightful heir to these districts, Kiwalao, in the early 1780s. This takes you to the village of **Napoopoo** on Keakalekua Bay. At the end of the road is a beach park by an old canoe landing on the south end of the bay. From here, rocky cliffs rise vertically from the ocean as far as the wooded spit which forms the north head of the bay. Midway on the spit, you can see a white pillar, monument to Captain James Cook, who died on the beach nearby in 1779. When Cook originally landed here the year before, he was welcomed by the Haw-

aiians as the god Lono, and relations between the ships' complements and those ashore were friendly. In February, 1779, Cook's ships *Discovery* and *Resolution* set sail from the bay but a few days later they returned with a broken mast to be repaired. The Hawaiians were disturbed that the god would return outside the sacred season. Then a ship's cutter was stolen and Cook took a party ashore to take Chief Kalaniopuu hostage until the cutter was returned. In an ensuing scuffle, Cook was clubbed and cried out. Immediately recognizing that this was no god but a mortal, warriors fell on him and stabbed him to death. The 27-foot **Captain Cook Monument** was erected in his memory in 1874; you can best see it from one of the cruises out of Kailua (see Cruises).

You can climb the steps onto **Hikiau Heiau**, at the water's edge, where Cook was proclaimed to be the god Lono when he first came ashore. It was at this temple that Cook himself conducted the Islands' first Christian burial service for one of his men less than a month before his own death.

On Napoopoo Rd heading uphill to SR 11, you come to the parking lot, marked by a profusion of multi-colored bougainvillea, for the **Royal Kona Coffee Mill and Museum** across the road. The smell of roasting coffee wafts in the air as you inspect the museum's graphic display illustrating the history and artifacts of more than 150 years of coffee growing. The slopes of Hualalai upland from here is the only area in the United States where coffee is grown commercially. An urn in the corner of the museum dispenses the coffee which Mark Twain described as having ' . . . a richer flavor than any other'. It is open from 8 am to 4.30 pm; free.

From here Napoopoo Rd winds back up between jacarandas and poinciana to rejoin SR 11, which along this coast is called the Kuakini Highway. Heading toward the resorts of Keauhou-Kona and

Kailua, you pass through towns with weathered storefronts, old woodframe hotels, restaurants and shops. Houses are set in gardens ablaze with bougainvillea, startlingly brilliant against the lava rock of this region. On the mountainside above are coffee farms, macadamia nut orchards, ranches (and hidden fields of marijuana) which flourish in the wetter climate of the higher altitudes.

Places to Eat

Manago Hotel Restaurant Venerable family-run hotel dining room serving Japanese and American food. (B)

Breakfast, lunch, dinner daily. Kuakini Highway (SR 11) at Captain Cook; tel 323-2642.

Keauhou-Kona

Stay on the lower road when the highway forks and a short distance along is Kamehameha III Rd, which leads down to Keauhou-Kona. This planned resort has grown in the last decade around a championship golf course and Keauhou Bay. Luxury hotels and condominiums set in well-kept lawns overlook the ocean, some from water's edge, others from higher up the slope.

This area is rich in history. Alii Drive, which runs along the shoreline to Kailua, winds down to a beach park at the southern end of the resort. The adjoining **burial ground** was scene of the December 1819 Battle of Kuamoo, when the king's cousin led dissidents opposed to the abolition of the *kapu* system, which Kamehameha II had proclaimed two months before.

Down on the pier at Keauhou Bay, you'll find a **memorial** almost buried in lush tropical growth marking the birthplace of Kamehameha III. And on the hill above, you might just be able to distinguish the path of the royal **Holua slide,** one of the 17 known such slides in the area from Manuka to Lapakahi. This royal sport was favored apparently only by Hawaiians and Maoris and this is the largest slide which has been located in either Hawaii or New Zealand. Participants would sled down the pili grass-covered rocky slide at speeds of up to 70 miles per hour; burial sites by many slides testify at what risk.

At the Kona Surf Hotel, on the south head of Keauhou Bay, you can see a collection of fine artworks from Pacific Rim culture which decorate the public areas.

The Keauhou Beach Hotel, further north on Alii Drive, has preserved remains of the apparently large settlement which once flourished in this area. On the hotel grounds are two restored *heiaus,* petroglyphs and the 150-foot spring-fed King's Bathing Pool. From it's beach, you can see remnants of a remarkable piece of ancient engineering: a breakwater constructed of huge boulders to enclose adjacent Kahuluu Bay.

Next door in the grounds of the Kona Lagoon Hotel are remains of a 16th century palace, several *heiaus* and more petroglyphs.

Ancient home sites, burial platforms, *heiaus* and petroglyphs are incorporated into **Kona Gardens,** a botanical and cultural park located across Alii Drive from the Keauhou Beach and Kona Lagoon hotels. The site has been landscaped with tropical trees and exotic flowers to complement the historical experience, and is open every day from 9 am to 5 pm; tours; admission charge.

Places to Eat

Keauhou-Kona Golf Course Restaurant Fine view Keauhou Bay and good food make this popular with locals. *Pupu* snacks and happy hour add to pleasure of stunning sunsets. Hawaiian entertainment. (B/M)

Breakfast, lunch, dinner daily. At Keauhou Golf Course; tel 322-3700.

Kahaluu Bay

There's good swimming and snorkeling at the vest-pocket beach park which shares this sheltered bay with the Keauhou Beach Hotel. It's a popular place for watching the superb Kona sunsets.

You should stop here, anyway, to visit tiny blue-and-white **St Peter's Catholic Church**, built in 1889 on the site of a *heiau*. It can hold 26 at its Saturday services. Historically services were held on Saturdays because in the early days priests had to travel from parish to parish. St Peter's Catholic Church still follows this tradition.

Along Alii Drive from here to Kailua six miles away, you pass seaside cottages which speak of a time before tourists discovered this sunny coast, and the numerous condominiums which have sprung up in the past 10 years.

Midway to Kailua, look for **White Sand Beach**. It is known locally as Disappearing Sands or Magic Sands because at times the surf carries away the sand, leaving only a jagged lava shoreline. At other times, it is a delightful stretch of white sand beach where you can sunbathe under the palms. Visitors are warned against swimming here, though, because of dangerous currents.

Kailua-Kona

The town of Kailua spreads around Kailua Bay. For the fishermen who throng to Kona to troll seas that have yielded the world's record Pacific blue marlin, focal point is Kailua Wharf. For shoppers, it is boutiques and souvenir shops in **World Square** and **Kona Inn Shopping Village**, converted from the popular 50-year-old inn. For those interested in history, Kailua's charm is accentuated by the opportunity to wander places which played a key role in Hawaii's past.

Premier amongst these is **Kamakahonu**, the royal residence grounds, and **Ahu'ena Heiau**, which you'll find in the gardens of the King Kamehameha Hotel around the beach from the wharf. Amfac restored them when it built the new hotel. Stop by the lobby of the hotel to view the paintings by Herb Kane, which depicts

Kamehameha at Kamakahonu. It was here that Kamehameha I spent his last seven years and here he died on May 8, 1819. And it was here five months later that Kamehameha II joined Queens Keopuolani and Kaahumanu at a feast, signalling the end of the *kapu* system. For information about the free tour of Kamakahonou and the hotel's ethno-botanic tour of the gardens, telephone 329-2911.

Kailua Wharf was landing point for the first missionaries. When the brig *Thaddeus* made landfall at Kawaihae after 159 days at sea, they were forced to wait aboard for a few more days before Kamehameha II gave permission for Asa Thurston and several others to land at Kailua while the rest went on to Honolulu.

Walk around the sea wall to Asa Thurston's **Mokuaikaua Church**, first Christian church in the Islands. The present structure superseded two earlier thatched churches and was dedicated in 1837. Coral from the sea, lava rock from the land and ohia and koa wood from the mountain were used by Reverend Thurston and his converts to build it. A member of the parish will greet you and show you around the interior, including pointing out a model of the *Thaddeus*.

Across the street, **Hulihee Palace** offers fascinating insight into the personalities of royal family members, through such items as Kamehameha I's pipe and his exercise ball, a 180-pound stone! Hulihee Palace was built in 1838 by Governor John Adams Kuakini and became a royal retreat until 1916. Kamehameha IV and Queen Emma spent much of his reign in Kailua but Hulihee was most popular with King David Kalakaua, who purchased and remodeled it in 1882. Today it is much as he left it, including a massive koa and kou wardrobe, handcarved for him by a Chinese prisoner, and other huge pieces befitting his reputedly larger-than-life nature. The Daughters of Hawaii, who restored and maintain the palace, conduct guided tours through it and the grounds, in which are several grass houses. It's open daily Monday to Friday 9 am to 4 pm; last tour 3.30 pm; admission charge; tel 329-1877.

Places to Eat

Eclipse Restaurant Continental cuisine, Polynesian ambience. Dinner dancing. (E)

Dinner nightly. Kuakini Highway, Kailua-Kona, opposite Foodland; tel 329-4686.

Quinn's Cheerful, friendly bar with garden dining, good food. (B)

Lunch, dinner daily. Across from King Kamehameha Hotel; tel 329-3822.

Ocean View Inn Large cafe facing sea wall and bay. Lacking in atmosphere but makes up for it with menu running gamut from hamburgers to Chinese, Japanese and Hawaiian dishes. (B)

Breakfast, lunch, dinner, closed Monday. Alii Drive, Kailua; tel 329-9998.

NORTH OF HILO TO KOHALA

SR 20 heads north along the Hamakua Coast toward Waimea (Kamuela) and Kohala. This is sugar cane country, its monotony broken from time to time by deep gulches. Take the time to stop at these and you'll see waterfalls tumbling down through dense rain forest whose many shades of green are splashed with the crimson of African tulip.

As you cross the Wailuku River leaving Hilo, look upriver to see **Maui's Canoe,** an oblong-shaped rock in the middle of the stream. Legend says that when the demigod Maui sensed his mother was in danger in her cave under Rainbow Falls, he crossed the channel from the island of Maui with two mighty strokes of his paddle. Reaching the mouth of the Wailuku he beached his canoe, which remains here where he left it as he rushed to rescue her.

HAMAKUA COAST
Akaka Falls

About four miles north of Hilo, a scenic drive lined with lofty Alexander palms loops off the highway to skirt Onomea Bay. Further up the highway, follow a spur road inland to these spectacular 420-foot waterfalls. From the parking lot, you stroll through a lush botanical garden, featuring many varieties of tropical plants and blooms to reach points overlooking the Akaka and Kahuna falls.

Laupahoehoe

The Hamakua Coast was scene of several battles during the early 1780s, when Kamehameha was pitted against Keawemauhili and Keoua in the struggle for supremacy over the island. After one fierce encounter, Kamehameha withdrew his forces to the peninsula at Laupahoehoe ('leaf of lava') to recoup.

Today this point is an attractive park, where picnic pavilions overlook surf crashing on craggy lava rocks. Hard as it is to imagine here an encampment of 18th century warriors, it is harder still to transpose on this peaceful scene the horror of April 1, 1946, when a tsunami swept in. A plaque at the end of the road memorializes 24 students and teachers who lost their lives that day. Down by the shore, you see clumps of *naupaka;* examine its small white flower and you'll find it's only half a bloom. Legend says a princess came down from the mountain to the shore and fell in love with a fisherman, but their love was doomed. So today for every half-flower on sea-level *naupaka,* there is a corresponding half-flower somewhere in the mountains, immortalizing their love.

If you'd like to glimpse the past in an old plantation town, detour off the highway to one of the villages such as **Papaaloa** or **Paauilo.** You'll be charmed by tiny wooden churches, weathered cottages with iron roofs, vintage movie houses and community stores.

Honokaa

Forty miles north of Hilo is Honokaa, gateway to the historic Waipio Valley. You must detour off the highway to reach Honokaa and the overlook for Waipio Valley which lies nine miles beyond; we definitely recommend that you do so, as the valley presents one of the island's loveliest sights.

Honokaa, a predominantly Portuguese town, offers another opportunity to sample macadamia nut products at **Hawaiian Holiday Macadamia Nut Factory,** which is open daily 9 am to 6 pm; free.

Stop by **Tex Drive-In,** too, and try their *loco moco* (a rice and hamburger mixture with egg which tastes infinitely better than it sounds!)

Waipio Valley

Continuing through Honokaa, you pass canefields and rural cottages en route to **Waipio Point.** Here you gaze down on one of nature's grandest creations, Waipio Valley. The Valley of Kings is a six-mile-deep canyon carved into the Kohala mountains. Vertical cliffs 2000-feet high seclude it from the surrounding land but a mile-long crescent of beach opens it to the ocean. Once a well-populated enclave of fertile taro farms, the valley was inundated by the 1946 tsunami. Now it is home to fewer than a dozen persons.

Waipio was one of ancient Hawaii's most sacred places. Kamehameha the Great spent part of his childhood here and it was in this valley that he received the war god Kukailimoku from Kalaniopuu and started on his road to conquest. Offshore he fought Hawaii's first naval battle using cannons against Maui King Kahekili's commander, Kaheiki. The 1791 battle went down in Hawaiian history as Kepuwahaulaula, 'the red-mouthed gun'.

Only four-wheel drive vehicles can negotiate the steep, curving road down into the valley. The recommended method to explore the valley floor is on **Waipio Valley Shuttle's** conducted hour-long tours. These take you down to the beach, then deep into the valley, following the river through jungle choked with banana and guava, breadfruit and mango trees, ferns and flowering fruit trees and bushes. All the while, the driver spins tales of historical and legendary lore.

The shuttles leave from the lookout as frequently as they have four passengers; reservations for parties over four can be made through Waipio Valley Shuttle, PO Box 4, Kukuihaele, HI 96727; telephone (808) 775-7121 or 775-7703. Cost at writing is $10 per person.

Kohala

At the turnoff for Honokaa, SR 19 turns inland to Waimea (Kamuela), center for Kohala's ranchlands. Kohala, which occupies the jutting northern tip of the island, is home of the famed Parker Ranch, largest privately-owned ranch in the United States.

North Kohala is little affected as yet by tourism; South Kohala is a burgeoning resort area which is destined probably to become one of Hawaii's top-drawing areas for affluent vacationers. People who take the time to explore these districts are rewarded with sites where Hawaii's past comes to life: historic *heiaus*, a centuries-old fishing village and the birthplace of Kamehameha the Great. The island's best beaches are here and country villages where life remains simple. Panoramas of windswept upland pastures, secluded coastal gorges and Maui's Haleakala looming across the Alenuihaha Channel make the drive more than worthwhile.

Waimea (Kamuela)

The town of Waimea spreads across the foothills of the Kohala Mountains, it houses clustered in groves of koa and eucalyptus. From a distance, the softly rounded mountains resemble scoops of mint icecream with trickles of chocolate running down their sides.

The US Postal Service designates this town as Kamuela, as it considers there are too many 'Waimea' post offices in the Islands. Whatever its name, this is visibly a 'cowtown', center for the *paniolos* (cowboys) who work the vast Parker spread. (The term *'paniolo'* came from *espanol* for the Latin American cowboys imported in the early 1800s.)

At the Parker Ranch Visitor Center, located near the rear of the shopping plaza on the main street, you can learn all about this remarkable enterprise.

The Parker Ranch

John Parker came to the Islands from New England in 1809 and became a friend of Kamehameha I, whose *haole* advisors John Young and Isaac Davis had inspired the king to seek other capable foreign aides. Parker was assigned to take charge of controlling wild cattle, which were over-running the area. (A 10-year *kapu* placed on a gift of five cows and a bull from Captain George Vancouver had resulted in extensive wild herds.) Eventually in January 1847, Kamehameha III granted Parker a two-acre parcel of land, genesis of the ranch which now covers 250,000 acres and runs 40,000 to 50,000 head of cattle. It is owned and operated by sixth-generation family member, Richard Smart.

At the **Parker Ranch Visitor Center** a museum depicts the life and times of the Parker family through the six generations; a 15-minute audio-visual details the operation of the ranch and highlights its history. There is also a small museum displaying medals, trophies and newsclips of Duke Kahanamoku, Hawaiian Olympic Gold Medalist who introduced surfing to Australia in 1912. It's open Monday to Saturday 9.30 am to 3.30 pm; admission charge; tel 885-7655.

You can sample the ranch's product at **Parker Ranch Broiler** in the shopping center, which serves ranch beef in turn-of-the-century surroundings.

A second fascinating museum in Waimea is the **Kamuela Museum**, where you can view an eclectic collection: Hawaiiana pertaining to the monarchy, Polynesian artifacts and oriental jade and ivory pieces are amongst the displays. This private collection has been gathered over more than half a century by its owner, a descendant of John Parker, who likely will entertain you with tales attached to the pieces. You'll find it at the junction of SR 19 and SR 250; open daily 8 am to 5 pm; admission charge; telephone 885-4724.

Driving through Waimea, you see several charming reminders of olden days: **Imiola Church,** built by early missionary Lorenzo Lyons in 1857, is on SR 19 as you enter town. Beneath its New England steeple is an Hawaiian interior, where koa wood is featured extensively in ceiling, walls and the altar. At the junction of SR 250, notice the carpenter's Gothic **Kahilu Theater** where live shows sometimes star Richard Smart, who has appeared on Broadway.

Being a 'cowtown', **rodeos** are a popular pasttime in Waimea. The two major functions are the three-day Labor Day Roundup and the July 4 rodeo, a family function limited to Parker Ranch paniolos' participation in the events. The popular Memorial Day rodeo is held in Honokaa.

NORTH KOHALA

SR 250 is the high road to North Kohala; SR 270 is the coast road and, with the stretch of SR 19 between Waimea and Kawaihae, they form a loop around this scenic peninsula.

SR 250 leaves town to climb through fields of lush pili grass, studded here and there with clumps of cactus. Tall eucalyptus and Norfolk pines form windbreaks for cattle grazing patures outlined with stone fences. Clearly visible from here are the three volcanoes, Mauna Kea, Mauna Loa and Hualalai. From 2000-foot elevation, the panorama embraces mountain peak to surf. You catch glimpses of Haleakala through ironwood trees lining the road at its 3564-foot crest, then descend into North Kohala. At the fork in the road, follow the top road into Kapaau.

Kapaau

Here in front of the north Kohala Civic Center stands the original **statue of Kamehameha**, once lost at sea then recovered. Its better-known near-replica stands across from Iolani Palace in downtown Honolulu.

Kamehameha was born near here and no doubt spent his childhood years as children do today playing in these fields, fishing the streams and hiking into the mountains. Many coves around this coast are designed as beach parks, where you'll find swimming risky but picnicking and fishing fine.

Several historic places of worship are worth investigation in Kapaau: the road alongside the Civic Center leads to a quaint **Buddhist temple**. Down an old carriage road arched with a canopy of royal palms and Norfolk pines is **Kalahikiola Church**, designed by missionary Elias Bond, who founded Kohala's first sugar plantation.

Pololu Valley

The road ends at a point overlooking a dramatic coastline. Pololu Valley is one of a series of steep-walled canyons indenting the coast; a two-mile trail leads down to the beach fronting the rugged cove.

Hawi

From the overlook, retrace your path through Kapaau to reach Hawi, an 1840s plantation town where you're likely to see oldtimers playing checkers across from Luke's Hotel, social center of the area.

Take the Upolu Airport turnoff to visit the **Mookini Heiau**. You'll find it left of the road facing the ocean (look for the HVB Warrior) – close the gate behind you and follow the dirt road for about half a mile. This vast *heiau* was originally built

around 480 AD. In the days of Paao, the 13th century *kahina nui* from Tahiti, it became a sacrificial temple of the highest rank, equal to the one at Wahaula. Descendants of the Mookini family serve as guardians of the temple, as they have done reputedly for 1500 years. Near the *heiau*, a stone tablet enveloped in a field of sugar cane marks the birthplace of Kamehameha.

SR 270 rounds the point and heads south toward Kawaihae. Now you pass from grassland that gleams silver-gray in the sunlight to a darker, more arid landscape speckled with kiawes, a tree of the mesquite family.

Lapakahi

In recent yeas, archeologists probing the land for its historic sites found the ruins of a 14th century fishing village, now part of the **Lapakahi State Historical Park** on the shore a few miles down the road. At the thatched-roofed Visitor Center, you can pick up a self-guided walking tour map and browse the village's house sites, shrines, canoe shed and games area on your own; allow 30 to 40 minutes. If you prefer, the knowledgeable women at the Visitor Center will accompany you, explaining how people worked and played here 600 years ago. When there are sufficient visitors, they give demonstrations of ancient games, fishing techniques and crafts.

Open daily except holidays from 8 am to 4.30 pm (entrance closes 4 pm); free; tel 889-5566.

Kawaihae

Kawaihae today consists of a gas station, several stores and some oil tanks. There is little to recall that this was an important harbor in the early days of the Hawaiian kingdom. Kamehameha I frequently sailed in and out during the years he was struggling to unify the Islands and it saw the arrival of the first missionaries from New England on March 30, 1820. Later, Parker Ranch cattle were swum out from here to be hauled aboard steamers heading for Oahu.

Puukohola Heiau

A short way down the road is perhaps the most revered site in all Hawaii. As you approach the turnoff for Spencer Park, you'll see a massive *heiau* on a hill overlooking the ocean and, below the road, a second *heiau* under the kiawes. The dominant temple is the famed Puukohola. When in the late 1780s Kamehameha had conquered Maui, Lanai and Molokai but had been unable to achieve dominion over his own island, he asked a famous prophet what he should do. The *kahuna* bade him build a great sacrificial *heiau* and dedicate it to his war god, Kukailimoku; only then would he have the power to unite the islands in one kingdom. For two years, Kamehameha labored alongside his men, building the 224 by 100 feet structure of water-worn lava rocks set without mortar. In the summer of 1791 it was finished. Kamehameha invited his rival, Keoua, to the dedication as a peace offering. Though he felt it meant certain death, Keoua accepted. On his arrival, as he stepped from his canoe in the cove below the *heiau*, a scuffle ensued and Keoua was killed. His body was offered as principal sacrifice to the war god. The prophecy was fulfilled. Within four years Kamehameha defeated Oahu and established his kingdom.

The **Puukohola Heiau National Historic Site** is run by the National Park Service. A road just past the *heiau* leads to the Visitor Center, where you can get a map and information. The park embraces Puukohola Heiau which, since it is still considered sacred by Hawaiians, cannot be entered; Mailekini Heiau, built by Kamehameha's ancestors, which John Young converted into a fort to protect Kawaihae; and several other sites which are being studied by archeologists. Follow the trail down from Mailekini Heiau and you'll see a stone slab leaning

post. Here an ancient chief leaned as he watched sharks devouring his offerings at a *heiau* dedicated to the shark gods, which is believed submerged in the cove. At the edge of the cove stood Pelekane, Kamehameha's residence, where Kamehameha II came after his father's death for purification in preparation for his role as king. Included in the complex also are the ruins of John Young's house, which was located above SR 270. *Olohana*, as Hawaiians called him, settled here under Kamehameha I's patronage and became a chief. His granddaughter, Emma, was to become Kamehameha IV's Queen Emma.

Puukohola was the last *heiau* built in Hawaii. Soon after his accession to the throne, Kamehameha II abolished the *kapu* system and the temples were abandoned. The complex is open daily from 7.30 am to 4 pm; free.

Spencer Beach Park

At the foot of the road between the *heiaus* is an attractive beach park and one of the island's best beaches. Spencer Beach is a golden sand crescent with water temperatures that average around 78°F. The cove offers fine snorkeling. A kiawe-shaded lawn provides a setting for picnics and camping. There are pavilions, changing rooms with showers, picnic tables and barbecue pits and even tennis courts. Beyond them is a pleasant park where you can camp under coconut palms. A county permit is needed from the Parks and Recreation Department, County of Hawaii, Hilo HI 96720 (tel (808) 961-8311).

From here, you can take SR 19 back to Waimea, if you are returning to Hilo. Or you can continue to the Kona Coast, either by the high road, SR 190, from Waimea, or along the coast on SR 19, Queen Kaahumanu Highway. The latter follows the coastline, somewhat inland, to Kailua-Kona. It traverses 19th century lava flows from Mauna Loa and Hualalai which endow the landscape with a savage beauty. Spur roads lead off to several fine beach parks, a petroglyph field and several exceptional resorts.

Mauna Kea Beach Hotel

A mile down the road is the prestigious resort originally built by David Rockefeller's Rockresorts and now part of Westin's chain of luxury properties. The hotel's alfresco corridors are a museum of fine art from the Pacific and the Orient as well as Hawaiiana, including a superb collection of Hawaiian quilts. The property fronts a beach occupied in ancient times by fishing villages, relics of which have been preserved and restored.

Hapuna Beach State Park

Accommodation is more mundane at Hapuna, but the beach is great: white sand at the base of landscaped bluffs, with picnic pavilions set on well-tended lawn. The ocean here can be rough, so exercise caution. Campers can use A-frame shelters uphill, which have electricity, cooking facilities (unequipped), central toilets and cold showers, but no bedding. Reservations should be made in person at the Department of Land and Natural Resources, State Parks Division, 75 Aupuni St, Hilo; tel 961-7200; cost of the shelters, which sleep four, is $7 per night.

Puako

Kiawe and pandanus trees line the approach to the beach at Puako, where three fields of interesting **petroglyphs** are located. Worth seeing is the restored 1860 **Hokuloa Church**. You'll find the first field of petroglyphs by walking inland from the church for about 10 minutes; the others are further in. New homes and the Puako Beach Resort Apartments signify changes to come for this picturesque old fishing village.

Mauna Lani

An acclaimed 18-hole championship golf course highlights the area's newest deluxe resort, the *Mauna Lani Bay Hotel*.

Sculpted out of the lava, the course's greens appear startling, like swaths of emerald velvet thrown across the chunky chocolate-colored lava. The resort offers tennis and watersports, too, in an atmosphere of luxury, not surprisingly at an appropriately exalted tariff.

Waikoloa

A little further down the highway is the third of South Kohala's elegant resorts, the *Sheraton Royal Waikoloa Hotel* on expansive Anaehoomalu beach. It is part of a 31,000-acre development which embraces two Robert Trent Jones Jr-designed golf courses, tennis courts, stables and condominiums. The hotel recognizes the historical significance of its site with displays of artifacts and art relics of old Hawaii. **Mamalahoa,** the olden King's Trail, followed this coastline and there are important petroglyphs in the environs. You can see some of them on Sheraton's self-guided interpretive walk, designed and signed by famed Hawaiian artist Herb Kane.

Each of these Kohala resorts offers numerous dining and entertainment opportunities, some with fine ocean views. Happy hours celebrate the spectacular sunsets that distinguish this coast.

Back on Queen Kaahumanu Highway, notice the modern-day version of petroglyphs on either side of the road. Countless passers-by have inscribed their names and other data with white rocks laid on the black lava, an improvement at least on most forms of graffiti.

Leaving the Waikoloa-Anaehoomalu junction behind, you enter North Kona. A short way down the road is a gatehouse, entrance to Kona Village Resort.

NORTH KONA

Kona Village Resort

Before the 1801 eruption of Hualalai, legend says, Pele wandered the coastal villages along here asking for food. At each she was refused, except at a village set in the kiawes at Kaupulehu. When she sent her torrents of molten lava down the slopes, she spared this village – you can see where the flow deviated, leaving an island of kiawes around the lagoon. Thatched-roof cottages of different Pacific islands' cultures sit here now, part of the secluded, paradisiacal Kona Village Resort. You can tour this unique resort on an hour-long guided walk Monday to Friday at 10 am or 11 am. Non-guests are welcome to dine in the longhouse restaurant, which serves very fine continental cuisine, and to join in their authentic luau held Friday evenings (tel 325-5555 for reservations).

The growing numbe of houses you see on the slopes of Hualalai signal that you are approaching Kailua, hub of the Kona Coast. The highway swings around past the area's airport at Ke-ahole and Honokohau boat harbor, site of a secluded nude beach, to join SR 190, the high road from Waimea, which takes you in to Kailua.

Things to See & Do

Most of the sailing and aquatic sports on the Big Island take place along the Kona Coast, where the most popular activities are game fishing and snorkeling cruises. Kailua is the home of the Hawaiian International Billfish Tournament and has earned a reputation as a sport fishing mecca.

Sport Fishing For sport fishermen who congregate at Kailua, the Pacific blue marlin is king; numerous fish over the 1000-pound mark have been boated by the sport fishing fleet which operates out of here. Other fish you'll see on the scales at Kailua Wharf late each afternoon when the catch is weighed in are *ahi* (tuna), *ono* (wahoo) and *ulua* (jack crevalle). Rates for charter boats average $375 to $450 for a full day, up to six persons $275 to $325 for a half-day; share boat per person runs $95 to $105 for a full day, $70 to $80 for a half day. Bookings can be made

through *Kona Activities Center,* PO Box 1035, Kailua-Kona, HI 96740 (tel 329-3171, toll free 800-367-5288); *Kona Seafari Sport* or *Kona Charter Skippers Association,* PO Box 806, Kailua-Kona, HI 96740 (tel 329-3600). Activities Center staffs desks at Kona Inn Shopping Village and in the lobby of the King Kamehameha Hotel in the village of Kailua. Kona Activities provides a one-stop source of information and reservations not only for fishing, but cruises, golf, tennis, hunting, horseback, flightseeing and other tours.

Sport fishing charters are also available at Keauhou and through the South Kohala resorts.

Cruises Most popular with visitors are the cruises which sail from Kailua and Keauhou piers down the Kona Coast to Kealakekua Bay. Here you can dive off to swim and snorkel in limpid water or laze in the sun, speculating perhaps whether one of thge cliff caves you see is actually the secret burial place of Kamahameha the Great. The cruiser, *Captain Cook VII* sails a three-hour cruise from Kailua at 9 am and 1 pm each day at a cost of $15 including snorkeling gear (tel 329-3811). A 50-foot trimaran *The Fair Wind* sails from Keauhu Bay twice daily; the 9 am sailing features a delicious BBQ cheeseburger lunch with snorkeling for $30 (Scuba, 1 tank plus gear $50) and the 1 pm sailing includes snacks and snorkeling for $18 (tel 322-2788).

Glass-bottom cruises for coral viewing are offered on Captain Bean's Polynesian-styled 85-foot power sailboat *Keana* which departs Kailua Pier four times daily for a one-hour cruise for $6. For schedule and reservations, contact Kona Activities Center (tel 329-3171), or Captain Bean's (tel 329-2955).

Sunset dinner cruise is offered nightly on Captain Bean's 300-passenger *Tamure,* cost $27.50.

There's free pick up and delivery at hotels for all cruises.

Scuba diving rates run around $45 for an introductory dive, $60 for two-tank and $225 for a five-day certification course. In Kona, contact *Gold Coast Divers* (tel 329-1328), *Sea Camp Hawaii* (tel 329-3388) and *Sea Paradise* (322-2500). *Pacific Sail & Snorkel* (tel 329-2021, 329-3171) run twice daily snorkeling tours for $20.

Windsurfing lessons are available through *Ocean Sports* – in Kona, tel 329-8844 and at the *Sheraton Royal Waikoloa*, tel 885-6064.

Golf & Tennis For landlubbers, there are golf courses and tennis courts on both sides of the island, some municipal and others at hotels where non-guests can play. The Hawaii Visitors Bureau will supply you with a current list; ring 935-5271 in Hilo, 329-7787 in Kailua-Kona.

Stables at Waikola and Mauna Kea Beach Hotel offer guided trail rides, the latter from the Waimea Headquarters of Parker Ranch. Contact *Waikoloa Stables* (tel 883-9335); Mauna Kea (tel 882-7222). On the Hilo side, call *Scheherazade Stables*, 965-7122. Rates are running $9 to $10 per hour.

Unusual trail **hiking** opportunities are offered by *Honua Hawaii*, an environmental center in Hilo's forest area (tel 959-6244 for information).

Tours
Gray Line (tel 935-2835; toll-free 800-367-2420) is among the major tour companies offering basic tours at standard prices: Hilo to Kona (or vice versa) via Volcanoes National Park and Ka'u $30; circle-island $33.50 to $53.50; four-hour Kona Historical tour $12 to $30; full-day Kohala Cultural tour, $28.

Flightseeing In Kona, *Kenai Air* helicopters offer flightseeing of Mauna Loa crater, $95; the Kona Coast $35 and the Kohala Coast $115; tel Sheraton Royal Waikoloa 883-6640, Kona Surf 322-931,

toll-free 800-367-5270. *Kona Helicopters* (329-2550) has similar tours.

Kona Flight Services offers single-engine flightseeing from Ke-Ahole Airport. The Kona Coast tour is $35 per person. A circle-island plane tour flies the Kona Coast to Ka'u and Volcanoes National Park, returning over Hilo, the Hamakua coast, Waipio Valley and the Parker Ranch lands; cost is $80. For reservations, telephone 329-2254 or 329-1474.

On the Hilo side, *Anuenue Aviation* has narrated air tours including the volcanoes from $45 per person, tel 961-5591. *Panorama Air Tours* operates an eight-island day tour for a minimum of six, $190 per person, and flightseeing when volcano is active; tel **Oahu** (808) 836-2122. Collect from Big Island; toll-free 800-367-2671.

Places to Stay
There's a range of accommodation available on both the leeward and windward coasts. In Hilo, hotels edging the bay along Banyan Drive include the top-rated *Naniloa Surf*. On the Kona Coast, the newer hotels and a number of condominiums are located in the Keauhou-Kona resort area seven miles from Kailua, while more condominiums line Alii Drive between Keauhou and Kailua. The *King Kamehameha* and *Kona Hilton* are the main hotels in the village of Kailua. The price range on the Kona Coast varies from the island's most expensive (Kona Village Resort, from $225 double which includes all meals) to the least expensive ($15 double at the old woodframe *Manago Hotel* in Captain Cook).

Rooms in private homes are available at varying rates through Go-Native Hawaii, 130 Puhili St, Hilo HI 96720; tel (808) 961-2080.

For a comprehensive listing of what's available, obtain the *Hawaii Visitors Bureau Member Hotel Guide*. Here are some samples:

Windward Side
Top End

Naniloa Surf (93 Banyan Drive, Hilo, HI 96720; tel (808) 935-0831; toll-free 800-367-5360). 389-room hotel on Hilo Bay; suites and deluxe rooms with balconies. Pool, shops, restaurants. Rates from $49 double.

Sheraton-Waiakea Village (400 Hualani St, Hilo, HI 96720; tel (808) 961-3041; toll-free 800-325-3535). 294 rooms in Polynesian-style buildings amidst lush garden on lagoon. Marketplace shopping bazaar. Pool, tennis courts. (Three-story without elevators, so ask for lower room if you can't climb stairs). Rates from $55 double.

Mid-Range

Volcano House (Hawaii Volcanoes National Park, HI 96718; tel (808) 967-7321; toll-free 800-325-3535.) Sheraton-operated historic hotel on rim of Kilauea crater; 11 rooms of total 37 have crater view. Restaurant, cocktails, shop. Rates from $37 double.

Hilo Bay Hotel (87 Banyan Drive, Hilo, HI 96720; tel (808) 935-0861, toll-free 800-367-5102 (mainland), 800-442-5841 (Hawaii). Well-known character 'Uncle Billy's' domain on Hilo Bay. 150 rooms, some kitchenettes. Pool, shops, restaurant and popular cocktail lounge. Rates from $32 double.

Budget

Hilo Hukilau Hotel (126 Banyan Drive, Hilo, HI 96720; tel toll-free 800-367-7000. On Hilo Bay; small, clean rooms. Pool, shop. Rates from $29 double.

Leeward Side
Top End

Kona Surf (Keauhou-Kona, HI 96740; tel (808) 322-3411; toll-free 800-367-5360). On point overlooking Keauhou Bay. Pacific Rim artworks in public areas; pools, tennis; golf nearby. Rates from $69 double.

Hotel King Kamehameha (75-5660 Palani Rd, Kailua-Kona, HI 96740; tel 329-2911.) On good beach at Kailua Wharf. Historical site and restoration. Pool, tennis. Rates from $55 double.

Kona Village Resort (PO Box 1299, Kailua-Kona, HI 96740; tel (808) 325-5555; toll-free 800-367-5290.) Individual Polynesian-style cottages in idyllic setting on Kaupulehu Beach. Pool, tennis. Renowned restaurant. Rates from $225 double, including meals.

Mauna Kea Beach Hotel (PO Box 218, Kamuela, HI 96743; tel (808) 882-7222.) Prestigious Westin hotel on beach near Kawaihae. Pool, tennis, golf, shops. Fine artworks in public areas. Rates from $250 double, including breakfast and dinner.

Mauna Lani Bay Hotel (PO Box 4000, Kawaihae HI 96743; tel (808) 885-6622, toll-free 800-367-2323). Elegant resort on beach with outstanding golf, tennis, pool, shops. Restaurants, cocktail lounges. Rates from $220 double.

Sheraton Royal Waikoloa (PO Box 5000, Waikoloa HI 96743; tel (808) 885-6789, toll-free 800-325-3535). Luxurious resort on historical site. Two golf courses, tennis, pool, exceptional beach. Lagoon-side cabanas. Restaurants, cocktail lounges. Rates from $85 double, $175 double for cabanas.

Mid-Range

Kona Seaside Hotel (75-5646 Palani Rd, Kailua-Kona, HI 96740; tel (808) 329-1655). Centrally located uphill from Kailua Bay. Popular with singles. Pools, shops, dining room and bar. Rates from $34 double, including rental car.

Kona Bay Hotel (75-5739 Alii Drive, Kailua-Kona, HI 96740; tel (808) 329-1393.) Once part of venerable Kona Inn; located across from bay. Run by 'Uncle Billy' Kimo's family. Complimentary continental breakfast. Rates from $37 double.

Bottom End

Kona Hukilau (75-5646 Palani Rd, Kailua-Kona, HI 96740; tel toll-free 800-

367-7000). Across from Kailua Bay sea wall. Modest rooms, popular restaurant, pool. Rates from $29 double.

Kona Tiki (PO Box 1567, Kailua-Kona, HI 96740; tel (808) 329-1425.) On waterfront one mile from Kailua, with lanais overlooking ocean. Complimentary continental breakfast. Pool. Three-day minimum. Rates from $26 double.

Camping The Big Island offers a number of county and state parks, as well as Volcanoes National Park, in which to camp. Some sites have cabins, too. For a free permit to camp in county parks, write 25 Aupuni St, Hilo, HI 96720 (tel (808) 961-8311); for state parks, write 75 Aupuni St, Hilo, HI 96720 (tel (808) 961-7200). Maximum stay permitted is one week and there is a fee for cabins in state parks. No permit is required to camp in the national park, but you must advise park rangers; a fee is required for cabins, and those at Namakani Palo campground must be booked through Volcano House (see above).

Fully-equipped campers are available from *Travel/Camp* (PO Box 11, Hilo, HI 96720 (tel (808) 935-7406); *Beach Boy Campers,* General Lyman Field, Hilo, HI 96720; (tel (808) 961-2022); and *Hawaii Campers,* 809 Leilani, Hilo, HI 96720 (tel (808) 935-8349). Rental rates run from around $31 per night for two persons. Recommended if you are planning on camping and hiking is a detailed package of information which you can obtain from Hawaii Geographic Society, PO Box 1698, Honolulu, HI 96806 (tel (808) 538-3952); cost $5.

Places to Eat
Dining choices on the Big Island may not be of the scope of those on Oahu, particularly in Hilo, but there are enough restaurants offering good food and pleasant atmosphere to please any taste. The finest are generally in the hotels, such as Kona Village's *Hale Moana,* Mauna Lani Bay's *Third Floor,* Kona Surf's *S S James*

Makee, Mauna Kea Beach's *Pavilion Dining Room* – all moderate to expensive.

Luaus
Scheduled luaus currently are offered only on the Kona side, where you can attend one each night of the week. Present prices run from $27, except for the gourmet luau Tuesdays at *Mauna Kea,* which costs $32.50. You can get a current schedule of luaus from the Hawaii Visitors Bureau's Hilo office.

Nightlife & Entertainment
For Hawaiian entertainment in Hilo, try Uncle Billy's *Kimo's Steak and Fish Restaurant,* where two shows a night entertain diners.

Polynesian entertainment accompanies the luaus on the Kona side. There's lively disco at the Keauhou Beach Hotel and quieter dancing at the Sheraton Waikoloa's *Tiare Lounge* and Kona Surf's *The Puka.*

Check *This Week on Big Island* for the current line-up in both Hilo and Kona.

Getting There
Air Visitors can fly into four airports on the Big Island, at Hilo, Kona, Waimea (Kamuela), and Waikoloa.

General Lyman Field, Hilo
This well-designed airport was planned for direct service between the Big Island and the mainland. Currently, however, it is sadly under-utilized with *United* running one flight a day between Hilo and Los Angeles.

The connection between the 'Overseas' section of the terminal and the 'Interisland' section is a great deal more simple than at Honolulu International, making this a good entry point for mainlanders en route to Maui, for instance. *Hawaiian Air, Aloha* and *Mid Pacific* operate their jets into the Interisland section; *Royal Hawaiian Air Service's* Cessnas use a separate terminal building beyond the overseas section.

Flying into Lyman Field, baggage collection is easy; carousels are located on street level. Car rental desks line the opposite side of the street, which is a one-way counterclockwise access to the airport complex. The airport is located just minutes away from downtown Hilo; Banyan Drive hotels are even closer.

There is no public transportation but *Gray Line* operates transfer service to hotels for $4 and taxis to Banyan Drive hotels run only about $5.50 plus baggage charge.

Ke-Ahole Airport, Kona

Ke-Ahole Airport is set in lava fields about a 15-minute drive from Kailua hotels, 20 minutes from Kohala resorts and a 25-minute drive from Keauhou-Kona hotels. It is served from the US mainland with direct service by United, and inter-island by *Aloha, Hawaiian Air, Mid Pacific* and *Royal Hawaiian*. Facilities include a visitor information desk, snack bar and cocktail lounge, car rental booths located across the road from the check-in area (again, access road is one-way counterclockwise).

Gray Line transfer to Kailua hotels costs $8.50 and to Keauhou-Kona hotels costs $10. Taxi cost to Kailua is running around $11 plus baggage charge at writing.

Waimea/Kohala Airport

This small strip one mile from Waimea (Kamuela) serves the South Kohala area. *Royal Hawaiian* and *Princeville Airways,* have daily flights into this airport.

Upolu Airstrip

Upolu strip in North Kohala is mostly devoted to general aviation but *Royal Hawaiian* will call in en route to and from Waimea on request.

Waikoloa airstrip

is served by Princeville Airways from Honolulu and Kauai's Princeville Airport.

Getting Around

Car Rental Most of the major car rental agencies are represented at Hilo's General Lyman Field, or they can be telephoned for pick up. Many are also stationed at Ke-Ahole. You can pick up a car at one airport and drop it off at the other but there is a drop-off charge, probably about $10. If you're planning on staying on the island long enough to really explore it, check into weekly rates.

Since rental agencies are reluctant to allow their cars on the Saddle Rd, you might prefer to rent a jeep if you want to ascend Mauna Kea; tel *Hawaiiana Rent-A-Jeep* 329-5077.

Motorbike rental Honda Express motorbikes are popular to tootle around the flat areas along the Kona Coast; *Bike Hi* offers them for $17 for 24 hours. You can also hire 10-speed bicycles for $8 per day from here (tel 329-2774).

In Hilo, try *Mike's Bike Rentals* on Mamo and Kamehameha Avenues (tel 935-9683).

Bus The county of Hawaii operates a service with brightly-painted buses known as *Hele on (hele* translates roughly as go). In Hilo, the *Hele-on Banyan Shuttle* loops between the Banyan Drive hotels and downtown areas from 9 am to 3 pm Monday through Saturday except holidays; fare is 50c per segment or $2 for a day's rides on the circuit. For rates and schedules of limited service across the island, telephone the County Transit System at 961-8343 or 935-8241.

On the Kona side, Hele-on runs on *Alii Shuttle* from Kailua to the Kona Surf hourly from 7 am to 6 pm daily except Sundays and holidays. Fare is 50c. In addition, a free double-deck London bus is operated from World Square shopping plaza to Keauhou-Kona hotels; current schedule is on the hour at 9 and 11 am, 1, 3, 5, 7 and 9 pm to Keauhou, return on the half-hour to Kailua.

Useful Addresses on Hawaii
Hawaii Visitors Bureau Kona Plaza Shopping Arcade, 75-5719 W Alii Drive, Kailua-Kona HI 96740; tel (808) 329-7787; Suite 104, Hilo Plaza, 180 Kinoole St, Hilo, HI 96720; tel (808) 935-5271.
Hawaii Island Chamber of Commerce (180 Kinoole St, Hilo, HI 96720.)
Keauhou-Kona Resort Association (78-7130 Kaleo Papa St, Kailua-Kona HI 96740; tel (808) 322-3866.)
Volcanoes National Park, HI 96718; (tel (808) 967-7311; eruption hotline (808) 967-7977.)
Interisland Airlines: Aloha Airlines 935-5771; Hawaiian Air 935-0811; Royal Hawaiian 935-2871. Mid Pacific 329-8047; Princeville Airways (800) 652-6541.
Visitor Information Center (General Lyman Field) 935-1018 daily 6.45 am to 8 pm; *(Ke-Ahole Airport)* 329-3432 daily 6.45 am to 8 pm.

Festivals & Events for all the Islands

January	*Hula Bowl college all-star football*, Oahu *Narcissus Festival*, Oahu (date depending on Chinese New Year)
February	*Great Waikoloa Horse Races & Rodeo*, Big Island *Mauna Kea Ski Meet*, Big Island (dependent on snow)
March	*Kona Stampede*, Honaunau, Big Island *Prince Kuhio Festival*, Kauai *Pan Am Hawaiian Windsurfing World Cup*, Kailua, Oahu
Easter	*Merrie Monarch Festival*, Hilo, Big Island
May	*May Day by the Bay*, Princeville, Kauai *Lei Day*, Kapiolani Park, Honolulu *Kona Gold Jackpot Fishing Tournament*, Kailua, Big Island *Paniolo Country Club Rodeo*, Waimea, Big Island *Haleiwa Sea Spree*, Haleiwa, Oahu
May-June	*50th State Fair*, Aloha Stadium, Oahu
June	*King Kamehameha Celebration*, all islands (Parades Oahu and Big Island)
July	*Annual Hilo Orchid Society Flower Show*, Big Island *Parker Ranch Horse Races & Rodeo*, Waimea, Big Island *Hanalei Stampede*, Princeville, Kauai
August	*Hula Festival*, Kapiolani Park, Honolulu *Hawaiian International Billfish Tournament*, Kona, Big Island *Augustfest*, Honokaa, Big Island

September	*Yacht Race Week*, Lahaina, Maui
	Parker Ranch Roundup, Waimea, Big Island
September-October	*Aloha Week*, all islands (different schedules)
October	*Kona Coffee Festival*, Kailua-Kona, Big Island
	Makahiki Festival, Waimea Falls Park, Oahu
	Ironman Triathlon, Kailua-Kona, Big Island
November	*Na Mele O Maui* (Hawaiiana Festival) *Lahaina, Maui*
	Kona Coffee Festival, Kailua-Kona, Big Island
November-December	*Hawaiian Pro-Surfing Championships*, North Shore, Oahu
December	*Festival of Trees*, Kailua-Kona, Big Island
	Festival of Trees, Neal S Blaisdell Center, Oahu

Appendix

ARIZONA

Flagstaff Chamber of Commerce, 101 West Santa Fe, Flagstaff 86001; (602) 774-4505.

Lake Havasu City Chamber of Commerce, 2074 McCulloch Boulevard, Lake Havasu City 86403; (602) 855-4115.

Phoenix and Valley of the Sun Convention and Visitors Bureau, 2701 East Camelback Rd, Suite 200H, Phoenix 85016; (602) 957-0070.

Metropolitan Tucson Convention & Visitors Bureau, 120 West Broadway Boulevard PO Box 3028, Tucson 85702; (6020 624-1817.

CALIFORNIA

Amador County Chamber of Commerce, 30 South Highway 49 and 88 PO Box 596 Jackson 95642; (209) 223-0340.

Anderson Valley Chamber of Commerce, PO Box 275, Boonville 95415;

Auburn Chamber of Commerce, 1101 High St, Auburn 95603; (916) 885-5616.

Avenue of the Giants Association PO Box 1000, Miranda 95553; (707) 946-2321.

Beverly Hills Chamber of Commerce, 239 South Beverly Drive, Beverly Hills, 90212; (213) 271-8126.

Bodega Bay Area Chamber of Commerce, PO Box 146, Bodega Bay 94923; (707) 875-3407.

Calaveras County Chamber of Commerce, 30 South Main PO Box 177, San Andreas 95249; (209) 754-1821.

Carmel Business Association, San Carlos (between Ocean & 7th Sts), Carmel 93921; (408) 624-2522.

Catalina Island Chamber of Commerce, Green Pleasure Pier PO Box 217, Avalon 90704; (213) 510-1520.

Del Norte County Chamber of Commerce, PO Box 246, Front & K Sts, Crescent City 95531; (707) 464-3174.

El Dorado County Chamber of Commerce, 542 Main St, Placerville 95667; (916) 626-2344.

Eureka Chamber of Commerce, 2112 Broadway, Eureka 95501; (707) 464-3174.

Fort Bragg-Mendocino Coast Chamber of Commerce, 332 N Main St PO Box 1141, Fort Bragg 95437; (707) 964-3153.

Grass Valley Area Chamber of Commerce, 6290 Sunset Boulevard, Suite 525, Hollywood 90028; (213) 469-8311.

Indio Chamber of Commerce, 82503 Highway III, Incio 92201; (714) 347-0676.

Laguna Beach Chamber of Commerce, 205 North Coast Highway, Laguna Beach 92651; (714) 494-1018.

Lakeport Chamber of Commerce and Visitors' Bureau, 875 Lakeport Boulevard, Lakeport 95453; (707) 263-6131.

Greater Los Angeles Visitors and Convention Bureau, 505 South Flower St, Los Angeles 90071; (213) 628-3101.

Monterey Peninsula Chamber of Commerce and Visitors and Convention Bureau, 380 Alvarado PO Box 1770, Monterey 93940; (408) 649-1770.

Nevada City Chamber of Commerce, 132 Main St, Nevada City, 95959; (916) 265-2692.

Palm Springs Convention & Visitors Bureau, Municipal Airport Terminal, Palm Springs 92262; (714) 327-8411.

Petaluma Chamber of Commerce, 314 Western Avenue, Petaluma 94952; (707) 762-2785.

Placerville County Chamber of Commerce Visitors Information Center, 661 Newcastle Rd, Newcastle 95658; (916) 663-2061.

Red Bluff Chamber of Commerce, 100 Main St, Red Bluff 96080; (916) 527-6220.

Redding Chamber of Commerce, 1345 Liberty St PO Box 1180, Redding 96001; (916) 449-5291.

Sacramento Convention & Visitors Bureau, 1100 14th St, Sacramento 95814; (916) 449-5291.

San Diego Convention & Visitors Bureau, 1200 Third Avenue, San Diego 92101; (714) 232-3101.

San Francisco Convention & Visitors Bureau, Hallidie Plaza, Powell and Market Sts, San Francisco 94102 PO Box 6977, San Francisco 94101; (415) 974-6900.

San Luis Obispo Chamber of Commerce, 1039 Chorro St, San Luis Obispo 93401; (805) 543-1323.

Santa Barbara Conference & Visitors Bureau, 1301 Santa Barbara St PO Box 299, Santa Barbara 93102; (805) 965-3021.

Santa Rosa Chamber of Commerce, 637 First St, Santa Rosa 95404; (707) 545-1414.

Shasta-Cascade Wonderland Association, S Market and Parkview Sts, PO Box 1988, Redding 96001; (916) 243-2643.

South Lake Tahoe Chamber of Commerce, 3066 Highway 50, PO Box 15090, South Lake Tahoe 95702; (916) 544-5050.

Solvang Visitors Bureau, 1623 Mission Drive, Solvang 93463; (805) 688-3317.

Tuolomne County Chamber of Commerce, 158 W Bradford Avenue, PO Box 277, Sonora 95350; (209) 532-4212.

Ukiah Chamber of Commerce, 495 E Perkins, Ukiah 95482; (707) 462-4705.

Willits Chamber of Commerce, 15 S Main, Willits 95490; (707) 459-4413.

HAWAII

Hawaii

Hawaii Island Chamber of Commerce, 180 Kinoole St, Hilo 96720.

Hawaii Visitors' Bureau, Suite 104, Hilo Plaza, 180 Kinoole St, Hilo 96720; (808) 935-5271.

Hawaii Visitors' Bureau, World Square, PO Box 367, Kailua-Kona 96740; (808) 329-1782.

Keahou-Kona Resort Association, 78-7130 Kaleo Papa St, Kailua-Kona 96740; (808) 322-3866.

Kona Coast Resort Association PO Box H, Hailua-Kona 96740; (808) 329-2714, 800-366-5072.

Kauai

Hawaii Visitors' Bureau, Suite 207, Lihue Plaza Building, 3016 Umi St, Lihue 96766; (808) 245-3971.

Maui

Hawaii Visitors' Bureau, Room 431-2, County Building, 200 High St, Wailuku 96793; (808) 244-9141.

Maui County Visitors' Association, PO Box 1738, Kahului 96732; (808) 877-7822.

Oahu

Hawaii Visitors' Bureau, 2285 Kalakaua Avenue, Honolulu 96815; (808) 923-1811.

Chamber of Commerce of Hawaii, 735 Bishop St, Honolulu 96813; (808) 531-1411.

MEXICO

Tijuana Convention & Visitors' Bureau, PO Box 1831, Tijuaha, Baja California, Mexico; (903) 385-8692.

NEW MEXICO

Albuquerque Chamber of Commerce, Convention Center, 401 Second St NW, Albuquerque 87102; (505) 842-0220.

Santa Fe Chamber of Commerce, 330 Old Santa Fe Trail, PO Box 1928, Santa Fe 87501; (505) 983-7317.

Taos County Chamber of Commerce, The Plaza/Drawer 1, Taos 87571; (505) 758-3873.

OREGON

Pacific Northwest Regional Tourism Project, 610 SW Broadway, Suite 305, Portland 97205; (503) 227-1263; 800-547-4901.

Portland Chamber of Commerce Visitors Information Center, 824 SW 5th Avenue, Portland 97204; (503) 228-9411.

Travel Information Section, Oregon State Highway Division, State Highway Building, Salem 97310; (503) 378-6309; 800-547-4901.

WASHINGTON

Seattle-King County Convention and Visitors Bureau, 1815 Seventh Avenue, Seattle 98101; (206) 447-7273.

Tourism Promotion and Development Division, Department of Commerce & Economic Development, General Administration Building, Olympia 98504; (206) 753-5600.

Index

Lonely Planet travel guides

Africa on a Shoestring
Australia – a travel survival kit
Alaska – a travel survival kit
Bali & Lombok – a travel survival kit
Burma – a travel survival kit
Bushwalking in Papua New Guinea
Canada – a travel survival kit
China – a travel survival kit
Hong Kong, Macau & Canton
India – a travel survival kit
Japan – a travel survival kit
Kashmir, Ladakh & Zanskar
Kathmandu & the Kingdom of Nepal
Korea & Taiwan – a travel survival kit
Malaysia, Singapore & Brunei – a travel survival kit
Mexico – a travel survial kit
New Zealand – a travel survival kit
Pakistan – a travel survival kit kit
Papua New Guinea – a travel survival kit
The Philippines – a travel survival kit
South America on a Shoestring
South-East Asia on a Shoestring
Sri Lanka – a travel survival kit
Thailand – a travel survival kit
Tramping in New Zealand
Trekking in the Himalayas
Turkey – a travel survival kit
USA West
West Asia on a Shoestring

Lonely Planet phrasebooks

Indonesia Prasebook
Nepal Phrasebook
Thailand Phrasebook

Lonely Planet travel guides are available around the world. If you can't find them, ask your bookshop to order them from one of the distributors listed below. For countries not listed or if you would like a free copy of our latest booklist write to Lonely Planet in Australia.

Australia
Lonely Planet Publications, PO Box 88, South Yarra, Victoria 3141.

Canada
Milestone Publications, Box 2248, Sidney British Columbia, V8L 3S8.

Denmark
Scanvik Books aps, Store Kongensgade 59 A, DK-1264 Copenhagen K.

Hong Kong
The Book Society, GPO Box 7804.

India & Nepal
UBS Distributors, 5 Ansari Rd, New Delhi.

Israel
Geographical Tours Ltd, 8 Tverya St, Tel Aviv 63144.

Japan
Intercontinental Marketing Corp, IPO Box 5056, Tokyo 100-31.

Malaysia
MPH Distributors, 13 Jalan 13/6, Petaling Jaya, Selangor.

Netherlands
Nilsson & Lamm bv, Postbus 195, Pampuslaan 212, 1380 AD Weesp.

New Zealand
Roulston Greene Publishing Associates Ltd, Box 33850, Takapuna, Auckland 9.

Papua New Guinea
Gordon & Gotch (PNG), PO Box 3395, Port Moresby.

Singapore
MPH Distributors, 116-DJTC Factory Building, Lorong 3, Geylang Square, Singapore, 1438.

Sweden
Esselte Kartcentrum AB, Vasagatan 16, S-111 20 Stockholm.

Thailand
Chalermnit, 1-2 Erawan Arcade, Bangkok.

UK
Roger Lascelles, 47 York Rd, Brentford, Middlesex, TW8 0QP.

USA
Lonely Planet Publications, PO Box 2001A, Berkeley, CA 94702.

West Germany
Buchvertrieb Gerda Schettler, Postfach 64, D3415 Hattorf a H.